# ROME

## AND ENVIRONS

# CONTENTS

|                                  | *Page* |
|----------------------------------|--------|
| PREFACE                          | 5      |
| EXPLANATIONS                     | 10     |
| HISTORICAL SKETCH OF ROME        | 11     |
| LIST OF ROMAN EMPERORS           | 19     |
| CHRONOLOGICAL LIST OF POPES      | 20     |

## PRACTICAL INFORMATION

| I    | APPROACHES TO ROME                       | 32 |
|------|------------------------------------------|----|
| II   | HOTELS AND PENSIONS                      | 34 |
| III  | RESTAURANTS AND CAFÉS                    | 36 |
| IV   | FOOD AND WINE                            | 38 |
| V    | TRANSPORT                                | 41 |
| VI   | USEFUL ADDRESSES                         | 43 |
| VII  | CHURCHES AND CHURCH CEREMONIES           | 45 |
| VIII | AMUSEMENTS                               | 46 |
| IX   | MUSEUMS, COLLECTIONS AND MONUMENTS       | 46 |
| X    | GENERAL HINTS                            | 51 |
|      | GLOSSARY OF ART TERMS                    | 52 |

## ROME

| *Route* |                                                                       | *Page* |
|---------|-----------------------------------------------------------------------|--------|
| 1       | PIAZZA VENEZIA AND THE CAPITOL                                         | 55     |
| 2       | FROM CORSO VITTORIO EMANUELE SOUTH TO THE TIBER                        | 74     |
| 3       | FROM PIAZZA VENEZIA TO PORTA SAN PAOLO AND SAN PAOLO FUORI LE MURA     | 85     |
| 4       | FROM CORSO VITTORIO EMANUELE NORTH TO THE TIBER                        | 95     |
| 5       | THE ROMAN FORUM                                                       | 108    |
| 6       | THE PALATINE                                                          | 125    |
| 7       | THE IMPERIAL FORA AND THE COLOSSEUM                                    | 135    |
| 8       | VIA DEL CORSO TO PIAZZA DEL POPOLO                                     | 147    |
| 9       | VILLA BORGHESE AND VILLA GIULIA                                        | 155    |
| 10      | FROM PIAZZA VENEZIA TO PIAZZA DI SPAGNA AND THE PINCIO                 | 167    |
| 11      | THE QUIRINAL AND THE QUARTERS N. AND N.E.                              | 175    |
| 12      | FROM PIAZZA VENEZIA TO THE MUSEO NAZIONALE ROMANO AND THE STATION      | 188    |
| 13      | FROM THE STATION TO THE UNIVERSITY AND SAN LORENZO FUORI LE MURA       | 197    |
| 14      | FROM PIAZZA VENEZIA TO SANTA MARIA MAGGIORE                            | 199    |
| 15      | FROM THE COLOSSEUM TO THE LATERAN AND THE PORTA MAGGIORE               | 207    |
| 16      | THE CAELIAN, THE BATHS OF CARACALLA AND THE APPIAN WAY                 | 218    |
| 17      | TRASTÉVERE, THE JANICULUM, THE BORGO AND CASTEL SANT'ANGELO            | 235    |

8                                    CONTENTS

18   FROM PIAZZA CAVOUR TO MONTE MARIO AND PONTE        255
       MILVIO
19   E.U.R.                                              258
20   THE VATICAN CITY. ST PETER'S. THE VATICAN PALACE    261


## ENVIRONS OF ROME

21   OSTIA                                               321
       A   Ostia Antica and the Isola Sacra             321
       B   Lido di Ostia                                333
       C   Porto and Fiumicino                          334
22   ANZIO AND NETTUNO                                   335
23   THE ALBAN HILLS                                     338
       A   Frascati and Grottaferrata                   339
       B   Via dei Laghi: Marino, Rocca di Papa, Nemi   343
       C   Castel Gandolfo, Albano, Genzano, Velletri   347
24   PALESTRINA                                          352
25   TIVOLI. HADRIAN'S VILLA. SUBIACO                    357
       A   Tivoli                                       357
       B   Hadrian's Villa                              362
       C   Subiaco                                      366
26   VIA FLAMINIA AND THE TIBER VALLEY                   370
27   VEIO AND LAKE BRACCIANO                             372
28   CÉRVETERI                                           375
     LIST OF PRINCIPAL ITALIAN ARTISTS                   381
     INDEX                                               391

9

# MAPS AND PLANS

| | |
|---|---|
| ATLAS (1-15) | *At the end of the book* |
| ENVIRONS OF ROME | 318-19 |
| BATHS OF CARACALLA | 223 |
| CAPITOLINE MUSEUM | 58-9 |
| CASTEL SANT'ANGELO | 248-49, 251, 253 |
| CERVÉTERI | 377 |
| DOMUS AUREA | 145 |
| GALLERIA NAZIONALE D'ARTE MODERNA | 165 |
| HADRIAN'S VILLA, TIVOLI | 365 |
| IMPERIAL FORA | 139 |
| MUSEO NAZIONALE ROMANO AND SANTA MARIA DEGLI ANGELI | 193 |
| OSTIA ANTICA | 331 |
| PALATINE | 130-31 |
| PALAZZO DEI CONSERVATORI | 63 |
| PALESTRINA | 355 |
| ROMAN FORUM | 120-21 |
| SAN CLEMENTE | 208-9 |
| ST JOHN LATERAN | 214 |
| SANTA MARIA MAGGIORE | 205 |
| ST PETER'S AND VATICAN GROTTOES | 272-73 |
| TIVOLI | 359 |
| VATICAN MUSEUMS | 308-9 |
| VATICAN MUSEUMS: GREGORIAN MUSEUM OF PAGAN ANTIQUITIES AND ETHNOLOGICAL MISSIONARY MUSEUM | 281 |
| VIA APPIA ANTICA AND THE CATACOMBS | 232-33 |
| VILLA GIULIA | 165 |

# EXPLANATIONS

**Type.** The main routes are described in large type. Smaller type is used for branch-routes and excursions, for historical and preliminary paragraphs, and (generally speaking) for descriptions of greater detail or minor importance.

**Asterisks** indicate points of special interest or excellence.

**Distances** in the environs of Rome are given cumulatively from the starting-point of the route or sub-route in kilometres. Heights are given in metres.

**Populations** are given in round figures according to the latest official figures (estimates of 1975 based on the census of 1971).

**Abbreviations.** In addition to generally accepted and self-explanatory abbreviations, the following occur in the guide:

| | |
|---|---|
| Abp | archbishop |
| Adm. | admission |
| Bp | bishop |
| C | century |
| c. | circa |
| C.I.T. | Compagnia Italiana Turismo |
| E.N.I.T. | Ente Nazionale Italiano per il Turismo |
| E.P.T. | Ente Provinciale per il Turismo |
| exc. | except |
| fest. | *festa,* or festival (i.e. holiday) |
| incl. | including |
| fl. | floruit (flourished) |
| km. | kilometre(s) |
| l. | lira (pl. lire); left |
| m | metre(s) |
| m. | sea miles |
| min. | minutes |
| P. | pension (i.e. board and lodging) |
| Pal. | Palazzo |
| Pl. | atlas plan |
| P.za | Piazza |
| r. | right |
| R. | room(s) |
| Rfmts. | refreshments |
| Rist. | ristorante (restaurant) |
| Rte | route |
| SS. | Saints (in English); Santissimo, -a (in Italian) |
| T.C.I. | Touring Club Italiano |

For abbreviations of Italian Christian names, see p. 381; for glossary of art terms, see p. 52.

References in the text (Pl. 1; 1) are to the 15-page Atlas at the back of the book, the first figure referring to the page, the second to the square. Ground plan references are given as a bracketed single figure or letter.

# HISTORICAL SKETCH OF ROME

Rome was founded—probably at least a century earlier than the traditional date of 753 B.C.—at the spot where the territories of the Latins, the Sabines, and the Etruscans met, and where the Isola Tiberina provided an easy crossing-place of the Tiber. The agricultural and pastoral community of the Palatine united with the inhabitants of the surrounding hills. Favoured by its central position in the Italian peninsula, by the neighbourhood of the sea, and by the bold character of its inhabitants, Rome grew rapidly in importance. Under its seven more or less legendary kings (Romulus, Numa Pompilius, Tullus Hostilius, Ancus Marcius, Tarquinius Priscus, Servius Tullius, and Tarquinius Superbus) it waged war, almost always successfully, with the Latins and Etruscans. Rome became a republic c. 510 B.C. and, though it was distracted by the long but not wholly barren internecine struggle between the Plebs and the Patricians, it was strong enough to conquer the Etruscans of Veii and Tarquinii, the Latins, and the Volscians. The Etruscans were defeated at the famous Battle of Cuma in 474 B.C. From almost total destruction by the Gauls in 390 B.C. Rome recovered to overthrow the Samnites in three campaigns and, after gloriously defeating Pyrrhus (275 B.C.), turned her arms against Magna Graecia and Sicily and challenged the naval power of Carthage (264 B.C.). Hannibal transferred the fight to Italy in the Second Punic War, and inflicted severe defeats on the Romans at the Ticinus, the Trebia, Lake Trasimene, and Cannæ; but, nothing daunted, the Republic achieved the conquest of Spain, carried the war once more into Africa, where it gained the famous victory of Zama (202 B.C.), and finally, in the Third Punic War, utterly reduced its dangerous rival (146 B.C.). The defeat of Carthage seems to have stimulated the ambition of the Romans, who now made themselves masters, not only of all Italy but also of Gallia Cisalpina, Illyria, Greece, and Macedonia, and finally proceeded to the conquest of the known world. The Teutons and Cimbri were defeated in 102-101 B.C.; the insurrection of the Italic peoples (the Social War) was put down in 89 B.C.; Asia Minor, Tauris, Syria, and Palestine were brought under Roman sway, and Julius Cæsar bore the Roman eagles to Gallia Transalpina and Britain. The civil strife between Marius and Sulla and between Caesar and Pompey, and the brief coalitions of the two triumvirates (Pompey, Cæsar and Crassus; Antony, Lepidus, and Octavian) resulted in the founding c. 27 B.C., of the Empire under Octavian (afterwards Augustus), marking the triumph of the democratic party over the old oligarchy, the centre of which was in the Senate. In spite of the moral degeneracy, the incapacity, and the tyranny of many of the emperors, the dominion of Rome continued to extend and reached its maximum expansion under Trajan (98-117). The language and the laws of Rome were accepted as standards by the world and the solidity and strength of the Roman state were still unbroken in the 3C A.D., although some provinces had been lost to the barbarians. The decline of Rome as capital of the world began under Diocletian (284), who divided the empire into a Western Empire and an Eastern Empire, and it was confirmed when Constantine transferred the seat of government to Byzantium (A.D. 330). In the 5C the barbarians descended upon Rome. The imperial city was sacked by Alaric the Goth in 410, by Genseric the Vandal in 455, and by Ricimer the Sueve in 472. Finally, in 476, Odoacer compelled Romulus Augustulus to abdicate and thus put an end to the Western Empire.

The Roman Church, persecuted until the reign of Constantine, but finally triumphant owing to its moral grandeur and the herosim of its martyrs, rescued Latin civilisation from ruin, and the moral supremacy of the bishop of Rome was gradually recognized by a Christianized world. Rome, the possession of which was disputed in the 6C by Goths and Byzantines, passed at the beginning of the 7C under the temporal protection of the Popes, a protection which was transformed into sovereignty by the force of circumstances and as a consequence of papal endowments. Pope Stephen III, threatened by the Lombards, appealed to Pepin the Frank, who defeated the enemy and bestowed upon the Pope a portion of Lombardy (A.D. 754). Thus began the temporal power of the popes over the States of the Church. On Christmas Day, 800, Charlemagne, son of Pepin, was crowned by Leo III in St Peter's as Augustus and Emperor, and thus began the 'Holy Roman Empire' which endured until the abdication of Francis II of Austria in 1806.

On the death of Charlemagne a turbulent period ensued, which clouded the fortunes of the papacy. Gregory VII, however, reasserted the papal authority although he was unable to prevent Robert Guiscard, the Norman, from devastating the city in 1084. Paschal II and Calixtus II did much to restore the city. A brief republican period which then ensued was terminated by Frederick Barbarossa, and Alexander III reassumed power. In 1309, a century after the glorious pontificate of Innocent III (d. 1216) and a few years after the solemn jubilee proclaimed by Boniface VIII, Pope Clement V fled from Rome to Avignon, where he enjoyed the protection of France. Rome meanwhile became the theatre of fierce struggles between the families of the Colonna, Caetani, and Orsini, and in 1347 witnessed the tragic failure of the tribune Cola di Rienzo, in his patriotic but utopian attempt to revive the ancient power and glory of the Imperial City. Gregory XI, at the instance of St Catherine of Siena, re-transferred the papal seat from Avignon to Rome in 1378, but the western schism still engaged the attention of the popes, and it was not until 1420 that Martin V began to restore the city, which had deteriorated sadly both physically and socially during the so-called 'Babylonish Captivity'. Under Julius II and Leo X Rome recovered brilliantly and became the centre of the Italian renaissance in art; but in 1527, under Clement VII, the ally of Francis I against Charles V, it was captured and ruthlessly sacked by German mercenary troops. The restoration and the further embellishment of the city occupied the attention of many succeeding popes. In Feb 1798, the French entered Rome and proclaimed a republic; Pius VI was carried as a prisoner to France, where he died in 1799. In 1809 Napoleon annexed the States of the Church, already mutilated, to the French Empire; in 1810 the French Senate proclaimed Rome to be the second capital; and in 1811 Napoleon conferred the title of King of Rome on his new-born son. On the fall of Napoleon, Pius VII returned to Rome, to which were restored, also, almost all the works of art that had been removed by the emperor. The city was keenly interested in the agitated period of the 'Risorgimento', or political renaissance of Italy. Pius IX issued a political amnesty in 1846, and in 1848 granted a 'Statuto' or constitution. He blessed the war against Austria and caused his troops to take part in it, but he soon withdrew from the enterprise, believing himself to be threatened by the liberals in his domains. He retired to Gaeta, and a republic was proclaimed at Rome, under the triumvirate of Mazzini, Saffi, and Armellini, who entrusted the defence of the city to Garibaldi. The army despatched by France to the aid of the pope entered Rome on 3 July 1849, and Pius IX returned in the following April. In 1859 the Romagna joined Piedmont; in 1860, after the defeat of the papal forces at Castelfidardo, Cialdini occupied the Marches and Umbria; and on 20 Sept 1870, the Italian army, under Raffaello Cadorna, entered Rome by a breach in the walls beside the Porta Pia. Shortly afterwards Rome was proclaimed the capital of united Italy. Since then the capital has seen its population rapidly increase and has prominently shared in all national events.

After the First World War (which had little direct effect on Rome), the movement known as *Fascismo,* organized by Benito Mussolini, rapidly developed. 28 October 1922, saw the 'March on Rome' of Mussolini and his myrmidons, after which the King, Victor Emmanuel III, invited Mussolini to form a government. Fascist rule prevailed until its overthrow on 25 July 1943, in the middle of the Second World War. In the period between the wars—on 11 February 1929—the Lateran Treaty (the 'Conciliazione') was signed. By its provisions the Vatican City became an independent sovereign state (see p. 261). Italy entered the Second World War on the Axis side on 10 June 1940. On 10 July 1943, the Allies landed in Sicily, and on 3 September the Allied invasion of the mainland began, when the British 8th Army landed in Southern Italy. The objective of the subsequent landings at Anzio and Nettuno (22 January 1944) was at length achieved on 4 June 1944, when elements of the American 5th Army entered the city of Rome by the Porta Maggiore from the Vie Casilina and Prenestina, and by the Porta San Giovanni from the Via Appia Nuova. On 28 April 1945 Mussolini was killed after his capture by Italian partisans while attempting to escape into Switzerland. On 9 May 1946, Victor Emmanuel III abdicated. Less than a month later a general election, with a referendum on the form of government, was held. The referendum favoured the establishment of a republic. The royal family left the country on 13 June and on 28 June a provisional President was elected. On 22 December 1947, the Constituent Assembly approved the new republican constitution.

## Growth of Rome

According to legend, supported by archæology, the first settlements were on the Palatine, where excavations have laid bare the remains of a hut village of the Early Iron Age. The Sabines settled on the Quirinal, while the Romans built a citadel on the Capitoline Hill. In the valley between the Palatine, the Capitoline, and the Esquiline—later the site of the Roman Forum—was the necropolis of the original settlers. Here have been discovered a cemetery of the Early Iron Age (10C-8C B.C.) and the Lapis Niger, possibly the burial-place of Romulus. King Ancus

Marcius is said to have built the Tulianum, or Mamertine Prison, and to have founded Ostia, the port of Rome. Tarquinius Priscus is credited with the building of the Temple of Jupiter Capitolinus and Servius Tullius with the building of the Servian Wall. Livy ascribes to Tarquinius Superbus, the last of the kings of Rome, the construction of the Cloaca Maxima, which still functions after 25 centuries.

Under the Republic the city grew in size and dignity. After the conquest of Greece in 146 B.C. the Roman architects were inspired by the developed forms of Greek art; but long before this they had been active. The Appian Way, dating from 312 B.C., became lined with tombs, among them the Tomb of the Scipios and the Tomb of Cecilia Metella. Some of the most ancient buildings in the Roman Forum were rebuilt or restored centuries later; among them are the Temple of Saturn, founded in 497 B.C. and rebuilt in the 1C B.C. and again in the 4C A.D.; the Temple of Castor (or Dioscuri), built in 484 B.C. and several times rebuilt; and the Temple of Concord, built in 366 B.C. and restored in the 2C B.C. On the ancient walls of the first citadel was erected the Tabularium in 78 B.C. The elegant Temple of Fortuna Virilis dates from the 3C B.C. On the left bank of the Tiber were built the great warehouses of the Emporia (193 B.C.). Julius Caesar adorned the Roman Forum with the Basilica Julia and he built the forum named after himself, first of the imperial fora.

Under the Empire the expansion and embellishment of the city went on apace. To Augustus are ascribed the Porticus of Octavia, the Temple of Julius Caesar, the Theatre of Marcellus, the Forum of Augustus, with its Temple of Mars Ultor, the emperor's house on the Palatine, his own Mausoleum, and the Ara Pacis Augustae. Augustus restored many buildings and there is truth in the boast that he found the city brick and left it marble. Rome, which he divided into 14 *Regiones,* had in his reign virtually attained the size that it preserved for centuries. M. Vipsanius Agrippa built the Pantheon, a temple of Neptune in celebration of naval victories, and the first thermae in Rome (19 B.C.).

Tiberius restored the Temple of Castor (or Dioscuri) and built the Temple of Augustus. Caligula is said to have united his palace on the Palatine with the Temple of Jupiter on the Capitol by means of a bridge, of which no traces survive. He also began in A.D. 38 the aqueduct which Claudius finished in 52. After the fire of A.D. 64, Nero began to rebuild the city on a regular plan and he erected his stupendous Golden House, which he adorned with a colossal statue of himself as the Sun. Vespasian rebuilt the Temple of Claudius. He began in 72, and his son Titus completed in 80, that masterpiece of Roman architecture, the Colosseum. Titus built his Thermae on the Oppian Hill and, with his brother Domitian, the Temple of Vespasian in the Forum. The Senate and Roman people commemorated his and Vespasian's victories in Judaea by erecting the Arch of Titus. Domitian erected his grandiose palace on the Palatine, rebuilt the Curia in the Roman Forum and began the Forum completed by Nerva in 97. Under Trajan the architect Apollodorus designed the Forum of Trajan, with its famous column and the spacious Basilica Ulpia.

Hadrian ordered the execution of several important projects. These included the Temple of Venus and Rome, overlooking the Colosseum and of vast dimensions, his Mausoleum, later the Castel Sant'Angelo, and the neighbouring Pons Aelius (Ponte Sant'Angelo). His most significant undertaking was the planning of his famous Villa near Tibur (Tivoli). Under Antoninus Pius the Senate decreed the erection of the Temple of Faustina, one of the most beautiful in the Roman Forum, dedicated also to him after his death. The victories of Marcus Aurelius were commemorated by his famous column (in Piazza Colonna).

From now on began the decadence of Roman architecture. The Arch of Septimius Severus (A.D. 203), despite its imposing mass and rich ornamentation, is inferior to earlier monuments. In 217, however, Caracalla erected his famous Thermæ, which eclipsed in size and magnificence all previous construction of this type. From the 3rd century date also the Arch of Janus, the Amphitheatrum Castrense, the Septizonium of Septimius Severus, demolished by Sixtus V, the Arch of Gallienus, and the so-called Temple of Minerva Medica. Aurelian (A.D. 270-275) built a new city wall which enclosed all the seven hills and part of the Janiculum across the Tiber. It was several times restored; most of it survives.

At the beginning of the 4C the Temple of Saturn (see above) was restored again. In 302 Diocletian began the erection of his Thermæ, the largest in Rome, which were completed by Constantine in 306. Maxentius built a temple and a circus in honour of his son Romulus Maxentius, and began the huge basilica in the Forum which Constantine completed. The Arch of Constantine, built close to the Colosseum in 315, is the last notable specimen of Roman architecture, but its statues and reliefs come from earlier works. The contemporary mausoleum of Constantine's daughter, Constantia, later became the church of Santa Costanza. The Portico of the Dii Consentes, erected in 367, is probably the last pagan monument of Rome.

Art for a time now died out in Rome. The city, devastated by barbarians and swept by conflagrations, became more and more depopulated and ruined, until a new force arose to carry on its history. The Christians, at first compelled to elude persecution by hiding in the Catacombs, used them as their cemeteries and places of worship; but after Constantine had granted liberty of worship in 313, and when the new creed became the State religion under Theodosius (d. 395), the Christians began to erect churches and baptisteries. A primitive oratory had been built c. A.D. 155 over the tomb of St Peter and the first basilica of St Peter was consecrated in November 326 (see p. 265). Other early Christian places of worship were the church of St Pudentiana, the chapel of St Petronilla, and the baptistery of St John. To the 4C are assigned also Santa Maria in Trastévere, Sant'Alessio, and Santa Prisca on the Aventine. To Constantine is attributed—in some cases on slender grounds—the foundation of St John Lateran, St Peter's, San Paolo fuori le Mura, Santa Croce in Gerusalemme, Sant'Agnese fuori le Mura, and San Lorenzo fuori le Mura.

The churches of the 5C include Santa Sabina, which retains the typical basilican form of the primitive Christian churches, Santo Stefano Rotondo, and San Teodoro. Santi Cosma e Damiano dates from the 6C. To the 7C belongs the oratory of San Venanzio, the apse-mosaics in which are the last expression of Roman art before it succumbed to Byzantine influence. Santa Maria Antiqua and the reconstructed church of Santi Nereo ed Achilleo, dating from the 8C;

and the rebuilt church of Santa Maria in Domnica, the chapel of St Zeno, and the church of Santa Cecilia in Trastévere, dating from the 9C, are all remarkable for their mosaics. The walls of the Leonine City likewise date from the 9C.

The characteristic portal of San Cosimato is of the 10C; so also are the puteal in the cloisters of St John Lateran and probably the Casa di Crescenzio. Santa Maria in Cappella was built in the 11C. The 12C saw, after the devastation of Robert Guiscard, the restoration of San Clemente, Santi Quattro Coronati, Santi Giovanni e Paolo, San Lorenzo in Lucina, Santa Maria in Cosmedin, Santa Maria in Trastévere, and Santa Maria Nova. In the same century were built the cloisters of San Cosimato, the campanile of Santa Cecilia in Trastévere, and the cloister of San Lorenzo fuori le Mura.

In the early 13C San Saba and San Giorgio in Velabro were rebuilt, and the Torre dei Conti and Torre delle Milizie were erected, together with a large number of similar towers, afterwards pulled down; the senator Brancaleone is said to have demolished 140 of them in 1257. From this century date also the present basilica of San Lorenzo fuori le Mura, the charming cloisters of St John Lateran and San Paolo fuori le Mura, the rebuilding of Santi Vincenzo ed Anastasio, the reconstruction of Santa Maria in Aracoeli in the Franciscan Romanesque-Gothic style, the portal of Sant'Antonio, and the Cosmatesque chapel of the Sancta Sanctorum. Santa Maria sopra Minerva, built near the close of the century, is the only church in Rome with a Gothic interior.

To the Renaissance, which appeared late in Rome, belong Palazzo Capranica and the severe Palazzo di Venezia, which still looks like a fortress despite its graceful 15C windows and portals. To the last part of the century belong also the House of Manlius, the Palazzi del Governo Vecchio, dei Penitenzieri, and Santacroce; the church of Sant'Agostino; the rebuilt Ponte Sisto; the hospital of Santo Spirito with its beautiful tower; the Sistine Chapel in the Vatican; the rebuilding of San Cosimato, Santa Maria del Popolo, and Santa Maria in Via Lata; and the façade of Santa Maria sopra Minerva. Palazzo della Cancelleria is the masterpiece of the 15C in Rome. In the latter half of the century Hadrian's Mausoleum began to be transformed into a fortress and Alexander VI made himself responsible for the Borgia Rooms in the Vatican.

Pope Julius II (1503-13), who laid the first stone of the new St Peter's and built Via Giulia, enlarged the Vatican Palace and employed Bramante, Michelangelo, and Raphael, the three greatest geniuses of the age, to carry out his plans. The golden age of Italian art lasted into the papacy of Leo X (1513-21). Among the monuments of the two reigns are the little temple of San Pietro in Montorio, Palazzo Cenci, Santa Maria dell'Anima, the cloister of Santa Maria della Pace, the Palazzo Torlonia, Santa Maria di Loreto, San Giovanni dei Fiorentini, Villa Farnesina, Palazzo Baldassimi, and Villa Madama.

From the 16C date Palazzo Massimo alle Colonne, Palazzo Farnese, perhaps the most dignified and impressive in Rome, the Porta Santo Spirito, the rearrangement of Piazza del Campidoglio by Michelangelo, Palazzo Spada, Villa Medici, Villa di Papa Giulio, the Palazzina of Pius IV, Michelangelo's transformation of the great hall of Diocletian's Thermæ into the church of Santa Maria degli Angeli and his building of the adjoining cloisters, Palazzo Regis, Santa Caterina dei Funari, the Gesù, Santa Maria in Vallicella, Palazzo del Collegio Romano, Palazzo del Quirinale (not completed until the reign of Clement XII), and many other public and private buildings.

The energetic pope Sixtus V (1585-90) did more than any of his predecessors to improve and adorn the city. He not only built new long and straight streets, but he completed the dome of St Peter's and brought the water of the Acqua Felice to the centre of Rome. Palazzo Borghese and the church of Sant'Andrea della Valle date from the end of the 16C.

It is to the 17C that Rome owes its Baroque aspect of today. Paul V (1605-21) completed St Peter's (consecrated by Urban VIII in 1626), and erected the great fountain on the Janiculum for the Acqua Paola, which he had brought to Rome. Urban VIII (1623-44) was the patron of Bernini, whose greatest work was the colonnade in the Piazza San Pietro. To this period belong also Palazzo Mattei, Palazzo Barberini, Sant'Ignazio, Villa Doria Pamphilj, Palazzo Pamphilj, now Palazzo Doria, the twin churches of Piazza del Popolo, the Palazzo Altieri, Palazzo di Montecitorio, and the remarkable fountains of Bernini, the most striking of which is in Piazza Navona. In the latter half of the 17C were built the façade of Santa Maria della Pace, and the church of Santa Maria in Campitelli. The chief exponent of the Baroque school was Borromini, who built the church and dome of Palazzo della Sapienza, the convent of the Filippini, and the campanile and apse of Sant'Andrea delle Fratte. Palazzo Doria is another striking Baroque edifice.

The flamboyant staircase and façade of the Trinità dei Monti date from the 18C, as do the façades of San Giovanni dei Fiorentini and St John Lateran. To the 18C belong also the Fontana di Trevi, Villa Torlonia (ex-Albani), Palazzo Corsini, Palazzo della Consulta, the façade of Santa Maria Maggiore, and Palazzo Braschi. The present appearance of Piazza del Popolo dates from the pontificate of Pius VII (1800-23). Leo XII (1823-29) began the rebuilding of San Paolo fuori le Mura, and Pius IX erected the Columns of the Immaculate Conception.

Since Rome resumed her place as the capital of Italy, much has been done to improve the amenities of the city, albeit at the expense of the picturesque. Old quarters such as those of the Campitelli and the Ghetto have been destroyed; new quarters have been built outside the walls to accommodate the ever-increasing population. New streets and squares have been built and vistas created. Existing parks and gardens have been improved and new ones opened. The obtrusive Victor Emmanuel monument (1911) presaged the 'Imperial' style of the Mussolini era. The climax of replanning was reached in the thirties of this century. The Capitol is now flanked by broad thoroughfares, both opened in 1933— Via dei Fori Imperiali on one side and Via del Teatro di Marcello on the other. Excavations in Rome, particularly on the Palatine, have yielded fruitful results. Beyond the Tiber, the Borgo was transformed by the building of Via della Conciliazione (1937), which leads direct from the Tiber to Piazza San Pietro. Of the other developments one of the most significant has been the construction of Esposizione Universale di Roma (E.U.R.), typical of the grandiose conception of Fascist Rome. Instead of five bridges spanning the Tiber there are now twenty-one, among the newest being the Ponte Flaminio (1951).

The vast complex of buildings of the University of Rome known as the Città Universitaria was completed in 1935. For the Olympic Games of 1960 the Foro Italico of 1931 was enlarged and modernized, and the Stadio Flaminio and the daring Palazzo dello Sport were built. Transport is well served by the main railway station, the Stazione di Termini, opened in December 1950 and claimed to be the largest in Europe. Its reconstruction was accompanied by the enlargement of Piazza dei Cinquecento.

The city of Rome emerged almost scatheless from the Second World War, although the surrounding country suffered much devastation. The only major damage in Rome was that to the church of San Lorenzo fuori le Mura, which was partly wrecked by bombing in 1943.

### The Walls of Rome

Rome has from time immemorial been a walled city. The earliest settlements on the Palatine, united, according to tradition by Romulus, to form the city in 753 B.C., were surrounded with a wall of tufa blocks. The area enclosed was more or less rectangular and became known as *Roma Quadrata*. Fragments of this wall, which had three gates, still are in existence. Little by little the inhabitants of Roma Quadrata obtained the mastery of the neighbouring hills and formed the city of the *Septimontium* by the union of the three summits of the Palatine (Palatium, Germalus, and Velia) with the four of the Esquiline (Oppius, Cispius, Fagutalis, and Subura).

After further acquisitions there arose the *City of the Four Regions*. The regions were the Palatine, the Subura (incl. the Cælian), the Esquiline, and the Collina (incl. the Quirinal). This area was eventually surrounded by a formidable line of fortifications c. 11 km. long, known as the **Servian Wall**. Its traditional creator was Servius Tullius, sixth king of Rome; it is now thought that the wall dates from about 378 B.C. There were 12 gates, the sites of some of which are conjectural. The wall ran S. from the Porta Collina (N. of the Baths of Diocletian) past the Porta Viminale and the Porta Esquilina (W. of the Stazione Termini) to the Porta Celimontana, near the present Porta San Giovanni. At this point the wall curved to the W. round the base of the Cælian to the Porta Capena, below the Palatine, the starting-point of the Appian Way (Rte 16). Thence it took an irregular course round the Aventine (several gates) to the Tiber, which it bordered as far as the Pons Aemilius (Ponte Rotto; p. 87). It then ran N. and N.E. past the W. side of the Capitol, and the W. and N. sides of the Quirinal to the Porta Salutare. Hence, after a slight detour, it bore E. to the Porta Collina.

After 87 B.C., during a period of civil strife between Marius and Sulla, a part of Trastévere was fortified. A new wall ran from the Pons Aemilius to the Porta Aurelia (Porta San Pancrazio), on the Janiculum, and another back to the Tiber, opposite the Aventine.

To Aurelian (emperor 270–275) is due the building of the **Aurelian Wall**, most of which survives to this day. Although Aurelian had defeated the invading Alemanni in two decisive battles, he was taking no chances, and he erected his wall immediately afterwards. The enceinte took in all the seven hills, the Campus Martius, and the previously fortified area of Trastévere. It was about 19 km. round and had 18 main gates and 381 towers. From the Porta Flaminia (now Porta del Popolo) it ran irregularly along the Pincio to the Porta Salaria. Thence it turned S.E., took in the Castro Pretorio and continued S.E. to the Porta Tiburtina (Porta San Lorenzo) and the Porta Prenestina (Porta Maggiore). Here describing an acute angle, it bent back past the Porta Asinaria (Porta San Giovanni; near the Porta Cælimontana; see above) to the Porta Metronia. It next ran S. past the Porta Latina to the Porta Appia (Porta San Sebastiano), thus enclosing part of the Appian Way within the city boundaries. From this point the wall turned W. to the Tiber. It now followed the left bank of the river. By the Pons Sublicius (the present Ponte Aventino) it crossed the river. Passing the Porta Portuense (Porta Portese) it ran N.W. to the Porta Aurelia (comp. above). Returning N.E. to the Porta Settimiana, it recrossed the Tiber, and followed the left bank of that river, skirting the Campus Martius, until it turned E. to reach the Porta Flaminia. Aurelian made a bridgehead of the Castel Sant'Angelo in his fortifications.

The walls were restored by Honorius and Arcadius in 403 A.D. They continued to be the defence of Rome until 1870 when the army of the Kingdom of Italy breached them with modern artillery, N.W. of the Porta Pia.

The walls are mostly well preserved and many of the gates are still in use under their modern names. Although the city has spread far beyond Aurelian's wall, most of its treasures are within its confines. One important exception is the basilica of San Paolo fuori le Mura; others are San Lorenzo and Sant'Agnese fuori le Mura.

## LIST OF ROMAN EMPERORS

| | | | |
|---|---|---|---|
| 27 B.C.-A.D. 14 | Augustus | 270-75 | Aurelian |
| 14-37 | Tiberius | 275-76 | Tacitus |
| 37-41 | Caligula | 276 | Florian |
| 41-54 | Claudius | 276-82 | Probus |
| 54-68 | Nero | 282-83 | Carus |
| 68-69 | Galba | 282-85 | Carinus |
| 69 | Otho | 283-84 | Numerian |
| 69 | Vitellius | 285-305 | Diocletian |
| 69-79 | Vespasian | 286-305 | Maximian |
| 79-81 | Titus | 305-06 | Constantius Chlorus |
| 81-96 | Domitian | 305-10 | Galerius |
| 96-98 | Nerva | 308-24 | Licinius |
| 98-117 | Trajan | 306-07 | Flavius Severus |
| 117-38 | Hadrian | 306-12 | Maxentius |
| 138-61 | Antoninus Pius | 308-14 | Maximinus |
| 161-80 | Marcus Aurelius | 306-37 | Constantine the Great |
| 161-69 | Lucius Verus | 337-40 | Constantine II |
| 180-92 | Commodus | 337-50 | Constans |
| 193 | Pertinax | 337-61 | Constantinus II |
| 193 | Didius Julianus | 350-53 | Magnentius |
| 193-211 | Septimius Severus | 361-63 | Julian |
| 211-17 | Caracalla | 363-64 | Jovian |
| 211-12 | Geta | 364-75 | Valentinian I |
| 217-18 | Macrinus | 364-78 | Valens |
| 218-22 | Heliogabalus | 367-83 | Gratian |
| 222-35 | Alexander Severus | 375-92 | Valentinian II |
| 235-38 | Maximinus | 378-95 | Theodosius I |
| 238 | Gordian I | | |
| | Gordian II | | WESTERN EMPIRE |
| 238 | Pupienus | | |
| | Balbinus | 395-423 | Honorius |
| 238-44 | Gordian III | 425-55 | Valentinian III |
| 244-49 | Philip I | 455 | Petronius Maximus |
| 247-49 | Philip II | 455-56 | Avitus |
| 249-51 | Decius | 457-61 | Majorian |
| 251-53 | Trebonianus Gallus | 461-65 | Libius Severus |
| 253 | Aemilian | 467-72 | Anthemius |
| 253-60 | Valerian | 472 | Olybrius |
| 253-68 | Gallienus | 473 | Glycerius |
| 268-70 | Claudius | 474-75 | Julius Nepos |
| 270 | Quintillus | 475-76 | Romulus Augustulus |

# CHRONOLOGICAL LIST OF THE POPES

Various points in early papal history must be regarded as still uncertain: thus the evidence for Dioscuros as legitimate pope is perhaps stronger than the evidence for Boniface II (No. 55); Leo VIII (no. 132) is an antipope if the deposition of John XII (No. 131) was illegal, and if Leo VIII was a legitimate pope, Benedict V (No. 133) is an antipope; and if the triple deposition of Benedict IX (No. 146) was illegal, Sylvester III, Gregory VI, and Clement II (Nos. 147, 149, 150) must rank as antipopes. Among the popes named John there was never a John XX. The title 'pope' was first assumed by John VIII (d. 882); the triple tiara first appears on the sepulchral effigy of Benedict XII (d. 1342). Adrian IV (d. 1159) was the only English pope, Gregory XI (d. 1378) the last French pope and Adrian VI (d. 1523) the last non-Italian pope, before John Paul II. [Anacletus II (d. 1138) was a converted Jew. 'Pope Joan' is placed between John V (d. 686) and Conon.]

The names of antipopes and of illegal occupants of the papal chair and particulars as to papal tombs imperfectly identified or no longer in existence are enclosed in square brackets [ ]. Conjectural dates are followed by a query (?). The title of each pope is given, together with the date of his consecration (for the early popes) or of his election (from Gelasius II onward; No. 162), the date of his death, the duration of his pontificate, and, as far as possible, his birthplace, family name, and place of interment. Martyred popes are indicated by the letter M. Most of the early tombs in the old basilica of St Peter were scattered or lost on the demolition of the church by Julius II; but some of the remains of the popes were collected in two ossuaries in the Grotte Vaticane.

St Peter's remains are preserved beneath the altar of the Confession in St Peter's and the thirteen following popes are believed to be interred close by. Churches mentioned below are in Rome, unless otherwise indicated.

|  |  | Began to reign |
|---|---|---|
| 1. | ST PETER; M.; 42-67 | 42 |
| 2. | ST LINUS of Tuscia (Volterra?); M.; 67-78 | 67 |
| 3. | ST ANACLETUS I, of Rome; M.; 78-90 (?) | 78 |
| 4. | ST CLEMENT I, of the Roman Flavian gens; M.; 90-99 (?). D. at Cherson (Crimea), relics in San Clemente | 90 |
| 5. | ST EVARISTUS, of Greece (or of Bethlehem); M.; 99-105 (?) | 99 |
| 6. | ST ALEXANDER I, of Rome; M.; 105-115 (?) | 105 |
| 7. | ST SIXTUS I, of Rome, M.; 115-125 (?) | 115 |
| 8. | ST TELESPHORUS, of Greece; M.; 125-136 (?) | 125 |
| 9. | ST IGINUS, of Greece; M.; 136-140 (?) | 136 |
| 10. | ST PIUS I, of Italy; M.; 140-155 (?) | 140 |
| 11. | ST ANICETUS, of Syria; M.; 155-166 (?) | 155 |
| 12. | ST SOTER, of Campania (Fundi?); M.; 166-175 (?) | 166 |
| 13. | ST ELEUTHERUS, of Epirus (Nicopolis?); M.; 175-189 | 175 |
| 14. | ST VICTOR I, of Africa; M.; 189-199 | 189 |
| 15. | ST ZEPHYRINUS, of Rome; M.; 199-217. Int. near the Cimitero di San Callisto | 199 |
| 16. | ST CALIXTUS I, of Rome; M.; 217-222. Int. in the Cimitero di Calepodio, on the Via Aurelia Vetus; relics in Santa Maria in Trastevere | 217 |
| [HIPPOLYTUS, 217-235] | | |
| 17. | ST URBAN I, of Rome; M.; 222-230. Int. in the Cimitero di San Callisto; relics in Santa Cecilia in Trastévere | 222 |
| 18. | ST PONTIANUS, of Rome; M.; 21 July 230-28 Sept 235. Int. in the Cimitero di San Callisto; relics in Santa Prassede | 230 |
| 19. | ST ANTERUS, of Greece; M.; 21 Nov 235-3 Jan 236. Int. in the Cimitero di San Callisto; relics in San Silvestro in Capite | 235 |
| 20. | ST FABIAN, of Rome; M.; 10 Jan 236-20 Jan 250. Int. in the Cimitero di San Callisto; relics in Santa Prassede (?) | 236 |

21. ST CORNELIUS, of Rome; M.; March 251-June 253. Int. near the    251
    Cimitero di San Callisto; relics in Santa Maria in Trastévere
[NOVATIAN, 251-258]
22. ST LUCIUS I, of Rome; M.; 25 June 253-5 March 254. Int. in the    253
    Cimitero di San Callisto; relics in Santa Cecilia in Trastévere
23. ST STEPHEN I, of Rome; M.; 12 May 254-2 Aug 257. Int. in the    254
    Cimitero di San Callisto; relics in San Silvestro in Capite
24. ST SIXTUS II, of Greece (?); M.; 30 Aug 257-6 Aug 258. Int. in the    257
    Cimitero di San Callisto; relics in San Sisto Vecchio
25. ST DIONYSIUS, of Magna Graecia (?); M.; 22 July 259-26 Dec 268.    259
    [Int. in the Cimitero di San Callisto]
26. ST FELIX I, of Rome; M.; 5 Jan 269-30 Dec 274. Int. in the Cimi-    269
    tero di San Callisto, afterwards in Santa Prassede
27. ST EUTYCHIANUS, of Luni; M.; 4 Jan 275-7 Dec 283. Int. in the    275
    Cimitero di San Callisto; relics in Sarzana cathedral
28. ST GAIUS, of Dalmatia (Salona?); M.; 17 Dec 283-22 April 296.    283
    Int. in the Cimitero di San Callisto
29. ST MARCELLINUS, of Rome; M.; 30 June 296-25 Oct 304. Int. in the    296
    Cimitero di Priscilla, Via Salaria
30. ST MARCELLUS I, of Rome; M.; 27 May 308-16 Jan 309. Int. in the    308
    Cimitero di Priscilla; relics in San Marcello
31. ST EUSEBIUS, of Greece; M.; 18 April 309-17 Aug 309 or 310. Int.    309
    in the Cimitero di San Callisto
32. ST MELCHIADES or *Miltiades,* of Africa; M.; 2 July 311-11 Jan 314.    311
    Int. near the Cimitero di San Callisto; relics in San Silvestro in
    Capite
33. ST SYLVESTER I, of Rome; 31 Jan 314-31 Dec 335. Int. in the Cimi-    314
    tero di Priscilla; relics in San Silvestro in Capite
34. ST MARK, of Rome; 18 Jan 336-7 Oct 336. Int. in the Cimitero di    336
    Santa Balbina, Via Ardeatina; relics in San Marco
35. ST JULIUS I, of Rome; 6 Feb 337-12 April 352. Int. in the Cimitero    337
    di Calepodio, Via Aurelia Vetus; relics in Santa Maria in Traste-
    vere
36. LIBERIUS, of Rome; 17 May 352-22 Sept 366. Int. in the Cimitero di    352
    Priscilla
[ST FELIX II, 355-22 Nov 365.] Tomb on the Via Aurelia Vetus
37. ST DAMASUS I, of Spain; 1 Oct 366-11 Dec 384. Int. in his family    366
    tomb, Via Ardeatina; relics in San Lorenzo in Damaso
[URSINUS, 366-367]
38. ST SIRICIUS, of Rome; 15 Dec 384-26 Nov 399. Int. above the    384
    Cimitero di Priscilla
39. ST ANASTASIUS I, of Rome; 27 Nov 399-19 Dec 401. Int. near the    399
    Cimitero di San Ponziano, Via Portuense
40. ST INNOCENT I, of Albano; 22 Dec 401-12 March 417. Int. near the    401
    Cimitero di San Ponziano
41. ST ZOSIMUS, of Greece; 18 March 417-26 Dec 418. Int. on the Via    417
    Tiburtina, near the tomb of St Laurence
42. ST BONIFACE I, of Rome; 29 Dec 418-4 Sept 422. Int. in the    418
    Cimitero di Santa Felicità
[EULALIUS, 27 Dec 418-3 April 419]
43. ST CELESTINE I, of Campania; 10 Sept 422-27 July 432. Int. above    422
    the Cimitero di Priscilla
44. ST SIXTUS III, of Rome; 3 July (?) 432-19 Aug 440. Int. on the Via    432
    Tiburtina, near the tomb of St Laurence
45. ST LEO I the Great, of Tusculum; 29 Sept 440-10 Nov 461. Int.    440
    under the portico of St Peter's; relics in St Peter's
46. ST HILARY, of Sardinia; 19 Nov 461-29 Feb 468. Int. on the Via    461
    Tiburtina, near the tomb of St Laurence

47. ST SIMPLICIUS, of Tivoli; 3 March 468-10 March 483. [Int. under    468
    the portico of St Peter's]
48. ST FELIX III (II), of Rome, of the Gens Anicia; 13 March 483-1    483
    March 492. [Int. in San Paolo fuori le Mura]
49. ST GELASIUS I, of Africa; 1 March 492-21 Nov 496. Int. under the    492
    portico of St Peter's
50. ST ANASTASIUS II, of Rome; 24 Nov 496-19 Nov. 498. Int. in St    496
    Peter's
51. ST SYMMACHUS, of Sardinia; 22 Nov 498-19 July 514. [Int. in St    498
    Peter's]
[LAURENTIUS, Nov 498-505]
52. ST HORMISDAS, of Frosinone; 20 July 514-6 Aug 523. [Int. under    514
    the portico of St Peter's]
53. ST JOHN I, of Tusculum; M.; 13 Aug 523-18 May 526. Died at    523
    Ravenna. [Int. under the portico of St Peter's]
54. ST FELIX IV (III), of Samnium (Benevento ?); 12 July 526-22 Sept    526
    530. [Int. under the portico of St Peter's]
55. BONIFACE II, of Rome; 22 Sept 530-7 Oct 532. [Int. under the    530
    portico of St Peter's]
[DIOSCUROS, 22 Sept 530-14 Oct 530]
56. JOHN II, of Rome; 2 Jan 533-8 May 535. [Int. under the portico of    533
    St Peter's]
57. ST AGAPETUS I, of Rome; 13 May 535-22 April 536. Died at Con-    535
    stantinople. [Int. under the portico of St Peter's]
58. ST SILVERIUS, of Frosinone; M.; 8 June 536-deposed 11 March 537.    536
    Died in exile on the island of Ponza 538 (?). [Int. on the island of
    Ponza]
59. VIGILIUS, of Rome; June 538 (?)-7 June 555 (but elected 29 March    538
    537). Died at Syracuse. Int. at Rome [in the Cimitero di Priscilla]
60. PELAGIUS I, of Rome; 16 April 556-4 March 561. [Int. under the    556
    portico of St Peter's]
61. JOHN III, of Rome; 17 July 561-13 July 574. [Tomb in St Peter's]    561
62. BENEDICT I, of Rome; 2 June 575-30 July 579. [Tomb in St Peter's]    575
63. PELAGIUS II, of Rome; 26 Nov 579-7 Feb 590. [Tomb in St Peter's]    579
64. ST GREGORY I the Great, of Rome, of the Gens Anicia; 3 Sept 590-    590
    13 March 604. Tomb and relics in St Peter's (Capp. Clementina)
65. SABINIANUS, of Tusculum; 13 Sept 604-22 Feb 606. [Tomb in St    604
    Peter's]
66. BONIFACE III, of Rome; 19 Feb 607-12 Nov 607. [Tomb in St    607
    Peter's]
67. ST BONIFACE IV, of Valeria de' Marsi; 25 Aug 608-8 May 615.    608
    Tomb in St Peter's; transferred to the new basilica, altar of St
    Thomas
68. ST DEODATUS I, of Rome; 19 Oct 615-8 Nov 618. [Tomb in St    615
    Peter's]
69. BONIFACE V, of Naples; 23 Dec 619-25 Oct 625. [Tomb in St Peter's]    619
70. HONORIUS I, of Campania; 27 Oct 625-12 Oct 638. (Int. in San-    625
    t'Agnese fuori le Mura)
71. SEVERINUS, of Rome; 28 May 640-2 Aug 640. [Tomb in St Peter's]    640
72. JOHN IV, of Dalmatia; 24 Dec 640-12 Oct 642. [Tomb in St Peter's]    640
73. THEODORE I, of Jerusalem (? or Greece); 24 Nov 642-14 May 649.    642
    [Tomb in St Peter's]
74. ST MARTIN I, of Todi; M.; 21 July 649-exiled 18 June 653-16 Sept    649
    655. Died at Sebastopol; relics in San Martino ai Monti
75. ST EUGENIUS I, of Rome, 16 Sept 655-2 June 657; consecrated 10    655
    Aug 654. [Tomb in St Peter's]
76. ST VITALIAN, of Segni; 30 July 657-27 Jan 672. [Tomb in St Peter's]    657
77. DEODATUS II, of Rome; 11 April 672-17 June 676. [Tomb in St    672
    Peter's]

78.  DONUS, of Rome; 2 Nov 676-11 April 678. [Tomb in St Peter's]        676
79.  ST AGATHO, of Sicily; 27 June 678-10 Jan 681. [Tomb in St Peter's]   678
80.  ST LEO II, of Sicily; 17 Aug 682-3 July 683. Tomb and relics in St   682
     Peter's (Cappella della Colonna)
81.  ST BENEDICT II, of Rome; 26 June 684-8 May 685. [Tomb in St          684
     Peter's]
82.  JOHN V, of Antioch; 23 July 685-2 Aug 686. [Tomb in St Peter's]      685
83.  CONON, of Thrace; 21 Oct 686-21 Sept 687. [Tomb in St Peter's]       686
[THEODORE, 22 Sept 687-Oct 687]
[PASCHAL, 687]
84.  ST SERGIUS I, of Palermo; 15 Dec 687-8 Sept 701. [Tomb in St         687
     Peter's]
85.  JOHN VI, of Greece; 30 Oct 701-11 Jan 705. [Tomb in St Peter's]      701
86.  JOHN VII, of Greece; 1 March 705-18 Oct 707. [Tomb in St Peter's]    705
87.  SISINNIUS, of Syria; 15 Jan 708-4 Feb 708                            708
88.  CONSTANTINE, of Syria; 25 March 708-9 April 715. [Tomb in St         708
     Peter's]
89.  ST GREGORY II, of Rome; 19 May 715-11 Feb 731. [Tomb in St          715
     Peter's]
90.  ST GREGORY III, of Syria; 18 March 731-10 Dec 741. [Tomb in St       731
     Peter's]
91.  ST ZACHARIAS, of Greece; 10 Dec 741-22 March 752. [Tomb in St        741
     Peter's]
92.  STEPHEN II, of Rome; 23 March 752-25 March 752. Burial place         752
     unknown
93.  ST STEPHEN III, of Rome; 26 March 752-26 April 757. [Tomb in St      752
     Peter's]
94.  ST PAUL I, of Rome; 29 May 757-28 June 767. [Tomb in St             757
     Peter's]
[CONSTANTINE II, 5 July 767-murdered 769]
[PHILIP, elected 31 July 768-abdicated 768]
95.  STEPHEN IV, of Sicily; 7 Aug 768-3 Feb 772. [Tomb in St Peter's]     768
96.  ADRIAN I, of Rome; 9 Feb 772-26 Dec 795 [Tomb in St Peter's];        772
     epitaph, dictated by Charlemagne, under the portico of St Peter's
97.  ST LEO III, of Rome; 27 Dec 795-12 June 816. Tomb and relics in      795
     St Peter's (Cappella della Colonna)
98.  ST STEPHEN V, of Rome; 22 June 816-14 Jan 817. [Tomb in St           816
     Peter's]
99.  ST PASCHAL I, of Rome; 25 Jan 817-11 Feb 824. [Tomb in St           817
     Peter's]
100. EUGENIUS II, of Rome; 21 Feb 824-27 Aug 827.                         824
101. VALENTINE, of Rome; Aug (?) 827-Sept (?) 827. Burial place un-       827
     known
102. GREGORY IV, of Rome; Oct 827-25 Jan 844. [Tomb in St Peter's]        827
103. SERGIUS II, of Rome; Jan 844-27 Jan 847. [Tomb in St Peter's]        844
[JOHN, 844]
104. ST LEO IV, of Rome; 10 April 847-17 July 855. Tomb and relics in     847
     St Peter's (Cappella della Colonna)
105. ST BENEDICT III, of Rome; 6 Oct 855-17 April 858. [Tomb in St        855
     Peter's]
[ANASTASIUS, 29 Sept 855-20 Oct 855]                                      855
106. ST NICHOLAS I, the Great, of Rome; 24 April 858-13 Nov 867.          858
     [Tomb in St Peter's]; epitaph in the Grotte Vaticane
107. ADRIAN II, of Rome; 14 Dec 867-14 Dec 872. [Tomb in St Peter's];     867
     epitaph in the Grotte Vaticane
108. JOHN VIII, of Rome, 14 Dec 872-16 Dec 882. [Tomb in St Peter's]      872
109. MARINUS I (MARTIN II) of Gallesium; 16 Dec 882-15 May 884.           882
     [Tomb in St Peter's]

110. St Adrian III, of Rome; 17 May 884-17 Sept 885. Tomb at Nonantola — 884

111. Stephen VI, of Rome; Sept 885-Sept 891. [Tomb in St Peter's] — 885

112. Formosus, bishop of Porto; 6 Oct 891-4 April 896. Thrown into the Tiber — 891

113. Boniface VI, of Gallesium; April 896 — 896

114. Stephen VII, of Rome; May 896-Aug 897. Strangled in prison — 896

115. Romanus, of Gallesium; Aug 897-end of Nov 897 — 897

116. Theodore II, of Rome; Dec 897-Dec 897 — 897

117. John IX, of Tivoli; Jan 898-Jan 900. [Tomb in St Peter's] — 898

118. Benedict IV, of Rome; Jan 900-end of July 903. [Tomb in St Peter's] — 900

119. Leo V, of Ardea; end of July 903-Sept 903. Deposed and imprisoned. [Int. in St John Lateran] — 903

[Christophorus, of Rome; 903, deposed in Jan 904]

120. Sergius III, of Rome; 29 Jan 904-14 April 911. [Tomb in St Peter's] — 904

121. Anastasius III, of Rome; April 911-June 913. [Tomb in St Peter's] — 911

122. Landonius, of Sabina; end of July 913-Feb 914 — 913

123. John X, of Ravenna; March 914-May 928. Strangled in prison. [Int. in St John Lateran] — 914

124. Leo VI, of Rome; May 928-Dec 928. [Tomb in St Peter's] — 928

125. Stephen VIII, of Rome; Jan 929-Feb 931 — 929

126. John XI, of Rome; son of Pope Sergius III and Marozia; March 931-Dec 935. Died in prison — 931

127. Leo VII; 3(?) Jan 936-13 (?)July 939 — 936

128. Stephen IX, of Germany (?); 14 (?) July 939-end of Oct 942 — 939

129. Marinus II (Martin III), of Rome; 30 (?) Oct 942-May 946 — 942

130. Agapetus II, of Rome; 10 May 946-Dec 955. [Int. in St John Lateran] — 946

131. John XII, Ottaviano, of the family of the Counts of Tusculum, aged 19 yr; 16 (?) Dec 955-deposed 14 May 964. [Int. in St John Lateran] — 955

132. Leo VIII, of Rome, 4 Nov 963-1 March 965 — 963

133. Benedict V, Grammatico, of Rome; 22 (?) May 964-expelled from the pontifical see 23 June 964; died at Bremen 4 July 966. Int. first in Bremen, afterwards in Rome (church unknown) — 964

134. John XIII, of Rome; 1 Oct 965-5 Sept 972. [Int. in San Paolo fuori le Mura] — 965

135. Benedict VI, of Rome; 19 Jan 973-June 974. Strangled in prison — 973

[Boniface VII, Francone, of Rome; June-July 974 for the first time]

136. Benedict VII, of the family of the Counts of Tusculum, of Rome; Oct 974-10 July 983. Tomb in Santa Croce in Gerusalemme — 974

137. John XIV, of Pavia; Dec 938-20 Aug 984; killed by Francone (Boniface VII). [Int. in St John Lateran] — 983

[Boniface VII, Francone; for the second time, Aug 984-murdered July 985]

138. John XV, of Rome; Aug 985-March 996 — 985

139. Gregory V, Bruno, of the family of the Counts of Carinthia; 3 May 996-18 Feb 999. Tomb (an ancient Christian sarcophagus) now in the Grotte Vaticane — 996

[John XVI, John Philagathus, of Greece; March 997-Feb 998]

140. Sylvester II, Gerbert of Aurillac, Auvergne; 2 April 999-12 May 1003. [Tomb in St John Lateran]; epitaph in the s. aisle — 999

141. John XVII, Sicco, of Rome; June (?) 1003-6 Nov 1003. [Tomb in St John Lateran] — 1003

142. John XVIII, of Rapagnano; Jan (?) 1004-July (?) 1009. [Tomb in San Paolo fuori le Mura]; epitaph in the convent — 1004

143. SERGIUS IV, of Rome; 31 July 1009-12 May 1012. [Tomb in St    1009
    John Lateran]; epitaph in the s. aisle
144. BENEDICT VIII, John, of the family of the Counts of Tusculum, of    1012
    Rome; 18 May 1012-9 April 1024
[Gregory, 1012]
145. JOHN XIX, of Rome, brother of Benedict VIII; April 1024-1032    1024
146. BENEDICT IX, Theophylact, of the family of the Counts of    1032
    Tusculum; elected (at 15 yr of age) for the 1st time in 1032-
    deposed in Dec 1044; elected for the 2nd time 10 March 1045-
    deposed 1 May 1045; elected for the 3rd time 8 Nov 1047-deposed
    17 July 1048. Tomb in the monastery of St Nilus at Grottaferrata
147. SYLVESTER III, John, bishop of Sabina; 20 Jan 1045-deposed 10    1045
    March 1045
148. GREGORY VI, Gratian, of Rome; 5 May 1045-banished 20 Dec    1045
    1046; died 1047
149. CLEMENT II, Suidger, bishop of Bamberg; 25 Dec 1046-died at    1046
    Pesaro 9 Oct 1047. Tomb in Bamberg Cathedral
150. DAMASUS II, Poppo, bishop of Bressanone; 17 July    1048
    1048-9 Aug 1048. Died at Palestrina. [Tomb in St John Lateran]
151. ST LEO IX, Bruno, of Germany, bishop of Toul; 12 Feb 1049-19    1049
    April 1054. Int. in St Peter's and transferred to the new basilica
152. VICTOR II, Gebhard, of Germany, bishop of Eichstätt; 16 April    1055
    1055-28 July 1057. Died at Arezzo; tomb at Florence
153. STEPHEN X, Frédéric, of the family of the Dukes of Lorraine; 3    1055
    Aug 1057-29 March 1058. Died and int. in Florence [in the
    church of Santa Reparata, afterwards in the crypt of Santa Maria
    del Fiore]
[Benedict X, of Rome; 5 April 1058-deposed 24 Jan 1059. Tomb in Santa
    Maria Maggiore]
154. NICHOLAS II, Gérard de Bourgogne; 24 Jan 1059-27 (?) July 1061    1059
155. ALEXANDER II, Anselmo of Milan; 30 Sept 1061-21 April 1073.    1061
    [Tomb in St John Lateran]
[Honorius II, appointed by Imperial Diet in Basle 1061-1072]
156. ST GREGORY VII, Hildebrand, di Bonizio Aldobrandeschi, of    1073
    Sovana; 22 April 1073-25 May 1085. Tomb in Salerno Cathedral
[Clement III, Ghiberto; 25 Jan 1080-Sept 1100]
157. B. VICTOR III, Desiderio Epifani, of Benevento; elected 24 May    1086
    1086, consecrated 9 May 1087-16 Sept 1087. Tomb at Monte
    Cassino
158. B. URBAN II, of Reims; 12 March 1088-29 July 1099. [Tomb in St    1088
    Peter's]
159. PASCHAL II, Rainiero, of Breda; 14 Aug 1099-21 Jan 1118. [Tomb    1099
    in St John Lateran]
[THEODORIC, Sept-Dec 1100; epigraph in the cemetery of La Cava]
[ALBERT, Feb-March 1102]
[SYLVESTER IV, 18 Nov 1105-12 April 1111]
160. GELASIUS II, Giov. Caetani, of Gaeta; 24 Jan 1118-28 Jan 1119    1118
    [Tomb at Cluny]
[GREGORY VIII, Maurice Bourdain, of Limoges, 8 March 1118-deposed
    April 1121]
161. CALIXTUS II, Gui de Bourgogne, of Quingey; 2 Feb 1119-13 Dec    1119
    1124. [Tomb in St John Lateran]
162. HONORIUS II, Lamberto Scannabecchi, of Fanano (Modena);    1124
    15 Dec 1124-13 Feb 1130. Died [and buried] in the monastery of
    Sant'Andrea

163. INNOCENT II, Gregorio Papareschi, of Trastévere; 14 Feb 1130-24   1130
Sept 1143. Int. in St John Lateran; transferred in 1617 to Santa
Maria in Trastévere (monument of 1849) where the original epi-
taph is under the portico

[ANACLETUS II, Pierleone, a converted Jew; 14 Feb 1130-25 Jan 1138]

[VICTOR IV, Gregorio da Monticelli, elected 15 March 1138, abdicated 29
May 1138]

164. CELESTINE II, Guido, of Città di Castello; 26 Sept 1143-8 March   1143
1144. [Tomb in St John Lateran]

165. LUCIUS II, Gerardo Caccianemici dell'Orso, of Bologna; 12 March   1144
1144-15 Feb 1145. [Tomb in St John Lateran]

166. B. EUGENIUS III, Bernardo Paganelli, of Montemagno (Pisa); 15   1145
Feb 1145-8 July 1153. [Tomb in St Peter's]

167. ANASTASIUS IV, Corrado, of the Suburra, Rome; 12 July 1153-3   1153
Dec 1154. Int. in St John Lateran, in the porphyry sarcophagus
of St Helena (now in the Vatican)

168. ADRIAN IV, Nicholas Breakspeare, of Bedmond (Hertfordshire,   1154
England); 4 Dec 1154-1 Sept 1159. Died at Anagni; tomb in St
Peter's; sarcophagus in the Grotte Vaticane (tablet, 1925)

169. ALEXANDER III, Rolando Bandinelli, of Siena; 7 Sept 1159-30 Aug   1159
1181. Died at Civita Castellana; tomb in St John Lateran; epitaph
in the s. aisle, on a monument commissioned by Alexander VII

[VICTOR IV (V), Ottaviano; 7 Oct 1159-20 April 1164]

[PASCHAL III, Guido da Crema; 22 April 1164-20 Sept 1168]

[CALIXTUS III, John of Strumio, a Hungarian, Sept 1168, abdicated 29
Aug 1178]

[INNOCENT III, Lando Frangipane of Sezze, elected 29 Sept 1179, deposed
in Jan 1180]

170. LUCIUS III, Ubaldo Allucingoli, of Lucca; 1 Sept 1181-25 Nov   1181
1185. Died in exile at Verona, int. in the cathedral of Verona
(tomb of 1383)

171. URBAN III, Uberto Crivelli, of Milan; 25 Nov 1185-20 Oct 1187.   1185
Died at Ferrara; int. in the cathedral of Ferrara (sarcophagus of
1305)

172. GREGORY VIII, Alberto di Morra, of Benevento; 21 Oct 1187-17   1187
Dec 1187. Int. in the cathedral of Pisa (sarcophagus destroyed in
1595)

173. CLEMENT III, Paolino Scolare, of Rome; 19 Dec 1187-March 1191.   1187
[Tomb in St John Lateran]

174. CELESTINE III, Giacinto Bobone Orsini, of Rome; 30 March 1191-8   1191
Jan 1198. [Tomb in St John Lateran]

175. INNOCENT III, Lotario dei Conti di Segni, of Anagni; 8 Jan 1198-16   1198
July 1216. Died at Perugia; remains transferred from Perugia
Cathedral to St John Lateran in 1891 (tomb by Giuseppe
Luchetti)

176. HONORIUS III, Cencio Savelli, of Rome; elected at Perugia, 18 July   1216
1216-died at Rome, 18 March 1227. Tomb in Santa Maria
Maggiore

177. GREGORY IX, Ugolino dei Conti di Segni, of Anagni; elected at the   1227
age of 86; 19 March 1227-22 Aug 1241. [Tomb in St Peter's]

178. CELESTINE IV, Castiglione, of Milan; 25 Oct 1241-10 Nov 1241.   1241
[Tomb in St Peter's]

179. INNOCENT IV, Sinibaldo Fieschi, of Genoa; 25 June 1243-7 Dec   1243
1254. Died and int. at Naples (monument in San Gennaro, Naples)

180. ALEXANDER IV, Orlando dei Conti di Segni, of Anagni; 12 Dec   1254
1254-25 May 1261. Died at Viterbo [and int. in Viterbo Cathedral]

181. URBAN IV, Hyacinthe Pantaléon, of Troyes; elected at Viterbo 29   1261
     Aug 1261; died at Perugia 2 Oct 1264. Tomb in the cathedral of
     Perugia
182. CLEMENT IV, Gui Foulques Le Gros, of St-Gilles; elected at Viterbo 1265
     5 Feb 1265-died at Viterbo 29 Nov 1268. Int. at Viterbo in Santa
     Maria in Gradi, afterwards in San Francesco (mon. by Pietro
     Oderisio)
183. B. GREGORY X, Teobaldo Visconti of Piacenza; elected at Viterbo   1271
     1 Sept 1271-died at Arezzo 10 Jan 1276. Tomb in the cathedral
     of Arezzo (monument ascribed to Agost. di Giovanni and Angelo
     di Ventura)
184. B. INNOCENT V, Pierre de Champagny, of the Tarentaise; 21 Jan   1276
     1276-22 June 1276. [Tomb in St John Lateran]
185. ADRIAN V, Ottobono de' Fieschi, of Genoa; elected at Rome 11   1276
     July 1276-18 Aug 1276. Tomb at Viterbo in San Francesco (mon.
     by Arnolfo di Cambio)
186. JOHN XXI, Pedro Julião, of Lisbon; elected at Viterbo 8 Sept 1276- 1276
     20 May 1277. Tomb in the cathedral of Viterbo (mon. of 1884)
187. NICHOLAS III, Giov. Gaetano Orsini, of Rome; elected at Viterbo   1277
     25 Nov 1277-died at Soriano nel Cimino 22 Aug 1280. Tomb in
     St Peter's (sarcophagus in the Grotte Vaticane)
188. MARTIN IV, Simon de Brion, of Montpincé in Brie; elected at   1281
     Viterbo 22 Feb 1281-died at Perugia 28 March 1285. Tomb in
     Perugia cathedral
189. HONORIUS IV, Iacopo Savelli, of Rome; elected at Perugia 2 April   1285
     1285-3 April 1287. [Tomb in St Peter's]; sarcophagus with re-
     cumbent statue, in Santa Maria Aracoeli
190. NICHOLAS IV, Girolamo Masci, of Lisciano di Ascoli; 15 Feb 1288- 1288
     4 April 1292. Tomb in Santa Maria Maggiore (mon. designed by
     Dom. Fontana)
191. ST CELESTINE V, Pietro Angeleri da Morrone; of Isérnia, 5 July   1294
     1294-abdicated 13 Dec 1294. Died in the Castello di Fumone near
     Alatri 19 May 1296. Int. at Sulmona, afterwards in Santa Maria
     Collemaggio, at Aquila (mon. by Girol. da Vicenza, 1571)
192. BONIFACE VIII, Benedetto Gaetani, of Anagni; 24 Dec 1294-11 or   1294
     12 Oct 1303. [Tomb in St Peter's]; sarcophagus, with recumbent
     figure, in the Grotte Vaticane
193. B. BENEDICT XI, Niccolò Boccasini, of Treviso; 22 Oct 1303-died at 1303
     Perugia 7 July 1304. Mon. in San Domenico, Perugia (mon. by
     Lorenzo Maitani or Nic. di Nuzzo)
194. CLEMENT V, Bertrand de Got, of Villandraut, near Bordeaux;   1305
     elected at Perugia 5 June 1305, died at Roquemaure 14 April
     1314. Int. at Uzeste, Gascony (tomb of 1359)
195. JOHN XXII, Jacques d'Euse, of Cahors; elected at Avignon 7 Aug   1316
     1316-died at Avignon 4 Dec 1334. Tomb in the cathedral of
     Avignon
[NICHOLAS V, Pietro da Corvara, 12 May 1328-30 Aug 1330]
196. BENEDICT XII, Jacques Fournier, of Saverdun, near Toulouse; 20   1334
     Dec 1334-25 April 1342. Tomb in the cathedral of Avignon (mon.
     by Jean Lavenier; destroyed)
197. CLEMENT VI, Pierre Roger de Beaufort, of Château Maumont,   1342
     near Limoges; 7 May 1342-6 Dec 1352. Tomb at La Chaise-Dieu,
     Auvergne (mon. destroyed, only the sarcophagus remains)
198. INNOCENT VI, Etienne d'Aubert, of Mont, near Limoges; 18 Dec   1352
     1352-12 Sept 1362. Tomb in the Chartreuse of Villeneuve-lés-
     Avignon (mon. partly destroyed)

199. B. URBAN V, Guillaume de Grimoard, of Grisac, near Mende in     1362
     Languedoc; Oct 16 1362-19 Dec 1370. Tomb in the Abbey of St
     Victor, Marseille (mon. partly destroyed; only the recumbent
     figure now remains)
200. GREGORY XI, Pierre Roger de Beaufort, nephew of Clement VI,     1370
     of Château Maumont, near Limoges; elected at Avignon 30 Dec
     1370-died at Rome 27 March 1378. Mon. in Santa Francesca
     Romana
201. URBAN VI, Bart. Prigano, of Naples; 9 April 1378-15 Oct 1389.   1378
     Tomb in St Peter's (mon. transferred to the Grotte Vaticane)
202. BONIFACE IX, Pietro Tomacelli, of Naples; 2 Nov 1389-1 Oct 1404. 1389
     [Tomb in St Peter's]
203. INNOCENT VII, Cosimo de' Migliorati, of Sulmona; 17 Oct 1404-6  1404
     Nov 1406. [Tomb in St Peter's]; sarcophagus in the Grotte Vati-
     cane
204. GREGORY XII, Angelo Correr, of Venice; 30 Nov 1406-abdicated    1406
     4 June 1415, died at Recanati 17 Oct 1417. Tomb in the cathedral
     at Recanati
     Popes at Avignon:
        [CLEMENT VII, Robert of Savoy, of Geneva; elected at Fondi 20 Sept
        1378-16 Sept 1394]
        [BENEDICT XIII, Pedro de Luna, of Aragon; 28 Sept 1394-23 May
        1423]
     Antipopes at Avignon:
        [CLEMENT VIII, Gil Sanchez Muñoz, of Barcelona; 10 June 1423-16
        July, 1429]
        [BENEDICT XIV, Bernard Garnier; 12 Nov 1425-1430 (?)]
     Popes at Pisa:
        [ALEXANDER V, Pietro Filargis, of Candia; 26 June 1409-3 May 1410.
        Tomb in San Francesco, Bologna; mon. by Sperandio]
        [JOHN XXIII, Baldassarre Cossa, of Naples; 17 May 1410, deposed
        29 May 1415-died at Florence 23 Dec 1419. Tomb in the Baptis-
        tery, Florence; mon. by Donatello and Michelozzo]
205. MARTIN V, Oddone Colonna, of Genazzano; elected (aged 50) at    1417
     Constance, 11 Nov 1417-20 Feb 1431. Tomb in St John Lateran
     (by Simone Ghini)
206. EUGENIUS IV, Gabriele Condulmero of Venice; elected (aged 48)   1431
     3 March 1431-23 Feb 1447. Int. in St Peter's; whence the mon.
     (by Isaia de Pisa) has been transferred to the refectory of the
     Congregation of San Giorgio in Alga, an ancient convent adjoin-
     ing San Salvatore in Lauro
[FELIX V, Amadeus, duke of Savoy; 5 Nov 1439-7 April 1449; d. 1451   1447
     at the Château de Ripaille, on the Lake of Geneva]
207. NICHOLAS V, Tommaso Parentucelli, of Sarzana; elected (aged 49) 1447
     6 March 1447-24 March 1455. Tomb in St Peter's (sarcophagus
     with recumbent figure and fragments of the monument in the
     Grotte Vaticane)
208. CALIXTUS III, Alfonso Borgia, of Xativa, in Spain; elected (aged 78) 1455
     8 April 1455-6 Aug 1458. Int. in Sant'Andrea near St Peter's
     (destroyed). The body was removed to Santa Maria di Monser-
     rato (mon. by F. Moratilla, 1881); cenotaph in the Grotte Vati-
     cane
209. PIUS II, Aeneas Silvius Piccolomini, of Corsignano (Pienza);    1458
     elected (aged 53) 19 Aug 1458-15 Aug 1464. Int. in St Peter's;
     in 1623 the mon. (by Niccolò della Guardia and Pietro da Todi)
     was reconstructed in Sant'Andrea della Valle

210. PAUL II, Pietro Barbo, of Venice; elected (aged 48) 30 Aug 1464-26  1464
     July 1471. Tomb in St Peter's; the mon. by Mino da Fiesole has
     been reconstructed in the Grotte Vaticane
211. SIXTUS IV, Fr. della Rovere, of Savona; elected (aged 57) 9 Aug     1471
     1471-12 Aug 1484. Int. in St Peter's. The tomb was violated
     during the sack of Rome, 1527; the bronze sarcophagus by Ant.
     Pollaiolo now in the Museo Storico Artistico in St Peter's
212. INNOCENT VIII, G. B. Cibo, of Genoa; elected (aged 52) 29 Aug
     1484-25 July 1492. Int. in St Peter's; the monument, by Ant. and  1484
     Pietro del Pollaiolo, is in the present basilica
213. ALEXANDER VI, Roderigo Lenzuoli-Borgia, Valencia, Spain;           1492
     elected (aged 62) 11 Aug 1492-18 Aug 1503. Int. in St Peter's,
     afterwards removed to the chapel of San Diego in Santa Maria di
     Monserrato (mon. by F. Moratilla, 1881)
214. PIUS III, Fr. Todeschini-Piccolomini, of Siena; elected (aged 64)  1503
     22 Sept, 1503-18 Oct 1503. Tomb in St Peter's; mon. by Pasquino
     da Montepulciano, reconstructed in Sant'Andrea della Valle
215. JULIUS II, Giuliano della Rovere, of Savona; elected (aged 60) 31  1503
     Oct 1503-21 Feb 1513. Int. in St Peter's, afterwards in the sarco-
     phagus of Sixtus IV (?); his remains were scattered in 1527. Parts
     of a projected mausoleum by Michelangelo are now in San
     Pietro in Vincoli.
216. Leo X, Giov. de' Medici, of Florence; elected (aged 38) 9 March    1513
     1513-1 Dec 1521. Tomb in Santa Maria sopra Minerva
217. ADRIAN VI, Adrian Florisz Dedel, of Utrecht; elected (aged 63) 9   1522
     Jan 1522-14 Sept 1523. Tomb in Santa Maria dell'Anima
218. CLEMENT VII, Giulio de' Medici, of Florence; elected (aged 45) 19  1523
     Nov 1523-25 Sept 1534. Tomb in Santa Maria sopra Minerva, by
     Ant. da Sangallo.
219. PAUL III, Aless. Farnese, of Camino (Rome) or of Viterbo (?),      1534
     elected (aged 66) 13 Oct 1534-10 Nov 1549. Tomb in St Peter's
     (mon. by Gugl. della Porta)
220. JULIUS III, Giov. Maria Ciocchi del Monte, of Monte San Savino,    1550
     near Arezzo; elected (aged 63) 7 Feb 1550-23 March 1555. Tomb
     in the Grotte Vaticane (sarcophagus)
221. MARCELLUS II, Marcello Cervini, of Montefano (Macerata);           1555
     elected (aged 54) 9 April 1555-30 April 1555. Tomb in the Grotte
     Vaticane (sarcophagus)
222. PAUL IV, Giov. Pietro Caraffa, of Capriglio, Avellino; elected     1555
     (aged 79) 23 May 1555-18 Aug 1559. Tomb in Santa Maria sopra
     Minerva (mon. by Tom. da Cerignola from designs by Pirro
     Ligorio)
223. PIUS IV, Giov. Angelo de' Medici, of Milan; elected (aged 60) 26   1559
     Dec 1559-9 Dec 1565. Int. in Santa Maria degli Angeli
224. ST PIUS V, Ant. Ghislieri, of Bosco Marengo, near Tortona; elected 1566
     (aged 62) 7 Jan 1566-1 May 1572. Tomb in Santa Maria Maggiore
225. GREGORY XIII, Ugo Boncompagni, of Bologna; elected (aged 70)       1572
     13 May 1572-10 April 1585. Tomb in St Peter's by Camillo
     Rusconi
226. SIXTUS V, Felice Peretti, of Grottammare; elected (aged 64) 24     1585
     April 1585-27 Aug 1590. Tomb in Santa Maria Maggiore
227. URBAN VII, G. B. Castagna, of Rome; elected (aged 69) 15 Sept      1590
     1590-27 Sept 1590. Tomb in Santa Maria sopra Minerva
228. GREGORY XIV, Niccolò Sfondrati, of Cremona; elected (aged 55) 5    1590
     Dec 1590-15 Oct 1591. Tomb in St Peter's (sarcophagus without
     mon.)

229. INNOCENT IX, Giov. Ant. Facchinetti, of Bologna; elected (aged 72) 1591 29 Oct 1591-30 Dec 1591. Tomb in the Grotte Vaticane (sarcophagus)

230. CLEMENT VIII, Ippolito Aldobrandini, of Fano; elected (aged 56) 1592 30 Jan 1592-3 March 1605. Tomb in Santa Maria Maggiore

231. LEO XI, Aless. de' Medici, of Florence; elected (aged 70) 1 April 1605 1605-27 April 1605. Tomb in St Peter's

232. PAUL V, Camillo Borghese, of Rome; elected (aged 53) 16 May 1605 1605-28 Jan 1621. Tomb in Santa Maria Maggiore

233. GREGORY XV, Aless. Ludovisi, of Bologna; elected (aged 67) 9 Feb 1621 1621-8 July 1623. Tomb in Sant'Ignazio (mon by Pierre Le Gros)

234. URBAN VIII, Matteo Barberini, of Florence; elected (aged 55) 6 1623 Aug 1623-29 July 1644. Tomb in St Peter's (mon. by Bernini)

235. INNOCENT X, G. B. Pamphilj, of Rome; elected (aged 72) 15 Sept 1644 1644-7 Jan 1655. Tomb in Sant'Agnese al Circo Agonale (mon. by Maini)

236. ALEXANDER VII, Fabio Chigi, of Siena; elected (aged 56) 7 April 1655 1655-22 May 1667. Tomb in St Peter's (mon. by Bernini)

237. CLEMENT IX, Giulio Rospigliosi, of Pistoia; elected (aged 67) 20 1667 June 1667-9 Dec 1669. Tomb in Santa Maria Maggiore, under the pavement (mon. in the nave by Guidi, Fancelli and Ercole Ferrata from designs by Carlo Rainaldi)

238. CLEMENT X, Emilio Altieri, of Rome; elected (aged 80) 29 April 1670 1670-22 July 1676. Tomb and mon. in St Peter's

239. INNOCENT XI, Bened. Odescalchi, of Como; elected (aged 65) 21 1676 Sept 1676-11 Aug 1689. Tomb in St Peter's (by Etienne Monnot from designs by Carlo Maratta)

240. ALEXANDER VIII, Pietro Ottoboni, of Venice; elected (aged 79) 6 1689 Oct 1689-1 Feb 1691. Tomb in St Peter's (mon. by Arrigo di San Martino from designs by Angelo de Rossi)

241. INNOCENT XII, Ant. Pignatelli, of Spinazzola (Bari); elected (aged 1691 76) 12 July 1691-27 Sept 1700. Tomb and mon. in St Peter's

242. CLEMENT XI, Giov. Fr. Albani, of Urbino; elected (aged 51) 23 Nov 1700 1700-19 March 1721. Tomb in St Peter's (beneath the pavement of the choir)

243. INNOCENT XIII, Michelangelo Conti, of Rome; elected (aged 66) 1721 8 May 1721-7 March 1724. Tomb in the Grotte Vaticane (no monument)

244. BENEDICT XIII, Vinc. Maria Orsini, of Gravina (Bari); elected 1724 (aged 75) 29 May 1724-21 Feb 1730. Tomb in Santa Maria sopra Minerva

245. CLEMENT XII, Lor. Corsini, of Florence; elected (aged 79) 12 July 1730 1730-6 Feb 1740. Tomb in St John Lateran

246. BENEDICT XIV, Prospero Lambertini, of Bologna; elected (aged 65) 1740 17 Aug 1740-3 May 1758. Tomb in St Peter's (mon. by Pietro Bracci)

247. CLEMENT XIII, Carlo Rezzonico, of Venice; elected (aged 65) 6 July 1758 1758-2 Feb 1769. Tomb in St Peter's (mon. by Canova)

248. CLEMENT XIV, Giov. Vincenzo Ganganelli, of Sant'Arcangelo di 1769 Romagna (Forlì); elected (aged 64) 19 May 1769-22 Sept 1774. Tomb in Santi Apostoli

249. PIUS VI, Angelo Braschi, of Cesena; elected (aged 58) 15 Feb 1775- 1775 29 Aug 1799. Died at Valence, France; int. in the Grotte Vaticane; mon. by Ant. Canova in the Confessio, St Peter's; the heart of Pius VI is preserved at Valence

250. PIUS VII, Giorgio Barnaba Chiaramonti, of Cesena; elected (aged 1800 58) at Venice; 14 March 1800-died at Rome, 20 Aug 1823. Tomb in St Peter's

251. LEO XII, Annibale della Genga, born at La Genga, near Foligno;   1823
     elected (aged 63) 28 Sept 1823-10 Feb 1829. Tomb in St Peter's,
     beneath the pavement of the chapel of St Leo the Great; mon. by
     Gius. Fabris, in the nave
252. PIUS VIII, Francesco Saverio Castiglioni, of Cingoli; elected (aged   1829
     69) 31 March 1829-30 Nov 1830. Tomb in St Peter's (mon. by
     Pietro Tenerani)
253. GREGORY XVI, Bart. Cappellari, of Belluno, elected (aged 66) 2   1831
     Feb 1831-1 June 1846. Tomb in St Peter's (mon. by Amici)
254. PIUS IX, Giov. Maria Mastai Ferretti, of Senigallia; elected (aged   1846
     54) 16 June 1846-7 Feb 1878. Tomb in the crypt of San Lorenzo
     Fuori le Mura
255. LEO XIII, Gioacchino Pecci, of Carpineto Romano, elected (aged   1878
     68) 20 Feb 1878-20 July 1903. Int. in St John Lateran (mon. by
     Giulio Tadolini)
256. ST PIUS X, Giuseppe Sarto, of Riese (Treviso); elected (aged 68) 4   1903
     Aug 1903-20 Aug 1914. Tomb in the Cappella della Presentazione
     (St Peter's); mon. in St Peter's by Pietro Astorri and Florestano di
     Fausto
257. BENEDICT XV, Giacomo della Chiesa, of Genoa; elected (aged 60)   1914
     3 Sept 1914-22 Jan 1922. Tomb in the Grotte Vaticane; sarco-
     phagus with recumbent effigy by Giul. Barberi (1924)
258. PIUS XI, Achille Ratti, of Désio (Milan); elected (aged 65) 6 Feb   1922
     1922-10 Feb 1939. Tomb in the Grotte Vaticane; mon. in St
     Peter's by P. Canonica.
259. PIUS XII, Eugenio Pacelli, of Rome; elected (aged 63) 2 March   1939
     1939-9 Oct 1958. Tomb in the Grotte Vaticane; mon. in St Peter's
     by Fr. Messina
260. JOHN XXIII, Angelo Roncalli, of Sotto il Monte, Bérgamo; elected  1958
     (aged 77) 28 Oct 1958-3 June 1963. Tomb in the Grotte Vaticane;
     mon. by Emilio Greco in St Peter's
261. PAUL VI, Giov. Battista Montini, of Brescia; elected (aged 65) 21   1963
     June 1963-6 August 1978. Tomb in the Grotte Vaticane
262. JOHN PAUL I, Albino Luciani, of Forno di Canale, Belluno;   1978
     elected (aged 66) 26 August 1978-29 September 1978. Tomb in
     the Grotte Vaticane
263. JOHN PAUL II, Karol Wojtyla, of Wadowice (Krakow), Poland;   1978
     elected (aged 58) 16 October 1978

# PRACTICAL INFORMATION

## I   APPROACHES TO ROME

The Approaches from the North are described in the 'Blue Guide to Northern Italy'.

**Information Bureaux.** General information may be obtained in London from the *Italian State Tourist Office (E.N.I.T., Ente Nazionale Italiano per il Turismo,* 201 Regent St., W.I., who distribute free an invaluable 'Traveller's Handbook' (revised c. every year), an annual list of hotels and pensions in Rome, a practical Guide and map to the city, etc. Their office in Rome is at No. 2 Via Marghera. The headquarters of the *Ente Provinciale per il Turismo di Roma* (E.P.T.) is at No. 11 Via Parigi; E.P.T. information offices at the main station (Termini), Fiumicino airport, and on the AI autostrada from Milan (service area 'Salaria-Ovest') and on the A2 autostrada from Naples (service area 'Frascati-Est')

**Travel Agents** (most of whom belong to the Association of British Travel Agents) sell travel tickets and book accommodation, and also organize inclusive tours and charter trips to Rome. These include: *C.I.T.,* 10 Charles II St., S.W.1. (agents for the Italian State Railways), *Thomas Cook & Son,* 45 Berkeley St., W.I., and other branches, *Americian Express,* 9 Suffolk Place, S.W.1., etc.

**Passports** or **Visitors Cards** are necessary for all British travellers entering Italy and must bear the photograph of the holder. American travellers must carry passports. British passports valid for ten years are issued at the Passport Office, Clive House, Petty France, London S.W.1., or may be obtained for an additional fee through any tourist agent. No visa is required for British or American travellers to Italy.

**Currency Regulations.** The allowance permitted by the British Government for pleasure travel outside the sterling area per yearly period (beginning on 1 Nov) varies from time to time. In 1979 it is £500 for each person, all of which may be held in foreign notes. There are also frequent variations on the amount of sterling notes which may be taken out of Britain, and of Italian lire notes which may be taken in or out of Italy. Since there are normally strict limitations, the latest regulations should be checked before departure. At present, only 100,000 in lire notes can be taken in or out of Italy, and £100 in sterling notes can be taken in or out of Great Britain.

**Money.** In Italy the monetary unit is the Italian lira (pl. lire). Notes are issued for 500, 1000, 2000, 5000, 10,000, 20,000, 50,000 and 100,000 lire. Coins are of 5, 10, 20, 50, 100, and 200 lire. The rate of exchange in 1979 is approximately 1,600 lire to the £ and 830 lire to the U.S. dollar.

**Police Registration.** Police Registration is required within three days of entering Italy. For travellers staying at a hotel the management will attend to the formality. The permit lasts three months, but can be extended on application.

## Airports

**Fiumicino** (*Leonardo da Vinci*), 26 km. s.w. of Rome, served by an autostrada, is the airport for both international and internal air serivces. The *Town Air Terminal* is in Via Giolitti, at the side of Termini Station (airport buses depart c. every hour). The taxi fare between the airport and the station is at least 10,000 l. (in 1979).—**Ciampino,** 13 km. s.e. of Rome, a subsidiary (used mainly for internal flights and international charter flights) of Fiumicino, is served by buses from P.za dei Cinquecento and Viale Carlo Felice (Pl. 10; 3).

## Railway Stations

**Stazione Termini** (Pl. 5; 4), Piazza dei Cinquecento, rebuilt 1938 50 and now one of the best-equipped in Europe, the main station for all services of the State Railways and for the Underground Railway. **Stazione Roma Tiburtina** is used by some fast trains which do not stop at Stazione Termini. Less central than the main station (comp. p. 357), it is well served by buses.—Suburban stations (of little interest to the tourist) include *Roma Tuscolana, Ostiense, Trastévere, San Pietro,* and *Prenestina.*

## Motoring

British drivers taking their own cars by any of the multitudinous routes across France, Belgium, Luxembourg, Switzerland, Germany, and Austria need only the vehicle registration book, a valid national driving licence (accompanied by a translation, issued free by the R.A.C., A.A., and E.N.I.T. offices), and an International Insurance Certificate (the 'Green Card'). A nationality plate (e.g. G.B.) must be affixed to the rear of the vehicle so as to be illuminated by the tail lamps. Motorists who are not owners of the vehicle must possess the owner's permit for its use abroad.

Membership of the *Automobile Association* (Fanum House, Leicester Square, London W.C.2), or the *Royal Automobile Club* (83 Pall Mall, London S.W.1.), the *Royal Scottish Automobile Club,* the *American Automobile Association,* or the *American Automobile Touring Alliance,* or other club accredited by the Automobile Club d'Italia (A.C.I.) or the Touring Club Italiano entitles motorists to many of the facilities of affiliated societies on the Continent and may save trouble and anxiety. The U.K. motoring organizations are represented at most of the sea and airports, both at home and on the Continent, to assist their members with customs formalities.

Temporary membership of the A.C.I. can be taken out on the frontier or in Italy. The headquarters of the A.C.I. is at 8 Via Marsala in Rome. Concessions gained from membership include parking facilities, legal assistance, and discounts on tolls and car hire. In case of breakdown, the nearest A.C.I. office can be contacted by telephone number 116. On the Autostrada del Sole (Milan-Rome), there is an emergency press button box on the right of the road every two kilometres.

The continental rule of the road is to drive on the right and overtake on the left. The provisions of the respective highway codes in the countries of transit, though similar, have important variations, especially with regard to priority, speed limits, and pedestrian crossings.

B

It is obligatory to carry a red triangle in the car in case of accident or breakdown. This serves as a warning to other traffic when placed on the road at a distance of 50 metres from the stationary car. It can be hired from the A.C.I. for a minimal charge, and returned at the frontier.

PETROL COUPONS. Foreign motorists in Italy with a vehicle registered outside the country are entitled to purchase a certain number of petrol coupons for c. 30 per cent of the market price of petrol in Italy. The normal cost of petrol in 1978 is 500 l. per litre. Petrol coupons can be purchased only outside Italy or at the frontier and cannot be paid for in Italian currency. In Britain they are available from the A.A., C.I.T., R.A.C., and Barclays Bank. A maximum allowance of 400 litres is allowed for up to two visits a year. Unused petrol coupons can be refunded at the frontier or by the issuing office.

ITALIAN MOTORWAYS (Autostrade). Italy has the finest motorways in Europe. Tolls are charged according to the rating of the vehicle and the distance covered. On some motorways (including the Autostrada del Sole) cars with foreign number plates may qualify for reduced tolls which correspond to the lowest tariff (applicable to motorcycles). Service areas are found on nearly all autostrade.

British drivers in Rome will find the speed of the traffic much faster than in Britain. Most of the centre of the city has been closed to private cars (including the Corso), and the main traffic arteries are, as a result, extremely congested. Rome has various car parks and garages, and the city is best explored on foot (using public transport).

## II   HOTELS AND PENSIONS

Most of the best hotels in Rome are in the Ludovisi Quarter, regarded as the Mayfair of Rome; its main thoroughfare, Via Vittorio Veneto, runs from Porta Pinciana to Piazza Barberini. Other good hotels are situated near Piazza di Spagna, the Pantheon, at the eastern end of Via Cavour, and near the main railway station. The leading hotels are first class establishments in every sense of the term and are of the type expected in any capital city; those of the second class are usually comfortable. Rooms should be booked in advance during the summer and the late season (which lasts from Easter to the end of May), and throughout October.

Information about hotels in Rome may be obtained in London from the E.N.I.T. office, and on arrival in Rome at the E.P.T. offices at the station, Fiumicino airport, and on the autostrade (see p. 32).

Every hotel or pension has its fixed charges agreed with the Provincial Tourist Board. In all hotels the service charges are included in the rates. V.A.T. is added at a rate of 9 per cent (14 per cent in De Luxe hotels). However, the total charge is exhibited on the back of the door of the hotel room.

Pension terms can be arranged for a stay of a week or more (sometimes less by agreement). 'Half-board' terms are also available at most hotels and pensions; this comprises room, breakfast, and one meal. Pensions that provide board are entitled to impose half-board terms.

There are five official categories of hotels and pensions in Italy: de

Luxe (**L**), first (**1** or **P1**), second (**2** or **P2**), third (**3** or **P3**) and fourth class. These are listed with charges in the annual (free) publication of the E.P.T. *Alberghi e Pensioni di Roma e Provincia*.

In the following list, the category of the hotel or pension has been given. Hotels with more than 100 rooms (100 R) have been indicated; hotels of the fourth-class and third-class pensions have not been included. Rome has over 600 hotels and pensions, and it has been thought necessary to give only a small selection; omission does not imply any derogatory judgement.

Hotels Meublés do not usually have restaurants. They often have larger rooms, and fewer public rooms.

Alberghi Diurni ('day hotels') are establishments provided with bathrooms, hairdressers, cleaning services, rest and reading rooms and other amenities, but no sleeping accommodation.


# ACCOMMODATION IN ROME AND ENVIRONS

Near Termini Station: **Grand Hotel et de Rome** (a; Pl. 4; 4), 3 Via V. E. Orlando, 180 R; **Mediterraneo** (c; Pl. 4; 4), 15 Via Cavour, 280 R, both **L**.—**Mondial** (ii; Pl. 4; 4), 127 Via Torino; **Atlantico** (e; Pl. 4; 4), 23 Via Cavour; **Massimo d'Azéglio** (f; Pl. 5; 6), 18 Via Cavour, 210 R; **San Giorgio** (g; Pl. 5; 6), 61 Via G. Améndola, 190 R; **Quirinale** (b; Pl. 4; 4), 7 Via Nazionale, 200 R, all **1**.—**Genova** (aa; Pl. 5; 6), 33 Via Cavour, 110 R; **Esperia** (bb; Pl. 4; 4), 22 Via Nazionale, 100 R; **Nord-Nuova Roma** (cc; Pl. 4; 4), 3 Via G. Amendola, 160 R; **Diana** (dd; Pl. 4; 4), 4 Via Principe Amadeo, 180 R; **Impero** (ee; Pl. 4; 4), 19 Via Viminale; **San Remo** (ff; Pl. 4; 4), 36 Via M. d'Azeglio; **Tirreno** (gg; Pl. 4; 6), 17 Via San Martino ai Monti; **Rex** (hh; Pl. 4; 4), 149 Via Torino, all these **2**.—**Ariston** (uu; Pl. 5; 6), Via Fil. Turati; **Igea** (vv; Pl. 5; 6), 97 Via Principe Amadeo, both **3**.

In the Ludovisi Quarter and near Piazza Barberini: **Ambasciatori Palace** (i; Pl. 4; 1), 70 Via Veneto, 140 R; **Excelsior** (j; Pl. 4; 1), 125 Via Veneto, 380 R; **Bernini-Bristol** (l; Pl. 4; 3), 23 P.za Barberini, 130 R, all **L**.—**Imperiale** (d; Pl. 4; 3), 24 Via Veneto; **Flora** (k; Pl. 4; 1), 191 Via Veneto, 180 R; **Majestic** (m; Pl. 4; 3), 50 Via Veneto, 100 R; **Regina Carlton** (n; Pl. 4; 1), 72 Via Veneto, 140 R; **Eliseo** (o; Pl. 4; 1), 30 Via di Porta Pinciana; **Savoia** (p; Pl. 4; 1), 15 Via Ludovisi, 110 R; **Victoria** (q; Pl. 4; 1), 41 Via Campania, 110 R; **Boston** (r; Pl. 4; 1), 47 Via Lombardia, 120 R, all these **1**.—**Alexandra** (jj; Pl. 4; 3), 18 Via Veneto; **Quattro Fontane** (ll; pl. 4; 3), 149a Via Quattro Fontane, both **2**.—**Dinesen** (kk; Pl. 4; 1), 18 Via di Porta Pinciana, **3**.

In the Parioli Quarter: **Parioli** (mm; Pl. 11; 3), 54 Via Bruno Buozzi, **2**.

Near Piazza di Spagna: **Hassler-Villa Medici** (s; Pl. 4; 1), 6 P.za Trinità de' Monti, 110 R, **L; De La Ville** (t; Pl. 4; 3), 69 Via Sistina, 200 R; **Plaza** (n; Pl. 3; 4), 126 Via del Corso, 210 R; **Marini Strand** (v; Pl. 3; 4), 17 Via del Tritone, 120 R, all **1**.—**Internazionale** (nn; Pl. 4; 3), 79 Via Sistina; **Auriga** (oo; Pl. 4; 3), 33 Via S. Andrea delle Fratte, both **2**.

Near Piazza Colonna and the Pantheon: **Milano** (w; Pl. 3; 4), 12 P.za Montecitorio; **Nazionale** (x; Pl. 3; 4), 131 P.za Montecitorio; **Raphael** (y; Pl. 2; 6), 2 Largo Febo, all **1**.—**Tiziano** (qq; Pl. 3; 6), 110 Corso Vitt. Emanuele, **2**.

Near the Vatican: **Michelangelo** (z; Pl. 1; 6), 14 Via Stazione di S. Pietro, 150 R, **1; Colombus** (ss; Pl. 1; 6), 33 Via della Conciliazione, 100 R, **2**.

Monte Mario: **Cavalieri Hilton** (tt; Pl. 15; 7), Via Cadlolo, 400 R, **L; Clodio** (rr; Pl. 15; 8), 10 Via Santa Lucia, **2**.

Hotels Meublés. Near Termini Station: *Columbia*, 15 Via Viminale; *Nizza*, 16 Via Massimo d'Azeglio; *Torino*, 8 Via Principe Amadeo, 100 R; *Touring*, 34 Via Principe Amadeo; *Patria*, 36 Via Torino, all **2**.—*Alba*, 12 Via Leonina; *Doria*, 4 Via Merulana; *Merulana*, 278 Via Merulana; *Capitol*, 77 Via Giov. Améndola; *Stazione*, 36 Via Gioberti; these **3**.

Near Piazza dei Spagna: *Lugano*, 132 Via del Tritone; *d'Inghilterra*, 14 Via Bocca di Leone, 100 R, both **2**.—*Concordia*, 15 Via Capo le Case; *Homs*, 71 Via della Vite, both **3**.

Near Piazza Colonna and the Pantheon: *Moderno*, 30 Via Marco Minghetti, 100 R., **1**.—*Bologna*, 4a Via Santa Chiara, 120 R; *Santa Chiara*, 21 Via Santa

Chiara; *Cesari*, 89a Via di Pietra; *del Senato*, 73 P.za della Rotonda; *Genio*, 28 Via G. Zanardelli; *Sole*, 63 P.za della Rotonda, all **2.**—*Abruzzi*, 69 P.za della Rotonda; *Portoghesi*, 1 Via dei Portoghesi, both **3.**

**Pensions.** Near Termini Station: *Terminus*, 47 P.za della Repubblica, **P1.**—*Adria*, 58 Via Venti Settembre; *Hanover*, 4 Via Venti Settembre; *Haeslin*, 30 Via Palestro; *Europa*, 83 Via V. E. Orlando; *Esquilino*, 29 P.za Esquilino; *Milani*, 7b Via dei Mille; *Alfa*, 196 Via Nazionale; *Aberdeen*, 48 Via Firenze; *Quisisana*, 107 Via Torino; *Magenta*, 39 Via Magenta; *Abadan*, 122 Via Torino; *Augustea*, 251 Via Nazionale; *Bel Soggiorno*, 117 Via Torino, all these **P2.**

In the Ludovisi Quarter and near the Piazza Barberini: *delle Legazioni*, 11 Via Barberini; *Merano*, 155 Via Veneto; *Waldorf*, 79 Via Boncompagni; *Amati*, 155 Via Veneto; *Bellavista Milton*, 16 Via di Porta Pinciana; *Priscilla*, 17 Via Calabria; *Daria*, 24 Via Sicilia, all **P2.**

In and near the Piazza di Spagna: *Ausonia*, 35 P.za di Spagna; *Suisse*, 56 Via Gregoriana; *City*, 97 Via due Macelli; *Elite*, 49 Via F. Crispi, these **P2.**

In the Parioli Quarter: *Paisiello Parioli*, 47 Via Paisiello, **P2.**

To the N., N.E., and E. of the Porta Pia: *Villa del Parco*, 110 Via Nomentana, **P1.** *Laura*, 109 Viale Ventuno Aprile; *Villa Fiorita*, 5 Via Bartolomeo Eustachio; *Villa Borghese*, 4 Via Sgambati; *Pilla*, Viale Ventuno Aprile, all **P2.**

Aventine: *Sant'Anselmo*, P.za Sant'Anselmo, **P2.**

**Alberghi Diurni:** *Stazione Termini; Cobianchi*, 295 Via del Corso (corner of Piazza Venezia); 136 Via Cola di Rienzo (in Trastèvere); *Casa del Passeggero*, 1 Via Viminale.

**Youth Hostels and Students' Hostels.** *Italian Youth Hostels Association* (Associazione Italiana Alberghi per la Gioventù), 61 Lungotevere Maresciallo Cadorna. A 'Guide for Foreign Students' giving detailed information on students' hostels, students' facilities, etc., can be obtained from the Italian Ministry of Education, Viale Trastevere (500 l.). *Ostello del Foro Italico*, 61 Viale delle Olimpiadi; *Pax Christi Hostel*, 21 Piazza Adriana (open only in summer). Enrolled university students can sometimes find accommodation at the *'Civus' International Students' House*, 5 Viale Ministero degli Affari Esteri, and the *Casa dello Studente*, 24 Via Cesare de Lollis (Città Universitaria). *Y.W.C.A.*, 4 Via Balbo.

Religious organizations run some pensions for students and visitors (list available from the E.P.T.).

**Camping.** A list and location map of camping sites in Rome and environs can be obtained free from the *Federazione Italiana del Campeggio e del Caravanning*, 11 Via Vittorio Emanuele II, Calenzano (Florence). Among the sites on the outskirts of Rome are: *Roma Camping*, Via Aurelia; *Pineta Arca*, Via Cristoforo Colombo; *Internazionale di Castelfusano*, Via Litoranea (Lido di Ostia; open 1 April-31 Sept); *Capitol*, 45 Via Castelfusano, Ostia Antica. In the environs there are sites at Anzio, Nettuno, Bracciano, Subiaco, and Tivoli.

HOTELS AND PENSIONS IN THE ENVIRONS OF ROME. **Fregene:** *Golden Beach*, 2; *La Conchiglia*, **P1.**—**Lido di Ostia:** *Belvedere, La Scaletta, Lido, Sirenetta*, all 3; *Bellavista*, **P3.**—**Castel Fusano:** *E.N.A.L.C.*, **1.**—**Albano Laziale:** *Nuova Albano*, 3; *Villa Venosa*, **4.**—**Anzio:** *Esperia e Parco, Golfo*, both 2; *La Bussola, La Tavernetta, Riviera*, all 3;—**Ariccia:** *Paradiso*, **P2.**—**Bracciano:** *Casina del Lago*, 3.—**Castel Gandolfo:** *Belvedere*, **4;** *Lucia*, **P3.**—**Frascati:** *Flora*, 2; *Bellavista*, 3. **Genzano:** *Belvedere*, **4.**—**Marino:** *Villa Svizzera*, **P2.**—**Nemi:** *Al Bosco*, 3; *Allo Specchio di Diana*, **4.**—**Nettuno:** *Astura*, 2.—**Palestrina:** *Stella*, 3.—**Rocca di Papa:** *Europa, Angeletto*, both 2; *Righi*, 3.—**Subiaco:** *Belvedere, Zia Lidia*, both 3.—**Tivoli:** *Torre Sant'Angelo*, 1; *Eden Sirene*, 3.

# III   RESTAURANTS AND CAFÉS

**Restaurants** (*Ristoranti, Trattorie*) of all kinds and categories abound in Rome, and the standard of cuisine is usually high. The least pretentious restaurant often provides the best value. Prices on the menu generally do not include a cover charge (*coperto*, shown separately on the menu) which is added to the bill. The service charge is now almost always automatically added at the end of the bill. Tipping is therefore not strictly necessary, but a few hundred lire are appreciated. The menu displayed outside the restaurant indicates the kind of charges the customer should expect. However, many simpler establishments do not offer a menu, and here, although the choice is usually limited the standard of cuisine is often very high. Lunch is normally around 1 o'clock, and is the main meal of the day, while dinner is around 8 or 9 o'clock.

Most quarters of the city have restaurants of all grades, the good ones not being concentrated (as in some cities) in a particular area.

**Cafés** (*Bar*), which are open from early morning to late at night, serve numerous varieties of excellent refreshments which are usually taken standing up. The customer generally pays the cashier first, and presents a receipt to the barman in order to get served. It has become customary to leave a small tip of 50 lire for the barman. If the customer sits at a table he must not pay first as he will be given waiter service and the charge will be considerably higher. Black coffee (*caffè* or *espresso*) can be ordered diluted (*alto* or *lungo*), with a liquor (*corretto*), or with hot milk (*cappuccino*). In summer, many customers take cold coffee (*caffè freddo*), or cold coffee and milk (*caffè-latte freddo*).

A selection of the most well-known restaurants grouped according to district is given below. In simpler trattorie the food is usually as good, and cheaper, but they are less comfortable and do not often have tables outside. Pizzas and other snacks are served in a *Pizzeria, Rosticceria,* and *Tavola Calda.*

Near Termini Station. *Peppino,* 70a Via Principe Amadeo.

In the Ludovisi Quarter. *Giggi Fazi,* 22 Via Lucullo; *Da Tullio,* 26 Via San Nicola da Tolentino; *George's,* 7 Via Marche.

Near Via Venti Settembre. *La Taverna Flavia,* 9 Via Flavia.

Near Piazza di Spagna. *Ranieri,* 26 Via Mario dei Fiori; *Otello alla Concordia,* 81 Via della Croce; *Hosteria 31,* Viale delle Carrozze; *dal Bolognese,* 1-2 P.za del Popolo; *Casina Valadier,* on the Pincio, with terrace overlooking western Rome and Trastévere (luxury class); *Casina delle Rose,* in Villa Borghese, near the Porta Pinciana (also luxury class).

Near the Pantheon. *Alfredo alla Scrofa,* 104 Via della Scrofa, noted for fettucine; *Hostaria dell'Orso,* 93 Via Monte Brianzo, near Ponte Umberto Primo, an ancient hostelry and now a celebrated restaurant of the highest class; *Il Passetto,* 14 Via G. Zanardelli; *Il Buco,* 8 Via Sant'Ignazio; *La Maddalena,* P.za della Maddalena; *La Pentola,* 20 P.za Firenze; *Host. 'La Maiella',* P.za S. Apollinare; *Tre Scalini,* 31 P.za Navona; *Mastrostefano,* 94 P.za Navona.

Between Largo Chigi and Via dei Fori Imperiali. *Taverna Ulpia,* 2 P.za Foro Traiano, in the remains of the Basilica Ulpia, with a view of Trajan's markets.

Near the Corso Vittorio Emanuele. *Angelino a Tormargana,* 37 P.za Margana (closed Sun); *Vecchia Roma,* 18 P.za Campitelli; *Biblioteca del Valle,* 7 Largo Teatro Valle, noted for the sparkling wine known as Acqua di Trevi; *da Pancrazio,* P.za Biscione (in ruins of Pompey's theatre); *Piperno,* 9 Via Monte dei Cenci, noted for carciofi alla giudia.

Near the Vatican. *al Girarrosto* (Tuscan), 56-60 Via Germanico; *Pierdonati,* 39 Via della Conciliazione.

In Trastévere. *Romolo,* 8 Via di Porta Settimiana; *La Cisterna,* 10-14 Via della Cisterna; *Pastarellaro,* 33 Via San Crisogono, noted for fettucine; *Galeassi* and *Sabatini,* 3 and 13 P.za Santa Maria in Trastévere; *Corsetti,* P.za San Cosimato, noted for seafood; *Checco e carettiere,* 13 Via Benedetta; *Scarpone,* 15 Via di San Pancrazio (on the Janiculum), and many trattorie.

Parioli quarter. *Ambasciata d'Abruzzo,* 26 Via Pietro Tacchini.

Outside the walls. To the N. and N.E.: *Belvedere delle Rose,* 455 Via Cassia; *Al Chianti,* 17 Via Ancona. To the S.; *Belvedere, Hostaria l'Archeologia, Quo Vadis,* 206, 139, and 38 Via Appia Antica; *Orazio,* 5 Via Porta Latina.

**Cafès and Tea Rooms.** *Caffè Greco,* 86 Via Condotti (a famous cafè, comp. p. 173); *Caffè de Paris,* 90, *Rosati,* 108a, *Carpano,* 118, *Doney,* 145, and *Strega,* 175

Via Veneto; *Casina Valadier,* on the Pincio; *Casina delle Rose,* Villa Borghese; *Giolitti,* 40 Uffici dei Vicario (well-known for its ice-creams); *Tre Scalini,* 31 P.za Navona, noted for its 'tartufi' (truffles) and ices; *Vanni,* Via Monte Zenio; *Babington* (English tea rooms), P.za di Spagna.

**Birrerie.** *Birreria Viennese,* 21 Via della Croce; *Albrecht,* 39 Via Fr. Crispi; *Dreher,* 53 P.za SS. Apostoli; *San Marco,* 8 Via Mazzarino.

## IV   FOOD AND WINE

**Food and Wine.** The chief speciality of Italian cookery is the *pasta asciutta,* served in various forms with different sauces and sprinkled with cheese. Rome has its specialities and some of its restaurants are famous for them. *Fettuccine* are ribbon noodles, often served with butter and cheese, or 'alla Matriciana', with a salt pork and tomato sauce. *Gnocchi alla Romana* is a heavy dish made from potato, flour and eggs. Young artichokes are served in many different ways; among them are *cariciofi alla giudia,* that is cooked in oil. An unexpected dish is *fichi col prosciutto,* green figs with Parma ham. *Zuppa di pesce,* fish stew, is almost a meal in itself. Among the main dishes is *Abbacchio,* roast sucking lamb, *Saltimbocca alla Romana,* veal escalope with ham and sage. *Trippa al sugo* is stewed tripe, served with a sauce and tomatoes. Another estimable dish is *Coda alla vaccinara,* oxtail cooked with herbs and wine. Cheese specialities include *ricotta,* made from ewe milk; *pecorino,* a stronger hard cheese made from ewe milk; *mozzarella,* made from buffalo milk, the cheese used in pizzas (also 'affumicato', smoked). Roman confectionary, cakes, pastries, and ices are renowned.

**Wines.** The most famous wines of Lazio are the Vini dei Castelli; preeminent among these are the white wines of *Frascati, Grottaferrata, Albano,* and *Genzano,* with their clear amber tint, their characteristic bouquet, and their occasionally piquant flavour. The red Castelli wines, of which *Marino* and *Velletri* are the most liked, are stronger. It is often advisable to accept the 'house wine' (white and red usually available) which is suggested at a restaurant. This varies a great deal, but is normally a 'vin ordinaire' of average standard and reasonable price.

The MENU which follows includes many dishes that are likely to be met with:

### Antipasti, Hors d'oeuvre

*Prosciutto crudo o cotto,* Ham, raw or cooked
*Prosciutto e melone,* Ham (usually raw) and melon
*Salame,* Salami
*Salame con funghi e carciofini sott'olio,* Salami with mushrooms and artichokes in
  oil.
*Salsicce,* Dry sausage
*Tonno,* Tunny fish
*Frittata,* Omelette
*Verdura cruda,* Raw vegetables
*Carciofi o finocchio in pinzimonio,* Raw artichokes or fennel with a dressing
*Antipasto misto,* Mixed cold hors d'oeuvre
*Antipasto di mare,* Seafood hors d'oeuvre

### Minestre e Pasta, Soups and Pasta

*Minestre, zuppa,* Thick soup
*Brodo,* Clear soup
*Stracciatella,* Broth with beaten egg

*Minestrone alla toscana,* Tuscan vegetable soup
*Spaghetti al sugo* or *al ragù,* Spaghetti with a meat sauce
*Spaghetti al pomodoro,* Spaghetti with a tomato sauce
*Penne all'arrabbiata,* Short pasta with a rich spicy sauce
*Timbalo,* A rich pasta dish cooked in the oven
*Tagliatelle,* Flat spaghetti-like pasta, almost always made with egg
*Lasagne,* Layers of pasta with meat filling and cheese and tomato sauce
*Cannelloni,* Rolled pasta 'pancakes' with meat filling and cheese and tomato sauce
*Ravioli,* Filled with spinach and ricotta cheese
*Tortellini,* Small coils of pasta, filled with a rich stuffing served either in broth or
   with a sauce
*Agnolotti,* Ravioli filled with meat
*Fettuccine,* Ribbon noodles
*Spaghetti alla carbonara,* Spaghetti with bacon, beaten egg, and black pepper
   sauce
*Spaghetti alla matriciana,* Spaghetti with salt pork and tomato sauce
*Spaghetti alle vongole,* Spaghetti with clams
*Cappelletti,* Form of ravioli often served in broth
*Gnocchi,* A heavy pasta made from potato, flour, and eggs
*Risotto,* Rice dish
*Polenta,* Yellow maize flour, usually served with a meat or tomato sauce


### Pesce, Fish

*Zuppa di pesce,* Mixed fish usually in a sauce (or soup)
*Fritto misto di mare,* Mixed fried fish
*Fritto di pesce,* Fried fish
*Pesce arrosto, Pesce alla griglia,* Roast, grilled fish
*Pescespada,* Sword-fish
*Aragosta,* Lobster (an expensive delicacy)
*Calamari,* Squid
*Sarde,* Sardines
*Coda di Rospo,* Angler fish
*Dentice,* Dentex
*Orata,* Bream
*Triglie,* Red mullet
*Sgombro,* Mackerel
*Baccalà,* Salt cod
*Anguilla (con piselli in umido),* Eel (stewed with peas)
*Sogliola,* Sole
*Tonno,* Tunny fish
*Trota,* Trout
*Cozze,* Mussels
*Gamberi,* Prawns
*Polipi,* Octopus
*Seppie,* Cuttlefish


### Pietanze, Entrées

*Vitello,* Veal
*Manzo,* Beef
*Agnello,* Lamb
*Maiale (arrosto),* Pork (roast)
*Pollo (bollito),* Chicken (boiled)
*Petto di Pollo,* Chicken breasts
*Pollo alla Cacciatora,* Chicken with herbs, and (usually) tomato and pimento
   sauce
*Bistecca alla Fiorentina,* Rib steak (grilled over charcoal)
*Costoletta alla Bolognese,* Veal cutlet with ham, covered with melted cheese
*Abbacchio,* Roast sucking lamb
*Costolette Milanese,* Veal cutlets, fried in breadcrumbs
*Saltimbocca,* Rolled veal with ham
*Bocconcini,* As above, with cheese
*Ossobuco,* Stewed shin of veal
*Coda alla vaccinara,* Oxtail cooked with herbs and wine
*Porchetta,* Roast suckling pig, with herbs, fennel, etc.

*Stufato,* Stewed meat served in slices in a sauce
*Polpette,* Meat balls (often served in a sauce)
*Involtini,* Thin rolled slices of meat in a sauce
*Coratella d'abbacchio,* Stew of young lamb's liver, heart, etc.
*Spezzatino,* Veal stew, usually with pimento, tomato, onion, peas, and wine
*Cotechino e Zampone,* Pig's trotter stuffed with pork and sausages
*Stracotto,* Beef cooked in a sauce, or in red wine
*Trippa,* Tripe
*Fegato,* Liver
*Tacchino arrosto,* Roast turkey
*Cervello,* Brains
*Bollito,* Stew of various boiled meats
*Fagiano,* Pheasant
*Coniglio,* Rabbit
*Lepre,* Hare
*Cinghiale,* Wild boar

## Contorni, Vegetables

*Insalata verde,* Green salad
*Insalata mista,* Mixed salad
*Pomidori ripieni,* Stuffed tomatoes
*Funghi,* Mushrooms
*Spinaci,* Spinach
*Broccoletti,* Tender broccoli
*Piselli,* Peas
*Fagiolini,* Beans (French)
*Carciofi,* Artichokes
*Asparagi,* Asparagus
*Zucchine,* Courgettes
*Melanzane,* Aubergine
*Melanzane alla parmigiana*
   Aubergine in cheese sauce
*Peperoni,* Pimentoes
*Finocchi,* Fennel
*Patatine fritte,* Fried potatoes
*Insalata di Puntarelle,* a typical
   Roman salad served with garlic
   and anchovies

## Dolci, Sweets

*Torta,* Tart
*Monte Bianco,* Mont blanc (with
   chestnut flavouring)
*Saint Honore,* Meringue
*Gelato,* Ice cream
*Zuppa inglese,* Trifle

## Frutta, Fruit

*Macedonia di frutta,* Fruit salad
*Fragole con panna,* Strawberries and
   cream
*Fragole al limone,* . . . with lemon
*Fragoline di bosco,* Wild
   strawberries (in May and June)
*Mele,* Apples
*Pere,* Pears
*Arance,* Oranges
*Ciliege,* Cherries
*Pesche,* Peaches
*Albicocche,* Apricots
*Uva,* Grapes
*Fichi,* Figs

# V  TRANSPORT

**Buses and Trams.** In the centre of Rome there are numerous bus routes; trams survive in the outskirts. Bus stops are marked *Fermata*. Passengers enter at the rear of the car, where tickets are obtained from the conductor (or a coin-operated machine), and leave at the front. Entrance and exit doors, operated by the driver, are opened at the stops and kept closed in transit. Although there is a frequent service on most routes, buses and trams are often crowded, especially during rush hours,of which there are four; morning and evening and twice during the lunch break. It is advisable for a passenger to work his way forward (saying 'permesso' as he moves) well before the bus arrives at his stop. Smoking is not allowed.

It should be noted that, owing to the great number of one-way streets, return journeys do not always follow the same routes as the outward.

Fares are 100 l. on trams and buses. Tourist tickets valid for seven days may be purchased for 3000 l. at the A.T.A.C. offices in Piazza dei Cinquecento or 65 Via Volturno.

A selection of the more important routes is given below; map (500 l.) and information from the A.T.A.C. Information Office in P.za dei Cinquecento (outside the station).

## Buses

**60** P.za Sonnino—Ponte Garibaldi—Largo Argentina—P.za Venezia—Via del Corso—P.za S. Silvestro—Via Barberini—Via XX Settembre—Porta Pia—Via Nomentana—P.za Sempione.

**64** Staz. Termini—P.za Venezia—Corso Vitt. Emanuele—S. Pietro.

**66** P.za Cavour—P.za Augusto Imperatore—Via del Tritone—Via Nazionale—Staz. Termini—Castro Pretorio—Staz. Tiburtina.

**67b** Staz. Termini—Via Nazionale—Traforo—Largo Tritone—P.za del Popolo—Lungotevere (Via Flaminia)—Ponte Duca d'Aosta—Foro Italico.

**70** Via Giolitti—S. Maria Maggiore—Via Nazionale—P.za Venezia—Corso Vitt. Emanuele—Corso Rinascimento—Ponte Cavour—P.za Cavour—Viale Giulio Cesare—Piazzale Clodio.

**71** Via Giolitti—Traforo Umberto I—P.za S. Silvestro.

**77** Staz. Termini—P.za Barberini—Via del Tritone—P.za Cavour—P.za Risorgimento.

**85** P.za Colonna—P.za Venezia—Colosseum—S. Giovanni in Laterano.

**87** Pantheon—P.za Venezia—Colosseum—S. Giovanni in Laterano—P.za Baronio.

**88** P.za Cavour—Corso—P.za Venezia—Colosseum—S. Giovanni in Laterano—P.za Tuscolo.

**89** P.za Venezia—Via Teatro Marcello—Terme di Caracalla—Porta Metronia—Via Macedonia.

**90** P.za del Fante—Ponte Matteotti—P.za del Popolo—P.za Colonna—P.za Venezia—Terme di Caracalla—Porta Metronia—P.za Zama.

**91** P.za Venezia—P.za Bocca della Verità—Lungotevere Aventino—Piazzale Ostiense—P.za Navigatori—Via Odescalchi.

**93** Staz. Termini—S. Maria Maggiore—S. Giovanni in Laterano—Porta Metronia—Terme di Caracalla—Via C. Colombo—Staz. E.UR.

**94** Pantheon—P.za Venezia—The Aventine—Via G. A. Sartorio.

**95** Piazzale Ostiense—Lungotevere Aventino—P.za Venezia—P.za del Popolo—Piazzale Flaminio.

**97** Viale della Tecnica (E.U.R.)—Viale Marconi—Viale Trastevere—P.za Sonnino.

**118** Colosseum—Terme di Caracalla—Porta Latina—Via Appia Antica.

**123** Basilica S. Paolo—E.U.R.

**218** S. Giovanni in Laterano—P.za Epiro—P.za Galeria—Via Appia Antica—Fosse Ardeatine.
**223** Basilica S. Paolo—Abbazia Tre Fontane.

## Trams

**30** Monteverde—Viale Trastevere—Ponte Sublicio—Porta S. Paolo—Colosseum—Porta S. Giovanni—Porta Maggiore—Piazzale Verano—Viale Regina Margherita—Piazza Ungheria—Viale Belle Arti—Ponte Matteotti—Viale d. Milizie—P.za Risorgimento.
**19** Centocelle—Via Prenestina—Porta Maggiore—Piazzale Verano—Viale Regina Margherita—P.za Ungheria—Viale Belle Arti—Ponte Matteotti—Viale d. Milizie—P.za Risorgimento.
**12** Largo Preneste—Porta Maggiore—Piazza Vittorio Emanuele—Via Farini—Stazione Termine.
**13** Largo Preneste—P.za Vitt. Emanuele—Colosseum—P.za Monte Savello—Monteverde.

## Night Service

Tram **30** operates throughout the night on a slightly modified route.
**60** P.za Sonnino—P.za Venezia—P.za Barberini—Via Nomentana—Tufello.
**75** (barred). Largo Argentina—Viale Trastévere—Monteverde.
**78** Piazzale Clodio—Piazzale Flaminio—P.za Cavour—Corso Rinascimento—P.za Venezia—Staz. Termini.

## Underground Railway

The first stage of the *Metropolitana* was completed in 1952, and runs s.w. from Stazione Termini to *Porta San Paolo,* in Piazzale Ostiense, where it comes to the surface just beyond the station of that name, running from there alongside the Rome-Lido railway as far as *Magliana,* beyond the Basilica of San Paolo fuori le Mura. It then runs underground (N.E.) to terminate at *Tre Fontane (Laurentina).* There are intermediate stations at *Via Cavour, Colosseo, Circo Massimo, Piramide (Porta San Paolo), Garbatella, San Paolo, Magliana,* and *E.U.R.*—A service also runs from Termini viâ San Paolo to *Ostia Antica* and *Ostia Lido.*

A second underground railway is nearing completion from Stazione Termini viâ P.za Vitt. Emanuele II, San Giovanni in Laterano, Via Appia Nuova, Via Tuscolana, Cinecittà, to Osteria del Curato. A third line is still under construction from Stazione Termini viâ P.za Barberini and P.za di Spagna to Viale Giulio Cesare (near the Vatican).

## Taxis

Taxis (yellow in colour) are provided with taximeters; it is advisable to make sure these are operational before hiring a taxi. They are hired from ranks: there are no cruising taxis. For Radio taxis dial 3570. In 1979 the initial charge was 460 l. and 60 l. for each succeeding 250 metres or 45 seconds waiting. Additional night charge (22-7) 500 l.; for each piece of luggage 100 l. Horse Cabs are now used exclusively by tourists. The fare must be established before starting the journey.

## Car Hire

The principal car-hire firms have offices at Fiumicino airport and at Termini station as well as in the centre of Rome. It should be noted that travellers hiring cars in Italy are not entitled to petrol coupons. The main car-hire firms include: *Automobile Club di Roma,* 261 Via Cristoforo Colombo, 375 Via Magliana; *Hertz,* 28 Via Sallustiana; *Maggiore,* 8 Via Po, 57 P.za della Repubblica; *Avis,* 1 p.za Esquilino, 38 Via Sardegna.

### Sight-seeing Tours of Rome and environs

Tours are organized by C.I.T. (starting in P.za della Repubblica 64), and other travel agencies. Four or more different itineraries of the city (one of Rome by night) are arranged. Tours of the environs include Tivoli; the Castelli Romani; Cervéteri and Tarquinia. Naples, Pompei, Sorrento, Capri, Amalfi, and Assisi, Perugia, Siena, etc. are included in long-distance excursions.

### Coach, tram, and train services in the environs

There is no central coach station in Rome; the coaches start from and return to various squares or streets. In some instances there is a booking office; in others, tickets are bought on board. The services are run by A.CO.TRA.L. (Azienda Consortile Trasporti Lazio), 25 Via Portonaccio (Tel. 780612). For further details about transport in the environs, see the beginning of Rtes 21-28. *Via Gaeta,* N.E. corner of P.za dei Cinquecento, for buses to *Tivoli; Roma Termini,* s.w. side of P.za dei Cinquecento, for *Colonna, Palestrina, Genazzano,* and *Fiuggi; Viale Castro Pretorio,* for *Frosinone, Subiaco, Palestrina,* and *Cervéteri; E.U.R.* underground station for *Castel Porziano, Anzio,* and *Nettuno; Viale Carlo Felice* (Pl. 10; 3) for the *Castelli, Terracina, S. Felice Circeo; Piazzale Flaminio* (Roma Nord station) for *Civitacastellana* and *Viterbo.*

TRAMWAY STATIONS. Services have been reduced to the following: *Roma Termini,* Via Giovanni Giolitti, adjoining the Stazione Ferrovie Laziali (see below) for trams to *Centocelle* and *Grotte Celoni.—Roma Termini,* Via Giovanni Améndola (corner of Via Viminale) for trams to *Cinecittà* and *Capannelle.*

TRAIN SERVICES. *Stazione Ferrovie Laziali,* an extension on the s.w. side of Stazione Termini, Via Giovanni Giolitti, facing Via Mamiani (Pl. 5; 6; reached also from the main station; long walk along Platform 22), for trains to *Palestrina, Genazzano,* and *Fiuggi.—Porta San Paolo* (Pl. 8; 7), Piazzale Ostiense, for trains to *Ostia Antica* and *Lido di Ostia.—Piazzale Flaminio* (Pl. 11; 7), for trains of the Ferrovie Roma Nord for *Castellana* and *Viterbo.*

# VI   USEFUL ADDRESSES

**Information Bureaux and Tourist Agents.** *E.N.I.T. (Ente Nazionale Italiano per il Turismo),* 2 Via Marghera (Tel. 49711); *E.P.T. (Ente Provinciale per il Turismo),* 11 Via Parigi (Tel. 461851); *C.I.T. (Compagnia Italiana Turismo),* 64 Piazza della Repubblica, Stazione Termini, etc.; *American Express Co.,* 38-40 P.za di Spagna; *Italturist,* 114 Via Quattro Novembre; *Agriturist,* 101 Corso Vittorio Emanuele.—STUDENT TRAVEL BUREAUX: *A.T.G.,* 23 Via dei Barbieri; *C.T.S.,* 16 Via Genova; *European Student Travel Centre,* 14 Via S. Agata dei Goti.

**Head Post Office** (Pl. 3; 4), Piazza San Silvestro, open weekdays 8.30-21; Sat 8-14 (open until 21 for the issue of mail addressed 'fermo posta' and for the acceptance of special delivery registered mail only). *Telegraph* and *Telephone Offices,* open always.

**Public Offices.** *Municipio,* Palazzo Senatorio; *Questura* (Central Police Station), 15 Via San Vitale.—Airports: *Fiumicino* (Tel. 4687); *Ciampino* (Tel. 600251).—Main Railway Station (*Termini*), Information (Tel. 4775); Lost Property Office (Tel. 4730).—City Transport: *A.T.A.C.,* 65 Via Volturno, & P.za dei Cinquecento (Tel. 4695).

**Motoring Organizations.** *Automobile Club d'Italia,* 8 Via Marsala; *Touring Club Italiano,* 7 Via Ovidio; *Rome Automobile Club,* 261 Via C. Colombo.—A.C.I. Breakdown service, Tel. 116.

**Airline Offices.** *Alitalia,* 13 Via Bissolati; *British Airways,* 48-54 Via Bissolati; *T.W.A.,* 59 Via Barberini; *Pan American,* 46 Via Bissolati; *Air France,* 89 Via Veneto; *K.L.M.,* 97 Via Barberini; *Canadian Pacific,* 63 Via Barberini.

**Hospitals.** For emergencies, Tel. 113. *San Giovanni,* Accident Hospital ('Pronto Soccorso'), for road accidents and other emergencies (Tel. 7578241). *Policlinico,* (Tel. 492856). Some chemists remain open all night and on holidays (listed in the daily newspapers).

**Banks** (usually open Mon-Fri, 8.30-13.30; Sat and holidays closed). *Banca Commerciale Italiana,* 226 Via del Corso; *Banca d'Italia,* 91 Via Nazionale; *Banco di Roma,* 307 Via del Corso; *Credito Italiano,* 374 Via del Corso; *Banca d'America e d'Italia,* 161 Largo del Tritone; *Banco di Santo Spirito,* 18 P.za del Parlamento; *First National City Bank,* 26 Via Boncompagni; *American Express Bank,* 79 Via Due Macelli, 5 P.za Mignanelli.

**Embassies.** The British Ambassador accredited to the Italian government resides at the Villa Wolkonsky, 25 Via Conte Rosso; the new embassy buildings, including the Consular section, adjoin Porta Pia (80 Via Venti Settembre). British Legation to the Holy See, 91 Via Condotti.—American Embassy (and Consulate) to Italy, 119 Via Veneto.

**Learned Institutions and Cultural Societies.** *British School at Rome,* 61 Via Antonio Gramsci (Valle Giulia); *British Council,* Palazzo del Drago, 20 Via delle Quattro Fontane; *American Academy,* 5 Via Angelo Masina; *French Academy,* Villa Medici, 1 Viale Trinità dei Monti; *Goethe Institut,* 267 Via del Corso; *German Archaeological Institute,* 79 Via Sardegna.—*Università degli Studi,* Viale dell'Università (Città Universitaria); *Istituto Nazionale di Archeologia e Storia dell'Arte,* Piazza San Marco (Palazzo di Venezia); *Accademia dei Lincei,* 10 Via della Lungara; *Società Italiana Dante Alighieri* (with Italian language courses), 27 P.za Firenze; *Istituto Centrale del Restauro,* 9 P.za S. Fràncesco di Paola; *Società Geografica Italiana,* 12 Via della Navecella (Villa Celimontana); *Accademia Filarmonica Romana,* 116 Via Flaminia; *Accademia Nazionale di Santa Cecilia,* 6 Via Vittoria.— *Associazione Italia Nostra,* 287 Corso Vittorio Emanuele; *Amici dei Musei di Roma,* Palazzo Braschi (P.za San Pantaleo).

**Libraries.** *Biblioteca Nazionale Centrale,* Viale Castro Pretorio; *Archivio di Stato,* 40 Corso Rinascimento; *Biblioteca Alessandrina Universitaria,* Città Universitaria; *Biblioteca Hertziana,* 28 Via Gregoriana; *Biblioteca Angelica,* 8 P.za Sant' Agostino; *Gabinetto Fotografico Nazionale,* 1 P.za di Porta Portese; *English Library,* 20 Via delle 4 Fontane; *American Library,* 62 Via Veneto.

# VII   CHURCHES AND CHURCH CEREMONIES

St Peter's and the other three great basilicas are open all day (7-19). Other churches are usually closed between 12 and 15.30, 16 or 17. Some churches, including several of importance, are open only for a short time in the morning and evening, but admission at other times may sometimes be obtained on application to the sacristan, who generally lives nearby. The sacristan will also show closed chapels, crypts, etc., and a small tip should be given. Many pictures are difficult to see without lights which are often coin operated (100 lire). During Passion Week and for part of Holy Week many works of art in churches are veiled and are not shown. Some churches now ask that sightseers do not enter during a service, but normally visitors may do so, provided they are silent and do not approach the altar in use. At all times they are expected to cover their legs and arms, and generally dress with decorum. Churches in Rome are very often not orientated. In the text the terms N. and s. refer to the liturgical N. (left) and s. (right), taking the high altar as at the E. end.

The four great or PATRIARCHAL BASILICAS are *San Giovanni in Laterano* (St John Lateran; the cathedral and mother church of the world), *San Pietro in Vaticano* (St Peter's), *San Paolo fuori le Mura,* and *Santa Maria Maggiore.* These, with the three basilicas of *San Lorenzo fuori le Mura, Santa Croce in Gerusalemme,* and *San Sebastiano,* comprise the 'Seven Churches of Rome'. Among minor basilicas rank *Sant'Agnese fuori le Mura, Santi Apostoli, Santa Cecilia, San Clemente,* and *Santa Maria in Trastévere.*

**Ave Maria** or **Angelus.** The ringing of the evening Ave Maria bell at sunset is an important event in Rome, where it signifies the end of the day and the beginning of the night. The hour varies according to the season.

**Roman Catholic Services.** On Sun and, in the principal churches, often on weekdays, Mass is celebrated up to 1 p.m. and from 5 p.m. until 8 p.m. High Mass, with music, is celebrated in the basilicas (see above) on Sun at 9.30 or 10.30 a.m. (10.30 in St Peter's). Confessions are heard in English in the four main basilicas and in the Gesù, S. Maria sopra Minerva, Sant'Anselmo, Sant'Ignazio, and Santa Sabina.

ROMAN CATHOLIC SERVICES IN ENGLISH take place in San Silvestro in Capite, St Thomas of Canterbury, and Santa Susanna; in Irish at St Patrick's, Sant'Isidoro, San Clemente and S. Agata dei Goti.

**Church Festivals.** On saints' day mass and vespers with music are celebrated in the churches dedicated to the saints concerned.—Octave of the Epiphany at Sant'Andrea della Valle.—Blessing the lambs at Sant'Agnese Fuori le Mura, 21 Jan c. 10.30.—Procession with the Santo Bambino at Santa Maria in Aracoeli, 6 Jan in the evening.—Holy Week liturgy on Wed, Thurs, and Fri in Holy Week, at St Peter's, St John Lateran, Santa Croce, and other churches.

**Audience of the Pope,** see p. 263.

**British and American Churches.** *All Saints* (Anglican), 153 Via del Babuino; *St Paul's* (American Episcopal), Via Nazionale; *St Andrew's* (Scottish Presbyterian), 7 Via Venti Settembre; *Methodist,* P.za Ponte S. Angelo; *Christian Science Society,* 42 Via dei Giardini.

**Jewish Synagogue.** Lungotévere dei Cenci.

## VIII  AMUSEMENTS

**Theatres.** *Argentina,* Largo di Torre Argentina; *Valle* (Pl. 3; 6), Via del Teatro Valle; *Eliseo,* 183 Via Nazionale; *Delle Arti,* 59 Via Sicilia; *Delle Muse,* 43 Via Forlì; *Parioli,* 20 Via G. Borsi; *Quirino,* 1 Via Marco Minghetti; *Goldoni,* 3 Vicolo di Soldati, and many others.

**Concert Halls.** *Accademia Nazionale di Santa Cecilia,* 7 Via dei Greci (chamber music; in summer at the Basilica of Constantine); *Auditorium del Foro Italico,* 26 Lungotévere Diaz; *Oratorio del Gonfalone,* 32 Via del Gonfalone; *S. Leone Magno,* 38 Via Bolzano; *Teatro Olimpico,* 17 P.za Gentile da Fabriano.—**Opera:** *Teatro dell'Opera* (Pl. 4; 4), Via del Viminale (Dec to May); in summer at Terme di Caracalla.

**Popular Festivals.** *Epiphany* (*Befana*), on the night of 5-6 Jan, celebrated in Piazza Navona; *Festa di San Giovanni,* on the night of 23-24 June, near the Porta San Giovanni; *Festa di San Giuseppe,* 19 March, celebrated in the Trionfale quarter; *Festa della Repubblica,* first Sun in June, military parade in the Via dei Fori Imperiali; *Anniversary of the birth of Rome,* 21 April celebrated on the Campidoglio; *Festa di Noantri,* celebrations in Trastévere for several weeks in July.

Sport. Horse Racing under the auspices of the *Federazione Italiana Sport Equestri (F.I.S.E.),* Foro Italico. At the racecourses of *Le Capanelle,* Via Appia Nuova, *Tor di Valle,* Via del Mare, *Tor di Quinto,* Viale Tor di Quinto, and *Piazza di Siena,* Villa Borghese (international horse-show in April-May).—Polo. *Campo del Roma Polo Club,* Viale dell'Acqua Acetosa.—Football. *Federazione Italiana Gioco Calcio,* 70 Viale Tiziano; ground in the Stadio Flaminio.—Golf. *Federazione Italiana Golf,* 70 Viale Tiziano; *Circolo del Golf di Roma,* Via Appia Nuova, near Acqua Santa.—Lawn Tennis. *Nuovo Circolo Tennis Club Parioli,* Via di Ponte Salario, Forte Antenne; *Federazione Italiana Tennis,* 70 Viale Tiziano. Tennis courts in the grounds of the Foro Italico, and in the *Centro Tre Fontane* at E.U.R.—Swimming. Baths (covered and open-air) in the *Foro Italico,* and *E.U.R.* (open-air).

## IX  MUSEUMS, COLLECTIONS AND MONUMENTS

Below will be found a table giving the hours of admission to the various museums, galleries, and monuments in Rome, in force in 1979. Many of the museums and galleries are closed on Mondays; on Sundays and public holidays some are open for two or three hours in the morning, when admission is usually free. *Opening times vary and often change without warning;* those given below should therefore be accepted with reserve. All museums etc. are closed on the main public holidays: 1 Jan, Easter, 1 May, 15 Aug, and Christmas Day. On other holidays (see p. 51) they open only in the morning (9-13). The seasonal variations in the opening times of all State-owned museums and galleries have been abolished and a standard time-table for the whole year established, namely weekdays 9-14, Sunday and fest. 9-13. Open-air excavations, parks, etc. are open daily from 9 to one hour before sunset. MUSEUM CARDS obtainable in England at the R.A.C., C.I.T., or Barclays Bank (40p) and International Student Identity Cards gain free admission to all State-owned museums and monuments. Membership of Italia Nostra or the Amici dei Musei (comp. p. 44) allows free entrance to most museums, etc. Admission charges usually vary from 150 l. to 350 l.; those with exceptionally high entrance fees are mentioned in the text.

Lecture tours of museums, villas etc. (sometimes otherwise closed to the public) are organized by the *'Amici dei Musei di Roma'*. These are advertised in the local press and on a duplicated sheet obtainable at most museums. Museum Week (*Settimana dei Musei Italiani*) has now become established as an annual event (usually in April or May). Entrance to most museums is free during the week, and some have longer opening hours, and private collections may be specially opened.

HOURS OF ADMISSION TO THE MUSEUMS, COLLECTIONS,
AND MONUMENTS IN ROME

| Name | Open (see Note x) | Page number |
|------|-------------------|-------------|
| Accademia di San Luca | Tues and Thurs 10-12 | 171 |
| African Museum | Closed for restoration | 160 |
| Alto Medio Evo, Museo dell' | Weekdays exc. Mon 9-14, Sun 9-13 | 260 |
| Antiquarium Comunale | Apply at Capitoline Museum | 70 |
| Antiquarium Forense | Daily exc. Tues 9.30-12.30 (opened only ev. half hr.) | 124 |
| Ara Pacis Augustae | (C) See note a | 106 |
| Arti e Tradizioni Popolari, Museo delle | Daily exc. Mon 9-14 Sun 9-13 | 259 |
| Auditorium of Maecenas | (C) See note b | 206 |
| Barberini Gallery | Daily exc. Mon 9-14 Sun 9-13 | 178 |
| Barracco Museum | (C) Daily exc. Mon 9-14; Tues and Thurs also 17-20; Sun 9-13 | 77 |
| Bersaglieri, Museo Storico dei | Tues & Thurs 10-12.30 | 182 |
| Bessarion, House of Card. | (C) See note a | 224 |
| Borghese Gallery | Daily exc. Mon 9-14, Sun 9-13 | 156 |
| Burcardo, Raccolta Teatrale del | Weekdays 9-13 (exc. Aug) | 75 |
| Calcografia Nazionale | Weekdays 9-13.30 | 171 |
| Canonica, Museo | (C) Daily exc. Mon 9-14; Sun 9-13 | 156 |
| Capitoline Museums | (C) Weekdays exc. Mon 9-14, Sun 9-13; Tues & Thurs also 17-20 & Sat 21-23.30 | 57 |

| Name | Open (see Note x) | Page number |
|---|---|---|
| Caracalla, Baths of | Daily exc. Mon 9 to one hr before sunset, Sun 9-13 | 222 |
| Castel Sant'Angelo | Weekdays exc. Mon 9-13, Sun 9-12 | 247 |
| Catacombs (see note e): | Daily 8.30-12 and 14.30 (or 15) to dusk Adm. fee 500 l. | 227 |
| Priscilla | | 185 |
| Sant'Agnese | closed Sun morning | 184 |
| San Callisto | closed Wed | 228 |
| San Domitilla | closed Tues | 230 |
| San Pancrazio | | 244 |
| San Sebastiano | closed Thurs | 229 |
| Civiltà Romano, Museo della | (C) Weekdays exc. Mon 9-14, Sun 9-13; Tues & Thurs also 17-20 | 260 |
| Colonna, Galleria | Sat only 9-13 | 168 |
| Colosseum | All day: upper galleries closed for restoration | 142 |
| Corsini Gallery | Closed for rearrangement; adm. Tues 9-13 on request | 240 |
| Diocletian, Baths of | See Museo Nazionale Romano | 190 |
| Domus Aurea of Nero | Daily exc. Mon 9-13 | 144 |
| Doria Pamphili Gallery | Sun, Tues, Fri, Sat 10-13 | 147 |
| Ethnographic and Prehistoric Museum (Luigi Pigorini) | Daily exc. Mon 9-13 | 259 |
| Farnese, Palazzo | Sun 11-12 | 81 |
| Folklore Museum | Daily exc. Mon 9-13 | 239 |
| Forum, Roman, and Palatine | Daily exc. Tues 9 to one hr before sunset; Sun 9-13 | 108 |
| Forum of Augustus, Forum of Nerva, Antiquarium, and Casa dei Cavalieri di Rodi | (C) See note a | 138 |
| Forum of Caesar | (C) Closed | 137 |
| Forum of Trajan | See Markets of Trajan | 136 |
| Galleria Comunale d'Arte Moderna | Temporarily closed (Wed & Sat 9-14) | 188 |
| Galleria Nazionale d'Arte Antica | See Barberini Gallery, and Corsini Gallery | 178, 240 |

| Name | Open (see Note x) | Page number |
|------|-------------------|-------------|
| Galleria Nazionale d'Arte Moderna | Weekdays exc. Mon 9-14, Sun 9.30-13 | 160 |
| Genio, Museo del | By appointment | 256 |
| Geologico, Museo del | Weekdays 9-13 | 181 |
| Goethe Museum | Daily exc. Mon 10-13, 16-19; Sun 10-13 | 153 |
| Istituto Centrale del Restauro | Adm. 9-13 by special request | 199 |
| Keats' House | 9-12.30 & 14.30-17 exc. Sat & Sun (see note d) | 173 |
| Maltese Villa, church and garden | Permission from the Cancelleria, 68 Via Condotti | 90 |
| Mamertine Prison | Daily 9-12.30, 15-18.30 | 110 |
| Markets and Forum of Trajan | (C) See note a | 137 |
| Mausoleum of Augustus | (C) Closed to public (see note b) | 106 |
| Medicine, National Museum of | Weekdays 9-13 | 247 |
| Museo Nazionale Romano, Baths of Diocletian | Weekdays exc. Mon 8-30-14, Sun 9-13 | 190 |
| Musical Instruments, Museum of | Daily exc. Mon 9-14; Sun 9-13 | 217 |
| Napoleonic Museum | (C) Daily exc. Mon 9-14; Sun 9-12.30; Tues & Thurs also 17-20 | 101 |
| Numismatico, Museo della Zecca | Weekdays 9-12 | 182 |
| Oriental Museum | Daily exc. Mon 9-14; Sun 9-13 | 206 |
| Palatine | See Roman Forum | 125 |
| Palatine Antiquarium | Daily exc. Tues 9.30-12.30 (opened at half-hourly intervals) | 133 |
| Pamphili, Palazzo | Temporarily closed for restoration | 103 |
| Pantheon | Daily 9 to one hr before sunset | 97 |
| Porta Maggiore, Basilica di | See note f | 217 |
| Poste e Telecomunicazioni, Museo Storico delle | Daily exc. Mon & fest. 9-13 | 255 |
| Quirinal | Adm. only by appointment after written application | 177 |

| Name | Open (see Note x) | Page number |
|------|-------------------|-------------|
| Risorgimento, Museo Centrale del | Wed, Fri & Sun 10-13 | 72 |
| Roma, Museo di | (C) Daily exc. Mon 9-14, Sun 9-13; Tues & Thurs also 17-20 | 100 |
| Rospigliosi, Casino | 1st of ev. month 10-12, 15-17 | 176 |
| Sepolcreto Ostiense | Closed to public (see note b) | 92 |
| Spada Gallery | Weekdays exc. Mon 9-14 | 82 |
| Tasso Museum | Weekdays 9-12 | 246 |
| Tomb of the Scipios | (C) See note a | 225 |
| Torlonia Museum | Closed indefinitely | 240 |
| Vatican Museums | See p. 276 | |
| Venezia, Museo del Palazzo | Daily exc. Mon 9-14, Sun 9-13 | 72 |
| Via Ostiense, Museo della | Temporarily closed | 91 |
| Villa Albani | See Villa Torlonia | 186 |
| Villa Farnesina | Weekdays 9-13; closed Sun | 242 |
| Villa Giulia | Daily exc. Mon 9-14 Sun 9-13 | 163 |
| Villa Medici | Garden only: temporarily closed for restoration, but normally open one day a week | 174 |
| Villa Torlonia (ex-Albani) | By special permit | 186 |
| Zoological Gardens | Daily 8.30-sunset | 159 |
| Zoological Museum | 8-13; Sun closed | 160 |

NOTES

a   1 June-30 Sept daily exc. Mon 9-13, 15-18; 1 Oct-31 May 10-16; Sun 9-13
b   Special permission sometimes given by the Soprintendenza Comunale ai Musei, Monumenti e Scavi, 3 P.za Caffarelli
c   Free last Sun of month; Sat 21-23.30
d   Summer 9-12, 16-18 (June-Sept)
e   The other catacombs may be visited by special permission only. Apply Pontificia Commissione di Archeologia Sacra, 1 Via Napoleone III
f   Special permission required from the Soprintendenza Antichità, 53 P.za S. Maria Nova.
x   The opening hours for Sundays apply also to holidays (giorni festivi)

# X GENERAL HINTS

**Season.** The climate of Rome is exceptionally good except in the height of summer and periodically in the winter. For tourists the best months are April, May, June, September, and October. In January and February it can be unexpectedly cold and at times very wet.

**Manners and Customs.** Attention should be paid by the traveller to the more formal manners of Italians. It is customary to open conversation in shops, etc., with the courtesy of *buon giorno* (good day) or *buona sera* (good evening). The deprecatory expression *prego* (don't mention it) is everywhere the obligatory and automatic response to *grazie* (thank you). The phrases *per piacere* or *per favore* (please), *permesso* (excuse me), used when pushing past someone (essential on public vehicles), *scusi* (sorry; also, I beg your pardon, when something is not heard), should not be forgotten. In shops and offices a certain amount of self-assertion is taken for granted, since queues are not the general rule and it is incumbent on the inquirer or customer to get himself a hearing. Shaking hands is an essential part of greeting and leave-taking. A visitor will be wished *Buon appetito!* before beginning a meal, to which he should reply *Grazie, altrettanto*. This pleasant custom may be extended to fellow passengers taking a picnic meal on a train. Social calls or telephone calls should not be made during the *'siesta'* period in the afternoon, between 1 and 3 or 4 o'clock.

**Photography.** There are few restrictions on normal photography, but permission should be obtained before photographing the interiors of churches, museums, etc. (which in some cases may be withheld), and particularly before photographing individuals, notably members of the armed forces and the police. Photography is forbidden on railway stations and civil airfields as well as in frontier zones and near military installations.

**Public Holidays.** The main holidays in Rome, when offices, shops, and schools are closed are as follows: New Year's Day, 25 April (Liberation Day), Easter Monday, 1 May (Labour Day), 15 Aug (Assumption), 1 Nov (All Saints' Day), 8 Dec (Conception), Christmas Day, and 26 Dec (St Stephen).

**Telephones and Postal Information.** Stamps are sold at tobacconists (displaying a blue 'T' sign) and post offices. There are numerous public telephones all over Rome in kiosks, bars, restaurants, etc. These are usually operated by metal disks known as 'gettone', rather than coins, which are bought (50 lire each) from tobacconists, bars, some newspaper stands, and post offices (and are considered valid currency). Most cities in Europe can now be dialled direct from Rome (prefix for London, 00441).

**Shopping.** The smartest shops are in Via Frattina and Via Condotti (the Bond Street of Rome), leading from Piazza di Spagna. A good shopping area (less expensive) is near the Pantheon. Chemists: *Internazionale Schirillo,* 129 Via Veneto; *Lepetit,* 417 Via del Corso (selling English and American medicines). Department Stores: *La Rinascente,* P.za Colonna; *Standa,* P.za Santa Maria Maggiore, Viale Trastévere; *Upim,* Via del Corso. Book Shops: *Rizzoli,* Largo Chigi,

Galleria Colonna, 76 Via Veneto; *Einaudi,* 56a and 58 Via Veneto; *Lion Bookshop,* 181 Via del Babuino, and *Economy Book Center,* 29 P.za di Spagna, the last two English and American. Antique shops in Via del Babuino and Via dei Coronari. Open air markets: *Porta Portese* (general 'flea market'; open Sun morning only); *Via Sannio* (Porta San Giovanni), new and second-hand clothes; *Campo dei Fiori, P.za Vitt. Emanuele II,* and *Via Andrea Doria,* all for food.

**Newspapers.** The most widely read Italian newspapers in Rome are *Corriere della Sera* (Roman edition), *Paese Sera, Messaggero, Il Tempo* and *La Repubblica.* Foreign newspapers and weekly publications in English giving news of events in Rome are obtainable at most kiosks, and always in Piazza di Spagna and Via Veneto.

**Working Hours.** Government and business offices usually work weekdays from 8-14 or 14.30. Shops are open from 8 or 9-13 and 16.30 or 17.30-19.30 or 20. For banking hours, see p. 44.

# GLOSSARY OF ART TERMS

AMBO (pl. *ambones*). Pulpit in a Christian basilica; two pulpits on opposite sides of a church from which the gospel and epistle were read.

AMPHORA. Antique vase, usually of large dimensions, for oil and other liquids.

ANTEFIX. Ornament placed at the lower corners of the tiled roof of a temple to conceal the space between the tiles and the cornice.

ANTIPHONAL. Choir-book containing a collection of *antiphonae*—verses sung in response by two choirs.

ANTIS. *In antis* describes the portico of a temple when the side-walls are prolonged to end in a pilaster flush with the columns of the portico.

APODYTERIUM. Dressing-room in a Roman bath.

ARCA. Wooden chest with a lid, for sacred or secular use. Also, monumental sarcophagus in stone, used by Christians and pagans.

ARCHIVOLT. Moulded architrave carried round an arch.

ATLANTES (or *Telamones*). Male figures used as supporting columns.

ATRIUM. Forecourt, usually of a Byzantine church or a classical Roman house.

ATTIC. Topmost story of a classical building, hiding the spring of the roof.

BADIA, *Abbazia.* Abbey.

BALDACCHINO. Canopy supported by columns, usually over an altar.

BASILICA. Originally a Roman building used for public administration; in Christian architecture, an aisled church with a clerestory and apse, and no transepts.

BORGO. A suburb; a street leading away from the centre of a town.

BOTTEGA. The studio of an artist: the pupils who worked under his direction.

BUCCHERO. Etruscan black terracotta ware.

BUCRANIA. A form of classical decoration—heads of oxen garlanded with flowers.

CALDARIUM or CALIDARIUM. Room for hot or vapour baths in a Roman bath.

CAMPANILE. Bell-tower, often detached from the building to which it belongs.

CAMPOSANTO. Cemetery.

CANEPHORA. Figure bearing a basket, often used as a caryatid.

CANOPIC VASE. Egyptian or Etruscan vase enclosing the entrails of the dead.

CARCERES. Openings in the barriers through which the competing chariots entered the circus.

CARDO. The main street of a Roman town, at right angles to the Decumanus.

CARYATID. Female figure used as a supporting column.

CAVEA. The part of a theatre or amphitheatre occupied by the row of seats.

CELLA. Sanctuary of a temple, usually in the centre of the building.

CHIAROSCURO. Distribution of light and shade, apart from colour in a painting.

CIBORIUM. Casket or tabernacle containing the Host.

CIPOLLINO. A greyish marble with streaks of white or green.

CIPPUS. Sepulchral monument in the form of an altar.

CISTA. Casket, usually of bronze and cylindrical in shape, to hold jewels, toilet articles, etc., and decorated with mythological subjects.

COLUMBARIUM. A building (usually subterranean) with niches to hold urns containing the ashes of the dead.

CONFESSIO. Crypt beneath the high altar and raised choir of a church, usually containing the relics of a saint.

CUNEUS. Wedge-shaped block of seats in an antique theatre.

CYCLOPEAN. The term applied to walls of unmortared masonry, older than the Etruscan civilization, and attributed by the ancients to the giant Cyclopes.

DECUMANUS. The main street of a Roman town running parallel to its longer axis.

DIPTERAL. Temple surrounded by a double peristyle.

DIPTYCH. Painting or ivory tablet in two sections.

EXEDRA. Semicircular recess.

EX-VOTO. Tablet or small painting expressing gratitude to a saint.

FORUM. Open space in a town serving as a market or meeting-place.

FRIGIDARIUM. Room for cold baths in a Roman bath.

GIALLO ANTICO. Red-veined yellow marble from Numidia.

GONFALON. Banner of a medieval guild or commune.

GRAFFITI. Design on a wall made with an iron tool on a prepared surface, the design showing in white. Also used loosely to describe scratched designs or words on walls.

GRISAILLE. Painting in various tones of grey.

HERM (pl. *hermae*). Quadrangular pillar decreasing in girth towards the ground, surmounted by a bust.

HEXASTYLE. Temple with a portico of six columns at the end.

HYPOGEUM. Subterranean excavation for the interment of the dead (usually Etruscan).

IMPASTO. Early Etruscan ware made of inferior clay.

INTARSIA (or *Tarsia*). Inlay of wood, marble or metal.

KRATER. Antique mixing-bowl, conical in shape with rounded base.

KYLIX. Wide shallow vase with two handles and short stem.

LACONICUM. Room for vapour baths in a Roman bath.

LOGGIA. Covered gallery or balcony, usually preceding a larger building.

LUNETTE. Semicircular space in a vault or ceiling often decorated with a painting or relief.

MATRONEUM. Gallery reserved for women in early Christian churches.

METOPE. Panel between two triglyphs on the frieze of a temple.

NARTHEX. Vestibule of a Christian basilica.

NAUMACHIA. Mock naval combat for which the arena of an amphitheatre was flooded.

NIELLO. Metalwork with an engraved and enamelled design.

NIMBUS. Luminous ring surrounding the heads of saints in paintings; a square nimbus denoted that the person was living at that time.

NYMPHAEUM. A sort of summer-house in the gardens of baths, palaces, etc., originally a temple of the Nymphs, and decorated with statues of those goddesses.

OCTASTYLE. A portico with 8 columns.

OINOCHOE. Wine-jug usually of elongated shape for dipping wine out of a krater.

OPUS ALEXANDRINUM. Mosaic design of black and red geometric figures on a white ground.

OPUS INCERTUM. Masonry of small irregular stones set in mortar.

OPUS QUADRATUM. Masonry of large rectangular blocks without mortar; in *Opus Etruscum* the blocks are placed alternately lengthwise and endwise.

OPUS·RETICULATUM. Masonry arranged in squares or diamonds so that the mortar joints make a network pattern.

OPUS SECTILE. Mosaic or paving of thin slabs of coloured marble cut in geometrical shapes.

OPUS SPICATUM. Masonry or paving of small bricks arranged in a herring-bone pattern.

OPUS TESSELLATUM. Mosaic formed entirely of square tesserae.

OPUS VERMICULATUM. Mosaic with tesserae arranged in lines following the design contours.

PALAZZO. Any dignified and important building.

PALOMBINO. Fine-grained white marble.

PAVONAZZETTO. Yellow marble blotched with blue.

PAX. Sacred object used by a priest for the blessing of peace, and offered for the kiss of the faithful, usually circular, engraved, enamelled or painted in a rich gold or silver frame.

PEPERINO. Earthy granulated tufa, much used in Rome.

PERIPTERAL. Temple surrounded by a colonnade.

PERISTYLE. Court or garden surrounded by a columned portico.

PIETÀ. Group of the Virgin mourning the dead Christ.

PISCINA. Roman tank; a basin for an officiating priest to wash his hands before Mass.

PODIUM. A continuous base or plinth supporting columns, and the lowest row of seats in the cavea of a theatre or amphitheatre.

POLYPTYCH. Painting or tablet in more than three sections.

POZZOLANA. Reddish volcanic earth (mostly from Pozzuoli, near Naples) largely used for cement.

PREDELLA. Small painting attached below a large altarpiece.

PRESEPIO. Literally, crib or manger. A group of statuary of which the central subject is the Infant Jesus in the manger.

PRONAOS. Porch in front of the cella of a temple.

PROPYLAEA. Columned vestibule approaching a temple.

PROSTYLE. Temple with columns on the front only.

PULVIN. Cushion stone between the capital and the impost block.

PULVINAR. Imperial couch and balcony on the podium of a theatre.

PUTTO (pl. *putti*). Figure sculpted or painted usually nude, of a child.

RHYTON. Drinking-horn usually ending in an animal's head.

SCHOLA CANTORUM. Enclosure for the choristers in the nave of an early Christian church, adjoining the sanctuary.

SINOPIA. Large drawing on a wall made in preparation for painting a mural. It was done on the rough coat of plaster, and retraced in a red earth pigment called *sinopia* (because it originally came from Sinope, a town on the Black Sea).

SITULA. Water-bucket.

SPINA. Low stone wall connecting the turning-posts (*metœ*) at either end of a circus.

STAMNOS. Big-bellied vase with two small handles at the sides, closed by a lid.

STELE. Upright stone bearing a monumental inscription.

STEREOBATE. Basement of a temple or other building.

STOA. A porch or portico not attached to a larger building.

STRIGIL. Bronze scraper used by the Romans to remove the oil with which they had anointed themselves.

STYLOBATE. Basement of a columned temple or other building.

TELAMONES, see *Atlantes*.

TEMENOS. A sacred enclosure.

TEPIDARIUM. Room for warm baths in a Roman bath.

TESSERA. A small cube of marble, glass, etc., used in mosaic work.

TETRASTYLE. Having four columns at the end.

THERMAE. Originally simply baths, later elaborate buildings fitted with libraries, assembly rooms, gymnasia, circuses, etc.

THOLOS. A circular building.

TONDO. Round painting or bas-relief.

TRANSENNA. Open grille or screen, usually of marble, in an early Christian church.

TRAVERTINE. Tufa quarried near Tivoli; the commonest of Roman building materials.

TRICLINIUM. Dining-room and reception-room of a Roman house.

TRIGLYPH. Small panel of a Doric frieze raised slightly and carved with three vertical channels.

TRIPTYCH. Painting or tablet in three sections.

VELARIUM. Canvas sheet supported by masts to protect the spectators in an open theatre from the sun.

ZOÖPHORUS. Frieze of a Doric temple, so-called because the metopes were often decorated with figures of animals.

# ROME

**ROME** (2,891,330 inhab.), in Italian **Roma,** the capital of Italy and the metropolis of the Roman Catholic church is situated on the Tiber, 35½ km. from its mouth, in the middle of an undulating plain lying between the Sabine Apennines and the Tyrrhenian Sea. Its average height above sea level is c. 48 metres, and its geographical position is lat. 41° 54′ N. and long. 12° 29′ E. The Eternal City, the 'Urbs' par excellence, to which all roads lead, the Alma Mater of Mediterranean civilisation, and the Caput Mundi, whence law and the liberal arts and sciences radiated to the confines of its vast empire, conterminous with the Western World, is exceptionally rich in treasures of art. In its monuments may be traced the history of 3000 years, from the primitive settlement of remote antiquity, down through the days of imperial and papal pride to the present time. The yellow Tiber divides the city into two unequal parts; but the Rome of the Republic and the early Empire was confined to the left bank, where rise the famous seven hills: the Palatine and Capitoline in the centre, the Aventine, Caelian, Esquiline, Viminal, and Quirinal (from S. to N.) in an arc to the E. The last two were known as *colles;* all the rest were *montes.*

## 1  PIAZZA VENEZIA AND THE CAPITOL

**Piazza Venezia** (Pl. 4; 5), a huge and busy square, is the focus of the main traffic arteries of the city. Towards it converge Via del Corso from the N., Via del Plebiscito (the continuation of the Corso Vittorio Emanuele) from the W. (and St Peter's), Via Battisti (the continuation of Via Quattro Novembre) from the E. (and the Station), and, from the S.E. and S.W. respectively, Via dei Fori Imperiali and Via del Teatro di Marcello. As an overpowering background to the piazza rises the great Victor Emmanuel Monument, opposite which opens the straight Via del Corso, over a mile long, with the obelisk of Piazza del Popolo at its end. A policeman regulates the traffic at the head of the Corso; from here can be seen (left) the Palazzo delle Assicurazioni Generali di Venezia (1907), with a fine winged lion from Padua, and (right) Palazzo di Venezia (see p. 72). Behind the Monument, to the right, rises the Capitoline hill, reached from Piazza d'Aracoeli in which is a fountain (1589) designed by Jacopo della Porta.

The **Capitoline Hill** (in Italian, *Campidoglio;* 50 m) is the smallest but most famous of the Seven Hills of Rome. It was the political and religious centre of Ancient Rome, and since the end of the 11C has been the seat of the civic government of the city.

It is now thought that the hill was already inhabited by the late Bronze Age. Its two summits are separated by a depression, occupied by Piazza del Campidoglio. On the S. summit (*Capitolium*) stood the Capitol proper, with the *Temple of Jupiter Optimus Maximus Capitolinus,* the most venerated in Rome, as Jupiter was regarded as the city's special protector. The consuls, accordingly, on taking office, repaired to his temple to make their vows, and here the victorious general, at the end of a solemn procession in his triumphal car, offered thanks (comp. p. 112). The temple, traditionally founded by Tarquinius Priscus and completed by Tarquinius Superbus, was dedicated in 509 B.C. It was destroyed in 83 B.C. during the civil wars, rebuilt by Sulla, destroyed again in A.D. 69, rebuilt by Vespasian and again by Domitian, and was still standing in the 6C. Remains of the earliest temple still exist (comp. pp. 64, 69). The N. summit (altered by the construction of the Victor Emmanuel Monument) was occupied by the *Arx*, or citadel of Rome. During a siege by the Gauls in 390 B.C. the Capitol was saved from a night attack by the honking of the sacred geese of Juno kept here, who alerted the Romans to the danger. In 345 B.C. a temple was erected to Juno Moneta; the name came to be connected with the Mint later established here. The site of the temple is now covered by the church of Santa Maria in Aracoeli (p. 70).

Formerly the Capitoline Hill was accessible only from the Forum but since the 16C the main buildings have been made to face the north, in conformity with the direction of the modern development of the city.

From Piazza d'Aracoeli the wide modern Via del Teatro di Marcello runs s. to the Tiber, past the w. base of the Capitoline Hill (see Rte 3).

Three approaches to the hill ascend from Piazza d'Aracoeli. On the left a long steep flight of 124 steps (dating from 1348) mount to the church of Santa Maria in Aracoeli, more easily reached from Piazza del Campidoglio (see p. 70). On the right, Via delle tre Pile (a carriage road of 1873 now used by motor traffic), winds up to the Capitol, passing fragments of temples and a stretch of archaic wall. The middle ascent, 'La Cordonata', in the form of a ramp, dating from 1536, is the one most frequently used. It is guarded by two Egyptian lions in black granite (veined with red) of the Ptolomaic period, from the Isaeum. In the garden on the left (traversed by another flight of steps shaded by a pergola), a statue of Cola di Rienzo marks the spot where he was killed in 1354, having been acclaimed by the people on the Capitol in 1347. Higher up is a cage which, until recently, contained a she-wolf, a symbol of Rome. At the top, a balustrade defines the open end of Piazza del Campidoglio, with colossal figures of the Dioscuri (much restored), late Roman works, found in the Ghetto in the 16C. Also adorning the balustrade are two trophies of barbarian arms (Flavian period), known as 'Trophies of Marius', statues of Constantine and Constans (from the Baths of Constantine), and two milestones, the first and seventh of the Appian Way (p. 226).

The stately \***Piazza del Campidoglio** (Pl. 4; 7), designed by Michelangelo and completed in the 17C, is bounded on three sides by palaces. At the back is Palazzo Senatorio; on the left is Palazzo del Museo Capitolino; facing it, on the right, Palazzo dei Conservatori. Behind the last, and invisible from the piazza, is Palazzo Caffarelli. In the centre of the piazza is the \**Equestrian Statue of Marcus Aurelius* (? A.D. 166), brought from the Lateran in 1537 by order of Paul III.

This superb bronze statue, which bears traces of gilding, is a rare surviving example of antique imperial statues of the kind, and probably owes its preservation to the medieval belief that it represented the Christian emperor Constantine the Great. The small and elegant base, by Michelangelo, is in keeping with the character of the architectural surroundings.

**Palazzo Senatorio** (Pl. 4; 7), the official seat of the Governor of Rome, was built over the remains of the ancient Tabularium (see below). In its medieval form it was a towered castle which Boniface IX (1389-1404) gave to the municipality of Rome. The present façade (1592), by *G. B. della Porta* and *Girol. Rainaldi,* is a modification of Michelangelo's design. In front is a double staircase, with converging flights, adorned by a fountain with two colossal statues (1C A.D.) of the Tiber (r.) and the Nile (l.); in the recess is a porphyry statue of Minerva, found at Cori and transformed into the Dea Roma. The palace is crowned by a bell-tower

(1582), with a clock, a statue of Rome, and a gilded cross; two bells (1803-4) replace the famous *Patarina*.

The INTERIOR is visible only by special permission, or on the anniversary of the founding of Rome (21 April), when the campanile can also be climbed. The entrance is in Via S. Pietro in Carcere. On the left of the entrance hall is a room with sculptural fragments, models, and inscriptions. On the first floor in the COUNCIL CHAMBER is a colossal marble statue of Caesar, of the period of Trajan, and in the antechamber, L'Aurora by *Pietro da Cortona*. The ROOM OF THE FLAG contains a fragment of the 14C flag of St George, from the church of San Giorgio in Velabro.—In the adjoining PROTOMOTECA is a large collection of busts of the famous, mostly dating from the 18C and 19C. The GREAT HALL also has a Canova monument, and from here there is access to a terrace with a remarkable view of the Forum.

The **Tabularium** or depository of the State archives lies under Palazzo Senatorio. It was erected in 78 B.C. by Q. Lutatius Catulus; the inscription stone can still be seen by one entrance on the left flank of Palazzo Senatorio. Beyond this, in Via S. Pietro in Carcere, is the arcaded gallery of the Tabularium with a splendid view of the Forum. Here, also, is part of the frieze from the Temple of Concord (p. 110), and in the adjoining gallery (seen through a closed iron gate) is part of the frieze from the Temple of Vespasian (p. 110), another section of which can be seen through the arch, still in position above three columns at the foot of the Capitol.

For admission to the rest of the Tabularium, apply at the Palazzo dei Conservatori. There are several entrances, as a gallery was constructed in 1938 under the Piazza and Palazzo Senatorio, connecting this with Palazzo dei Conservatori and Palazzo del Museo Capitolino. Numerous inscriptions, some in Greek, have been arranged along the gallery.

The Tabularium had a rectangular plan, with a central court and two stories. The upper story is the most interesting; the lower level was used as a medieval prison, and is now a store. Here are considerable remains of the *Temple of Veiovis*, erected first in 196 B.C., and rebuilt after fire in the 1C B.C. The pronaos is orientated towards Via del Campidoglio, and the podium and cella are well preserved. The external wall of the Tabularium may be seen on two sides; a small gap was left between it and the Temple. Behind the Temple is a colossal marble statue of Veiovis (1C A.D., after a 5C B.C. Greek type), found in the cella.—To the right is a perfectly preserved staircase of the Republican period, leading steeply down to the Forum. It was blocked at the bottom by a tufa wall (still in place) when the Temple of Vespasian was built.

The assemblage of art treasures housed in the Palazzi del Museo Capitolino, dei Conservatori, and Caffarelli is grouped under the comprehensive title of *Capitoline Museums. The title is somewhat confusing, as one of the museums is called the Capitoline Museum (see below).

The nucleus of the exhibits is the oldest collection in the world, and dates from 1471, when Sixtus IV made over to the people of Rome a valuable group of bronzes, which were deposited in Palazzo dei Conservatori. Later, up to the foundation of the Pius-Clementine Sculpture gallery in the Vatican, this nucleus was enriched with discoveries in Rome and various acquisitions, the most noteworthy of which was the collection of Card. Alessandro Albani. New discoveries occasioned by the expansion of Rome in the 1870s led to the opening of a second Museum in 1876. Adm., see p. 47.

58

## CAPITOLINE MUSEUM

Palazzo del Museo Capitolino (Pl. 4; 5), built in the reign of Innocent X (1644-55), contains the *Capitoline Museum, an extremely interesting collection of antique sculpture, begun by Clement XII and added to by later popes. It was opened to the public in 1734, during the pontificate of Clement XII.

Ground Floor. Inner Court (R. II). Fountain, by *Giac. della Porta,* with a colossal figure of a river-god, known as 'Marforio', probably of the 2C A.D. found at the foot of the Capitol (one of Rome's talking statues; see p. 101). In the side niches are two figures of Pan (telamones), from the Theatre of Pompey.—Portico (III): Egyptian sculptures from the Isaeum Campense, including two apes from the tomb of Nectanebes II (358-341 B.C.).—Corridor (I). 2. Colossal statue of Minerva, from a

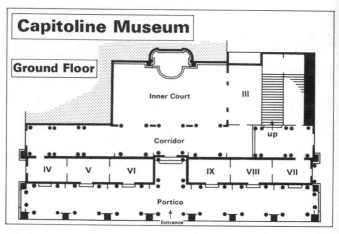

5C original.—At the left end is the entrance to three rooms (sometimes closed; apply at entrance gate), containing monuments of Oriental cults. Room IV. Three representations of Mithras; Base dedicated to the Magna Mater, with reliefs representing the Miracle of the Vestal Claudia, who with her girdle drew the ship bearing the image of the goddess to Rome (205 B.C.). In the centre is an altar to Sol Sanctissimus, the God of the Sun. Statue of a Gaul (early 3C A.D.), formerly at Wilton House near Salisbury.—R. V. 12. Bust of a young boy, follower of the cult of Isis (3C A.D.); 14. Bust of Serapis.—R. VI. Sculptures relating to the cult of Zeus Dolichenos.

At the right end of the corridor: (17, 14.) Two statues of women, after Kalamides' Aphrodite Sosandra, with portrait heads of the 2-3C A.D.; colossal statue of Mars, dating from the Domitian period. Here is the entrance to three more rooms (if closed apply at entrance gate): R. VII. Heads, busts, and fragments of calendars from the Palatine and Ostia, including a finely preserved Order of Precedence of the citizens of Ostia (temp. Emp. Pertinax).—R. VIII. 1. Roman head from the period of Trajan; *4. Celebrated Amendola Sarcophagus, with reliefs representing a battle between Gauls and Romans, showing a remarkable affinity with the Pergamene school; 10. Cippus of the master-mason Titus Statilius Aper, with his tools.—R. IX. Colossal double *Sarcophagus, formerly supposed to be that of Alexander Severus, a remarkable work of the 3C A.D., with portraits of the deceased and reliefs representing the story of Achilles; Cippus of Vettius Agorius Praetextatus, pro-consul of Achaia.—Opposite the colossal statue of Mars is the staircase.

FIRST FLOOR. Beyond the gallery (see below) is ROOM I. *Dying Gaul, an admirably modelled figure of a Celtic warrior who lies wounded on the ground awaiting death. It was discovered in the gardens of Sallust and is a copy of the Roman period of one of the bronze statues dedicated at Pergamon by Attalos I in commemoration of his victories over the Gauls (239 B.C.).

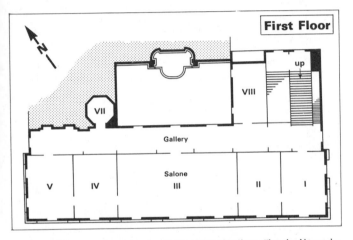

This figure was long erroneously called the Dying Gladiator, "butcher'd to make a Roman holiday", in Byron's phrase. Nearly all the other statues in this room were found at Hadrian's Villa, near Tivoli.

Round the room: 1. Amazon, a Roman work after an original attributed to Pheidias (wrongly restored); 2. Colossal head of Alexander the Great; 3. Hermes, Hadrianic version of a 4C original; 4. Lycian Apollo, copy of a work by Praxiteles; 6. Head of a youth; *7. Satyr Resting, an admirable replica of an original by Praxiteles (the 'Marble Faun' of Hawthorne's romance; other replicas in the Vatican); *8. Head of Dionysos; 9. Greek cynic philosopher, Roman copy in marble of a bronze original; 10. Head of a general, a Pheidian type; 11. Priestess of Isis, period of Hadrian; 12. Eros and Psyche, Hellenistic work.

ROOM II. In the centre, *1. Laughing Silenus, in red marble, of the Imperial period from a Hellenistic bronze; 2. Alabaster bust of unknown Roman, period of Gallienus; 5. Sarcophagus depicting the Hunt of the Calydonian Boar; 8. Child with mask, a Hellenistic work; 11. Sarcophagus with figures of Endymion and Selene (early 3C A.D.); 16.

Herm of Hercules (2C A.D.); 17. Boy with goose, copy of a bronze by Boethos of Chalcedon (2C B.C.); Sarcophagus (2C A.D.) with the life of Dionysos including his birth, a graceful work.

On the wall is a bronze plaque on which is inscribed the *Lex Regia* of Vespasian, the historic decree conferring sovereign power on that emperor; it was first brought to notice by Rienzo, whom it served as a text for demonstrating the greatness and the rights of Rome.

ROOM III (SALONE). In the centre, 1, 5. Statues of Zeus and Asklepios, both from originals of the 4C B.C.; 2, 4. Young or laughing centaur, Old or weeping centaur, two vigorous works from Hadrian's Villa, signed by his contemporaries Aristeas and Papias of Aphrodisias in Caria; 3. Infant Hercules, a colossal ugly figure in green basalt, of the late Imperial epoch, on a base decorated with scenes from the myth of Zeus.

Round the room (l. to r.): 7. Colossal statue of Apollo (the head does not belong); 11. Hera, from an original attributed to Agorakritos (5C B.C.), badly restored with a portrait head; 13. Hadrian as Mars; 20. Archaic statue of Apollo, copy of the so-called Omphalos Apollo in Athens; 21. Statue of a young Roman of the time of Hadrian as Hermes; *22. Old woman in terror, a striking example of the Hellenistic period; 23. Muse, once probably representing Hera, from a 4C original; 24. Colossal statue of Demeter, restored as Hera, from an Attic original of the 4C B.C.; 27. Huntsman, head of the period of Gallienus on a body of the late-Archaic type; 28. Statue of Harpocrates, period of Hadrian; *30. Apollo, from a work of the first half of the 5C; 31. Pothos, from an original by Skopas; 33. Wounded Amazon, signed by the copyist Sosicles, from a 5C original; 34. Roman couple as Mars and Venus, period of Septimius Severus; 36. Athena Promachos, a 4C type from the Villa d'Este.

ROOM IV. The identifications of the busts of philosophers, poets, and others in this room are not all certain. Those whose identity is most probable are Socrates (various types), Theon (17), Sophocles (22-23), Chrysippos (27), Euripides (30-31), Homer (39-41), Demosthenes (43), Aeschines (50), Metrodorus (51), *Double portrait of Epicuros and Metrodorus (52), Epicuros (53), Antisthenes (55), Cicero (56), Theophrastus (74). In the centre, 75. Seated figure ('Marcellus') from an original of the 4C B.C. (head modern). On the walls are fragments of a frieze, perhaps from the Porticus of Octavia, with sacrificial instruments and parts of ships, and Greek votive reliefs.

ROOM V contains a rich collection of Roman imperial busts, interesting as portraits and also in some cases because of the precious materials used. (On columns): *Augustus, wearing a wreath of myrtle; *15. Woman of the late Flavian period; 20. Domitia; 21. Plotina, wife of Trajan, considered her best portrait; 24. Matidia; 32. Faustina the Younger; 39. Julia Domna; *55. Heliogabalus. On the walls are reliefs, two of which are works of great delicacy, executed in the first centuries of the Empire and following Hellenistic types: F. Perseus rescuing Andromeda; H. Sleeping Endymion. In the centre: 59. Helena, mother of Constantine, a beautiful seated figure inspired by the Aphrodite of Pheidias.

GALLERY. 35. Colossal head of an Emperor, 4C A.D.; 36. Portrait of Marcus Aurelius as a boy; 53. Colossal head of Aphrodite, perhaps an original of the Hellenistic period; 57. Sarcophagus of the 3C A.D. with reliefs of the rape of Persephone; 61. Roman matron of the Flavian period in the guise of Venus; 65. Torso of the Discobolos of Myron, badly restored by Monnot as a fighting gladiator; 67. Cupid as archer, a good copy of the celebrated work by Lysippos; 68. Hercules slaying the Hydra (so restored by Algardi: and the antique model he used can be seen beside it. It was more probably intended to represent Hercules capturing the hind). 4a. Relief of a man and wife, probably reading a will; 7. Leda and the Swan, replica of a work attrib. to Timotheos (4C B.C.); 8. Head of Marsyas, probably a Hellenistic original; 10. Drunken old woman, perhaps after Myron the Younger, a Pergamene sculptor of the end of the 3C B.C.; 22. Psyche winged, from a Hellenistic original; 24. Head of Dionysos, a good copy from a 4C B.C. original; 31. Minerva, copy of a bronze of c. 400 B.C.; 34. Decorative vase (krater) of the 1C A.D., resting on a *Well-Head from Hadrian's Villa, with archaistic decoration representing the procession of the twelve gods Dii Consentes).

ROOM VII (CABINET OF VENUS), contains the celebrated *Capitoline Venus, found in the 17C in a house near San Vitale, a superbly modelled statue of Parian marble. It is a Roman replica of a Hellenistic original, derived from the Cnidian Aphrodite of Praxiteles.

R. VIII (HALL OF THE DOVES) is named from a delicate *Mosaic (9) from Hadrian's Villa, after a work by Sosias of Pergamon; 8. Sarcophagus with the story of Prometheus (3C A.D.); 23. Herm of Hermes Propylaios; 37. Diana of Ephesus; 52. Front face of a sarcophagus, with the Triumph of Bacchus. In glass cases: 53. Tabula Iliaca or Trojan Tablet, a plaque with small reliefs representing the Trojan cycle, by Theodorus (1C A.D.); 76. Piece of a shield of Achilles by the same sculptor. In the centre of the room is a charming little statue of a child protecting a dove, a Roman copy of a Greek work of the 2C B.C. (wrongly restored with a snake).

# PALAZZO DEI CONSERVATORI

The **Palazzo dei Conservatori** (Pl. 4; 7) was rebuilt by Nicholas V about 1450 and remodelled after 1564 by *Giacomo Della Porta* from a design by Michelangelo. It contains the **Sale dei Conservatori,** the **Museo del Palazzo dei Conservatori,** and the **Pinacoteca,** or picture gallery. The first two are situated on the first floor, and the Pinacoteca on the second floor. Adjoining the building, and reached from the Museo del Palazzo dei Conservatori, is the **Museo Nuovo,** which is at ground level.

From the piazza is the entrance to the interior COURT. On the right are fragments of a colossal statue of Constantine the Great, including the head, which were brought from the Basilica of Constantine in 1486. Near the head is an inscription of the time of Boniface VIII. On the left are bases and transennæ with sculptured representations of provinces and nations subject to Rome, which once decorated the Temple of Hadrian in the Piazza di Pietra. Above is an inscription from the arch erected in A.D. 51 on the Via Lata to celebrate the conquest of Britain by Claudius. Beneath the portico at the farther end, a figure of Roma of the time of Trajan or Hadrian, and statues of Barbarians. 1st LANDING: Four reliefs from triumphal arches, three being from one erected to Marcus Aurelius; to the right, Sacrifice before the Temple of Jupiter Capitolinus. 2nd LANDING: Hadrian, relief from the demolished Arco di Portogallo (p. 152); statue of Charles of Anjou, attrib. to Arnolfo di Cambio. From this landing, at the top of the stairs, open the Sale dei Conservatori.

## SALE DEI CONSERVATORI

ROOM I, SALA DEGLI ORAZI E CURIAZI. Frescoes by *Giuseppe Cesari,* known as the Cavalier d'Arpino, representing episodes from the reigns of the early kings. *Urban VIII, marble statue, a studio work begun by *Bernini;* *Innocent X, bronze by *Algardi.*

R. II, SALA DEI CAPITANI. Handsome doors in carved wood (17C); further frescoes from Roman history, by *Tom. Laureti,* and 16-17C statues, including one of Alessandro Farnese and of Marcantonio Colonna.

R. III, SALA DEI TRIONFI DI MARIO. Frieze by *Mich. Alberti* and *Giac. Rocchetti* representing the triumph of Emilius Paulus over Perseus of Macedon. The most famous of the bronzes presented to the Conservatori by Sixtus IV are exhibited here. In the middle is the celebrated *Spinario, or Boy plucking a thorn from his foot.

This was formerly known as the 'Fedele Capitolino', because it was thought to be the portrait of Marcius, a Roman messenger who would not delay the execution of his mission though tortured by a thorn in his foot. It is a delicate Hellenistic composition in the eclectic style of the 1C B.C.

Bronze *Head, known as L. Junius Brutus, of Etruscan or Italic workmanship of the 3C B.C.; Camillus, or acolyte (1C A.D.); Bronze krater with an inscription, the gift of King Mithridates to a gymnastic association, part of the booty from a Mithridatic war, found at Anzio; fine sarcophagus front (3C A.D.).

R. IV, SALA DELLA LUPA, with more frescoes from Roman history. On the wall opposite the windows are fragments of the Fasti Consulares et Triumphales, from the inner walls of the Arch of Augustus in the Forum, in a framing designed by *Michelangelo.* These are records of Roman magistrates and of triumphs of the great captains of Rome in 13 B.C.-A.D. 12. In the middle is the *She-wolf sacred to Rome, thought to be an Etruscan bronze of the late 6C or early 5C B.C., probably belonging to the school of Vulca, an Etruscan sculptor of Veii.

This formerly stood on the Capitol and may be the wolf which was struck by lightning in 65 B.C., when the hind feet are said to have been damaged. The twins are the work of *Ant. Pollaiolo* (15C).

R. V, SALA DELLE OCHE, an interesting example of a 17C apartment, contains various works of art, among which may be mentioned a figure of Isis and two 'Geese', more likely ducks (antique bronzes), a bronze bust of Michelangelo, and a marble Head of Medusa, by *Bernini;* in the centre: Mastiff in rare green marble.

R. VI, SALA DELLE AQUILE. Sleeping Eros, after a Hellenistic type; Head of a charioteer (1C A.D.). From here opens R. XVIII of the Museo del Palazzo dei Conservatori (see below).

R. VII, SALA DEGLI ARAZZI. Tapestries executed for the municipality; one shows the goddess Roma, the others represent the Birth of Romulus and Remus (from the painting by Rubens in the Capitoline Gallery), the Vestal Tutia, and the 'defeatist' schoolmaster of Falerii punished by Camillus.—From here there is access to RR. XVI-XVIII of the Museo del Palazzo dei Conservatori (comp. p. 63).

R. VIII, CAPPELLA NUOVA. On altar, Madonna in glory with SS. Peter and Paul, by *Avanzino Nucci.*

R. IX, SALA DELLE GUERRE PUNICHE, is adorned with frescoes by *Giac. Ripanda.* In the middle, Two girls playing, Hellenistic work.

R. X, CAPPELLA VECCHIA. On the ceiling, Frescoes and stuccoes, by *Alberti* and *Rocchetti;* on the walls, Madonna and angels, by *Ant. da Viterbo.*

R. XI, CORRIDOR. 16C Flemish tapestry; Roman scenes by *Gasp. Vanvitelli.*— The Corridor leads back to the landing, where, to the right, is the entrance to the—

MUSEO DEL PALAZZO DEI CONSERVATORI

RR. XII, XIII, XIV, SALE DEI FASTI MODERNI. These rooms contain lists of the chief magistrates of Rome since 1640, and a collection of busts and herms. R. XII. 8. Fragment of a group of a giant fighting with two satyrs, deriving from the Gigantomachia of Pergamon.—R. XIII. 2. Cow, Roman copy, thought to be derived from the Cow of Myron; 4. Bust of Faustina, wife of Antoninus Pius; 5. Sarcophagus, depicting a Dionysiac ceremony; 6. Bust of Sabina, wife of Hadrian.—R. XIV. 4. Panther and wild boar in combat; Roman imperial busts.—From the gallery (see below) is the entrance (right) into—

R. XV, SALA DEGLI ORTI LAMIANI, containing sculptures found in the Lamiani Gardens, on the Esquiline. 3. Old fisherman; 5. Old woman with a lamb, two Hellenistic statues of great realism; 4. Seated girl, a graceful figure of the Hellenistic period; 7. Centaur's head, probably an original of Pergamene art; (in the second part of the gallery) 12. Bust of Commodus as Hercules, a work of considerable refinement; 13, 14. Tritons, perhaps its supporters; 15. Female statue, after an original of the 4C B.C.—In the centre, *29. Esquiline Venus, a young girl probably connected with the cult of Isis, an eclectic work of the school of Pasiteles, 1C B.C.

Beyond a pavement in marble and alabaster from the Esquiline can be seen R. XVI. At present it is necessary to return through the museum to the landing and re-enter the Sale dei Conservatori, from Room VII (comp. p. 62) of which there is access to RR. XVI-XVIII.

R. XVI SALA DEI MAGISTRATI (comp. the Plan, p. 65). 2, 5. Roman umpires starting a race in the time of Constantine; column of rare green breccia from Egypt; inscriptions recording the conferment of Roman citizenship on Petrarch, Michelangelo, Titian, and Bernini; 4. Artemis, from a 4C original, restored to represent Christian Rome; 6. The emperor Decius as Mars.

RR. XVII-XVIII, *SALE DEI MONUMENTI ARCAICI. In the centre, *10. Torso of an Amazon (late 6C B.C.), designed for the angle of the temple pediment of Apollo Daphnephoros at Eretria. 2. Headless female statue from a bronze original c. 460 B.C.; 4. Fragment of a stele (5 or 4C B.C.); 5. Latona, from a 5C original; 7, 9. Two young initiates of the Eleusinian mysteries.—R. XVIII. 6, 7. Korai in the Archaizing style of the early Imperial era; 8. Nike, probably from a 5C original; 10. Fragment of a stele of Attic workmanship; 11. Head of a lion (5C); 12. Stele representing a girl with a dove (late 6C); *13. Charioteer mounting, after a 5C original: wrongly restored, possibly intended to represent Theseus.

GALLERY. 14. Colossal foot, probably of the Rhodian school; 35. Copy of the 'Grande Ercolanese' (original formerly at Dresden); 41. Relief of a 'Scaenae frons' (1-2C A.D.); 44. Aedicula, or shrine, dedicated to the Earth Mother; 53, 54. Athletes, from 4C types; 56. Fragment of a relief from the Auditorium of Maecenas; 58. Claudia Justa as Fortune (2C A.D.); 68. Youth, perhaps from an original of the Polykleitan school.

The GARDEN (reached from the gallery) contains decorative sculpture.

From the beginning of the gallery is the entrance to RR. XIX, XX, SALE CRISTIANE. Sarcophagi with the Good Shepherd; inscriptions; 13. Head of a Roman matron (5-6C A.D.).

R. XXI, SALA DEL CAMINO, with remains of a chimneypiece (camino) of the Conservatori. 1. Sarcophagus, with the Calydonian boar hunt. In glass cases: Greek red- and black-figure vases, and antefixes from Capua (6-5C); in a case towards the gallery, Tragliatella oinochoe (7C B.C.) with paintings and graffiti, and below, Attic kylix of 470 B.C. from Cerveteri.

R. XXII, PRIMA SALA CASTELLANI, contains part of the collection presented by Augusto Castellani, the fruit of excavations between 1860-66 in S. Etruria and Latium. In glass cases along the walls: Etruscan, Italic and Faliscan vases. In the centre of the room: *Capitoline Tensa, reconstruction of a triumphal chariot overlaid with bronze, which carried the images of the gods at the opening of the Circensian games; Etruscan statuette in terracotta from Cerveteri (end of 7C B.C.).

R. XXIII, SECONDA SALA CASTELLANI. In glass cases along the walls: Corinthian and Attic vases, with red and black figures (6C B.C.) including (No. 64) the Amphora of Nikosthenes. In the middle of the room: *Krater of Aristonothos, with Odysseus and the Cyclops (7C); (No. 132) hydria from Ceretani; three sides of an Etruscan funerary bed, with animal reliefs.

R. XXIV, SALA DEI BRONZI. 2, 3, 8. Head, hand, and globe from a colossal statue of Constans II; 5. Rear half of a colossal bull, of finest workmanship; 6. Globe which originally adorned the Vatican Obelisk, damaged by a musket shot during the Sack of Rome in 1527; *10. Horse, copy of a work of the school of Lysippos; *11. Bed with exquisite decoration, of the 1C A.D.; *12. Litter, composed of bronze, found on the Esquiline by Castellani. In a glass case, to the r. of the door to R. XXV, statuette of a Lar, with rhyton and patera; statuette of Hecate.

R. XXV. SALA DEGLI ORTI MECENAZIANI, containing sculptures found in the Gardens of Maecenas on the Esquiline. 2. Statue of Hercules, from an original by Lysippos; 3. Eros (?), from an early 4C B.C. original; 6. Punishment of Marsyas, in Phrygian marble, probably of the Rhodian school; 7. Head of Augustus; 8. Hygieia, Roman copy of a Hellenistic original; *9. Dancing Maenad, in relief, from an original by Kallimachos; 10. Headless statue of Aphrodite, a fine copy of an Ionic Greek original; *11. Head of an Amazon, from an original by Polykleitos; 18. Rhyton, part of the decoration of a fountain, by Pontios of Athens, in the neo-Attic style of the 1C A.D.

## BRACCIO NUOVO

At the end of the gallery is (left) the PASSAGE OF THE ROMAN WALL (contents, see below), a tufa wall belonging to the Temple of Jupiter Capitolinus (6C B.C.; comp. p. 55). Here is the entrance to the New Wing, arranged between 1950 and 1952 and devoted to finds from more recent excavations. On the floor and walls of the first three rooms may be seen remains of the foundations of the Temple of Jupiter Capitolinus (clarified by a plan in R. II).

R. I. 1. Portrait of a man (1C B.C.); 2. Base dedicated to Hercules by the dictator Minucius, colleague of Q. Fabius Maximus, in 217 B.C.; *35. Fragment of a fresco from a tomb of the early 3C B.C. The subject is possibly Q. Fabius Rullianus, consul in 322, and this example is the earliest known of Roman painting; 36. (in front of the window), Relief of

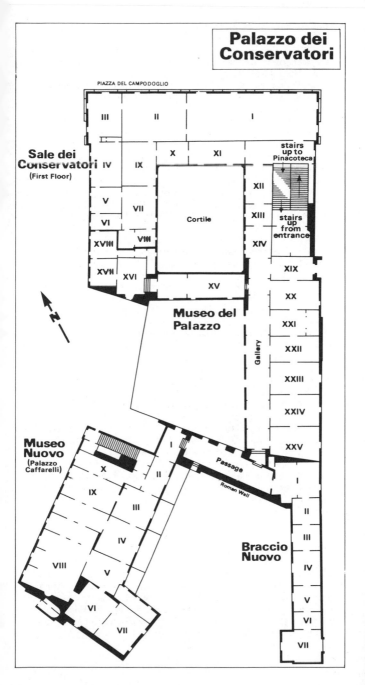

# Palazzo dei Conservatori

PIAZZA DEL CAMPODOGLIO

III  II  I

X  XI

stairs
up to
Pinacoteca

**Sale dei Conservatori** IV  IX
(First Floor)

XII

V  VII

XIII

stairs
up
from
entrance

VI

Cortile

XIV

XVIII  VIII

XIX

XVII  XVI

XV

XX

**Museo del Palazzo**

XXI

XXII

Gallery

XXIII

XXIV

XXV

**Museo Nuovo**
(Palazzo Caffarelli)

I

X  II

Passage

I

IX

Roman Wall

II

III

III

IV

IV

**Braccio Nuovo**

VIII  V

V

VI

VI

VII

VII

N

C

Marcus Curtius riding into the abyss (1C B.C.); 37. Sarcophagus cover of the Etruscan type (4C B.C.).

R. II. Further works of the Republican period. 1, 12. Two fragments of a frieze of a triumphal procession; 2, 3, and 4. Pediment with frieze from a Republican tomb; 13-19. Terracotta group of statues for the pediment of a temple; 5, 6. Two funerary statues; 7-10. Fragments of a sepulchral monument, finely executed; 11. Fragment of a frieze with a ritual dance.

R. III. Roman portraits. 7. Statue of a man, holding two busts of his forebears, 1C A.D.; 9. Agrippa; 10. Claudius; 11. Domitian, one of the few portraits of him extant; 15. Trajan; 25. Lucilla, daughter of M. Aurelius; 32. Fresco (2-3C A.D.), found during the construction of the Metro; in the centre, 31. Round base with Bacchic dance, neo-Attic.

R. IV. *3. Apollo shooting an arrow, a Greek statue of the first half of the 5C B.C., perhaps by Pythagoras of Rhegion; brought to Rome and altered, it was placed in the Temple of Apollo Sosianus. 2. Head of Hercules, after an original by Polykleitos; 4. Head of an Amazon, from an original by Kresilas, with a subtle expression of pain; 5, 6. Two replicas of Pothos, from an original by Skopas (No. 5 is particularly fine); *8. Aristogeiton, the best replica of one of the two statues of the tyrannicides by Kritios and Nesiotes (477-476 B.C.) which stood in the Agora at Athens.

R. V. 1, 4, 7, and 8. Four fragments of a richly decorated frieze (1C B.C.); Head of a youth, after the Kyniskos of Polykleitos; 2. Head of a girl, Archaic style, found on the Appia Antica; 14. Warriors in combat, metope of the 4C B.C., probably from the Temple of Poseidon at Isthmia; 17. Headless statue of Aphrodite, from an original of the Rhodian school; 18. Archaic base of a candelabrum with the divinities of Delos; on the floor, polychrome mosaic (1C B.C.).

R. VI. 2. Sarcophagus with winged victories, and a frieze of animals (3C A.D.); 9. Sarcophagus with the myth of Apollo and Marsyas of 2C A.D.; 13. Neo-Attic relief of the contest between Apollo and Marsyas.

R. VII. On the floor, coloured Mosaic of the Rape of Proserpina, with personifications of the seasons (late 2C A.D.); 4, 7, 8, and 10. Colossal female head, arm, and two feet of a cult statue from the Area Sacra of the Largo Argentina; 3, 5. Two altars, with bucrania; 1, 2, 6, 12, and 13. Frieze from the Temple of Apollo Sosianus, 1C B.C.; 9. Frieze of cupids with the arms of Mars, from the Temple of Venus Genetrix (c. 113 A.D.); Statue (fountain) of a reclining river-god, with a beautiful head. Dating from the late 2C or early 3C A.D., the statue was recently found in the centre of Rome.

## MUSEO NUOVO

The collection of sculptures comprising the Museo Nuovo is exhibited in the **Palazzo Caffarelli,** which rises at the S.W. end of the Palazzo dei Conservatori, on the other side of the garden. This palazzo was built for Giovanni Pietro Caffarelli in 1580 by *Gregorio Canonico.* Formerly the German Embassy, it was taken over by the Italian Government in 1918, and, after restoration, was opened as a museum in 1925. For some time it was known as the Museo Mussolini. (The numbering of the exhibits is in course of alteration.)

To reach the museum, it is necessary to return to the PASSAGE of the Roman Wall. 11. Inscribed base of a statue of Cornelia, mother of the Gracchi, from the Porticus of Octavia (p. 84); 12. Inscription from the beaked column erected in honour of the Consul C. Duilius after his naval victory off Mylae over the Carthaginians; 9. Cinerary stele of Agrippina the Elder.

ROOM I. 1. Funerary relief from the Baker's tomb at the Porta Maggiore (see p. 219), depicting the baker and his wife; 2-6. Fragments of a pediment, with pastoral subjects (1C A.D.); Cinerary urns.—R. II. 1. Sarcophagus with tritons and nereids (4C A.D.); behind glass, Busts and statuettes, among which, (12.) Head of a young boy, a Greek original of the early 5C.—R. III. Archaizing and neo-Attic sculpture. 2. Headless statue of a youth, showing traces of colour; 18. Priapus.

R. IV. Hellenistic art. In the centre, *24. The Muse Polyhymnia; 1. Head of Isis-Nechbet-Aphrodite, perhaps an Alexandrian original of the 2C B.C.; 4. Head of a youth; 7. Isis (?), an Antonine copy of a 4C B.C. original; 11. Torso of Hercules, from an original attributed to Skopas; *17-21. Groups of satyrs, maenads, and hermaphrodites, after a work at Pergamon by Kephisodotos the Younger.

R. V. In the centre, 18. Praying woman in grey basalt, from a bronze of the early 4C; 6. Votive relief to Asklepios and Hygieia (?), 4C original; 10. Aphrodite, from the same original as the Arles Aphrodite in the Louvre (? Praxiteles), the only copy preserving an arm; 15. Icarus, reworking of a Polykleitan original in the 2C A.D.; 16. Herm of Hercules replica of a work by Skopas; 17. Athena from the Castro Pretorio, copy of a work by Kephisodoros, once in Piraeus.

GARDEN. Fragments of fluted columns from the Temple of Jupiter, dating from a rebuilding in the time of Domitian. In the centre, *Group of a lion attacking a horse.

RR. VI, VII. Roman art. 1. Funerary altar from the Porta Salaria, of Q. Sulpicius Maximus, an infant prodigy who won a poetic contest at the age of 11 in the reign of Domitian (A.D. 94); 8. Stele of the shoemaker, Julius Aelius, with an expressive portrait-bust (Flavian period); 11. Sarcophagus, with relief of a battle between the Romans and Barbarians, and a fine relief above, of hunting scenes (end of 2C A.D.).—R. VII (left). 5. Lower part of a marble neo-Attic bowl, beautifully decorated; 10. Corbulo, the celebrated general, father-in-law of Domitian, and conqueror of the Germans and Parthians (d. A.D. 67); 12. Portrait of a girl, a charming work of the early Empire; 21. Fragment of a relief with an Ionic temple (this and Nos. 17 and 23 were found together with the reliefs incorporated into the façade of the Villa Medici, and were probably all part of the Ara Pietatis); 24. Domitian, the best portrait bust of this emperor; 26. Bust of a man, a vivid study from the end of the 3C A.D.; 27. Fragment of a marble fountain adorned with a ship's prow (1C A.D.).

R. VIII. Reproductions of Greek sculpture of the 5C B.C. This room was formerly the chapel of the German Embassy; it was partly built over the cella of the Temple of Jupiter. In the pavement, fragments of the original building. *18. Colossal statue of Athena, fine reproduction of an original by Kresilas; 1. Torso of Perseus (?) of mid-5C B.C. type; 2. Statue of Demeter, from a mid-5C original; 3. Discobolos resting, perhaps by Naukydes, son of Polykleitos (much restored); 5, 6. Athena

Parthenos, fragmentary reduced reproductions of the statue by Pheidias: No. 6 is particularly interesting, with part of the shield decorated with reliefs still intact; 7. Head of Ares, after an original attrib. to Alkamenes; 8. Head of Diomedes (c. 420 B.C.); 9. Head of the type of the Tyrannicides (c. 475 B.C.); 11. Poseidon, of the early 5C type; 15. Herm of Anacreon, perhaps taken from a bronze statue by Pheidias (c. 450 B.C.); 16. Head of Perseus, from a mid-5C B.C. original (perhaps belonging to the torso No. 1); 17. Statue of a woman, from an original attrib. to Kalamides; 19. Asklepios, Attic original of the late 5C B.C.—R. IX. 9. Torso of Apollo Kitharoidos (from a 5C original); the head of Apollo to the left (No. 11) is probably from the same original; 8. Head of a young athlete, from an original by Polykleitos.—R. X. 17-18. Fragments of a sarcophagus of Asiatic type; portraits of the Imperial period.

## PINACOTECA CAPITOLINA

The **Capitoline Picture Gallery,** founded in 1749 by Benedict XIV, was based on the Pio and Sacchetti collections, formed respectively by Prince Gilberto Pio of Savoy and Card. Sacchetti. In the 19C it lost some of its treasures to the Vatican Picture Gallery and to the Accademia di San Luca. More recently it was enriched by the Cini bequest, which included some interesting 14-15C paintings from the Sterbini collection, as well as the bronzes and ceramics of that collection. The Pinacoteca has noteworthy examples, native and foreign, of artists of the 16C, 17C, and 18C.

The gallery is on the second floor. On the LANDING: Apotheosis of Sabina, relief from the Arcdo di Portogallo (comp. p. 152); Head of a priest of Isis (?); Bull attacked by a tigress, two examples of marble intarsia work from the basilica of Junius Bassus on the Esquiline (4C A.D.).

ROOM I. 4. *School of Ferrara,* Portrait of a girl; 5. *Dosso Dossi,* Holy Family; 7. *Mazzolino,* Christ and the Doctors; *10. *Emilian School* (1513), Madonna and Child with Saints; *Garófalo,* *14. Annunciation, 21. Madonna in Glory (being restored in 1978), 22. Holy Family; 17. *Fr. Francia* (?), Presentation in the Temple; 23. *Scarsellino,* Adoration of the Magi.

R. II. *Paolo Veronese,* 1. Strength, 3. Temperance, 6. Rape of Europa; *2. *Girol. Savoldo,* Portrait of a lady with the attributes of St Margaret; 4. *Gentile Bellini* (attrib.), Portrait of a man; *5. *Giov. Bellini,* Portrait of a young man; *8. *Palma Vecchio,* Woman taken in adultery; *9. *Titian,* Baptism of Christ; 10. *Lor. Lotto,* Man with crossbow; *Domenico Tintoretto,* 11-13. Scourging of Christ, Crown of Thorns, Baptism of Christ, *17. St Mary Magdalene.

R. III. *Bart. Passarotti,* 1, 7. Two portraits of unknown men; 5. Portrait of a man with dog; *Van Dyck,* 2. The engravers Pieter de Jode, father and son, 10. The painters Luke and Cornelius de Wael; 3. *Anon.* (taken from a painting by Jacopino del Conte), Michelangelo; 4. *Guido Reni,* Self-portrait; 6. *Rubens,* Romulus and Remus fed by the wolf (finished by pupils); 8. *Federico Zuccari,* Self-portrait; *11. *Velazquez,* Portrait of a man (? Bernini); *Salvator Rosa,* 13. Soldier, 15. The witch; *17. *Jean Leclerc,* Christ with the doctors; 18. *Carlo Maratta,* Holy Family; 19, 21. *Il Borgognone,* Two battle scenes; 20. *Simon Vouet,*

Allegory; 23. *Luca Cambiaso*, Madonna and Child; 22. *Metsù*, Crucifixion; 25. *Guercino*, Holy Family; 26. *Denis Calvaert*, Marriage of St Catherine.

R. IV. Mainly 14C and 15C. *1. *Cola dell'Amatrice*, Death and Assumption of the Virgin; *5. *Macrino d'Alba*, Madonna and saints; *8. *Barnaba da Modena*, Ascension; 11. *G. A. Sogliani*, Madonna and Child; 12-16. *Central Italian master* (1376), Annunciation, Nativity, Presentation in the Temple, Flight into Egypt, Massacre of the Innocents; 17, 19. *Follower of P. Lorenzetti*, St Mary Magdalene and St Bartholomew; 18. *Nic. di Pietro Gerini*, Trinity.

To the right is R. V (the CINI GALLERY), containing part of the bequest of Count Giuseppe Cini (1881), and including a noteworthy collection of bronzes and ceramics. In glass cases: *Ceramics from various sources, including excellent Saxon porcelain, clocks, and tobacco boxes. 17. *Caravaggio*, St John the Baptist, a replica of one in the Galleria Doria.

At the end of the gallery is the *Medagliere*, or Cabinet of Medals (adm. by special permission), containing a rich collection of Roman, medieval, and modern coins and medals.

R. VI. *Pier Fr. Mola*, 1. Diana and Endymion, 7. Esther and Ahasuerus; *Pietro da Cortona*, 3. Rape of the Sabines, 12. Sacrifice of Polyxena, 14. Triumph of Bacchus; 6. *Pietro Testa*, Joseph sold into bondage; 9. *G. M. Bottalla*, Meeting of Esau and Jacob; 10, 11. *Crescenzio Onofri*, Landscapes.—(Above window), Bust of Benedict XIV; inlaid 17C cabinets. Hercules in gilt bronze, found in the time of Sixtus IV in the demolition of the Ara Maxima, near the Forum Boarium.

R. VII. (to r. of R. V.). 1. *Domenichino*, Sibyl; 2. *Guercino*, St John Baptist; 3. *Giov. Lanfranco*, Herminia among the shepherds; *Guido Reni*, 5. Magdalen, 6. Anima Beata; *Guercino*, 12. St Petronilla, a vast canvas, formerly in St Peter's, 14. Antony and Cleopatra, 16. St Matthew and the angel, 22. Persian Sibyl; 10. *Elisabetta Sirani*, Ulysses and Circe; 17. *Fr. Albani*, Nativity of the Virgin; *19. *Caravaggio*, Gipsy fortune-teller.

R. VIII. 3. *Pietro da Cortona*, Madonna and Child; 9. *Veronese*, Mary Magdalene; 10. *School of Tintoretto*, Pentecost; 15. *Guido Reni*, Christ Child and St John; 16, 18. *Agostino Tassi* (?), two landscapes; 17. *Poussin*, Triumph of Flora (replica of a painting in the Louvre).

R. IX. *Garófalo*, 3. Holy Family, 5. Marriage of Catherine; 7. *Guido Reni*, Madonna and Child with SS. Albert and Cecilia; 8. *Fr. Albani*, Madonna and Child; 9. *Ann. Carracci*, Madonna and Child; 11. *Lod. Carracci*, Head of a boy, a very fine early work; 18. *Ann. Carracci*, St Francis adoring the Crucifix.

From Piazza del Campidoglio, to the left of Palazzo dei Conservatori, a staircase ascends to a portico named after Vignola. Beyond it is Via del Tempio di Giove. Here are remains of the Temple of Jupiter (p. 55). This street leads into Via del Monte Tarpeo and the *Belvedere Monte Tarpeo*, a terrace commanding an extensive *View of Rome to the s. and s.e., including the Roman Forum. The precipice below the terrace was for long presumed to be the *Tarpeian Rock* (comp. p. 86).

Here is the rear entrance of the Palazzo Caffarelli, in which a selection of exhibits from the **Antiquarium Comunale** (adm. p. 47) have been arranged. This was founded in 1885 for objects found during excavations in Rome. The contents include finds from the Esquiline necropolis, and from excavations near Sant'Omobono and on the Campidoglio.

**Santa Maria in Aracoeli** (Pl. 4; 5), an austere brick-built church, dating from before the 7C, when it was already considered ancient, stands on the highest point of the Capitoline Hill. It is approached by a monumental flight of steps (comp. p. 56), but from the top of the hill it is more easily reached by steps to the E. of the Capitoline Museum. The church occupies the site of the Roman citadel, where, according to medieval tradition, the Tiburtine Sibyl foretold to Augustus the imminent coming of Christ in the words, "Ecce ara primogeniti Dei": hence the name Aracoeli, Church of the Altar of Heaven. In the 10C the church belonged to the Benedictines; in 1250 Innocent IV handed it over to the Franciscans, who rebuilt the exterior in the Romanesque style. The façade, overlooking the great staircase from Piazza d'Aracoeli, was never completed. The staircase was built in 1348 as a thank-offering for deliverance from a plague.

In the Middle Ages the church was the meeting-place of the Roman Council. Here Rienzo frequently addressed the assembly after the events of Whitsun 1347; Charles of Anjou held his parliament of the Romans; and Marcantonio Colonna celebrated his triumph after the battle of Lépanto. It was also in this church, as Gibbon "sat musing amidst the ruins of the Capitol, while the friars were singing vespers, that the idea of writing the Decline and Fall of the City first started to his mind" (5 Oct 1764).

In the tympanum of the s. door is a mosaic of the Madonna and two angels attributed to *Pietro Cavallini.*

The INTERIOR has been freely restored but has retained its grandeur and severity. The ceiling of the NAVE, with naval emblems and much gold ornamentation, dates from 1575 and commemorates the victory of Lépanto (1571). The lower part of the nave is divided from the aisles by 22 antique columns of varying sizes and styles, taken from pagan buildings; the 3rd on the left bears the inscription 'a cubiculo Augustorum'. It has a Cosmatesque pavement in which are set many tombs. To the right of the central door is the *Tomb of Cardinal d'Albret (Lebretto in Italian), by *Andrea Bregno* (1465), and the *Tomb slab of the archdeacon Giovanni Crivelli (1432; very worn), signed by *Donatello;* on the left is the tomb of the astronomer Lodovico Grato Margani (1531), of the school of *Andrea Sansovino,* who himself executed the figure of Christ.

SOUTH AISLE. 1st chapel (Bufalini): *Frescoes from the life of St Bernardino, ranking among the finest works of *Pinturicchio* (c. 1484; restored by Camuccini); between the 2nd and 3rd chapels, colossal statue of Gregory XIII, by *Pier Paolo Olivieri;* just inside the s. door (r.), Monument of Pietro da Vicenza, attributed to *Andrea Sansovino.* In the crossing, on the pilasters facing the high altar, are two *Ambones, by Lorenzo and Giacomo Cosmas (c. 1200).—SOUTH TRANSEPT. Savelli Chapel, containing two fine *Tombs with decorations by the Cosmati (13C and 14C); on the right-hand tomb is a statue of Honorius IV, on the other, an antique sarcophagus. The Cappella di Santa Rosa (seen through the Cappella del SS. Sacramento, to the right) has a fine mosaic of the 13C.—CHOIR. The high altar, over which is now a small Byzantine

Madonna, was graced from 1512 to 1565 by Raphael's 'Madonna of Foligno' (p. 285), commissioned by Sigismondo Conti, whose tomb is in the pavement near the stalls on the s. side. In the APSE, on the left, is the fine monument of Giov. Battista Savelli (school of *And. Bregno,* 1498).—In the centre of the NORTH TRANSEPT is the little Temple of St Helena, or Santa Cappella, a shrine with eight columns, said to stand on the site of the altar erected by Augustus in fulfilment of the Sibyl's prophecy. At the end of the transept is the beautiful Cosmati *Tomb of Cardinal Matteo di Acquasparta (d. 1302), mentioned by Dante ('Paradiso', xii, 124), with a fresco attrib. to Pietro Cavallini. To the r. is the entrance to the Cappella del Santissimo Bambino, which contains a figure of the Infant Christ, reputed to have been carved from the wood of an olive tree in the Garden of Gethsemane and an object of immense veneration (see below).—NORTH AISLE, 5th chapel, St Paul, by *Girol. Muziano,* and the fine tomb of Filippo Della Valle (1494; l.), by *Michele Marini;* 3rd chapel, St Antony, by *Benozzo Gozzoli,* and the Renaissance tomb of Antonio Albertoni (1509; r.); between the 3rd and 2nd chapels, a statue of Paul III. The 2nd chapel (Cappella del Presepio) is open only during the Christmas festival, when the Christ Child is exhibited (from the Cappella del Santissimo Bambino; see above). Every afternoon, children of from 5 to 10 years of age recite little poems and speeches before its crib, a charming ceremony.

Piazza Venezia is dominated by the **Monument of Victor Emmanuel II,** called the 'father of his country', which symbolizes the achievement of Italian unity. This overwhelming memorial by *Giuseppe Sacconi* (d. 1905) begun in 1885, was inaugurated in 1911. Familiarly known as 'the wedding-cake', it is built of dazzling white Botticino marble from Brescia, in the Graeco-Italian style. Its total height is c. sixty-four metres.

At the sides of the monument are fountains representing the seas of Italy: on the right, the Tyrrhenian Sea, by *Canonica,* on the left, the Adriatic, by *Quadrelli.* Beside the latter are the remains of the tomb of Gaius Publicius Bibulus, dating from the latter part of the Republic. The steps of the monument, 41 m wide, are closed by a handsome grille which is lowered into the ground during the day. At the foot of the steps are two colossal groups in bronze, Action by *Jerace* on the right, and Thought, by *Monteverde,* on the left; midway are two winged Lions, by G. *Tonnini;* and at the top, bases for flagstaffs, sculptured with Victories (in bronze) by *E. de Albertis* (right) and *E. Rubino* (left). Above the stylobate are four sculptural groups: from right to left, Law, by *Ximenes;* Sacrifice, by *Bistolfi;* Concord, by *Pogliaghi;* Strength, by *Rivalta.* The grave of Italy's Unknown Soldier (il Milite Ignoto), guarded by sentinels, lies at the foot of the Altare della Patria, by *Zanelli,* with a figure of Rome enshrined in the pedestal and triumphal processions at the sides: the Triumph of Patriotism (r.), and the Triumph of Labour (l.). The steps to the right and left lead up to the Museo del Risorgimento (see below). Above, on either side of the triforium, are sculptures: to the right, War, by *Maccagnani,* and Revolution, by *Ferrari;* to the left, Philosophy, by *Maccagnani,* and Politics, by *Cantalamessa-Papotti.* Staircases flank the equestrian statue of Victor Emmanuel II, in gilt bronze, 12 m high, which is the work of *Enrico Chiaradia,* slightly retouched by *Gallori.* Around the base are figures by *Maccagnani* representing historic towns of Italy; (from centre to left) Turin, Florence, Naples, Amalfi, Pisa, Ravenna, Bologna, Milan, Genoa, Ferrara, Urbino, Mantua, Palermo, and Venice; and on the pedestal are military emblems. From here there is a view of the upper stylobate, with its eight large bases for statues; above are the sixteen columns of the portico, and the elegantly designed propylaea on which have been placed the Quadrigae of Liberty, by *Paolo Bartolini* (right), and of Unity, by *Carlo Fontana* (left). Above the columns are a fine frieze with eagles and a cornice with lions' heads and sixteen colossal statues,

symbolizing the Italian provinces. In front of the propylæa are the four columns of
the Victories. The portico has a frieze with a design of swords and shields and
commands a fine *Panorama of Rome.

The **Museo Centrale del Risorgimento** is entered on the right flank of the
monument, or in Via di S. Pietro in Carcere (adm. see p. 50). It contains exhibits
illustrating the story of Italy's struggle for independence. It has a section devoted to
the First World War. The *Archives* contain a collection of documents and
autographs of the period of the Risorgimento. Also in the building is the *Museo
Sacrario delle Bandiere della Marina Militare* (adm. 9.30-13.30, weekdays only)
with material relating to naval history.

Across Piazza Venezia (l.) is the **\*Palazzo di Venezia,** originally
*Palazzo di San Marco.* The first great Renaissance palace in Rome, it
was perhaps designed by Leon Battista Alberti or Giuliano da Maiano
(or by Bern. Rossellino, according to Venturi). It was begun in 1455,
enlarged in 1464, and finally finished in the 16C. It was built, partly of
stone from the Colosseum, for the Venetian Cardinal Pietro Barbo,
afterwards Paul II (1464-71), the first of the great Renaissance popes.
Barbo is said to have built the palace in order to view the horse-races in
the Corso. It later became a papal residence, and was often occupied as
such even after it had been given by Pius IV (1559-65) to the Venetian
Republic for its embassy. From the Treaty of Campoformio in 1797
until 1915 it was the seat of the Austrian ambassador to the Vatican. In
1917 Italy resumed possession and the palace was restored. During the
Fascist régime it was occupied by Mussolini, who had his office in the
Sala del Mappamondo, and on occasion addressed the citizens of Rome
from the balcony overlooking the Piazza di Venezia. The building is
stately and impressive, with battlements and arched windows and
doorways. The door in the piazza, which is finely carved and attributed
to Giuliano da Maiano, serves as a second entrance to the church of San
Marco. The inner court (reached from No. 49, Piazza di San Marco), is
silent and picturesque with its tall palm trees, and has a large unfinished
15C loggia on two sides, of beautiful proportions. In the centre, is a
fountain by Carlo Monaldi (1730).

Adjoining the palace and facing the Via and Piazza di San Marco, to
the s. and e., is the **Palazzetto di Venezia.** This was originally (c. 1467) in
Piazza di Venezia, but was removed to its present position in 1911
because it obstructed the view of the Victor Emmanuel Monument. To
see the beautiful court and garden, special permission is needed (apply at
No. 49, Piazza di San Marco).

The **\*Museo del Palazzo di Venezia** occupies several of the papal
apartments and many rooms in the Palazzetto di Venezia as well. In
addition to the paintings, some of which are important, there is a
noteworthy collection of Romanesque wood sculptures, bronzes,
Romanesque and 14C ivory, Italian and Hispano-Moresque majolica,
17C and 18C silverware, 15-17C tapestries, and a valuable series of
cassoni. A considerable section of the palace is reserved for temporary
exhibitions, for which the main entrance in Piazza Venezia is used, while
the museum proper is entered from Via del Plebiscito. Adm., see p. 50. A
large part of the museum has been closed while the collections are being
re-arranged in sections. So far, only Rooms 1-10 have been opened.
They display the collection of arms and armour (left to the State by the
Odescalchi in 1976), tapestries, wood sculpture, silver, and ceramics.

Room 1 (to the right at the top of the entrance stairs), the Sala Regia, has a fine display of *Tapestries (German, Flemish, and Italian) including The Last Judgement, and Story of Judith and Holofernes (Tournai c. 1515). The arms and armour of Italian and German manufacture date from the 9C-17C.—R. 2, SALA DEL CONCISTORO. 16-17C tapestries and arms and armour.—R. 3., SALA DEL MAPPAMONDO, so called from a large map, mentioned in 1534. 17-18C tapestries and fire arms.—R. 4, SALA DELLE FATICHE D'ERCOLE, named from the painted frieze by the school of Mantegna. Among the fine examples of wood sculptures here are the *Cassa di Terracina, a rare example of wood intaglio; the Madonna di Acuto (13C), so called from its place of origin; and a Madonna attrib. to *Pietro Alamanno.*—RR. 5 & 6 contain the silver collection. R. V. (centre case) *Orsini Cross (Naples, 1334); (adjacent cases) Triptych of Alba Fucense (14C), and Pantocrator (13C Byzantine enamel). In the case between the windows, the bronze back of an episcopal seat by a German master of the late 12C. R. 6 has silversmiths' and goldsmiths' work from Russia, Britain, Germany, etc.—At the entrance to R. 7 is a statue of a pope, attrib. to *Arnolfo di Cambio.* The collection of ceramics is arranged chronologically in RR. 7-10; it includes examples from the Italian workshops of Ca' Pirota (Faenza), Casteldurante, and Montelupo, and Hispano-Moresque majolica.

The rest of the museum is still in the course of rearrangement. Below are listed (in no particular order) some of the contents of the collections of paintings, sculpture, and applied arts.

**Paintings.** *Giov. Bellini,* *Portrait of a young man; *Giorgione* (?), Double Portrait; *Nicolò de' Barberi,* Woman taken in adultery; *Giov. Cariani,* Lovers in a landscape, Portrait of a devotee; *Rocco Marconi,* Woman taken in adultery; *Lelio Orsi,* Pietà; *Bachiacca,* Lady as St Mary Magdalene, Vision of St Bernard; *Fed. Zuccari,* Scenes in the life of Taddeo Zuccari; *Benozzo Gozzoli,* The Redeemer (part of a fresco); *Dom. Puligo,* Madonna; *Gius. Maria Crespi,* David and Abigail, Finding of the infant Moses; *Donato Creti,* Nymphs dancing; *Girol. da Cremona,* Nativity and Annunciation (triptych); *School of Giovanni Bellini,* Moses rescued from the water, Meeting of the Madonna and St Anne; 13C Crucifix from the church of S. Tommaso dei Cenci; *Giov. da Modena,* Crucifixion; *Ottaviano Nelli,* Madonna; *Segna di Tura,* Madonna and Child; *Paolo Veneziano,* Angelic choir; *Bened. Diana,* Redeemer; *Garófalo,* St Jerome; *Guercino,* St Peter; *Sassoferrato,* St Francis; *Cornelius Johnson,* Child with a puppy; *Jacob Cuyp,* Portraits of a woman and of a man; *Ciro Ferri,* Marriage of St Catherine; *Sim. Canterini,* Madonna; *Fr. Solimena,* Marriage feast at Cana; *Carlo Maratta,* Cleopatra.

**Sculpture.** *Nicola Pisano,* Head of a woman; *Bened. da Maiano,* Madonna and Child; *Mino da Fiesole,* Scenes from the life of St Jerome; *Giov. Dalmata,* Bust of Paul II; *Baccio da Montelupo,* Christ (terracotta); *Aless. Vittoria,* Bust of Doge Marino Grimani (1595-1605); small bronzes by *Iac. Sansovino, Aless. Vittoria, Algardi, Riccio, Giambologna, Leoni, Tacca, Mochi,* and *Susini.* *Bozzetti in terracotta by *Bernini, Algardi, Duquesnoy,* and others. *School of Bernini,* Head of young Bacchus; wood sculpture by the school of Brabant.

**Applied Arts.** 11C Byzantine ivories; 15C ivory and bronze engravings; medieval bronzes and crosses from the Abruzzi; 15C Florentine cassoni; Venetian glass; stained glass from Switzerland and the Rhineland; 16C Florentine embroidery; Venetian damask; Renaissance plaques and medals.

The palace is also the seat of the *Istituto Nazionale di Archeologia e Storia dell'Arte* (entered at No. 49, Piazza San Marco), founded in 1922. The library (reached from the main entrance of the Palazzo Venezia) comprising c. 250,000 volumes, may be visited on week-days 9-13 and 16-20 by permission of the Director.

At the corner of Piazza San Marco is a colossal mutilated bust of Isis, known as 'Madama Lucrezia' and formerly used for the display of satirical comments and epigrams like those of Pasquino and Marforio; in the garden in front (right) is a fountain (1927) with a pine-cone, the emblem of this quarter, the Rione della Pigna.

In Piazza San Marco is the church of **San Marco** (Pl. 3; 6), which forms part of the Palazzo di Venezia. Said to have been founded in 336 by St Mark the Pope, it was restored in 833, rebuilt in 1468, and again restored in the 17C and in 1744. The campanile is Romanesque, and the Renaissance façade is attributed to Giuliano da Maiano or L. B. Alberti. Under the portico are sculptural fragments and inscriptions, and over the central door is a relief of St Mark the Evangelist enthroned, by *Isaia da Pisa* (1464).

The INTERIOR, with nave and aisles divided by columns of Sicilian jasper, is richly decorated in the Baroque style and has a fine Renaissance ceiling and the remains of a Cosmatesque pavement (E. end). South side: 1st chap., *Palma Vecchio*, Resurrection; 3rd chap., *Carlo Maratta*, Adoration of the Magi; chap. r. of high altar, *Melozzo da Forlì*, St Mark the Pope. In the apse a *Mosaic (833) represents Christ with saints and Gregory IV offering a model of the church. In the sacristy (ring on the l., in the church porch), is a tabernacle by *Mino da Fiesole* and *Giov. Dalmata,* and *St Mark the Evangelist, by *Melozzo.*


# 2   FROM CORSO VITTORIO EMANUELE SOUTH TO THE TIBER

The CORSO VITTORIO EMANUELE (Pl. 3; 5, 6), one of the main arteries of Rome, dates from 1876. It runs w. from Piazza Venezia, and its first section is called Via del Plebiscito. On the left is Palazzo di Venezia and on the right the s. façade of Palazzo Doria, the *Palazzo Grazioli* and the *Palazzo Altieri* (1670; with an interesting court). Opposite (l.), in Piazza del Gesù, rises the *Gesù (Pl. 3; 6), the principal Jesuit church in Rome and the outstanding type of the sumptuous style to which the Order has given its name. It was built between 1568 and 1575 at the expense of Alessandro Farnese. Both the façade (by *Giacomo della Porta*) and the interior (by *Vignola*) are important to the development of the design of Baroque churches in Rome.

The INTERIOR has a longitudinal plan, with an aisleless nave and lateral chapels, and is decorated, almost to excess, with coloured marbles, sculptures, paintings, bronzes, and gilding. On the vaulting is a striking and original *Fresco by *Baciccia* representing the Triumph of the Name of Jesus (sketch in the Galleria Spada, p. 82). This bold and vivid composition, with its intense lights and marvellous effects of foreshortening, seems impatient of the limitations of its space, and almost as if it were breaking over the cornice. The frescoes of the cupola and the tribune are by the same artist.—SOUTH TRANSEPT. Altarpiece from a sketch by *Pietro da Cortona* with the Death of St Francis Xavier, by *Carlo Maratta.* Over the high altar, gorgeous with coloured marbles, the Circumcision, by *Aless. Capalti.* In the main apse, a bust of Card. Roberto Bellarmine, by *Bernini,* was placed in a neo-classical setting after the tomb was destroyed during rebuilding in 1843.—NORTH TRANSEPT, *Altar-tomb of St Ignatius, by *And. Pozzi* and others (1696-1700), resplendent with marble and bronze; the columns are encrusted with lapis lazuli and their bronze decorations are by *And. Bertoni.* The statue of St Ignatius is a copy by *Tadolini* of the original by *Legros* (melted down during the French Revolution). Above is a group of the Trinity by *Bern. Ludovisi* and *Lor. Ottoni,* with a terrestrial globe formed of a splendid block of lapis lazuli, the largest known. In front of the altar is a magnificent balustrade, and at the sides are marble groups: Religion triumphing over Heresy, by *Le Gros* (r.), and Barbarians adoring the Faith, by *J. Théodon* (l.).—The singing of a solemn Te Deum in this church annually on 31 Dec is a magnificent traditional ceremony.

Via d'Aracœli leads from Piazza del Gesù (with the headquarters of the Christian Democrat Party) to Piazza d'Aracœli and the Capitol. On the right, in Via delle Botteghe Oscure (with the headquarters of the Italian Communist Party) are remains of a temple probably dating from the IC B.C., and recently identified as a Temple of Nymphs.

The Corso Vittorio Emanuele next reaches the Largo di Torre Argentina, usually known as LARGO ARGENTINA. On the left of this open space is a group of **Four Republican Temples,** excavated in 1926-35 (entrance, usually closed, in Via di San Nicola dei Cesarini, on the E. side; for adm. apply at Piazzale Caffarelli 3), an area which abounds in cats.

All the temples face a courtyard to the E. paved with travertine. It is not yet known with certainty to whom they were dedicated. The first temple ("A") is peripteral and hexastyle; the tufa columns and stylobate are largely preserved. In the Middle Ages the church of St Nicholas was built over it; the apses of the church (otherwise demolished) may still be seen. The second temple ("B"), the most recent, is circular, and six columns survive, as well as the original flight of steps and the altar. A podium behind this temple near Via di Torre Argentina, almost certainly belongs to the Curia Pompei where Caesar was murdered.—The third temple ("C"), oldest of the four, was built at a lower level; it dates from the end of the 4C or the beginning of the 3C B.C. In the Imperial era the cella was rebuilt and the columns and podium covered with stucco. In 1935 the altar, with an inscription relating to c. 180 B.C., was discovered; even this antique was a replacement of an older altar.—The fourth temple ("D"), in travertine, is the largest; it has not been completely excavated as part of it is under Via Florida, to the S.

Facing the temples, on the w. side of the Largo Argentina, is the *Teatro Argentina,* dating from 1730 (restored in 1971). Here in 1816 was held the first performance of Rossini's 'Barber of Seville', and in 1851 that of Verdi's 'Rigoletto'. It is now noted for prose productions and the 'Teatro di Roma' is the resident company. Just beyond, Via del Sudario leads left past the s. façade of the *Palazzo Vidoni* (formerly belonging to the Caffarelli), designed by Raphael (1515). The *Chiesa del Sudario* (1604), opposite, was the court church of the House of Savoy from 1870 to 1946. Adjoining is the delightful *Casa del Burcardo,* built in 1503 by Bp. Hans Burchard or Burckhardt.

He was author of a remarkable account of the papal court under Innocent VIII and Alexander VI, and called the house the Torre Argentina, which in turn became the name of the piazza. The back doors of the Teatro Argentina (see above) open on to the court. It now houses a theatrical museum and library. Adm. see p. 47.

Beyond is the side wall of the church of *Sant' Andrea della Valle (Pl. 3; 6: entrance to r.), built in 1591 from a design by *Fra Fr. Grimaldi* and *Giac. della Porta,* and crowned by a fine dome (by *Carlo Maderno*), the largest in Rome, after that of St Peter's. The ornate façade is by *Carlo Rainaldi.*

The aisleless INTERIOR is immense and sumptuous. The lofty barrel-vault, the spacious apse, the small altar, and the bright lighting and the gay effect of the gold-framed frescoes, give the impression of a great reception hall rather than of a house of prayer. The 2nd chapel on the right (Cappella Strozzi) is attributed to *Michelangelo* and contains reproductions of his Pietà and of his statues of Leah and Rachel. At the end of the nave, high up, are the monuments of two popes of the Piccolomini family: on the right, Pius III (d. 1503), by *Fr. Ferrucci* and his son *Sebastiano;* on the left Pius II (d. 1464), by *Paolo Taccone* and a follower of *And. Bregno.* In the dome is the Glory of Paradise, by *Lanfranco;* in the pendentives, the *Evangelists,* by *Domenichino* (1623), who painted also the Six Virtues and the Scenes from the life of St Andrew, in the apse. The gigantic frescoes in the tribune are by *Calabrese.* In the s. transept, Sant'Andrea Avellino, by *Lanfranco.*

A short detour may be made to the s., turning from the noisy Corso Vittorio Emanuele down Via de' Chiavari, to the right of the façade of

Sant'Andrea della Valle (with a good view of the dome). This leads into the semicircular Via Grotta Pinta, following the line of the auditorium of the *Theatre of Pompey* (55 B.C.; Rome's first stonebuilt theatre); to the E. of it formerly stood the great Porticus of Pompey, off which opened the Regia (see p. 75) where Julius Caesar was murdered (15 March, 44 B.C.) at the foot of a statue of Pompey (comp. p. 82). The modern Teatro dei Satiri is in the adjoining Piazza dei Satiri. A dark passage to the r. of the old chapel of S. Maria di Grottapinta leads under a frescoed archway into Piazza di Biscione. On the l. rises *Palazzo Pio (Righetti)* built over the ruins of Pompey's theatre. To the r. is a small house with a painted façade. Nearby opens the CAMPO DEI FIORI (Pl. 3; 5) which became one of the most important piazze in Rome in the 15C. Executions were occasionally held here; the fine monument (by Ettore Ferrari; 1889) to Giordano Bruno, in the centre, stands on the spot where he was burned alive in 1600. It is now an attractive open market-place, with old stalls and canvas shades. At the N. corner is Piazza della Cancelleria which leads back to the Corso Vitt. Emanuele.

On the left of this piazza is the pure and simple façade of the \***Palazzo della Cancelleria** (Pl. 3; 5), a masterpiece of the Renaissance, built for Card. Raff. Riario by an unknown architect. It is thought that Bramante may have helped at a late stage, possibly designing the beautiful court; it is also probable that And. Bregno was involved in the building. It belongs to the Papacy, and is the residence of the Cardinal-Vicar of Rome.

The palazzo was probably begun in 1486, and the long main façade shows Florentine influence, with a double order of pilasters. The magnificent \*Court has double loggias with antique columns. Inside the palace (special permit required) is a chapel decorated by Fr. Salviati, and a salone, said to have been painted by Vasari in a hundred days.

Incorporated into the palace is the church of **San Lorenzo in Damaso** (entered by a doorway in the main façade, r.). The ancient basilica was finally demolished c. 1484; the present church (built on part of the site) is contemporary with the palazzo, although it was entirely restored in 1868-82. It has a double atrium, and over the fine doorway in the r. aisle is a lunette fresco of angel musicians by *Cav. d'Arpino* (detached; formerly in the nave). The adjoining chapel has a 14C crucifix in wood. At the end of the l. aisle is the tomb of Card. Ludovico Trévisan (1505), and over the high altar is the Coronation of the Virgin, with Saints, by *Fed. Zuccari.*

The Corso Vittorio Emanuele widens on the right into Piazza di San Pantaleo. Facing the square is the elegant \***Piccola Farnesina,** called also the *Farnesina dei Baullari* and *Palazzo Regis.* This gem of the Renaissance was built in 1523 to the order of the French prelate Thomas Le Roy (hence the name Palazzo Regis); the architect was almost certainly *Ant. da Sangallo the Younger.*

Le Roy, who held important posts at the pontifical court, played a noteworthy part in the concordat of 1516 between Leo X and Francis I of France. For his services he was ennobled and permitted to augment his coat of arms with the lilies of France. This heraldic privilege is recorded in the architectural details of the palace: the three floors are divided horizontally by projecting bands displaying the Le Roy ermines and the Farnese lilies, which were substituted for the lilies of France and gave the palace the name of Piccola Farnesina by which it is best known. It has no connection with the Villa Farnesina in Trastévere.

The Piccola Farnesina was built to face Vicolo dell'Aquila, to the s. The construction of the Corso Vittorio Emanuele left exposed the N. side of the palace, which backed on houses that had to be pulled down to make room for the new street. A new façade on the Corso was accordingly built in 1898-1901; the architect was Enrico Gui, who also modified the side of the palace facing Via dei Baullari.

Since 1948 the palace has contained the \***Museo Barracco,** a museum of ancient sculpture. The collection, not large but choice and well arranged, was formed by Senator Giovanni Barracco (1829-1914), and by him presented to the city of Rome in 1902. The entrance to the museum is in the Via dei Baullari. Admission, see p. 47.

COURTYARD. Bust of Giovanni Barracco, by *Giuseppe Mangionello* (1914). Below, the foundation inscription of the palace (found during rebuilding). Headless Egyptian sphinxes.—ATRIUM. 245. Christian sarcophagus (4C). Stairs lead up to the first floor. ROOM I (straight ahead). Egyptian sculpture from the beginning of the 3rd millennium to the end of the Roman era. 2. Bas-relief of 5th Dynasty, with a cow being milked and other scenes; \*21. Head of a youth (?Rameses II), with a blue chaplet (1299-1233 B.C.); 1. Fragment of a relief of Nofer, a court official (3rd Dyn., 2778-2723 B.C.); 33. Painted stucco head of a mummy (Roman era); 30. Head of a Greek; 15. Head of a prince (18th Dyn., 1580-1320 B.C.); \*31. Head of a priest wearing a diadem, once thought to be a portrait of Julius Caesar, an interesting example from Roman Egypt; 13. Sphinx of a queen, perhaps Hatshepsut, with the seal of Thutmosis III (1504-1450 B.C.).—R. II. Assyrian and Phoenician Art. 58. Relief of Assyrian huntsmen with a horse; 59. Alabaster lion mask, Phoenician, found in Sardinia; 60. Statue of the Phoenician god Bes, from a villa in the Alban Hills; 48. Assyrian relief of five women prisoners in a palm grove (period of Sennacherib, 705-681, or Assurbanipal, 669-626 B.C.); 47. Assyrian relief of a winged deity, from the N.W. palace of Assurnasirpal (884-860 B.C.); 57. Relief of an Assyrian archer.

Off the loggia, at the top of the stairs, is R. III (sometimes closed). Greek art to the middle of the 5C B.C.; sculptures from Cyprus and elsewhere. \*97. Head of Marsyas, replica of the head of the famous statue by Myron; 64. Head of a bearded priest wearing a chaplet, showing traces of colour (Cyprus, end of 5C); 115, 116. Statuettes in rosso antico of hydrophorai (girls carrying water-vessels); 101. Head of a girl (5C); 83. Upper part of a statue of Hermes Kriophoros, possibly derived from the statue of Kalamis at Tanagra (c. 480 B.C.); 76. Statuette of a woman wearing a chiton (early 5C); 77. Statuette of a woman in a peplos (c. 470 B.C.); 88. Attic head (early 5C); 66. Colossal head of a priest (Cyprus, 6-5C); 79. Head of a general (Attica; 490-480 B.C.); 81. Head of Athena, 5C original from Greece or Southern Italy; 80. Archaic head of a youth (Aeginetan, early 5C); 73. Fragment of an Attic sepulchral stele (early 5C; original found in Rome).—FIRST-FLOOR LANDING. 205. Head of a woman, part of a tomb-decoration found near Bolsena; 204. Head of a woman, from a tomb found near Orvieto; both Etruscan, 3C B.C.; 78. Archaic statue of Minerva.

SECOND FLOOR. R. IV (straight ahead at the top of stairs). Greek 5C art at its zenith. \*102. Upper part of a statue of the Amazon of Polykleitos, after the original in the Temple of Diana at Ephesos; 103. (in the window corner), Part of a leg of this statue; 130. Sepulchral relief (Attica, 4C); \*92. Head of Apollo, after an original by Pheidias, possibly the bronze statue seen by Pausanias near the Parthenon (Athens, before

450 B.C.); *109. Statuette of Hercules, after a work of Polykleitos; 113. Head of a girl (Argive-Sikyonian school); 127, 128. Attic funeral lekythoi (4C B.C.); 108. Head of the Doryphoros of Polykleitos, good copy of the original bronze; 135. Fragment of an Attic sepulchral relief; 96. Herm of Pericles, replica of that in the Vatican; 110. Head of an athlete in the style of Polykleitos; 134. Fragment of a relief of a horseman stroking the mane of his horse, from a representation of the Dioscuri (4C, Greco-Italian); 107. Head of the Diadumenos of Polykleitos, after the original bronze. In the middle of the room; *99. Replica of the Westmacott athlete in the British Museum, after an original by Polykleitos, possibly a portrait of Kyniskos, victor at Mantinea.

R. V. Greek art of the 4C B.C. *131. Head of Apollo Kitharoidos, the best existing replica of the statue by Praxiteles; 143. Head of an old man, possibly Demosthenes; 160. Bust of Hermes (replica of a 4C original). GLASS CASE A. Upper Shelf. 44, 45. Sumerian bronze statuettes (3rd millennium B.C.). 155. Bust of Epicurus, after an Ionian original, 270 B.C.; *129. Votive relief to Apollo (early 4C). GLASS CASE B. Greek and Italiot vases from the 8th to the 3C B.C. 132. Head of a veiled woman, part of an Attic sepulchral relief; *139. Bitch licking her wounds, perhaps a replica of the masterpiece by Lysippos, formerly in the Temple of Jupiter on the Capitol.

R. VI. Hellenistic sculpture. 176. Archaistic relief, depicting the cave of Pan; *151. Statuette of Neptune, from a 4C Greek original; 157. Head of Alexander the Great or Mithras, in the style of Leochares (330-300 B.C.).—R. VII. Roman art. 190. Bust of a young Roman (probably period of Tiberius); 195. Head of Mars (period of Trajan); *194. Head of a Roman boy, perhaps C. Cæsar, nephew of Augustus.—SECOND-FLOOR LANDING. 206, 249, 250. Sepulchral reliefs (Palmyra, 3C B.C.); 140. Head of Demosthenes, from an original attributed to Polieuctes.

In the basement of the Piccola Farnesina (no adm.) are remains of a late-Roman building, with columns, which is now under water. The frescoes, discovered in 1899 during the reconstruction of the palace, have been detached.

Opposite is Palazzo Braschi, now the Museo di Roma (see p. 100), and right, the church of *San Pantaleo,* dating from 1216, rebuilt in 1681, and given its present façade by Valadier in 1805. At the angle of the piazza rises *Palazzo Massimo alle Colonne,* skilfully set in a narrow, irregular site, by Baldassarre Peruzzi. Inside the convex façade is a beautiful portico decorated with stuccoes, and a charming Renaissance courtyard with a frescoed loggia, and Baroque fountain.

At the back of the second court was the *Palazzetto Massimi,* to which Pannartz and Sweynheim transferred their press (from Subiaco; comp. p. 368) in 1467 and issued the first books printed in Rome.

From Piazza della Cancelleria, the Chiesa Nuova (p. 79) may either be reached directly viâ the Corso (in which No. 217 is Palazzo Sora, 1503-9), or viâ the more picturesque and peaceful route through the old streets to the S. of the Corso (described below).

Via del Pellegrino skirts the back of the Cancelleria, with shops set into the façade on the street level, and has interesting old houses and courtyards on the left. Vicolo del Bollo diverges left. Across Via dei

Cappellari (a beautiful old narrow street leading l. to the Campo dei Fiori) Via di Montoro continues to Via di Monserrato. Just to the r. is the church of **Santa Maria di Monserrato**, the Spanish national church, begun by *Ant. da Sangallo the Younger* (1518) but altered later, with a façade by *Fr. da Volterra.* Within, the 1st chapel on the r. contains a San Diego, by *Ann. Carracci,* and the tombs of the two Borgia popes, Calixtus III (d. 1458) and Alexander VI (d. 1503), and of Alfonso XIII (d. 1941). In the 3rd chap. l. is a statue of St James, by *Iac. Sansovino,* and two fine wall tombs attrib. to *And. Bregno;* in the 1st chap. a group of the Madonna and Child with St Anne, by *Tom. Boscoli,* and a ciborium (behind wooden doors) attrib. to *Luigi Capponi.*

In the court, reached through the Sacristy at the end of the nave on the r. (or at No. 151 Via Giulia), are several fine tombs, notably that attrib. to *And. Bregno* of Card. Giov. de Mella. In a room off the courtyard is the monument to Pedro de Foix Montoya; this incorporates a remarkable portrait bust, an early work (c. 1621) by *Gian Lorenzo Bernini.*

Via di Monserrato continues past Piazza Ricci, with its 16C palazzo (badly faded painted façade), and No. 20 with a tiny but charming courtyard. Beyond is the Largo della Moretta (named after the pharmacy, founded in the 15C; a modern chemist shop occupies the old site), out of which runs Via dei Banchi Vecchi. At the church of S. Lucia del Gonfalone (belonging to the ancient confraternity of the Gonfalone), Vicolo Cellini (r.; the sculptor is known to have frequented this area) leads back to the Corso Vittorio Emanuele. The **Chiesa Nuova**, or *Santa Maria in Vallicella* (Pl. 3; 5) was built under the inspiration of St Philip Neri. Among the architects were *Matteo Bartolini da Città di Castello* and *Martino Longhi the Elder* (1575-1605), but the façade is by *Fausto Rughesi.*

Born in Florence in 1515 St Philip Neri came to Rome c. 1530. He was an outstanding figure of the Counter Reformation and founded an 'Oratorio'. In recognition of the Order Gregory XIII gave him Santa Maria in Vallicella in 1575 which he proceeded to rebuild.

The vault, apse, and dome were decorated by *Pietro da Cortona* (1664), and the whole interior is brilliantly gilded. In the sanctuary are three *Paintings by *Rubens* (1608), of superb colouring: over the high altar, Madonna and angels; to the right, SS. Domitilla, Nereus, and Achilleus; to the left, SS. Gregory, Maurus, and Papias. On the right of the apse, under the organ, is the Cappella Spada, designed by *C. Rainaldi,* with an altarpiece by *C. Maratta* (Madonna between SS. Charles and Ignatius). St Philip Neri is buried beneath the altar of the sumptuous chapel of St Philip, on the left of the apse; his portrait in mosaic is copied from a painting by Guido Reni. In the N. transept, Presentation, by *Barocci.*—In the fine sacristy, with a ceiling painted by *P. da Cortona,* is a statue of St Philip, by *Algardi.* From here there is access to another chapel and the Rooms of St Philip Neri (works by *Guercino, Pietro da Cortona, Guido Reni, Garófalo,* etc.) with mementoes of the saint.

In the neighbouring *Oratorio dei Filippini,* rebuilt by *Borromini* (1637-50), St Philip instituted the musical gatherings which, becoming known as oratorios, gave their name to a form of musical composition. The façade, between that of a church and a palace, has a subtle design. The delightful clock tower can be seen from Via dei Banchi Nuovi, on the right. The convent buildings, likewise by Borromini, are now occupied by the Vallicelliana Library (history of Rome), the Municipal Archives, and various learned societies.

On the s. side of the Corso is Piazza Sforza Cesarini, named after the Palazzo, the s. side of which (with a 15C courtyard) faces on to Via dei

Banchi Vecchi. Farther along Via dei Banchi Vecchi, Vicolo Sugarelli leads left to the long and straight *VIA GIULIA* (Pl. 3; 5), once the most beautiful of Roman 16C streets, which was built by Julius II (1503-13). At the end of this street (l.), is **San Giovanni dei Fiorentini** (Pl. 2; 5), the church of the Florentines. Leo X ordered a competition for its erection. Raphael and Peruzzi were among the contestants; but *Iac. Sansovino* was successful and began the work. It was continued by *Ant. da Sangallo the Younger* and completed by *Giac. della Porta; Carlo Maderno* added the transept and cupola. The façade is by *Aless. Galilei* (1734).

INTERIOR. In the s. transept, SS. Cosmas and Damian at the stake, by *Salvator Rosa.* On either side of the door into the Sacristy is a portrait bust; that on the left by *Pietro Bernini* (1614), and that on the right by his son *Gian Lorenzo* (1622). The high altar was begun by *Pietro da Cortona*, and completed by Borromini and C. Ferri. Beneath is a crypt sepulchre of the Falconieri family, a fine late work by *Borromini.*

Opposite Vicolo Sugarelli (comp. above) stands *Palazzo Sacchetti* at No. 66 built by Sangallo the Younger (1543). Farther on is the small church of S. Biagio della Pagnotta, and, still on the r., several large rough blocks of masonry protruding into the street, which were intended for a great court of justice designed for Julius II by Bramante but never finished. Just beyond another church, Santa Maria del Suffragio (the façade by G. Rainaldi), a street leads to the *Oratorio di S. Lucia del Gonfalone* (entrance in Vicolo della Scimmia) with frescoes by the Tuscan-Emilian school of the late 16C including Jacopo Bertoia, Raffaellino da Reggio, Federico Zuccari, Livio Agresti, and Marco Pino. The fine ceiling is by Ambr. Bonazzini. Concerts are given here regularly by the Coro Polifonico Romano.

On Via Giulia are the *Carceri Nuove*, built in 1655 and long considered a model prison. The *Museo Criminologico*, entered on Via del Gonfalone, has been opened here (adm. 9-13 exc. fest.). Some way farther on, a street on the r. leads to the church of *SANT' ELIGIO DEGLI OREFICI*, a masterpiece built from a design by *Raphael* (open 10-13 exc. fest; ring at No. 9 Via di Sant' Eligio). The cupola is in restoration. From the Lungotevere dei Tebaldi, close by, a beautiful view may be obtained of the Janiculum, the dome of St Peter's, and the Villa Farnesina.

Via Giulia continues: just before an archway (comp. below) is (r.) *Palazzo Falconieri*, by Borromini, distinguished by the giant falcons' heads on its façade. To the left is Palazzo Farnese, whose rear façade added by Giac. della Porta can be glimpsed above the wall.

The design of Michelangelo to connect the palace with the Villa Farnesina (p. 242) by a bridge across the Tiber was never carried out, but a single arch of the viaduct to the bridge spans Via Giulia at this point. The fountain in the wall on the left, the 'Mascherone', was erected by the Farnese; both the colossal mask and the porphyry basin are Roman.

Via dei Farnese, passing a charming small palazzo at No. 83, leads into PIAZZA FARNESE (closed to traffic), in which is beautifully set the main façade of the Palazzo Farnese. Here are two huge baths of Egyptian granite brought from the Baths of Caracalla in the 16C and used by the Farnese as a type of 'royal box' for the spectacles which were held in the piazza. They were adapted as fountains (using the Farnese Lilies) in 1626.

The *Palazzo Farnese (Pl. 3; 5), now the *French Embassy,* is the most magnificent Renaissance palace in Rome. It was begun by *Ant. da Sangallo the Younger* for Card. Aless. Farnese, afterwards Paul III. He began the piazza façade and the two sides, and after his death in 1546, Michelangelo continued the upper stories and added the superb entablature.

The palace is entered through *Sangallo*'s *VESTIBULE, with its beautiful colonnade and stuccoed ceiling, to the *COURT. This was also designed by Sangallo on the first two stories; the upper story is by *Michelangelo.*

INTERIOR (adm., see p. 48). At the top of the stairs, to the right, is the huge SALON d'HERCULE, named after the gigantic statue (copy to r. of the entrance to the room) of the Farnese Hercules. When the palace passed into the hands of the Bourbons, the magnificent Farnese collection of sculpture was transferred to Naples. The Salon has a fine wood ceiling by Sangallo. The two statues on either side of the fireplace of Piety and Abundance, by *Giac. della Porta,* were designed (but never used) for the tomb of Paul III in St Peter's.—At the end of the loggia is the GALLERIA, with *Frescoes by *Ann. Carracci* of mythological scenes. The ingenious treatment of the angles, and the magnificent over-all scheme centring on the Triumph of Bacchus, demonstrate the great imagination of the artist, who here created the model for subsequent Baroque ceiling paintings. Carracci was assisted by his brother *Agostino,* and (in the frescoes above the doors and niches) by *Domenichino.*

Via di Monserrato leads out of the piazza to Piazza di S. Caterina della Rota with three churches. On the right of the street is the English College, and the church of ST THOMAS OF CANTERBURY, rebuilt by *Poletti* and *Vespignani* in 1888.

The college and church can be entered just beyond the piazza at No. 45 Via di Monserrato; the ground on which they stand has been the property of English Catholics since 1362, when it started as a hospice for pilgrims, and the record of visitors shows the names of Thomas Cromwell (1514), Harvey (1636), Milton (1638), Evelyn and Manning. The church contains the simple and beautiful tomb of Card. Bainbridge (1514), and in the gallery are paintings of English martyrdoms, and in the college, of which Card. Howard and Card. Wiseman were rectors, are portraits of English cardinals.

On the left of the piazza is the church of SAN GIROLAMO DELLA CARITÀ (open 8-11 only; when closed ring at No. 63 Via S. Girolamo).

The 1st chapel on the right is one of the last works of *Borromini.* His adaptation of a cramped space into a beautiful funerary house for the Spada is masterly. The next chap. has a wood crucifix of 15C. To the left of the high altar is a decorative chapel (1710) dedicated to S. Filippo Neri, by Fil. Iuvarra (light to left).

From the other side of Piazza Farnese (comp. above) Vicolo de'Venti leads into Piazza di Capo di Ferro, in which (r.) is **Palazzo Spada** (Pl. 3; 5), probably built by *Giulio Mazzoni* for Card. Girol. Capo di Ferro (1540). The palace was acquired by Card. Bernardino Spada (1594-1661) and is now the seat of the Council of State.

The court and façade are by *Giulio Mazzoni* (or *Girol. da Carpi*) and are outstanding examples of stucco decoration. *Borromini* later restored the palazzo, and added an ingenious *trompe-l'oeil* perspective on the s. side of the palace (reached through a door into the garden, r. of stairs leading up to the gallery).

This makes use of waste space between the Spada garden and the adjoining Palazzo Massari. The dimension of the tunnel is perspectively multiplied more than four times through the use of light and spacing of the columns.

The *State Rooms on the first floor can be seen (with special permission) in the afternoon, if they are not being used, and if the porter is available. The GENERAL COUNCIL CHAMBER has magnificent trompe l'oeil frescoes by the 17C Bolognese artists, *Agostino Mitelli* and *Michelangelo Colonna*, with birds and figures peering into the room from around columns and window ledges. The colossal statue of Pompey is traditionally the one at the foot of which Cæsar was murdered. The decoration in the next room is extremely fine, with frescoes and stucco in high relief. The last room on this side of the palazzo has another fine ceiling. From here is the entrance to the CORRIDOR OF STUCCOES, a delightful work, complemented by the ornamentation of the façade of the court seen through the windows. Further rooms lead to the MERIDIANA, a corridor decorated by *G. B. Ruggeri*, mapping the times at various places in the world. The eight Hellenistic reliefs of mythological subjects of 2C A.D. are very fine, and in a good state of preservation.

Reached by a staircase from a corridor at the back of the palace is the *Galleria Spada, a collection of paintings formed by Card. Bernardino Spada, and augmented by successive generations of the Spada family. Acquired by the State in 1929, it comprises a small but important assemblage of 17C and 18C works of art. There are also some interesting Roman sculptures of the 2C and 3C A.D. The four rooms in which the collection is shown are planned, in their decoration, furnishings, and arrangement, to give the effect of the collection of a patrician Roman family. Adm., see p. 50.

R. I. *Guido Reni*, 8. Lucretia; *25. Card. Bernardino Spada, 35. Judith; 38. *Guercino,* Card. Bernardino Spada.

R. II. 85. *Fiorenzo di Lorenzo*, St Sebastian; 72. *Marco Palmezzano*, Way to Calvary, Eternal Father; 73. *G. B. Bertucci*, Madonna and Child with St John; 75. *16C Florentine School*, Madonna and St John the Baptist; 180. *Lavinia Fontana*, Cleopatra; 84. *15C Umbrian school*, Madonna and Child; 78. *Parmigianino* (?), Three heads (fresco); *86. *J. van Scorel*, Young Man; 82. *Hans Dürer*, Young Man; 53. *And. del Sarto*, Visitation; 56. *Titian*, musician (unfinished), 74. Paul III (copy). 16C Tabernacle in carved and gilded walnut, with a bas-relief of the Annunciation. On the two long walls, fragments of a larger painted frieze by *Perin del Vaga*, originally intended for the wall below Michelangelo's 'Last Judgment' in the Sistine Chapel.

R. III. 87. *Ciro Ferri*, Vestals; 88. *Nicolo dell' Abate*, Landscape; 94. *David Teniers the Younger*, Winter Scene; *Pietro Testa*, 96. Iphigenia, 97. Massacre of the Innocents; 100. *Ann. Carracci*, Young Man; 102. *Fr. Trevisani*, Antony and Cleopatra; 105. *Sophonisba Anguissola*, Young girl; *Baciccia*, *108. Sketch for the vaulting of the Gesù. 115. Christ and the woman of Samaria; 109. *Guercino*, Death of Dido; 118. *Fr. Furini*, St Lucy; *121. *Rubens*, Portrait of a cardinal; 124. *Ann. Carracci*, Portrait of young boy; *J. F. Voet*, 123. Gentlewoman, 130, 135. Portraits of Urbano and Pompeo Rocci; 127. *Nic. Tornioli*, Cain and Abel; 132. *P. Snayers*, Sack of a village; 138. *Jan ('Velvet') Breughel*, Landscape with windmills.—Among the Roman sculpture are a Seated Philosopher, and a bust of a woman of the 2C A.D.

R. IV. 139. *Mattia Preti*, Christ tempted by the devil; *Michelangelo Cerquozzi*, 141. At the water-trough; 146. Death of the donkey; *149. Market-place at Naples during the revolt of Masaniello; 166. Traveller and shepherds; 144. *Orazio Gentileschi*, David; 145. *Anon* 17C, Boy with plumed hat; 151. *Dom. Fiasella*, Holy Family; 153. *Mich. Sweerts*, Market; 156. *A. Bauguin*, Still-life; 158. *Bart. Cavorozzi*, Madonna; 160. *Orazio Borgianni*, Pietà; 161. *Nic. Renieri*, David; 162. *School of Caravaggio*, Madonna and St Anne; 163. *School of Carlo Saraceni*, Christ scourged; 168. *Theodore Rombouts* (?), Topers; 169. *Il Valentin*, Holy Family; 173. *Artemisia Gentileschi*, St Cecilia; 174. *School of Gherardo delle Notti*, Betrayal of Christ.—Sculptures: Bust of a boy, of the Julio-Claudian era; two Roman statuettes of a boy one donning the lion-skin of Hercules, and another donning the philosophic pallium.

Via Capodiferro leads into Piazza dei Pellegrini, with the church of the *Santissima Trinità dei Pellegrini* (1603-16; open 7-8 only, and 11-12 on Sun), with an altarpiece (the Trinity) by Guido Reni. In the neighbouring *Hospice* (1625) the poet Goffredo Mameli, author of the national hymn which bears his name, died in 1849 at the age of 22 from wounds received in fighting for the Roman Republic (comp. p. 245). On the opposite side of the piazza is the back of the *Monte di Pietà* (now a bank), with a long history as a pawn-shop.

The entrance can be reached by Via dell' Arco del Monte di Pietà, and inside is a fine domed CHAPEL (admission on request) by Carlo Maderna (1641; restored 1725). It contains high reliefs by Domenico Guidi, R. Le Gros, and Giov. Théodon. The clock tower on the imposing façade was added by Borromini.

From Piazza dei Pellegrini (comp. above) Via dei Pettinari, to the r. of the church, leads to the *Ponte Sisto* over the Tiber, which has a beautiful view of the Janiculum and the tree-lined river, passing on the r. the church of *San Salvatore in Onde* of ancient foundation, with an interesting crypt.

Via S. Paolo alla Regola leads from Piazza dei Pellegrini to the *Casa di San Paolo*, a towered medieval house, now used as offices. To the left is the church of *Santa Maria in Monticelli*, with a 12C campanile.

In the apse is a mosaic head of Christ, and fragments of mosaic decoration dating from the 12C. In the second chap. to the r. is a Flagellation (detached fresco) by Ant. Carracci; opposite is a 13-14C wooden crucifix.

Via S. Maria in Monticelli continues to Piazza Cairoli, with the church of **San Carlo ai Catinari** (Pl. 3; 6), by *Rosati* (1612), with a façade by *G. B. Soria*.

In the pendentives of the cupola are the Cardinal Virtues, by *Domenichino;* over the high altar, San Carlo carrying the sacred Nail to the plague-striken, by *Pietro da Cortona;* in the inner choir, reached through the sacristy which has a bronze crucifix by *Algardi*, is a fresco by *Guido Reni* of San Carlo praying.—Opposite is the 15C Palazzo Santacroce.

Across the busy Via Arenula, Via Falegnami leads to Piazza Mattei, with the charming *\*Fontana delle Tartarughe*, by Taddeo Landini (1584), on a design by Giac. della Porta (restored in 1658 perhaps by Bernini, when the tortoises were added; these have been temporarily removed for restoration in 1978). At the s.w. angle of the piazza is *Palazzo Costaguti* (no admission), with ceilings on the first floor painted by Albani, Domenichino, Guercino, Lanfranco, and others. On the N. side is the *Palazzo Mattei* (Pl. 3; 6), which comprised five palaces of the 16C and the 17C.

The fine façades, in Via dei Funari and Via Michelangelo are by Carlo Maderna. In the piazza, Nos. 19 and 17 open on to courts, and a third door gives access to a staircase (l.), finely decorated with stucco and antique reliefs. Inside are frescoes by Domenichino, Lanfranco, and Albani. Part of the buildings are now used by the Centro Italiano di Studi Americani.

Immediately to the E. of the Palazzo Mattei is *Santa Caterina dei Funari*, a church with a fine façade (being restored in 1978) by Guidetto Guidetti (1564), and an original campanile. From here Via dei Funari leads to Piazza Campitelli, a picturesque square with the Palazzo Cavaletti (No. 1), and a fountain probably designed by Jacopo della Porta in 1589.

The charming façade of **Santa Maria in Campitelli** (Pl. 3; 8) was erected by *C. Rainaldi* when the church was rebuilt (1662-67) in honour of a miraculous Madonna, which was believed to have halted an outbreak of a pestilence.

The INTERIOR is remarkable for its perspective effect. In the 2nd chapel on the right is a St Anne, by *Luca Giordano;* in the midst of the ornate high altar, the

Miraculous Virgin, a 13C image in pietra dura. In the 1st chapel on the left, are two tombs of the Altieri family, inscribed respectively 'Nihil' and 'Umbra'; in the left . transept, *Baciccia*, Birth of St John the Baptist (comp. p. 172).

The narrow Via della Tribuna di Campitelli and Via Sant'Angelo in Pescheria lead from here to the **Porticus of Octavia,** erected by Augustus in honour of his sister, and restored by Septimius Severus (A.D. 203). To the s. of this building is the Theatre of Marcellus (see p. 85).

The Porticus of Octavia was rectangular, with about 300 columns, which enclosed the temples of Jupiter and Juno. The entrances consisted of two propylaea with 8 columns and 4 piers. The southern extremities of the porticus area have been exposed, and one monumental entrance (an arch was added, and the pediment repaired in medieval days). Remains of columns to the w., and the stylobate to the E. can also be seen. Inside the porticus is the church of *Sant'Angelo in Pescheria,* where from 1584 until the rule of Pius IX the Jews were forced to listen to a Christian sermon every Saturday. In the N. aisle is a Madonna enthroned with angels, attrib. to Benozzo Gozzoli or his school. From this church Cola di Rienzo and his followers started to seize the Capitol on the night of Pentecost, 1347.

In the quarter to the w. of this point formerly lay the **Ghetto,** where from 1556 onwards the Jews were segregated and subject to various restrictions on their personal freedom, although to a less degree than in other European countries. In Via del Portico d'Ottavia may be seen remains of medieval and Renaissance dwellings. No. 1 is the *Casa di Lorenzo Manilio,* dating from 1468 (2221 A. U. C.), decorated with ancient fragments, an inscription carved in bold stone lettering, and the patriotic invocation 'Have Roma'; No. 13 has a fine court with loggie. Via della Reginella on the r. is also an interesting old street.—A further detour may be made to the left along the wide Via del Progresso to *Palazzo Cenci,* formerly belonging to the Crescenzi, built at the beginning of the 16C. The palace belonged to the family of Beatrice Cenci.—Near the river rises the *Synagogue* (Pl. 3; 8), built in 1874, and at No. 2 Lungotevere Cenci is a Jewish *Museum* (adm. 10-16 or 18, exc. Sat & fest.).

The area between P.za Cairoli and the Theatre of Marcellus, and Via del Portico d'Ottavio and the Tibur is now thought to be the site of the *Circus of Flaminius* (221 B.C.)

The **Ponte Fabricio,** or 'dei Quattro Capi' (because of the two herms of the four-headed Janus on the parapet), with an inscription over the arches recording the name of the builder, L. Fabricius and the date, 62 B.C., here crosses an arm of the Tibur to the **Isola Tiberina.** The island, which provides an easy crossing place on the Tibur, is thought to have been settled early in the history of Rome. A temple of Aesculapius was dedicated here in 293 B.C. and ever since the island has been associated with the work of healing. On the right is the modern hospital of the Fatebenefratelli (of ancient foundation), and on the left a tall medieval tower, formerly part of an 11C fortress, and Piazza San Bartolomeo. The island was formerly encircled with a facing of travertine, a portion of which still remains at the extremity, which can be reached through the archway on the left of the piazza. It is in the form of a ship with the serpent of Aesculapius carved upon it in relief. The church of *San Bartolomeo,* on the site of the temple of Aesculapius, was built in the 10C in honour of St Adalbert, Bishop of Prague, and several times restored, notably by Orazio Torriani in 1624; the tower is Romanesque. The interior contains 14 antique columns, and an interesting sculptured well-head on the chancel steps, probably from the original church.—The s. side of the Isola Tiberina is joined to Trastevere by the **Ponte Cestio,** built by L. Cestius in 46 B.C., restored in A.D. 370, and rebuilt in 1892 (the centre arch to its original design and measurements).

Across Piazza di Monte Savello (at the end of Ponte Fabricio) Via del Teatro di Marcello leads back to Piazza Venezia.

# 3   FROM PIAZZA VENEZIA TO PORTA SAN PAOLO AND SAN PAOLO FUORI LE MURA

This itinerary involves a somewhat circuitous route to Porta San Paolo. The direct route viâ Porta San Paolo to the basilica of San Paolo fuori le Mura is followed by bus No. 95 which, starting from Piazzale Flaminio, runs along the Corso, past Piazza Venezia and Via del Teatro di Marcello, to Piazzale Ostiense (Porta San Paolo). Thence bus No. 23 or 18 goes direct to the basilica, from which bus No. 223 (destination Cecchignola) goes on to the Monastery of Tre Fontane.

The *Underground Railway* (see p. 42) runs from Stazione Termini to Porta San Paolo, San Paolo fuori le Mura, E.U.R., and Tre Fontane.

On the right of the Victor Emmanuel Monument, in Piazza Venezia, lies Piazza Aracoeli (Pl. 8, l.) at the foot of the Capitol hill. At this point begins the broad VIA DEL TEATRO DI MARCELLO, opened in 1933. It was at first known as *Via del Mare,* as it eventually led to the sea but this name has now been given to a highway farther s. (p. 95). The street skirts the w. base of the Capitoline Hill. On the right is the severe façade of the *Monastero di Tor de' Specchi* (open to visitors on 9 March each year), founded in 1425 by St Francesca Romana. The Oratory is decorated by Antoniazzo Romano.

On the right rise the majestic remains of the \***Theatre of Marcellus** (Pl. 8; 1), begun by Julius Cæsar. It was dedicated in B.C. 13 or 11 by Augustus to the memory of his nephew and son-in-law who had died in B.C. 23. The exterior was restored in 1932. It originally had at least two tiers of 41 arches, the first with Doric and the second with Ionic pillars probably crowned by an attic stage of the Corinthian order. Only 12 arches in each of the two tiers survive; the upper stage has disappeared in the course of the various alterations. The building was despoiled in the 4C for the restoration of Ponte Cestio. In the 12C it was made into a fortress by the Fabi. In the 16C it was converted into a palace by Baldass. Peruzzi for the Savelli, and later passed in turn to the Orsini and the Sermoneta families. The palace garden is the site of the cavea, which held c. 15,000 spectators. The debris from the demolitions became known as Monte Savello: hence the name of the piazza to the s. of the theatre.

In front of the theatre are three Corinthian columns of the *Temple of Apollo,* built in 433 B.C. and restored by the consul C. Sosius, in 33 B.C.

Via del Teatro di Marcello now traverses the area of the *Forum Holitorium,* or vegetable market, which extended from the Capitoline Hill to the Tiber. Beyond (r.) in Piazza di Monte Savello is the church of *San Nicola in Carcere* (Pl. 8; 1). This 12C church was remodelled in 1599 by Giac. della Porta and detached from the surrounding buildings in 1932. It occupies the site of three *Temples* in the Forum Holitorium, thought to have been dedicated to *Janus, Juno Sospita,* and *Spes.* The first, to the r. of the church, was Ionic hexastyle, with columns on three sides only, the remains of which can be seen incorporated in the s. wall of the church; the second, now incorporated in the church, was Ionic hexastyle peripteral; the third, on the left of the church was Doric hexastyle peripteral.

The INTERIOR of the church has fine antique columns from the temples with diverse capitals. At the end of the l. aisle is an altarpiece of the Ascension, by Lor. Costa.

On the other side of Via del Teatro di Marcello, opposite the church, Vico Jugario leads past the Capitoline Hill to Piazza della Consolazione.

On the left can be seen arcades of a portico built of peperino. On the right, around the church of *Sant' Omobono,* is the **Area Sacra di Sant' Omobono** (adm. 9-14, exc. Mon). Excavations in the 1960s revealed interesting remains on seven different levels, the oldest dating from the 9C-8C B.C. where traces of hut dwellings similar to those on the Palatine (comp. p. 128) were found. Two archaic temples (mid 6C B.C.) have been attributed to Fortuna and Mater Matuta traditionally founded by Servius Tullius. These rest on an artificial mound c. 6 metres high in which were found Bronze Age and Iron Age sherds and imported Greek pottery of the 8C B.C. In front of the temples are two archaic altars, possibly dedicated to Carmenta. The most conspicuous remains mostly date from after 213 B.C. when the temples were reconstructed. The material found on the site, which has provided new light on the origins of Rome, is exhibited in the Antiquarium Comunale (comp. p. 70).

In Piazza della Consolazione beyond, is the church of S. MARIA DELLA CONSOLAZIONE. The façade is by *Longhi* (1583-1606); the upper part was added in the same style in the 19C. In the 1st chap. to the right are frescoes by *Taddeo Zuccari* (1556) of the life of Christ (including the *Flagellation) and the Crucifixion (much damaged). In the apse, Birth of Mary and the Assumption by *Pomarancio,* and over the altar, the Madonna della Consolazione, a 14C fresco repainted by *Antoniazzo Romano.* In the 1st chap. on the left, is a marble relief of the Marriage of St Catherine by *Raffaello da Montelupo* (1530).

The cliff above, on the Capitoline Hill, is thought to be the notorious Tarpeian Rock from which condemned criminals were flung in ancient Rome although it has also been connected with the N. side of the hill (comp. p. 69).

Via del Teatro di Marcello continues to Piazza della Bocca della Verità, and then turns right to end in the Lungotévere Aventino. The *PIAZZA DELLA BOCCA DELLA VERITÀ, one of the most attractive open spaces in Rome, occupies part of the site of the *Forum Boarium,* or cattle-market, the oldest market of ancient Rome. In the piazza the ancient temples of Vesta and Fortuna Virilis and the medieval church of Santa Maria in Cosmedin form a picturesque group. The fine Baroque fountain in the centre of the square is by C. Bizzaccheri (1717).

On the right of the piazza is the **Casa dei Crescenzi,** erroneously called the *House of Cola di Rienzo,* a unique example of a Roman seignorial mansion of the mid-medieval period. Another name for it is *Casa di Pilato,* because it formed one of the Stations of the Cross in the passion plays. It was probably at first a tower to guard the passage of the river. It is constructed mainly from fragments of classical buildings. The bricks of the lower portion are formed into half-columns, with rudimentary capitals. An inscription over a door states that the house was erected by Nicholas, son of Crescentius and Theodora, who were probably the most powerful clan in Rome at the end of the 10C. The Casa dei Crescenzi is now the *Centro di Studi per la Storia di Architettura,* and is used occasionally for concerts.

Opposite, to the s., is the so-called ***Temple of Fortuna Virilis,** more probably dedicated to Portunus, god of harbours. It dates from the end of the 2C B.C. In 872 it was consecrated as the church of *Santa Maria Egiziaca.* This pseudoperipteral temple, with four fluted Ionic columns in front of the portico and two at the sides, escaped alteration in the Imperial epoch and remains a precious example of the Greco-Italian temples of the Republican age. It has been disengaged, without undue restoration, from the buildings which formerly surrounded it.

Farther s. and close to the Lungotévere Aventino, is the little round temple erroneously called the ***Temple of Vesta** (Pl. 8; 3). It also dates from the end of the 2C B.C. (restored under Tiberius) and is the oldest marble edifice to survive in Rome. The recent discovery of an inscription makes it likely that it was dedicated to Hercules Victor.

This charming little building consists of a circular cella of solid marble, surrounded by 20 fluted columns; one of these is missing on the N. side but the base is left. In the Middle Ages the temple became the church of *Santo Stefano delle Carrozze* and later *Santa Maria del Sole*. The existing roof is not the original; the ancient roof and entablature have vanished.—The entrance to a side conduit of the Cloaca Maxima (see below) can be seen under a travertine lid in front of the temple.

On the S. side of the piazza is *Santa Maria in Cosmedin** (Pl. 8; 3), an admirable example of a medieval Roman church.

The site was occupied by a porticoed hall of the Flavian era (some of the columns of which have been incorporated into the church), once identified with the Statio Annonæ or market inspector's office. Nearby was a monumental altar and a temple, both dedicated to Hercules, the latter restored by Pompey. The basilica, built in the 6C and much enlarged by Adrian I (772-95), was assigned to Greek refugees driven from Constantinople by the iconoclastic persecutions, and became known as the *Schola Græca*. Its other appellation, 'in Cosmedin', from a Greek word meaning decoration, refers to the embellishments of Adrian. At that period it had galleries reserved for women and three apses. Nicholas I altered the building, and Gelasius II and Calixtus II restored it (12C), closing the galleries and rebuilding the portico. The Romanesque tower is a fine and typical structure of seven stories (although unfeelingly restored). The church was restored and the 18C alterations removed in 1894-99, and in 1964.

Beneath the portico, to the left, is the **Bocca della Verità** proper, a large cracked marble disk representing a human face, the open mouth of which was believed to close upon the hand of any perjurer who faced the ordeal of placing it there. In reality it is a slab that once closed an ancient drain. To the right is the tomb of Cardinal Alfano, chamberlain of Calixtus II (see above). The principal doorway is the work of Johannes de Venetia (11C).

The INTERIOR, dark and strikingly pictorial in effect, with a nave and two aisles each ending in an apse, closely reproduces the 8C basilica, with some 12C additions. The arcades are supported on antique columns grouped in threes between piers; the capitals repay study. High up on the walls are the remains of frescoes of the 11C. The schola cantorum, rood-loft, paschal candelabrum, episcopal throne, and pavement (1123) are the *Work of the Cosmati. The baldacchino over the high altar (an antique porphyry bath) is by Deodatus, third son of the younger Cosmas (1294). The paintings in the apses are restored. Columns of the Roman hall (comp. above) survive in various parts of the building; in the sacristy, to the right of the entrance, are also some fragments of a mosaic of 706 on a gold ground, representing the Adoration of the Magi, formerly in the oratory of John VII at St Peter's. In the chapel to the left, over the altar, is a Madonna and Child attributed to the late 15C Roman school. The tiny crypt, reached from either aisle, was built into part of the altar dedicated to Hercules, the columns of which remain.

From the Lungotévere Aventino, w. of Piazza della Bocca della Verità, the iron *Ponte Palatino* crosses the Tiber to Trastévere (Rte 17). In the bed of the Tiber, upstream, is a single arch of the *Pons Aemilius*, the first stone bridge over the Tiber (the piers were built in 179 B.C., and were connected by arches in 142 B.C.). From the 13C onwards it was repaired numerous times, and has been familiarly known as the *Ponte Rotto* since its final collapse in 1598. From the parapet of the Ponte Palatino the mouth of the Cloaca Maxima (see below), may be seen under the quay of the left bank, when the river is low.

On the E. side of Piazza della Bocca della Verità is Via del Velabro, which perpetuates the name of this ancient quarter of Rome. The *Velabrum*, once a stagnant marsh left by the inundations of the Tiber, extended between the river and the Palatine, and included the Forum Boarium (p. 84). The derivation of the name is in dispute. The Velabrum is famous in legend as the spot where the shepherd Faustulus found the twins Romulus and Remus.

It was drained by the **Cloaca Maxima,** which was an extensive system serving the valleys between the Esquiline, Viminal, and Quirinal hills, as well as the Roman Forum. At first a natural watercourse to the Tiber, it was later canalized, and arched over in c. 200 B.C.; it is still in use.

In Via del Velabro (Pl. 8; 3) is situated the massive four-sided **Arch of Janus,** which formed a covered passage at a cross-roads (quadrivium) and served as a shelter for the cattle-dealers. It is a work of the decadence, dating perhaps from the reign of Constantine, and is built partly of ancient fragments, with numerous niches for statues. To the left is \*San Giorgio in Velabro (Pl. 8; 1), a church dating from the 6C or possibly earlier. The campanile and portico are of the 12C or 13C, when the church was restored. It was further restored in 1926.

The Ionic portico has square pillars of the 7C. The cool grey interior is basilican, with nave and aisles separated by sixteen antique columns. The curious irregularity of the plan can be seen from the wood ceiling. In the apse is a fresco by P. Cavallini (1295; repainted) of the Madonna with St Peter, St Sebastian, and St George. The altar, with some Cosmatesque decoration, and the canopy, date from the 13C.

To the left of the church is the ornate little *Arcus Argentariorum* (A.D. 204), which was erected by the money-changers (argentarii) and cattle-dealers in honour of the emperor Septimius Severus, Julia Domna, and their children. The portrait and name of Geta were effaced as a mark of his disgrace.

To the left of the arch, a street leads to the church of **San Giovanni Decollato** (ring at No. 22). The interior has fine stucco and fresco decoration dating from 1580-90. The altarpiece of the decapitation of St John is by *Vasari*. In front of the w. door is the entrance to the Oratory with remarkable \*Frescoes by the 16C Roman Mannerists, Jacopino del Conte, Fr. Salviati, Pirro Ligorio, and others. There is also a 16C Cloister. On the other side of the road, reached by a raised pavement, is *Sant'Eligio dei Ferrari* with an interesting Baroque interior.

A detour may be made to the N.E. by Via San Teodoro, which corresponds to the ancient *Vicus Tuscus,* skirting the Palatine on the w. On the right is the small round church of **San Teodoro** (Pl. 8; 2; open 16-18), beside which the she-wolf of the Capitol was found (p. 62). The church (recently restored) was built during the last days of the Empire on the site of the great warehouse known as the *Horrea Agrippiana.* Inside is an early medieval mosaic (Christ and saints), much restored.

From Piazza della Bocca della Verità Via dei Cerchi runs S.E. On the left, in Piazza di Sant'Anastasia (reached also from Via di San Teodoro; see above) is the church of *Sant'Anastasia,* dating from 492 and several times restored. The classical façade is by L. Arrigucci. Inside, under the high altar, is a recumbent statue of St Anastasia, begun by Fr. Aprile and finished by Ercole Ferrata. Beneath the church are remains of an Imperial building. Via dei Cerchi skirts the N.E. side of the **Circus Maximus** and ends in Piazza di Porta Capena. From the street a good view is obtained from below of the ancient buildings on the s. of the Palatine (Rte 6).

Via del Circo Massimo borders the Circus Maximus on the s.w. Half-way along its course the street broadens into the Piazzale Romolo e Remo, in which is a seated bronze statue, by Ettore Ferrari, of Giuseppe Mazzini, unveiled at the centenary (1949) of the Roman Republic.

The **Circus Maximus** lies in the Valle Murcia, between the Palatine and the Aventine, and was the first and largest circus in Rome. According to Livy, it dates from the time of Tarquinius Priscus (c. 600 B.C.), who is said to have here inaugurated a display of races and boxing-matches after a victory over the Latins; but the first factual reference to the circus is in 329 B.C. The circus was altered and enlarged on several occasions. In the time of Julius Cæsar its length was three stadia (1875 Roman feet), its width one stadium, and the depth of the surrounding buildings half a stadium. The resultant oblong was rounded at one end and straight at the other. Tiers of seats were provided all round except at the straight end; here were the *carceres,* or stalls for horses and chariots. In the centre, running lengthwise, was the *spina,* a low wall terminating at either end with a *meta* or conical pillar denoting the turnings of the course. The length of a race was 7 circuits of the *spina.* Though primarily adapted for chariot races, the circus was used also for athletic contests, wild-beast fights, and (by flooding the arena) sea battles. The accommodation varied with the successive reconstructions from 150,000 to 385,000. The circus was destroyed by fire under Nero (A.D. 64) and again in the time of Domitian. A new circus was built by Trajan; Caracalla enlarged it and Constantine restored it after a partial collapse. The last games were held under the Ostrogothic king Totila in A.D. 549.—The extant remains belong to the Imperial period. Some seats and part of the substructure of the stairways may be seen at the curved E. end, near Piazza di Porta Capena, as well as some shops. In the centre of this curve can be seen fragmentary decorative columns of a triumphal arch commemorating Titus's conquest of Jerusalem in A.D. 80-81, which formed the entrance gate. The obelisks now in Piazza del Popolo and outside the Lateran once stood in the circus.

The Aventine hill rises on the s.w. side of the Circus. A secluded residential area with beautiful trees and gardens, it is one of the most peaceful spots in the centre of Rome.

The **Aventine** (40 m), the southernmost of the Seven Hills of Rome, was at first not included within the precincts of the city and remained outside the *pomoerium,* or line of the walls, throughout the republican era. For centuries it was scantily populated. The hill has two summits: the Aventine of antiquity, which extends s.w. of Via del Circo Massimo in the direction of the Tiber, and the Little Aventine, to the s. These two eminences are separated by Viale Aventino, which runs s.w. from the Porta Capena towards the Testaccio.—It was to the Aventine that C. Gracchus, after failing to secure his re-election as tribune, withdrew with his colleague Fulvius Flaccus for their last stand against the Senate. In the Imperial era the Aventine became an aristocratic quarter.

From Via del Circo Massimo, Clivio dei Publici or Via di Valle Murcia mount the hill to Via di Santa Sabina. At the top of the rise the road passes (r.) the walled garden (open) known as the *Parco Savello,* delightfully planted with orange trees, and with a good view of Rome to the N. and N.W. (steps in the far corner lead down to the Tiber). A door in the wall leads into Piazza Pietro d'Illiria, with a splendid wall fountain. Here is the church of \***Santa Sabina** (Pl. 8; 3), one of the most beautiful churches in Rome of the basilican type. It was built by Card. Peter of Illyria (422-32) on the presumed site of the house of the sainted Roman matron Sabina, near a temple of Juno. It was restored in 824 and in 1216. In 1219 Honorius III gave it to St Dominic for his new Order. It was disfigured in 1587 by Dom. Fontana and skilfully restored by A. Muñoz in 1919, and by Berthier in 1936-39.

The church has a small 15C portico, and a door on the left leads into a vestibule, which contains the famous wooden \**Door* of the early 5C, with 18 panels carved with Scriptural scenes, probably not in the original order. These include one of the oldest representations of the Crucifixion in existence.

The INTERIOR is the sole remaining example at Rome of a 5C basilica of the Ravenna type. Of its mosaic decoration, however, only one portion remains, above the doorway, showing seven hexameters in gold lettering on a blue ground, with the founder's name (430), and, at the sides, figures of the Church of the Jews (ex circumcisione) and the Church of the Gentiles (ex gentibus). The wide nave is divided from the aisles by 24 fluted Corinthian *Columns from a neighbouring temple. The arches are adorned with a splendid 5C marble inlay in 'opus sectile'. In the centre of the NAVE is the mosaic tombstone of Muñoz de Zamora (d. 1300), perhaps by *Iac. Torriti*. The schola cantorum, ambones, and bishop's throne (in the choir) have been reconstructed from ancient fragments.—The RIGHT AISLE contains an antique column, older than the church. Adjacent to it, the Chapel of St Hyacinth, is frescoed by the *Zuccari;* and at the end of the aisle is the tomb of Card. Valentino Ausi da Monreale (1485), of the school of *And. Bregno*. Beneath the nave excavations have revealed remains of a small temple and an edifice of the early Imperial period with a fine marble pavement.—The Baroque Elci Chapel, in the LEFT AISLE, contains, over its altar, the *Madonna of the Rosary with SS. Dominic and Catherine, by *Sassoferrato*. The beautiful windows, 34 in all, have their transennae of varied design based on original fragments.

In the convent is St Dominic's room, now a chapel. The beautiful *Cloister* (1216-25), with 103 columns, is open on Sat and Sun 8-12.30, 15.30-17.

Farther on is the church of **Sant' Alessio** (Pl. 8; 3; until 1217, *San Bonifacio*), near which the Crescentii built a convent in the 10C. The interior of the church (if closed, ring at the door on the left) was modernised by *Tom. de Marchis* in 1750, but two tiny mosaic columns remain on either side of the wooden bishop's throne in the apse. At the w. end of the left aisle, set in a modern altar, is a portion of the wooden staircase beneath which St Alexis lived and died.

The street ends at the delightful Piazza dei Cavalieri di Malta, with elaborate decorations by G. B. Piranesi, seen against a background of cypresses and palms. He also designed the monumental entrance in the square to the **Priorato di Malta,** or *Maltese Villa* (Pl. 8; 5), the residence of the Grand Master of the Knights of Malta. A remarkable view of the dome of St Peter's at the end of an avenue may,be seen through a keyhole in the doorway. The villa (adm. rarely granted; see p. 49), contains a Chapter Hall with portraits of the Grand Masters, from Gerard (1113) onwards, and an altarpiece from the church by And. Sacchi. The beautiful garden, graced with palm trees and bay hedges, has a superb view from a terrace looking over the Tiber towards the Monte Mario.

On the left, a drive leads to the back of the villa and the church of **Santa Maria del Priorato,** or *Aventinense* (adm. see Villa), a Benedictine foundation once incorporated in the residence of the patrician senator Alberic, who was the virtual ruler of Rome in 932-54. It passed into the hands of the Templars, and thence to the Knights of Malta. It was rebuilt in 1765 by Piranesi. The fine façade of a single order crowned with a tympanum, has rich decorative details.

The harmonious INTERIOR is striking, with fine stucco decoration; the Rococo high altar by *Tom. Righi* is cleverly lit. On the right is the tomb of Card. Spinelli, an antique sarcophagus with reliefs of the Muses, beyond which is a statue of Piranesi by *Gius. Angelini*. In the left aisle is the tomb of Bart. Carafa (d. 1405) by *Paolo Salviati,* and a medieval marble reliquary, in the form of a pagan cinerary urn (? 10-12C).

On the w. side of the Priorato, facing Via della Marmorata, is the ancient brick *Arco di San Lazzaro,* which may have had some connection with the storehouses (*Emporia*) in this neighbourhood (comp. p. 94).

In Piazza di Sant' Anselmo, just s. of the Priorato, is the large *Benedictine Seminary* (1892-96), with the church of Sant' Anselmo, built in 1900 in the Lombard Romanesque style, and noted for its Gregorian chant (9.30 on Sun).

From P.za Sant' Anselmo, Via di S. Anselmo and Via Icilio (l.) lead towards S. Prisca (beyond P.za Albinia; comp the Plan). The church of **Santa Prisca** (Pl. 8; 5), possibly dating from the 4C, is said to occupy the site of the house of Aquila and Prisca, who entertained St Peter.

INTERIOR. Pretty frescoes in the nave, by *Fontebuoni,* follower of the Zuccari brothers. Right aisle: Baptismal font made from a large Doric capital, with a bronze cover and the Baptism of Christ, by *Ant. Biggi.* Left aisle (near entrance door): Fragment of a 15C Tuscan fresco (Annunciation). In the sacristy are three detached 17C fresco fragments by the school of Maratta.—Beneath the church, besides a Nymphæum (with a small museum) and the Crypt, is a MITHRAEUM, found in 1958. The interesting remains include frescoes and a statue of Mithras slaying the Bull and the lying figure of Saturn.

Via di S. Prisca continues down to the wide and busy Viale Aventino. In Piazza Albania (r.) are extensive remains of the Servian wall (p. 18). Across the square Via S. Saba leads up to the 'Piccolo Aventino' (see p. 89) and the church of **San Saba** (Pl. 8; 6), with a little walled forecourt. Beneath the church were found fragments of frescoes (now exhibited in the sacristy corridor), belonging to the first church founded in the 7C by Palestinian monks fleeing the Eastern invasions. The present church may date from c. 900, although it has been rebuilt several times and was restored in 1943. In 1463, under Card. Piccolomini, the loggia was added above the portico and the four original windows bricked in.

In the portico are sculptural fragments, some Oriental in character (rider and falcon), also a large Roman sarcophagus with figures of a bridegroom and Juno Pronuba. The fine doorway is by Giacomo, the father of Cosma, who also probably executed the floor. In the right aisle are the remains of a schola cantorum, a patchwork of Cosmatesque ornament. On the left-hand side of the church is a short fourth aisle, formed by wide decorated arches, within which are remains of 13C frescoes of St Nicholas of Bari. High up on the arch over the apse is an Annunciation, also added for Card. Piccolomini. In the apse, above the Bishop's throne is a fine Cosmatesque marble disk and a 14C fresco of the Crucifixion.

From Piazza Bernini (with a tiny market), behind the church, Via Palladio leads to Viale Giotto. Flanked on its s. side by the Aurelian Wall (this stretch heavily restored during the Renaissance) the Viale leads r. to the busy Piazza della Porta San Paolo. In the middle of the square rises the **Porta San Paolo** (Pl. 8; 7), the former *Porta Ostiensis.* The inner side, with two arches, is of the time of Aurelian; the outer side, rebuilt by Honorius in 402, has been restored. The gate houses the *Museo della Via Ostiense* (adm. see p. 50), which illustrates the history of the road to Ostia. It includes milestones and reliefs (some only casts), together with models of Ostia and its port in Imperial times. Among the tomb paintings are three frescoed lunettes from a tomb of the Servian period. On the s. side of the gate the square is called Piazzale Ostiense, an important traffic centre, where seven streets converge.

Via della Marmorata comes in from the N. and Via Ostiense leads s. to San Paolo fuori le Mura and to the highway for Ostia and Lido di Roma. Here, also, are the terminus of the electric railway to Ostia and Lido di Roma, and a station of the Underground.—From Porta San Paolo to Porta San Sebastiano, see p. 226.

On the w. side of the square, across the line of the city wall, is the \*Pyramid of Gaius Cestius (d. 12 B.C.), prætor, tribune of the plebs, and member of the college of the Septemviri Epulones, who had charge of solemn banquets. This is a tomb in the form of a tall pyramid of brick faced with marble, 27 m high with a base 22 m square. An inscription records that it was built in 330 days.

Beyond the pyramid to the left extends the so-called **Protestant Cemetery** (Pl. 8; 7; open 7 till dusk; visitors ring at No. 6, Via Caio Cestio), romantically set with dark green cypresses. The earliest recorded grave dates from 1738.

It was of the *Old Cemetery* (left of the entrance), that Shelley wrote "it might make one in love with death to think that one should be buried in so sweet a place". The tomb in the far corner is that of John Keats (1796-1821; "Here lies one whose name was writ in water"); close by lies his friend Joseph Severn (1793-1879); behind, John Bell (1763-1820), the surgeon. In the *New Cemetery* lie the ashes of P. B. Shelley (1792-1822; 'cor cordium'), with a monument by Onslow Ford (1891). Close by lies his friend Edw. Trelawny (1792-1881). Here are buried also J. Addington Symonds (1840-93), the historian of the Renaissance; John Gibson (1790-1886), the sculptor; William Howitt (1792-1879) and his wife Mary (1799-1888), R. M. Ballantyne (1825-94), and Julius Goethe (d. 1830), the only son of the poet.

Just beyond the Protestant Cemetery, at the end of Via Caio Cestio, and across Via Nicola Zabaglia is the **Rome British Military Cemetery,** where 429 members of the three Services lie at rest. The cemetery is beautifully situated along the line of the city wall. The gate remains unlocked; caretaker at No. 81 Via Mastrogiorgio.

To the N. of the British Military Cemetery and W. of Via Nicola Zabaglia rises the curious **Monte Testaccio** (Pl. 8; 7), an isolated mound 54 m high and some 1000 m round, entirely composed of potsherds (testæ) dumped here from the neighbouring EMPORIA, or storehouses, which anciently lined the Tiber between Ponte Testaccio and Ponte Sublicio. The store-houses were served by the landing-stage of the Marmorata, long since vanished. Among the finds here was a hoard of amphoræ, used to import oil from Spain, with official marks scratched on them, which are of fundamental importance to our knowledge of the economic history of the late Republic and early Empire. The top of Monte Testaccio (entered from the corner facing Via Galvani and Via Zabaglia) commands a fine view. The neighbourhood was the scene of jousts and tournaments in the Middle Ages.

In Via della Marmorata, on the E. side near Piazza di Porta San Paolo, is the Ostiense branch post office, a striking modernistic building, by De Renzi and Libera. The street goes on towards the Tiber, ending in Piazza dell'Emporio. Hence the *Ponte Aventino* or *Ponte Sublicio* crosses the river to Trastévere (Rte 17), near the Porta Portese. The original bridge at this point, the *Pons Sublicius*, was the first bridge across the Tiber; it is said to have been built by Ancus Marcius, fourth king of Rome, to connect the Janiculum with the city.

From Piazzale Ostiense the broad uninteresting VIA OSTIENSE leads almost due S. through a depressing part of the town. It is not recommended to walkers; buses 23 and 18 follow it to (2 km.) the basilica of San Paolo. It crosses under the Pisa railway; beyond, to the left, are the Mercati Generali and, to the right, the headquarters of the Gas Works. Some distance farther, on the left, is the site of an oratory marking the spot where, according to tradition, St Peter and St Paul greeted each other on the way to martyrdom. To the E. extends the modern *Quartiere della Garbatella.* In the middle of the road just before San Paolo is a small necropolis known as the *Sepolcreto Ostiense,* which contained pagan and perhaps Christian tombs. The site, seen through railings (adm. only by special permission) extended over a wide area; another part is visible left of the road.

Here the narrow Via delle Sette Chiese, passing the *Catacombs of Commodilla* (adm. by special permit), branches off to join Via Ardeatina and the Appian Way (Pl. p. 232).

*San Paolo fuori le Mura (Pl. 8; beyond 7), or *Basilica Ostiense,* 2 km. from Porta San Paolo, is the largest church in Rome after St Peter's, and is more noteworthy for its interior decoration than for its external appearance. One of the four great patriarchal basilicas (see p. 45), it commemorates the martyrdom of St Paul and is believed to contain the Apostle's tomb. The present building, third on the site, is a 19C construction replacing the ancient basilica virtually destroyed by fire in 1823. San Paolo fuori le Mura is one of the three basilicas enjoying extraterritoriality.

The first basilica was erected by Constantine to replace an oratory in the vineyard of the Roman matron Lucina that had been built over the spot where she had buried the body of the Apostle. In 386 a much larger basilica was begun by Valentinian II and Theodosius the Great; it was enlarged by the latter's son Honorius and adorned with mosaics by Galla Placidia, sister of Honorius. The basilica was further embellished by Leo III (Pope, 795-816) and it became the largest and most beautiful church in Rome. In the 9C it was pillaged by the Saracens and John VIII (872-82) enclosed it in a fortified village known as *Giovannipolis.* It was restored c. 1070 by Abbot Hildebrand, later Gregory VII. The façade, overlooking the Tiber, was preceded by a colonnaded quadriporticus. Before the Reformation the King of England was *ex officio* a canon of San Paolo and the abbot, in return, was decorated with the Order of the Garter. This great basilica was almost entirely destroyed by fire on the night of 15-16 July 1823.

Leo XII (1823-29) ordered the reconstruction, which was directed by Pasquale Belli, Bosio, and Camporese, and afterwards by Luigi Poletti. In their enthusiasm for the work of rebuilding the architects pressed on with new materials and disregarded much of the old work that could have been preserved after repair. The transept was consecrated by Gregory XVI in 1840 and the complete church by Pius IX in 1854. In plan and dimensions, if not in spirit, the new basilica follows the old one almost exactly. Its history since 1854 has not been completely unchequered. In 1891 an explosion in a neighbouring fort broke most of the stained glass; its place has been taken by slabs of alabaster. Here in March 1966 took place a service performed by Pope Paul VI and Dr Ramsey, Abp of Canterbury, when they issued a joint declaration of amity.

EXTERIOR. Before entering the church, it is worthwhile walking round the left (N.) side to see the façade on the Tiber. In front of it is a great QUADRIPORTICUS, designed by *Giuseppe Sacconi,* with a row of ten enormous monolithic columns of red Baveno granite constituting a portico before the façade, and three other rows of columns, of Montórfano granite, on the remaining sides. In the middle of the quadriporticus is a statue of St Paul and four palm trees.—The FAÇADE is adorned with elaborate mosaics dating from 1885. The central doorway has a bronze door by *Ant. Maraini* (1928-30). The general effect of the exterior is impressive, if frigid.—The *Campanile,* at the other end of the church, in front of the apse, is disappointing. It was built by Poletti to replace a Romanesque campanile, which was pulled down to make way for it.—In front of the N. porch is the Portico Gregoriano. On one of the nearest columns, close under the frieze, is a 4C inscription of Pope Siricius (384-99).

INTERIOR. The nave and transept form in plan a tau or Egyptian cross, 132 m by 65 m; the height is 30 metres. The view of the interior from near the main door is remarkable.—The NAVE, with double aisles separated from one another by eighty columns of Montórfano granite, is the new part of the basilica. In the centre of the ceiling, which is richly decorated with stuccoes in white and gold, are the arms of Pius IX. The paintings between the windows depict scenes in the life of St Paul; under these (and in the aisles), forming a frieze, are the portraits in mosaic of all the 263 popes from St Peter to Paul VI. In the outermost aisles are niches with statues of the Apostles. The six huge alabaster columns beside the doors were presented by Mohammed Ali of Egypt. Between the Porta Santa and the central door are the recently restored bronze *Doors which belonged to the old basilica. They were made at Constantinople by Staurakios in 1070, inlaid with silver in 54 panels of scenes from the Old and New Testament. Near the E. end of the nave are statues of St Peter (by *Iacometti*) and of St Paul (by *Revelli*).

The *TRIUMPHAL ARCH, a relic of the old basilica, is supported by two colossal granite columns. Its mosaics (much restored) are due to Galla Placidia. They represent Christ blessing in the Greek manner, with angels; Symbols of the Evangelists; the Elders of the Apocalypse; SS. Peter and Paul. On the other side of the arch are the remains of mosaics by *Pietro Cavallini.*—Over the high altar, supported by four porphyry columns, is the famous *Tabernacle, by *Arnolfo di Cambio* and his companion *Pietro* (*Oderisi?*, 1285). The old tradition which places the tomb of St Paul beneath the altar is well-founded. Excavations before the rebuilding in 1823, revealed a 1C tomb, surrounded by Christian and some pagan burials. When the grating of the Confessio is opened, the inscription 'Paolo Apostolo Mart', dating from the time of Constantine, may be seen. To the right of the high altar is a huge 12C paschal *Candlestick by *Nicolò di Angelo* and *Pietro Vassalletto.*

The magnificent ceiling of the transept is decorated with the arms of Pius VII, Leo XII, Pius VIII, and Gregory XVI, as well as with those of the basilica (an arm holding a sword). The walls are covered with rare marbles.—The Corinthian pilasters are made up of fragments of the old columns.—The great *Mosaic of the APSE was executed c. 1220 by Venetian craftsmen sent by Doge Pietro Ziani at the request of Pope Honorius III. The subjects are Christ blessing in the Greek manner, with SS. Peter, Andrew, Paul, and Luke; at the feet of Christ, Pope Honorius III; below this, a gem-studded Cross on the altar, angels and apostles. On the arch sides, Virgin and Child with St John blessing Pope John XXII.

At either end of the transept is an altar of malachite and lapis lazuli, presented by Nicholas I of Russia. Over the left-hand altar, *Vinc. Camuccini,* Conversion of St Paul; over the other, mosaic copy of the Coronation of the Virgin, by *Giulio Romano.* Both altars are flanked by statues.—To the left of the apse: Chapel of St Stephen, with a statue of the saint by *Rinaldi,* and paintings of his expulsion from the Sanhedrin, by *Coghetti,* and of his stoning, by *Podesti.* Chapel of the Crucifix, by *Carlo Maderna* (the only chapel salved in the fire); on the altar, Crucifix attrib. to *Tino da Camaino.* In a niche to the right of the door, statue of St Bridget by *Stef. Maderna;* to the l., statue of a Saint in wood. In this chapel, in 1541, St Ignatius de Loyola and the first Jesuits took the corporate oaths formally establishing their society as a religious order.—To the right of the apse: Chapel of the Choir or of St Laurence, by *Gugl. Calderini;* 15C marble triptych, frescoes by *Viligiardi.* Chapel of St Benedict, a sumptuous yet severe work of Poletti, who has reproduced in it the cella of an antique temple; the 12 fluted columns are from Veii.

The door to the r. in the s. transept leads to the SALA DEL MARTIROLOGIO (sometimes closed, but with glass doors), with badly damaged 13C frescoes, and a bust of Poletti. The door to the left in this transept leads past the Baptistery (r.; designed by Arnaldo Foschini in a Greek cross in 1930) to the Vestibule preceeding the s. door of the church, which contains a colossal statue of Gregory XVI by Rinaldi, and 13C mosaics from the old basilica. A door to the r. off the vestibule leads to the *Cloisters (open daily 9-11.45, 14-Ave Maria) belonging to the old Benedictine convent. They have coupled colonnettes of different forms decorated with mosaics, with tiny couchant animals (most of which have now disappeared) between the columns. In the centre is a rose garden. The cloisters were begun under Abbot Pietro da Capua (1193-1208) and finished before 1214, and are the work, at least in part, of the Vassalletti. Along the walls are placed inscriptions and sculptured fragments: XIV. Statue of Boniface IX; XVII. Sarcophagus with the story of Apollo and Marsyas; XIX. An inscription recording the suicide of Nero (probably a 17C forgery); XX. Statue of a prophet. The painted wood roof is noteworthy.—Off the Cloister is the Chapel of Reliquaries, with a gilded silver cross, and the Pinacoteca, with works by Antoniazzo Romano and Bramantino (Flagellation).

From San Paolo the road continues s. After a short distance, a road to the right leads viâ Viale Marconi to Via del Mare (for Ostia and Lido di Roma; Rte 21).— For E.U.R. and the Monastery of Tre Fontane (Rte 19) Via Laurentina forks left from Vla Ostiense under the railway, and soon joins Via Cristoforo Colombo.

## 4 FROM THE CORSO VITTORIO EMANUELE NORTH TO THE TIBER

This itinerary covers part of the ancient **Campus Martius**, or Plain of Mars, which was the N.W. portion of the low-lying ground in the bend of the Tiber. It was not included in the walls of Rome until Aurelian built his famous wall round the city (270-75). After the 2C B.C. it was adorned with temples, laid out with gardens and pleasure-grounds, and devoted to the exercises and amusements of the Roman youth. Originally the property of the Tarquins, it was dedicated to Mars on the expulsion of the kings. The s. part of the Campus Martius was the Prata Flaminia, with the Circus of Flaminius.

The narrow Via del Gesù (Pl. 2; 8) runs N. from Piazza del Gesù (p. 74), which unites Via del Plebiscito with the Corso Vittorio Emanuele.

At No. 85, where the street enters the little Piazza della Pigna, is a beautiful Renaissance doorway. In the piazza is the Baroque church of *S. Giovanni della Pigna* (with interesting tomb slabs inside the entrance wall), and, at No. 6, the house where Mussolini met Card. Gasparri in 1923 to initiate discussions on the Conciliation between the Church and the Italian State. In Via della Pigna is the *Palazzo Marescotti* (Vicariato di Roma), built by Giacomo della Porta at the end of 16C (altered later). Beyond Via dei Cestari, in Via dell' Arco della Ciambella, part of the circular wall of the central hall of the *Baths of Agrippa* is charmingly incorporated into the street architecture. These were the first public baths in the city, begun by Agrippa in 25 B.C.

Via dei Cestari or Via del Gesù lead N. to Piazza Minerva. Here is a bizarre but delightful work by Bernini (1667), a marble elephant supporting a small obelisk which belonged to the ISAEUM CAMPENSE, or *Temple of Isis,* that formerly stood near here. Other relics from the temple are in the Capitoline Museum, in the Viale delle Terme (p. 196), and in the Egyptian Museum in the Vatican. The hieroglyphic inscription on the obelisk relates to Apries, the last of the independent Pharaohs of Egypt (the Hophrah of the Bible), who was the ally of Zedekiah, king of Judah, against Nebuchadnezzar (6C B.C.).

*Santa Maria sopra Minerva (Pl. 2; 6), on the E. side of the piazza, is an ancient church on the site of a temple of Minerva. It was rebuilt in 1280, apparently by Fra Sisto and Fra Ristoro the architects of Santa Maria Novella in Florence, and was long the church of the Florentines. It is the only old church in Rome in the Gothic style. 'Classicized' by Maderno in the 17C, it was restored in 1847 to something like its original form. On the right side of the simple façade (attributed to *Meo del*

*Caprina;* 1453) small marble plaques register the heights reached by floods on the Tiber before it was canalized.

The INTERIOR (good light essential; best in the afternoon) contains some important works of art and a number of Baroque monuments. The vault, the rose-windows, and the excessively colourful decorations date from the 19C restoration. On the right of the central door is the tomb of Nerone Diotisalvi, a Florentine exile (d. 1482), and, on the right of the s. door, that of Virginia Pucci Ridolfi (1567), the latter with a fine bust by an unknown Florentine.

SOUTH AISLE. By 1st chap., tomb of the archivist Castalio, with a fine portrait.—5th chap. (Chapel of the Annunciation, by *C. Maderna*). *Antoniazzo Romano,* Altarpiece, representing (on a gold ground) the Annunciation, with Card. Johannes de Turrecremata (uncle of Tomás de Torquemada, the inquisitor) presenting three poor girls to the Virgin, commemorating the Confraternity of the Annunziata, founded in 1460 to provide dowries for penniless girls; on the left, tomb of Urban VII, by *Ambr. Buonvicino.*—6th chap. Frescoed ceiling by *Cherubino Alberti;* altarpiece, by *Barocci;* at the sides, tombs of the parents of Clement VIII, by *Giac. della Porta,* and (in a niche to the left) a statue of Clement VIII. A statue of St Sebastian has recently been removed from a niche and placed in the centre of the chapel since its attribution to Michelangelo. Probably made as a model for his Christ (see below), it may have been finished by *N. Cordier.*—7th chap. On the r., tomb of Card. Diego de Coca (1477), by *And. Bregno,* with a fresco by *Melozzo da Forlì;* on the l., tomb of Bened. Sopranzi, Bp. of Nicosia (d. 1495), by the school of A. Bregno.

SOUTH TRANSEPT. 1st chap., wooden crucifix (early 15C); *2nd chap., at the end (Cappella Carafa or di San Tommaso), with a fine marble arch (by Florentine sculptors) and a beautiful balustrade. Within are celebrated *Frescoes by *Filippino Lippi* (1489; light, 100 l.): over the altar, Annunciation and St Thomas Aquinas presenting Card. Olivieri Carafa to the Virgin; altar wall, Assumption; right wall, below, St Thomas confounding the heretics, the central figures being Arius and Sabellius (the two youths in the right-hand group are probably the future Medici popes, Leo X and Clement VII, both buried in this church). On the left wall, monument of Paul IV (d. 1559) by *Giac.* and *Tom. Cassignola,* from a design by Pirro Ligorio. In the vault, Four sibyls, by *Raffaellino del Garbo.*—To the left of this chapel, *Tomb of Guillaume Durand (d. 1296), bishop of Mende, by *Giov. di Cosma,* with a beautiful 13C mosaic of the Madonna and Child.—3rd chap., *C. Maratta,* Madonna and saints.—4th chap., Frescoed ceiling by *Marcello Venusti;* on the right, tomb of Card. Capranica (1458).

CHOIR. At the foot of the steps, on the left, is the famous *CHRIST BEARING THE CROSS by *Michelangelo* (1514-21), commissioned at a cost of 200 ducats by Metello Vari and P. Castellani. The bronze drapery is a later addition. Under the modern high altar rests the body of St Catherine of Siena (see below). In the apse are the tombs of Leo X (l.) and Clement VII, designed by Ant. Sangallo the Younger, with statues by *Raff. da Montelupo* and *Nanni di Baccio Bigio* respectively. In the pavement is the slab-tomb of Card. Pietro Bembo (1547), secretary to Pope Leo X from 1512-20, and friend of Michelangelo, Raphael, and Ariosto.

NORTH TRANSEPT. To the left of the choir, in a passageway which serves as an exit, are several large monuments, including those of Card. Alessandrino, by *Giac. della Porta,* and of Card. Dom. Pimentel, designed by *Bernini.* Surrounded by a modern bronze fence is the *Tomb-slab of Fra Angelico, with some charming lines composed by Pope Nicholas V.—2nd chap. to the l. of the choir, Tomb of Giov. Arberini (d. c. 1470) by a Tuscan sculptor (*Agost. di Duccio*?), who has introduced a Roman copy of a Greek *Bas-relief of the 5C B.C., representing Hercules and the lion. To the left is the entrance to the sacristy, behind which is the room in which St Catherine of Siena died in 1380; it was brought from Via di Santa Chiara by Card. Barberini. The frescoes, in poor preservation, are by *Antoniazzo Romano* and his school (1482).—At the end of this transept is the Cappella di San Domenico, with the Baroque monument of Benedict XIII (d. 1730). At the corner of the nave and transept is the small tomb of And. Bregno (1421-1506). On the 2nd pillar is the tomb of Maria Raggi, a colourful work by *Bernini.*

NORTH AISLE. 3rd chap. Tiny altarpiece (the Redeemer), attrib. to *Perugino* or to *Pinturicchio;* on the right, statue of St Sebastian, attrib. to *Mich. Marini;* on the left, St John the Baptist, by *Ambr. Buonvicino;* against the side-walls, tombs of Benedetto and Agostino Maffei, attributed to *L. Capponi* (15C).—1st chap. Bust of Girol. Bottigella, perhaps by *Iac. Sansovino.*—Near the door is the tomb of Francesco Tornabuoni (1480), by *Mino da Fiesole,* and above is that of Card. Tebaldi (1466), by *And. Bregno* and *Giov. Dalmata.*

The monastery was once the headquarters of the Dominicans, in which Fra Angelico died (1455) and Galileo was tried (1633). A small *Museum* (opened on request) contains icons from Jugoslavia (17-19C), ecclesiastical vestments, a detached fresco of the Madonna and Child (late 13C or early 14C), etc.

Via della Minerva skirts the side of the Pantheon to reach PIAZZA DELLA ROTONDA. In the centre of the square is a fountain (1575), on a model of Jacopo della Porta, surmounted by an obelisk of Rameses the Great, formerly belonging to the Temple of Isis (p. 95) and erected here in 1711.

The **Pantheon (Pl. 2; 6), which became in time the church of *Santa Maria Rotonda* or *ad Martyres,* is one of the best preserved monuments of Roman antiquity. A pedimented pronaos precedes a gigantic domed rotunda, and a rectangular feature as wide as the pronaos and as high as the cylindrical wall is inserted between the two. This combination of a pronaos and rotunda gives it a special place in the history of architecture. Admission, see p. 49.

HISTORY. The original temple was built apparently of travertine, during the third consulate of Agrippa (27 B.C.), son-in-law of Augustus, to commemorate the victory of Actium over Antony and Cleopatra. It was injured by fire in A.D. 80 and was restored by Domitian; but in spite of the dedicatory inscription on the pediment of the pronaos (*M. Agrippa, L. F. Cos. tertium fecit*), which was restored by G. Baccelli in 1894, the existing temple is not that of Agrippa, but a new one built and probably also designed by Hadrian of brick, on a larger scale and on different lines. It has been conclusively proved (by examination of the brick stamps) that the whole building including the pronaos was constructed under Hadrian. This second building, begun in A.D. 118 or 119 and finished between A.D. 125 and 128, received and retained the name of Pantheon, though it was conceived as much as a secular Imperial monument as a shrine. It stood and remains the most magnificent symbol of the Empire.

D

It was restored by Septimius Severus and Caracalla. Closed and abandoned under the first Christian emperors and pillaged by the barbarians, the Pantheon was given to Boniface IV by the Byzantine emperor Phocas (whose column is in the Forum; see p. 115). Boniface IV consecrated it as a Christian church in 609; it was dedicated to Santa Maria ad Martyres in allusion to the martyrs' bones—no less than twenty-eight wagon-loads, according to tradition—which were transferred here from the catacombs. In 663 Constans II, emperor of Byzantium, despoiled the temple of what the Goths had left, and, in particular, stripped off the gilded roof-tiles (probably of bronze). Benedict II (684) restored it, Gregory III (735) roofed it with lead; in 1153 Anastasius IV built a palace at the side. During the residence of the popes at Avignon the Pantheon served as a fortress in the struggles between the Colonna and the Orsini; but in 1435 Eugenius IV isolated the building, and from that time it was the object of such jealous veneration that the Roman Senator on taking office swore to preserve 'Maria Rotonda' intact for the pontiff, together with the relics and sacred treasures of the City. The Renaissance admired and revered the monument; Pius IV caused the bronze door to be repaired, and practically re-cast (1563). Urban VIII (Barberini), however, employed Bernini to add two clumsy turrets in front, which became popularly known as the 'ass-ears of Bernini'. Urban VIII also melted down the bronze ceiling of the portico to make the baldacchino at St Peter's and cannon for the Castel Sant' Angelo, an act of vandalism that prompted Pasquino's stinging gibe, "Quod non fecerunt barbari fecerunt Barberini". Alexander VII had the portico restored by Giuseppe Paglia (1662) and the level of the piazza lowered, so that the façade of the building should be seen to better advantage; Clement IX surrounded the portico with an iron railing (1668); Benedict XIV employed Paolo Posi (1747) to restore the interior and the atrium. The first two Kings and the first Queen of Italy are buried here. The incongruous turrets added by Bernini were removed in 1883.

The PORTICO (being restored in 1978) is nearly 34 m wide and 15½ m deep, and has 16 monolithic Corinthian columns of red or grey granite, without flutings, each 12½ m high and 4½ m in circumference. The superb capitals and the bases are of white marble. The three columns on the E. side are replacements, one by Urban VIII (1625), the others by Alexander VII (1655-67); the armorial bearings of these popes may be seen in the decoration of the capitals. Eight of the columns stand in front, and the others are disposed in four rows, so as to form three aisles, the central one leading to the bronze door, which dates from Pius IV, and the others to the two great niches which may formerly have contained colossal statues of Augustus and Agrippa.

The visual impact of the *INTERIOR is unforgettable. The use of light from the opening in the dome displays the genius of the architect. The height and diameter of the interior are the same—43.3 m. The great dome has five rows of coffers diminishing in size towards the circular opening in the centre, which measures almost 9 m across. The intricate design of the coffers is mainly responsible for the effect of space and light in the interior. They were probably ornamented with gilded bronze rosettes. The diameter of the dome exceeds by more than 1 m that of the dome of St Peter's. Its span, which contains no brick arches or vaults, begins at the level of the highest cornice seen on the outside of the building, rather than, as it appears in the interior, at the top of the attic stage.

The cylindrical wall is 6 m thick; and in its thickness are contrived seven great niches, or recesses, each, except the central apse preceded by two Corinthian columns of giallo antico, and flanked by pilasters. The apse instead has two free-standing columns. Between the recesses, which originally contained statues, are eight shrines (aediculae), those flanking the apse and entrance with triangular pediments, and the others with segmented pediments. They are supported by two Corinthian columns in giallo antico, porphyry, or granite. Above the recesses is the entablature with a beautiful cornice, and still higher is an attic, unfortunately restored in 1747, making this stage more pronounced than was intended. Part of the original decoration can be seen over the recess to the right of the apse: between the rectangular openings (fitted with grilles) were shallow pilasters of reddish marble alternating with three marble panels. In antiquity the interior would have been more colourful, although more than half of the original coloured marble sheets on the walls are still in place. The floor, though restored, retains its original design.

In the 1st chap. on the right, *Annunciation, a fresco attrib. to *Melozzo da Forlì*. 2nd chap. on the right, tomb of Victor Emmanuel II, first king of Italy (d. 9 Jan 1878), who succeeded to the Sardinian crown after the defeat of Novara, and ultimately led the Italian armies to the Capitol. The tomb, which is simple and austere, was designed by *Manfredi*. Opposite is the tomb of Humbert I, who was assassinated at Monza on 29 July 1900. It was designed by *Gius. Sacconi*. Below Humbert's tomb is that of Margherita di Savoia, first queen of Italy (d. 5 Jan 1926).

To the right of the tomb of Humbert I is the *TOMB OF RAPHAEL, inscribed with the famous distich of Bembo, translated by Pope in his Epitaph on Sir Godfrey Kneller ("Living, great Nature feared he might outvie Her works, and dying, fears herself may die"). On the altar is the statue of the Madonna del Sasso, by *Lorenzetto*, probably with the help of *Raff. da Montelupo*, from Raphael's original design. The bronze bust is by De Fabris. Below the empty niche on the right is the short epitaph of Maria Bibbiena, niece of Cardinal Dovizi da Bibbiena, who was betrothed to Raphael and died before him. To the right, in the next chap., is a monument by *Thorvaldsen*, to Card. Consalvi (d. 1824), secretary of Pius VII, who represented the Holy See at the Congress of Vienna. Among other artists buried in the Pantheon are Giov. da Udine, Perin del Vaga, Taddeo Zuccari, Ann. Carracci, and Bald. Peruzzi.

A door on the left of the pronaos leads to a staircase to the cupola (extensive views; permit to be obtained from the Director-General, Accademia di Belle Arti).

Behind the Pantheon, in Via della Palombella, are remains of Agrippa's *Basilica of Neptune*, reconstructed by Hadrian.

To the N. of Piazza della Rotonda, Via del Pantheon (with a hotel at No. 63 on the right where Ariosto stayed in 1513; plaque), leads to the small and charming Piazza della Maddalena. Here the church of the **Maddalena** has a Rococo façade (1735) by *G. Sardi*. The INTERIOR, on an original plan, is the work of various 17C artists including, *Carlo Fontana, Carlo Quadrio*, and *Giov. Ant. de Rossi*. It contains frescoes by *Seb. Conca, Mich. Rocca*, and *Baciccia*, and a fine organ. The Sacristy (1741) of unique design (restored in 1968) is entered from the left aisle.

Via delle Colonnelle (which passes the r. side of the church dating from the late 17C) leads to Piazza Capranica, which is dominated by the *Palazzo Capranica*, partly Gothic and partly Renaissance in style. The tower has a delightful loggia.

Behind the Pantheon Via della Palombella leads into Piazza Sant' Eustachio, where the church of *Sant' Eustachio* preserves its campanile of 1196. The charming palazzo on the corner opposite has fine windows, a pretty cornice and remains of its painted façade. In the same square is a palazzo (No. 83) built by Giulio Romano for the Maccarani. From here there is a good view of the campanile of St Ivo (comp. below). From the piazza Via degli Staderari leads past the N. side of Palazzo della Sapienza (and a tiny wall fountain) to the modern Corso del Rinascimento. Here on the left is the entrance to the palace.

The **Palazzo della Sapienza** (Pl. 2; 6), the seat until 1935 of the University of Rome, was founded by Boniface VIII in 1303. The present building houses the *Archivio di Stato*, where exhibitions are held in a library designed by Borromini. The fine Renaissance façade is by Giac.

della Porta. Through the door can be seen the beautifully shaped *Court by Borromini, which has porticoes on three sides, and the church of *St Ivo at the far end. Built for the Barberini pope, Urban VIII, both the courtyard and the church incorporate his device (the bee) into their design. The church (shown by the porter) is a masterpiece of Baroque architecture, with a remarkable light interior. The dome is crowned by an ingenious spiral campanile (copied many times, especially in Germany).

On the w. side of the Corso del Rinascimento Via de'Canestrari leads into the s. end of Piazza Navona (p. 103) and is continued by Via di Pasquino. In this street is the N. façade of *Palazzo Braschi*, by Cosimo Morelli (after 1792), now housing the **Museo di Roma.** The entrance is behind in Piazza San Pantaleo (adm. see p. 50).

The museum was founded in 1930 to illustrate the history and life of Rome from the Middle Ages to the present day. Many of the works of art come from demolished buildings. The collection is undergoing rearrangement.

Off the courtyard is the train built in Paris in 1858 for Pius IX, and the carriage of Leo XIII. To the left is the Vestibule at the foot of the stairs with a colossal statue of Christ and St John by *Fr. Mochi*. Here are four rooms (opened on request) which house part of the Pinacoteca of the Accademia dell' Arcadia (see p. 243) which contains portraits of illustrious members including Vittorio Alfieri and Isaac Newton. The magnificent staircase ascribed to Valadier (1802-04) and decorated by Luigi Acquisti leads to the first floor.

ROOM I. *Fr. Mochi*, Bust of Carlo Barberini; ceiling fresco of the Annunciation of the school of *Zuccari*.—R. II. *Baciccia*, Portrait of Card. Ginnetti.—(r.) R. III. Three large 16C paintings of tournaments in Rome.—R. IV. Ceiling *Frescoes of the fable of Psyche by *Cigoli*. These were detached from a room, since demolished, in the Palazzo Rospigliosi. In the cases, wooden corbels from 12-17C.—R. V. The oval ceiling is painted in the form of a pavilion. In the centre, tabernacle by *Girolamo da Carpi*. Bust of Clement XII by *Filippo Valle*.—R. VI. Fragments of frescoes, those on the large wall from a house belonging to Card. da Carpi. The others are by *Polidoro da Caravaggio* and *Maturino da Firenze*.—R. VII. Detached *Frescoes from the Papal hunting lodge at Magliana; attributed to *Lo Spagna* (early 16C), they represent Apollo and the Nine Muses.—R. VIII. Tournament in Piazza Navona, and the Visit of Urban VIII to the Gesù, both by *Andrea Sacchi*. Investiture of Taddeo Barberini by *Agostino Tassi*. Urban VIII, portrait by *Pietro da Cortona*. The three adjacent rooms are to exhibit Medieval frescoes.—R. IX (with a fine view of P.za Navona). 17C cabinet with a series of miniature scenes of Rome, and on the walls, paintings of Piazza S. Pietro and Piazza del Popolo.—In the large GALLERY are Gobelins tapestries. The room is designed by *Valadier*, who also designed the adjoining CHAPEL (opened on request), with a fine stucco vault. It contains a St Francis, attrib. to *Guido Reni*, and on the altar an 18C ivory crucifix. Beyond R. XI, R. XII has a pretty majolica floor and fine *Paintings by *Pompeo Batoni* (portraits of Pio VI, and John Staples, Self-portrait, and Woman at her toilet) and *Giov. Paolo Pannini* (Portrait of Benedict XIV and a Cardinal).—R. XIII. *And. Sacchi*, Portrait of Card. Dom. Ginnasi. Works by *Canova* are exhibited in R. XIV, including the original plaster model for his Self-portrait, two bozzetti, and a painted Self-portrait. Beyond R. XV with church furniture, R. XVI exhibits weights and measures. A corridor leads back to R. I and the staircase.

SECOND FLOOR. Many of the rooms have ceilings decorated by *Liborio Coccetti* (early 19C). In the Vestibule are three huge paintings illustrating the story of Helen and Paris, by *Gavin Hamilton*. Beyond R. I with works by *Fr. Gai*, R. II contains fresco fragments from Palazzo Caffarelli. In R. III begins the collection of water-colours of old Rome by *Ettore R. Franz* (1845-1907; continued in R. VI). Beyond an oval room, R. V. contains fresco fragments (end of 13C) and *Mosaics from the old façade of St Peter's. An interesting series of views of Rome in the nineteenth century, by *Ippolito Caffi*, and a portrait of Piranesi are to be exhibited on this floor.

The Third Floor is still in the course of arrangement. The exhibits will include a collection of drawings and water-colours of Roman costumes by *Bart. Pinelli*, scenes of Rome by *Dom. Morelli* and *De Sanctis*, and other 19C works from the GALLERIA COMUNALE D'ARTE MODERNA (comp. p. 188). Also on this floor is the

*Archivio Fotografico Comunale.*—Sculptures by *Pietro Tenerani* are to be arranged on the Fourth Floor.

Via di Pasquino leads to Piazza Pasquino, at the corner of which is the famous fragment of a marble group really representing Menaleus supporting Patroclus, but known since the 16C as **Pasquino.**

It became the custom to affix witty or caustic comments on events of the day to this group or its pedestal, and the credit for originating this method of public satire was, rightly or wrongly, ascribed to a certain Pasquino, a tailor in the vicinity: hence the name of the statue and the origin of the term 'pasquinade'. Pasquino used often to maintain animated dialogues with Marforio (p. 58), before the incarceration of the latter on the Capitol.

The itinerary described immediately below, as far as the church of Santa Maria della Pace (p. 102), leads through various old and narrow Roman streets. The church may be reached more directly by Via dei Lorenesi which leads out of the N. end of Piazza Navona.

From Piazza Pasquino the narrow Via del Governo Vecchio, an ancient papal thoroughfare, with many traces of the early Renaissance, leads W. On the right (No. 39) is the PALAZZO DEL GOVERNO VECCHIO, built by Card. Stefano Nardini, created Governor of Rome by Paul II; the magnificent porch dates from the Renaissance. Opposite is the remarkable *Palazzo Turci* (early 16C), once attributed to Bramante. The street ends in Piazza dell' Orologio. Via degli Orsini leads right to reach Via di Monte Giordano, in which, opposite, is the 18C *Palazzo Taverna* (Pl. 2; 5) formerly *Gabrielli,* with a beautiful fountain by Antonio Casoni (1615) in the court.

The palace stands on Monte Giordano, the name of which is derived from Giordano Orsini (13C), whose legendary fortress stood here. Dante mentions the 'Monte' ('Inferno', xxviii, 12) in the description of the pilgrims crossing the Ponte Sant' Angelo on the occasion of the jubilee of 1300.

Via di Panico leads towards the river; to the r. diverges *VIA DEI CORONARI* (Pl. 2; 5), a beautiful straight street (closed to traffic), with many antique shops. It traverses a region with Renaissance houses. Near the beginning, on the right (Nos. 122-23) stands the presumed House of Raphael. In the piazza on the left is *San Salvatore in Lauro* a church with a Palladian interior by Mascherino (1594). To the left of the church (No. 15) is the entrance to the fine Renaissance cloister (in poor repair). A small courtyard beyond has two Renaissance portals. The refectory contains the *Tomb of Eugenius IV (d. 1447) by *Isaia da Pisa,* one of the earliest sepulchral monuments to exhibit the characteristic forms of the Renaissance.—The next road left skirts the side of *Palazzo Lancellotti* (no adm.), which was begun by Fr. da Volterra and finished by Carlo Maderna. Via della Maschera d' Oro leads on to Piazza Fiammetta, with the fine *Palazzo Sacripante Ruiz* (attrib. to Bart. Ammannati), where Via Giuseppe Zanardelli diverges on the left for Ponte Umberto I.

In the Piazza Ponte Umberto I is Palazzo Primoli, in which is the **Napoleonic Museum** (reopened in 1977), presented to the city of Rome in 1927 by Count Joseph Primoli. The collection belonged to Count Joseph and his brother Louis, who were sons of Carlotta Bonaparte. In the seventeen period rooms of the museum are paintings, statues, and relics of the Bonaparte family, with special reference to the Roman branch. The more important works include paintings by *David* of Zenaide and Carlotta, daughters of Joseph, king of Naples, by *Gerard* of Elisa Baciocchi, by *Wicar* of Louis, king of Holland, by *Winterhalter* of Napoleon III and the Empress Eugénie; sculptures by *Canova, Bartolini, Carpeaux* and

*Thorvaldsen;* miniatures by *Isabey;* prints illustrating the contest between Napoleon and Pius VII; State robes; autographs, inc. the marriage contract of Napoleon and Marie Louise. Admission, see p. 49.

Near by, on the corner of Via di Monte Brianzo, is the *Osteria dell' Orso.* The Medieval building was altered c. 1460, and it first became a hotel in the 16C. Rabelais, Montaigne, and Goethe were among its patrons. It is now a celebrated restaurant.

Via Sant' Apollinare leads to the piazza of the same name (Pl. 2; 6), passing *Palazzo Altemps,* begun c. 1480 for Girolamo Riario and completed by Martino Longhi the Elder, with a charming belvedere in the form of a turret. The *Teatro Goldoni,* which adjoins the palace, preserves its 17C decoration.

To the s.w., by Via Tor Sanguigna, is *Santa Maria dell' Anima (Pl. 2; 6), the German church, which dates from 1500-23. The portals are by *And. Sansovino;* the bell-tower on the s. side is attributed to *Bramante.*

The Virgin above the principal door, which is also by *And. Sansovino,* is a copy of a highly venerated representation of the Madonna between two souls in purgatory, which was formerly in the church and was the origin of its name.

INTERIOR (if closed, ring at the door of the Hospice behind the church). The painting of the vault and walls is by *L. Seitz* (1875-82), who designed also the window over the central door. S. side. 1st chap., San Benno, by *C. Saraceni;* 2nd chap., Holy Family, by *Gimignani;* 4th chap., Pietà, by *Nanni di Baccio Bigio,* in imitation of Michelangelo (comp. p. 269). In the sanctuary, Holy Family with saints, by *Giulio Romano,* over the high altar; on the right, the magnificent tomb of Adrian VI (d. 1523; of Utrecht), the last non-Italian pope, designed by *Bald. Peruzzi,* with sculptures by *Michelangelo Senese* and *Nic. Tribolo;* on the left, Tomb of the Duke of Cleves (d. 1575), by *Gilles de Rivière* and *Nicolas d' Arras* (a bas-relief from this tomb is in the corridor leading to the sacristy).—N. side. 4th chap., Descent from the Cross and frescoes, by *Fr. Salviati;* 3rd chap., Life of St Barbara, frescoes by *Michiel Coxie;* 1st chap., Martyrdom of St Lambert, by *C. Saraceni.*

Vicolo della Pace, on the right, leads to the beautiful church of *Santa Maria della Pace* (Pl. 2; 6) built by Sixtus IV (1471-84), in honour of a miraculous image of the Virgin which bled on being struck by a stone. The architect is believed to have been Baccio Pontelli. The church was partly rebuilt in 1611 and again by Alexander VII, under whose auspices the façade and the lovely little semicircular porch with Tuscan columns were erected by Pietro da Cortona; his design of the piazza and the surrounding area were never completed.

INTERIOR (in 1978 open 7-8.30 only; custodian at No. 5 Vicolo dell' Arco della Pace). The building consists of a domed octagon preceded by a simple rectangular nave. Above the arch of the 1st chapel on the s. side are the famous *SIBYLS of *Raphael* (1514), majestic yet graceful figures, executed for Agostino Chigi, founder of the chapel. They represent (beginning on the left) the Cumæan, Persian, Phrygian, and Tiburtine Sibyls, to whom the future is being revealed by angels, and their varying shades of awe and wonder are skilfully conveyed in look and gesture. The paintings were restored in 1816 by Palmaroli. Above them are four Prophets, by *Timoteo Viti* (Raphael's pupil): on the left, Daniel and David, on the right, Jonah and Hosea. On the altar, Deposition, a fine bronze by *Cosimo Fancelli.*—The 2nd chapel was designed by *Ant. da Sangallo the Younger,* and has remarkable marble decoration by *Simone Mosca* (16C), the material for which was taken from the temple of Jupiter on the Capitol.—N. side: 1st chap. Over the altar is a magnificent \*Fresco of the Virgin, SS. Bridget and Catherine, and the donor Ferdinando Ponzetti, by *Bald. Peruzzi,* who painted also the small frescoes of Old Testament subjects on the vaulting. At the sides of the chapel are tombs of the Ponzetti family (1505 and 1509). 2nd chap. Altarpiece, Madonna and saints, by *Marcello Venusti* from a design by Michelangelo.—OCTAGON. Above the high altar, by *Carlo Maderna,* is the highly venerated image of the Madonna della Pace. The beautiful marble tabernacle in the chapel of the Crucifix (l.) is attributed to *Pasquale da Caravaggio.*

The \*Cloisters (well restored in 1971), entered from the sacristy, are among *Bramante's* finest works in Rome (1504). They have two rows of arcades one above the other, the columns of the upper row rising from the centres of the arches in the lower row. The tomb of Bp Bocciaccio (1497) on the right is of the school of *Luigi Capponi.*

\*PIAZZA NAVONA (Pl. 2; 6) is reached either by Via dei Lorenesi or by Via dell' Anima and Via Sant' Agnese (left; on the right is the *Torre Millina*). It occupies the site of the ancient stadium of Domitian, preserving its form and name (*agone, n'agona, navona*). Historic festivals, jousts, and open-air sports were held here, and from the 17C to the late 19C the piazza was flooded every week-end in August, for the entertainment of the Romans (the nobles enjoyed the spectacle from their carriages). During the Christmas festival, statuettes for the Christmas crib are sold here, and the fair and toy-market of the Befana, or Epiphany is held. In the total absence of wheeled traffic it remains the most animated piazza in Rome.

Three splendid fountains embellish the piazza. At the s. end, the *Fontana del Moro,* begun in 1575 by Jacopo della Porta was altered by Bernini who designed the central figure known as 'Il Moro'.—The \**Fontana dei Fiumi,* or Fountain of the Rivers, in the middle of the Piazza, one of Bernini's finest and most imposing creations, was begun in 1648. The mass of rockwork and grottoes is surmounted by a tall obelisk, a Roman erection in the Egyptian style, which was moved here by Innocent X from the Circus of Maxentius (p. 231) and bears the names of Vespasian, Titus, and Domitian in hieroglyphics. At the four corners are colossal figures, by pupils of Bernini, of the rivers Danube, Ganges, Nile, and Plate, representing the four quarters of the globe. Alluding to the rivalry between Bernini and Borromini, a popular jest has it that the Nile is covering his eyes so that he may not see the façade of Sant'Agnese (see below).—The fountain at the N. end representing Neptune struggling with a marine monster, Nereids, and sea-horses, is by Antonio della Bitta and Zappalà (1878).

Remains of the N. curve of the stadium, with the entrance gate, may be seen at the bottom of Via Zanardelli, N. of the piazza.

On the w. side of the piazza is Sant' Agnese in Agone, an ancient little church built on the ruins of the stadium, possibly on the spot where St Agnes was exposed (see p. 183). The church was reconstructed by C. Rainaldi (1652), to whom are due the lantern of the dome and the two towers; the Baroque façade is by Bernini's rival, Borromini (1653-57).

INTERIOR. The cupola is covered by a crowded fresco, by *Ciro Ferri* and *Corbellini;* the consoles are by *Baciccia.* Above the seven altars marble bas-reliefs take the place of paintings, in the 17C Baroque manner. The high altarpiece is a Holy Family by *Dom. Guidi.* 2nd chap., N. side, St Sebastian, an antique statue altered by *Paolo Campi.* Above the entrance is the monument of Innocent X, by *G. B. Maini.* In a subterranean chapel a bas-relief by *Algardi* represents the miracle of St Agnes's hair.

To the s. of the church is Palazzo Pamphilj (sometimes called *Palazzo Doria*) started by *Girolomo Rainaldi,* and completed by *Borromini* for

Innocent X, in the mid-17C. It was later occupied by the sister-in-law of Innocent, the notorious Olimpia Maidalchini. It is now the Brazilian Embassy (closed to the public for restoration in 1978).

INTERIOR. At the top of the stairs is the SALA PALESTRINA. This is a magnificent example of *Borromini*'s secular architecture, using the minimum of surface decoration. The busts are by *Alles. Algardi.* It has had an interesting history as a music room, since the first performance of the Concerti Grossi of Corelli took place here in the 17C.—To the right are the State rooms overlooking Piazza Navona, decorated with delightful friezes, all painted between 1634 and 1671. In the first room, Bacchic scenes, by *Giacinto Brandi* or *Andrea Camassei.* R. II (to the right), *Agostino Tassi,* seascapes. R. III. *Gaspard Dughet,* landscapes. R. IV. *Giacinto Gemignani,* scenes from Roman history. R. V. *Camassei,* episodes in Ovid's Metamorphoses.—The long *GALLERY* (designed by *Borromini*), has a magnificent fresco of the story of Aeneas by *Pietro da Cortona.* His organization of the long vault is masterly. The charming papal bedroom also has a ceiling fresco by Cortona.

On the opposite side of the piazza, is the church of the MADONNA DEL SACRO CUORE, formerly *San Giacomo degli Spagnoli,* which was rebuilt in 1450 and restored in 1879. The entrance from the piazza is by a side door at the E. end. On the S. side the choir-gallery is by *Pietro Torregiani;* the chapel off the N. side is by *Ant. da Sangallo the Younger.*

From Piazza Navona, Corsia Agonale leads into Corso del Rinascimento (p. 100). On the E. side of the Corso is **Palazzo Madama** (Pl. 2; 6), which since 1871 has been the seat of the Italian Senate. Originally this was a house belonging to the Crescenzi, which passed to the Medici in the 16C as part of the dowry of Alfonsina Orsini. In the 17C the building was enlarged and decorated by Lod. Cardi and Paolo Marucelli, who are responsible for the heavy but interesting Baroque façade. It owes its name to the residence there of 'Madama' Margaret of Parma, natural daughter of Charles V, who married first Alessandro de' Medici and afterwards Ottavio Farnese, and was Regent of the Netherlands from 1559 to 1567 (comp. p. 256). Benedict XIV bought the palace in 1740, and it became successively the residence of the Governor of Rome and the seat of the Ministry of Finance (1852-70), before it became the Palazzo del Senato. The right wing was added in 1931. The public are not admitted to the interior.

In Piazza San Luigi dei Francesi, to the N. of Palazzo Madama, are *Palazzo Giustiniani,* by G. Fontana and Borromini, and **San Luigi dei Francesi** (Pl. 2; 6; closed Mon and Thurs afternoon), the French national church (1518-89). The façade, attrib. to *Giac. della Porta,* with two superimposed orders of equal height, was over-restored in 1977.

The INTERIOR is decorated by Ant. Dérizet (1756-64). The chapels are exceedingly ornate. South Aisle. By the 1st pillar is the monument to the French who fell in the siege of Rome in 1849.—2nd chap., *Frescoes (recently damaged by restoration) by *Domenichino;* to the right, St Cecilia distributing garments to the poor, and St Cecilia and her betrothed crowned by angels; to the left, St Cecilia refusing to sacrifice to idols, and her martyrdom; on the ceiling, St Cecilia in Paradise. The altarpiece is a copy by *Guido Reni* of Raphael's St Cecilia at Bologna.—4th chap., Altarpiece by *Iacopino del Conte,* Oath of Clovis; to the right, Army of Clovis, by *Pellegrino Tibaldi;* to the left, Baptism of Clovis, by *Girol. Sermoneta.* The high altarpiece is an Assumption of the Virgin by *F. Bassano.*—North Aisle. 5th chap. (light on r.; 100 l.) *Paintings by *Caravaggio* (1597-1602): (l.) Calling of St Matthew, (r.) his Martyrdom, and (altarpiece) St Matthew and the Angel. On the 1st pillar is a monument to Claude Lorrain (1600-82) by *Lemoyne.*

From Piazza San Luigi dei Francesi Via della Scrofa runs N. A
turning to the left, Via di Sant' Agostino, leads to the church of **Sant'**
**Agostino** (Pl. 2; 6), which was built for Card. d'Estouteville by Giac. da
Pietrasanta (1479-83). It is dedicated to St Augustine, author of the
Confessions. The severely plain façade is one of the earliest of the
Renaissance.

The INTERIOR, renovated by L. Vanvitelli (1750), is adorned with some
noteworthy frescoes by *P. Gagliardi* (1855). Immediately to the right of the
principal entrance is the *Madonna del Parto, by *Iac. Sansovino* (1521), an image
which is greatly venerated and the object of innumerable votive offerings. On the
3rd pillar on the N. side of the nave is the *PROPHET ISAIAH, by *Raphael,* which,
notwithstanding its restoration by Daniele da Volterra, shows how greatly the
painter was influenced by Michelangelo's frescoes in the Sistine Chapel.—Right
Aisle, 2nd chap. Madonna della Rosa, a copy by Avanzino Nucci of the original
painting by *Raphael* which was stolen from Loreto and subsequently
disappeared.—4th chap., Christ giving the keys to St Peter, sculpted by *G. B.
Cotignola.*—Right Transept. Chap. of Sant'Agostino, altarpiece by *Guercino* and
side panels by his school; Baroque tomb of Card. Renato Imperiali, by *Paolo Posi.*
On the high altar, by *Bernini,* is a Byzantine Madonna brought from
Constantinople. In the chapel to the left of the choir is the tomb of St Monica
(mother of St Augustine), by *Isaia da Pisa.*—Left Aisle, 4th chap., St Apollonia, by
*Girol. Muziano;* 2nd chap., Madonna and St Anne, a group by *And. Sansovino;*
1st chap., *Our Lady of Loreto, by *Caravaggio.*—In the little vestibule at the N.
door are Four Doctors by *Isaia da Pisa,* statues belonging to the tomb of St
Monica, and a crucifix by *L. Capponi* (15C).

In Via delle Coppelle, to the r. off Via della Scrofa, is (No. 35) *Palazzo
Baldassini,* a smaller version of Palazzo Farnese, by *Ant. Sangallo the Younger*
(1514-23), with a gracious courtyard and loggia. Garibaldi lived here in 1875.

Farther up Via della Scrofa on the left is Via dei Portoghesi, at the end
of which can be seen a delightful 15C doorway and tower, and the ornate
façade of the church of *Sant'Antonio dei Portoghesi* (17C). It contains a
painting of the Madonna and Child with SS. Anthony and Francis, by
Antoniazzo Romano.

On the other side of Via della Scrofa, Via della Stelletta leads to the piazza and
church of **Santa Maria in Campo Marzio.** The church, of ancient foundation, was
rebuilt in 1685 by G. Ant. De Rossi. on a Greek cross plan, with a good portico and
court (reached from inside the church). Over the high altar is a Madonna, part of a
triptych probably of the 12-13C.

Via della Scrofa ends in Piazza Nicosia, with a fountain by Giac. della
Porta (1573), and is continued as Via di Ripetta (the name of which is a
reminder of the old river bank and port) to Piazza del Popolo (p. 153).
To the right Via del Clementino, with a view of the Trinità dei Monti in
the distance, leads to Piazza Borghese (Pl. 2; 6, 4), with the celebrated
**Palazzo Borghese** called from its shape the 'harpsichord of Rome'. It
was begun perhaps by Vignola (c. 1560) and completed by Flaminio
Ponzio, who designed the beautiful terrace on the Tiber front. The
palace was acquired by Card. Camillo Borghese, who became Pope Paul
V in 1605, and was renowned for its splendour. For nearly two centuries
it contained the paintings from the Galleria Borghese (p. 156); they were
restored to their former residence in 1891.

The interior **Court** is very picturesque with its long lines of twin columns in two
stories. It is adorned with colossal antique statues representing Ceres and the
empresses Sabina and Julia; a garden beyond contains fountains and antique
sculpture.

Via Borghese leads back to Via di Ripetta. Across Via Tomacelli is Largo degli Schiavoni. This was the quarter of the Serbs (Schiavoni) who came here as refugees after the battle of Kossovo (15 June 1389). Here are the church of *San Girolamo degli Schiavoni* (sometimes called S. Girolamo degli Illirici, or S. Girolamo dei Croati), rebuilt in 1587, and *San Rocco*. This has a neo-classical façade by Valadier (1834), and contains (in the sacristy) an early altarpiece by Baciccia. In the s.e. corner of the Largo degli Schiavoni is the apse of San Carlo (p. 153).

In the spacious PIAZZA AUGUSTO IMPERATORE, lined with ungainly modern buildings, is the **\*Mausoleum of Augustus,** or *Tumulus Cæsarum* (no admission; part of the interior can be seen through the entrance on the s. side of the piazza). This was the tomb of Augustus and of the principal members of his family, the gens Julia-Claudia, and was one of the most sacred monuments of Roman antiquity. The last Roman emperor to be buried here was Nerva in A.D. 98. Erected in 28 B.C., it is a circular structure 87 m in diameter. It was originally surmounted by a tumulus of earth some 44 m high, planted with cypresses and crowned, it is believed, with a statue of the emperor.

Excavations carried out in 1926-30 by G. Q. Giglioli and A. M. Colini have freed the crypt of the mausoleum from the debris that surrounded and partly buried it, and restored as far as possible its original appearance. The circular base, of opus reticulatum, has a series of large niches on the outside. The plan of the interior has been made clear by excavation. From the entrance a passageway leads past a series of 12 compartments arranged in a circle to an outer ring-passage, at the entrance to which are fragments of statues; beyond is an inner ring and finally the sepulchral cella, with walls of travertine blocks, a central pillar, and three niches. In the central niche were found the cinerary urns of Augustus and of his wife Livia; on either side were those of his nephews Gaius and Lucius Cæsar (right) and of his sister Octavia (left), with an inscription to his beloved nephew Marcellus.

Before the entrance were originally inscriptions setting forth the will of Augustus, a copy of which was found at Ancryra, in Asia Minor, now Ankara, capital of Turkey, and two obelisks, one of which is now in the Piazza del Quirinale (p. 176) and the other in Piazza dell' Esquilino (p. 204).

In the Middle Ages the tomb became a fortress of the Colonna. Later it was despoiled to provide travertine for other buildings and after further vicissitudes a wooden amphitheatre was built into it. Goethe watched beast-baiting here in 1787. Later still it was converted into a concert hall and was used as such until 1936.

To the w. of the Mausoleum, between Via di Ripetta and Lungotévere in Augusta, is a platform approached by a flight of steps at either end. Here a building with glass walls protects the **\*Ara Pacis Augustæ,** reconstructed in 1937-38 from scattered fragments and from reproductions of other fragments not available. This monumental altar is a splendid example of Roman sculpture, influenced by Greek Classical and Hellenistic art. Adm., see p. 47.

The Ara Pacis Augustæ was consecrated in the Campus Martius on 4 July 13 B.C., and dedicated four years later after the victorious return of Augustus from Spain and Gaul, in celebration of the peace that he had established within the Empire. This much is known from the document (*Res gestoe Augusti*) which the emperor caused to be engraved on bronze tablets in Rome a year before his death in A.D. 14. A copy of this has been engraved in bronze letters on the wall of the modern building.

In 1568, during excavations for the foundations of the Palazzo Fiano (p. 152), nine blocks belonging to the frieze of the altar were found and bought by Card. Ricci da Montepulciano for the Grand Duke of Tuscany. To facilitate transport, each block was sawn into three. These went to the Uffizi Gallery in Florence. The cardinal overlooked two other blocks unearthed at the same time. One of these eventually passed to the Louvre in Paris; the other to the Vatican Museum (p. 305).

In 1859, during a reconstruction of the Palazzo Fiano, the contractors found the base of the altar, with the left half of the relief panel of the sacrifice of Aeneas and other architectonic and decorative elements. These were acquired in 1898 by the Italian Government for the Museo Nazionale Romano. In 1903 excavations brought to light further fragments: these included most of the basement of marble cubes supporting the altar, portions of the acanthus frieze (see below) and the right half of the relief of the sacrifice of Aeneas, in which Augustus himself appeared. There was also found a panel with two *Flamines* (priests), but this could not then be dislodged.

Finally, in 1937, the Italian Government decided on further excavations with a view to complete reconstruction. The work involved digging down to a depth of 10½ m and freezing the subsoil water. This difficult task was successfully accomplished. Outlying fragments were recovered from the Museo Nazionale and the Uffizi Gallery; those in the Louvre, the Vatican, and the Villa Medici were copied. Thus the monument has recovered, so far as is humanly possible, its original form and appearance.

The monument, built throughout of Luni marble, has a simple base with two horizontal bands. On the base is an almost square-walled enclosure, with two open and two closed sides. The open sides are 11½ m and the closed sides 10½ m long. The two openings are each 3½ m square; one of them is approached by a flight of steps. The external decoration of the enclosure is in two zones divided by a horizontal Greek key-pattern border. The lower zone is covered with an intricate and beautiful composition of acanthus leaves on which are swans with outstretched wings. In the upper zone is the frieze of reliefs, with a decorated cornice above it. Between the jambs of the main or w. entrance are scenes illustrating the origins of Rome. The left panel (almost entirely lost) represented the *Lupercalia;* the right panel shows *Aeneas sacrificing the white sow. The panels of the E. entrance depict *Tellus, the earth goddess (l.), and Rome (r.), much damaged. Mythology and allegory give way to realism in the subjects of the side panels, which represent the ceremony of the consecration of the altar. In procession are seen Augustus, members of his family including children, State officials, and priests. The interior of the enclosure is also in two zones; in view of the nature of the operations here, the lower part has no decoration other than simple fluting. The upper zone, however, is adorned with beautifully carved bucrania.

The altar is an exact reconstruction of all recovered fragments. Approached by a flight of steps, it has a back and two side walls; a further flight, of narrow steps, leads up past the walls to the altar proper. The cornice and the anta of the left side wall have been the best preserved; the reliefs indicate the *Suovetaurilia,* or sacrifice of a pig, a sheep, and an ox. Little else of the decoration survives.

Via del Corso, E. of Piazza Augusto Imperatore, returns to Piazza Venezia.

# 5   THE ROMAN FORUM

Admission, see p. 48. The admission ticket includes the Palatine (Rte 6). The entrance is in Via dei Fori Imperiali, opposite the end of Via Cavour. In the following description the exit is along the Sacra Via behind the Arch of Titus. A full exploration of the Forum and the Palatine requires more than a single day.

The **Roman Forum** is not only the heart of ancient Rome; it is also the mirror of its history. Here is reflected almost every event of importance in the city's development from the time of the kings through the Republican and Imperial eras to the twilight of the Middle Ages. The ruins stand in the centre of modern Rome as a romantic testament to her past greatness. The plants and shrubs which now surround them add to their charm. However, the visible remains are difficult to understand in detail without preparatory study and constant reference to the plans (pp. 120-21).

Before entering the Roman Forum, it is a good plan to skirt its western side and ascend to the Belvedere of Monte Tarpeo (p. 110), from which there is a comprehensive view of its extent. This preliminary walk takes in some monuments of the Forum outside the precincts (see below); the entrance to the enclosure is close to the Basilica Aemilia (Pl. 8; 2; p. 111).

The Forum runs w.n.w. and e.s.e., following the direction of the Capitoline end of the Sacra Via and that of the Nova Via. In the following description it is taken as running w. and e., the left side, looking towards the Colosseum, being n. and the right side s. The plans are thus orientated.

**History.** The site of the Forum was originally a marshy valley lying between the Capitoline and Palatine Hills. It was bounded on the n. and e. by the foothills of the Quirinal and Esquiline and by the low ridge of the Velia, which connected the Palatine with the Esquiline. In the Iron Age it was used as a necropolis. Buildings arose on it after the union of the Latin villages of the Palatine with the Sabines of the Quirinal, which is traditionally said to have followed the battle of Romans and Sabines on the Palatine slopes. To the period of the kings are ascribed the first monuments of the Forum, such as the Lapis Niger, the Vulcanal, the Temple of Janus, the Regia, the Temple of Vesta, and the Curia. The Tarquins made the area habitable by canalizing its stagnant waters into the Cloaca Maxima and it became the market-place (Forum) of Rome, where farmers exposed their produce and merchants offered their wares.

The original Forum was a rectangle bounded at the w. by the Lapis Niger and the Rostra, on the e. by a line through the site of the Temple of Julius Cæsar, and on the n. and s. by two rows of shops (*Tabernæ*) approximately on the line of the Basilica Aemilia (n.) and the Basilica Julia (s.). The area thus contained was about 115 m by 57 m. Adjacent, on the n.w., was a second rectangle including the Comitium, reserved for the assemblies of the people, or *Comitia Curiata*. Here also were the Curia, or senate-house, and the Rostra, or orators' tribune. Beyond the limits of this second square, to the e., were the Regia, seat of the Pontifex Maximus, the Temple of Vesta, and the House of the Vestals. In this direction ran the *Sacra Via*. Other streets were the *Argiletum* to the n., the *Vicus Jugarius* and the *Vicus Tuscus* to the Velabrum, the *Clivus Argentarius,* which ran between the Capitol and the Quirinal to the Via Flaminia and the Campus Martius, and the *Nova Via,* on the s. side, dividing the Forum from the Palatine.

Three distinct areas of the Forum thus became defined—the Comitium, or political centre, the religious centre of the Regia, and the Forum proper. This last gradually lost its character of market-place and became a centre of civic importance and the scene of public functions and ceremonies (comp. p. 112). The greengrocers and other shopkeepers were banished to the Velabrum and replaced by money-changers (argentarii), but their vacated shops did not long survive.

In the 2C b.c. there was introduced a new type of building, the basilica. Its function was mainly for judicial hearings and public meetings. The new construction involved the demolition of private dwellings behind the tabernæ. The first basilica was the Basilica Porcia, built by the censor Cato in 185 B.C. and destroyed in 52 B.C. Others were the Basilica Aemilia (179 B.C.), and the Basilica Sempronia (170 B.C.), built by T. Sempronius Gracchus, father of the tribunes, and later replaced by the Basilica Julia. The latest is the Basilica of Constantine (4C A.D.; p. 123).

In 133 Tib. Gracchus was killed in the Forum. After Julius Caesar's assassination on the Ides of March, 44 B.C., his body was cremated in the Forum on the spot where now stands his temple. He had begun the enlargement of the Forum which Sulla had planned some years before. It was left to Augustus to complete the work. Between 44 and 27 B.C. the Basilica Julia, Curia, and Rostra were completed, the Temple of Saturn and the Regia restored, the Temple of Julius Caesar dedicated, and the Arch of Augustus erected. So thoroughly was the work of building and embellishment carried out that, in the words of Suetonius, Augustus found the city brick and left it marble.

By this time the area of the Forum had become inadequate for the growing population and the emperors were obliged to build their own Fora (see Rte 7). A fire in the old Forum in the 3C A.D. caused much damage, which was repaired by Diocletian, but the area shared in the general decay of the city. Temples and sanctuaries were neglected under Christian rule and robbed of most of their treasures. The few that remained were finally despoiled in the barbarian invasions and the abandoned buildings were further damaged by earthquakes.

The medieval Roman barons, notably the Frangipani family, used the loftiest of the ruined buildings as foundations for their fortress-towers, and a few churches were constructed. But for the most part grass grew in the silent squares, and the Forum became the *Campo Vaccino,* or cattle-pasture. Its monuments were used as quarries and its precious marbles were burned in lime-kilns.

The awakening interest in the monuments of the past, aroused by Rienzo, came too late to save the buildings and their works of art; but the Forum inspired the artists of the Renaissance and suggested the plans of their great constructions of the 15-18C, to which only too often ancient relics were sacrificed. A new archæological movement at the end of the 18C brought about the systematic excavation of the site, continued with little interruption through the 19C, especially after 1870. The distinguished archæologist, Giacomo Boni, after 1898, conducted the excavations with more enlightened knowledge; digging always deeper, he reached the ancient foundations of archaic monuments of supreme interest, a discovery which threw much light upon the primitive history of Rome. After his death in 1925 the work was continued by Alfonso Bartoli. The most recent excavations have been in the area of the Temple of Vesta, the Curia, and the Regia.

From Piazza Venezia **Via dei Fori Imperiali** runs in a straight line to Piazza del Colosseo. This thoroughfare, 850 m long and 30 m broad, lined with trees and flower gardens, was opened in October 1933 as the Via dell' Impero. Passing the Victor Emmanuel Monument on the right, it traverses the entire length of the Roman Forum on the right and the Imperial Fora on either side. The Colosseum is in view for the whole of its length. Towards the end it passes the N. side of the Basilica of Constantine, the imposing bulk of which is seen to great advantage here (see also p. 123). Half-way along the street, opposite the W. end of Via Cavour, is the entrance to the Roman Forum.

At the beginning of Via dei Fori Imperiali Via del Tulliano leads right. This street, which partly follows the Clivus Argentarius (p. 108), runs between the Forum of Caesar (Rte 7) on the right and the church of **San Luca e Santa Martina** on the left (Pl. 8; 2; open Sun 10-11 only). This church was built before the 8C on the Secretarium Senatus (p. 113), and rebuilt in 1640 by Pietro da Cortona. The two stories, the upper dedicated to St Luke and the lower to St Martina, have an original and complex design. The façade, built of travertine, and the dome are particularly fine. The church of St Luke has a centralized Greek cross plan. The lower church of Santa Martina is reached by a staircase to the left of the High Altar.

In a well-designed chapel (l.) are the tombs of SS. Martina, Epifanio, and Concordio, and a tabernacle by *Pietro da Cortona.* The side chapel with a restrained scallop motif has a fine terracotta group of the three saints by *Aless. Algardi.* In the corridor is the tomb of Pietro da Cortona, and in the vestibule, statuettes by *Cosimo Fancelli,* and a bas-relief of the Deposition by *Algardi.*

Nearly opposite is the little church of *San Giuseppe dei Falegnami* (closed), built in 1598, perhaps by G. B. Montano, above the *Tullianum,* or **San Pietro in Carcere,** later called the **Mamertine Prison** (adm. see p. 49).

This is thought originally to have been a cistern, like those at Tusculum and other Etruscan cities. On the lower level, the form can be seen of a round building which may have had a tholos (which could date it as early as the 6C B.C.). A spring still exists in the floor. The building was used as a dungeon in Roman times for criminals and captives awaiting execution. Jugurtha, Vercingetorix, the accomplices of Catiline, and, according to Christian tradition, St Peter were confined here, and since the 16C it has been called San Pietro in Carcere.
Via San Pietro in Carcere climbs from Via dei Fori Imperiali above the Tullianum to the Capitol.

On the right of the church a flight of steps leads up to the Capitol. Via del Foro Romano skirts the w. side of the Forum and cuts off some of its monuments from the main enclosure. On the left rise the Arch of Septimius Severus and the Temple of Saturn (p. 114). On the right, immediately past the Capitol steps, are the remains of the **Temple of Concord.** This was a reconstruction by Tiberius (7 B.C.-A.D. 10) of a sanctuary built by Camillus in 366 B.C. to commemorate the concordat between the patricians and the plebeians, and rebuilt in 121 B.C. by the consent of Opimius after the murder of Gracchus. It became a museum and gallery of paintings and sculptures by famous Greek artists. Only the pavement remains in situ; part of the frieze is in the Tabularium (p. 57).

Just beyond the Temple of Concord are three lofty columns, all that remains of the hexastyle pronaos of the rich and elegant **Temple of Vespasian,** erected in honour of that emperor at the foot of the Tabularium staircase by his sons Titus and Domitian after his death in A.D. 79. Beyond is the **Portico of the Dii Consentes,** still preserving twelve white columns forming an angle; the original seven columns are in marble, the restorations in limestone. Rebuilt by the prefect Vettius Prætextatus in A.D. 367, on the pattern of a Flavian structure, it is perhaps the last monument of the pagan religion. The portico was reconstructed in 1858.

Via del Tempio di Giove (pedestrians only; Via di Monte Tarpeo is used by cars) ascends the Capitol hill; it partly follows the line of the *Clivus Capitolinus,* the flint pavement of which has been laid bare. This ancient street, was the w. continuation of the Sacra Via (p. 111) in the Forum, and the only way up to the Capitol. It was used for triumphal and other processions from the Forum to the Temple of Jupiter on the Capitol (see p. 55). Above is the *Belvedere di Monte Tarpeo* (p. 69), with its incomparable *View.

The panorama takes in the whole of the valley of the Forum, with Via dei Fori Imperiali on the left and the green slopes of the Palatine on the right. Immediately below are the Portico of the Dii Consentes and the three columns of the Temple of Vespasian. Within the precincts of the Forum are seen the portico of the Temple of Saturn and, on the left, the Arch of Septimius Severus. Behind, partly masked by the arch, is the Curia, with the cupola of the church of Santi Luca e Martina. In the middle distance, from right to left, are the remains of the Basilica Julia, the lofty Column of Phocas, and the Basilica Aemilia. Farther away are seen the tall columns of the Temple of the Dioscuri, the Temple of Vesta, and the Temple of Antoninus and Faustina, with the façade of the church of San Lorenzo in Miranda. Still farther are the so-called Temple of Romulus and the Basilica of Constantine. On the eminence of the Velia rise the Arch of Titus on the right and the campanile of Santa Francesca Romana on the left. The view is closed by the overpowering bulk of the Colosseum.

It is now necessary to return to Via dei Fori Imperiali to reach the entrance to the Forum Romanum. Beyond the entrance gate, a broad path descends between the Temple of Antoninus and Faustina (left; see p. 122) and the Basilica Aemilia on the level of the Forum.

The **Basilica Aemilia** was built by the censors M. Aemilius Lepidus and M. Fulvius Nobilior in 179 B.C., restored by members of the Aemilia gens in 78 B.C. and rebuilt in the time of Julius Caesar. It was rebuilt in A.D. 22 after a fire and nearly destroyed by another fire during Alaric's sack of Rome in 410. On the side towards the Forum it faces the Sacra Via; on its w. side is the *Argiletum,* once one of the Forum's busiest streets, which led N. to the quarter of the Subura through the Forum of Nerva (p. 138).

This ancient building was for the most part demolished during the Renaissance for the sake of its marble. It comprised a vast rectangular hall 70 m by 29 m, divided by columns into a central nave and aisles, single on the s. side and double on the N. In the fine pavement of the hall, in coloured marble, are embedded some coins that fused with the bronze roof-decorations during the fire of 410. Casts of fragments of the entablature have been assembled below the terrace at the N.E. corner. On the s. side, facing the Forum, was a two-storied portico covering a row of shops, the *Tabernæ Novæ,* still in a fair state of preservation. The portico was restored during the late empire; evidence of this restoration is claimed in the three granite columns that have been set up in front of the Basilica. On the w. side are remains (covered) of the earliest basilica.

The open space in front of the Basilica Aemilia is the original **Forum;** through it runs the Ima Sacra Via (see below). As the meeting-place of the whole population, the Forum was kept free of obstructions in Republican days. Here took place all important ceremonies and public meetings. Orators harangued the people from the Rostra, where magistrates' edicts, legal decisions, and official communications were published; farmers spread out their produce and merchants plied their trade. All the main religious festivals were held here; triumphal and other processions passed through. Political offenders were executed; the funeral ceremonies of illustrious personages were enacted; it was in the Forum that the body of Julius Caesar was cremated. Under the Empire the Forum lost its original character. New buildings encroached upon the area, which became merely an official centre, while the crowds migrated to the rival attractions of the Imperial Fora.

The **Sacra Via,** the oldest street in Rome, traverses the length of the Forum and extends beyond it on either side. It received its name, according to tradition, from the fact that it was the scene of the peace treaty between Romulus and the Sabine king Titus Tatius. A more likely explanation is that it was lined with important sanctuaries. Its oldest section is that between the Temple of Castor and the Velia. The section through the original Forum as far as the Temple of Julius Caesar was called the *Ima Sacra Via;* thence to the point where it begins to climb to the Arch of Titus it was called the *Media Sacra Via;* the actual rise to the Arch was the *Clivus Sacer* or *Summa Sacra Via.* On the w. side it was continued as the *Clivus Capitolinus,* which climbed round the Portico of the Dii Consentes to the Temple of Jupiter on the Capitol. On the E. side the road was continued in late Imperial times beyond the Arch of Titus to the Arch of Constantine, near the Colosseum.—It was along the Sacra Via that a victorious general accorded a triumph passed in solemn procession to the Capitol to offer sacrifice in the Temple of Jupiter. He rode in a chariot drawn by four horses, preceded by his captives and spoils of war, and followed by his soldiers.—Roughly parallel with the Sacra Via, on the s., runs the *Nova Via,* which separates the Forum from the Palatine (see p. 122).

In the Sacra Via, by the s.e. corner of the Basilica Aemilia, is a dedicatory inscription to Lucius Caesar, grandson and adopted son of Augustus, set up in 2 B.C.: here was built a portico to him and his brother Gaius.

On the s. side of the Sacra Via is the **Temple of Julius Caesar,** the site of which marks the E. limit of the original Forum. It was dedicated in 29 B.C. by Augustus in honour of Divus Julius over the place where his body was burned (after the Ides of March, 44 B.C.), and where his will was read by Mark Antony. Here Tiberius gave a funeral oration over the body of Augustus before it was buried in his mausoleum (p. 106) in A.D. 14.

This temple (probably Corinthian prostyle hexastyle) was preceded by a terrace which was an extension of the podium. This was called the *Rostra ad Divi Julii,* from the beaks of the Egyptian ships taken at Actium which adorned it. Nothing remains save the central block of the podium and the round altar (under cover), marking the spot where Caesar was cremated. Fragments, thought to belong to the frieze, are in the Antiquarium Forense (p. 124). Remains of foundations on the N. and s. sides of the temple are thought to be those of the arcaded *Porticus Julia,* which surrounded the temple on three sides.

About 50 m farther w., near the steps of the Basilica Aemilia, are the foundations of the circular *Shrine of Venus Cloacina,* which stood on the point where the Cloaca Maxima entered the Forum. This great drain crossed the Forum from N. to s. on its way to the Tiber (see p. 87). It was beside the shrine that the maiden Virginia is said to have been killed by her father to save her from the advances of the decemvir Appius Claudius Crassinus.—At the w. end of the Basilica Aemilia is the presumed site of the *Shrine of Janus,* whose bronze doors were closed only in peace-time. This is said to have occurred only three times in the history of Rome.

To the w., in front of the Curia building (p. 113) lies the area of the COMITIUM, the place where the *Comitia Curiata,* representing the 30 Curiae into which the city was politically divided, met to record their votes. The earliest political activity of the Republic took place here and this was the original site of the Rostra. During the Empire the Comitium was restricted to the space between the Curia, and the Lapis Niger; under the Republic the area was much more extensive. Here, protected by a roof, is the **Lapis Niger** with the oldest relics of the Forum. The Lapis Niger was a pavement of black marble laid to indicate a sacred spot. Tradition placed here the tomb of Romulus or of the shepherd Faustulus or of Hostus Hostilius, father of the third king of Rome. The pavement was discovered in 1899 and, with it, the monuments below it. These are now reached by a flight of iron steps. They comprise the base of a truncated column (possibly the base for a statue), an altar, and a square stele with inscriptions on all four sides. These afford the most ancient example of the Latin language (6C or early 5C B.C.) and, though not fully deciphered, are generally understood to refer to a lex sacra, i.e. a warning against profaning a holy place. In the space between the pavement and the monuments were found, mixed with profuse ashes (indicating a great sacrifice), bronze and terracotta statuettes, fragments of 6C vases and later material; these relics are now in the Antiquarium Forense.

Excavations to the E. of the Lapis Niger have revealed some remains of the Republican *Rostra*, dating partly from 338 B.C., and partly (the curved front and steps) from Sulla's time.

At the N. end of the Comitium rises the *Curia, or *Senate House*. The existing building, known as the *Curia Julia*, was begun by Sulla in 80 B.C., and rebuilt after a fire by Julius Caesar in 44 B.C. It replaced the original *Curia Hostilia* said to have been built by Tullus Hostilius and several times rebuilt. Fifteen years after Caesar's death the Curia Julia was completed by Augustus, who dedicated a statue of Victory in the interior. The Senate House was restored by Domitian and rebuilt by Diocletian. In 638 it was converted into the church of *Sant' Adriano*. In 1935-38 Alfonso Bartoli restored to it the form it had under Diocletian. The brick façade was originally covered with marble in the lower and with stucco in the upper courses; it was preceded by a portico. The existing doors are copies of the originals, removed by Alexander VII to St John Lateran. A simple pediment with travertine corbels crowns the building.

The austere interior, 27 m long and 18 m wide and 21 m high, is enlivened by a beautiful pavement in opus sectile, revealed by the removal of the floor of the church. On either side is a series of three marble-faced steps, extending along the whole length; here were seats for c. 300 senators. At the end, by the president's tribune, is a brick base which may have supported the golden statue of Victory presented by Augustus. The side walls were partly faced with marble and were and still are adorned with niches. Two doors at the rear end opened into what was probably a columned portico. Here was found a headless porphyry statue, possibly of Hadrian. Connected to the Senate House was the *Secretarium Senatus* used by a tribunal set up in the late Empire to judge senators.

The Curia houses the *Plutei of Trajan, or *Anaglypha Trajani*, two finely sculptured balustrades or parapets, found in the Forum between the Comitium and the Column of Phocas.

On the inner faces are depicted the animals offered up at public sacrifices (suovetaurilia), a pig, a sheep, and a bull; on the outer faces are famous deeds of the emperor. The first represents the emperor burning the registers of outstanding death duties, an event which took place in 118, during Hadrian's reign; in the second an emperor standing on a Rostra with a statue of Trajan, is receiving the thanks of a mother for the founding of an orphanage. The architectural backgrounds show the buildings on the W., S., and E. sides of the Forum systematically depicted. From the right of the 1st panel to the left of the 2nd: Temple of Vespasian, an arch without decoration, Temple of Saturn, the Vicus Iugarius, and the arcades of the Basilica Julia. The arches are continued on the 2nd panel, followed by an interval for the Vicus Tuscus (?), Temple of Castor, Rostra of the Temple of Julius Caesar (on which the emperor is standing); his attendants mount the ramp of the Rostra through the Arch of Augustus. On both sides is shown the statue of Marsyas beside the sacred fig-tree (see p. 115).

Between the Lapis Niger and the Imperial Rostra (see below) is a large marble column base bearing an inscription of Diocletian to commemorate the decennial games of A.D. 303; the reliefs on the other sides depict scenes of sacrifice. Close by is the marble base of an equestrian statue which celebrated the victory of Arcadius and Honorius over the Goths in 403.

On the N.W. side of the Forum rises the triple **Arch of Septimius Severus,** nearly 21 m high and over 23 m wide, erected in A.D. 203 in honour of the tenth anniversary of the emperor's accession, and dedicated by the senate and the people to Severus and his sons Caracella and Geta in memory of their victories over the Parthians, Arabs, and Adiabenians of Assyria.

The name of Geta, elder son of Severus, who was murdered by Caracalla in 212, was replaced by an inscription in praise of Caracalla and his father, but the holes made for the original letters are still visible. The proportions of the arch are good, but the sculptural decoration is heavy. The four large reliefs depict scenes from the two Parthian campaigns; in the small friezes are figures symbolic of the homage paid by the Orient to Rome; and at the bases of the columns are captive barbarians. A small interior staircase admits to the four chambers of the attic.

To the s. of the Arch of Severus are the ruins of the **Imperial Rostra,** or orator's tribune brought from its original site in front of the Curia during Caesar's restoration. It is 3 m high, 24 m long and 12 m deep.

The original structure (see above), of very early date, was adorned with the 'rostra' or iron beaks of the ships captured at the battle of Antium (338 B.C.). On the platform rose columns surmounted by commemorative statues, and its parapet was probably decorated with the sculptured plutei of Trajan. In front, on the right, are the *Rostra Vandalica,* an extension of the 5C A.D.; the name is due to an inscription commemorating a naval victory over the Vandals in 470.

At the back of the Rostra is a semicircular wall (*Hemicyclium*), formed by alterations during the building of the Arch of Septimius Severus. At its N. end, by the Arch, is a cylindrical construction, the *Umbilicus Urbis* (? early 4C), supposed to mark the centre of the city. Opposite the other end of the wall is the site of the *Millarium Aureum,* the 'golden milestone', a bronze-covered column set up by Augustus as the starting-point of all the roads of the Empire, with the distance from Rome to the chief cities engraved in gold letters on its base.

Immediately behind the Umbilicus, protected by a roof, is a quadrangular area identified as the *Volcanal,* or Altar of Vulcan, part of a larger area dedicated to the god, of ancient foundation. By it grew, in Republican times, two trees—a lotus and a cypress—said to be older than the city itself.

From the s.w. corner of the original Forum, the *Vicus Jugarius* runs s. to the Velabrum between the Basilica Julia on the left (see below) and the Temple of Saturn on the right, close to the modern Via del Foro Romano.

The *\*Temple of Saturn,* one of the most ancient sanctuaries in the Forum, was traditionally founded in 497 B.C. in honour of the mythical god-king of Italy, whose reign was the fabled Golden Age. Saturn taught his people the art of husbandry; the earth brought forth abundantly; war, slavery, and private property were alike unknown. The temple was rebuilt, after several previous reconstructions, by L. Munatius Plancus in the year of his consulship, 42 B.C. It was again restored after a fire in the 4C A.D. There survive the high podium, dating from Plancus, and eight columns of the pronaos, with part of the entablature, dating from the restoration. The columns are nearly 11 m high. Six of them, in grey granite, are in front; the other two, in red granite, are at the sides. The temple was the State treasury. In the vaults were kept gold and silver ingots, coined metal, and other treasures. The room (*Aerarium*) E. of the narrow stairway of the temple could be locked (the holes for the lock can still be seen). The 'Saturnalia' was celebrated here every year on 17 Dec.

Opposite the Temple of Saturn, near the N.W. corner of the Basilica Julia, is a concrete base, believed to be part of the *Arch of Tiberius,* erected in A.D. 16 in honour of the emperor and of his nephew Germanicus, who avenged the defeat of Varus in the Teutoburg Forest (A.D. 9) by his victory over the German tribes at Idisiavisus (on the Weser).

I he scanty but extensive ruins of the **Basilica Julia** occupy the area between the Vicus Jugarius and the Vicus Tuscus (see below). The basilica, built on the site of the Basilica Sempronia (170 B.C.), was begun by Julius Caesar in 54 B.C., and finished by Augustus. After fire, it had to be reconstructed and re-dedicated by Augustus in A.D. 12. It was again damaged by fire in A.D. 284 and restored by Diocletian in 305. It suffered yet again in Alaric's sack of 410 and was restored for the last time by Gabinius Vettius Probianus six years later. The Basilica Julia was the meeting-place of the four tribunals of the *Centumbiri,* who dealt with civil cases. In the Middle Ages the church of *Santa Maria in Cannapara* was built on its W. side. The surviving remains mostly date from the restoration of 305; the brick piers of the central hall are modern reconstructions.

The basilica, even larger than the Basilica Aemilia, measured 101 m by 49 m. It had a central hall 82 m long and 18 m wide, bordered all round by a double row of columns which formed aisles. On the long side, facing W., was a colonnade of arches and piers with engaged columns; this contained a row of shops. On the steps here can be seen graffiti in the marble used as 'gaming boards'.
The *Vicus Tuscus* was so called either from its Etruscan shopkeepers or from a colony of Veientine workmen who built the Temple of Jupiter Capitolinus.

In front of the Basilica Julia is a row of seven brick bases, dating from the 4C. These mark the S. limit of the original FORUM which was first paved in the Etruscan period. The surviving pavement was laid by L. Surdinus in the Augustan period (as the restored inscription records). On the bases stood columns bearing statues of citizens who had deserved well of the State. Two of the columns have been re-erected. In front, towards the W. rises the **Column of Phocas,** not only a conspicuous feature of the Forum but the last of its monuments. It was set up in 608 by Smaragdus, exarch of Italy, in honour of the centurion Phocas who had seized the throne of Byzantium; its erection may have been a mark of gratitude for the emperor's gift of the Pantheon to Boniface IV (see p. 99). The fluted Corinthian column, probably taken from some building of the best Imperial era, is 13½ m high. It stands on a lofty base, formerly faced with marble and surrounded by steps. On the top was originally a statue of the usurper.

To the N. of the column of Phocas were placed the Plutei of Trajan (now in the Curia; p. 113). In the intervening pavement is a small square unpaved space, where once stood the statue of Marsyas next to the sacred fig-tree, the olive, and the vine (all recently re-planted here), tended with superstitious diligence. In one of the pavement slabs is incised the name of L. Naevius Surdinus, praetor peregrinus in the time of Augustus, who may have had his tribunal here. This legal dignitary had to deal with cases involving peregrini, i.e. individuals not Roman citizens.

To the E. is the paved area of the *Lacus Curtius,* with the substructure of a puteal (covered), surrounded by a twelve-sided structure of peperino blocks. The original of the relief found here of M. Curtius riding his horse into the abyss is now in the Pal. dei Conservatori (p. 66; a cast is shown in situ). The lake must have been a relic of the marsh drained by the Cloaca Maxima. According to one tradition, there opened here in 362 B.C. a great chasm which the soothsayers said could be closed only by throwing into it Rome's greatest treasure. On this, Marcus Curtius, a noble youth, mounted his horse and, declaring that Rome possessed no greater treasure than a brave and gallant citizen, leaped into the abyss, which promptly closed.

In the S.E. corner of the Forum are the bases of two equestrian statues. Part of the base of the *Equus Constantini* (probably dedicated in A.D. 334) survives; of the *Equus Domitiani* (A.D. 91), there survive the three travertine blocks to which the legs of the colossal bronze horse were attached.

At the E. end of the original Forum is the Temple of Julius Caesar, described on p. 112. To the S. are the foundations of the *Arch of Augustus,* erected in 29 B.C. to commemorate the victory over Antony and Cleopatra at Actium two years earlier. A second triple arch was erected in 19 B.C., after the standards captured by the Parthians had been returned. The structure was of unusual design. Only the central portion had an arch, properly so called; the side-passages, which were lower and narrower, were surmounted by pediments. Recent research has established that the consular and triumphal registers (*Fasti*) were placed inside these lateral passageways, and not on the outside of the Regia (p. 122). Fragments of the records are now in the Sale dei Conservatori, on the Capitol.

Near the S. pier foundation of the arch a rectangular monument in the shape of a well-head was found in 1950. This is a remnant of the *Puteal Libonis,* a monument which stood beside the tribunal of the Prætor Urbanus, who dealt with cases involving Roman citizens.

Beyond the Arch and facing the E. end of the Basilica Julia across the Vicus Tuscus is the *Temple of Castor, or *Temple of the Dioscuri.* It was built according to tradition, in 484 B.C. by the dictator Aulus Postumius in honour of the twin heroes Castor and Pollux, whose miraculous appearance at the battle of Lake Regillus (496 B.C.) secured victory for the Romans over the Tarquins and their Latin allies. The temple was several times rebuilt; the most important reconstructions were by L. Caecilius Metellus in 117 B.C. and by Tiberius during the reign of Augustus (A.D. 6). Peripteral in plan, it had eight Corinthian columns at either end and eleven at the sides. The wide pronaos was approached by a flight of steps. Three of the columns, which are 12½ m high, survive, with their beautifully proportioned entablature. They are generally accepted as among the most characteristic features of the Forum. The Roman knights regarded the Dioscuri as their patrons; every year, on 15 July, they staged an impressive parade before the temple. Fragments of statues of the Dioscuri found here, are now in the Antiquarium of the Roman Forum (p. 124).

On the E. side of the temple is the *Lacus Juturnæ,* or Basin of Juturna, inextricably connected with the story of the Dioscuri. It was here, immediately after they had turned the tide of battle at Lake Regillus, that they were seen watering their horses. Juturna, the nymph of healing waters, was venerated in connection with the springs that rise at this spot. The fountain has a square basin of opus reticulatum lined with marble; at its centre is a rectangular base, probably of a statue. On the parapet is a small marble altar (replaced by a copy; the original is in the Antiquarium Forense), with reliefs of the Dioscuri and their sister Helena on two of its sides, and of their parents Jupiter and Leda, on the other two. In the 4C the Lacus Juturnæ was the seat of the city's water administration. In the late Empire a series of rooms was built presumably to accommodate invalids who came to take the waters. These rooms contain fragments of statues of gods and other sculptures. To the s. is the shrine proper, an aedicula, restored in 1953-55, with the front built into the brick walls, and with two columns. Before the front of the aedicula is a marble puteal, with a dedicatory inscription to Juturna by the curule aedile M. Barbatius Pollio. In front again is a marble altar, with a relief of Juturna and her brother Turnus.

Adjoining the shrine, on the s., is an apsidal building of the late Empire, converted into the *Oratory of the Forty Martyrs* and preserving remains of 8-9C frescoes (seen through the locked gate). The forty were soldiers martyred at Sebaste, in Armenia,by being frozen to death in an icy pool. The building closes the w. end of the Nova Via.

To the s. of the Oratory are the considerable remains of the church of *Santa Maria Antiqua* (closed indefinitely because of lack of custodians), the oldest and most important Christian building in the Forum. It includes the adjacent rectangular hall, commonly called the *Temple of Augustus,* of which it was once presumed to be the library. Recent investigations have led to the belief that the building was not an annexe of the Temple of Augustus (which is now placed elsewhere, in the area of Piazza della Consolazione), but a monumental vestibule erected by Domitian to his palace on the Palatine. It was part of the general reconstruction of the Palatine begun by Domitian and completed by his successors; this included an ambitious bridge, probably of wood, built by Caligula, whereby the emperor was able to go from his palace to the Capitol without having to descend into the Forum.

The transformation into a church appears to have taken place as early as the 6C. Pope John VII (705-7) restored the church and adorned it with paintings, which were renovated under Zacharias (741-52) and Paul I (757-67). Following a series of disasters to the building, caused by earthquakes and landslides and perhaps also by the Saracens, Leo IV (847-55) transferred the diaconate to Santa Maria Nova (p. 140) and rebuilt the church completely. In the 12C a further rebuilding was found necessary, perhaps on account of more earthquakes, and the church was renamed *Santa Maria Liberatrice.* In 1702 a restoration brought to light the remains of the original church, and in 1901-2 Santa Maria Liberatrice, by that time entirely modernized, was pulled down.

The church comprises a quadrangular atrium, a quadriporticus, nearly square, and a presbytery, with three chapels, the central chapel being apsidal. On the right is the so-called Temple of Augustus; on the left a ramp leading up to the Palatine.

The ATRIUM, the oldest part, is perhaps the atrium of Caligula's palace, but dates more probably from the time of Domitian. It was used as the vestibule of the church and preserves its impluvium. It has (on the walls) Byzantine frescoes, and fragments of ancient and medieval sculptures. Beyond the narthex is the central hall converted into a church.

Four Corinthian columns with traces of painting divide it into a nave and two aisles. In the nave are the low brick walls of the schola cantorum. The 7-8C *Wall-paintings are of the highest importance in the history of early Christian art, although they are very ruined. On the walls dividing the hall from the presbytery: left, Annunciation (period of Martin I; 649-53); right, *Mother of the seven martyred Maccabees (2 Mac. 7; period of John VII; 705-7). Left aisle: paintings in four bands:

second band, Christ enthroned with the doctors of the Church (Byzantine influence; Paul I; 757-67); above, two series of panels with Latin inscriptions depicting scenes from the Old Testament. Right aisle: detached fresco from the atrium, showing the Virgin enthroned between saints and a pope with a square nimbus (indicating that he was alive at the time of the painting). Some of the sarcophagi in the hall are of pagan origin. Doors on the right lead into the vast 'Temple of Augustus'.

PRESBYTERY. To the right, on the continuation of the schola cantorum, two panels showing Isaiah at the death-bed of Hezekiah and David with the vanquished Goliath. On the side walls are heads of the Apostles; above, in two bands, scenes from the New Testament. In the *Apse* and on the wall to the right are the remarkable *Palimpsests, superimposed layers of painting from the 6C to the 8C; especially noteworthy are a Madonna enthroned (lowest layer; 6C), an Annunciation (second layer), with a beautiful angel head, and (third layer; period of John VII), Fathers of the Church (Greek lettering).— *Right Chapel* (of SS. Cosmas and Damian): figures of saints, in a poor state of preservation.—*Left Chapel* (of SS. Cyriac and Julitta): in niche above rear wall, *Crucifixion, with Christ on the Cross, the Virgin and St John, St Longinus and the soldier holding the sponge dipped in vinegar. The painting below, with the Virgin between SS. Peter and Paul, SS. Cyriac and Julitta, Pope Zacharias and the dean Theodotus, has been detached, and is now in the Antiquarium Forense (p. 124). On the other walls are eight paintings with scenes from the life of SS. Cyriac and Julitta, the Virgin adored by a family, possibly that of Theodotus (note the square nimbi of the two children), Theodotus kneeling, and the pathetic representation of four unknown saints, with the inscription *quorum nomina Deus scit.*

Near Santa Maria Antiqua, beyond the 'Temple of Augustus', is a vast brick building known as the *Horrea Agrippiana.* This was a warehouse of three courtyards, each provided with three stories of rooms. The church of San Teodoro (p. 88) stands on the second courtyard.

Vicus Tuscus returns N. between the Basilica Julia and the Temple of Castor, and then E., past the Arch of Augustus (p. 116), to reach the religious centre of the Forum. Here are the Temple of Vesta, the House of the Vestals, and the Regia.

The *Temple of Vesta,** where the vestals guarded the sacred fire, is a circular edifice of 20 Corinthian columns. Its present appearance is the result of a partial reconstitution of the ruins in 1930 by Alfonso Bartoli. The circular form recalls the Latin hut and the first temple on this site was possibly made, like the hut, of straw, and wood. Vesta goddess of the hearth, protected the fire, which symbolized the perpetuity of the State. The task of the vestals was to keep the fire for ever burning. Its extinction was the most fearful of all prodigies, as it implied the end of Rome. The origin of the cult is supposed to go back to Numa Pompilius, second king of Rome, or even to Aeneas, who brought from Troy the eternal fire of Vesta with the images of the penates.

The temple was burned down several times, notably during Nero's fire of A.D. 64 and in 191. It was rebuilt as often, the last time by Septimius Severus and his wife Julia Domna. It was closed by Theodosius and was in ruins in the 8C. For centuries until 1930 all that remained was the circular basement surmounted by tufa blocks and architectonic fragments. In the interior was an adytum, or secret place containing the unknown pledges of the duration of Rome (*pignora imperii*). These included the *Palladium,* or statue of Pallas Athena, supposedly carried off from Troy by Aeneas. No one was allowed inside the adytum except the vestals and the Pontifex Maximus and its contents were never shown. The Palladium was an object of the highest veneration, as on its preservation depended the safety of the city. At least one attempt was made to steal it; Gibbon reminds us (Chapter 6) that the Emperor Elagabalus (Heliogabalus) "broke into the sanctuary of Vesta, and carried away a statue, which he supposed to be the Palladium; but the vestals boasted that, by a pious fraud, they had imposed a counterfeit image on the profane intruder" (comp. p. 135). The cult statue of Vesta was kept, not in the temple, but in a small shrine near the entrance to the House of the Vestals.

Immediately E. of the Temple of Vesta is the **\*House of the Vestals,** or *Atrium Vestoe.* This is a large rectangular structure arranged round a spacious courtyard. It dates from Republican times, but was rebuilt after the fire of Nero in A.D. 64, and was last restored by Septimius Severus; remains of both structures can still be seen.

The **Vestals,** or virgin priestesses of Vesta, numbered only six. At first they were chosen by the king; during the Republic and Empire by the Pontifex Maximus. Candidates had to be between six and ten years old, sound in body and mind, daughters of freeborn parents and resident in Italy. On election the vestal was taken in hand by the Pontifex Maximus and led to the Atrium Vestæ, where she lived thereafter. The period of service was thirty years; ten learning her mysterious duties, ten performing them, and ten teaching novices. During this period she was bound by the solemn vow of chastity. At the end of the 30 years she was free to return to the world and even to marry; few, however, availed themselves of this concession. The senior among them was called *Vestalis Maxima* or *Virgo Maxima.* If a vestal was so careless as to let out the sacred fire, she was scourged by the Pontifex Maximus, and he rekindled the fire by the friction of two pieces of wood from a *felix arbor.* The vestals' other duties included periodic offerings to Vesta, sprinkling her shrine daily with water from the Egerian fount, assisting at the consecration of temples and other public ceremonies, and guarding the Palladium. Maintained at the public expense, they had many privileges, such as an exalted order of precedence, and the right of intercession. Wills—even the emperor's will— and solemn treaties were entrusted to their keeping. If a vestal broke her vow of chastity the punishment was barbarous: she was stripped of her badges of office, scourged, and immured alive in the Campus Sceleratus (p. 197); her paramour was publicly flogged to death in the Forum.

The building is seemingly too large for the accommodation of six vestals, and part of it may have been reserved for the Pontifex Maximus, whose official residence in the Regia (see below) was scarcely habitable. The House of the Vestals is remarkable for its courtyard, which is 61 m long and 20 m wide. In the middle are three ponds irregularly spaced and unequal in size. The central pond is the largest; at one time it was partly covered by an octagonal structure of unknown purpose. A charming rose-garden has been planted among the ruins. Along the sides of the courtyard are statues and statue-bases of vestals who had deserved well of the State; they date from the 3C A.D. onwards. Near the entrance is a base from which the name of the vestal has been removed, possibly for apostasy.

The portico surrounding the courtyard was of two stories. In the middle of the short E. side is a large hall paved with coloured marbles and flanked on either side by three small rooms, thought to be the sacristy of the priestesses. Behind this hall, towards the Palatine, are an open courtyard with a fountain, and other rooms. Along the S. side, which abuts on the Nova Via, is another series of rooms (no adm.) opening out of a corridor. In the first of these are the remains of a mill; the second is

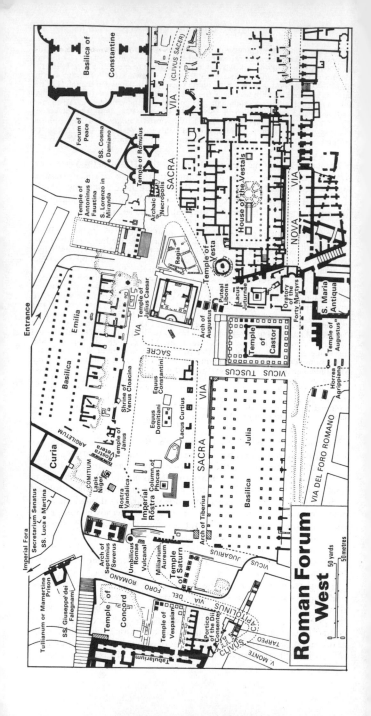

# Roman Forum
## West

Entrance

Basilica of Constantine

(CLIVUS SACER)

VIA SACRA

Forum of Peace

SS. Cosma e Damiano

Temple of Romulus

Temple of Antoninus & Faustina

S. Lorenzo in Miranda

Archaic Necropolis

House of the Vestals

Temple of Vesta

VIA NOVA

Regia

Puteal Libonis

Temple of Julius Caesar

Lacus Juturnae

Oratory of the Forty Martyrs

S. Maria Antiqua

"Temple of Augustus"

Basilica Emilia

Arch of Augustus

VIA SACRA

Temple of Castor

Shrine of Venus Cloacina

Equus Constantini

VICUS TUSCUS

Temple of Janus

Equus Domitiani

Lacus Curtius

Horrea Agrippiana

VIA DEL FORO ROMANO

ARGILETUM

Curia

COMITIUM

Postra Vetera

Lapis Niger

Basilica Julia

VIA SACRA

Rostra Vandalica

Imperial Rostra

Column of Phocas

Arch of Tiberius

Secretarium Senatus

SS. Luca e Martina

Imperial Fora

Arch of Septimius Severus

Umbilicus Romae

Vulcanal

Miliarium Aureum

VICUS JUGARIUS

Tullianum or Mamertine Prison

SS. Giuseppe dei Falegnami

VIA DEL FORO ROMANO

Temple of Concord

Temple of Saturn

Temple of Vespasian

Portico of the Dii Consentes

CLIVUS CAPITOLINUS

V. MONTE TARPEO

0    50 yards

0    50 metres

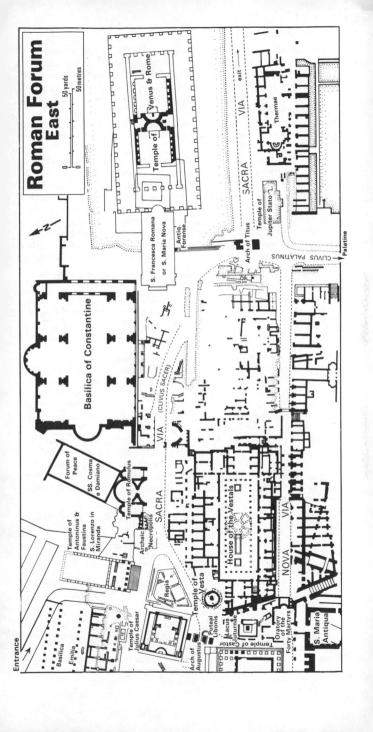

# Roman Forum East

50 yards
50 metres

Entrance

Basilica Emilia

Temple of Julius Caesar

Arch of Augustus

Regia

Temple of Vesta

Archaic Necropolis

SACRA

Temple of Antoninus & Faustina

S. Lorenzo in Miranda

Temple of Romulus

SS. Cosma e Damiano

Forum of Peace

Basilica of Constantine

VIA (CLIVUS SACER)

Puteal Libonis

Lacus Iuturnae

Temple of Castor

House of the Vestals

Oratory of the Forty Martyrs

S. Maria Antiqua

NOVA VIA

CLIVUS PALATINUS

Palatine

Arch of Titus

Temple of Jupiter Stator

Antiq. Forense

S. Francesca Romana or S. Maria Nova

Temple of Venus & Rome

SACRA VIA

exit

Thermae

Temple of

probably a bakehouse. On this side staircases lead to the upper floor and to the Nova Via. Near the last staircase is a small shrine. In the middle of the w. side is a large room, perhaps the dining-room, leading to the kitchen and other rooms. The n. side of the building is less well preserved. It certainly had more than two stories, as stairways are found on the second floor.

The *Nova Via* (not accessible) runs parallel with the Sacra Via along the s. side of the Forum. It was built to provide a means of communication with the buildings on the slopes of the Palatine.

To the n. of the Temple of Vesta and e. of the Temple of Julius Caesar are the remains of the **Regia** (under cover), the traditional palace of Numa Pompilius and the official residence of the Pontifex Maximus. As it was too small for a residential palace, the Pontifex Maximus probably lived in part of the House of the Vestals, called the *Domus Publica,* and used the Regia as his official headquarters. Destroyed by fire in 36 B.C. it was rebuilt by Domitius Calvinus. Scattered fragments of his building may be recognized by the elegance of their architectural style. Other portions date from a reconstruction of the time of Septimius Severus.

The Regia may have been the depository of State archives and of the *Annales Maximi,* written by the Pontifex Maximus. It also included the Sacrarium of Mars, with the *Ancilia,* or sacred shields which had fallen out of the skies, and the spears which trembled when war was about to break out. Here also was the chapel of Ops, goddess of plenty. It is now established that the consular and triumphal *Fasti* were placed, not here, but on the Arch of Augustus.

At the s.e. corner of the Regia have been discovered the foundations of the arch, erected in 121 B.C. by Q. Fabius Maximus Allobrogicus to span the Sacra Via.

To the n. of the Regia rises the **Temple of Antoninus and Faustina,** near the main entrance to the excavations. One of the most notable buildings of Imperial Rome, it was dedicated by the Senate in A.D. 141 to the memory of the Empress Faustina and, after his death in 161, to Antoninus Pius also. The temple was converted into the church of *San Lorenzo in Miranda* before the 12C, and given a Baroque façade in 1602. There survive, reached by a reconstructed flight of steps, the pronaos, of Corinthian cipollino columns, six in front and two on either side, the architrave and frieze of vases and candelabra between griffins, and the side walls of the cella, of peperino blocks, originally faced with marble. Sculptures placed in the pronaos include a female torso. The dedication of the church commemorates the trial of St Laurence, who may have been brought before his judges in this temple.

To the e. of the temple is the **Archaic Necropolis,** discovered in 1902. This was the cemetery of the ancient inhabitants of the Esquiline or of the original settlement on the Palatine, and dates back to the Early Iron Age, before the date of the traditional foundation of Rome. Tombs were found for both cremated and buried bodies. The cremated ashes were discovered, in their urns and with their tomb-furniture, in small circular pits. The buried bodies had been placed in tufa sarcophagi, hollowed-out tree-trunks, or trenches lined with tufa slabs. Recent excavations have discovered an extension of the necropolis in the vicinity of the Temple of Julius. The yields are in the Antiquarium Forense.

Here the Sacra Via begins to ascend the Velia and this portion, as far as the Arch of Titus, is known as the *Clivus Sacer.* On either side of the road are the ruins of private houses and shops, including one once wrongly called the Carcer, or prison.

On the left is the so-called **Temple of Romulus** (no adm.), a well-preserved 4C structure formerly thought to have been dedicated to Romulus, son of Maxentius who died in A.D. 309. It is a circular building built of brick and covered by a cupola flanked by two rectangular rooms with apses, each originally preceded by two cipollino columns (only those on the right survive). The pronaos has two porphyry columns and an architrave taken from some other building; the splendid antique bronze *Doors are a remarkable survival. Behind is a rectangular hall, part of the *Forum of Peace* built by Vespasian in A.D. 70 (see p. 138; previous ascriptions are considered erroneous). This hall was converted in the 6C into the church of SS. Cosmas and Damian (p. 140), the temple serving as a vestibule. In the Forum of Peace were probably kept the city plans, cadastral registers, and other documents. On the wall towards Via dei Fori Imperiali was affixed the plan of Rome, or *Forma Urbis,* fragments of which are in the Antiquarium Comunale (p. 68).

Beyond tower the remains of the ***Basilica of Constantine,** or **Basilica of Maxentius** (no adm.; but visible through railings), the largest monument in the Forum and one of the most impressive examples of Roman architecture in existence. The skill and audacity of its design have served as a model to later architects: it is said that Michelangelo closely studied it when he was coping with the problems of the dome of St Peter's. The three arches of the N. side, which still dominate the Forum, have inspired many Renaissance builders, many of whom, not content with copying, were not averse from despoiling the fabric. It was begun by Maxentius (306-10) and completed by Constantine, who considerably modified the original plan. The Basilica is open (entrance on Via dei Fori Imperiali) in the summer for concerts given by the Accademia di Santa Cecilia.

The huge building is a rectangle 100 m long and 65 m wide, divided into a nave and two aisles by massive piers supported by buttresses. As first planned, it has a single apse, on the w. side. Against the central piers were eight Corinthian columns 14½ m high; the only survivor was moved by Paul V (1605-21) to the Piazza Santa Maria Maggiore. The original entrance was from a side road on the E.; Constantine added on the s. side a portico opening on the Sacra Via. The portico had four porphyry columns, partly surviving. In the middle of the N. wall Constantine formed a second apse, which was shut off from the rest of the building by a colonnaded balustrade; within the enclosure thus formed the tribunal probably held its sittings. The interior walls, decorated with niches, were faced with marble below and with stucco above. The three arches of the N. aisle are 20½ m wide, 17½ m deep, and 24½ m high: the arches of the nave, whose huge blocks have fallen to the ground, were 35 m high and had a radius of nearly 20 m. Parts of a spiral staircase leading to the roof can be seen on the ground, having been flung down in an earthquake. A tunnel was built under the N.W. corner of the basilica, to allow a thoroughfare to pass (which had been blocked by its construction). The entrance to the tunnel (walled up since 1566) can still be seen.

In the w. apse was found in 1847 a colossal statue of Constantine, fragments of which are now in the courtyard of the Palazzo dei Conservatori. The bronze plates of the roof were removed in 626 by Pope Honorius I to cover Old St Peter's.

On the opposite side of the Sacra Via is a mass of ruins, among which is a massive *Portico,* the vestibule to the Golden House of Nero (p. 144). Domitian used this to build the *Horrea Piperataria,* a bazaar for Eastern goods, pepper and spices, to the N. of the Sacra Via. Later, the s. part became commercialized. Domitian's building was finally destroyed in 284. A small circular base with a relief of a Mænad and an inscription recording restoration by Antoninus Pius, in front, on the Sacra Via, may be the remains of a *Sanctuary of Bacchus.*

On the ascent to the Arch of Titus is the church of Santa Francesca Romana, or Santa Maria Nova (p. 140). The former convent of this church is now the seat of the *Ufficio degli Scavi del Foro Romano e del Palatino,* and contains the **Antiquarium Forense** (adm., see p. 47; guided visit every ½ hr). The collection occupies several rooms on two floors of the cloister and between the cloister and the cella of the Temple of Venus and Rome.

In the first room is tomb-furniture from the Archaic Necropolis, and a model. RR. II & III: objects found near the House of the Vestals; yields from wells, Italo-geometric and Etrusco-Campanian vases, votive objects, glass ware, bones, and lamps.—R. IV (beyond R. II) has a good view of the cella of the Temple of Venus and Rome (comp. p. 141). Here are displayed objects from the area of the Lapis Niger, Comitium, Cloaca Maxima, Regia, and Basilica Aemilia.—R. V. Contents of various wells and a model of the Arch of Augustus area of the forum.

UPPER FLOOR. R. VI. Fragment of a statuette of Aphrodite (in the case on the right). R. VII. Portrait of young M. Aurelius; large capital from the Temple of Concord.—PORTICO: inscriptions and architectonic fragments; red porphyry statue (headless) of the 2C A.D. R. VIII. Large marble basin reconstructed from original fragments found near the Lacus Juturnæ; fragments of the frieze of the Basilica Aemilia. R. IX (the ancient refectory of the convent): sculptures from the Lacus Juturnæ, including a headless statue of Apollo from a Greek original of the 5C B.C.; fragments of a group of the Dioscuri with their horses; marble heads and architectural decoration from the Basilica Aemilia, including two fragments of low relief, beautifully executed: Apollo and Nike (Hadrianic), and a Neo-Attic relief of dancers (Augustan). On the r. wall is part of the *Fresco removed from the chapel of SS. Cyriac and Julitta in Santa Maria Antiqua: it shows the Virgin enthroned and Child between SS. Peter and Paul and SS. Cyriac and Julitta. At the sides, wearing square nimbi (see p. 118) are Pope Zacharias and the ecclesiastic Theodotus.

Dominating the summit of the Clivus Sacer is the *Arch of Titus, erected under Domitian (A.D. 81) in honour of the victories of Titus and Vespasian in the Judæan War, which ended with the sack of Jerusalem (A.D. 70). In the middle ages the Frangipani (p. 109) incorporated the arch in one of their strongholds, but the encroaching buildings were partly removed by Sixtus IV (1471-84) and finally demolished in 1821. Restoration of the arch was then undertaken by Gius. Valadier, travertine being used instead of marble to repair the damaged portions.

The beautiful single archway, in perfect proportion, is covered with Pentelic marble; its columns are of the Composite order. The two splendid reliefs within the arch are of the highest interest (although in poor repair). On one side is Rome guiding the imperial quadriga in which are seen Titus and Victory; opposite is the triumphal procession bearing the spoils from Jerusalem, including the altar of Solomon's temple adorned with trumpets, and the seven-branched golden candlestick. In the centre of the panelled vault is the Apotheosis of Titus, who is carried heavenward by an eagle. On the exterior frieze is another procession in which may be seen the symbolic figure of the vanquished Jordan, borne on a stretcher.

The Forum can usually be left by the gate beyond the Arch of Titus. Beyond the gate the path descends the last extension of the Sacra Via with the Temple of Venus and Rome (p. 141) on the left. At the bottom is the Piazzale del Colosseo.; Piazza Venezia may be reached by Via dei Fori Imperiali.

# 6   THE PALATINE

Admission, see p. 49 and Rte 5. To reach the Palatine, visitors go in by the entrance gate to the Roman Forum on Via dei Fori Imperiali, descend the path to the level of the Forum, turn left into the Sacra Via, and ascending the Clivus Sacer past the Arch of Titus, enter the precinct by the *Clivus Palatinus*. Other ways in from the Forum (by the ramp on the side of the church of Santa Maria Antiqua and from a stairway at the s.w. corner of the House of the Vestals) have been closed indefinitely. The most convenient entrance (in Via S. Gregorio, a portal by Vignola and Rainaldi) is now also locked.

The topography of the Palatine is intricate, one level after another of multi-story buildings having been erected on and through the previous levels. Several of the more interesting sites are apt to be fenced off, because of fresh excavations or damage of some kind. Visitors may, therefore, have to make their own adjustments to the description given below. The custodians are informed and helpful.

The **Palatine** (Pl. 4; 7) is a four-sided plateau s. of the Forum rising to a height of 40 m above it and 51 m above sea-level. It is about 1740 m in circuit. If the Forum is the heart of Rome, the Palatine is its cradle; it was here that the primitive city was founded and it is on these slopes that the most ancient relics may be found. Apart from its archæological interest, which ranges from prehistoric remains to the ruined splendour of the imperial palaces, the Palatine is now a beautiful park which abounds in wild flowers and fine trees. On all sides the hill commands splendid views.

**History and Topography.** At the present day the Palatine has the appearance of a plateau, the intervening hollows having been filled in by successive constructions in imperial times. In antiquity it had three summits—the *Palatium,* towards the s. and overlooking the Circus Maximus, the *Germalus,* on the w. and n. (now largely occupied by the Farnese Gardens) looking towards the Capitol, and the *Velia,* which continues as the saddle connecting the Palatine through the Forum Romanum with the Esquiline. The name of Palatium is said to be derived from Pales, the divinity of flocks and shepherds, whose festival was celebrated on 21 April, the day on which (in 754 or 753 b.c.) the city of Rome is supposed to have been founded. Long before that date, however, the hill was settled, according to legend, from Greece. Sixty years before the Trojan War (traditional date 1184 b.c.), Evander, son of Hermes by an Arcadian nymph, led a colony from Pallantion, in Arcadia, and built at the foot of the Palatine Hill near the Tiber a town which he named after his native village. At all events, traces of occupation going back to the 9C b.c. have certainly been discovered.

When the twins Romulus and Remus decided to found a new city, the honour of naming it was accorded to Romulus by the omen of twelve vultures which he saw on the Palatine. Some time after its foundation on the hill, the city was surrounded by a strong wall forming an approximate rectangle: hence the name *Roma Quadrata.* Three gates were provided in the walls—the Porta Mugonia on the n.e., the Porta Romanula on the n.w., and the Scalae Caci at the s.w. corner overlooking the valley of the Circus Maximus.

Under the Republic many prominent citizens lived on the Palatine. They included Q. Lutatius Catulus, the orator Crassus, Cicero, the demagogue Publius Clodius, the orator Hortensius, and the triumvir Antony. Their houses were all concentrated on the Germalus and they were demolished when Tiberius and Caligula began to build the imperial palaces. Augustus was born on the Palatine; he acquired the house of Hortensius and enlarged it. His new buildings included the Temple of Apollo, renowned in antiquity, with Greek and Latin libraries attached. Part of his palace is in the process of being excavated. The example of Augustus was followed by later emperors and the Palatine tended to become an imperial reserve. The emperors' residences became more and more magnificent: etymologists scarcely need reminding that the word palace is derived from Palatine.

Tiberius built a new palace, the Domus Tiberiana, in the n.w. of the Germalus, destroying all the private houses on the site. Caligula extended it towards the Forum, adapted a hall near it, the Aula of Isis, and built a bridge over the tops of the buildings in the Forum to connect the palace with the Capitol. Nero (or possibly Claudius) began a palace—the Domus Transitoria—which was destroyed in the fire of A.D. 64. Over the ruins Nero built the outworks of his immense Domus Aurea, and added the Cryptoporticus. The whole of the Palatium, with the depression uniting it to the Germalus, was reserved for the constructions of the Palace of Domitian, which comprised the official palace, the emperor's residence, and the Stadium. Additions to this complex included a Temple of Augustus, which became a shrine of the deified emperors, or Aedes Caesarum. Another accretion was the so-called Temple of Augustus in the Forum, probably a monumental entrance to the palace from the Forum (see p. 117). To provide a water supply, Domitian extended the Aqua Claudia from the Caelian to the Palatine. Hadrian preferred to live on his estate near Tivoli, but he extended the Domus Tiberiana and carried out other works on the Palatine.

A new spate of building was begun by Septimius Severus (193-211). He increased the area of the hill to the s. by means of a series of arcades. Other noteworthy achievements were the emperor's box overlooking the Circus Maximus and the monumental Septizonium. Heliogabalus built a new temple by the Aedes Caesarum, in which he placed the most venerated treasures of Rome.

Odoacer, first king of Italy after the extinction in 476 of the Western Empire, lived on the Palatine; so for a time did Theodoric, king of the Ostrogoths, who ruled Italy from 493 to 526. The hill later became a residence of the representatives of the Eastern Empire. From time to time it was favoured by the popes. Christian churches made their appearance; a Greek monastery flourished here in the 12C.

In the course of time, after a period of devastation, the Frangipani and other noble families erected their castles over the ruins. In the 16C most of the Germalus was laid out as a villa for the Farnese which, as the Orti Farnesiani, became renowned. Systematic excavations began about 1724, shortly after Duke Francis I of Bourbon Parma had inherited the Farnese Gardens. He charged Francesco Bianchini with the work, which was mainly concentrated in the area of the Domus Flavia. Little more was done till 1860; in that year the gardens were bought by Napoleon III, who entrusted the direction of the excavations to Pietro Rosa. After 1870, when the Palatine was acquired by the Italian Government, Rosa continued with the work. In 1907 D. Vaglieri began to explore the Germalus; he was succeeded by Giac. Boni, who worked on the buildings below the Domus Flavia. Alfonso Bartoli later carried out valuable research under the Domus Augustana and elsewhere and brought to light much information about the earliest habitations. Excavations now in progress are revealing important remains of the House of Augustus.

The Clivus Palatinus ascends from the Forum passing the Nova Via (p. 122) on the right. Hereabouts was the *Porta Mugonia*, one of the three gates of Roma Quadrata, but its exact location is unknown. On the right of the ascent is a modern flight of steps leading towards the *Farnese Gardens, laid out by Vignola in the middle of the 16C for Card. Alexander Farnese, nephew of Paul III. They extended from the level of the Forum, then much higher, to the summit of the Germalus; the various terraced levels were united by flights of steps. Vignola's work was completed by Girol. Rainaldi at the beginning of 17C. The modern stairs lead up to the first terrace (formerly approached by a monumental ramp from the Nova Via in the Forum) with a Nymphaeum. Above another terrace with a fountain stand the twin pavilions of the Aviary on the highest level of the gardens, overlooking the Forum. The classical *Viridarium* instituted by Alexander Farnese was replanted here by the archaeologist Giac. Boni (1859-1925). The gardens are still beautifully maintained. Boni's tomb stands beneath a palm-tree in the part of the gardens overlooking the Forum. Delightful paths continue through the gardens to the w. side of the hill. To the s. is an ancient palm-tree beneath which is a box-hedge maze reproducing that in the peristyle of the Domus Flavia.

The gardens cover the site of the **Domus Tiberiana**, or *Palace of Tiberius,* very little of which has been excavated. An atrium was traced in the course of excavations in the 18C and 19C, but it has been covered up again. The only visible remains are an oval fishpond in the s.e. corner near the stairs leading down to the Cryptoporticus and a series of rooms with brick vaults on the s. slope overlooking the Temple of Cybele. These rooms (no adm.) are of much later date than the rest of the palace, as they were built by the Antonines for the accommodation of the Prætorian Guard; graffiti in them indicate their occupation by soldiers. The w. side of the Domus Tiberiana faced the Clivus Victoriae; here the façade was altered by Domitian. Trajan and Hadrian made further additions on the N. side, so that it reached the Nova Via.

The *Clivus Victoriæ,* leading from the Velabrum (p. 88), was in antiquity the principal means of access to the Palatine. It derived its name from a Temple of Victory founded (it is said) by Evander, the site of which is undetermined. The road skirted the w. side of the Germalus and led past the Horrea Agrippiana to the so-called Temple of Augustus in the Forum (Santa Maria Antiqua), joining the top of the ramp on the w. side of the church. Near here was the *Porta Romanula* (p. 125). Stairs (no adm.) lead down to the Clivus Victoriae from the w. side of the Farnese Gardens.

From the s. side of the gardens a modern flight of steps descends past (left) considerable remains of the Domus Tiberiana (comp. above). On the right are the remains of the **Temple of Cybele** (*Magner Mater*) covered by a thicket of ilex. The temple was built in 204 B.C., and consecrated in 191 B.C. in obedience to a prophecy of the Sibylline books. Thirteen years earlier, during a critical period of the second Punic War, the oracular books had stated that the tide of battle would be turned only if the Romans obtained from Phrygia the black stone, attribute of the goddess. This was done. Matters improved immediately and a temple was built to accommodate the statue. The temple, raised on a high podium, had six Corinthian columns in antis. It was burned in 111 B.C. and rebuilt by Q. Cæcilius Metellus, consul in 109. It was restored again in the reign of Augustus (A.D. 3). It is depicted on a relief in the garden façade of the Villa Medici (p. 174)—one of those belonging to the Ara Pietatis Augustæ. The podium and the walls of the cella survive: the statue of Cybele and fragments of a marble lion found here have been placed under an arch of the Domus Tiberiana.

Cybele, the Magna Mater, mother of the gods, was the great Asiatic goddess of fertility. The town of Pessinus, in Phrygia (Asia Minor), was regarded as the principal seat of her worship, and it was from this town that the statue was brought to Rome. The goddess was the beloved—some say the mother—of Attis, and she was served by priests who, following the example of Attis, mutilated themselves on entering her service. The festival of Cybele and Attis was celebrated annually (22-24 March) with barbarous orgies.

To the E. of the temple is a smaller building, restored by Hadrian. Formerly identified as the *Auguratorium,* it is now thought by some experts to be a Sanctuary of Juno Sospita. Farther E. are two *Archaic Cisterns* (under cover) dating from the 6C B.C., one of which is particularly well preserved. It is circular in form, with a beehive vault of cappellaccio blocks laid in gradually diminishing courses until the top could be closed with a single slab. The construction recalls the Mycenean *tholos.*

The area to the s. is the most ancient part of the hill. Here are traces of a wall of tufa and the site of the *Scalæ Caci,* one of the three gates of Roma Quadrata. Cacus was the giant who stole the oxen from Hercules, and according to legend, had his den in the Forum Boarium (p. 86), at the foot of the hill, and was slain there by Hercules. A tradition which survived till the 4C A.D. placed in the vicinity the *House of Romulus,* or rather the hut of Faustulus where the twins were brought up after their discovery by the shepherd. Excavations begun here in 1907, and resumed in 1948-49, have revealed the traces of a HUT VILLAGE of the Early Iron Age (9C B.C.). On the rocky level of the hill are numerous holes and channels indicating the plan of three huts. In the holes were placed poles supporting the roofs. The channels were used to carry away the rain-water from the roofs.

In this part of the hill was the **Lupercal,** the cave sanctuary where Romulus and Remus were nurtured by the she-wolf. It contained an altar and was surrounded by a grove sacred to the god Lupercus. Here every year, on 15 February, was held the feast of the *Lupercalia.* The Luperci, priests of the god, assembled and sacrificed goats and young dogs. Two noble youths were led naked to the priests: one priest touched their foreheads with the blood of the victims; others wiped off the blood with wool dipped in milk. Thereupon the two youths were obliged to shout with laughter. After a feast, at which much wine was taken, the youths cut up the skins of the sacrificed goats: with some of the pieces they covered parts of their bodies; other pieces they cut into thongs. Holding these improvised whips in their hands, they ran through the streets of the city striking with them all they met, especially women who believed that the castigation made them fruitful. The act was a symbolic purification: the name of the month in which the festival was held— February—means purification and expiation. Mark Antony, during his consulate became one of the Luperci. Shakespeare, confusing the office, makes Julius Caesar tell him not to forget to touch Calpurnia ('Julius Caesar', i, 2).

The part of the hill between the Scalae Caci and the Temple of Apollo (see below) has been fenced off while excavations (begun in 1961) of the **House of Augustus** (not to be confused with the Domus Augustana, comp. 133) are in progress (adm. with special permission from the Office of Excavations in the Antiquarium Forense, p. 124).

In the W. wing of the house, thought to be the private quarters of the Emperor, have been found two rooms with paintings of the highest interest: the first has a charming frieze of pine cones, and the second architectural and theatrical motifs. To the W. are a series of larger rooms (still being excavated) probably used for public ceremonies and including two libraries, and a little fountain decorated with shells. The wall paintings here are remarkable for their vivid colour and intricate design (and refined figure studies). Considerable fragments of the stuccoed vaults and pavements of marble inlay have also come to light.

To the S.E. of the House of Augustus are the scanty remains once called *Temple of Jupiter Victor.* It was given this name by Pietro Rosa, who identified it with the temple built to this divinity by Q. Fabius Rullianus in 295 B.C. after his victory over the Samnites at Sentinum. This identification is now thought to be erroneous, as a building of the late Republican era was discovered underneath. The remains are, instead, considered to be those of the famous **Temple of Apollo** vowed by Augustus in 36 B.C. and dedicated eight years later. A corridor which is thought to have connected the Temple to the House of Augustus is being excavated in 1978. Fragments of a colossal statue of Apollo were found near the site of the temple, although they do not belong to the renowned statue of Apollo by Skopas known to have been placed here. All that survives is the basement of the temple 44 m by 24 m reached on the S. side by a long flight of steps (no adm.; the existing flight is a modern reproduction). On one of the landings is a round marble altar which is an intruder: it recalls a dedication of a building vowed by C. Domitius Calvinus after a victory in Spain in 53 B.C. The Temple of Apollo was surrounded by the *Portico of the Danaids,* on which were statues of the fifty daughters of Danaus. Some magnificent painted terracotta panels (now in the Palatine Antiquarium) were found here. Near by were the renowned Greek and Latin libraries, rebuilt by Domitian.

To the N. of the House of Augustus is the so-called **\*House of Livia,** famous for its wall-paintings. When it was discovered by Pietro Rosa in 1869, the finding of some lead pipes bearing the inscription *Iulia*

*Augusta* suggested its identification as the house of Livia, wife of Augustus. Other authorities thought that its owner was Germanicus or Tiberius Claudius Nero, first husband of Livia. It is now considered to be part of the house of Augustus himself (comp. above). The masonry dates from the 1C B.C.; the mural paintings are Augustan. The house is shown by a custodian.

An original staircase descends into the rectangular *Courtyard*, in which there are two pillar bases and architectural paintings. The most important rooms open onto it. In front are the three rooms of the *Tablinum*, or reception suite; on the right is the *Triclinium*, or dining-room. (Some authorities hold these ascriptions to be arbitrary.) The decorations of the tablinum are in the so-called second Pompeian style (1C B.C.), which imitates in painting the marble of Greek and Roman domestic architecture and introduces figures. The paintings have recently been detached but are exhibited in situ. The paintings in the central room are the best preserved, especially that on the right wall of this room. It has panels separated by columns of fantastic design in a free interpretation of the Corinthian style. In the central panel Hermes is seen coming to the rescue of Io, the beloved of Zeus, who is guarded by Argus of the hundred eyes; in the left panel is a street scene; the right panel is lost. In the intercolumniations are small panels with scenes of mysterious rites. The central painting on the rear wall of this room, now almost obliterated, shows Polyphemus pursuing Galatea into the sea; on the left wall, which lost its paintings in antiquity, are fixed the lead pipes which gave the house its name (see above).

In the room on the left the decoration, which is in a poor state, is architectural, with panels of griffins and other fantastic creatures. The room on the right is also architectural in its decorative scheme. The yellow frieze depicts with much delicacy small landscapes and genre scenes. Below is the representation of a Corinthian portico; between the columns are rich festoons of fruit and foliage. In the *Triclinium* (no adm.) the decorations are likewise mainly architectural. On the wall opposite the entrance is a portico with an exedra; in front is a trophy with spoils of the chase, and below is a pond with ducks. Above are branches of trees.

To the N. of the House of Livia is one of the most interesting features of the Palatine. This is the \*Cryptoporticus, a vaulted passage 128 m long, skirting the Farnese Gardens and the Domus Tiberiana. Decorated in the vault with fine stuccoes (replaced by casts; originals in the Antiquarium) for part of its length, it receives light and air from windows set high on the E. side. It was built by Nero to connect the Domus Aurea with the palaces of Augustus, Tiberius, and Caligula. A branch corridor was later added to link it with the Domus Flavia. The Cryptoporticus may be reached also by stairs leading down from the Farnese Gardens.

To the E. extends the vast area of the **Palace of Domitian,** which occupies nearly the whole of the Palatium and the former depression between it and the Germalus. This vast collection of buildings was planned for Domitian by the architect C. Rabirius, who levelled the central part of the hill to fill up the depression on the W. In the process he demolished or buried numerous earlier constructions, from private houses to imperial palaces; some of these have been revealed by excavations (see below). The complex includes the Domus Flavia, or official palace, the Domus Augustana, or imperial residence, and the Stadium. Originally it was reached from the N. by a monumental staircase of three flights.

The splendour of the \*Domus Flavia, northernmost of the constructions, was praised with nauseating flattery by Roman poets. On the N. side it has a portico of cipollino columns which may have served as a loggia. In the centre of the palace is the spacious *Peristyle* with an

E

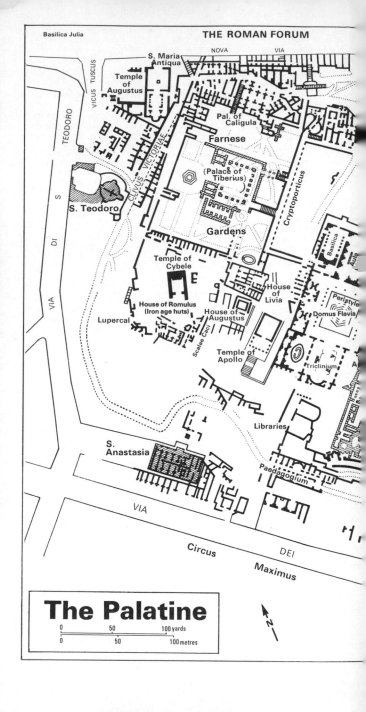

Basilica Julia

# THE ROMAN FORUM

S. Maria Antiqua

Temple of Augustus

Pal. of Caligula

Farnese

(Palace of Tiberius)

S. Teodoro

Gardens

Temple of Cybele

House of Romulus (Iron age huts)

Lupercal

House of Augustus

House of Livia

Peristyle

Domus Flavia

Scalae Caci

Temple of Apollo

Triclinium

Libraries

Basilica

Aula

S. Anastasia

Paedagogium

VIA

Circus

Maximus

DEI

VICUS TUSCUS

TEODORO

S

DI.

VIA

CLIVUS VICTORIAE

Cryptoporticus

NOVA

VIA

# The Palatine

| 0 | 50 | 100 yards |
| 0 | 50 | 100 metres |

N

SACRA VIA

Arch of Titus

Arch of Constantine

entrance

Thermae

CLIVUS  PALATINUS

S. Sebastiano

Aedes
Cæsarum

VIA  DI  S.  GREGORIO

S. Bonaventura

Domus
Augustana

arium

Stadium

Aqueduct

Palace of
Septimius Severus

CIRC

impluvium in the form of an octagonal maze surrounding a fountain. A box-hedge reproduction of this maze is in the Farnese Gardens. The peristyle was a favourite promenade of Domitian. In his constant dread of assassination he had the walls covered with slabs of Cappadocian marble whose mirror-like surface enabled him to see anyone approaching. On the w. side is a series of small rooms with apses, statue-bases, and baths; on the E. side are traces of three more rooms.

To the N. of the peristyle are three large halls (fenced off) facing N. onto an open space identified with the Area Palatina. The central hall is the *Aula Regia,* or throne room, originally decorated with 16 columns of pavonazzetto and with 12 black basalt statues: two of the statues were found in 1724 and are now in the Museo at Parma. In the apse was placed the imperial throne where the emperor sat when he presided over meetings of his council and received foreign ambassadors. To the E. is the so-called *Lararium* (under cover), in fact thought to be another room used for public ceremonies. To the w. is the *Basilica Jovis,* divided by two rows of columns of giallo antico; it has an apse at the farther end, closed by a marble screen. It may have been used as an Auditorium. A flight of steps leads down from the Basilica to the Cryptoporticus.

To the s. of the peristyle is the *Triclinium,* or banqueting hall. This is almost certainly the well-known *Coenatio Jovis.* It has an apse reached by a high step; in this was placed the table where the emperor, whose person was too sacred to risk close contact with the other diners, took his meals apart. The hall was paved with coloured marbles, which are well preserved in the apse. Leading out of the hall on either side was a court with an oval fountain. Around the fountain on the w. side, which is well preserved, is a magnificent pavement in opus sectile belonging to the Domus Transitoria of Nero. Here, too, is a pavilion constructed by the Farnese as part of their gardens (comp. p. 126), with a double loggia looking N.W. and decorations attrib. to the Zuccari.

Behind the triclinium is a row of columns (partly restored) belonging to the Domus Flavia. Farther s. are two rooms with apses, which are doubtless Domitian's reconstruction of the famous *Greek and Latin Libraries* of the Temple of Apollo (p. 128). It is now thought that Augustus used the libraries as reception rooms for legates.

The Domus Flavia covers several earlier constructions of considerable interest which have been unearthed. Various underground areas are shown by the custodian; for adm. apply at the Antiquarium (9-13). Beneath the Lararium is the *House of the Griffins, named from two griffins in stucco which decorate a lunette in one of the rooms. It is the oldest Republican building preserved on the Palatine (2C or 1C B.C.). Its wall-paintings, like those in the House of Livia, are in the second Pompeian style. The house is on two levels; the decorations are on the lower level. Of the several rooms reached by the staircase, the large hall is the best preserved. The pavement is in opus sectile. The mural paintings simulate three planes of different depth; the columns imitate various marbles. Round the top of the room runs a cornice and the ceiling is stuccoed. Paintings from two of the rooms have been detached and are now in the Palatine Antiquarium. Beneath the Basilica is the **Aula of Isis** (closed indefinitely), a large rectangular hall, with an apse at one end. The mural paitings have been detached and are now exhibited in a room of the Domus Augustana (see below).

Steps lead down from the triclinium to part of the *Domus Transitoria of Nero* (formerly called the Baths of Tiberius). At the foot of the steps is a court with a partly restored nymphæum, adorned with rare marbles. Other rooms have traces of pavements with fine marble inlay. Small paintings of Homeric subjects found in a room leading off the court have been removed to the Antiquarium. Beneath the Peristyle is the so-called *Palatine Mundus* (no adm.; a grate now covers the entrance to the stairs), a pit with a well at one end. This was thought by Boni, when it was discovered, to be the Mundus of Roma Quadrata, but it was more probably a silo. In 1952, on the wall of a building—one of the many destroyed when the Domus Flavia was built—was found a Christian inscription, believed to refer to the celebration of the Eucharist in A.D. 78 and, if so, the earliest yet discovered.

Overlapping the Domus Flavia on the E. are the vast remains of the **Domus Augustana**. This was the private residence of the emperor, 'the Augustus', not that of the Emperor Augustus. It was built on two levels. There are two peristyles on the upper and one on the lower level. Only the bases of the columns survive. The first peristyle, towards Via di San Bonaventura, was open. In the middle of the second peristyle is a large basin with a quadrangular shrine, possibly dedicated to Vesta. Around the court are remains of rooms, one of which has been identified by Bartoli with the 4C *Oratory of St Cæsarius*. Close by is the Palatine Antiquarium (see below). In another of the rooms is a graceful 16C loggia decorated with grotesques, formerly part of the Villa Mattei. Here are exhibited the *Paintings detached from the Aula of Isis (comp. above).

Dating from the Republican period these were painted before the edict of 21 B.C. banning Isis-worship. The fantastic architectural paintings have panels with scenes of the cult of Isis and the fragments of the ceiling decoration are especially interesting. When the hall, with the House of the Griffins, was discovered in 1720-22, the paintings, which were in much better condition than they are now, were copied by Gaetano Piccini and by Fr. Bartoli. Bartoli's water-colours are now in the Topham Collection at Eton.

Another peristyle of the Domus Augustana is on a much lower level (no adm. but well seen from above). In the middle is the basin of a fountain. Beyond are rooms with pavements of coloured marbles. A doorway in the bottom wall leads to the exedra of the palace overlooking the Circus Maximus; this was originally adorned with a colonnade.

A good view of the buildings at the s. end of the Palatine can be enjoyed from Via dei Cerchi, which skirts the Circus Maximus (see p. 89).

The **Palatine Antiquarium** occupies the former Convent of the Visitation between the Domus Flavia and the Domus Augustana. It was formed with the material collected in 1860-70 from the excavations instituted by Napoleon III in the Farnese Gardens and amplified by Pietro Rosa. It lost its most important sculptures on the opening of the Museo Nazionale Romano. The exhibits are in five rooms (adm. see p. 49).

In the room to the left are wall decorations from a Republican house, near the House of Livia, and from the Domus Transitoria; a fresco of Apollo, found near the Scalæ Caci; paintings, including a charming frieze from a house dated 130 B.C. found beneath the Baths of Caracalla; paintings from the Schola of the Præcones (p. 134), dating from the 3C A.D., and graffiti from the Pdagogium (p. 134), including the notorious *Graffito of Alexamenos,* discovered in 1855. This is a caricature of the Crucifixion and shows a youth standing before a cross on which hangs a figure with the head of an ass; the legend says in Greek 'Alexamenos worships his god'. In the small room opposite are fragments of the stuccoed vault of the Cryptoporticus. In the vestibule, two fragments of marble intarsia from the pavement of the Domus Tiberiana (early 1C A.D.) and an archaic altar of an unknown god. The second room on the left contains torsoes of Mercury (copy of a Greek 5C original) and Diana (Roman copy of a Greek original), and two heads of Attis. Also, *Painted terracotta panels from recent excavations near the Temple of Apollo (p. 128). The rooms to the right (closed in 1978) contain objects found beneath the Domus Flavia, and from the Temple of Cybele, and finds (with a model) from the area of the Hut Village (p. 128).

To the E. of the Domus Augustana lies the *Stadium. This is an enclosure 146 m long, with a series of rooms at the N. end and a curved wall at the S. The interior had a two-storied portico with engaged columns covering a wide ambulatory or cloister. The arena has a semicircular construction at either end, presumably once supporting a turning-post (*meta*). In the centre are two rows of piers of a portico of the late Empire. Towards the S. end are the remains of an oval enclosure of the early Middle Ages which blocked the curved end of the Stadium. On the surface of the arena lie columns of granite and cipollino, Tuscan, Corinthian, and Composite capitals, and fragments of a marble altar with figures of divinities. In the middle of the E. wall is a wide exedra shaped like an apse, of two stories, and approached from the outside by a curved corridor. This structure is usually called the *Imperial Box*. Its existence strengthens the view that the Stadium was, as its name implies, used for races and athletic contests commanded by the emperor, though some authorities think it may have been his private garden.

Behind the Stadium was the so-called **Domus Severiana**, which was built over a foundation formed by enlarging the S. corner of the hill by means of enormous substructures that extended almost as far as the Circus Maximus. The scanty remains include part of the *Baths*. To the N. is the *Aqueduct* built by Domitian to provide water for his palace; it was an extension of the Aqua Claudia which ran from the Cælian to the Palatine. The aqueduct was restored by Septimius Severus.

To the S. is the site of the imperial box built by Septimius Severus, from which he watched the contests in the Circus Maximus. In the S.E. corner of the Palatine is the probable site of the *Septizonium* or *Septizodium,* built by Septimius Severus in A.D. 203 to impress visitors to Rome arriving by the Appian Way. Here in 1241 the cardinals, imprisoned in filth by Matteo Orsini, were forced to elect Celestine IV, who, with three of the cardinals, died as a result of the conditions. It was demolished by Sixtus V at the end of the 16C. Renaissance drawings of this building show that it had three floors, each adorned with columns; the façade was divided vertically into seven zones, the number corresponding either to that of the planets or to the days of the week; hence the uncertainty about the name. The columns and other material from this ornate structure were used for various purposes in different churches in Rome; the blocks of marble and travertine and the columns all found new homes.

Beyond the Severian arches, the S. end of the Stadium, and the exedra of the Domus Augustana, lies the **Pædagogium** (no adm.), halfway down the hill and facing the Circus. The Pædagogium is so called because it is supposed to have been a training school for the court pages. The name keeps on recurring in the numerous graffiti scratched on the walls; the best-known one is the graffito of Alexamenos, now in the Antiquarium (see p. 133). The building dates from the 1C or 2C A.D.; the graffiti are later.

Other rooms (inaccessible) are situated on the edge of the hill above Via dei Cerchi; these are believed to comprise the *Schola of the Prœcones,* or College of Auctioneers; some have been ascribed, without foundation, to the *Domus Gelotiana,* the house of a private citizen incorporated in the palace of Caligula. The paintings are in the Antiquarium.

To leave the Palatine it is necessary to return across the Domus Augustana and descend by the Clivus Palatinus (comp. the Plan) to the exit at the Arch of Titus in the Forum.

Outside the arch (and not included in the Palatine enclosure) Via di San Bonaventura ascends between remains of the *Temple of Jupiter Stator* (founded in

294 B.C. on the site of an ancient sanctuary), to the N.E. summit of the Palatine. Here, approached by a 17C portal in the wall of the former Barberini vineyard is the small medieval church of *San Sebastiano al Palatino;* its apse has interesting 11C paintings. Excavations in the churchyard have unearthed the probable site of the **Aedes Caesarum,** the temple erected by Tiberius to the deified Augustus and later consecrated to all emperors who were accorded deification. Heliogabalus added a *Temple of the Sun,* in which he placed the treasures rifled from various shrines in Rome, including (as he imagined) the Palladium (see p. 119): hence the medieval name of this area, *Palladii* or *in Pallara,* which was given also to the church of St Sebastian. The last section of Via di San Bonaventura (which ends at the church) is flanked by terracotta Stations of the Cross (18C).

# 7   THE IMPERIAL FORA AND THE COLOSSEUM

The **Imperial Fora** were built between the N. side of the Roman Forum and the lower slopes of the Quirinal and Viminal. They are now traversed by the wide Via dei Fori Imperiali, constructed in 1932-33. There were five imperial fora: of Caesar, of Augustus, of Vespasian, of Nerva, and of Trajan; all have been partly or wholly excavated and their limits traced. On the way from Piazza Venezia to the Colosseum, Via dei Fori Imperiali passes on the left the Fora of Trajan and Augustus, and on the right the Forum of Caesar. It then crosses over the Fora of Nerva and of Vespasian. They are all clearly visible from the road outside (with the exception of the Forum of Vespasian), but sometimes access is restricted.

With the ever-increasing population of the city, the Roman Forum had become, in the last days of the Republic, too small for its purpose, congested as it was with buildings and overcrowded by citizens and by visitors from abroad. There was no alternative to expansion and the only direction in which expansion was possible was to the N. As this area also was encumbered with buildings, their demolition was inevitable.

The purpose of any new forum was to be the same as that of the Roman Forum, namely to serve, with its basilicas, temples, and porticoes, as a judicial, religious, and commercial centre. Such a construction, while easing the administration of the city's affairs, could not fail to dazzle the eyes of the alien visitor to the metropolis of the world.

The first step was taken by Julius Caesar, who built his Forum during the decade before his death in 44 B.C. In it he placed the Temple of Venus Genetrix in commemoration of the victory of Pharsalus (48 B.C.). His example was followed by his successors, most of whom erected temples in memory of some outstanding event in Roman history for which they took the credit. The Forum of Augustus, with the Temple of Mars Ultor, commemorated the battle of Philippi (42 B.C.); the Forum of Vespasian had its Temple of Peace erected with the spoils of the campaign in Judaea (A.D. 70); and the Forum of Trajan, completed by Hadrian, had a temple to the deified Trajan in honour of his conquest of Dacia (A.D. 106). The Forum of Nerva had a Temple of Minerva which, however, does not appear to have commemorated any noteworthy achievement of arms. All the fora were connected and the whole area was arranged in conformity with a definite plan, which has only recently been brought to light.

This centre of precious monuments suffered greatly from medieval despoilers. During the Renaissance it was raided for its marbles and bronzes; the sites were built over and the whole plan became obliterated. Until the 20C nothing was visible of the imperial fora save parts of the Fora of Trajan and Augustus and the so-called Colonnacce (p. 138). In 1924 the clearance of the area was begun, under the direction of Corrado Ricci, and by 1933, when Via dei Fori Imperiali was opened, the clearance was virtually completed.

From Piazza Venezia, between Palazzo delle Assicurazioni Generali (l.) and the Victor Emmanuel Monument (r.) opens the Largo del Foro

Traiano. Here are two domed churches of similar design. The first, *Santa Maria di Loreto* (1507), is surmounted by a curious *Lantern by Giac. del Duca (1582). It contains an altarpiece attrib. to Marco Palmezzano, and a statue of St Susanna by Fr. Duquesnoy (1630). The second church, dedicated to the *Nome di Maria* is by Ant. Dérizet (1738).

In front of the churches extends the *Forum of Trajan, the latest and most splendid of the imperial fora. It was designed by the imperial architect Apollodorus of Damascus (entrance, see below). It is in the form of a rectangle 118 m by 89 m, with a portico and exedra on each of the long sides. At the w. end, occupying the whole of its width, was the Basilica Ulpia. Adjoining, on the w., were the Greek and Latin libraries, with Trajan's Column between them, and, still farther w., beneath the area of the two churches, the Temple of Trajan. In the opinion of ancient writers these constructions made up a monumental group unequalled in the world. At the e. end of the forum was the Arch of Trajan, and, near it, the equestrian statue of the emperor. To the N. of the forum and virtually adjoining it is the semicircle of the Markets of Trajan.

*Trajan's Column, still almost intact, and the most conspicuous monument of the imperial fora, was dedicated to Trajan in 113 in memory of his conquest of the Dacians, the inhabitants of what is now Rumania. The statue of St Peter now on the top of the column was put there in 1588 in place of that of Trajan. A good view of the column may be obtained from the balustrade; another from the level of the forum.

The column is 100 Roman feet (29.7 m) high, or with the statue, 39.8 m; it is constructed of a series of marble drums. Around the column shaft winds a spiral *Frieze 200 m long and between 0.89 m and 1.25 m high, with some 2500 figures illustrating the most notable exploits of the Dacian campaigns (101-102 and 105-106). The relief carving constitutes a masterpiece of sculptural art (details may be studied in the casts in the Museo della Civiltà Romana; p. 260). A spiral stair of 185 steps (no adm.) carved in the marble ascends to the top of the Doric capital on which once stood the statue of Trajan. The ashes of the emperor, who died in Cilicia in 117, and of his wife Plotina, were enclosed in a golden urn and placed in a vault below the column. An inscription at the base has been interpreted to indicate that the top of the column reached to the original ground-level, thus giving an idea of the colossal excavations necessary for the construction of the forum.

Steps by the column descend to the level of the forum (when this entrance is closed, it is necessary to use the main entrance in Via Quattro Novembre, reached up the steps of Via Magnanapoli). On the left of the column is the *Latin Library* and on the right the *Greek Library,* both of them rectangular, with wall niches surmounted by marble cornices to hold the manuscripts. These can be seen (usually illuminated) through railings; the area to the l. is particularly interesting with many architectural fragments from the forum. Behind the column is a fragment of a colossal granite column (with its marble capital), virtually all that remains of the huge *Temple of Trajan* erected after his death in 117 by Hadrian.

The area in front of the column has extensive remains of the **Basilica Ulpia,** dedicated to the administration of justice; it was one of the largest in Rome. Though not so spacious as the Basilica of Constantine (p. 123), it was longer (120 m), not counting the apses at either end); its width was 60 m. It was divided by rows of columns into a nave and four aisles. On each short side was an extensive apse; the N. apse was found under the Palazzo Roccagiovine beside the Via Magnanapoli. The front of the basilica, towards the interior of the forum, had three doors; at the back, towards Trajan's Column, there were two doors. Part of the pavement in coloured marbles has survived; also a fragment of the entablature, with reliefs depicting scenes of sacrifice and candelabra.

An underground passage leads into the main area of the Forum, where excavations have revealed the site of the *North Portico.* This, made up of precious marbles, was razed to the ground by medieval and later despoilers. There survive the remains of three steps of giallo antico, a column base, traces of the polychrome marble pavement, and a column of the apse. Behind the apse was the wall of the enceinte; part of this is visible on the left. The site of the *South Portico* is under Via dei Fori Imperiali. On the E. side of the forum little has been discovered: here was the *Arch of Trajan*. In the centre of the forum was the equestrian statue of the emperor.

Behind the N. portico and conforming to its semicircular shape is the conspicuous agglomeration of the ***Markets of Trajan,** built before the Forum of Trajan, at the beginning of the 2C A.D. The markets consisted of 150 individual shops, used for general trading.

They form a large semicircle of three superimposed rows of shops with arcaded fronts, built on the slopes of the Quirinal. The semicircle ends on either side in a well-preserved apsidal hall (only the one on the left can be visited). The portico of the fourth shop on the left of the bottom row has been reconstructed. Staircases lead to the top of the building, from the roof (sometimes closed) of the apse on the right there is an excellent view of the imperial fora. The apsidal buildings on the second floor are particularly well preserved. At the back of the semicircle an ancient road, the Via Biberatica, leads from the 13C Torre del Grillo under an arch through the markets, and is now blocked by the Via Quattro Novembre. The exit from the markets is through a rectangular *Hall* of two stories, with six shops on each floor; on the upper story is a large covered hall which may have served as a bazaar.

The *Torre delle Milizie* (reached from the r. of the Hall) rising behind the Markets of Trajan, dates from the 13C. It is a massive brick-built leaning tower, now only two-thirds of its original height. It is popularly known as Nero's Tower, from the tradition that from its top Nero watched Rome burning. It has been closed indefinitely: the view from the top is, however, excellent.

At the beginning of Via dei Fori Imperiali, beyond the Victor Emmanuel Monument and the steep Via di San Pietro in Carcere (which diverges right to climb past the Tullianum to the Capitol), a bronze statue of Julius Caesar stands in the gardens lining the road. This is a reproduction of a marble original in the Palazzo Senatorio on the Capitol. Behind it are the remains of the Forum of Caesar.

The **Forum of Caesar** (no adm.), first of the imperial fora, is said by Dio Cassius to have been more beautiful than the Roman Forum. It contained the Temple of Venus Genetrix, from whom Julius Caesar claimed descent. The temple, dedicated in 46 B.C., two years after the battle of Pharsalus, was adorned with a statue of the goddess by Arcesilaus, a statue of Julius Caesar, and two pictures by Timomachus of Byzantium (1C B.C.) of Ajax and of Medea. Here also Caesar, with questionable taste, placed a statue of his paramour Cleopatra. In front of the temple stood a bronze figure of a horse—supposed to be Bucephalus—by Lysippos. Trajan added the Basilica Argentaria, or exchange, and five large shops over which was an extensive public lavatory or Forica.

The entrance to the ruins is by a staircase near the church of San Luca e Santa Martina (p. 109). Beyond (r.) the remains of the *Forica,* the level of the Forum is reached. On the left are the shops; at the end is the *Basilica Argentaria.* In the middle is the lofty base of the **Temple of Venus Genetrix,** shorn of its marble facing; three of its Corinthian columns have been re-erected. In front of the basilica are the remains of the piers of a triumphal arch of the late Empire.

On the other side of Via dei Fori Imperiali, in front of their respective fora, are modern bronze statues of Trajan, Augustus, and Nerva. Adjoining the Forum of Trajan is the ***Forum of Augustus,** built to commemorate the victory of Philippi (42 B.C.) and dedicated to Mars Ultor (the Avenger). Its whole extent is seen from the railings along Via dei Fori Imperiali; but the entrance is at the back, in Piazza del Grillo. This can be reached by the raised walk-way (Via di Campo Carleo), which leads out of Via dei Fori Imperiali, and passes between the Markets of Trajan and the Forum of Augustus. The entrance gives access to the FORUM OF AUGUSTUS, FORUM OF NERVA, and the CASA DEI CAVALIERI DI RODI; adm., see p. 48.

From Piazza del Grillo a modern stairway descends to the arcaded entrance to the Forum. From there a wide antique staircase leads on to the podium of the Temple of Mars Ultor.

The octastyle *Temple of Mars Ultor, dedicated in 2 B.C., had columns on three sides. It had a large pronaos and an apsidal cella. A centre of solemn ceremonies and the Imperial sanctuary, it became a museum of art and miscellaneous relics; among these were the sword of Julius Cæsar and the Roman standards surrendered by the Parthians in 20 B.C. Three columns at the end of the right flank are still standing. Of the eight Corinthian columns in front four (the two middle and the two end ones) have been partly reconstructed from antique fragments. A broad flight of steps ascends to the capacious pronaos. In the cella, where the effect of undue width is lessened by a colonnade on either side, are the stepped bases of the statues of Mars, Venus, and perhaps Divus Julius. Behind is the curve of the large apse. A stairway (usually closed) on the left descends to an underground chamber once thought to be the temple treasury.

On either side of the temple, marble steps lead up to the site of a *Basilica*. These twin basilicas were almost completely destroyed during the Renaissance for their marble; each had a great apse, which Augustus embellished with statues of famous Romans, from Aeneas onwards (some of the niches can still be seen). On the ground between the surviving columns of the temple and the right-hand basilica are architectural fragments of great interest. Behind these is the *Arch of Pantanus*, formerly the entrance to the forum. The left-hand basilica had an extension at the N. end known as the *Hall of the Colossus*, a square room which held a colossal statue of Augustus or of Mars, the base of which remains. Two ancient columns have been re-erected at the entrance.

At the E. end of the Forum of Augustus is the **Forum of Nerva,** or *Forum Transitorium,* so called because it led into the Forum of Vespasian. Nerva's Forum, which was begun by Domitian, was, in effect, a development of the *Argiletum,* the street that led from the Roman Forum to the Subura (p. 199). In the middle rose the *Temple of Minerva,* the ponderous basement of which remains in place. The temple was still standing at the beginning of the 17C, when it was pulled down by Paul V to provide marble for the Fontana Paolina on the Janiculum. Beyond the temple and close to the enceinte wall are two enormous Corinthian columns (temporarily covered for restoration), the so-called *Colonnacce,* now excavated down to their bases. In the attic between the columns is a high-relief of Minerva, after an original of the school of Skopas. In the rich frieze of the entablature Minerva (Athena) is seen teaching the arts of sewing and weaving and punishing Arachne, the Lydian maiden who excelled in the art of weaving and had dared to challenge the goddess. In front of the Colonnacce is a section of the Argiletum.

To the E. of the Forum of Nerva extended the **Forum of Vespasian** or *Forum of Peace,* built in A.D. 70 with the spoils of the Judan War. Excavations have revealed and identified a shrine under the Torre dei Conti, some prone columns, and remains of a pavement in opus sectile; a large hall was converted in the 6C into the church of Santi Cosma e Damiano (see below).

From Piazza del Grillo (comp. above) is the entrance to the **Casa dei Cavalieri di Rodi,** ancient seat of the Roman priorate of the Order of the Knights of St John of Jerusalem (Hospitallers, Knights of Rhodes, or

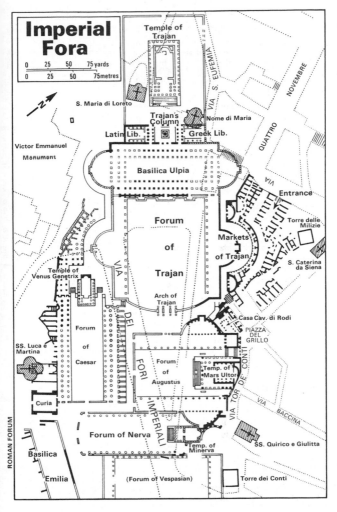

Knights of Malta). The house was built over a Roman edifice at the end of the 12C, and restored c. 1470. It has recently regained a 15C appearance. It has a well-preserved colonnaded Atrium, dating from the time of Augustus; the roof is a Renaissance addition. It is now used as a chapel by the Knights of St John. The atrium leads into the *Antiquarium of the Forum of Augustus* (temporarily closed), arranged in three Roman shops. The exhibits include: Room I. Fragments of sculpture: *Head of Jupiter from the frieze of one of the basilicas; R. 2. Medieval fragments from the churches in the area; R. 3. Model of the Forum; capitals and other architectural fragments; foot of a bronze statue.

To the left, at the top of a flight of Roman stairs (restored) is a fine Renaissance hall, off which are several contemporary rooms; one of these, the Sala del Balconcino contains part of the attic story of the portico of the Forum of Augustus, with caryatids. Stairs lead up to a loggia with fine views over the fora. It has been temporarily closed while the frescoes on the walls are being detached and cleaned.

Via di Campo Carleo leads back to Via dei Fori Imperiali which continues towards the Colosseum, passing the entrance to the Roman Forum. A stairway on the left of the entrance leads to the church of San Lorenzo in Miranda (p. 122). Farther on is the church of **Santi Cosma e Damiano.** This church occupies a large rectangular hall (probably a library) of the Forum of Vespasian, which St Felix IV adapted in 527, adding an apse. The so-called Temple of Romulus in the Roman Forum (p. 122) serves as a vestibule to the church. It was rebuilt in 1632, when the pavement was added to make it a two-storied building. The church is reached through the early 17C cloisters of the adjoining convent with contemporary frescoes (much damaged) by *Fr. Allegrini.*

The INTERIOR is celebrated for its 6C *Mosaics, copied in several Roman churches (especially in the 9C). On the triumphal arch is the Lamb enthroned, surrounded by seven candlesticks, four angels, and the symbols of the Evangelists. In the apse, SS. Cosmas and Damian presented to Christ by St Peter and St Paul; on the right, St Theodore; on the left St Felix IV (restored) presenting a model of the church; also, palms and the phoenix, the symbol of resurrection. Below the Lamb on a mount from which four rivers (the Gospels) flow, and twelve other lambs (the Apostles) issuing from Bethlehem and Jerusalem.

The ceiling of 1632 has a fresco by *Marco Montagna,* who also painted frescoes in the nave. The Baroque altar by *Domenico Castelli* (1637) is adorned with a 13C Madonna and Child.

In the 1st chap. in the right aisle, is a striking fresco of Christ encrowned on the Cross, derived from the Volto Santo in Lucca. It dates perhaps from the 13C, but more probably from a repainting in the 17C by an unknown Lucchese artist. In the vault are frescoes by *G.B. Speranza.* In the 2nd chap. paintings by *Giov. Baglione.* The 3rd chap. has an altarpiece of St Anthony of Padua by *Spadarino,* and frescoes by *Allegrini* (who also painted the frescoes in the 2nd chap. in the left aisle).

From the cloisters, a doorway to the l. leads to the vestibule which contains a complex 18C Neapolitan presepio. The models and figures in wood, terracotta, and porcelain are of exceptionally fine workmanship.

Via dei Fori Imperiali next passes on the right the colossal ruins of the Basilica of Constantine. Here, on a brick wall facing the street, is an interesting series of four relief *Maps* of the Roman dominion at various stages in history: in the 8C B.C.; in 146 B.C., after the Punic Wars; in A.D. 14, after the death of Augustus; and in the time of Trajan. A.D. 98-117.

Adjoining the Basilica of Constantine (and reached by a flight of steps from Via dei Fori Imperiali) is the church of **Santa Maria Nova,** more commonly known as **Santa Francesca Romana** (Pl. 8; 2). It is on the summit of the Velia and encroaches on the Temple of Venus and Rome (see below); a fine stretch of ancient Roman road is conspicuous on the approach to the W. door.

The church incorporates an Oratory of SS. Peter and Paul formed in the 8C by Paul I (757-67) in the W. portico of the Temple of Venus and Rome. In the 9C, after grave structural damage to the church of Santa Maria Antiqua in the Forum, that church was abandoned and the diaconate was transferred to the oratory, which became *Santa Maria Nova.* During the reconstruction by Honorius III in 1216 the delightful *Campanile, adorned with majolica plaques, was erected. The façade, designed by Carlo Lombardi, was added during his reconstruction in 1615.

Santa Francesca Romana (Francesca Buzzi; 1384-1440), wife of Lorenzo Ponziani, founded here in 1421 the Congregation of Oblates, which she herself joined after her husband's death in 1436. Canonized in 1608, she is the patron saint of motorists and on her feast day (9 March) the street between the church and the Colosseum is thronged with the cars of those seeking benediction. The painter Gentile da Fabriano was buried in the church in 1428.

INTERIOR. In the vestibule of the side entrance (r.), Tombs of Card. Martino Vulcani (d. 1394) and of Ant. da Rio (or Rido), castellan of Castel Sant' Angelo (c. 1450). S. transept, Tomb of Gregory XI, by *Olivieri,* set up in 1585 by the Roman people in honour of the pope who restored the seat of the papacy from Avignon to Rome (1377). Let into the s. wall (behind grilles) are two flagstones of the Sacra Via on which are shown the imprint of the knees of St Peter, made as the saint knelt to pray for the punishment of Simon Magus, who was demonstrating his wizardry by flying. The legendary site of Simon's consequent fall is in the neighbourhood.—From here stairs lead down to the crypt with a bas-relief of St Francesca Romana and an angel (17C). The confessio, designed by *Bernini* has a marble group of the same subject, by *G. Meli* (1866).

In the apse, *Mosaics, the Madonna and saints (probably completed in 1161), and on either side, statues of angels of the school of Bernini. Above the altar, a 12C Madonna and Child, revealed in 1950 and detached from an earlier painting found beneath it. The earlier painting, dating from the end of the 6C and one of the most ancient Christian paintings in existence, is now kept in the Sacristy (temporarily removed for restoration). Also in the sacristy, Paul III and Card. Reginald Pole (l. wall) attrib. to *Perin del Vaga;* fragments of medieval frescoes. On the entrance wall, Madonna enthroned between St Benedict and Santa Francesca Romana, by *Girolamo da Cremona;* Madonna enthroned with Saints, by *Sinibaldo Ibi* of Perugia (1545); Miracle of St Benedict, by *Subleyras.*

The former conventual buildings now contain the Antiquarium Forense (p. 124).

Beyond the church is the summit of the Velia, transformed into a terrace, the area of which (145 m by 100 m) virtually coincides with that of the enormous *Temple of Venus and Rome.* The temple was built by Hadrian, who chose to place it on the site of the vestibule of the Domus Aurea, which had been adorned by Nero with a colossal bronze statue of himself as the Sun. The statue had therefore to be moved (see p. 144). The temple was built in honour of Venus, the mother of Aeneas and the ancestor of the gens Julia, and of Roma Aeterna, whose cult appears to have been localized on the Velia. It was dedicated in 135, damaged by fire in 283, and restored by Maxentius (307). It is said to have been the last pagan temple which remained in use in Rome, as it was not closed till 391 (by Theodosius). It remained virtually entire till 625, when Honorius I carried off to Old St Peter's the bronze tiles of its roof.

To counteract the unevenness of the ground, it was necessary to build a high basement; this was of rubble, with slabs of peperino and marble-faced travertine. The temple was amphiprostyle peripteral, with ten granite Corinthian columns at the front and back and twenty on each of the sides. It had two apsidal cellae placed back to back; that facing the Forum was the shrine of Rome and the other that of Venus. The two apses, with diamond-shaped coffers, are still standing. That facing the Forum has been partly restored. The brick walls were formerly faced with marble and provided with niches framed with small porphyry columns. Within the apse is the base of the statue of the goddess. The floor is of coloured marbles. In 1935 the surviving columns and column-fragments were re-erected; the line of the missing columns is indicated by the arrangement of the terrace, which is laid out as a garden.

From the terrace of the temple steps descend into the Piazzale del Colosseo (recently closed to traffic on its s. side), which lies in a valley between the Velia on the w., the Esquiline on the N. and the Cælian on the s. Here rises the **\*\*Colosseum** (Pl. 5; 7) the most stupendous monument of ancient Rome and the emblem throughout the ages of her eternity. The original designation, *Flavian Amphitheatre,* commemorates the family name of Vespasian, who began the building, and of his son Titus, who completed it. The popular name of the amphitheatre first occurs in the writings of the Venerable Bede (c. 673-735), who quotes a prophecy of Anglo-Saxon pilgrims: "While the Coliseum stands, Rome shall stand; when the Coliseum falls, Rome shall fall; when Rome falls, the world shall fall." This name is probably due to the size of the building, though some authorities think it is derived from the proximity of Nero's colossal statue (p. 144). It may be entered from the side facing the Roman Forum or on the s. side (adm. times see p. 48). Access to the upper stories has been closed since restoration work began in 1973; its interest is greatly reduced as a consequence. Little idea of the grandeur of the building can be gained without seeing it from above.

**History.** The amphitheatre, begun by Vespasian between A.D. 70 and 76 on the site of the lake in the gardens of Nero's Domus Aurea, was completed by Titus in 80. The inaugural festival lasted 100 days, during which many gladiators and 5000 wild beasts were killed. The amphitheatre was restored c. 230 under Alexander Severus and in 248 the thousandth anniversary of the foundation of Rome was celebrated here. According to tradition, the first of many martyrdoms in the Colosseum was that of St Ignatius of Antioch (c. 110), although there is no historical basis for the tradition that Christians were martyred in the arena. Gladiatorial combats were suppressed in 407 and fights with wild beasts in 523. The damage wrought by the earthquake of 422 was probably repaired by Theodosius II and Valentinian III. The building suffered further damage from earthquakes in 1231 and 1349. It was later converted into a stronghold by the Frangipani, from whom it passed to the Annibaldi.

In 1312 the Colosseum was presented to the senate and people of Rome by the Empeor Henry VII. By the 15C it had become a recognized quarry for building material. The Palazzi di Venezia, della Cancelleria, and Farnese, and the Quay of Ripetta were built of its travertine. Later it was further despoiled to the advantage of St Peter's and the Palazzo Barberini. In 1749, however, Benedict XIV dedicated the Colosseum to the Passion of Jesus and pronounced it sanctified by the blood of the martyrs. The work of destruction ceased. Pius VII, Leo XII, Gregory XVI, and Pius IX carried out the work of restoration, erecting buttresses and other supports. In 1893-96 it was freed from encumbering buildings by Guido Baccelli, and the interior structures laid bare. Further clearances were effected after the construction in 1933 of Via dei Fori Imperiali, which ends in Piazzale del Colosseo. Restoration work was resumed in 1973.

EXTERIOR. The elliptical amphitheatre is built of travertine outside and of brick and tufa within. The travertine blocks were originally fastened together with iron tenons; these were torn out in the Middle Ages and their sockets are conspicuous. Despite the pillage of the centuries, the Colosseum preserves an aspect of indescribable grandeur and the N.E. side appears almost undamaged. The mighty exterior wall, which supports the complicated interior, has four stories. The lower three have rows of arches adorned with engaged columns of the three orders superimposed: Doric on the lowest sory, Ionic on the middle, and Corinthian on the top. The fourth story, dating from the restoration of Alexander Severus, has no arches but is diversified with slender Corinthian columns. Statues originally occupied the arches of the second and third stories. The exterior dimensions are: length 186 m, breadth 155 m, circumference 527 m, height 57 m.

There were 80 entrance arches. All were numbered except the four main entrances at the ends of the diameters of the ellipse, situated N.E., S.E., S.W. and N.W. That on the N.E. (between arches XXXVIII and XXXIX), which was without a cornice and was wider than the others, opened into a hall ornamented with stuccoes; it was reserved for the emperor. The numbered arches led to the concentric vaulted corridors giving access to the staircases. Each spectator entered by the arch corresponding to the number of his ticket, ascended the appropriate staircase and found his seat in the cavea by means of one of the numerous passages.

INTERIOR. This was divided into three parts—the Arena, the Podium, and the Cavea. The *Arena* measures 76 m by 46 m. It was so called from the sand with which it was covered to prevent combatants from slipping and to absorb the blood. It could be flooded for sea-fights, or naumachiae (comp. p. 89). The *Cross* replaces an earlier one which commemorated the martyrs of the Colosseum. The arena was surrounded by a wall c. 5 m high to render the spectators safe from the attacks of wild beasts. At the top of this wall was the *Podium.* This was a broad parapeted terrace in front of the tiers of seats, and on it was placed the imperial couch, or pulvinar. The rest of the terrace was reserved for senators, pontiffs, vestals, foreign ambassadors, and other very important persons. The *Cavea* was divided into three tiers, or *Moeniana.* The lowest tier was reserved for the knights, the middle one for the wealthier citizens, and the top one for the populace. The tiers were separated by landings (*Proecinctiones*), reached by several staircases. Each tier was intersected at intervals by *Vomitoria,* 160 in all, passages left between the seats, and a section between any two such passages was called a *Cuneus,* or wedge, from its shape. Above the topmost tier was a colonnade, to which women were admitted. At the very top was the narrow platform for the men who had to attend to the *Velarium,* or awning; the holes for the supporting poles may still be seen. It is estimated that the building could hold 50,000 spectators.

Excavation has revealed the subterranean passages used for the arrangement of the spectacles, the dens of the wild beasts, and the space for the mechanism whereby scenery and other apparatus were hoisted into the arena.

Access to the upper stories (closed during restoration work in 1978) is gained through the second arch on the left of the main entrance; a modern staircase ascends. From the central of the three curving corridors of the first story an interesting idea of the construction of the building may be gained. Above the entrance on the side towards the Palatine another staircase ascends to the second and (l.) the third floors. From the latter a flight of steps mount to a gallery commanding a magnificent *View of the city, in which the salient features are the Forum and the Amphitheatre itself, backed by the green slopes of the Palatine and the more distant whiteness of the Victor Emmanuel Monument. Though practically two-thirds of the original building have been removed, and the rows of seats in the cavea are missing, the magnificence of the amphitheatre seen from above more than justifies its widespread renown.

In Piazzale del Colosseo, between the Colosseum and the end of Via dei Fori Imperiali, travertine slabs let into the roadway indicate the site of the large square base of the *Colossus of Nero* as god of the Sun. This statue 35 m high, executed in gilt bronze by Zenodorus, was moved here from the vestibule of the Domus Aurea (see below) by Hadrian when he built the Temple of Venus and Rome. Decrianus, the architect assigned to the task of removal, made use of 24 elephants to shift the statue. The emperor's intention to erect a companion statue of Luna does not appear to have been carried out.—Also in the square, between the Arch of Constantine (see below) and the end of the Sacra Via (p. 111), a circular plaque in the roadway marks the site of the *Meta Sudans,* a marble-faced fountain erected by Domitian and restored by Constantine. It received its name from its resemblance to the turning-post (meta) of a chariot race in the circus, and from the fact that it 'sweated' water through numerous small orifices. It was surrounded by a circular basin. Its remains were demolished in 1936 by order of Mussolini.

At the s. end of Piazzale del Colosseo, facing Via di San Gregorio, rises the triple \***Arch of Constantine,** erected in A.D. 315 in honour of Constantine's victory over Maxentius at Saxa Rubra (p. 371). This arch, disinterred from the fortifications of the Frangipani in 1804, is made up of fragments from older monuments, skilfully arranged in an architectural framework and producing an impression of considerable power—though Gibbon describes it as "a melancholy proof of the decline of the arts, and a singular testimony of the meanest vanity".

The two large reliefs which adorn the inside of the central archway and the two above on the sides of the arch come from the frieze of a monument commemorating Trajan's victories over the Dacians. The statues of barbarians on the attic are from the same source. The eight medallions on the two façades, depicting hunting-scenes and pastoral sacrifices, belonged to a monument of Hadrian. The eight high reliefs let into the attic have been taken (like the three in the Pal. dei Conservatori, p. 61) from a monument to Marcus Aurelius, and represent a sacrifice, orations to the army and to the people, and a triumphal entry into Rome. The small bas-reliefs of the frieze and the victories and captives at the base of the columns are of the period of Constantine.

To the N.E. of the Colosseum rises the **Oppian Hill,** one of the four summits of the Esquiline and one of the seven hills of the primitive Septimontium of Rome (p. 18). On its slopes is the PARCO OPPIO, with its main entrance in Via Labicana. Near the entrance of the park are traces of the *Baths of Titus* and the extensive ruins of a wing of the **Domus Aurea** of Nero, overlaid by those of the *Baths of Trajan.* Excavations have unearthed the vast ramifications of the palace buildings which were buried by the construction of the baths. These subterranean rooms were known to and visited by artists of the Renaissance, who examined the murals and scratched their names on the walls. The type of decoration known as 'grottesques' takes its name from the Domus Aurea, and clearly inspired Raphael when decorating his Logge in the Vatican.

Nero already had one palace, the Domus Transitoria on the Palatine, which was destroyed in the fire of A.D. 64. Even before its destruction he had planned to build another palace (the Domus Aurea) which, with its outbuildings and gardens, was to extend over part, or all of the Palatine, much of the Cælian and part of the Esquiline hills, an area of about 50 hectares. He is reputed to have commented when it was completed that at last he was beginning to be housed like a human being. He employed Severus as architect, and Fabullus as painter, and produced what has been called the first expression of the Roman revolution in architecture. The understanding and use of vaulted spaces in the palace was quite new. It is thought that nearly all the rooms were vaulted, although some of the ceilings in the wing that survives are no longer intact. The atrium or vestibule, with the colossal statue of the emperor (comp. p. 144), was on the summit of the Velia; the Cryptoporticus (still extant) united the various palaces of the Palatine; the gardens, with their lake, were in the valley now occupied by the Piazzale del Colosseo.

This grandiose edifice did not long survive the tyrant's death in 68, as succeeding emperors demolished or covered up his buildings. In 72 Vespasian obliterated the lake to build the Colosseum; Domitian (81-96) buried the constructions on the Palatine (except the Cryptoporticus) to make room for the Flavian palaces. Trajan (98-117) overwhelmed the dwellings on the Oppian to build his baths; and Hadrian (117-38) destroyed the atrium in favour of the Temple of Venus and Rome, and moved the statue.

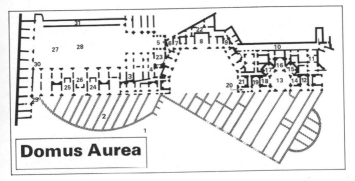

Domus Aurea

Of the *Baths of Titus*, which occupied the s.w. corner of the Oppian Hill, scarcely anything remains. The much larger *Baths of Trajan* are better preserved. There survive some remains of the central hall towards the s.e., with exedræ and parts of the wall that surrounded the establishment. A well-preserved feature was formerly part of the Domus Aurea, adapted by Trajan; this is a reservoir called *Le Sette Sale*, in the Brancaccio Gardens (p. 206). The architect of the baths was Apollodorus of Damascus, whose designs were a model for later builders of imperial baths.

A VISIT TO THE DOMUS AUREA (adm., see p. 48) is necessarily confusing, and it is difficult to obtain a clear idea of the layout from the buildings uncovered, which formed only a small part of the vast palace complex. A further difficulty is created by the intrusion of the baths of Trajan at many points. However, it may assist the visitor to consider that the rooms which remain probably formed four main areas, and that the design of each of these groups of rooms appears to have been more important to the architect than the way they were joined together. The areas suggested are: I. The rooms around the large room (8) and the five-sided court to the south. II. The complex of rooms around the octagonal hall (13). III. The rooms around the Imperial bedrooms (24 and 25). IV. The internal courtyard (27), which would have included in its design the nymphæum (5). The other rooms tend to have less intricate design and are often connecting corridors, or subsidiary service rooms. Groups are conducted every half hour by a custodian; the order given in the description below is not always followed, and all the rooms are not always shown.

In the small garden (1) is the semicircular wall of the great exedra of the Baths of Trajan. The present entrance passes through the wall (2). A passage leads r. past remains of Republican houses recently excavated. At the end of a corridor (4; l.) is a Nymphæum (5). This has an interesting vault mosaic (the only one surviving in the rooms of the palace so far excavated) depicting Ulysses and Polyphemus. On the walls are the remains of a shell decoration, and an opening in the east wall provided for a cascade of water. This formed part of the interior court design to the west (see below, 27). From here there is access into an irregularly-shaped room (6) with traces of red decoration on the walls and vault, and (7) a room with paintings of birds. From here is the entrance to the first designed complex of rooms (see above), centred around the large room (8), and the open courtyard to the South. Beyond is a small room (9) with a painted false window, and the long Cryptoporticus (10) decorated with grotesques, with signatures of 16C artists on the vault (usually difficult to see because of the damp). At the end (r.) is a room (11) which has well-preserved frescoes of complicated perspective design, with scenes of Rome, and a mosaic floor.

The most important group of rooms (12-19) are designed around an octagonal atrium (13). The southern prospect of the rooms would have opened on to an extensive garden, looking across the valley where the Colosseum now stands. The openings from the southernmost rooms were blocked up by Trajan, but their outline can still be seen clearly. The Laocoön (now in the Vatican) was found in the apsidal hall (12) in 1506. The atrium has an entirely original design and structure. The light effect is masterly both from the wide central opening in the dome, and from the side rooms. There is an opening for a cascade (16), and good painted stucco decoration (17). Beyond the second apsidal hall (19; compare 12), a corridor (r; 20) has a double-vaulted ceiling, and to the left (21) a room has a well-preserved mosaic floor. Beyond several more rooms is one (22) with more artists' signatures, and (23), an apsidal hall partly open to the sky, which was perhaps a temple. From here the entrance may be regained.

The west wing is reached to the left of the entrance (2). It contains the rooms, called the Imperial bedrooms (24 and 25) and the triclinium (26) which opened on to an interior garden (27), but which was later enclosed by walls of Trajan's baths. Here was found (28) the great porphyry vase now in the Circular Hall of the Vatican. The different building methods and materials used by Nero and Trajan can here be seen clearly. The southern prospect of these rooms (as in rooms 12-19) opened on to the valley, probably beyond a Colonnade. The bases of two columns which could have formed part of the colonnade can be seen in a room beyond (29). A long corridor (30) leads N. to another cryptoporticus (31; compare 10).

# 8  VIA DEL CORSO AND PIAZZA DEL POPOLO

**Via del Corso** (Pl. 3; 6, 4, 2), usually called simply *Il Corso,* is a straight and fairly narrow street nearly a mile long connecting Piazza Venezia with Piazza del Popolo. It has recently been closed to private traffic and yet remains one of the busiest streets in Rome. It contains a large number of fashionable shops, particularly between Piazza Venezia and Via Condotti. The pavements are hardly wide enough to accommodate the almost incessant stream of pedestrians in either direction during working hours.

The Corso corresponds to the *Via Lata* of ancient Rome, so called because of its width, exceptional in antiquity. As the main road leading to northern Italy it became the 'Regina Viarum', supplanting the Appian Way when Rome's intercourse with the East became of secondary importance. Its present name is derived from the horse-races, which took place there in the Middle Ages. The street afterwards became the theatre of the gay Roman Carnival; princely palaces and churches were built along it, and in the 18C this remarkable thoroughfare had assumed its present appearance. The straightness of its line between Piazza Venezia and Piazza Colonna was perfected by Alexander VII, when he took down the two triumphal arches that formerly spanned it. From 1900 to 1947 the street was called Corso Umberto I.

The Corso runs N. from Piazza Venezia. At its left corner is the so-called *Palazzo Bonaparte* (now Palazzo Misciatelli), by Giov. Ant. dei Rossi (17C), where Letizia Ramolino, mother of Napoleon I, died in 1836. On the right beyond Vicolo del Piombo, are *Palazzo Salviati,* by C. Rainaldi (1662), and *Palazzo Odescalchi,* of the 17-18C, but with a façade (1887-88) in the Florentine 15C style.

On the opposite side of the Corso is **Palazzo Doria** (Pl. 3; 6), which dates from 1435, but has suffered many vicissitudes. The façade towards the Corso, by Gabriele Valvassori (c. 1734), is perhaps the finest and most balanced specimen of the Rococo style in Rome. The s. façade (p. 74) is by Paolo Ameli (1743); that on the N. in Piazza del Collegio Romano, is by Ant. Del Grande (c. 1660), with two very fine wings. At No. 1A in the piazza is the entrance to the Gallery.

The **\*Galleria Doria Pamphilj,** the most important of the Roman patrician art collections, dates from the period of splendour in the house of Pamphilj. The collection was initiated by Olimpia Maidalchini, the acquisitive sister-in-law of Innocent X, in her palace in Piazza Navona (Palazzo Pamphilj, later Palazzo Doria, p. 103); it was increased by the Aldobrandini and Doria bequests. The paintings are mainly of the 16C and 17C. Visitors enter on the first floor. The best light is about midday. Admission, see p. 48.

1ST GALLERY. 10. *Titian,* Spain succouring Religion; 15. *Tintoretto,* Portrait of a Man; 17. *Bern. Licinio* (?), Portrait of a Man; *20. Correggio,* Triumph of Virtue (unfinished sketch for the painting now in the Louvre); \*23. *Raphael* (attrib.), Navagero and Beazzano (?), Venetian savants; \*26. *Lor. Lotto,* St Jerome; 28. *Paris Bordone,* Venus, Mars, and Cupid; \*29. *Titian,* Herodias; and, to the l. of the door, through which the State apartments can be seen: 38. *Carlo Saraceni,* St Roch and the angel; *Caravaggio,* 40. Mary Magdalene, \*42. Rest on the flight into Egypt, 44. Young St John the Baptist; 46. *Lo Spagnoletto,* St Jerome; 48. *Mattia Preti,* Jesus pays tribute; I. *Aless. Algardi,* Bust of

Olimpia Maidalchini; and, to the r. of the door, 53. *Sassoferrato, Virgin.*—SALONE ALDOBRANDINI. Antique sculptures, and four Brussels tapestries of the battle of Lépanto. The paintings include: 77. *Guercino, Herminia and Tancred;* and 103. *Mattia Preti,* Concert. The two marble reliefs (VII and VIII) of Sacred and Profane Love, and Bacchanalia of Putti are by *Franc. Duquesnoy.*—2ND GALLERY. 120. *Ann. Carracci,* St Jerome; 122. *Sassoferrato,* Holy Family; and on the wall behind, 131. *Dom. Fetti,* Mary Magdalene; behind, IV. *Algardi,* Bust of Innocent X; 135. *Lod. Carracci,* St Sebastian; 136. *Guido Reni,* Madonna; 137. *Ann. Carracci,* Pietà.

ROOM II. 172. *Giov. Bellini,* Madonna and Child with St John; *Giov. di Paolo,* 174. Marriage of the Virgin, *176. Birth of the Virgin; *Nic. Rondinelli,* 178, 182. Madonnas; 180. *Ortolano,* Nativity; 183. *Bicci di Lorenzo,* St Christopher and St John the Baptist; 185. *Vinc. Catena,* Circumcision; *186. *Boccaccino,* Madonna and Child; 187. *Marco Basaiti,* St Sebastian; 191. *Nic. Frangipani,* Christ and St Veronica; 194. *Iac. Bassano,* Adam and Eve in Earthly Paradise.—R. III. 195. *School of And. del Sarto,* Madonna and Child with St John; 207. *Parmigianino,* Madonna and Child; *Garófalo,* 208. Visitation, *Dosso Dossi,* 209. Portrait of Girolamo Beltramonte, 211. Dido; 212. *And. del Sarto,* Holy Family with St John; *Mazzolino,* 216. Jesus in the Temple, 217. Massacre of the Innocents, 219, Pietà; 231. *Garófalo,* Holy Family adored by saints.—In the next two rooms, Dutch and Flemish schools. R. IV. *237. *Thos. de Keyser,* Portrait of a lady; 252. *Wijbrand de Geest,* Portrait of a man; 244. *Jan Lievens,* Sacrifice of Abraham; 258. *Adriano Isenbrandt,* Mary Magdalene; 266. *David Ryckaert III,* Rural feast; 277. *David Teniers the Younger,* Fête Champêtre; 278. *P. Brill,* Creation of Man; 279. *Jan Scorel,* Agatha van Schoenhoven; 280. *P. Brueghel the Younger,* Vision of St John in Patmos.—R. V. *J. F. van Bloemen,* Seven Landscapes; *Paul Brill,* 287, Landscape with huntsmen; *Nicolas Juvenel,* 288, 294. Portraits; 290. *Q. Massys,* Usurers; *291. *Rubens,* Franciscan; 295. *Jan Brueghel the Elder,* Earthly Paradise; 306. *Herri met de Bles,* Ascent to Calvary; 316. *P. Brueghel the Younger,* Snow scene; 317. *P. Brueghel the Elder,* Battle in the Bay of Naples.—1ST CABINET. 17C Dutch and Flemish schools.

3RD GALLERY. 337. *School of Raphael,* Joan of Aragon, princess Colonna.—2ND CABINET. *339. *Velazquez,* Innocent X (1650), the gem of the collection.—VII. *Bernini,* Bust of Innocent X.—4TH GALLERY. *Claude,* *343. The Mill, 346. Rest on the flight into Egypt, 348. Sacrifice at Delphi, 351. Meeting with Diana, 352. Mercury runs away with the oxen of Apollo; 357. *Fr. Albani* and *Ann. Carracci,* Assumption; *School of Ann. Carracci,* *359. Flight into Egypt, 362. Christ carried to the sepulchre; 365. *Bart. Torregiani,* River estuary; 381. *Aless. Allori,* Christ on the road to Golgotha; *Gasp. Vanvitelli,* 384, 385. Two views of Venice.

The guided visit (arranged at 11 and 12 o'clock) to the *Private Apartments** begins with the WINTER GARDEN, adorned with antique busts, a 16C Brussels tapestry, and an 18C sedan chair. Next is the FUMOIR, containing a large polyptych, with gold background, of the early 15C Tuscan school (Virgin and Child with saints and angels); a triptych of the Madonna between St John Baptist and St Bernardine by *Sano di Pietro;* and a 16C Brussels tapestry depicting the month of

February. Off this is a room furnished in 19C style. In the ROOM OF ANDREA DORIA a glass case contains some of his possessions, while two Brussels tapestries show further scenes of Lépanto. The SMALL DINING ROOM contains a bust of Princess Emily Doria by *Canonica,* a collection of Trápani corals, ambers, and ivories, and a 19C frieze showing the fiefs of the Doria-Pamphilj family. Next is the GREEN SALON, containing a Madonna, by *Beccafumi;* Deposition, by *Hans Memling;* large mid-15C Tournai tapestry with the medieval legend of Alexander the Great; bronze bust of Innocent X, by *Algardi;* *Portrait (perhaps of himself), by *Lor. Lotto.* In the centre, rare 18C cradle in carved and gilded wood.—In the recess to the left: Portraits of And. Doria, by *Seb. del Piombo,* and of Gianetto Doria, attrib. to *Bronzino;* tender *Annunciation, by *Filippo Lippi.* From the Gallery the APPARTAMENTO DI RAPPRESENTANZA is reached, the ceiling of which is decorated with a fresco of Venus and Aeneas (18C Roman), and containing a 17C Florentine marble table with a carved and gilded wooden base in the shape of four dolphins. In the charming BALL ROOM is a Gobelins tapestry woven for Louis XIV from a 16C Flemish design, representing the month of May. The altar of rare marbles in the CHAPEL is 17C work. Tapestries of the signs of the Zodiac by *Claude Audran* in the YELLOW ROOM were executed to Louis XV's order, and two exquisite Ming vases are displayed here. The ceiling fresco is by *Conca.* The SMALL GREEN DRAWING ROOM is in the elegant 18C Venetian style, with three Venetian scenes attrib. to Longhi. Lastly, in the SMALL RED DRAWING ROOM are a 17C Gobelins tapestry, four allegorical paintings of the Elements and Seaons by *Jan Brueghel the Elder,* and a portrait of James Stuart, the Old Pretender, by *A. S. Belle.*

On the N. side of Piazza del Collegio Romano (Pl. 3; 6) is the **Collegio Romano,** formerly *Collegio dei Gesuiti,* a large building erected in 1585 by order of Gregory XIII for the Jesuits. The architect is thought to have been Bartolomeo Ammannati, or, possibly, the Jesuit Giuseppe Valeriani. The founder of the Jesuit College was St Francis Borgia, duke of Gandia, third in succession after Ignatius Loyola as General of the Jesuits. Its pupils included eight popes: Urban VIII, Innocent X, Clement IX, Clement X, Innocent XII, Clement XI, Innocent XIII, and Clement XII. The building used to house the *Museo Preistorico Etnografico Luigi Pigorini* which was moved to E.U.R. (comp. p. 259). The Jesuit library founded here formed the nucleus of the *Biblioteca Nazionale Centrale Vittorio Emanuele* which has recently been moved to new premises near the Castro Pretorio (p. 197). Part of the Jesuit library has remained here in its original bookcases. Some of the rooms in the building are now used by the Ministry of Culture and Environment.

On the s. side of the piazza is the former church of *Santa Marta* (restored in 1966 as an exhibition centre), by Carlo Fontana, with a good doorway. Inside (closed when not in use) is a good vault decoration designed by Baciccia, with paintings by him and Paolo Albertoni.—Just beyond, on the left of Via del Piè di Marmo, in Via di S. Stefano del Cacco, is a colossal marble foot (perhaps from an antique statue of Isis).

In the Corso, beyond Palazzo Doria, rises **Santa Maria in Via Lata,** a small church of ancient foundation, rebuilt in the 15C. The graceful façade and vestibule are by Pietro da Cortona (1660).

INTERIOR (open 7.30-9, & 17-23). At the end of the left aisle is the tomb (1776) of the poet Ant. Tebaldeo (1463-1537), tutor of Isabella d'Este, secretary of Lucrezia Borgia, courtier of Leo X, and friend of Raphael (who painted his portrait in the Vatican, a copy of which is placed here). The church also contains tombs of the families of Joseph and Lucien Bonaparte.

The lower level (ring on l. of the façade of the church) has remains of a Roman public building, and of earlier churches built in the 7C and in the 11C. Interesting frescoes (7-9C) discovered here have been detached because of the humidity and removed for restoration. A tradition that St Paul was guarded here on his second visit to Rome, led to excavations as early as the 17C. The high relief over the main altar of the saints Peter, Paul, Luke, and Matthew by *Cosimo Fancelli* dates from this period. Also to be seen: an ancient well (still in use) and a column inscribed with words of St Paul, and an altar (derived from a pagan cult altar) in a chap. to the right.

Here the Corso was spanned by the *Arch of Diocletian* (demolished in 1491). Nearby was the Ara Pietatis erected by Claudius in A.D. 43; remains, p. 67 & p. 174.

In the Corso, beyond Via Lata, the Banco di Roma now occupies *Palazzo Simonetti* (No. 307), once the property of the Boncompagni-Ludovisi and for years the residence of the splendour-loving Card. de Bernis, ambassador of Louis XV at the papal court.

Low down on the corner of this Palazzo in Via Lata is the *Fontanella del Facchino* with a sturdy porter holding a barrel; water issues from the bung-hole. Water-sellers are supposed to have resold Tiber or Trevi water from their barrels. 'Il Facchino' ('the porter') used to indulge in satirical conversations with Pasquino (p. 101), Madame Lucrezia (p. 73), etc.; and, with his flat beret, was long popularly supposed to be a caricature portrait of Martin Luther, though it is more likely Abbondio Rizio, an immoderate drinker. In 1751, Vanvitelli attributed the sculpture to Michelangelo.

Opposite Palazzo Simonetti is **San Marcello** (Pl. 3; 6), a very old church, rebuilt by Iac. Sansovino after a fire in 1519, with a facade by Carlo Fontana (1683) and a richly frescoed interior.

INTERIOR. to the left of the entrance, Tomb of Card. Michiel (d. 1503) and his nephew Bp Orso (d. 1511), by *Iac. Sansovino*. On the ceiling of the 4th chap. on the right are frescoes begun by *Perin del Vaga* (Creation of Eve, St Mark, and St John the Evangelist), completed after the sack of Rome by *Daniele da Volterra* and *Pellegrino Tibaldi.*—It was in front of this church that the body of Rienzo was exposed after his murder on the Capitol steps in 1354.

Via del Caravita diverges to the left for the delightful Piazza di Sant'Ignazio, a 'theatrical' masterpiece by Fil. Raguzzini (1728). The Jesuit church of **\*Sant'Ignazio** (Pl. 3; 6), rivals the Gesù in magnificence. It was built between 1626 and 1650 by Card. Ludovisi to celebrate the Canonization of St Ignatius de Loyola, the design, by Carlo Maderna and others, being carried out by Orazio Grassi. The fine façade is broad and simple in its lines.

The spacious aisled INTERIOR is sumptuously decorated. In the vaulting are paintings by *Padre Pozzo* representing St Ignatius entering Paradise, and the Four Quarters of the World, the latter a wonderful piece of perspective but decidedly theatrical in effect. It is best seen from the small disc let into the pavement about the middle of the nave. In the ornate chapels of the transepts are large marble high reliefs: on the s. side, the Glory of St Louis Gonzaga, by *Le Gros,* with a lapis-lazuli urn containing the remains of the saint; on the N. the Annunciation by *Filippo Valle,* and another lapis-lazuli urn with the relics of St John Berchmans (d. 1621).

Farther on in the Corso is (No. 239, on the right) *Palazzo Sciarra-Colonna,* a severe looking edifice of the late 16C by Flaminio Ponzio, under which, in 1887, was found part of the Acqua Virgo. Opposite is the *Savings Bank,* by Cipolla (1874). The street here was once spanned by the triumphal *Arch of Claudius* (fragments in Palazzo dei Conservatori). Via delle Muratte diverges (r.) for the Fontana di Trevi (see p. 170).

In Piazza di Pietra, a few metres to the left of the Corso by Via di Pietra, are the remains of the **Temple of Hadrian,** built by Antoninus Pius in 145 and dedicated to his father. The wall of the cella and the peristyle of the right side with eleven fluted Corinthian *Columns (15 m high) remain. They are incorporated in the façade of the *Borsa.*

The Corso next reaches **Piazza Colonna** (Pl. 3; 4), which for centuries was the centre of the city. On the N. side rises the great flank of PALAZZO CHIGI, begun by Carlo Maderna and finished by Felice Della Greca, once the residence of the Austro-Hungarian ambassador, now the official residence of the Prime Minister (no adm.; but the interesting court can be seen through the entrance). The famous Chigi library, founded by Alexander VII, was presented by the State to the Vatican in 1923. The main façade of the palace faces the Corso and *Largo Chigi* from which the busy Via del Tritone leads to Piazza Barberini (p. 180). On the other side of the palace Via dell'Impresa leads past the E. flank of Palazzo Montecitorio to Piazza del Parlamento (p. 152).—The E. side of the piazza is closed across the Corso, by the *Galleria Colonna,* with shops and cafès in an interior arcade in the form of a Y. On the opposite side of the piazza is the façade of *Palazzo Wedekind* (1838), incorporating on the ground floor a handsome portico, with 12 Ionic marble columns, brought from a Roman building at Veio.

The little church on the s. side is *San Bartolomeo dei Bergamaschi* (1561). At the beginning of Via del Tritone (comp. above) is *Santa Maria in Via* rebuilt in 1594, with a good Baroque front, completed in 1670.

In the centre of the piazza, beside a graceful fountain, designed by Giac. della Porta (the dolphins, etc., are a 19C addition by Achille Stocchi), rises the monument from which it derives its name, the majestic *Column of Marcus Aurelius.* It was erected in honour of his victories over the Germans and Sarmatians (A.D. 169-76), and dedicated to the Emperor and his wife, Faustina.

Like Trajan's Column (p. 136), by which this was inspired, it towered, if not in the middle of a true Forum, at all events in the centre of an important group of monuments of the Antonine period. In the vicinity were the *Ustrina Antinorum* (that of Marcus Aurelius under Palazzo del Parlamento, and that of Antoninus Pius s. of the column of Antoninus Pius), the *Temple of Hadrian* in Piazza di Pietra (see above), and the *Porticus Vipsanioe* (on the other side of the Corso, in the area of Palazzo della Rinascente). The column, which was erected between 180 and 193, is made entirely of marble from Luni, and is formed of 27 blocks. The ancient level of the ground was nearly 4 m lower than at present. The shaft measures 100 Roman feet (29.6 m), and the total height of the column, including the base and the statue, is nearly 42 metres. The ancient base was decorated with Victories, festoons, and reliefs. In 1589 Dom. Fontana restored it, and a statue of St Paul was placed on the summit, where there were originally figures of Marcus Aurelius and Faustina. Around the shaft a bas-relief ascends in a spiral of 20 turns, interrupted half-way by a Victory; the lower part of the relief commemorates the war against the Germanic tribes (169-173), the upper that against the Sarmatians (174-176). In these heroic struggles, which delayed the barbaric invasion for several centuries, the philosopher-emperor was always to be found at the head of his troops. On the third spiral (E. side) the Roman solders are represented as being saved by a rain storm, which in the 4C was regarded as a miracle brought about by the prayers of the Christians in their ranks. Casts of the reliefs are in the Museo della Civiltà Romana (p. 260). The summit is reached by 203 steps lit by 56 tiny windows, in the interior of the column. Permission to ascend may be obtained from the Ufficio del Comune, 3 P.za Campitelli.

A little farther w. is Piazza di Montecitorio, with the old façade of **Palazzo di Montecitorio,** which, since 1871, has been the seat of the Italian *Chamber of Deputies.* The original palace was begun for the Ludovisi family in 1650 by *Bernini,* who was responsible for the general plan of the building and for the notion of enhancing the effect of the façade by giving it a convex, slightly polygonal form. The N. façade of the palazzo is in Piazza del Parlamento (see below).

In 1918 it was enlarged and given its new façade by E. Basile; the principal entrance is now on this side. The Art Nouveau red-brick front is in contrast to the prevailing style of architecture. The Chamber, also of this period, is panelled in oak and brightly illuminated from above by a row of windows pierced in the cornice. Below the cornice is an encaustic frieze by Aristide Sartorio, representing the development of Italian civilization. The fine bas-relief in bronze in honour of the House of Savoy is by Davide Calandra.

The **Obelisk** (22 m high) in the centre of the piazza was originally erected at Heliopolis by Psammetichus II (c. 590 B.C.), and was brought to Rome by Augustus to celebrate his victory over Cleopatra, and set up in the Campus Martius, where it served as the gnomon of an immense sundial. In 1748 it was discovered underground in the Largo dell' Impresa (an open space N. of the palazzo) and in 1792 it was placed on its present site; it was restored in 1966.

In the Corso, beyond Largo Chigi, stands *Palazzo della Rinascente* and (l.) *Palazzo Verospi* where Shelley lived in 1819 (plaque). On the right again are *Palazzo Marignoli* (1889) and the *Caffè Alemagna,* formerly *Aragno,* once the chief rendezvous of journalists and politicians. From this point Via delle Convertite leads (r.) to Piazza San Silvestro, with the central **Post and Telegraph Office** (Pl. 3; 4); the building has another entrance in Via della Vite, on its N. side. The adjoining church of SAN SILVESTRO IN CAPITE (rebuilt in 1690), originally erected by Pope Stephen III (752-7) on the site of Aurelian's *Temple of the Sun,* was bestowed upon the English Roman Catholics by Leo XIII in 1890. It has a campanile of the 12C or 13C.

Farther along the Corso, beyond Piazza del Parlamento (comp. above), is *Palazzo Fiano* (l.), built over the remains of the *Ara Pacis Augustæ* (p. 106). Here once stood the Roman Arco di Portogallo, demolished in 1662 by order of Alexander VII. A small square opens out just beyond, opposite the pretty Via Frattina, the first of several long straight pedestrian streets which open off this side of the Corso and end in Piazza di Spagna (comp. p. 172). In the square, on the left, is **San Lorenzo in Lucina** (Pl. 3; 4), a church dating perhaps from the 4C, rebuilt in the 12C, and again in 1650. Of the 12C church there remain the campanile (restored) which has several rows of small loggie with colonnettes, the portico with six Ionic columns, and the doorway.

Inside, by the 2nd pillar on the s. side, is the tomb of Nicolas Poussin (1594-1665) by *Lemoyne,* which was erected by Chateaubriand in 1830. The high altarpiece (Crucifixion) is by *Guido Reni.* In the 1st chapel on the s. side is preserved a portion of the gridiron on which St Lawrence was martyred; and the 4th chap., designed by Bernini for Innocent X's doctor Gabriele Fonseca, has a fine portrait bust by him. Pompilia (in Browning's 'The Ring and the Book') was married in this church.

Beyond *Palazzo Ruspoli* (No. 418A; l.), by Ammannati, with a great marble staircase by Martino Longhi the Younger, Largo Carlo Goldoni is reached. Here three streets converge on the Corso: Via Condotti, with its fine shops, leading past *SS. Trinità dei Spagnoli,* with an eliptical interior of the 18C, to Piazza di Spagna (p. 172), Via Fontanella di

Borghese, ending in Piazza Borghese (p. 105), and Via Tomacelli, which leads to *Ponte Cavour,* an important bridge over the Tiber leading to the Prati Quarter (p. 255). Farther on, where the street widens, stands **Santi Ambrogio e Carlo al Corso** (Pl. 3; 4) built in 1612 by Onorio Longhi, completed by his son Martino. The fine cupola is by Pietro da Cortona. The unprepossessing façade is by G.B Menicucci and Fra Mario da Canepina (1690). The altarpiece (poorly lit; the Madonna presenting San Carlo to Christ) is one of *Carlo Maratta's* best works, and on an altar behind it is a rich urn containing the heart of St Charles Borromeo.

In the neighbouring *Oratory of Sant'Ambrogio* (at No. 437, to the left of the church; ring for the porter), on the site of the old church built by the Lombards in 1513 on a piece of land granted them by Sixtus IV, is a marble group of the Deposition, by Tom. della Porta (1618)

In Via Vittoria off the Corso (r.) is the renowned Accademia Musicale di Santa Cecilia (comp. p. 46). Farther N. the Corso passes (l.) the church of *San Giacomo in Augusta* (so called from its proximity to the Mausoleum), with a façade by Maderna; it is known also as *San Giacomo degli Incurabili* from the adjoining hospital. Opposite is the small church of *Gesù e Maria,* with a façade by G. Rainaldi who was also responsible for the interior decoration completed c. 1675. On the left (Nos. 518-19) is the former *Palazzo Sanseverino,* with an imposing double porch, now a bank. Opposite (No. 20) the *Goethe Museum* (adm. see p. 49) occupies the house where the poet lived in 1786-88. It contains interesting material relating to his travels in Italy.

*Piazza del Popolo (Pl. 3; 2), at the end of the Corso, is a spacious oval formed of two hemicycles, harmonious in effect and interesting for its monuments. For motorists approaching the city by Via Flaminia, as did most travellers in the days of the 'grand tour', before the opening of the railway, it forms a nobly impressive entrance into the centre of Rome.

The piazza was designed by Gius. Valadier after the return of Pius VII from France in 1814. Three streets converge on it from the s; Via di Ripetta (p. 105) on the left, Via del Corso in the middle, and Via del Babuino (from Piazza di Spagna) on the right. The ends of the streets are separated by a pair of decorative Baroque churches, *Santa Maria dei Miracoli* (left) and *Santa Maria in Montesanto* (r.), by Bernini and Fontana (1675-78), after Carlo Rainaldi. On the N. side of the piazza is the monumental Porta del Popolo, adjoined by the church of Santa Maria del Popolo (see below). In the centre of each hemicycle is a fountain with marble groups (on the left, Neptune with two Tritons, on the right, Rome between the Tiber and the Anio) and at the ends are neo-classical statues of the Four Seasons. In the centre of the piazza, between four fountains with lions by Valadier (1823; to 16C designs by Dom. Fontana), is an *Obelisk* (24 m) the hieroglyphs on which celebrate the glories of the pharaohs Rameses II and Merenptah (13-12C B.C.); Augustus brought it from Heliopolis after the conquest of Egypt, and it was dedicated to the sun in the Circus Maximus. Domenico Fontana removed it to its present site in 1589, as part of the urban plan of Sixtus V. On the w. side of the piazza Via Ferdinando di Savoia comes in from *Ponte Margherita.* On the E. side a winding road, designed by Valadier and now known as Viale Gabriele d'Annunzio, descends from the Pincio (p. 174).

Across the piazza rises the flank of **Santa Maria del Popolo** (Pl. 3; 2), erected by Paschal II in 1099 over the tombs of the Domitia family, which were popularly believed to be the haunt of demons, because Nero was buried there. The Pope solemnly cut down a walnut tree that was supposed to shelter them. The church was rebuilt in 1227 and again under Sixtus IV (1472-77). The early Renaissance façade is attributed to And. Bregno.

The **Interior** (lights in each chapel and the apse) was renovated by *Bernini* and is a veritable museum of works of art.

SOUTH AISLE. 1st chap. (Della Rovere), *Frescoes by *Pinturicchio* (1485-89): over the altar, the Adoration of the Child; in the lunettes, scenes from the life of St Jerome; on the right, tomb of Card. De Castro (1506), perhaps by *Ant. da Sangallo the Younger;* on the left, the tomb of Cardinals Crist. and Dom. Della Rovere (1477) by *Mino da Fiesole* and *And. Bregno.*—The 2nd chapel (Cybo) is well designed; the architecture is by *C. Fontana* and its marbles are especially rich and varied. The altarpiece (Assumption and Four Doctors of the Church) is by *Carlo Maratta;* at the sides are the tombs of the Cybo family, and of Bp Girol. Foscari (d. 1463), with a bronze statue attrib. to Vecchietta.— 3rd chap., frescoed by the school of *Pinturicchio* (1504-7); over the altar, the Virgin, four saints, and the Eternal Father; in the lunettes, scenes from the life of the Virgin; on the left, the Assumption. To the right is the tomb of Giovanni Della Rovere (1483; school of And. Bregno). The majolica pavement should be noticed.—4th chap. (Costa), altarpiece, SS. Catharine, Vincent, and Anthony of Padua (1489), in the manner of *Giov. Dalmata.* On the right, tomb of Marcantonio Albertoni (1485); on the left, tomb of the founder, Card. Giorgio Costa (1508). In the lunettes, frescoes by the school of *Pinturicchio,* the Fathers of the Church (1489).

SOUTH TRANSEPT. On the right, tomb of Card. Lodovico Podocataro of Cyprus (1508). A corridor, passing an altar from the studio of *And. Bregno,* leads to the Sacristy which contains a *Tabernacle by *Bregno,* with a painted Madonna of the early Sienese school, and the monuments of Bp Rocca (d. 1482) and Abp Ortega Gomiel of Burgos (d. 1514).

The APSE of the church, by *Bramante,* contains *Frescoes (high up in the vault) by *Pinturicchio* (1508-9); Coronation of the Virgin, Evangelists, Sibyls, and Four Fathers of the Church. The stained glass, commissioned by Julius II, is by Giullaume de Marcillat. At the sides are the splendid *Tombs of Card. Girol. Basso Della Rovere (1507) and Card. Ascanio Sforza (1505), signed by *And. Sansovino.* Over the high altar is a notable 13C Madonna.

NORTH TRANSEPT. In the 1st chap. to the left of the choir (right wall), *Crucifixion of St Peter, and (l. wall) *Conversion of St Paul, both by *Caravaggio.* In the chap. at the end of the transept, Tomb of Card. Bernardo Lonati (late 15C).

NORTH AISLE. 3rd chap., to the right of the altar, tomb of Card. Pietro Mellini (1483, a small but gracious work).—The octagonal *Chigi Chapel,** founded by the great banker Agostino Chigi (1465-1520), was built from a design by *Raphael,* who prepared also the cartoons for the *Mosaics in the dome, executed by Luigi Di Pace, a Venetian, in 1516. These represent God the Father as creator of the firmament, surrounded by symbols of the seven planets, each of which is guided by an angel as in Dante's conception. The frescoes depicting the Creation and the Fall, between the windows, and the medallions of the Seasons, are by *Salviati.* The altarpiece (Nativity of the Virgin) is by *Seb. del Piombo;* the bas-relief in front (Christ and the Woman of Samaria) by *Lorenzetto.* Statues of Prophets: by the altar, *Jonah (l.), designed by *Raphael,* executed by *Lorenzetto,* and Habakkuk (r.) by *Bernini;* by the entrance, Daniel and the lion, by *Bernini,* and Elijah, by *Lorenzetto.* At the sides are the tombs of Agostino Chigi and of his brother Sigismondo (d. 1526). The much criticized pyramidal form of these tombs is now believed to have been dictated by Raphael's architectural scheme. The figure of Death in the mosaic pavement was probably an addition of Bernini's.—On the l., of the chap. is a curious funerary monument, erected in 1771 in memory of Princess Odescalchi. In the baptistery are two ciboria by *A. Bregno*, and the tombs of Cardinals Fr. Castiglione (r.; 1568) and Ant. Pallavicini (1507).

The former Augustinian convent adjoining the church was the residence in Rome of Martin Luther during his mission there in 1511.

Beside the church stands the monumental and historic **Porta del Popolo** (Pl. 3; 2), which occupies almost the same site as the ancient *Porta Flaminia*. The inner face of the gate was executed by Bernini in 1655, on the occasion of the entry into Rome of Queen Christina of Sweden; the outer face (1561) is by Nanni di Baccio Bigio, who followed a design by Michelangelo. The two side arches were opened in 1879.

On the N. side of Porta del Popolo is *Piazzale Flaminio,* a spacious and busy square and the starting-point of Via Flaminia (Rte 18).

# 9   THE VILLA BORGHESE AND THE VILLA GIULIA

Immediately N. of the Aurelian wall is the *Villa Borghese,* or *Villa Umberto I* (Pl. 11; 8), a magnificent park, with a circumference of six kilometres. The main entrance is on the w., from Piazzale Flaminio, just outside Porta del Popolo. There are four other entrances: s., from Piazzale Brasile, outside Porta Pinciana; s.e., from Via Pinciana; n.e., from Via Mercadante; and n. from Viale delle Belle Arti (see below). Traffic is excluded from the main area of the park.

The Villa owes its origin, in the 17C, to Card. Scipione Borghese, Paul V's nephew, called 'Rome's Delight' because of his fine manners and splendid hospitality. In the 18C Prince Marcantonio Borghese (father of Prince Camillo Borghese who married Pauline Bonaparte) employed Jacob More from Edinburgh to design the gardens. Early in the 19C the property was enlarged by the addition of the Giustiniani Gardens and in 1902 it was bought by the State and handed over to the city of Rome. The Villa (c. 688 hectares) is now connected with the Pincio and the Villa Giulia, so that the three form one great park, intersected in every direction by avenues and paths, with fine oaks, giant ilexes, umbrella pines and other trees, as well as statues, fountains, and terraces.

From the classical main gateway, by Canina (1835), Viale Washington ascends to the Fountain of Aesculapius with an antique statue. From here a road leads (r.) to the *Portico Egiziano,* another imposing entrance, in the form of pylons. Straight on is a monument to Victor Hugo (1905), presented by the Franco-Italian League. On the left of the avenue is the *Giardino del Lago,* with shady interlacing alleys. Here are several fountains, and statues of four Tritons (1575) by Jacopo della Porta moved here from his fountain in Piazza Navona (comp. p. 105) in 1874 where they have been replaced by copies. On an island in the little lake is a Temple of Aesculapius. From Piazza delle Canestre, farther on, the broad Viale delle Magnolie, connecting the Villa with the Pincio, runs s.w., and Viale San Paolo del Brasile runs s.e. past a monument to Goethe (by Eberlein) to Piazzale Brasile. Here is a monument, in Carrara marble, to Byron after Thorvaldsen (1959). Beyond is Porta Pinciana.—From Piazza delle Canestre an avenue leads N.E. to the attractive *Piazza di Siena,* a rustic amphitheatre with lofty pine trees (where equestrian events are held), beside it is a monument to Humbert I, by Calandra. At the end of the avenue is a reproduction of the Temple of Faustina.

On the left *'La Fortezzuola'* dates from the 16C. The crenellations were added in the 19C. In 1926 it became the studio of the sculptor and musician Pietro Canonica (born 1869) who lived here until his death in 1959. He left the house and a large collection of his sculpture to the Commune of Rome, and it is now open to the public (admission, see p. 47) as the MUSEO CANONICA.

The first room contains portraits of Donna Franca Florio (1903) and Princess Emily Doria Pamphili (1901), and 'Dopo il Voto', a statue of a young nun exhibited in Paris in 1893. Room II has the model for a monument to Alexander II of Russia (destroyed in the Revolution of 1917), and various funerary monuments. Room III. Equestrian statue of Simon Bolivar (1954), and the King of Irak (1933), and several war memorials. The gallery at the r. of the entrance contains original models of portraits, notably Lyda Borelli (1920), Alexander II of Russia (1913), Luigi Einaudi (1948), the Duke of Portland (1896), Margaret of Savoy (1903), and casts of portraits of the English royal family made in 1902-22. The house and small studio are also shown, with some fine works of art collected by Canonica (some from Palazzo Reale in Turin).

A road leads right past the 18C *Fontana dei Cavalli Marini,* by Christopher Unterberger, a marble basin supported by four seahorses. A road to the left leads to the Casino Borghese.

The direct approach to the Casino from Porta Pinciana, follows Viale del Museo Borghese.

The **Casino Borghese** was built by Jan van Santen (Giov. Vasanzio) of Utrecht in 1613-16, and later transformed by Asprucci and Unterberger in the 18C; the interior decoration dates from 1782. The Casino contains the *Galleria Borghese,* a collection of sculpture and paintings founded by Card. Scipione Borghese. Though added to by later members of the family, it was partly despoiled during the empire of Napoleon I, when Camillo Borghese gave up a large proportion of its contents for a fief in Piedmont and a valuable consideration. It was bought by the State in 1902. The number and importance of the surviving paintings, which include examples of almost every school, make this one of the chief Roman galleries. For nearly two centuries the paintings were housed in the Palazzo Borghese, near Via del Corso; they were brought here in 1891. Admission, see p. 47. The Museum of Sculpture is on the ground floor, the Picture Gallery on the first floor. The beautiful formal garden behind the Casino is seen to advantage from the first-floor windows.

**Ground Floor.** Roman numerals are used for the sculptures, arabic numerals for the paintings exhibited here. PORTICO. XXV. Fragments of a triumphal frieze of Trajan (not from the arch of Claudius).—SALONE. Ceiling fresco by *Mariano Rossi* (1774), representing M. Furius Camillus at the Capitol breaking off peace negotiations with Brennus; on the pavement, five fragments of a Roman mosaic (early 4C) depicting fights of gladiators and bestiarii (found in 1834 at Torre Nuova, near Rome); XXXVI. Colossal figure of a satyr; XXXVII. Colossal head, possibly of Juno; XLI. Augustus; XLVIII. Colossal head of Hadrian; XLIX. Bacchus; L. Colossal head of Antoninus Pius.

Most of the ceilings on this floor were decorated by *G. B. Marchetti,* with numerous assistants, under Marcantonio Borghese (c. 1750-60).

R. I (SALA DELLA PAOLINA). *LIV. Pauline Borghese, sister of Napoleon, as Venus Victrix, by *Canova* (1805), justly one of his best known works; *CCLXXI. St John the Baptist, plaster sketch by *J. A. Houdon* for a colossal marble statue, never executed, which was to have been a pendant to his St Bruno in Santa Maria degli Angeli; CCLXXII. Bust of Clement XII, by *Pietro Bracci.*

R. II (SALA DEL DAVIDE). LXXIX, XCV. Panels of a sarcophagus representing the Labours of Hercules and the birth of Apollo and Diana; LXXX. Frieze depicting the arrival of the Amazons at Troy; *LXXVII. David, by *Bernini* at the age of 25 (1623-24); the face is a self-portrait.— Paintings. 23. *Ann. Carracci,* Samson in prison, 6. *Nicolò Dell' Abate,* Landscape with deer hunt; 8. *Girol. da Carpi,* Landscape with procession of magicians; 180. *Guido Reni,* Moses; 192. *Pier Fr. Mola,* Liberation of St Peter.

R. III (SALA DI APOLLO E DAFNE). *CV. Apollo and Daphne, by *Bernini,* executed in 1624; the dramatic moment of capture is well portrayed.—14. *Cigoli,* Joseph and Portiphar's wife; 15. *Giov. Baglioni,* Judith and Holofernes; and, over the doors, two landscapes by *P. Brill.*—In the CHAPEL, frescoed by *Deruet* (d. 1660): 16. *Giov. Lanfranco,* Norandino and Lucilla surprised by the ogre.

R. IV (SALA DEGLI IMPERATORI). Busts of Roman emperors, in porphyry and alabaster, carved in the 17C. The decoration of the room is a notable example of 18C skill and taste in the ornamental arrangement of a great variety of precious marbles, and the incorporation of bas-reliefs and paintings into the design. CXLVII, CL, CLIII, CLVI. Vases in marble from Luni (Carrara), with the Seasons, by *Maximilien Laboureur; Bernini,* CCLXVIII. Rape of Proserpine, another youthful masterpiece (formerly in the Villa Ludovisi), 7386. Neptune, bozzetto in bronze for a fountain group now in the Victoria and Albert Museum, London; CXXXI. Two alabaster columns; CCXLIX. Farnese Bull, bronze by *Ant. Susini,* after the group now in the Museo Nazionale at Naples.

R. V. (SALA DELL' ERMAFRODITO). CLXXII. Hermaphrodite, a replica of the famous Hellenistic prototype; in niche above. Alabaster vase on red porphyry base; CLXXI. Bust of Titus; CLXXIV. Sappho, after a 5C Greek original. On the floor: Roman mosaic of a fishing scene, and above the doors, landscapes by *P. Brill.*

R. VI (SALA DELL' ENEA ED ANCHISE). *CLXXXI. *Bernini,* Aeneas and Anchises, carved at the age of 15 (1613) jointly with his father (Pietro Bernini); Colossal figure of Truth (on loan from the Bernini estate), sculptured by *Bernini* for the vestibule of his palace in Via del Corso, but left unfinished.—22. *Dosso Dossi,* SS. Cosmas and Damian; 347. *Garófalo,* Conversion of St Paul.

R. VII (SALA EGIZIANA). Paintings by *Tom. Conca* representing the gods and religions of ancient Egypt. CC. Youth riding on a dolphin, intended for a fountain (period of Hadrian); *CCXVI. Young girl, archaic Greek statue (head restored).

R. VIII (SALA DEL FAUNO DANZANTE). *CCXXV. Dancing faun, discovered in 1824 at Monte Calvo (Sabina) and restored under the superintendence of Thorvaldsen.—*G. Honthorst,* 27. Susanna and the

Elders; 31. Concert; 271. *Giorgio Vasari,* Nativity; 398. *Taddeo Zuccari,* Deposition; 464. *Perin del Vaga.* Holy Family.—From R. IV, a spiral staircase leads to the first floor.

**Upper Floor.** Here too arabic numerals are used for the paintings and Roman numerals for the sculptures.

LANDING. Above the door, 346. *Sassoferrato,* Copy of Titian's Three Ages of Man; 123. *Luca Cambiaso,* Venus and Cupid.

R. IX. Ceiling decoration by *Antonio von Maron,* Story of Aeneas. *433. *Lor. di Credi,* Madonna and Child; 348. *Botticelli,* Madonna and Child with the infant St John and angels (studio piece); 375. *And. del Sarto,* Pietà with saints, an early predella; 439. *Fra Bartolomeo,* Holy Family; *Raphael,* *369. Descent from the Cross (recently restored), signed and dated 1507, executed for Atalanta Baglioni of Perugia in memory of her dead son, *371. Lady with a unicorn, *397. Portrait of a man; 401. *Perugino,* Madonna; 343. *Piero di Cosimo,* Madonna and Child with St John and angel musicians; *377. *Pinturicchio,* Christ on the Cross, with SS. Jerome and Christopher.

R. X. Ceiling panels by *Crist. Unterberger,* Scenes in the life of Hercules.—*461. *Andrea Salario,* Christ carrying the Cross; *Sodoma,* 459. Holy Family, 462. Pietà; 335. *Alonso Berruguete,* Madonna and Child and Saints; 88. *And. del Brescianino,* Portrait of a woman; *334. *Andrea del Sarto,* Madonna and Child with St John; 399. *Ridolfo del Ghirlandaio,* Portrait of a young man; 435. *Marco d'Oggiono,* Christ blessing; 514. *Master of the Pala Sforzesca* (16C Lombard), Head of a woman; 287. *School of Dürer,* Portrait of a man; 326. *Lucas Cranach,* Venus and Cupid (harshly restored); 328. *Puligo,* Mary Magdalene; *444. *Bronzino,* Youthful St John the Baptist; 332. *Rosso Fiorentino,* Holy Family.—Beyond R. IX is:

R. XI. *Lor. Lotto,* *185. Self-portrait, *193. Madonna and Child with saints; *Savoldo,* 139. Portrait of a boy, *547. Tobias and the angel; 163. *Palma Vecchio,* Madonna and Child, with saints.

R. XII. 364. *Pietro da Cortona,* Portrait of Marcello Sacchetti; 542. *Pompeo Batoni,* Madonna and Child; 515. *Ann. Carracci,* Jupiter and Juno; 549. *Sim. Cantarini,* Holy Family; 318. *Carlo Dolci,* Madonna and Child; 231. *Cavalier d' Arpino,* Flight into Egypt; *55. *Domenichino,* Music (formerly known as the Cumæan Sibyl); 81. *Lavinia Fontana,* Portrait of a young boy; 382. *Sassoferrato,* Madonna and Child; 83. *Ann. Carracci,* Head of a young boy laughing.

R. XIII. *Guglielmo della Porta,* Bas-relief of the Crucifixion, in wax; *Scipione Pulzone,* 313. Holy Family, 80. Portrait of a woman; 432. *Dom. Puligo,* Holy Family; 458. *Franciabigio,* Madonna and Child with St John; 320. *Giulio Romano* (?), Madonna and Child.

R. XIV. This large room was formerly a loggia (until 1786). Ceiling frescoes by *Giov. Lanfranco* of the gods on Olympos, restored by Dom. Corvi (who was responsible for the lunettes).—Opposite the windows, *Fr. Albani,* 35, 40, 44, 49. Mythological scenes (Venus, Adonis, Vulcan, Diana); above the door, 42. *Guercino,* Return of the prodigal son; 110. *Caravaggio,* *Madonna of the Serpent, painted for the Palafrenieri, who placed it in St Peter's, whence it was later removed for what was considered its excessive realism; 41. *Lionello Spada,* Concert; *Caravaggio,* *455. David with the head of Goliath, 136. Boy with basket of fruit, 534. Boy crowned with ivy, 56. St Jerome; 53. *Domenichino,*

Diana the huntress; 43. *Ant. Carracci*, Burial of Christ; *Caravaggio*, 267. St John the Baptist.—Sculpture. *Bernini*, *cxviii. Young Jupiter with the goat Amalthea; ccLxv, ccLxvi. Portraits of Card. Scipione Borghese; *ccLxix. Terracotta sketch for the equestrian statue of Louis XIV; the statue, which is less fine than the sketch, was altered to represent Q. Curtius Rufus and is in the park at Versailles; *clx. *Aless. Algardi*, Sleep, an admirably carved figure of a boy, in nero antico, asleep, with a dormouse by his side.

R. XV. On the ceiling, *Gaetano Lapis*, Allegory of Aurora. *411. *Rubens*. Descent from the Cross (formerly attributed to Van Dyck); *Bernini*, 554, 545. Two self-portraits, 555. Portrait of a boy; *376. *Andrea Sacchi*, Clemente Merlini; 403. *Fed. Barocci*, St Jerome.

R. XVI. On the ceiling, *G. B. Marchetti*, Flora; *Iac. Bassano*, *26. Nativity, 144. Last Supper, 120. Ewe and lamb, 565. Adoration of the Magi, 127. Holy Trinity; 30. *Girol. da Treviso*, Venus.

R. XVII. On the ceiling, *Gius. Cades*, Story of Walter of Angers, returning unrecognized to his daughter's house. *Garófalo*, 240. Madonna and Child; *Lod. Mazzolino*, 247. Nativity, 451. Magi, 223. Christ appearing to Thomas; *Fr. Francia*, 57. St Francis; 390. *Ortolano*, Descent from the Cross; *Fr. Francia*, 65. St. Stephen, 61. Madonna and Child; *Lod. Mazzolino*, 218. Adoration of the Magi; and above, *Scarsellino*, 222. Madonna and Child, 169. Christ in the house of the Pharisee, 226. On the road to Emmaus, 219. Venus bathing.

R. XVIII. Dutch and Flemish Schools. Ceiling decoration by *Bénigne Gagneraux*, Antiope and Jupiter. *253. *Frans Francken*, Picture dealers; 272. *Pieter Codde*, Guardroom; 291. *David Teniers the Younger*, Topers; 284. *Tilborgh*, Inn interior; 277. *Rubens*, Susanna and the Elders; 279. *Abraham Cuylenborch*, Bath of Diana; 354. *Paul Brill*, Harbour scene.

R. XIX. The ceiling of this room was decorated by the Scots painter *Gavin Hamilton* (1723-98), Story of Paris. *Dosso Dossi*, *217. Circe, 1. Apollo, 220. Adoration of the Shepherds, *304. Diana and Callisto; *125. *Correggio*, Danaë; *Marco Basaiti*, 129. Adam, 131. Eve; 85. *Parmigianino*, Portrait of a man.—Sculpture. *Aless. Algardi* (?), *ccLxx. Bust of Card. Domenico Ginnasi, ccLxvii. Vincenza Danesi.

R. XX. Ceiling paintings by *P. Ant. Novelli*, Mythological subjects. *Titian*, **147. Sacred and Profane Love, the masterpiece of the painter's youthful period. The subject is somewhat ambiguous, as both women have identical portraits. 188. *Titian*, St Vincent Ferrer (previously regarded as the portrait of St Dominic), *396. *Antonello da Messsina*, Portrait of a man; 450. *Vitt. Carpaccio*, Portrait of a woman; 445. *Palma Vecchio*, Portrait of a man; 170. *Titian*, Venus blindfolding Cupid; *Paolo Veronese*, *137. Preaching of the Baptist; 101. St Anthony preaching to the fishes; 194. *Titian*, Scourging of Christ; 157. *Palma Vecchio*, Virgin and Saints; 132. *Giorgione* (?), The Passionate shepherd; *176. *Giov. Bellini*, Madonna and Child.

Behind the Casino is the Garden of Venus, with the picturesque Venus Fountain. A short road leads s.e. to Via Pinciana, with one of the subsidiary entrances to the park. Viale dell'Uccelliera runs n.w. to Viale del Giardino Zoologico, in which is the entrance to the **Zoological Gardens** (Pl. 11; 6), established in 1911 and enlarged in 1935. The gardens (Rest.) cover an area of about 12 hectares. The collection is strong in bears and large cats. Admission, see p. 50.

In Via Ulisse Aldovrandi, on the N. side of the Zoological Gardens, and accessible thence also are the *Zoological Museum* (1932) and the *African Museum.*

Viale del Giardino Zoologico continues to the exit of Villa Borghese on Viale delle Belle Arti. In this Avenue, on the right, is the **Palazzo delle Belle Arti** (Pl. 11; 5), by Cesare Bazzani (1911; enlarged 1933). It contains the *****Galleria Nazionale d'Arte Moderna** ( *National Gallery of Modern Art*), the most important collection extant of 19-20C Italian art. Founded in 1883, the gallery now fills no fewer than 73 rooms. Important exhibitions are frequently held. Adm., see p. 49.

Rooms numbered I-XXXV contain mainly works by Italian 19C artists. To the left is the Corridor (R. I). Neo-classicism. *Teodoro Matteini,* Portrait of two gentlemen.—R. II. *And. Appiani,* Portrait of Vincenzo Monti; *Fil. Agricola,* Portrait of Costanza Monti Perticari; *Vinc. Podesti,* Still Life; *Natale Schiavoni,* Portraits; *Henry Raeburn,* Portrait; *George Romney,* The Tempest.—Sculpture. *Pietro Tenerani,* Self-portrait; *Ant. Canova,* Sketch for the monument to Vittorio Alfieri.—R. III. Purists. *Emile J. H. Vernet,* Portrait of Bariatinsky; *Tom. Minardi,* Blind Homer and the shepherd.—Sculpture by *Pietro Tenerani* and *Lor. Bartolini.*—R. IV. Neapolitan school. *Dom. Induno,* Two Portraits, News of the Peace of Villafranca, Genre scene; *Giacinto Gigante,* Sea scene, landscapes, and views of Naples; *Ipp. Caffi,* View of Rome from Monte Mario; *Massimo d'Azeglio,* Landscape, Azalea; *Fr. Hayez,* The Bather; *Giov. Carnovali (Il Piccio),* three *Portraits; *Gius. Molteni,* Portrait of a girl.—RR. V-VII. Neapolitan school. Works by *Fil. Palizzi.*—R. VII. (r.). *Gioacchino Toma.* In the convent, Luisa Sanfelice in prison, (on the screen) Portrait, sea scene, Villa Garzoni; *Mich. Cammarano,* Portrait, landscapes, Roman Scene, Piazza San Marco; *Dom. Morelli,* Portrait of David Wonviller, Half-length study of a woman, Head of an angel, *Portraits, Self-portrait, Embalming of Christ, Christ walking on the waves.

R. VIII is dedicated to the group of Tuscan artists known as the *Macchiaioli. Ant. Puccinelli,* Portrait of Nerina Badioli; *Giov. Fattori,* Battle of Magenta; *Gius. Abbati,* Oxen by the sea; *Giov. Fattori,* *Portrait of his first wife; *Silvestro Lega,* *The visit; *Odoardo Borrani,* Two landscapes; *Fattori,* Portrait of Patrizio Senese; *Vinc. Cabianca,* Village scenes, Study of a woman; *Christiano Banti,* Tuscan country girl; *Adriano Cecioni,* Two interior scenes; *Telemaco Signorini,* Florence ghetto, Rain in summer, Interior scene, A street in Ravenna; *Fattori,* Battle scenes; (on screen) *Giov. Boldini,* Interior with figure; *Gius. Abbati,* Tuscan road; *Vito d' Ancona,* Signora with umbrella; *Cabianca,* Two landscapes; *Odoardo Borrani,* Ponte alle Grazie, Florence.—Sculpture. *Adriano Cecioni,* Bust of Giosué Carducci, Mother; *Valmone Gemignani,* Giovanni Fattori.

RR. IX-XI. Historical paintings, including works by *Gius. Camino, Dom. Morelli, Napoleone Nani, Fed. Faruffini, Ipp. Caffi* (by the stairs), and *Massimo d' Azeglio.*—R. XI. *Tranquillo Cremona,* Marco Polo; *Fr. Hayez,* Sicilian vespers.—Sculpture. *Giov. Duprè,* Sappho; *Ant. Allegretti,* Fallen Eve.—RR. XII and XIII. Works from the studio of *Dom. Morelli.*—Sculpture. *Giulio Monteverde,* Edward Jenner experimenting on his son; *Alf. Balzico,* Cleopatra.— R. XIV. Academicism and Eclecticism. Works by *Ces. Mariani, Niv. Barabino, Enrico Gamba* and others.—R. XV (l.). Risorgimento Room. *Giov. Fattori,* Battle of Custoza 1880; *Fil. Palizzi,* Battle scenes, Forest of Fontainebleau; *Mich. Cammarano,* Battle of San Martino 1883, Battle of Dogali; *Girol. Induno,* Portrait of Garibaldi.—Sculpture. *Ercole Rosa,* Bust and head of Garibaldi.— Returning downstairs, and to the left, R. XVI. Lombard school. *Ant. Fontanesi,* Bath of Diana, The Po, Landscapes and country scenes; *Giac. Favretto,* After the bath, Waiting for the bride; *Tranquillo Cremona,* Two cousins; *Luigi Conconi,* Midnight variations, Sick child.—Sculpture. *Paolo Troubetzkoy,* Indian, My wife, *Mother and child.—R. XVII is devoted to *Sculpture by *Medardo Rosso.*—R. XVIII. Divisionists. Landscapes by *Eugenio Gignous, Giov. Segantini, Gius. Pellizza* and others.—R. XIX (r.) Northern Italian school. *Mosè Bianchi,* Chioggia Canal; *Fil. Carcano,* Sea scene; *Ces. Tallone,* Portrait of a child; *Emilio Gola, Pietro Fragiacomo,* Various paintings.—Sculpture. *Giov. Focardi,* Sweet Rest; *Ernesto Bazzaro,* The widow; *Giov. Mayer,* The Convalescent; *Giov.*

*Prini,* Bust of a woman.—R. XX (which leads upstairs). *Alberto Bonomi,* Val d'Adige; *Adriano Baracchini,* Sunset; *Ces. Maggi,* Nevaio 1908.—R. XXI. Northern Italian school. *Emma Ciardi,* Swallows and butterflies.

RR. XXII-XXIII. Realistic and Social art.—R. XXII. *Adolpho Tommasi,* Country scene.—Sculpture. *Rodin,* Bust of the sculptor Dalou, *Bronze Age, Bozzetto for a ballerina.—R. XXIII. *Fr. Gioli,* Procession; *Nic. Cannicci,* Sowing grain in Tuscany; *Aless. Milesi,* Venetian marriage, Portrait of an old woman.—Sculpture. *Urbano Nono,* Il turbine; *Vinc. Vela,* Victims of work; *Achille d'Orso,* *Proximus Tuus (weary tiller), Head of a sailor.—R. XXIV. Italian artists in Paris.

Galleria Nazionale
d'Arte Moderna

*Marco Calderini,* Winter sadness; *Fed. Zandomeneghi,* House at Montmartre; *Giov. Boldini,* Two portraits of women, *Portrait of Giuseppe Verdi; *Gius. de Nittis,* *Bois de Boulogne; *Eduardo Gordigiani,* Portrait of a woman.—R. XXV. *Michetti* and the late 19C in Southern Italy. *Fr. Paulo Michetti,* Il voto, Studies, *Head of a child.—Sculpture. *Costantino Barbella,* April; *Giov. Battista Amendola,* Autumn.—R. XXVI. *Ant. Mancini,* Various paintings, including *Portraits.—Sculpture. *Achille d'Orsi,* Two statuettes; *G. B. Amendola,* Three terracottas.—R. XXVII. Artists inspired by the Pre-Raphaelites. *Luigi Galli,* *Portraits, Galatea, Holy Family; *Norberto Pazzini,* Landscapes; *Luigi Serra,* St Bonaventura and St Francis, Entering Prague 1880; *Gius. Ferrari,* Two portraits; (on screen) *Nino Costa,* Landscapes; *Luigi Serra,* Venetian scenes.—Sculpture. *Dan. de Strobel,* Boy and Death; *Fil. Cifariello,* Arnold Böcklin.—R. XXVIII. (1) Artists of the Roman Campagna. Works by *Achille Vertunni, Gius. Raggio, Alf. Ricci* and others.—R. XXIX. Modernism. Works by *Aristide Sartorio, Ettore Tito* and others.—Sculpture. Works by *Carlo Fontana; Ercole Rosa,* *Diana; *Dom. Trentacoste,* Nude woman; *Adolfo Wildt,* Atte.—R. XXX. Works by *Gaetano Previati,* and sculpture by *Leon. Bistolfi.*

R. XXXI. European 19C prints and drawings from the collection of Luigi Sprovieri, including works by: Hogarth, Gillray, Cruickshank, Rowlandson, Blake, *Goya, Flaxman, Richter and German artists, Horoshige, Outamoro, and Hokusai.—R. XXXII. 19C European prints and drawings. Including works by: Prud'hon, Géricault, Delacroix, Ingres, Corot, Millet, Courbet, Fantin-Latour, Rodin, Manet, Degas, Sisley, Renoir, Pissarro, Toulouse-Lautrec, Gauguin, Edward Münch, Egon Schiele, Whistler, Beardsley, Burne-Jones, William Morris, Fattori, and Signorini.—R. XXXIII. Early 20C works. *Lloyd Llewelyn,* Dead chestnut; *Mario Puccini,* Landscapes; *Felice Casorati,* The old; *Mario de Maria,*

Moonlight.—Sculpture. *Amleto Cataldi,* Nude woman.—R. XXXIV. Foreign artists. *John Sargent,* Portrait of Mancini; *Frank Brangwyn,* Boys bathing.—R. XXXV (returning to the entrance). Drawings and *Sculpture by *Vincenzo Gemito:* (small bronze) Water-carrier, Portrait of Verdi, Head of Anna Gemito, Self-portrait.

On the right of the entrance hall is the part of the gallery which shows the development of 20C art. R.XXXVI. Early 20C Divisionists. *Cam. Innocenti,* *The Visit, Portrait, Late, Illustrated magazines.—R. XXXVII. *Armando Spadini,* Music on the Pincio, Various portraits.—R. XXXVIII. European masters of the late 19C and early 20C. *D. G. Rossetti,* *Mrs William Morris, 1874; *Gustav Klimt,* Three Ages of Man; *Claude Monet,* Lilies; *Vincent Van Gogh,* L'Arlesienne (removed for restoration); *Edgar Degas,* After the bath; *Paul Cézanne,* Track between rocks, Landscape with Rocks (double water-colour); *Modigliani,* Portrait, Nude; *Kees van Dougen,* Woman in white; *Maurice Utrillo,* *The Seine.—R. XXXIX. Divisionism and Futurism. *Leonarde Dudreville,* Morning over the Apennines; *Giac. Balla,* Portrait in the open, Villa Borghese; *Umberto Boccioni,* Landscape, Silvia, Portrait of the Master Busoni; *Gino Severini,* Dynamism of forms, light in space.—Sculpture. *Boccioni,* Ungracious portrait.—R. XL. Futurists. *Ant. Marasco,* Composition.—Sculpture by *Roberto Melli, Enrico Prampolini,* and *Alexander Archipenko.—R. XLI. *De Chirico,* Piazza d'Italia (temporarily removed), Gladiator fight, Self-portrait, Still-life; *Gino Severini,* Still-life.

R. XLII. *Gino Rossi,* Young girl reading; *Felice Casorati,* *Sleeping children, Still-life, *Portraits, Apples, Hospital, Provincial hotel; *Arturo Martini* (sculptures), Shepherd, Bust of a young boy, Orpheus, The drinker, Homage to Manet.—R. XLIII. *Arturo Tosi,* La Madonna di Nosarico; *Giorgio Morandi,* Landscapes, Still-lifes; *Fil. de Pisis,* Still-life, Paris scenes (also on screen); *Ottone Rosai,* Landscapes, Red table, *Café (all on screen); *Carlo Carra,* Landscapes and figures; *Massimo Campigli,* *Sailors' wives, Mother and child; *Alberto Savinio,* various works.—R. XLIV. Roman artists of the 'novecento'. Artists include *Fausto Pirandello.—R. XLVa. Roman school of 1930. Works by *A. Raphael Mafai,* and *Scipione (Gino Bonichi).—R. XLVb. Later Futurist works by *Prampolini* and *Roberto Melli.—R. XLVI. Sculpture by *Marino Marini.—R. XLVII. Neo-primitive painters.—R. XLVIII. Works by the six painters of Turin; *Enrico Paulucci, Carlo Levi, Gigi Chessa, Franc. Menzio, Piero Martina, Nicola Galante.—R. XLIX. Abstract artists of Milan (1930-40). Including works by *Enrico Prampolini* and *Alberto Magnelli.—R. L. *Renato Guttoso,* Flight from Etna; Sculpture by *G. Manzù:* Bust of Carla, Bust of a woman, bas-reliefs.—R. LI. Italian sculptors and painters of the immediate post-war years.

R. LII. Foreign painters and sculptors. Paintings by *Wassily, Kandinsky, Jean Miro, Klee, Max Ernst.* Sculpture by *Alberto Viani* and *Jean Arp.—Garden. Sculpture by Italian and foreign artists of the 1960s.—R. LIII. Italian paintings of the 1950s.—R. LIV. Paintings (variations on a theme) by *G. Capogrossi.—R. LV (l.) Relief paintings by *Alberto Burri.—R. LVI. Paintings by *Lucio Fontana.—LVII. Works by *Victor Pasmore, Henry Moore, Alberto Giacometti* and others.—R. LVIII. Sculpture by *Ettore Colla.—R. LIX. Spanish art, and sculpture by *Umberto Mastroianni.*

RR. LX-LXVI. Italian and foreign contemporary art.—RR. LXVII-LXIX. Kinetic art.—R. LXX. Latest acquisitions.—LXXI. Works of the 1960s. In the Corridor, Colossal group by *Canova* of Hercules and his servant Lichas.—RR. LXXII-LXXIII. Exhibition rooms.

Outside the Gallery Viale delle Belle Arti widens into Piazza Thorvaldsen, in which, on the right, is a copy of Thorvaldsen's Jason, the gift of the city of Copenhagen. Above the steps is a statue of Simon Bolivar (1934).

On the hill above, in Via Antonio Gramsci, is the *British School at Rome* (Pl. 11; 5), established in 1901 as a School of Archæology. After the 1911 International Exhibition of Fine Arts in Rome, the site where the British Pavilion had stood was offered to the School by the Commune of Rome. The pavilion designed by Sir Edwin Lutyens, with a façade based on the west front of St Paul's Cathedral, was to be reproduced in permanent materials. In 1912, the School widened its scope to the study of the Fine Arts, Literature, and History of Italy. Scholarships are awarded, and an annual exhibition is held in May of the artists' work. The researches of the School are published annually in 'The Papers of the British School'. This region is known as the VALLE GIULIA, and is favoured by other schools and academies. On the left of Viale delle Belle Arti are the Belgian, Dutch, and Swedish Academies; on the right, in Via Gramsci, beyond the British School, is the *Scuola Superiore di Architettura.*

Farther along Viale delle Belle Arti stands **Villa Giulia,** or correctly Villa di Papa Giulio (Pl. 11; 5), built in 1550-55 for Pope Julius III by Vignola and Bart. Ammannati, with some help from Michelangelo and Vasari. Since 1889 it has been the home of the *Museo Nazionale di Villa Giulia,* devoted mainly to pre-Roman antiquities from Latium, Umbria, and Southern Etruria; admission see p. 50.

The façade is of two orders, Tuscan on the ground floor and Composite above. The porch, in rusticated masonry, leads to an ATRIUM, with Corinthian columns and niches for statues. This opens into a semicircular PORTICO, with Ionic columns and arches, a frescoed ceiling and painted wall-panels. Beyond lies the COURTYARD, enclosed by walls with Ionic columns, niches, and reliefs. At the end of the courtyard is the LOGGIA, with delicate stucco decorations by Ammannati, which separates it from the NYMPHAEUM. This is on two levels. Two curved staircases lead down from the loggia to the first level, with fountains adorned with statues symbolizing the Tiber and the Arno. On the lower level are a ceiling relief of the miraculous finding of the Acqua Vergine and four marble caryatids. Behind the portico is an aedicula or shrine, with a statue of Hygieia, a Roman copy of a 5C Greek original.

The garden extends on either side of the courtyard. On the r. is a reconstruction of the Temple of Aletrium (Alatri) by Count Adolfo Cozza, according to the account of Vitruvius and the evidence of the remains (see below). The garden is flanked by modern galleries: on the right are RR. 29-34 and on the left RR. 1-9.

The entrance to the museum is on the left of the entrance portico. Rooms 1-5 contain finds from Vulci.

ROOM 1. Two pieces of Archaic sculpture: man astride a sea monster, and a Centaur.—R. 2. The four cases to the left contain Villanovian material including hut models and (2nd case) bronze statuette of a warrior in prayer with pointed helmet, large shield, and long plaits (late 8C). In the central cases, material relating to the Tomb of the Bronze carriage, etc.—R. 3. Attic vases, including one (last case on the left) with black figures showing women at a fountain; finds from Vulci.—R. 4. Bucchero ware from Vulci.—R. 5. Three terracotta models of a temple, a stoa, and a tower, terracotta heads and figurines from Hellenistic Vulci, forming part of a *Stipe* (trench for a votive offering). Recent finds include seated figures of children.—Stairs lead down to the reconstruction of a *Tomb from the necropolis at Cervéteri, with two chambers, containing beds and the belongings of the dead.

R. 6. Tomb furniture from Bisenzio-Visentium, including a small rustic chariot, and a vase, covered and decorated with figurines (late 8C).—R. 7. Celebrated group of *Apollo and Herakles, discovered in 1916 and 1939 in the area of the *Southern Sanctuary* at Veii. These statues (restored), of painted terracotta, formed part of a votive group representing the contest between Apollo and Herakles for the Hind in the presence of Hermes and Artemis, and are an impressive and vigorous example of Etruscan sculpture of the late 6C or early 5C B.C. They were probably the work of Vulca, a celebrated sculptor of Veii, who is said to have been summoned to Rome by Tarquinius Superbus to execute the statue and decorations for the Temple of Jupiter Capitolinus (p. 55). Of the other figures in the group there remain only the Hind and the *Head of Hermes.—Statue of a goddess holding a child. From the same temple is an antefix with the head of a gorgon.

RR. 8-10 house finds from the necropolis at Caere (Cervéteri; 7-1C).—R. 8. Terracotta votive heads, sarcophagus called 'dei Leoni'.—R. 9. Terracotta *Sarcophagus (6C), representing a husband and wife feasting upon a couch; this remarkable and rare specimen bears witness to the skill of the Etruscan artists, evident in the expressive rendering of the features, especially the hands and feet.—R. 10. The glass cases contain a collection of skyphoi (drinking cups), kylixes (cups on stems), vases for perfume and wine, and amphoræ (7C-2C). *Glass Case 2.* Protocorinthian skyphoi, with geometric decoration, and a Corinthian krater, with warriors on horseback and chariots. *Case 3.* Bronze work. *Case 6.* Collection of small aryballoi (vases for perfume). *Cases 7-10.* Rare Attic kylix, with lively figures of satyrs dancing, Story of Polyphemus, Vine motif, etc. *Cases 14-17.* Small red-figured kylix, showing two exploits of Theseus and a young cithara player. *Case 19.* Attic red-figured psykter (global vase with cylindrical support), showing Zeus enthroned on one side, and Theseus fighting the Minotaur on the other. *Case 20.* Attic red-figured krater, with hoplite running, and, on the neck, athletes, and Herakles struggling with Kyknos. *Cases 21-24.* Etruscan and Faliscan vases; silver-painted vases from Bolsena.

UPPER FLOOR. R. 11. Embossed bronze mask of Achelous, from Tarquinia; bronze plates from a triumphal chariot, with hoplites and horsemen fighting (6C); buckles.—R. 12. Ploughman at work, found at Arezzo; bronze votive statuettes.—RR. 13 and 14 contain a collection of bronzes, armour, mirrors, candelabra, and cistæ (see below). R. 15. *Glass Case 4.* *CHIGI VASE found at Formello (Veii), of exquisite workmanship and the finest extant example of the Protocorinthian style (first half of the 6C B.C.); among the subjects depicted are a lion-hunt, a hare-hunt, a troop of soldiers, and the Judgment of Paris.—R. 16. Vases.—R. 17. Terracotta masks of comic and tragic types. Fragment of a krater of Assteas, depicting a comic scene: Ajax, fleeing from Kassandra, clings to the statue of Pallas Athena.—R. 18. Sarcophagi.

The AUGUSTO CASTELLANI COLLECTION, housed in the semicircle of RR. 19-23, was amassed by Augusto Castellani, a member of a firm of goldsmiths renowned in Rome in the 18C. The rooms have a good view of the courtyard and garden of the villa. *Glass Case I.* Alabaster vases imported from Greece and Cyprus, Etruscan vases showing Oriental influence.—*Case 2.* Black- and red-figure vases, many decorated with animals.—*Case 3.* Two pitchers, one with the rape of Persephone, the other with Herakles and the dog Cerberus before Eurystheus.—*Case 4.* Black-figured Attic vases; Laconian krater decorated with lotus-flowers.—*Case 5.* Two amphoræ signed by Nikosthenes (540-510 B.C.)—*Case 6.* Group of miniature kylixes.—*Case 7.* Amphora with large handles, red and black figured.—*Case 8.* Red-figured Attic vases; pitcher with two young men and leveret.—*Case 10.* Red-figured Attic vases, and pelike showing Dionysus, Satyrs, and Mænads.—*Case 11.* Examples of Faliscan, Campanian, and Apulian ware.—*Case 12.* Ceramics from Egnatia in Apulia, white- and yellow-figured.

R. 24. Urns and sarcophagi from the Ager Faliscus. The Falisci were an Italic people akin to the Latins but much influenced by their Etruscan neighbours.—R. 25. Etrusco-Campanian *Dish with a war elephant, evidence of the impression made in Italy by the elephants of Pyrrhus. Three huge bronze shields, decorated with quadrupeds and floral motives, from Narce. Vases, mirrors, and other relics from Corchiano and Monte Sant'Angelo.

RR. 26-28 are devoted to the necropolis of Falerii Veteres (Civita Castellana).—R. 26. Cinerary urn in the form of a small house. Psykter (wine-cooler) showing the fight of the Centaurs and the Lapiths. Krater

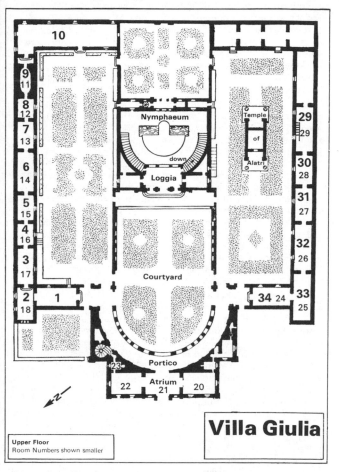

with scenes of the devastation of Troy. Oinochoe, with a battle of Amazons, and Actæon being devoured by his hounds; two similar bowls, with Dionysos and Ariadne and a Faliscan inscription (resembling Latin): 'Today I drink wine, tomorrow I shall have none'. *Amphora with volutes, showing Eos and Kephalos and Boreas and Orithyia. Large stamnos (two-handled jar) with two men feasting, a girl fluteplayer, and two young men, drunk, in the background (c. 440 B.C.);

twin stamnoi with Dionysos carrying the Thyrsos, and Eros, with a nude girl seated on a panther skin.—R. 27. Black-figured kylix with Dionysos and Maenads on the outside; red-figured kylix, with men and boys conversing, signed by Hieron. *Rhytons (drinking horns) shaped respectively like a knuckle-bone and a dog's head, masterpieces of Greek ceramic art of the first half of the 5C B.C.; the first is signed by Syriskos and the second attributed to Brygos. Large *Krater (mid-5C) with girls dancing; krater from S. Italy with Bellerophon and the Chimaera.—R. 28. Amphorae and stamnoi from Volsinium (Bolsena), painted and with floral decoration. Stamnos, with a scene from the worship of Dionysos Perikonios at Athens. Red-figured *Krater with Herakles and the Nemean lion; *Krater of the end of the 5C, with Herakles being received into Olympos.

In R. 29, on two levels, are sculptures and architectonic terracottas from temples near Falerii Vetres. To the right: part of the decoration from the *Temple of Apollo* at Lo Scasato (4C-2C), with notable antefixes of Persian Artemis and a winged genius. To the left: Decoration of the pediment and entablature from one or both temples in the neighbourhood of Sassi Caduti, and decorative cover-slab from the temple which replaced them, including a representation of flute-players.

Below are large figured terracottas which decorated the pediments of each temple. They offer striking examples of the influence of Greek sculpture, and especially good are: *Apollo; fine head of Mercury; female head. In glass cases are excellent examples of temple decoration and cult statues: antefixes with heads of Maenads, of Silenus, and part of an acroterion with two warriors, from Sassi Caduti (early 5C); portraits from the *Stipes* of the Temple at Vignale, the acropolis of Falerii Veteres; female head in peperino, crowned in bronze-leaf, from Celle; head of Zeus from Scasato.

R. 30 contains material from the *Temple of Diana at Nemi* (4C-2C B.C.), the famous sanctuary of the Golden Bough in the sacred wood beside the lake: lower portion of a cover-slab in gilded bronze, votive objects, terracotta pediment of the temple. Male head from Antemnae (late 4C).—R. 31. Coffin formed from the trunk of an oak-tree (from Gabii); Antefix with maenad's head, from Lanuvium; terracotta model, perhaps of a temple, from Velletri.—R. 32. Collection from the Tomba delle Ambre, at Satricum in the territory of the Volsci.—R. 33. ANTIQUITIES FROM PRAENESTE, comprising the *Barberini* and *Bernardini Tombs,* two important examples of the Oriental period (7C B.C.). The *BARBERINI COLLECTION was formed of objects unearthed between 1855 and 1866 from tombs in the locality of Colombella, just s. of the town of Palestrina (p. 353), which was built on the site of the ancient Praeneste. Praeneste was a flourishing centre of Latin and Volscian civilization and, as the trade and industry of Etruria and Latium were derived from the same sources, the culture here naturally had much in common with the Etruscan. This will be evident from an inspection of the exhibits displayed in this room. The Barberini Collection, acquired by the State in 1908, may be regarded (apart from certain additions) as divided into two main groups; the contents of a large tomb covered with marble slabs of the Oriental period (7C B.C.) and the contents of deep-laid tombs of the 4C-2C B.C. THE *BERNARDINI TOMB, discovered in 1876, a trench-tomb lined with tufa and covered by a tumulus, exactly corresponds with the style of the Barberini tombs and with that of the Regolini-Galassi tomb in the Vatican.

The tombs of the Oriental period yielded gold and silver articles, bronzes and ivories, in which Egyptian, Assyrian, and Greek art are mingled. Notable among the goldsmith's work: two *Pectorals, or large buckles, of gold granulated work, decorated with cats'heads, chimæras, and sphinxes; Patera in silver-gilt with Pharaoh in triumph, horses, and an Assyrian king's hunt; Caldaia, for heating or cooling water, in silver-gilt, with six serpents on the brim, and decorated with horsemen, foot-soldiers, farmers and sheep attacked by lions. Ivories: cups; lion with dead man on his back; mirror-handles (?) shaped like arms. Bronzes: conical vase-stand with fantastic animals in repoussé; throne in sheet-bronze, with ornamental bands and figures of men and animals.

The contents of the 4C-2C tombs include a full collection of bronze mirrors and CISTAE, which contained the mirrors, strigils, spatulæ and other implements for the care of the body. The cistæ are usually cylindrical, with engraved decoration in repoussé or pierced work, lids adorned with small figures, and feet and handles of cast metal. These toilet boxes were virtually peculiar to Præneste (comp. p. 353). Among them is the *CISTAE FICORONI, the largest and most beautiful yet discovered. It is named after Francesco Ficoroni who bought it and gave it to the Kircher collection (now incorporated in the Prehistoric and Ethnographic Museum; p. 259). On the body of the cista is a representation of the boxing match between Pollux and Amykos, king of the Bebryces, an elaborate design pure in its lines and evidently inspired by some large Greek composition, possibly a wall-painting contemporary with those by Mikon in the Stoa Poikile at Athens. The names of both the maker and the buyer of the cista are recorded in an archiac Latin inscription: *Novios Plautios med Romai fecid, Dindia Macolnia fileai dedit;* and it was no doubt a wedding present.

R. 34. Goldsmith's work; bronze helmet inlaid with silver, from Todi; Attic *Bowl signed by Pampheios, showing Odysseus evading Polyphemos; head from Cagli.

Beyond the Villa Giulia Viale delle Belle Arti goes on past Via Flaminia to Piazzale delle Belle Arti, close to Ponte del Risorgimento. On the left of the avenue is the red-brick church of *Sant'Eugenio* (1951), built to celebrate the 25th anniversary of the episcopal consecration of Pius XII in 1942, and, beyond it, the elegant *Palazzina of Pius IV,* attributed to Pirro Ligorio, who designed the Casina of Pius IV in the Vatican gardens. Via Flaminia leads back to Piazza del Popolo.

# 10   PIAZZA VENEZIA TO PIAZZA DI SPAGNA AND THE PINCIO

From Piazza Venezia Via Cesare Battisti (comp. p. 175) leads to the long thin Piazza dei Santi Apostoli (l.), the scene in recent years of political demonstrations. On the w. side of the piazza is *Palazzo Odescalchi,* which extends to the Corso (see p. 147); the façade on the piazza is by Bernini, with additions by Nic. Salvi and L. Vanvitelli (1750). On the E. side is the huge complex of the **Palazzo Colonna** (Pl. 4;

5) which is bounded s. by Via Quattro Novembre, E. by Via della Pilotta, and N. by Via del Vaccaro and Piazza della Pilotta. On the side facing Piazza dei Santi Apostoli the palace embraces the church of the Santi Apostoli.

The palace was built by Martin V (Oddone Colonna) and rebuilt in 1730. Here, on 4 June 1802, after the cession of Piedmont to France, Charles Emmanuel IV of Savoy, king of Sardinia, abdicated in favour of his brother Victor Emmanuel I, exchanging his royal robes for the habit of the Jesuits. Four arches spanning Via della Pilotta connect the palace with the Villa Colonna (no adm.) which has a beautiful garden (part of which can be glimpsed from the Galleria Colonna; see below). In the garden are the remains of a temple, believed to be the Temple of Serapis, built in the time of Caracalla.

The palace contains the magnificent *Galleria Colonna, begun in 1654 by Card. Girolamo I Colonna, who employed the architect Antonio Del Grande, but it was not completed till nearly fifty years later. On Del Grande's death in 1671, Girol. Fontana took over direction. In 1703 the palace was opened by Filippo II Colonna. One of the most sumptuous of the patrician houses in Rome, it is open to the public only on Saturday (9-17); adm., see p. 48. The entrance is at No. 17 Via della Pilotta.

From the entrance stairs mount to the VESTIBULE. The paintings here, of relatively minor importance, include examples of the schools of Van Dyck, Murillo, Lor. Lotto, etc.

HALL OF THE COLONNA BELLICA. A 16C column of rosso antico, surmounted by a statue of Pallas Athena, gives the room its name. Ceiling frescoes by *Gius. Chiari,* Reception into heaven of Marcantonio II Colonna. 46. *Pietro Novelli,* Isabella Colonna with her son Lorenzo Onofrio; 48. *Palma Vecchio,* Holy Family, with St Peter and donor; 51. *Van Dyck* (attrib.), Lucrezia Tomacelli Colonna; *53. *Bonifazio Veronese,* Holy Family, with SS. Jerome and Lucy; 55. *After Hieronymus Bosch,* Temptation of St Jerome; *56. *Bronzino,* Venus with Cupid and a satyr; 57. *Agost. Carracci,* Card. Pompeo Colonna; 58. *Moretto,* Portrait of a man; 59. *Dom. Tintoretto,* Adoration of the Sacrament; *60. *Scipione Pulzone,* Pius V; 62. *Dosso Dossi* (formerly attrib. to Giorgione), Giacomo Sciarra Colonna; *64. *Lor. Lotto,* Card. Pompeo Colonna; 65. *Girol. Muziano,* Vittoria Colonna, Italy's most famous poetess; 70. *Iac. Tintoretto* or *Paolo Veronese,* Narcissus; 71. *Fr. Salviati,* Venus and Cupid.—Sculpture: 61. Hercules; 67. Bacchus; 71. Head of Antinous. On the steps leading down to the Great Hall is preserved a cannon ball which fell here on 24 June 1849, during the siege of Rome.

The GREAT HALL is superbly decorated. The ceiling paintings, by *Giov. Coli* and *Fil. Gherardi,* depict incidents in the life of Marcantonio II Colonna, who commanded the papal contingent at Lépanto (1571); the central panel illustrates the battle. On the walls are four Venetian mirrors with flower paintings by *Mario de' Fiori* and *Giov. Stanghi,* and paintings of children by *Carlo Maratta.*— *Salvator Rosa,* *73. The artist as St John Baptist, 78. Preaching of St John Baptist; 75. *Iac. Bassano* (attrib.), Christ in the house of the Levite; 76. *G. F. Romanelli,* St Irene taking the arrows from St Sebastian; 79. *Tintoretto,* Double portrait; *Pier Fr. Mola,* 82. Hagar and Ishmael, 87. Rebecca at the well; 83. *Scipione Pulzone,* Family of Alfonso Gonzaga, Count of Novellara; *84. *Van Dyck* (attrib.), Carlo Colonna, duke of Marsi; *Giov. Lanfranco,* 90. Magdalen in glory, 95. St Peter delivered from prison by the angel; *91. *Nic. da Foligno (L'Alunno),* Madonna del Soccorso (the Virgin rescuing a child from a demon); 92. *Matt. Rosselli,* The fine arts; 94. *Guido Reni,* St Francis of Assisi with two angels; 96. *Enea Salmeggia,* Martyrdom of St Catherine; 97. *Guercino,* St Paul the Hermit; 99. *Aless. Allori,* Descent into hell; 100. *Sustermans* (attrib.), Federico Colonna, viceroy of Valencia; 102. *Ribera,* St Jerome; 103. *Bart. Passarotti* (formerly attrib. to Ann. Carracci), Family of Lodovico Peracchini; *104. *Rubens,* Assumption of the Virgin.—Sculptures. 97. Dancing faun; 118. Marcus Aurelius; 131. Gladiator. Fine bas-reliefs and sarcophagi fragments are set into the walls beneath the windows, and into statue pedestals.

The ROOM OF THE DESKS derives its name from two valuable *Desks displayed here. The first, in ebony, has 28 ivory bas-reliefs by Francis and Dominic Steinhard after drawings by Carlo Fontana; the central relief is a copy of Michelangelo's Last Judgment, the other 27 are copies of works by Raphael. The second desk, in sandalwood, is adorned with lapis lazuli, amethysts, and other semi-precious stones; in front are 12 small amethyst columns and at the top gilt bronze statuettes representing the Muses and Apollo seated under a laurel tree.—The ceiling frescoes, by *Seb. Ricci,* are of the battle of Lépanto. In this room is a noteworthy series of *Landscapes by *Gaspard Poussin* (105, 106, 108, 120, 128, 130, 132, 133, 134, 136, 139, 140), and a further series by *J. F. van Bloemen,* with figures by *Placido Costanzi* (109, 115, 123, 125).—*Philip Wouwermans,* 110. Stag hunt, 116. Battle scene; 112. *Claude,* Ruins of the palace of the Caesars; *114. *Nic. Poussin,* Apollo and Daphne; 117. *'Velvet' Brueghel* or *Paul Brill,* Landscape with figures; 118. *Paul Brill* (attrib.), Antigone recovering the bodies of her brothers; 121. *Lambert Zustriz,* Noli me tangere; *Salvator Rosa,* 122. Seascape, 126. The good Samaritan; 131. *Canaletto,* Venice. Sculpture, 149. *Susini,* copy in bronze of the Farnese bull; two antique fire irons in polished bronze; bronze group of a centaur and a female figure.

ROOM OF THE APOTHEOSIS OF MARTIN V. This room takes its name from the subject of the ceiling painting by *Benedetto Luti.* Above the windows, *Pietro Bianchi,* Fame crowning victory. Above the end wall, *Pompeo Batoni,* Time discovering truth.—142. *Pier Fr. Mola,* Cain and Abel; *Tintoretto,* 143, 144. Portraits; 147. *Sassoferrato* (?), Virgo purissima; 148. *Guido Reni,* St Agnes; 150. *Guercino,* The Angel Gabriel; 152. *Mabuse,* Man with clasped hands; 155. *Bronzino,* Madonna and Child with SS. John and Elizabeth; 156. *Titian* (?), Onofrio Panvinio, the Augustinian; *Fr. Salviati,* *158. Self-portrait, 166. Raising of Lazarus; 159. *Fr. Albani,* Rape of Europa; 160. *Guercino,* Tobias and the Archangel; 161. *Pietro di Giov. Spagna,* St Jerome; 162. *Iac. Tintoretto,* Spinet player; 163. *Puligo,* Madonna and Child; 164. *Bartolomeo Passarotti* (formerly attrib. to Annibale Carracci), Greedy peasant; 165. *Paris Bordone,* Holy Family with SS. Jerome and Sebastian; *170. *Paolo Veronese,* Man in Venetian costume.—Sculpture, 148. *Orfeo Buselli,* Bust of Card. Jerome I Colonna; two Roman marble busts.

The THRONE ROOM is reserved, as in other princely houses, for the Pope in the event of a visit from His Holiness; the chair is turned to the wall so that no one else shall sit in it. 199. *15C Venetian School,* Portrait of Martin V, Oddone Colonna; 196. *Scipione Pulzone,* Portrait of Marcantonio II Colonna; 197. *Pietro Novelli,* Portrait of Felice Colonna Orsini. In this room also are (198) a nautical chart presented by the Roman people to Marcantonio II and (200) a parchment diploma given him by the Roman senate after the battle of Lépanto. French clock by I. Godet of Paris.—Sculpture, 153, 154. Statuettes in bronze of a Satyr and Aphrodite; (marble busts) 151. Zeus, 152. Woman.

ROOM OF MARIA MANCINI. 201. *Fr. Cozza,* Nativity of the Virgin; 203. *Pietro da Cortona* (attrib.), Ascension, with members of the Colonna family; 206. *School of Roger van der Weyden,* Christ appearing to His Mother and St John after the Resurrection; *209. *Bart. Vivarini,* Madonna enthroned; 210. *Luca Longhi,* Madonna with St John Baptist and St Benedict; *Fr. Albani,* 212, 213. Herminia among the shepherds; *215. *Giul. Bugiardini,* Madonna; *216. *Melozzo da Forlì* (attrib.), Guidobaldo della Rovere, duke of Urbino; 217. *Iac. degli Avanzi,* Crucifixion; 227. *Lorenzo di Credi* (?), Madonna and Child; 219. *Sermoneta,* Madonna with the infant St John; *221. *Stef. da Zevio,* Madonna del Roseto; 213. *Botticelli* (workshop), Madonna and Child; *224. *Caspar Netscher,* Maria Colonna Mancini, the niece of Card. Mazarin; 225. *Simone Cantarini,* Holy Family; 226. *Rubens,* Reconciliation of Esau and Jacob; 218. *Jacopo del Sellaio,* Apostle St James; 229, 231. *Bernard van Orley,* The seven joys and seven sorrows of Mary; 230. *Inn. da Imola,* Holy Family with St Francis; 232. *Guercino,* Moses with the tables of law.—Sculpture. Two marble busts.

The church of the **Santi Apostoli** (Pl. 4; 5) was probably built by Pelagius I in 560 to commemorate the defeat and expulsion of the Goths by Narses. It was restored and enlarged in the 15C and 16C and almost completely rebuilt by Carlo and Fr. Fontana in 1702-14. It was given a neo-classical façade by Valadier in 1827. The 15C apse was covered with frescoes by Melozzo da Forlì; portions are preserved in the Quirinal (p.

177) and in the Pinacoteca of the Vatican (p. 284). From the piazza only the upper part of the church is visible, as the stately portico of nine arches, closed by a grille, is surmounted by a Baroque story giving it the appearance of a palace.

THE PORTICO, the oldest part of the church, was erected by Baccio Pontelli at the cost of Card. della Rovere, afterwards Pope Julius II. On the left, tomb of the engraver Giov. Volpato, by *Canova* (1807). On right, *Bas-relief of the 2C A.D., representing an eagle holding an oak-wreath in his claws; lion, signed by *Bassallectus.* Two Byzantine lions flank the entrance.

The Baroque INTERIOR is on a vast scale, with a nave 18 m broad. The effect of immensity is enhanced by the manner in which the lines of the vaulting continue those of the massive pillars, and the lines of the apse those of the nave. From the end near the entrance the surprising effect of relief attained by *Giov. Odazzi* in his contorted group of Fallen Angels, on the vault above the high altar, is seen to advantage. On the ceiling are the Triumph of the Order of St Francis, by *Baciccia,* and the Evangelists, by *Luigi Fontana.*—Against the second pillar of the s. aisle is a monument to Clementina Sobieska, queen of James III (comp. below), by *Fil. Valle,* and at the end of the aisle is a chapel with eight columns of the 6C church.— The main altarpiece is the Martyrdom of SS. Philip and James, by *Dom. Muratori* (1704), the largest picture in Rome. On the right, tombs of Count Giraud de Caprières (1505) and Card. Raffaele Riario, perhaps to a design by Michelangelo; on the left, the beautiful monument of Card. Pietro Riario, of the *School of And. Bregno,* with a Madonna by *Mino da Fiesole.*

In the CRYPT (in the chap. ahead to the l.), is the fine tomb by the school of And. Bregno, of Raffaele della Rovere (d. 1477), brother of Sixtus IV and father of Julius II. Foundations of the earlier church can be seen here.—North Aisle. At the E. end, *Mausoleum of Clement XIV, by *Canova;* 2nd chapel: St Joseph of Copertino, by *Gius. Cades,* between two columns of verde antico, which are the largest known.—In the Corridor beside the church (accessible also from the piazza, No. 51) are the tomb of Card. Bessarion (1389-1472), the illustrious Greek scholar, and a monument to Michelangelo, whose remains, now in Santa Croce at Florence, were originally interred here.

The little Baroque *Palazzo Balestra* (formerly *Muti*), at the end of the piazza, was presented by Clement XI to James Stuart, the Old Pretender, on his marriage in 1719. Here were born his sons Charles, the Young Pretender (1720), and Henry, Cardinal York (1725); and here died James, in 1766, and Charles, after many wanderings, in 1788.

At the N. end of Piazza dei Santi Apostoli Via del Vaccaro leads right into Piazza della Pilotta. At the E. end of the square is the large modern *Università Gregoriana Pontificia* (1930). From here the narrow Via dei Lucchesi runs N. past (r.) Via della Dataria, leading up to Piazza del Quirinale, and (l.) Via dell' Umiltà, leading to the Corso. Beyond the cross-roads the street, now called Via di San Vincenzo, continues to Piazza di Trevi, filled by the most monumental of all Rome's fountains, the *Fontana di Trevi (Pl. 4; 3).

Its waters are those of the 'Acqua Vergine', which Agrippa brought to Rome for his baths in 19 B.C., and which feed also the fountains of Piazza di Spagna, Piazza Navona, and Piazza Farnese. The aqueduct, which is nearly 20 km long, runs through the Villa Giulia. The original fountain was a simple and beautiful basin by L. B. Alberti; it was restored by Urban VIII, who is said to have obtained the necessary funds by a tax on wine. Later, Clement XII employed Nic. Salvi to construct the present grandiose erection; the design appears to have been based on a design by Bernini, and the whole was completed in 1762. The background is formed by the s. side of Palazzo Poli. Two giant Tritons, one blowing a conch, conduct the winged chariot of Neptune. In the side niches are figures of Health (r.) and Abundance (l.); the bas-reliefs above represent the Maiden of the legend from which the water took its name pointing out the spring to the Roman soldiers, and Agrippa approving the plans for the aqueduct. The four statues above these typify the Seasons with their gifts. At the summit are the arms of the Corsini family, with two allegorical figures. The water, which forms an essential part of the design, fills the little piazza with its noise. There is a tradition that the departing traveller who throws a coin into the fountain will return to Rome.

Opposite is the church of *Santi Vincenzo ed Anastasio,* rebuilt in 1630, with a Baroque façade by Martino Longhi the Younger. In the crypt of this church, the parish church of the neighbouring pontifical palace of the Quirinal, are preserved the hearts and lungs of almost all the popes from Sixtus V (1590) to Leo XIII (1903).

From Piazza di Trevi Via delle Muratte leads w. to the Corso. In Via della Stamperia, which runs N. to the right of the fountain, is the **Calcografia Nazionale** or *Calcografia di Roma,* the most important collection of copper-plate engravings in the world. Adm., see p. 47.

The collection was formed in 1738 by Clement XII and moved in 1837 to its present site; the building is by Valadier. It contains almost all the engravings of G. B. Piranesi (1432 plates) and examples of the work of Marcantonio Raimondi, Rossini, Pinelli, and many others. It has a total of more than 19,600 plates. Exhibitions are often held, and any items not on display can be seen on request.

The street opens out into Piazza dell'Accademia di San Luca. Here is *Palazzo Carpegna,* seat of the **Accademia di San Luca,** moved from the neighbourhood of the Roman Forum when Via dei Fori Imperiali was built. The academy, founded in 1577 by the painter Girol. Muziano of Brescia, incorporated the 15C Università dei Pittori whose members used to forgather in the little church of San Luca. Muziano's successor, Fed. Zuccari, gave the academy its first statutes, and it soon became famous for its teaching and for its prize competitions. The eclectic **\*Galleria dell' Accademia di San Luca** is formed of gifts and bequests from its members, together with donations from other sources. Adm., see p. 47.

The collection is arranged on the third floor (lift).

ROOM I. 1. *Baciccia,* \*Portrait of Clement IX; 2. *Girolamo* and *Giov. Battista Bassano,* Shepherds and sheep; 3. *Pier. Fr. Mola,* Spinster; 4. *Titian* (attrib.), St Jerome; 6. *Raphael,* \*Child, fragment of a fresco (1512); 8. *Iac. Bassano,* Annunciation to the shepherds; 9. *Marcello Venusti,* Deposition; 10. Presumed mask of Michelangelo; 12. *Carletto Caliari,* Venus with a mirror; 15. *Seb. Conca,* La Vigilanza; 14. *Carlo Maratta,* Death of Sisera; 15. *Poussin* (copy of Titian), Triumph of Bacchus; 16. *Titian* (attrib.), Portrait of Marino Cornaro.

R. II. Donation of Baron Michele Lazzaroni. 1. *Paris Bordone,* Seduction; 2. *Titian* (attrib.), \*Portrait of Ippolito Rimanaldo; 3. *G. B. Piazzetta,* Judith and Holofernes; *Cavalier d'Arpino,* 6. Perseus and Andromeda, 17. Taking of Christ; 7. *School of Matt. di Giovanni,* Madonna and Child with St Catherine; 8. *Fed. Barocci,* Rest during the flight into Egypt; 9. *School of Lorenzo di Credi,* Annunciation; 10. *Baciccia,* Madonna and Child; 11. *Florentine school of 15C,* Madonna and Child; 12. *Flemish school of 17C,* Portrait of a woman; 23. *Fed. Zuccari,* \*Self-portrait; 15. *Bronzino,* Portrait of a woman; 16. *Francesco di Giorgio Martini,* Madonna and Child.

R. III. Works of the 18C and 19C. *Dom. Pellegrini,* 1. Augustus Frederick, duke of Sussex, 2. Self-portrait, 3. Hebe; *Gius. Grassi,* 8, 18. Portraits of the architect Henry Wood and of Vinc. Camuccini; 9. *Mme. Brossard de Beaulieu,* Niobe; 12. *Angelica Kauffmann,* Hope; 14. *Anton Wiertz,* Portrait of the architect Angelo Uggeri; 17. *Mme. Vigée le Brun,* \*Self-portrait; *Alessandro d'Este* (?), Bust of Canova.

R. IV. 3. *Michiel Sweerts,* Jacob's Dream; 5. *Nicholas Berchem,* Cattle and shepherds in the Roman Campagna; *P. van Bloemen,* 6. Cattle scene, 8. Horses; 9. *Sweerts,* Genre scene; 13. *Giov. van Bloemen,* Pastoral scene.—Terracottas. *Vinc. Pacetti,* Achilles an Penthesilea; *Manuel Olive,* Creusa and Aeneas.—*Sweerts,* 14. Interior scene, 15. Drinker, 16. Genre scene, 18. Woman combing her hair; 19. *Giov. van Bloemen,* Pastoral scene.

R. V. 3. *Guido Cagnacci,* Tarquin and Lucretia; 4. *Canaletto,* Architectural perspective; *Giov. Paolo Pannini,* 6, 10. Landscapes with Roman ruins; 8. *Van Dyck,* \*Madonna and Child with angels; 9. *Rubens,* Nymphs crowning Abundance; 11. *John Parker,* Landscape; 12. *Jan Asselijn,* Roman Campagna; 13.

*Palma Giovane,* Susanna; 14. *Philip Wouwermans,* White horse; 15. *Jan van Mytens,* Admiral Neewszom Kostenaer; 16. *Salvator Rosa* (?), Study of cats' heads; 19. *Philip Peter Roos (Rosa da Tivoli),* Shepherd and animals; 21. *Van Dyck,* Madonna and Angels (drawing for No. 8, see above).

R. VI. (GALLERY). *Fr. Trevisani,* Scourging of Christ, St. Francis; *Bened. Luti,* Mary Magdalene at the feet of Christ, *Self-portrait; *Anton von Maron,* Portraits of academicians Raphael Mengs, Teresa Mengs von Maron, Vincenzo Pacetti, Caterina Cherubini Preciado, Thomas Jenkins; 37. *G. B. Canevari,* James II as a child, partial copy of Van Dyck's portrait of the children of Charles I in the Galleria Sabauda in Turin; *And. Locatelli,* 46, 45. Two genre scenes, 48, 53. Two landscapes; 52. *Guercino,* Venus and Cupid (detached fresco); 51. *Claude Joseph Vernet,* *Seascape; *Gasp. Vanvitelli,* 57. View of Tivoli, 56. Porto di Ripa Grande.—Sculpture. 50. *Clodion* (?; formerly attrib. to Bernini), *Bust of a young girl; *Canova,* 6. Self-portrait; 16. Bust of Napoleon; 1. *Tribolo,* Allegorical figure of a river (terracotta).

R. VII. 2. *Seb. Conca,* Marriage of St Catherine; 3. *Baciccia,* Sketch for the Birth of St John Baptist in Santa Maria in Campitelli; 8. *Sassoferrato,* Madonna and Child; 14. *Conca* (?), St Cecilia; 5. *Batoni,* Madonna and sleeping Child, 10. Nativity; 11. *Ribera,* *St Jerome and the Sadducees; 12. *J. F. de Troy,* Faustulus finding Romulus and Remus; 16. *Guido Reni,* L'Addolorata; 18. *Ciro Ferri,* Martyrdom of St Luke.

R. VIII. Terracottas from prize competitions held in the 18C. *Pierre Legros the Younger,* The arts paying homage to Clement XI; *Michelangelo Slodtz,* St Theresa transfixed by an angel.

STAIRCASE. *Aristide Sartorio,* Monte Circeo; *Fr. Hayez,* Il Vincitore; *Pietro da Cortona,* Copy of Raphael's Galatea; *Guido Reni,* Fortune, Bacchus and Ariadne; *Pietro Bracci,* Sketch in terracotta.

GROUND FLOOR. RR. IX and X. Paintings and sculpture by 20C academicians, donated by the artist or his family, including works by: Giorgio Morandi, Fausto Pirandello, Felice Casorati, and Emilio Greco.

The SALE ACCADEMICHE are no longer open to the public, except on St Luke's Day (18 Oct). They contain more important works from 15C to the present day.

Just N. of the Accademia is the busy VIA DEL TRITONE. This street ascends gradually from Largo Chigi in the Corso, to Piazza Barberini. Half-way is *Largo del Tritone,* entered from the N. by Via Francesco Crispi and Via Due Macelli. On the S. side Via del Traforo leads to the *Traforo Umberto I* (Pl. 4; 3), a tunnel under the Quirinal Gardens to Via Nazionale (p. 189). This tunnel, 347 m long, was built in 1902-5.

On the N. side of Via del Tritone, Largo del Tritone, is the narrow and animated Via Due Macelli, which runs N.W. In the first street to the left, Via Capo le Case, is the church of *Sant' Andrea delle Fratte,* which belonged to the Scots before the Reformation. Here in 1678 Aless. Scarlatti was married.

The rugged (unfinished) tower, and refined fantastical campanile, both by *Borromini,* were designed to make their greatest impression when seen from Via Capo le Case.

INTERIOR. In the 2nd chapel on the right is the tomb of Miss Falconet (1856), with a recumbent figure by the American artist *Harriet Hossmer.* In the vestibule of the side door is the tomb of Angelica Kauffmann (1741-1807). By the high altar are two *Angels by *Bernini,* intended for the adornment of the Ponte Sant'Angelo but replaced on the bridge by copies.

Via Due Macelli leads into the long and irregular **Piazza di Spagna** (Pl. 4; 1) favoured by visitors and at one time the centre of the English colony. Keats died in the square; the British consul formerly had his office here; and there is a well-known English tea-room. In the neighbouring Via del Babuino is the English church. The piazza takes its name from the *Palazzo di Spagna,* residence of the Spanish ambassador to the Vatican; the architect was Ant. del Grande (1647). At the point of emergence of Via Due Macelli is the *Collegio di Propaganda Fide,* with a façade in Via di Propaganda by Borromini (1662). The detailed friezes are particularly fine. The college, which has the privilege of extraterritoriality, was founded for the training of missionaries (including young foreigners) by Urban VIII as an annex to the Congregazione di Propaganda Fide established by Gregory XV in 1622. In the middle of the s. section of the piazza rises the *Column of the Immaculate Conception* (1857), commemorating the establishment by Pius IX in 1854 of the dogma of the Immaculate Conception of the Virgin Mary. On the E. side is the small Piazzetta Mignanelli.

In the narrow centre of the piazza is the *Fontana della Barcaccia,* the masterpiece of Pietro Bernini, father of a more famous son. The design (a leaking boat) is well adapted to the low water pressure of the fountain. On the right rises the scenographic *\*Scalinata della Trinità del Monti,* a famous flight of 137 steps built in 1721-25 by Aless. Specchi and Fr. De Sanctis. It is known by the English as the *Spanish Steps.* The double flight converges on a landing, and then separates, to converge again at the top. The steps used to be a haunt of artists' models. Every day there is a gorgeous display of flowers for sale at the foot, and the steps are covered with magnificent tubs of azalias at the beginning of May.

On the right looking up, is the **House of John Keats** (tablet), in which the poet died on 23 Feb 1821. He is buried in the Protestant Cemetery (p. 92). The house is now a Keats-Shelley memorial and museum (adm., see p. 49), with a library, and relics of Keats, Shelley, Byron, and Leigh Hunt.—The wide N. section of the piazza is adorned with tall palm trees.

The fashionable streets leading out of the w. side of Piazza di Spagna are all pedestrian precincts and lined with elegant shops. In Via Condotti, named after the conduits of the Acqua Vergine (p. 170), is the famous *Caffè Greco,* once the resort of almost every notable foreigner in Rome, and since 1953 a national monument. It is decorated with personal mementoes, self-portraits, etc. of its famous patrons. Farther down is the 17C palace of the Grand Master of the order of the Knights of St John of Jerusalem. At the N.W. end of the piazza Via della Croce leads to Via Bocca di Leone in which (r.), at the corner of Vicolo del Lupo, was the Brownings' Roman residence. Via del Babuino passes other streets in which many artists still have their studios, and ends at Piazza del Popolo (p. 153). This street also has many attractive shops. On the left, half-way, is the Gothic English church of **All Saints** (Pl. 3; 2), by G. E. Street (comp. p. 189). On the right, near Vicolo Alibert, was the studio of which Thorvaldsen succeeded Flaxman as occupant; and parallel on this side, is Via Margutta, Rome's 'street of artists' and, more recently, Rome's 'Carnaby street', with studios, art galleries, and shops.

The steps of the 'Scalinata' mount to *Piazza della Trinità dei Monti.* From the balustrade at the top there is a famous view of Rome. In the centre of the square is an *Obelisk,* probably brought to Rome in the 2C or 3C A.D., when the hieroglyphs were incised (copied from those on the obelisk in Piazza del Popolo), and set up here in 1788 by Pius VI. Dominating the terrace is the church of the **Trinità dei Monti** (Pl. 4; 1), attached to the French Convent of the Minims, begun in 1493 by Louis XII. It was restored after damage caused by Napoleon's occupation by F. Mazois in 1816 at the expense of Louis XVIII.

The INTERIOR (when closed, ring at the door of the small side staircase on the left) is divided by a grille into two parts, only one of which may ordinarily be visited. South side. 3rd chap., \*Assumption, by *Daniele da Volterra,* the best pupil of Michelangelo, whose likeness is seen in the last figure on the right of the picture, which has a remarkable design. The whole chapel is decorated to his design by pupils; 2nd chap., North side, \*Descent from the Cross, an especially fine work (although very damaged) by the same painter, possibly executed from a design by his master.—The other part of the church contains \*Frescoes by *Perin del Vaga,*

*Giulio Romano* and others, in finely decorated chapels. The 4th chap. on l. (N. transept) has the Assumption and Death of the Virgin by *Taddeo Zuccari*, finished by his brother *Federico*. The vault is painted by *Perin del Vaga*. In another chap.: Massacre of the Innocents, by *Alberti*.

From Piazza della Trinità dei Monti *Via Sistina* descends S.E. to Piazza Barberini (p. 180). In this street most of the illustrious visitors to Rome between the days of Napoleon and 1870 seem to have lodged. Nikolai Gogol (1809-52), the Russian writer, lived at No. 126; No. 48 housed in succession G. B. Piranesi, the engraver (1720-78), Bertel Thorvaldsen, the Danish sculptor (1770-1844), and Luigi Canina, the architect and archæologist (1795-1856).

Viale della Trinità dei Monti leads N. along the edge of the hill. On the right is the **Villa Medici** (Pl. 4; 1), now officially the *Académie Nationale de France*. Here French students who win the Prix de Rome at the École des Beaux-Arts in Paris for painting, sculpture, architecture, engraving, or music are sent to study for three years at the expense of their Government. The grounds are open to the public, on two days in the week for limited periods (adm., see p. 50); important exhibitions are held in the Villa.

The palace, built by Annibale Lippi for Card. Ricci da Montepulciano, c. 1540, was bought by Card. Aless. de' Medici in 1605, and afterwards sold to Leo XI, from whom it was inherited by the Grand Dukes of Tuscany. In 1801 it was bought by Napoleon and the French Academy, founded in 1666 by Louis XIV, was transferred here in 1803. Velazquez was a tenant in 1630; Galileo was confined here by the Inquisition from 1630 to 1633. The outer façade is bare, but the inner, or garden front, in the design of which Lippi is supposed to have been aided by Michelangelo, has both grace and grandeur. Fragments of the *Ara Pietatis* (see p. 150) are incorporated into the façade.

The **Garden** (16C) is beautiful, with long vistas through hedged walks, and fine views over Rome. The formal garden has several fountains and fragments of ancient sculpture, including the head of Meleagar, by Skopas.

The *Fountain among the ilexes in front of the Villa Medici dates from 1587.

It comprises an antique red granite vase, and a cannon ball said to have been shot from Castel Sant'Angelo by Queen Christina of Sweden, when late for an appointment with the painter Charles Errard who was staying at the French Academy.

The gently sloping Viale della Trinità dei Monti ends in an open space, in which is a work by Ercole Rosa (1883), a *Monument to the Brothers Cairoli,* who fell at Villa Glori (p. 257) in Oct 1867 in an attempt to rouse the people against the papal government. From this point Viale Gabriele d'Annunzio descends to Piazza del Popolo while Viale Mickiewicz ascends to the Pincio.

The *Pincio (46 m; Pl. 3; 2) was laid out as a park by Giuseppe Valadier in 1809-14 on the Pincian Hill. The first and most magnificent of the monumental gardens of ancient Rome, this was part of the site of the villa of L. Licinius Lucullus, which was built after 63 B.C. The only remains so far found of this vast edifice lie under the Biblioteca Hertziana in Via Gregoriana. Here, in the same villa, later the property of Valerius Asiaticus, Messalina, the third wife of the Emperor Claudius, murdered its owner. In the 4C it was owned by the Pinci, from whom its present name is derived. Adjoining the Villa Borghese (p. 155), it forms the largest public garden in the centre of Rome and it is especially crowded on holidays. Miss Thackeray (Lady Ritchie), the novelist's novelist daughter, remarked that on Sunday afternoons it was a fashionable halo of sunset and pink parasols.

Viale Mickiewicz opens out into the wide *Piazzale Napoleone.* The *View from its terrace is renowned at sunset: the domes, columns, and obelisks of Rome are silhouetted against the sky, and the great cupola of St Peter's dominates the scene.

Piazzale Napoleone may be reached also by a fairly steep broad path which rises from the right-hand (N.E.) side of Viale della Tinità dei Monti near the Cairoli monument. At the top of the path is a terrace on which is the *Casina Valadier* (1817-20), a fashionable restaurant and open-air café. Among the habitués of its most sumptuous period have been Richard Strauss, Mussolini, Farouk, Gandhi, and Chaing Kai-Shek. The view from its terrace is even better than that from Piazzale Napoleone, into which the pathway leads.

The park is intersected by broad avenues passing between magnificent trees, many of them remarkable specimens of their kind. One of these avenues, Viale dell'Obelisco, runs E. to join Viale delle Magnolie in the Villa Borghese (see p. 155). The obelisk which gives the avenue its name was placed in it in 1822; it was originally erected by Hadrian on the tomb of his favourite Antinous, the location of which is unsure, possibly Via Labicana. Throughout the park are busts of celebrated Italians from the days of ancient Rome to the present time. Of the fountains, the most noteworthy are the Water Clock, in Viale dell'Orologio, and the Fountain of Moses, reached thence by a subsidiary walk.

The Pincio is bounded on the N. and E. by massive walls, which define its limits by a right angle. Part of these walls is the *Muro Torto,* or *Murus Ruptus,* the only portion of Aurelian's wall that was not fortified by Belisarius against the Goths. The wall has for centuries seemed on the point of collapsing. When Belisarius proposed to fortify it, the Romans prevented him, saying that it would be defended by St Peter. Viale del Muro Torto, at the foot of the Pincio, is an important thoroughfare running outside the wall from Piazzale Flaminio to Porta Pinciana.

# 11   THE QUIRINAL AND THE QUARTERS N. AND N.E.

From Piazza Venezia Via Cesare Battisti leads E. This short street, named after the hero of Trent hanged by the Austrians in 1916, passes on the right Palazzo delle Assicurazioni Generali (p. 55) and *Palazzo Valentini* (1585), now the seat of the Prefecture, in the court of which are antique statues. Opposite this building is *Piazza Santi Apostoli,* with Palazzo Colonna (see Rte 10).

At this point begins Via Quattro Novembre, a street which makes two right angles in its short course. As far as the first bend the left-hand side is bounded by Palazzo Colonna; the picturesque Via della Pilotta (l.) passes under the arches joining the palazzo to its garden of tall cypresses. On the right is the *Waldensian Church.* The street now makes its first turn, to the right. The tower (r.) is the *Torre Colonna,* relic of a medieval fortress. Via Quattro Novembre now makes its second turn, to the left, and beyond steps down (r.) to the Forum of Trajan (p. 136), passes (r.) the entrance to the Markets of Trajan (p. 137), and ends at Largo Magnanàpoli (Pl. 4; 5). In the centre of the square is a little group of palm trees, with some remains of the *Servian Wall* (p. 18); in the ancient *Palazzo Antonelli* (No. 158; recently restored) are other remains in several rooms off the courtyard, including an arch for a catapult. On the right, behind the church of *Santa Caterina da Siena,* with a good Baroque interior, rises the conspicuous Torre delle Milizie, described on p. 137.

At the beginning of Via Panisperna, high up on the right, is the church of **Santi Domenico e Sisto,** reached by a fine staircase (1654) by *Vincenzo della Greca.* Inside is a huge scenographic fresco (1674-75) by the Bolognese, *Domenico Canuti,* and in the 1st chap. on the r. a sculpture group (Noli me tangere) by *Ant. Raggi.*

On the other side of Largo Magnanàpoli is the beginning of Via Nazionale (Rte 12). To the N. Via Ventiquattro Maggio goes up to the Quirinal. This street, formerly Via Quirinale, was renamed to commemorate the day on which in 1915 Italy declared war on Austria. Near the beginning, on the left, is the church of SAN SILVESTRO AL QUIRINALE (rebuilt 1524), from which the cardinals used to march in procession to shut themselves in the Quirinal when a conclave was held in summer. In one of the neighbouring houses the poetess Vittoria Colonna held intellectual converse with Michelangelo and others.

INTERIOR (reached by stairs through a door to the left of the façade). The plan is a Latin cross; the entrance is in the left transept. In the nave, the 1st chapel on l. has Della Robbian pavement tiles, and two fine landscapes by *Maturino* and *Polidoro da Caravaggio*, who also painted the St Catherine and Mary Magdalene flanking the altar. In the vault, frescoes by *Cavalier d'Arpino*.—2nd chap. on l. *Marcello Venusti,* Nativity.—In the chap. opposite, *Geminiani Gemignani,* Pius V and Card. Alessandrino, with, in the centre, a 13C Madonna and Child by a Roman artist.—The domed Bandini chapel at the end of the l. transept contains tondi by *Domenichino,* and statues of Mary Magdalene and St John the Evangelist by *Aless. Algardi* (1628; probably his first Roman commission). The altarpiece of the Ascension is by *Scipione Pulzone.*

The street ascends between two of the most attractive of Rome's princely residences. On the left is the entrance to the *Villa Colonna,* the garden dependency of the Palazzo Colonna (p. 175); on the right (behind a high wall), on the site of the *Baths of Constantine,* is **Palazzo Rospigliosi** (Pl. 4; 5), built by Card. Scipio Borghese in 1603. It later passed to Card. Mazarin, who employed Carlo Maderna to enlarge it. The *Galleria Pallavicini* on the first floor contains some important paintings (no adm.).

In the dependent **Casino Rospigliosi Pallavicini** (open on the 1st of each month, 10–12, 15–17) is *Guido Reni's* celebrated *Fresco of Aurora scattering flowers before the chariot of the Sun, which is escorted by the Hours; a work remarkable in Rome for its classical restraint and fine colouring.

At the top is the spacious and dignified PIAZZA DEL QUIRINALE, with its two palaces: the Quirinal in front, and Palazzo della Consulta, to the right. The balustrade on the w. side, overlooking Via della Dataria, commands a view across roof-tops to the dome of St Peter's in the distance.

The piazza occupies the summit of the **Quirinal** (61 m), the highest of the Seven Hills. It received its name from a Temple of Quirinus, or from *Cures,* an ancient Sabine town N.E. of Rome from which, according to legend, the Sabines under their king Tatius settled on the hill. The name of Quirinus was a title of Romulus, after he had been deified; the festival in his honour was called *Quirinalia.*

In the middle of the square, on a high pedestal, flanking an obelisk (see below), are two colossal groups of the **Dioscuri** (Castor and Pollux), standing by their horses. Their height is over 5½ m. They are Roman copies, dating from the Imperial era, of Greek originals of the 5C B.C.

The two groups were found near by in the Baths of Constantine and placed here by Dom. Fontana under Sixtus V (1585–90), who was responsible for the recutting of the false inscriptions on the bases, 'Opus Phidiæ' and 'Opus Praxitelis', which probably date from c. A.D. 450. At one time the statues were supposed to represent horse-tamers and they were so called for a long time; from this ascription the square received its alternative name of *Monte Cavallo.*—The obelisk (shaft 14½ m), originally in front of the Mausoleum of Augustus, was brought here by Pius VI in 1786; Pius VII added the great basin (now a fountain) of dark grey granite, till then used as a cattle-trough in the Roman Forum.

At the corner of Via Ventiquattro Maggio, where Via della Dataria begins, is a part of the *Scuderie Pontificie,* or Papal Stables, built in 1722. The **Palazzo della Consulta,** the seat of the supreme court of the Papal States (Santa Consulta) and later of the Italian Ministry of Foreign Affairs, is now the seat of the Corte Costituzionale, a supreme court for matters concerning the constitution. The façade is by Ferd. Fuga (1739).

The stately front of the **Palazzo del Quirinale** (Pl. 4; 5, 3), the official residence of the President of the Republic since 1947, projects into the piazza, while its flank, known as the 'manica lunga' ('long sleeve'), is in Via del Quirinale. The palace was begun in 1574 by Flaminio Ponzio and Ottavio Mascherino, under Gregory XIII, on the site of a villa belonging to Card. d'Este, and was continued by Dom. Fontana, Carlo Maderno, Bernini (who worked on the 'manica lunga'), and Fuga, being completed in the time of Clement XII (1730-40). The principal entrance is by Maderna; the tower on the left of it was added in the time of Urban VIII.

The Quirinal was the habitual summer palace of the popes. Sixtus V died here in 1590; many official ceremonies have taken place and occasional concaves (p. 262) have been held in it. From this palace Pius VII issued as the prisoner of Napoleon, and from its balcony Pius IX blessed Italy at the beginning of his pontificate. From 1870 to 1947 it was the royal residence. Victor Emmanuel II died here on 9 Jan 1878.

INTERIOR (admission only by appointment after written application). The guided tour takes over an hour, but the most important work can be seen at the start of the tour, half-way up the grand staircase. This is *Melozzo da Forlì*'s magnificent *Fresco of Christ in Glory, with angels, formerly in the church of the Santi Apostoli. At the top of the stairs is the SALA REGIA, decorated in 1616-17, with a frieze designed by Agostino Tassi and executed by *Lanfranco* and *Saraceni.* This and the adjoining CAPPELLA PAOLINA are by *Carlo Maderna.* The chapel has fine stucco decoration by *Martino Ferabosco.*

Visitors are now shown through a series of lavishly decorated rooms, containing works of lesser importance, the exceptions being the CAPPELLA DELL'ANNUNCIATA and the GALLERY of Alexander VII. The chapel was decorated between 1609-12, under the direction of *Guido Reni* (who executed the scenes of the life of the Madonna and the prophets, in the pendentives), by *Lanfranco, Francesco Albani,* and *Antonio Carracci.*—The GALLERY has frescoes carried out under the direction of *Pietro da Cortona* (1656-57) by *Grimaldi, Lazzaro Baldi, Ciro Ferri, Mola* (Joseph and his brothers, which is considered his most successful fresco), *Maratta, Gaspare Dughet, Ant. Carracci* and others.—The extensive garden, designed by Mascherino, is not open to the public.

Via del Quirinale skirts the 'manica lunga' (see above) of the palace. On the right, beyond a public garden with an equestrian statue of Charles Albert by Romanelli (1900) rises the church of **\*Sant'Andrea al Quirinale,** a masterpiece by *Bernini* (1678). The simple façade of a single order balances the fine domed elliptical interior, decorated with gilding and stucco. Cherubim look down from the lantern.

The high altarpiece of the Crucifixion of St Andrew is by *Borgognone* and is surmounted by a splendid group of angels and cherubim sculpted by *Raggi.* The fine 17C altarpieces include works by *Baciccia, Giacinto Brandi,* and *Carlo Maratta.* The Sacristy has a pretty frescoed ceiling by *Giovanni De La Borde* (approved by Bernini). The lavabo here is attrib. to *Bernini.*

Beyond, on the right, is another small oval church, **\*San Carlo alle Quattro Fontane** (*San Carlino*), a masterpiece by *Borromini* offering a strong contrast to the former church by Bernini. The tall curving façade (1665-68) is well adapted to the difficult site on the corner of a narrow street.

The INTERIOR (1638; if closed ring at door of the convent, r.) has convex and concave surfaces in a complicated design using triangles (from the theme of the Trinity) in a unifying scheme. In the fine chapel to the l. of the altar: Rest on the flight into Egypt, attrib. to *Ann. Carracci* or *G. F. Romanelli.*

The small \*CLOISTER which can be entered from the church is also designed by Borromini. From here is the entrance to the \*CRYPT, recently restored (and temporarily closed), designed in a fantastical play of curves linked by a heavy continuous cornice. It is thought Borromini intended this as the place of his own burial.

At this point Via del Quirinale ends at the carfax known as the **Quattro Fontane** (Pl. 4; 4), with its four vistas ending in Porta Pia and the obelisks of the Quirinal, Pincio, and Esquiline, typical of the Rome of Sixtus V. The four small fountains (whence the name), dating from 1593, typify Fidelity, Strength, the Nile, and the Tiber. Via delle Quattro Fontane leads right to Via Nazionale and left to Piazza Barberini.

Via Venti Settembre leads straight on, beyond the cross-roads, past *Palazzo del Drago,* by Fontana (1600), and the large *Ministry of Defence,* to Piazza San Bernardo (p. 181), where this route is rejoined after a detour to the N.W. At No. 7 in this street, on the left, is the Scottish presbyterian church of *St Andrew,* with a war memorial (1949) to the London Scottish.

To the left Via delle Quattro Fontane descends all the way to Piazza Barberini. Half-way down, on the right, is \***Palazzo Barberini** (Pl. 4; 3), one of the grandest palaces in Rome. It was begun by Carlo Maderna for Urban VIII in 1624. The windows of the top story, the stairs, and some doorways were clearly executed from a design by *Borromini.* The central block is attributed to *Bernini.* The garden flanks one side of the street and the iron grille, by *Azzurri,* deserves especial notice. In 1949 the palace became the property of the State, and now houses the **Galleria Nazionale.** This is part of the NATIONAL GALLERY OF ANCIENT ART, which is divided into two sections. Here are paintings of the 13-16C. Adm., see p. 47. The other section is in Palazzo Corsini. The two collections are undergoing re-arrangement.

After the State had purchased the Palazzo Corsini (p. 240) with the picture-gallery of Card. Neri-Corsini, it was presented with the collections of Prince Tommaso Corsini and later acquired the Torlonia and other collections. The combined collections, opened to the public in 1895, are pre-eminent in Italian Baroque painting; there are also some good examples of the 15-16C, and a large selection of foreign works.

A door on the left beneath the portico leads into the palace. Stairs mount to the first floor.

ROOM I (left). *Giov. da Rimini* and *Giov. Baronzio,* two paintings of scenes in the life of Christ; *Bonaventura Berlinghieri,* Crucifixion; *Nic. di Pietro,* Apostles, Coronation of Mary; *Michele Giambono,* Madonna and Child; *13C Tuscan School,* Crucifixion; *Simone Martini* (?), Madonna and Child; *Maestro dell' Incoronazione dell'Urbino,* Birth of St John the Baptist.

R. II. *Fra Angelico,* \*Triptych (Last Judgment, Ascension, Pentecost); *Piero di Cosimo,* \*St Mary Magdalene; *Filippo Lippi,* \*Annunciation and donors, Madonna and Child.

R. III. *Perugino,* St Nicholas of Tolentino (late work); *Antoniazzo Romano,* \*St Sebastian and donors; *Niccolò l'Alunno,* Madonna and Child, with Saints; *Antoniazzo Romano,* Madonna and Child with SS. Paul and Francis.

R. IV. *Giac. Francia,* Pietà; *Lor. Lotto,* Portrait of a young man,

Madonna with Child and saints; *Anon. 15C,* SS. Sebastian and Catherine, a peculiar work, perhaps from southern Italy; *Fr. Bianchi-Ferrari,* Agony in the garden; *Fr. Francia,* St George and the dragon; *Bart. Veneto,* *Portrait of a Nobleman; *And. Solario,* Lute player. Beyond the hall is R. VI. *Baldassare Peruzzi,* Bust of Ceres; *Dom. Beccafumi,* Madonna and Child with St John; *Sodoma,* Rape of the Sabines (youthful work; front of a cassone), Marriage of St Catherine, The three Fates.

R. VII. On the ceiling, Divine Providence, by *And. Sacchi.—And. del Sarto,* Madonna, Holy Family; *Tom. di Stefano,* Madonna and Child with St John; *Sermoneta,* Francesco II Colonna; *Bronzino,* Stef. Sciarra-Colonna; *Fr. Foschi,* Portrait of a young man; *Fra Bartolomeo,* Holy Family with St John; *Franciabigio,* Portrait. The Chapel (sometimes closed) contains frescoes of New Testament scenes by *Pietro da Cortona* and *Giov. Fr. Romanelli.*—R. VIII. *Raphael,* *La Fornarina; *Scipione Pulzone,* Cardinals Ricci and Savelli; *Fed. Zuccari,* Portrait of a gentleman; *Ventura Salimbeni,* Martyrdoms of SS. Peter and Paul; *Marcello Venusti,* Madonna of Silence; *Master of the Madonna of Manchester,* Pietà; *Venusti,* Agony in the Garden, Annunciation; *Fed. Barocci,* Self-portrait, Madonna and Child; *Giulio Romano,* Madonna and Child.

R. IX. *El Greco,* *Nativity, *Baptism of Christ; *Iac. Tintoretto,* Woman taken in adultery; *Titian,* Philip II; *Dom. Tintoretto,* St Jerome.—R. X. *Titian and pupils,* Venus and Adonis; *Luca Cambiaso,* Death of Adonis; *Iac. Bassano,* Adoration of the shepherds.—R. XI. *Garófalo,* The vestal Claudia, St Cecilia, Picus transformed into a woodpecker; *Girol. da Carpi,* Portrait of a gentleman; *Nic. dell'Abate,* Portrait of a young man; *Scarsellino,* Raising of Lazarus, Noli me tangere, Agony in the Garden, Pietà; *Bart. Passarotti,* Whistler (being restored in 1978), Fish-market, Meat-market.

R. XII. *Quinten Massys,* *Erasmus; *Hans Hoffmann,* Hare; *Simone Marmion,* Crucifixion; *16C Dutch School,* Old Woman; *Master of the Death of Mary* (? *Joos van Cleve*), *Bern. Clesio, prince-bishop of Trent; *Hans Maler,* Portrait of Wolfgang Tanvelder.—R. XIII. *Holbein,* *Henry VIII; *Marten van Heemskerk,* Deposition; *J. Heintz,* Diana and Actaeon; *15C Westphalian School,* Adoration of the Magi, Circumcision; *Jan Massys,* Judith.

R. XIV contains 18C French paintings. *Louis Bailly,* Fête du grandpère; *F. Boucher,* Mill, Petite Jardinière, Farmhouse scene; *Hubert Robert,* Maison Carrée de Nîmes, Fontaine Monumentale, Le Débarcadère, Grand Canal.—R. XV. *Greuze,* Girl with scarf; *N. Lancret,* Le Faucon, Family group, Rendezvous; *Fragonard,* Annette et Lubin; *A. Le Nain,* Petits Chanteurs; *Bern. Bellotto,* Place de Dresde; *F. Guardi,* Landscape and ruin, Venice.—If an exhibition is being held in the Salone and adjoining rooms, it is necessary to retrace ones steps to the entrance, and enter the rooms described below to the left.

R. XVI. Works by *Vouet, Valentin, Manfredi, Carlo Saraceni,* and *Caravaggio* (Judith).

On the left of the entrance hall is the SALONE. Here, on the ceiling, is *THE TRIUMPH OF DIVINE PROVIDENCE, by *Pietro da Cortona,* his main work, painted between 1633 and 1639 to celebrate the glory of the Papacy and the Barberini family. It is a *tour de force,* particularly in the organization of the space, and the reduction of the composition into the angles. On the walls are hung cartoons of the school of Pietro da Cortona, showing scenes from the life of Urban VIII.

Other rooms (usually closed) contain the exceptionally valuable *Numismatic Collection,* made by Victor Emmanuel III.

On the SECOND FLOOR (temporarily closed during re-arrangement) are five rooms containing the DUSMET COLLECTION which was left to the State in 1949.—R. I. 16C majolica from Asia Minor.—R. II. 17-18C Chinese porcelain, and a Tien Lungli vase; 16C Flemish tapestries. R. III. *Neri di Bicci* (attrib.), Death of the Virgin, Madonna and Child (tabernacle); *14C Sienese school,* Diptych of San Vescovo and San Monaco; *14C artist from the Marches,* Bishop Saint.—R. IV. Terracotta works: *Leone Leoni,* Deposition; *Francavilla,* statuettes of Moses and Aaron; *16C Florentine school,* Pietà; *Susini,* Christ in the Garden.—R. V. 16C Flemish tapestries. *Guercino* (attrib.), Visitation of St Julian; *Ann. Carracci,* Self-portrait; *Lor. Costa,* Annunciation.

In Via Rasella, which descends to the E. opposite the palace gates, 32 German soldiers of the SS. were killed, on 23 March 1944, by an explosion caused by men of the Resistance Movement. It was by way of reprisal for this that 355 Italians were killed at the Fosse Ardeatine (p. 230).

On the next corner opposite the palace is the site occupied by the *Scots College* in 1604-1962. Except for the church of St Andrew (1645-76) the buildings date from 1869. In the church are paintings by Gavin Hamilton (high altar) and Jamieson, including the foundress marchioness of Huntly. The college has now moved to Via Cassia (Rte 27).

Via delle Quattro Fontane ends in **Piazza Barberini,** one of the busiest traffic centres in the city. Here converge Via del Tritone (from the Corso), Via Sistina (from the Pincio), Via Vittorio Veneto, Via San Nicolò da Tolentino, and Via Barberini. In the centre of the square is Bernini's masterpiece, the **\*Fontana del Tritone** (1642-43), with four dolphins supporting a shell on which is seated a triton who blows water through a shell held up in his hands; on the N. side is the *Fontanella delle Api,* built by Bernini a year later, bearing the Barberini device of the bee and with an inscription stating that the water is for the use of the public and their animals. Here begins the broad and tree-lined VIA VITTORIO VENETO, which climbs in two sweeping curves to the Porta Pinciana. The street, with its great mansions, its fashionable hotels and cafés, and its ambiance of 'la dolce vita', passes through the aristocratic LUDOVISI QUARTER, the Mayfair of Rome.

On the right is the church of the **Cappuccini** or **Santa Maria della Concezione** (Pl. 4; 3), architecturally simple and unpretending in accordance with Franciscan ideals and in strong constrast to the Baroque works of the time (1624). Its founder was Card. Ant. Barberini.

INTERIOR. South side, 1st chap., *G. Reni,* St Michael; to the left, *Honthorst,* Mocking of Christ; 3rd chap., *Domenichino,* St Francis in Ecstasy, and Death of St Francis; 5th chap., *And. Sacchi,* St Anthony raising a dead man. An inscription on the pavement (Hic jacet pulvis, cinis et nihil) marks the grave of Card. Barberini in front of the high altar. North side, 5th chap., *A. Sacchi,* The Virgin and St Bonaventura; 1st chap., *Pietro da Cortona,* Conversion of St Paul.—A CEMETERY (entered down the stairs to the r. of the church) has five subterranean chapels lined with the bones and skeletons of over 4000 Capuchins, arranged in patterns. On the floor of two of these chapels is earth brought from Palestine. On All Souls' Day (2 Nov) these strange and gruesome chambers are illuminated.

Opposite, a street with steps descends to *Sant'Isidoro,* a Baroque church (1620) to which was attached a college for Irish students, founded by Luke Wadding (1588-1657), the distinguished Irish Franciscan, who instigated the Irish rebellion of 1641 against the confiscation of Ulster. His tomb is in the church.

Farther up the street, by its second curve (r.), is PALAZZO MARGHERI-
TA, a noble building in the classical style by Gaetano Koch (1866-90),
standing in a garden with a stately approach. The palace was built for the
Prince of Piombino, Rodolfo Boncompagni-Ludovisi, to supersede the
*Villa Ludovisi*, built in the early 17C for Card. Ludovico Ludovisi,
nephew of Gregory XV, and for ten years it contained the famous
Ludovisi Collection of antiquities, now in the Museo Nazionale Romano. From 1900 to 1926 the palace was the residence of Queen Margherita; it is now the United States Embassy. On the opposite side of the
street, at No. 62, is the *United States Information Service Bureau.*

On the right, just beyond, is Via Boncompagni, and on the left Via Ludovisi. In
Via Lombardia, farther on (left), is a relic of Villa Ludovisi, namely the *Casino
dell'Aurora*, noted for ceiling paintings by Guercino, showing Aurora and Fame
(no adm.). The street ends at *Porta Pinciana*, a handsome fortified gateway erected
by Honorius c. 403; opposite is one of the entrances to the Villa Borghese (Rte 9).
On the city side of Porta Pinciana, Via di Porta Pinciana branches left from Via
Vittorio Veneto and, passing the grounds of the Villa Medici, runs into Via
Francesco Crispi, which ends in Largo del Tritone. Beyond the gate, the broad
*Corso d'Italia*, skirting the Aurelian wall, runs past Piazza Fiume, site of the
demolished Porta Salaria, to Porta Pia.

From Piazza Barberini (comp. above) the modern Via Barberini
ascends. On the left, in a side street called after it, is the church of *San
Nicolò da Tolentino* (1599). Via Barberini ends at Largo Santa Susanna,
another traffic centre, where it is joined on the left by Via Leonida
Bissolati, a centre of tourist agencies. The square is dominated by the
building of the *Ufficio Geologico*, containing the *Geological Museum*
(weekdays 9-13), with a collection of minerals, marbles (archaeological
and modern), and fossils.

Adjoining Largo Santa Susanna on the S.E. is the busy *Piazza San
Bernardo*, with its fountain and three churches. It is, in effect, a widening
of Via Venti Settembre. On its N.W. side is the church of *Santa Susanna*
(Pl. 4; 4), a Paulist church, dating from the 3C, restored in 795 and
remodelled in 1475. It is now the American National church. The façade
is by Maderna (1603), and is by many considered his masterpiece; in the
rich Baroque interior are large mural frescoes by Baldass. Croce.
Opposite, at the beginning of Via Torino, is the round church of *San
Bernardo alle Terme*, once a hall flanking the exedra of the Baths of
Diocletian (p. 189). Inside are eight stucco statues of saints, by Camillo
Mariani.

The **Fontana dell'Acqua Felice** is fed by an aqueduct (1585-87) from Colonna in
the Alban Hills. The fountain dates from the time of Sixtus V and is by Dom.
Fontana; the unhappy figure of Moses is attrib. to Prospero Antichi or Leonardo
Sormani. The bas-relief of Aaron is by G. B. della Porta, and that of Gideon by
Flaminio Vacca and P. P. Olivieri; the four lions are copies of Egyptian antiques
removed by Gregory XVI to the Egyptian Museum founded by him in the
Vatican.—Via Orlando runs S.E. from the piazza to Piazza della Repubblica (p.
189).

At the beginning of the second reach of Via Venti Settembre, on the
left, is the church of *Santa Maria della Vittoria (Pl. 4; 4), a fine edifice
by Maderna (1620), with a façade by G. B. Soria. Originally dedicated to
St Paul, it was renamed from an image (burned in 1833) of the Virgin
that gave victory to the Catholic army over the Protestants at the battle
of the White Mountain, near Prague, on 8 Nov 1620 (Thirty Years War).

The INTERIOR is considered one of the most complete examples of Baroque decoration in Rome, rich in colour and glowing with costly marbles. South side, 2nd chapel. The altarpiece (Madonna and St Francis) and the frescoes (Vision of St Francis, and St Francis and the Stigmata) are by *Domenichino*.—North side. *4th chapel (THE CORNARO CHAPEL), by *Bernini*, a splendid architectural achievement, using the shallow space to great effect. Over the altar is St Theresa, rapt in an ecstasy of love for the Saviour, receiving in her heart a dart aimed by a smiling angel, a group in Bernini's most affected manner. At the sides are expressive portraits of the Venetian family of Cornaro, by pupils and followers of Bernini. The last half-hidden figure on the left is said to be a portrait of Bernini.—The fresco, by *L. Serra* (1885), in the apse of the church, commemorates the triumphal entry into Prague of the Catholic army.

The next part of this route follows Via Venti Settembre and, outside Porta Pia, Via Nomentana. A bus (No. 36, 37, 60, 62, 63, or 137) is recommended for at least part of the way as both roads are uninteresting and traffic-ridden, and the first important buildings are Sant'Agnese fuori le Mura and Santa Costanza (comp. p. 184) which lie some 3 km from Largo Santa Susanna.

In Via Venti Settembre, on the left, is the *Ministry of Agriculture and Forests;* on the right, farther on, the colossal *Ministry of Finance,* containing a *Numismatic Museum* (weekdays, 10-12). Interesting is a collection of wax seals by Benedetto Pistrucci, who designed the St George and dragon on the English sovereign.

The short Via Servio Tullio, opposite, leads N. to *Piazza Sallustio,* where, behind Villa Maccari (r.), is a considerable fragment of the Villa in the *Gardens of Sallust,* laid out in 40 B.C., on which the historian C. Sallustius Crispus lavished the wealth he had accumulated during his African governorship. The foundations of the Trinità dei Monti obelisk here show its medieval position. Beyond the piazza the street goes on as Via Nerva to Via Boncompagni, a straight and pleasant street which is continued to the left, beyond Via Vittorio Veneto, by Via Ludovisi.

Just beyond the end of the Ministry of Finance Via Piave leads N. (left) to the site of Porta Salaria and Via Salaria (p. 184). On the same side, near the end of Via Venti Settembre, is the *Villa Paolina,* once the home of Pauline Borghese (p. 157). The garden of the villa is beautiful and characteristic. Opposite, on the site where the former British Embassy, the *Villa Torlonia,* was damaged by a terrorist's bomb on 31 Oct 1946, new embassy buildings, designed by Sir Basil Spence, were opened in 1971. The ambassador continues to reside in the Villa Wolkonsky (p. 216). The lofty isolated arch of the **Porta Pia** (Pl. 12; 8), which closes the street, was erected by Michelangelo (his last architectural work) at the instance of Pius IV in 1561; the exterior face is by Vespignani (1868).

It was by this gate that the Italian troops under Gen. Raffaele Cadorna entered Rome on 20 Sept 1870, thus brining about the end of the temporal power of the popes. The actual breach was, however, a few steps to the left of the gate, in Corso d'Italia (commemorative stones). In the small courtyard of the gateway is the *Museo Storico dei Bersaglieri.* Adm. see p. 47.

Outside the gate, in Piazzale di Porta Pia, is the lofty *Monument to the Bersaglieri,* by Mancini and Morbiducci (1932). To the left is Corso d'Italia; to the right Viale del Policlinico, leading to the Policlinico (p. 197) past Piazza della Croce Rossa. In this square, on the right, is the ancient *Porta Nomentana,* walled up by Pius IV; the N. tower has been preserved. Here also is the entrance to the *Ministry of Transport.*

The wide *Via Nomentana* runs N.E. from Porta Pia, traversing a residential area of the city. It follows the line of the ancient consular road to Nomentum, now Mentana, c. 20 km. N.E. of Rome. To the right, at the beginning of the road, is the *Ministry of Works,* with the Ministry of Transport behind it (entrance in Piazza della Croce Rossa). The initial section of Via Nomentana is flanked by palaces and villas with beautiful gardens.

On the right, in Via dei Villini, at No. 32, are the *Catacombs of Nicomedes,* named after a martyr of the reign of Domitian.

The road traverses Viale Regina Margherita, a straight and spacious avenue running from N.W. to S.E. On the N. side, at No. 4 Via Cornelio Celso, are the offices of the *Commonwealth War Graves Commission* (Southern Region). A little farther on (r.) is the garden of the **Villa Torlonia** (Pl. 12; just beyond 8), after 1929 the private residence of Mussolini. It has been acquired by the Commune of Rome and recently opened as a public park (13½ hectares; adm. 9-dusk). Beneath the house and grounds are the 2C or 3C *Jewish Catacombs of the Via Nomentana,* formerly of vast extent (over 9 km. of galleries) but now mostly caved in. For the other Villa Torlonia, see p. 186.

About 2 km. from Porta Pia, beyond further villas, stands the church of *\*Sant'Agnese fuori le Mura,* probably built between 337 and 350 by Constantia, daughter or grand-daughter of Constantine, above the catacombs in which the martyred St Agnes was interred in 304. The church was rebuilt by Honorius I (625-38), and restored many times, notably in 1479 by Giul. Della Rovere (Julius II), by Card. Varallo after the sack of 1527, and by Pius IX in 1856. It incorporates the *Convento dei Canonici Lateranensi,* the buildings of which face the street (note the campanile and the small colonnaded front). Remains of the original basilica can be seen beyond Santa Costanza to the W. (see below).

St Agnes was a Christian maiden of the time of Diocletian who, having spurned the advances of a prætor's son, was exposed in the Stadium of Domitian, where her nakedness was covered by the miraculous growth of her hair. The presumed site of the miracle is now occupied by the church of Sant'Agnese in Agone, in Piazza Navona. She was then condemned to be burned at the stake, but the flames refused to touch her. After that she was beheaded. The *Pallium* worn by the Pope is made of the wool of lambs blessed annually on the day of her festival, 21 Jan.

A more direct entrance is in Via Sant'Agnese, which runs alongside the church; but it can also be entered by the convent gate across a court, on the right of which is a hall (originally a cellar) into which, during a visit in 1855, Pius IX and his suite were precipitated, though without injury, by the collapse of the floor of the room above. The incident is commemorated in a wall-painting by Toietti. Beyond a fine tower is the entrance to the basilica reached by a staircase of forty-five white marble steps (1590), the walls of which are covered with inscriptions from the catacombs, including St Damasus's record of the martyrdom of St Agnes (on the right near the bottom).

In the INTERIOR of the church (best light in the afternoon) the nave and aisles are separated by fourteen antique columns of breccia and pavonazzetto. There is a narthex for the catechumens, and a matroneum was built over the aisles and the W. end in 620. In the 2nd chapel on the right, over a Cosmati altar, is a fine relief of St Stephen and St Laurence, by *And. Bregno* (1490), and a bust of Christ once attributed to Michelangelo and probably the work of Nic. Cordier. On the high altar, in which are preserved the relics of St Agnes and St Emerentiana, her foster-sister, is an antique torso of Oriental alabaster restored in 1600 as a statue of St Agnes, beneath a baldacchino (1614) supported on four porphyry columns. On the left of the altar is a 4C candlestick. In the apse is the original plain marble decoration and an ancient episcopal throne. Above, a Byzantine \*Mosaic (625-38), representing St Agnes between Popes Symmachus and Honorius I, two restorers of the basilica, a model of which is held by Honorius. The simplicity of the composition, against a dull gold background is striking. In the left aisle is the entrance to the *Catacombs of St Agnes (comp. p. 227), the best-preserved and among the most characteristic Roman catacombs (adm. see p. 48; apply at the Sacristy. Visitors are conducted. The atmosphere in these catacombs, not normally visited by travellers in large groups offers a striking contrast to that in the more famous catacombs on the Appian Way (comp. pp. 228-29) which are always crowded with tours. These contain no paintings but there are numerous inscriptions and many of the loculi are intact. They may date from before 258 but not later than 305; the oldest zone extends to the left of the basilica. A chapel was built where the body of St Agnes was found, and a silver coffer provided in 1615 by Pope Paul V.

On the other side of the entrance court a path leads to the round church of *Santa Costanza (favoured for weddings; if closed apply at sacristy in Sant'Agnese), erected in c. 350 as a mausoleum for Constantia, and perhaps also Helena, daughters of Constantine. Constantia's porphyry sarcophagus is now in the Vatican; the one in the church is a reproduction.

The charming INTERIOR is annular in plan, twenty-four granite columns in pairs with beautiful Corinthian capitals, supporting the dome, which is 22½ m in diameter. Sixteen clerestory windows provide light. On the barrel-vaulting of the encircling ambulatory are early-Christian *Mosaics (4C), which are on a white ground, and are designed in pairs. In character they follow pagan models.

Those flanking the entrance have a geometric design, and the next, a circular motif with animals and figures. Vintage scenes and vine tendrils with grapes follow, and the 4th pair have roundels with a leaf design, busts, and figures. On either side of the sarcophagus are leaves, branches, amphoræ and exotic birds. Over the sarcophagus only a fragment remains of a mosaic with a star design. The two side niches also have fine mosaics (5C or 7C).

Beyond the church of Sant'Agnese Via Nomentana continues N.E. towards the river Aniene. On the right, incorporated in the garden wall of the *Villa Blanc,* is a 2C circular tomb looking like a small copy of the Mausoleum of Cecilia Metella on the Appian Way. The gardens of the Villa are destined to become a public park. Farther on, to the left, in Via Asmara (No. 6), is the entrance to the *Catacombs of the Cimitero Maggiore,* with interesting frescoes. The road crosses the river Aniene by the modern *Ponte Tazio.* The Aniene, the ancient *Anio,* rises near Tivoli, where it falls in cascades on its way to the Campagna. Here the river is quiescent. On the right of the new bridge is the ancient *Ponte Nomentano, rebuilt by Narses and bearing a medieval watch-tower. Beyond the river is the dismal modern QUARTIERE DI MONTE SACRO, named after the *Mons Sacer* (37 m), which rises to the right. This was the scene in 494 B.C. of the first secession of the plebs, who were induced to return to Rome by the fable of the belly and its members recited to them by Menenius Agrippa. From the top of the hill there is a good view.

To reach Via Salaria (see below), it is necessary to take Via di Sant'Agnese to Piazza Annibaliano and Corso Trieste (l.) to Piazza Istria; or to turn back towards the city and take the first turning to the right, Via di Santa Costanza, direct to Piazza Istria. From here Via Panaro leads to Piazza Volsinio, with the entrance to the *Parco Virgiliano,* opened in 1930 to commemorate the bimillenary of the birth of Virgil (15 Oct, 70 B.C.). Across the park, beyond Piazza Crati Via di Priscilla leads on to Piazza di Priscilla, on Via Salaria.

The **Via Salaria** (Pl. 12; 7, 5, 4, 2), so called from its association with the salt trade between the Romans and the Sabines, is one of the oldest of the Roman roads. It starts from Piazza Fiume, on the site of the ancient *Porta Salaria.* This gate no longer exists but the bases of two tombs in the square define its width. The road, now Highway 4 (comp. Rte 26), runs viâ Rieti and Antrodoco to Ascoli Piceno and the Adriatic near San Benedetto del Tronto.

On the left (w.) side of Via Salaria, near the piazza, at No. 430 is the entrance to the *Catacombs of Priscilla (Pl. 12; 2), the most ancient and among the most interesting in Rome (adm., see p. 48). Visitors are taken in groups by an English-speaking nun. The tour is on the road level, although there are further catacombs (unlit) below. The exit is usually on the other side of Via Salaria.

A chapel contains the oldest known painting of the Virgin and Child (with Isaiah), dating from the second half of the 2C. Beside this, a scene of the Good Shepherd with two sheep beneath a tree shows an unusual technique of stucco combined with painting. In a 3C chapel is a painting of the consecration of a maiden to the service of God. Several parts of the catacombs were found to have a layer of lime, formed after centuries of earth had been packed against the walls. This has been removed in some places, and the frescoes beneath saved. One such chapel has a painting of the Annunciation on the vault.

A pagan cryptoporticus and nymphæum, later converted by Christians, can also be seen. The cryptoporticus has cross-vaulting, and the remains of Pompeian style frescoes. From here is the entrance to the Greek chapel with 2C frescoes of New Testament scenes and good stucco decoration.

To the N., Via Salaria crosses the Aniene, near its confluence with the Tiber, by the ancient but much restored *Ponte Salario,* nearly 4 km from Piazza Fiume. Close by is the traditional spot where, in 360 B.C., Titus Manlius Torquatus slew the gigantic Gaul in single combat and stripped him of his torque or collar. Just short of the bridge a by-road leads left to a hill (62 m; military zone) commanding a view of the confluence of the Tiber and Aniene. This was the site of the ancient Sabine town of *Antemnoe,* said to have been founded by the Siculi. It had probably already disappeared by the time of the kings, leaving as its chief memorial the story of the rape of the Sabines.

From the Catacombs of Priscilla Via Salaria (bus No. 35, 56, or 57 along the parallel Via Nemorense) returns towards the city. On the right is the vast expanse of the *Villa Ada* (formerly *Savoia*), once the private residence of Victor Emmanuel III. The villa is now the embassy of the United Arab Republic; part of the grounds is owned by the Commune of Rome, and is a public park. The wall extends along Via Salaria, and the entrance gate to the villa is a considerable way towards the city. Via Panama on the r. continues the line of the wall, and the Salaria now widens with a line of pines down the centre. Soon after St George's English School (r.), there is an important road junction. On the left is Viale Regina Margherita (p. 183); on the right Viale Liegi, leading to Viale dei Parioli, in the fashionable PARIOLI QUARTER.

Farther on Via Scarlatti leads on the right to Piazza Verdi, in which is the building of the Government Printing Works (1930). To the w. of Piazza Verdi, at the corner of Via Spontini and Via Giovanni Paisiello, are the *Catacombs of Panfilo.* In Via Bertolini (a continuation of Via Paisiello) are the *Catacombs of Sant'Ermete,* with a large underground basilica, containing an 8C fresco of the Madonna and angels with SS. Hermes and Benedict, the earliest known painting of the last.

At the corner of Via Salaria and Via Taro is the entrance to the *Catacombs of Trasone,* among the deepest in Rome, while at No. 2 Via Simeto, farther along, is that of the *Catacombs of Santa Felicità,* with a small underground basilica. Only the last is open to the public; for adm. to the others, see p. 48.

In 1923, at the corner of Via Po, which cuts across Via Simeto, and Via Livenza, was discovered a 4C *Hypogeum,* 9 m below ground level, containing frescoes and mosaics.

Beyond the junction of Via Salaria with Via Po, on the right, is the circular *Mausoleum of Lucilius Peto,* dating from the time of Augustus and somewhat resembling the Mausoleum of Augustus. On the left, the road skirts the grounds of Villa Torlonia and come to its entrance at the corner of Via di Villa Albani.

*Villa Torlonia (Pl. 12; 7), formerly *Albani,* was built in 1760 by Carlo Marchionni for Card. Aless. Albani, whose valuable collection of classical sculpture was here arranged by Winckelmann in 1765. By order of Napoleon 294 pieces of this collection were removed to Paris; after Waterloo nearly all of them were sold at Munich instead of being returned. The original collection, however, continued to increase. In 1852 it passed into the possession of the Chigi and in 1866 it was bought, with the villa, by Princess Aless. Torlonia (p. 240).—Visitors are sometimes admitted, but only after previous written application to the Amministrazione Torlonia, 30 Via della Conciliazione.

There are two villas of the same name, the one described here, and the former residence of Mussolini, in Via Nomentana (p. 183).

From the entrance gate a magnificent avenue leads to a rotunda surrounded by umbrella pines, on which converge several other avenues; all of them are lined with boxwood hedges. One leads on the left direct to the **Casino.** This comprises a main building with a portico, and two re-entrant wings, likewise with porticoes, defining an elegant garden. In front is a *Hemicycle,* with 40 Doric columns; in its centre is a hall called *Sala del Canopo* or *Caffè.* In the garden are busts and antique fragments; small fountains play in front of the wings.

**Ground Floor.** PORTICO. In the niches are busts of Roman emperors. From the left, 52. Herm of Mercury; 54. Tiberius; 55. 60. Colossal masks; 58. Ptolemæus, last king of Numidia; 64. Trajan; 65. Altar with Hecate and the Four Seasons; 69. Bowl of Karystian marble; 74. Altar with Eleusinian divinities; 87. Statue of a man in armour (head of Augustus added).—From the Portico is access (l.) into the ATRIUM OF THE CARYATIDS. 16, 24. Kanephoroi (baskets modern); 19. Bacchante in the style of the 5C with a caryatid head from another statue by Kriton and Nikolaos of Athens; below (20) a relief, the so-called Kapaneus struck dead by Zeus (5C).—In the adjoining FIRST GALLERY, Collection of herms. The following ascriptions are mostly conjectural: 27. Themistocles; 29. Epicurus; 30. Hamilcar; 31. Leonidas; 32. Xenophon; 40. Hannibal; 43. Agrippa; 45. Scipio Africanus.—Beyond an antechamber on the left is the STAIRCASE. In front, on the left, 9. Rome, a relief dating from the reign of Trajan; 11. Sepulchral relief of Tiberius Julius Vitalis, sausage vendor. On the landings: 885. Frieze of Diana slaying the Niobids, possibly reproduced from the composition of Pheidias for the throne of Zeus Olympios; 889. The robber Sinis; 891. Thanatos; 898, 899. Bacchantes.

**First Floor.** OVAL HALL. Ceiling painting of Aurora, by *Ant. Bicchierari.* 905. Apollo with the tripod, the omphalos, and a crouching lion; *906. Statue of athlete, signed by Stephanos, pupil of Pasiteles (1C B.C.); 915. Cupid bending his bow; above the door, 921. Mithraic relief.—GREAT HALL, on the right, with a ceiling painting of *Parnassos* by *Raphael Mengs.* Numerous low reliefs. 1014. Apollo, Artemis, and Leto before the Temple at Delphi, archaistic votive offering of a victor in the Pythian games; 1007. Bacchante; 1008. Hercules in the garden of the Hesperides; 1009. Dædalus and Icarus; 1011. Ganymede; 1018. Antoninus Pius, Faustina, and Rome; *1012. Albani Pallas, wearing the diplax or folded mantle with a clasp (the head, from another statue, has a wolf's head headdress), Attic School; 1015, 1016. Sphinxes, Roman copies; 1017. Alabaster tripod; 1019. Jupiter; 1026. Messalina; 1029, 1030. Silenus; antique mosaic frieze.

RIGHT WING. ROOM 1. In the ceiling, *Ant. Bicchierari,* Venus and Cupid; *Paolo Anesi,* Landscapes. 1033. So-called Sappho, a Pheidian head of Aphrodite; *1031. Orpheus and Eurydice, and Hermes, at the moment when Orpheus turns round, replica of a 5C original in the Pheidian style; 1034. Theophrastos; 1036. Hippocrates.—R. 2. Paintings. 35. *Luca Signorelli* (attrib.), Madonna with saints and donor; 36. *Nic. da Foligno,* Madonna and saints (signed and dated 1475); 37. *Perugino,* Polyptych: Adoration of the Shepherds, Crucifixion, Annunciation and Saints; 46, 47. *Giov. Paolo Pannini,* Arch of Constantine.—R. 3. 51. *Honthorst,* Decapitation of John the Baptist; 52. *Pompeo Batoni,* Madonna and Child; 55. *Van Dyck,* Crucifixion; 56. *Taddeo Zuccari,* Deposition of Christ; 60. *Tintoretto,* Crucifixion; 64. *Ribera,* Head of an old man ('The thinker'); 73. *Guercino,* St Luke.

LEFT WING. ROOM 1. In the ceiling, *Bicchierari,* Saturn devouring his children; low reliefs by *Thorvaldsen,* \*994. Antinöus, a celebrated relief from Hadrian's Villa, the only piece brought back from Paris in 1815 (see p. 186); 995, 996. Herms in Oriental alabaster; 997. Female satyr playing the flute; 100. Bowl of green porphyry.—R. 2. 967. Dancing girls, relief possibly after an original by Kallimachos; 970. Minerva, archaistic; \*980. So-called Leucothea, relief of the beginning of the 5C B.C.; \*985. Battle-scene, admirable 5C relief, characteristic of Pheidias; 998. Fragment of frieze in the archaic style of the Dii Consentes; 991. Relief made up of two fragments found at Tivoli.—R. 3. Paintings. 17, 18. Sketches by *Giulio Romano* of the story of Psyche in the Palazzo del Te at Mantua (see the 'Blue Guide to Northern Italy'); 21. *Holbein* (attrib.), Sir Thomas More; 23. 24. *Philip Roos,* Landscapes; 28. *Borgognone,* Battle-scene.—R. 4. Ceiling by *Bicchierari* and *Lapiccola.* 931. Diana; 933. Herakles, bronze copy of an original by Lysippos; 942. Diogenes; 944. Hecuba; \*952. Apollo Sauroktonos, antique copy after Praxiteles; \*953. Bust of Quintus Hortensius; \*957. Apotheosis of Hercules, in the style of the Tabula Iliaca in the Capitoline Museum; 960. Persius (?); \*964. Aesop (so called), an admirably naturalistic nude statue of a hunchback, possibly a portrait of a court dwarf of the time of Hadrian.—Paintings. *Luca Giordano,* Caritas Romana, in the Flemish style; 5. *Marco David,* Portrait of Innocent XII; 6, 7. *Gaspare Vanvitelli,* Landscapes.—From the Oval Hall stairs lead down to the ground floor.

**Ground Floor** (continued). Beyond the portico is the ATRIO DELLA GIUNONE. 90. Pertinax; 91, 97. Kanephoroi; 93. Juno (?); 96. Marcus Aurelius.—GALLERY. \*103. Bacchante with nereids; 106. Faun and the youthful Bacchus; 110. Faun; 112. Numa, 115. Pindar, 122. Persius (attributions of these three conjectural); 120. Gaius Caesar.—The STANZA DELLA COLONNA is a room with 12 fine antique columns (one fluted, in alabaster). \*131. Sarcophagus, marriage of Peleus and Thetis, considered by Winckelmann to be one of the finest in existence; 132. Lucius Verus; 135. Hippolytus leaving for the chase; 137, 138. Alabaster lion masks; 139, 140. Sarcophagus, Rape of Proserpine.—R. 1. 146. Aesculapius and Hygieia, votive relief; 157. Polyphemus and Cupid; 161. Alexander visiting Diogenes; 164. Daedalus and Icarus, relief in rosso antico; terracottas.—R. 2. 185. Leda and the swan.—R. 3. 204. Theseus and the Minotaur; 212. Recumbent statue of a man; 213. Bacchic procession.—R. 4. 216. Sleep, low relief.

An ilex avenue leads from the Casino to the BIGLIARDO (billiard pavilion), which contains sculptures of little importance. Beyond is the HEMICYCLE. 594. Alcibiades (?), after the original in the Museo Torlonia; 596. Mercury; 604. Mars; 607. Antisthenes; 610. Chrysippos; 612. Apollo in repose; 617. Hadrian; 628. Caryatid; 633, 634. Caligula; 636, 647. Actors removing their masks after applause.— Beyond the door into the Hall: 721. Homer; 725. Caryatid; 737. Bust, of Jupiter or Neptune; \*749. Proserpine, a beautiful copy of a bronze by Pheidias; 754. Commodus; 757. Bacchus; 753. Venus, of the type of the Capuan Venus; 741. Herakles, copied from a bronze original perhaps by Praxiteles; 744. So-called Peisistratos, in the style of Myron.—From the middle of the Hemicycle is the entrance to a VESTIBULE. 711. Iris; 706. Theseus and Aethra; 641. Marsyas bound to the tree; 639. Venus and Cupid; statues of comic actors.—SALA DEL CANOPO or CAFFÉ. Elegant low reliefs reproducing famous antiques; paintings by *Lapiccola* and *Paolo Anesi.* In the pavement antique mosaic. 659. Diana of the Ephesians; 662. Artemis (5C B.C.); 663. Mosaic of seven philosophers; 676. Colossal head of Jupiter Serapis, in black basalt; 678. Boy with comic mask; 682. Ibis, in rosso antico; 684. Atlas supporting the heavens; 691. Canopus, rare sculpture in green basalt, with reliefs of Egyptian gods; 696. Hercules freeing Hesione, fine mosaic; 700. Diana of the Ephesians; 702. Caracalla; 704. Silenus; 706. Theseus, low relief.

Via Salaria returns to Piazza Fiume and the centre of Rome.

# 12   FROM PIAZZA VENEZIA TO THE MUSEO NAZIONALE ROMANO AND THE STATION

From Piazza Venezia to Largo Magnanàpoli, see Rte 11. From here the broad **Via Nazionale** runs N.E. At its junction with Largo Magnanàpoli, on the right, is the extensive garden of the *Villa Aldobrandini,* built in the 16C for the Duke of Urbino, acquired by Clement VIII (Ippolito Aldobrandini), and given by him to his nephews.

The social centre of Napoleonic Rome, the villa is now Government property, and contains an international law library. It gave its name to the *Aldobrandini Marriage,* the famous Roman painting of a marriage scene found on the Esquiline in 1605 and kept in one of the garden pavilions until 1838, when it was moved to the Vatican.

Via Nazionale skirts the villa wall as far as Via Mazzarino, in which (r.) is an open gate and steps which lead up past impressive 2C ruins to the garden. Farther on in Via Mazzarino, to the left, is the church of *Sant'Agata dei Goti* (if closed, ring at No. 16), built in 462-70, but much restored. The Byzantine plan remains, with antique columns and decorative capitals with pulvins. In the apse is a well-preserved 12-13C Cosmatesque tabernacle. An ancient well stands in the court. The original fabric of the church can be seen on leaving the church by the door in the r. aisle.

The hilly Via Panisperna continues left to the church of *San Lorenzo in Panisperna,* the traditional site of the martyrdom of the saint, in a delightful court of old houses, and a villa to the l. (part of the Ministero dell'Interno). The interior of the church contains a vast fresco of the martyrdom by Pasq. Cati. The shortest way back to Via Nazionale is viâ Via Milano which rejoins the main road at the Palazzo dell'Esposizione (see below).

Farther along Via Nazionale, on the right, is the neo-classical head office of the *Banca d'Italia* by Gaetano Koch (1886-1904). On the left is the *Teatro Eliseo.* A little farther on Via Milano is crossed; to the left this street leads to the Traforo Umberto I (p. 172). Just beyond Via Milano rises the monumental *Palazzo dell'Esposizione* (Pl. 5; 5), erected in 1878-82 to a design by Pio Piacentini. It is used as an exhibition centre.

The **Galleria Comunale d'Arte Moderna** is entered from Via Milano (adm., see p. 48). The ground floor is reserved for exhibitions, with the exception of the passage leading to the lift for the main collection. This has sculpture by *Attilio Torresini, Mich. Guerrisi, Giov. Prini, Achille Stocchi* and others.
The collection on the second floor contains works by Italian and some foreign artists from the beginning of the 20C to the present day. ROOM I. *Rodin,* Head of a man, Bust of a woman.—R. II. 3. *Guglielmo de Sanctis,* Portrait of Adele Castellani; *Mich. Cammarano,* 8. 12. Landscapes; 10. *Vannutelli Scipione,* S. Onoforio; 13. *Vinc. Cabianca,* Palestrina.—R. III. 4. *Norberto Pazzini,* Self-portrait. 1924.—R. IV. 5 *G. Aristide Sartorio,* Terracina.—R. VI. *G. Ballà,* 2. Portrait of Nathan, 3. Doubt.—R. VII. *Arturo Noci,* Oranges.—R. VIII. *Sartorio,* The Wise and Foolish Virgins. Sculpture: 19. *Attilio Torresini,* Aphrodite.—SALONE. *Amer. Bertoli,* 7. Circus, 8. Portrait of Longhi; *Ant. Donghi,* Landscapes; *Fausto Pirandello,* Roman landscape, Frightened figure, The bathers; *Roberto Melli,* Various works; 21. *Renato Guttuso,* Self-portrait. Sculpture by *Tom. Bertolino,* Langour, Female nude (half-length).—R. IX. 5. *A. Marasco,* Night at Sea.—R. XII. 3. *Renato Guttoso,* Roman roofs; 5. *Carlo Levi,* Carrubo.—R. XVI. *Giacomo Manzù,* Female head, 1941; *Giorgio Morandi,* Two engravings (still-lifes).—R. XXI. *Pietro Annigoni,* Girl; *R. Guttoso,* Head of a woman.—GALLERY. Engravings and drawings.

Part of the ANTIQUARIUM COMUNALE (comp. p. 70) is also displayed here, including finds from the Forma Urbis, frescoes, mosaics, bronzes, and objects relating to the every-day life of the Romans.

Beyond the palazzo, on a much lower level, is the little church of *San Vitale,* dedicated in 416 and several times restored; it has carved 17C doors, and damaged frescoes by Gaspard Poussin (r.) and by Cav. d'Arpino (l.).—Farther on is a cross-roads: on the left is the end of Via delle Quattro Fontane, which leads to Piazza Barberini; on the right Via Agostino Depretis leads to Piazza dell' Esquilino and Santa Maria Maggiore. In this street, on the right, is the large *Palazzo del Viminale* (1920), now the Ministry of the Interior.—Just beyond Via Napoli (r.) is the American episcopal church of *St Paul's,* a Gothic structure by G. E. Street (1879), containing a mosaic by Burne-Jones. The next street to the right, Via Firenze, leads to Via Viminale, in which is the *Teatro dell' Opera* (1880), acquired by the State in 1926, and restored and enlarged by Marcello Piacentini. It is the most important lyric theatre in Rome.

Via Nazionale crosses Via Torino (with a glimpse to the right of Santa Maria Maggiore) and ends in the spacious and busy PIAZZA DELLA REPUBBLICA (Pl. 5; 3), formerly *dell' Esedra* (from the exedra of the Baths of Diocletian, the buildings of which may be seen on the opposite side). The semicircular porticoed fronts of the palazzi on either side of the entrance to the piazza (by Koch; 1896-1902), follow the line of the exedra. The lofty jet of the *Fountain of the Naiads* (1870) is supplied by the Acqua Marcia (see p. 217). Four groups of reclining nymphs and the central Glaucus were sculpted by Mario Rutelli (1901-11). Via delle Terme di Diocleziano comes into the piazza from the S.E. (Pl. 5; 4), and Via Orlando from the N.W.

The *Baths of Diocletian, or Thermæ of Diocletian were built in 298-306 by Diocletian and Maximian. The largest of all the ancient Roman baths, they could accommodate over 3000 people at once. They covered a rectangular area, c. 380 m by 370 m, corresponding to that now bounded S.E. by Piazza dei Cinquecento, S.W. by Via Torino, N.W. by Via Venti Settembre, and N.E. by Via Volturno. The main buildings included the Calidarium, the Tepidarium, and the Frigidarium. The Calidarium, which survived into the late 17C, occupied part of the present piazza. The Tepidarium and the huge central hall of the baths are now occupied by the church of Santa Maria degli Angeli (see below). The Frigidarium was an open-air bath behind this hall. Numerous large and small halls, nymphaea, and exedræ were located within the precincts, but the exact purpose of some of them is conjectural. The only entrance to the baths was on the N.E. side, near the present Via Volturno. On the S.W. side the closed exedra was flanked by two circular halls: one of these is now the church of San Bernardo alle Terme (p. 181); the other is at the corner of Via Viminale and Via delle Terme. A third (octagonal) hall survives on the corner of Via Parigi at the N.W. angle of the main complex (it is now occupied by a Planetarium). In the 16C a Carthusian convent was built in the ruins (see below). Much damage was done to the baths in the 16-19C by architects and builders who used the materials for other purposes. After the opening in 1889 of the Museo Nazionale Romano the process of spoliation was halted, and numerous encroaching buildings were removed.

Along the modern Via Parigi stand conspicuous remains of buildings demolished to make way for the Baths. At the beginning of the street is a Roman column surmounted by a caravel, a gift from Paris (1961).

*Santa Maria degli Angeli (Pl. 5; 3) occupies the great central hall of the baths, converted into the church of the Carthusian convent. The work of adaptation was carried out in 1563-66 at the instance of Pius IV by *Michelangelo,* who may also have designed the cloisters and other conventual buildings. Michelangelo placed the entrance of the church at the short S.E. side of the rectangle and thus had at his disposal a nave of vast proportions. The effect was spoiled by *Vanvitelli* who, instructed by the Carthusian fathers in 1749, altered the orientation. He made the entrance in the long S.W. side and so converted the nave into a transept. To compensate for the loss of length, he built out on the N.E. side an apsidal choir, which broke into the monumental S.W. wall of the Frigidarium. The façade on Piazza della Repubblica, with Vanvitelli's doorway, incorporates an apsidal wall—all that is left of the Calidarium. Excavations during the restoration of the floor in 1970 revealed further remains of the baths.

INTERIOR. The circular VESTIBULE stands on the site of the Tepidarium. Here are the tombs of Carlo Maratta (d. 1713; r.) and Salvator Rosa (d. 1673; l.). By the entrance into the transept is (r.) a fine colossal statue of St Bruno, by *Houdon* (1766). The vast and impressive TRANSEPT is nearly 100 m long, 27 m wide and 28 m high. The eight monolithic columns of red granite, nearly 14 m high and 1½ m in diameter, are original; the others, in brick, were added when the building was remodelled.—Right transept: in the pavement, a meridian dating from 1703; tomb, by *Ant. Muñoz,* of Marshal Armando Diaz (d. 1928), Italian commander-in-chief in the First World War.—Left transept: Mass of St Basil, by *Subleyras;* Fall of Simon Magus, by *Pompeo Batoni.*—In the Choir, on the right, *Romanelli,* Presentation in the Temple; *Domenichino,* Martyrdom of St Sebastian; left, *Pomarancio,* Death of Ananias and Sapphira (painted on slate); *C. Maratta,* Baptism of Christ. In the apse, on the left, Monument of Pius IV, from Michelangelo's design, which inspired also the monument of Card. Serbelloni opposite.—The door to the Sacristy in the l. transept leads to impressive remains of the frigidarium (see above).

The *Museo Nazionale Romano (Pl. 5; 4) is one of the great museums of the world. Founded in 1889, it contains sculptures and other antiquities found in Rome since 1870, part of the Kircherian collection formerly in the Collegio Romano, and the treasures of the Ludovisi collection originally in the Villa Ludovisi (this, however, has been closed indefinitely for extensive rearrangement). The museum occupies part of the Carthusian convent. Adm., see p. 49. The official guide is outstanding. Parts of the Museum are closed without notice, when custodians are not available.

Before entering the museum proper the eleven Rooms of the Baths are visited. They contain an unrivalled series of sarcophagi, as well as other objects of interest. They were closed for rearrangement in 1976, but are expected to reopen shortly. The entrance is in Viale delle Terme.

## THE BATHS

The stark grandeur of the interior, with its high and massive walls and daring vault, make an indelible impression on the visitor. Seven of the rooms surround the S.E. or right transept of the church of Santa Maria degli Angeli. Four more are located in and near the Frigidarium.

ROOM I. On the floor, Mosaic with volutes and animals; three

sarcophagi depicting respectively the Three Graces, a Bacchic procession, and the story of Phædra.—R. II. Against the wall, Plaster
reconstruction of the base of the temple of Hadrian erected A.D. 141 by
Antoninus Pius (comp. p. 151). In front, Sarcophagus with figures of
Muses and two other sarcophagi; funerary altars; architectural fragments.—R. III. Polychrome mosaics; Christian sarcophagi, among
them that of Marcus Claudianus, with scenes from the Old and New
Testaments. From R. I is the entrance to—

R. IV. On the wall, in which was Michelangelo's entrance to the
church of Santa Maria degli Angeli, is a dedicatory inscription of the
Baths of Diocletian (reconstituted). Nilotic mosaic with a landscape
with pygmies, hippopotami, and crocodiles (from Collemancio, near
Assisi); colossal statue, Artemis of Ariccia, copy of an original attrib. to
Alkamenes; reconstruction of a small tetrastyle temple from Torrenova
on the Via Casilina (2C A.D.); sarcophagi, including one to the r. of the
temple, with a magnificent battle scene.—R. V. So-called group of Mars
and Venus, said to represent the emperor Commodus and his wife
Crispina; to left, Shaft of an oriental alabaster column, on a white
marble base, found, with other architectural fragments, during the
building of the extension to the Chamber of Deputies; sarcophagi.—R.
VI. On left of entrance, against the wall of the church, Plaster reproduction of the door of the Temple of Augustus and Rome at Ancyra
(Ankara); on this temple was engraved the *Monumentum Ancyranum;*
(on a pedestal) statue of Jupiter, after a Hellenistic original; polychrome
mosaic of Charioteers (found in 1939); *Dancers of the Via Prenestina, a
cylindrical drum of 9 marble slabs (two missing); Sarcophagi, one with a
Bacchic procession.—R. VII. Mosaics, inscriptions, etc.

Beyond the cluster of rooms round the church lies the FRIGIDARIUM
(R. VIII). This was the swimming pool of the Baths, open to the sky and,
with an area of 2500 sq. m, it was as large as a small lake. It was bounded
on the long N.E. side by a garden and had porticoes on both short sides.
The S.W. side was bounded by a monumental wall with five pedimented
niches. alternately rectangular and curved, and adorned with statues.
Most of the adornment had disappeared when Vanvitelli broke through
the centre of the wall to build his apisdal choir out into the middle of the
area. It had already been diminished by the construction of the small
cloister of the Carthusian convent (this now houses the Ludovisi
collection; see below), and the combination of these intrusions has
naturally robbed the Frigidarium of its character. The architectural
fragments along the walls of the baths, and in front of the modern wall of
the small cloister, were found during the extension of the Chamber of
Deputies.

To the right is R. IX, with a double exedra; here is a sarcophagus of
Egyptian style.—R.X. Reconstructed tomb of G. Sulpicius Platorinus
and of his family; inside are niches for cinerary urns; chamber tomb of
the 2C A.D., with pictorial decoration on the walls and ceiling, found in
1951 at the foot of the hill of Monteverde.—R. XI. Roman mosaics:
Hercules wrestling with Achelous (from Anzio); Nereids riding on sea-
monsters (from Casalotto, on the Via Cornelia); Rampant panthers
(from the Stazione Termini, Rome).—From R. X is the entrance to the
*Garden* looking on Piazza dei Cinquecento. In it is a colossal marble
fountain-basin shaped like a flower calyx. On the N.E. side the garden is

bounded by the ancient perimeter wall of the Baths. A modern flight of steps leads down through an arch cut in the wall to the *Forica,* with niches for statues and a floor mosaic. Along the curved wall were ranged some thirty lavatory seats, separated by marble slabs.—In the left (W.) corner of the garden is the entrance to the Museum.

## THE MUSEUM

PORCH. On the left, Telamon in the form of a young satyr, Roman copy of a Hellenistic original; polychrome mosaics.—ENTRANCE HALL. On column shafts, twelve busts of Roman personages of doubtful authenticity; herm of Mercury; mosaics, including one of a *Skeleton with inscription in Greek, 'Know thyself'.

On the left a door leads to the **Ludovisi Collection.** This has been closed for many years, and the date of reopening is still uncertain. The famous Ludovisi throne has been removed, and is now exhibited in Room 2 (see below). The collection was formed by Card. Ludovico Ludovisi, nephew of Gregory XV (Alessandro Ludovisi; pope 1621-23). It was originally housed in Villa Ludovisi and was moved to the new palace in Via Vittorio Veneto (now Palazzo Margherita; p. 181) on its completion in 1890. In 1901, after the palace had become the residence of Queen Margherita, the State bought the collection from the Prince of Piombino, Rodolfo Boncompagni-Ludovisi, and it was placed in the Museo Nazionale. It occupies the small cloister mentioned above. Notable are the Hermes Ludovisi, the god as orator, copy of a 5C original, and the Ludovisi Hera, a colossal head, copy of a 4C original. Many of the sculptures have been poorly restored.

Opposite the entrance to the cloister is the first of a series of eight rooms, containing an important collection of Greek and Hellenistic sculptures.

ROOM I. Floor mosaic depicting the head of Pan and four satyrs; (l.) fragments of a large neo-Attic rhyton, (r.) marble neo-Attic fountain cover. Cinerary urns from the tomb of C. Sulpicius Platorinus (p. 191).—R. II. In an impluvium, Polychrome mosaic with head of Oceanus and sea-monsters. 106164. Statue, from a Herakles after Polykleitos, from the baths of Caracalla; *608. Apollo of the Tiber, school of Pheidias, or perhaps by Kalamis, found in the Tiber; *124697. Aura of the Palatine, believed to have been the central acroterion of the Temple of Apollo Epikourios at Bassæ (430 B.C.); 1085. Head of Hygieia, in the style of the 4C B.C.; *124696. Dancer of the Palatine, wearing a chiton (5C B.C.); 124667. Peplophoros, probably a Greek original of the first half of the 5C B.C., found in Piazza Barberini; *51. Juno of the Palatine, possibly the portrait of an empress as the goddess; 55051. Colossal head of Athena, an acrolith; 124665. Torso of Minotaur, copy of a 5C bronze original.

R. III contains the most outstanding examples. *56039. DISCOBOLOS OF CASTEL PORZIANO, copy of a bronze statue by Myron; *72274. DAUGHTER OF NIOBE, from the Gardens of Sallust, a Greek original of the 5C B.C. of the school of Kresilas; **72115. VENUS OF CYRENE, an original Greek work of the 4C B.C., possibly by a predecessor of Praxiteles, representing the goddess just risen from the sea; near her right leg is her cloak, supported by a dolphin; the head and arms are missing. The statue was found in the Baths at Cyrene; *1075. EPHEBUS OF SUBIACO, Roman copy of an orginal of the 4C B.C., probably one of the

Niobids, found in Nero's villa at Subiaco; *Torso Valentini (no number) a hero or athlete, a remarkable work of the early 5C B.C., formerly in the court of Palazzo Valentini (p. 175); 124680. Head of Hypnos, attrib. to Praxiteles, from Hadrian's Villa; 1049. Bronze statue of a young man leaning on a lance, perhaps Pollux or one of the Seleucids, in the identical pose as the Alexander the Great of Lysippos; *1055. Boxer resting, a magnificent work signed by Apollonius; his coarse face is scarred and his body is relaxed as if he were very tired after his fight;

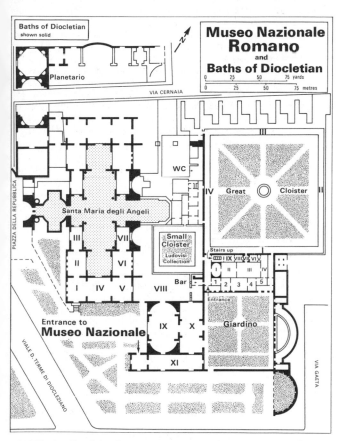

121302. Apollo of Anzio, by an unknown Attic predecessor of Praxiteles; **50170. MAIDEN OF ANZIO, a masterpiece of Greek art dating from the end of the 4C or beginning of the 3C B.C. by a sculptor of the school of Lysippos who had come under the influence of Praxiteles. It represents a young girl approaching an altar and carrying implements for a sacrifice. It was discovered in the imperial villa at Anzio in 1878; *126371. DISCOBOLOS EX-LANCELOTTI, the finest and best-preserved replica of the statue of Myron. In defiance of Italian law it was sold to Hitler in 1938, but was restored to Italy ten years later; 124679. Head of the goddess of Butrinto, discovered in 1929 at Butrinto in Albania (the arrangement of the hair somewhat resembles that of the Apollo of Anzio). Of the polychrome floor mosaics the best is that of a whirling wheel with 14 carved spokes (from Settecamini. on the Via Tiburtina).

R. IV. 607. Charis, or Grace, from a type by Kallimachos, similar in style to the Venus Genetrix by Arcesilaus; *108596. Dancer of Tivoli, Roman copy of a Hellenistic original; 124678. Riding Amazon charging a barbarian, of the school of Pergamon; *499. Young satyr turning round to look at his tail, Hellenistic; 121315. Young satyr laughing, Roman copy of a Hellenistic original; 60750, 108597. Crouching Venus, two replicas of the work by the Bithynian sculptor Doidalsas; on the wall, *Mosaic with volutes and a shield adorned with the head of Medusa; *12. Seated Muse, found in the Palatine Stadium; *121987. Goddess personifying a seaport, accompanied by a child merman (1C B.C.; recalling 4C); 124722. Muse or Nymph, found in the Palatine Stadium, possibly along with No. 12 (above). It was part of a group of the Muses, Apollo, and Marsyas by Philiscos of Rhodes (3C B.C.).

R. V. ROMAN DECORATIVE ART. To the right, marble *Altar (1C A.D.) found near Ponte Sant'Angelo, the front and sides with plane-branch decoration surmounted by a bull's head. To the left, *Sepulchral altar, comprising an ossuary and a cippus; on the front of the cippus is a relief depicting a nuptial scene; on the other sides are figures of mænads dancing and of youths carrying implements for a sacrifice.—RR. VI and VII. ROMAN PORTRAITS. *56230. Augustus as Pontifex Maximus, one of the finest portraits of the emperor, found in the Via Labicana; 618. Head of Nero, the best of his portraits; 124493. Head of an old woman of the early Empire; *639. Half-length figure of a chief Vestal, from the House of the Vestals in the Roman Forum.—R. VII. In the middle of the room, *Altar from Ostia, with reliefs of the origins of Rome (Mars and Rhea Silvia, Romulus and Remus suckled by the she-wolf, etc.); the altar is dated 1 Oct A.D. 124; 1043. Head of a maiden, with hair in tight curls, from the tomb of Sulpicius Platorinus; 124129. Head of a princess of the Julio-Claudian gens wearing a diadem, possibly Agrippina, mother of Nero; 1219. Antoninus Pius as a young man; 124489. Commodus as a youth; 629. Head of Sabina, wife of Hadrian (with traces of colour still visible); 124491. Head of Hadrian, from the Stazione Termini; *330. Head of Vespasian, from Ostia, one of the best surviving Roman portraits; 106538. Head of Nerva (emperor 96-98).

R. VIII. 126732. Sarcophagus of Acilia, badly damaged, with figures in high relief on front and sides (3C A.D.); 125802. Sarcophagus with pastoral scenes; 58561. Bearded head of Lucius Verus (emperor 161-69); *1119. Head of a young girl, an exquisite work of great tenderness and refinement, from the Palatine; 644. Bearded head of Gallienus (emperor 253-68), found in the House of the Vestals; 124486. Bust of a bearded personage (3C A.D.), from the Piazza della Chiesa Nuova; 56199. Bust of Constantius II (emperor 337-61).—R. IX. Mosaics, including a polychrome mosaic from a Republican villa on the Via Nomentana; 15826. Herakles, a colossal torso of the 2C A.D.; 168186. Sarcophagus of a child from Grottarossa.

From the corridor (comp. above) five more rooms are reached, containing less important works.

R. 1. 108518. Maiden as Diana, from Ostia; 30067. Archaic Kore, Roman replica of one of the series on the Acropolis at Athens.—R. 2. *Ludovisi Throne (exhibited here, while the rest of the Ludovisi collection is closed to the public, see above).

This is a large throne probably intended for the statue of a divinity, an original work of the 5C B.C. found in the Villa Ludovisi. The back and sides are adorned with reliefs. The central subject is apparently the birth of Aphrodite, who rises from the sea supported by two Seasons; on the right side is the representation of a young woman sitting clothed on a folded cushion; she is taking grains from a box and burning them in a brazier; on the left side is a naked flute girl, also sitting on a folded cushion, playing a double pipe. These three exquisite reliefs are among the masterpieces of classical sculpture.

1059. Statuette of young athlete, in green basalt, probably Autolykos, winner of the pankration in 422 B.C. (copy of a 5C original); 108604. Peplophoros, resembling the caryatids of the Erechtheion in Athens; further examples of peplophori; 52575. Head of a caryatid from Via del Cardello in Rome. R. 3. Attic torso from the Via della Spinola; *622. Dionysos, from Hadrian's Villa, Hadrianic copy of a 4C Greek original; 108595. Athena, also from Hadrian's Villa; 75675. Apollo or Eros, after a bronze original, from Palazzo Chigi.

R. 4. 125375. Mænad holding a goat by the horn, Hadrianic relief; 1087. Sleeping hermaphrodite, copy of a Hellenistic work; 1194. Young girl or nymph sleeping, from Nero's villa at Subiaco; *603. Head of a dying Persian, of the school of Pergamon, one of a series of sculptures set up at Pergamon to commemorate the victory of Attalos I over the Gauls.—R. 5. Against the wall, polychrome mosaic, with figures of the seasons, and, in the centre, Apollo punishing Marsyas (5C A.D.); 124495. Colossal statue of a seated veiled goddess, possibly Roma; 124482. Colossal statue of a Dacian; 115164. Marble and alabaster equestrian statue of a boy.

*GREAT CLOISTER. Built in 1565 (date on a pilaster : ; the entrance), this cloister is ascribed to Michelangelo, who died the year befo. e. It has a perimeter of 320 m, and the arcades, having alternate square and oval windows, are supported by 100 travertine columns. The fountain in the cloister garden gates from 1695; it is shaded by four cypresses, one of which is the original. Seven colossal heads of animals (probably from the Forum of Trajan) surround the fountain. In the cloister and garden are sculptures and inscriptions of relatively minor importance.

WING I. Four statues of Roman generals, three with breastplates; group of seated man and woman; nude youth, possibly the emperor Heliogabalus; altar with six girls dancing; three female statues.—WING II. Near the angle with Wing I, Granite slab with relief of Egyptian deities.—At the corner of WING III, *Pilasters with inscriptions relating to the Ludi Sæculares, celebrated in the reigns of Augustus (17 B.C.) and of Septimius Severus (A.D. 204). The earlier inscription records the festival ordained by Augustus, during which the Carmen Sæculare of Horace was sung at the Capitol. Between the pilasters, Nilotic mosaic.—WING IV. Statue of Jupiter standing with chlamys over his left arm; headless Herakles with club and lion-skin, after Lysippos; athlete, after Polykleitos.—In the garden, along the cloister wings, Inscriptions; Base from the Temple of Hercules at Tivoli; landmarks delimiting the land bordering the Tiber, with records of the consuls, censors, and *curatores alvei et riparum Tiberis;* other landmarks.

From the corridor a staircase leads to the **First Floor.** At the top are exquisite mosaic fragments of animals and fish, most found in Rome.— On the left, off the Sala degli Stucchi (see below) is the *SALA DEGLI AFFRESCHI DELLA VILLA DI LIVIA A PRIMA PORTA. This is a reconstruction of a rectangular room from the Imperial Villa of Livia, wife of Augustus, the walls of which are decorated with frescoes of a fruit and flower garden. It constitutes the masterpiece of naturalist decoration of the second style of Roman painting. Restored in 1952-53 and moved to the museum from Prima Porta, the painting was saved just in time from complete decay.

In the Sala degli Stucchi and the Sale dei Dipinti Murali are displayed the stucco and painted decoration of a building of the Augustan age discovered in the grounds of the Villa Farnesina near the banks of the Tiber. These are works of high artistic value, and the paintings are second in importance only to those from Pompeii and Herculaneum, now in the Museo Nazionale at Naples. In the SALA DEGLI STUCCHI are *Ceilings decorated in stucco, masterpieces of their kind, from three of the rooms (Cubicula B, D, and E). The friezes are decorated with festoons and cupids, interspersed with landscapes and mythological scenes.

At the end of the hall a door (l.) leads into the SALE DEI DIPINTI MURALI containing the painted decoration, arranged according to the rooms of the Augustan house, known as Cubicula B, C, D, and E. The paintings are in the second and third Pompeian styles: the former (1C B.C.) imitating marble decoration and introducing figures, the latter (early 1C A.D.), the best period, introducing more figures.—R. I. Paintings detached from Cubiculum E, with aediculae surmounted by fantastic cornices and paintings in which love-scenes and winged genii recur.

The next three sections contain the finest paintings found in the Roman house.—R. II. In Cubiculum B the prevailing colour is cinnabar red. The decorations include aediculae and caryatids. The paintings are of mythical subjects, including one of Aphrodite seated on a throne, attended by one of the Graces and by young Eros.—R. III. Room C has the largest painting of the series, a frieze 8½ m by 2 m, with scenes from the legend of the Egyptian king Bocchoris, the wise and noble judge. The walls have a black background.—R. IV. Cubiculum D, like its twin B, has walls mainly of red. Here is a representation of a seated female figure to whom a girl on tiptoe is offering a gift. Paintings of male and female figures issuing from flower petals show Egyptian influence. In the frieze are charming pictures of seated nymphs. On a column is inscribed the name (in Greek) of the artist, Seleukos.—R. V (closed indefinitely) contains paintings from two corridors (F and G).

Off the landing, opposite the staircase, are two rooms (usually closed) containing mosaics from Rufinello, near Tusculum, from Genazzano, and from the Villa of Septimius Severus at Baccano.

Beyond the garden to the right of the Museo Nazionale Romano lies the vast Piazza dei Cinquecento. In the garden is the Monument to the Fallen at Dogali, by Azzurri, erected in memory of 548 Italian soldiers ambushed at Dogali, Eritrea, in 1887. It incorporates an Egyptian obelisk found in the Isaeum Campense (p. 95; its companion is in Florence) inscribed with hieroglyphs recording the glories of Rameses the Great or Sesostris, the Pharaoh of the time of Moses. (The monument, first erected in front of the old railway station was moved here in 1924; in 1936-44 it was decorated with the Lion of Judah plundered from Addis Ababa.)—The **Piazza dei Cinquecento,** by far the largest square in Rome, is the terminus or junction of many urban bus and tram services and the starting-point of numerous bus and coach services to the environs.

The **Stazione di Termini** (Pl. 5; 4), on the S.E. side of the square, with its 12 main and numerous subsidiary platforms, is one of the largest and most modern in Europe. Its reconstruction, begun in 1938 and delayed by war, was completed 12 years later, and it was formally opened on 20 Dec 1950. Strictly functional in design, the station extends from Via Giovanni Giolitti on the S.W. to Via Marsala on the N.E. The façade is a plain white rectangular block, pierced horizontally by nine continuous lines of windows. In front is a gigantic quasi-cantilever construction sweeping upwards and outwards and serving as a portico for vehicles. The older and more conventional wings had been partly completed when the war stopped building operations in 1942. A covered way through the station connects the streets on either side. The Stazione di Termini is also the starting-point of the Underground railway.

In front of the station (l.), is the best preserved fragment of the so-called *Servian Wall*, formed of massive blocks of tufa. This wall was actually built after the invasion of the Gauls in 390 B.C. and was restored in the last days of the Republic (for a note on the walls of Rome, see p. 18). Further fragments of the wall were unearthed during the reconstruction of the station. Beneath the station have been found also remains of a private house and of some baths, with good mosaics, dating from the 2C A.D.

The area farther E. is described in Rte 13.

## 13   FROM THE STATION TO THE UNIVERSITY AND SAN LORENZO FUORI LE MURA

In front of the station, Via Solferino leads N.E. from Piazza dei Cinquecento to *Piazza dell' Indipendenza,* centre of the QUARTIERE DELL' INDIPENDENZA. The quarter is so called because its streets are named after battles of the War of Independence. It has a more sinister association as it is the site of the *Campus Sceleratus,* where vestals who had forgotten their vows of chasitity were buried alive.—From the piazza Via San Martino della Battaglia leads N.E. to Viale Castro Pretorio. Opposite is the **Castro Pretorio** (Pl. 6; 1), anciently the quarters of the Præetorian Guard.

The *Proetorioe Cohortes,* or emperor's bodyguard, originally nine or ten cohorts (9000-10,000 men), were instituted by Augustus and concentrated into a permanent camp at this spot by Sejanus, minister of Tiberius in A.D. 23; some portions of his building survive. In later Imperial times the Præetorian Guard acquired undue influence in the conduct of affairs of state. As Gibbon pointed out, emperor after emperor had to bribe them on his accession with a 'donative'; on one occasion, after the death of Pertinax in 193, they put up the Roman Empire for sale by auction; it was bought by Didius Julianus, who enjoyed his purchase for 66 days. Centuries later the Castro Pretorio passed into the hands of the Jesuits, who renamed it *Macao,* after their most successful foreign mission. It was again used as barracks in this century. It is now the site of the new buildings opened in 1975 of the *Biblioteca Nazionale Centrale Vittorio Emanuele II* (comp. p. 149). Founded in 1877 with the contents of the library of the Jesuit Collegio Romano, and later enriched with the books of 70 monastic libraries, it now has about 2,500,000 volumes (nearly 1900 incunabula) and 6200 manuscripts.

On the N. and E. sides the Castro Pretorio is bounded by Viale del Policlinico, which bends at a right angle to the right and then passes between the back of the library and the front of the **Policlinico** (Pl. 6; 1, 3), a large training hospital, designed by Giulio Podesti (1893), which provides free medical treatment.

On its E. side the Policlinico is bordered by Viale Regina Elena, in which the *Istituto Superiore di Sanità* has a research centre for chemical microbiology.

Viale del Policlinico ends in Viale dell' Università. This broad avenue, with a dual carriageway, runs to the right to join the winding Viale Castro Pretorio, passing (l.) the modern building of the *Air Ministry* (Pl.

6; 3) by Roberto Marino. In the other direction the avenue borders the **Città Universitaria,** built by Marcello Piacentini and others. This extensive series of buildings, formed into a 'city', was completed in 1935, in which year the seat of the University of Rome was translated from its cramped quarters in Palazzo della Sapienza in the Corso del Rinascimento (p. 99). From Viale dell' Università Viale delle Scienze leads s. In this street is (l.) the main entrance to the Città Universitaria.

From the monumental entrance a broad road leads to the *Foro Universitario,* in which is a water tank, adorned with a statue of Minerva, by A. Martini. Behind the statue rises the Rectorial Palace, with various faculties and the University Library. In the Faculty of Letters is the *Museo dei Gessi,* with reproductions of Greek and Hellenistic statuary. The road passes (r.) the faculties of Orthopaedy and Chemistry, and (l.) those of Hygiene, Physics, Mineralogy, and Geology. A side turning to the left leads to the church of *Divina Sapienza* (1947). To the right of the Rectorial Palace is the School of Mathematics and, behind it, the faculties of Botany, General Physiology, Anthropology, and Psychology.

To the s., at the junction of Viale delle Scienze with Via dei Marrucini, is the building of the *National Council of Research,* by Ortensi.

**Via dei Marrucini,** ends at Via Tiburtina, an ancient Roman road from Rome to Tibur (now Tivoli). To the left is Piazzale del Verano, in which is **Campo Verano** (Pl. 6; 4), the chief cemetery in Rome. Just beyond, to the left, is Piazza San Lorenzo, where several streets converge, with a statue of the saint, by Stef. Galletti.

At the entrance to the cemetery are four large allegorical figures. Among the tombs is that of Goffredo Mameli (d. 1849), the soldier-poet (first avenue to the left). On the high ground beside Via Tiburtina is a memorial of the battle of Mentana (1867). In the zone of the new plots is a memorial to the fallen of the war of 1914-18, by *Raff. De Vico.*

The basilica of ***San Lorenzo fuori le Mura*** (Pl. 6; 4) on the E. side of its piazza, is one of the seven pilgrimage churches of Rome and consists of two churches placed end to end. The original church of *San Lorenzo,* to the E., was built by Constantine in 330 and rebuilt in 579 by Pelagius II; the church of the *Madonna* dates from the time of Sixtus III (pope, 432-440). These churches were united in 1216, when Honorius III demolished their apses; they were skilfully restored in 1864-70. San Lorenzo was the only church in Rome to suffer serious damage during the Second World War, having been partly destroyed in an air raid on 19 July 1943. The façade and the s. wall of the church of the Madonna were rebuilt after the war, and the basilica was reopened for worship in the summer of 1949.

The simple Romanesque CAMPANILE dates from the 12C.—The façade of the church was formerly adorned with paintings of its builders and restorers; the reconstructed PORTICO of six antique Ionic columns has a carved cornice and a mosaic frieze. Inside are two curious tombs, a tablet (1948) commemorating repairs ordered by Pius XII after war damage, and a monument to Alcide De Gasperi (d. 1954), the statesman, by Manzù; the 13C frescoes depict the lives of SS. Laurence and Stephen.

The basilican INTERIOR has a chancel and no transept. Twenty-two Ionic columns of granite support an architrave, and the floor is paved with a 12C Cosmatesque mosaic. On the right of the entrance is the tomb of Card. Fieschi, a large Roman sarcophagus converted to its present use in 1256; it was rebuilt from the original fragments after the bombardment. Near the end of the nave on the right is a Cosmatesque ambone and the twisted stem of a paschal candlestick.— The baldacchino in the CHOIR is by *Augusto* and *Sassone,* sons of the mastermason Paolo (1147; upper part modern). The episcopal throne dates from the 13C. Within the triumphal arch is a 6C mosaic of Christ with saints, and Pelagius offering the

Church, reset during the Byzantine revival.—The *CHANCEL has Corinthian columns supporting an entablature of antique fragments, and above, an arcaded late-6C gallery.

Stairs lead down to the level of the original BASILICA OF CONSTANTINE, with some of the original pillars. In its former choir, now beneath the high altar, are preserved the remains of SS. Laurence, Stephen, and Justin. The original narthex, at the end, is now the Mausoleum of Pius IX (d. 1878), rebuilt by *Cattaneo* in 1881 and decorated by *Lod. Seitz.* The lunette mosaics are noteworthy; the coats of arms commemorate the families that subscribed to the tomb.—In the Sacristy, off the right aisle, is the entrance to the beautiful *CLOISTER of c. 1200, with varied columns, and inscriptions and fragments on the walls, and pagan sarcophagi.— The cloister gives access to the extensive *Catacombs of St Cyriaca,* where the body of St Laurence is said to have been placed after his death in 258.

For the continuation of Via Tiburtina to *Tivoli,* see Rte 25A. From the piazza the 30 tram returns to the Colosseum.

# 14   FROM PIAZZA VENEZIA TO SANTA MARIA MAGGIORE

From Piazza Venezia Via dei Fori Imperiali leads to the beginning of Via Cavour, opposite the entrance to the Roman Forum (Rte 5). **Via Cavour** (Pl. 8; 2), an important modern street, nearly parallel to Via Nazionale (Rte 12), runs direct to Piazza dei Cinquecento and Stazione Termini. Immediately after its start it opens out into Largo Corrado Ricci, from which Via Tor de' Conti leads left to the entrance to the Forum of Augustus (p. 138). At the beginning of this street, on the left, is the base of the *Torre dei Conti,* all that remains of a lofty tower erected at the beginning of the 13C by Riccardo dei Conti, brother of Innocent III. The tower was partly brought down by an earthquake in 1348 and was reduced to its present state by Urban VIII (1623-44).—Via Cavour now passes through the ancient *Subura,* a low-lying quarter once of equivocal reputation. The scarcely noticeable hill of the Subura was one of the four summits of the Esquiline included in the Septimontium, the city that succeeded Roma Quadrata (p. 125). The district was connected to the Roman Forum by the Argiletum.

At a cross-roads Via dei Serpenti, on the left, leads to the *Madonna dei Monti,* a church (1580; by Giac. della Porta) containing the tomb of the mendicant saint, Benoit Labre (d. 1783); on the right, Via degli Annibaldi affords an interesting glimpse of the Colosseum. Beyond the cross-roads a flight of steps ascends to the right called Via San Frances-co di Paola, on the site of the ancient Via Scelerata, so called from the impious act of Tullia, who drove her chariot over the dead body of her royal father Servius Tullius.

To the right is Piazza San Francesco di Paola, with a large 17C palazzo which houses the *Istituto Centrale del Restauro* (adm., see p. 49). This is a centre for the restoration of paintings, frescoes, bronzes and sculpture; visitors are shown the laboratories, and can see works which have not been fit to return to their original sites, such as the frescoes from the lower churches in S. Maria in Via Lata (exhibited in the class-room to the r. of the entrance hall; see p. 150), and the 8C Madonna from S. Maria in Trastevere (with many later additions and restorations). An exhibition is usually held during Museum Week (see p. 47).

The steps pass beneath an archway above which is an attractive Doric loggia, once part of the house of Vannozza Catanei, mother of Lucrezia Borgia.

At the top is Piazza San Pietro in Vincoli, with the church of *San Pietro in Vincoli (Pl. 5; 7), or *Basilica Eudoxiana,* traditionally founded in 442 by the Empress Eudoxia, wife of Valentinian III, as a shrine for the chains of St Peter. The church was restored in 1475 under Sixtus IV by *Meo del Caprina,* who was responsible for the façade, with its beautiful colonnaded portico. During 1956-59 remains of previous buildings, some going back to Republican times, were discovered beneath the church.

The two chains with which St Peter had been fettered were left in the Tullianum after his confinement there, and are said to have been recovered and taken to Constantinople. In 439 Juvenal, Bishop of Jersusalem, gave them to the Empress Eudoxia, wife of Theodosius the Younger. She placed one of them in the basilica of the Apostles at Constantinople, and sent the other to Rome for her daughter Eudoxia, wife of Valentinian III. The younger Eudoxia gave the chain to St Leo I (pope 440-61) and built the church of San Pietro in Vincoli for its reception. Later the second chain was sent to Rome. On being brought together, the two chains miraculously united.

The basilican INTERIOR, much affected by restoration, preserves its twenty columns with Doric capitals (the Ionic bases were added in the 17C). The NAVE, almost four times as wide as the aisles, has a ceiling-painting by *G. B. Parodi,* representing the cure of a demonaic by the touch of the holy chains. SOUTH AISLE. 1st Altar, *Guercino,* St Augustine; 2nd altar, *Domenichino* designed the tomb on the left and painted the portraits above both tombs; the altarpiece is a copy of his Deliverance of St Peter, now in the sacristy. At the end of the aisle is the TOMB OF JULIUS II, the unfinished masterpiece of *Michelangelo,* who was so harassed while working on the monument that he called it 'tragedy of a sepulchre'. Hindered by his quarrels with Julius and by the jealousy of that pope's successors, the artist left his task unfinished, and the great pontiff, who had contemplated for himself the most splendid monument in the world, lies uncommemorated in St Peter's. Some of the 40 statues which were to adorn the tomb are in Paris, some in Florence. No idea of the original design of the monument (for which many drawings survive) can be gained from this very unsatisfactory grouping of statues and niches. Only a few magnificent fragments remain, notably the powerful figure of *Moses,* Michelangelo's most strongly individualized work, in whose majestic glance is seen the prophet that spoke with God. The beautiful flanking figures of Leah and Rachel, symbols of the active and contemplative life (Dante, 'Purgatorio', xxvii, 108), are also by *Michelangelo.* The rest is his pupils' work; an ineffectual effigy of the Pope, by *Maso del Bosco;* a Madonna, by *Aless. Scherano;* a Prophet and Sibyl, by *Raff. da Montelupo.*

In the last chapel of this aisle, St Margaret, by *Guercino.*—The bishop's throne in the APSE, which is frescoed by *Giac. Coppi,* is a marble chair brought from a Roman bath. The baldacchino over the high altar is by *Virginio Vespignani* (19C). In the confessio below are the Chains of St Peter, displayed in a tabernacle with beautiful bronze doors attributed to *Caradosso* (1477). Stairs lead down to a tiny crypt, in which is a fine late 4C Roman sarcophagus with figures representing scenes from the New Testament, containing the relics of the seven Maccabee brothers.—NORTH AISLE. 2nd altar, 7C mosaic of the bearded St Sebastian, well preserved; 1st altar., *Pomarancio,* Descent from the Cross; (near the w. wall) *And. Bregno,* Tomb of Card. De Cusa, with a colourful relief (1465).—On the end wall to the right of the entrance door, is the Tomb of the brothers Pollaiuolo, by *Capponi*. Above is a fresco of the Plague of 1476, by un unknown 15C artist. Near the tomb, is an early fresco of the Head of Christ (behind glass).—The CLOISTER (entrance at No. 16 Via Eudossiana, on the right, now the University Faculty of Engineering), is attributed to *Giul. da Sangallo*. The arches have sadly been enclosed, but the lovely well-head by *Simone Mosca* remains.

The narrow Via delle Sette Sale, which leads out of the piazza on the left of San Pietro in Vincoli, is named after the reservoir of the Baths of Trajan (p. 206). The street passes between two of the summits of the Esquiline, the *Cispius* (l.) and the *Oppius* (r.).

The Esquiline (65 m), the highest and most extensive of the Seven Hills of Rome, was formerly a region of vineyards and gardens, and had few inhabitants. Even today, it is not wholly built over. Of its four summits, the *Oppius* or *Oppian Hill* is largely taken up by a park, the Parco Oppio, on which were built the Baths of Titus and of Trajan and the Golden House of Nero. The *Cispius,* extending to the N.E., is crowned by the basilica of Santa Maria Maggiore. The other two summits—the *Subura,* above the low-lying quarter of that name, and the *Fagutalis*—are insignificant. According to the erudite Varro, the name of Esquiline was derived from the word *excultus,* in reference to the ornamental groves planted on the hill by Servius Tullius—such as the Querquetulanus (oak grove) and Fagutalis (beech grove), the latter giving its name to one of the four summits.

Although the hill was generally unhealthy, part of it was a fashionable residential quarter. This was called the *Carinoe* and stretched from the site of the Tor de' Conti to the slopes of the Oppian Hill. Here lived Pompey, in a small but famous house, occupied after his death by Antony. The villa of Mæcenas was situated on the ground afterwards occupied by the Baths of Titus. The villa was eventually acquired by Nero, who incorporated it in his fabulous Golden House. Virgil had a house near the gardens of Mæcenas. Propertius lived in the quarter and Horace may have done so: he was certainly a constant visitor at the villa of his patron.

At the end of Via delle Sette Sale, by its junction with Viale del Monte Oppio, is the church of **San Martino ai Monti** (Pl. 5; 5, 6), the church of the Carmelites, built in 500 by St Symmachus and dedicated to SS. Sylvester and Martin. It replaced an older church founded in the 4C by Pope St Sylvester I, who came from Mount Soracte to cure Constantine of an illness. It was rebuilt c. 1650; the existing structure stands on the remains of the old church and incorporates part of some Roman baths, possibly the Baths of Trajan, which spread over the neighbouring Oppian Hill.

In this church were proclaimed, in the presence of Constantine, the decisions of the Council of Nicæa, and the heretical books of Arius, Sabellius, and Victorinus consigned to the flames.—The broad NAVE is divided from the aisles by 24 antique Corinthian columns. In the s. aisle, Frescoes of the Life of Elijah, by *Gaspard Poussin;* in the N. aisle, Interiors of St John Lateran and St Peter's before reconstruction, and the Council of Pope Sylvester, by an unknown 16C artist. The tribune, with a double staircase, leading to the high altar, and the tabernacle are by *Pietro da Cortona.* From the confessio stairs descend past the elaborate crypt to (left) a private chapel of the 3C, with traces of frescoes and mosaics, incorporated in eight large halls of the Baths of Trajan.

Behind the apse of San Martino, on the other side of Via Giovanni Lanza (in which are two fine medieval towers), is the church of **Santa Prassede** (Pl. 5; 6), entered from Via Santa Prassede, a turning (l.) out of Via San Martino ai Monti. An oratory, said to have been erected here about A.D. 150 by St Pius I, is known to have been in existence at the end of the 5C. The present church was built by St Paschal I in 822 and was restored in 1450, 1564, 1832, and 1869.

The building is dedicated to Praxedes, sister of Pudentiana (p. 204) and daughter of Pudens, in whose house St Peter first found hospitality at Rome. Here in 1118 the Frangipani assailed Pope Gelasius II with arrows and stones, driving him to exile in France, where he died.

The NAVE has an architrave with 16 granite columns and six piers. About 9 m from the door a porphyry disc and an inscription indicate the well where St Praxedes hid the bones of Christian martyrs. In the s. aisle is the *CHAPEL OF ST ZENO (lights on l.), a remarkable Byzantine structure, built by St Paschal as a mausoleum for his mother, Theodora. The entrance is flanked by two antique columns of dark granite with 6C Ionic capitals which support a rich cornice from some pagan temple, elaborately sculptured; on this rests an antique marble urn. Above is a double row of 9C mosaic busts; in the inner row, the Virgin and Child, SS. Praxedes and Pudentiana, and other saints; in the outer, Christ and the Apostles, and four saints (the lowest two perhaps added in the 13C). The vaulted interior, the solitary instance in Rome of a chapel entirely lined with mosaics, was known as the 'Garden of Paradise.' The pavement is perhaps the oldest known example of opus sectile. Over the door, SS. Peter and Paul uphold the throne of God; on the right, SS. John the Evangelist, Andrew, and James, and Christ between St Paschal and Valentine (?); inside the altar-niche, Madonna between SS. Praxedes and Pudentiana; on the left, SS. Praxedes, Pudentiana, and Agnes, and four female half-lengths including Theodora (with the square nimbus). In the vault, Christ and four angels. The four supporting columns have unusual bases. In a niche on the right are fragments of a column brought from Jerusalem after the 6th Crusade (1228), and said to be that at which Christ was scourged. In the adjoining chapel is the Tomb. of Card. Alain Cétive (1474) by *And. Bregno.* Outside, on a nave pillar, is the tomb of G. B. Santoni (d. 1592), one of the earliest works of *Bernini.* At the E. end of the aisle a chapel contains the Cosmatesque tomb of Card. Ancherus of Troyes (d. 1286) and architectural fragments.

NORTH AISLE. At the w. end, marble slab on which St Praxedes is said to have slept; 3rd chap., frescoes by *Cav. d'Arpino;* Christ bearing the Cross, by *Fed. Zuccari;* and the chair and table of St Charles Borromeo. In the Sacristy, Flagellation, attrib. to *Giulio Romano.*—To the r. a spiral staircase leads up to the campanile with 9C wall paintings.

The CHOIR is approached by steps of rosso antico. The *Mosaics date from the 9C (lights on r.): on the entrance-arch (outer face) the New Jerusalem, whose doors are guarded by angels, (inner face) Christ and saints; on the apse-arch, the Agnus Dei with the seven golden candlesticks, the symbols of the Evangelists, and 24 Elders; in the semi-dome, Christ between (r.) SS. Peter, Pudentiana, and Zeno, and (l.) SS. Paul, Praxedes, and Paschal; below, the Lamb, the flock of the Faithful and a dedicatory inscription; above, the monogram of Paschal I.—In the Confessio beneath are sarcophagi, including one with the remains of SS. Praxedes and Pudentiana, and a 13C Cosmatesque altar, with a damaged fresco above.

A short distance to the N. is *Piazza Santa Maria Maggiore,* occupying the highest point (55 m) of the Cispian summit of the Esquiline. In the square rises a fluted cipollino column 14½ m high, a relic of the basilica of Constantine. It was set up here in 1613 by Paul V and crowned with a statue of the Virgin. The fountain was designed by Carlo Maderna. Dominating the square is the ornate porticoed façade of *Santa Maria Maggiore (Pl. 5; 6), or *Basilica Liberiana,* which, more completely than any other of the four partriarchal basilicas (p. 45), retains its original interior magnificence. Santa Maria Maggiore has the privilege of extraterritoriality.

According to a 13C tradition, the Virgin Mary appeared on the night of 4-5 Aug 352, to Pope Liberius and to John, a patrician of Rome, telling them to build a church on the Esquiline on the spot where they would find in the morning a patch of snow covering the exact area to be built over. The prediction fulfilled, Liberius drew up the plans and John built the church at his own expense. The original title was therefore Santa Maria della Neve. The church was afterwards called *Santa Maria del Presepe,* after a precious relic of the Crib of the Infant Jesus. The church was rebuilt by Sixtus III in 432-40. Eugenius III (pope, 1145-53) and Nicholas IV (1288-92) enlarged and restored it, Clement X (1670-76) rebuilt the apse, and Benedict XIV (1740-58) added the main façade.

Two important ceremonies are held here annually. On 5 Aug the legend of the miraculous fall of snow is commemorated in a pontifical Mass in the Borghese Chapel (see below). On Christmas morning occurs the procession in honour of the Santa Culla, or Holy Crib, which culminates in the exposure of the relic on the high altar.

In 366 supporters of the antipope Ursinus barricaded themselves in the church and surrendered only when the partisans of Pope Damasus I took off the roof and pelted them with tiles. In 1075 Gregory VII (Hildebrand) was carried off from Mass by the rebel Cencio, but was rescued next day by the people. In 1347 Rienzo was crowned here as Tribune of Rome.

**Exterior.** The unsatisfactory MAIN FAÇADE, masking one of the 12C, was designed by *Fuga* (1743); it is approached by steps and is flanked by two grandiose wings. The portico is surmounted by a loggia of three arches, above which are statues. Five openings admit to the portico, on the right of which is a statue of Philip IV of Spain, after *Bernini*. In the loggia may be seen the mosaics of the earlier façade, dating from the time of Nicholas IV (apply to the sacristan), which depict the Legend of the Snow (see above) and saints, by *Filippo Rusuti* (c. 1320); the lower part was probably completed by assistants. Of the five doors which lead into the basilica that on the left is the *Porta Santa* (comp. p. 262).—The fine CAMPANILE, the loftiest in Rome, was given its present form in 1377 by Gregory XI.—The APSIDAL FAÇADE, completed c. 1673, is approached by an imposing flight of steps from Piazza dell'Esquilino. The right-hand section, with its dome, is by *Flaminio Ponzio;* the central and left sections by *Carlo Rainaldi;* the left-hand dome by *Dom. Fontana.*

The vast but well-proportioned **Interior** (86 m long), which still preserves the basilican form, is divided into nave and aisles by 36 columns of shining Hymettian marble and 4 of granite, all with Ionic capitals supporting an architrave adorned with mosaics, the whole discreetly rearranged and regularized by *Fuga.* Over the triumphal arch and above the arches of the nave are *Mosaics, set up by Sixtus III (432-440). On the left, scenes from the life of Abraham, Jacob, and Isaac; r., scenes from the life of Moses and Joshua (restored: in part painted); over the arch, the life of Mary. The coffered *Ceiling, attributed to *Giul. da Sangallo,* is said to have been gilded with the first gold brought from America by Columbus, presented to Alexander VI by Ferdinand and Isabella. The fine Cosmatesque pavement dates from c. 1150. Near the right-hand door (A) is the monument of Clement IX (1670), by C. Rainaldi, and others. On the left (B) that of Nicholas IV (1574), by *Dom. Fontana* and others. The Confessio (C), reconstructed in the 19C by *Vespignani,* contains a kneeling statue of Pius IX by *Iacometti.* The baldacchino over the high altar, with four porphyry columns, is by *Fuga;* a porphyry urn which contains the relics of St Matthew and other martyrs serves as the high altar; the fragment of the Crib of the Infant Jesus is kept below in the Confessio in a reliquary adorned with reliefs and silver statuettes.—The mosaic of the APSE (O) dating from the time of Nicholas IV (1288-94), by *Iac. Torriti,* represents the *Coronation of the Virgin, with angels, saints, Nicholas IV, Card. Iac. Colonna, etc. It is the culminating point of all the mosaics in the church, which commemorate the declaration at the Council of Ephesus (5C) that the Virgin was the Mother of God (Theotókos). The Virgin is seated on the same throne as Christ, a composition probably derived from the 12C mosaic in the apse of Santa Maria in Trastévere. Below, between the windows, are more mosaics by Torriti of the life of the Virgin, notably, in the centre, the Dormition of the Virgin. The four reliefs, below the windows, are from the old ciborium by *Mino del Reame*.

RIGHT AISLE. From the Baptistery (E), with a bas-relief by *Pietro Bernini*, is the entrance to the Sacristy (F), designed, like the Baptistery, by *Ponzio* (early 17C), with a tomb by *Aless. Algardi*. In the vault of the Cappella San Michele (G; usually closed) are traces of 15C frescoes. A column in the adjoining courtyard celebrates the conversion of Henry IV of France. On the s. aisle is the entrance to the Cappella delle Reliquie (H) with ten porphyry columns. The *SIXTINE CHAPEL, or *Chapel of the Holy Sacrament* (J), is a work of extraordinary magnificence by *Dom. Fontana*. It is a veritable church in itself, decorated with statues and frescoes, and contains the sumptuous monuments of Sixtus V, with statue by *Valsoldo*, and of Pius V, with statue by *Leon. Sormani*. The temple-like baldacchino in the centre covers the original little Cosmatesque chapel of the relics, redesigned by *Arnolfo di Cambio* (late 13C). The ceiling paintings are by Mannerists of the late 16C.—Near the door at the end of the aisle is the beautiful *Tomb of Card. Consalvo Rodriguez (d. 1299), a masterpiece by *Giov. Cosmati* (K). The mosaic of the Madonna enthroned, with saints, fits well the architectonic lines of the tomb, which was completed by the beginning of the fourteenth century.

LEFT AISLE. Balancing the Sixtine Chapel is the even more sumptuous BORGHESE CHAPEL, or *Cappella Paolina* (L). This chapel, built by Paul V on the plans of *Flaminio Ponzio* (1611), is frescoed by *Cigoli, Cav. d' Arpino, Guido Reni*, and *Lanfranco*. On the altar, decorated with lapis lazuli and agate, is a Madonna and Child with crossed hands, now attributed to an artist before the 10C. The tombs of Clement VIII and Paul V, with statues by *Silla Longhi*, are on either side.—The SFORZA CHAPEL (M), erected by Giac. della Porta, perhaps to a design by Michelangelo, contains an Assumption, by *Girol. da Sermoneta*. In the next (N) the CESI CHAPEL, by *Guidetto Giudetti*, are two tombs, by *Gugl. della Porta* and a St Catherine, by *Sermoneta*.—The tomb of the Cardinals Filippo and Eustachio de Levis (1489), above the Porta Santa (P) is in the style of *Giov. Dalmata*.

The doors on either side of the apse lead out on to *Piazza dell'Esquilino*. In the centre of the square is an obelisk, nearly 15 m high, set up by Sixtus V in 1587. Like its twin in Piazza del Quirinale it once stood outside the entrance to the Mausoleum of Augustus. Via Cavour (comp. p. 199) cuts across the piazza. Opposite Santa Maria Maggiore Via Agostino Depretis runs N.W. to Via Nazionale (p. 188). Via Urbana, on the left, leads in a few metres to **Santa Pudenziana** (Pl. 5; 5), one of the oldest churches in Rome; it is dedicated to Pudentiana, sister of Praxedes (see p. 201). The tradition that it was founded on the site of the house of the senator Pudens where St Peter lodged in Rome has been disproved. The church was rebuilt by Pope St Siricius (384-99) and several times later, notably in 1589.

The façade was rebuilt and decorated in the 19C; the campanile dates from the late 12C. A few steps descend to the entrance through a fine doorway, with a beautiful medieval frieze in relief.

The nave and aisles in the severe INTERIOR are divided by antique columns built up into piers. The dome was painted by *Pomarancio*. The precious *Mosaic in the apse (390) was damaged by a 16C restoration, which removed the two outermost Apostles at each end and cut the others in half. It depicts Christ enthroned holding an open book, with SS. Pudentiana and Praxedes offering crowns. At the back is a hill with a cross, and buildings (houses, thermæ, and a basilica) which were perhaps the property of Pudens; above are the symbols of the Evangelists. The Roman character of the figures is noticeable; the magisterial air of Christ recalls the representations of Jupiter, and the Apostles, in their togas, resemble senators.—In the chapel at the end of the left aisle an altar, presented by Card. Wiseman, encloses part of the legendary communion-table of St Peter; the rest of it is in St John Lateran. The marble group of Christ entrusting the keys to St Peter is by *G. B. della Porta*. The Cappella Caetani, opening off the aisle is a rich Baroque

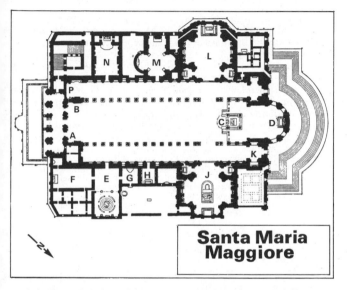

**Santa Maria Maggiore**

work, by *Franc. da Volterra,* finished by *Carlo Maderna.* The altar relief is by *P. P. Olivieri.* Behind the apse are fragments of frescoes and a statuette of the Good Shepherd.

Through a door in the l. aisle (apply to sacristan, but usually closed) is a courtyard, showing part of 2C baths, and, up some stairs, the *Oratorium Marianum,* containing 11C frescoes and brick stamps of Hadrian's time, discovered during excavations. The building incorporates part of the baths said to have been erected by Novatian and Timotheus, the brothers of Pudentiana and Praxedes, above the so-called house of Pudens. The baths extend on to the pavement in Via Balbo; the frescoes are also visible from here. Excavations under the church in 1933 revealed Republican mosaics and walls, with a 2C house; these, however, have been closed since 1970 when they were badly flooded.

From Piazza Santa Maria Maggiore, Via Carlo Alberto passes the churches of (l.) *Sant'Antonio Abate,* the church of the Russo-Byzantine rite, with its Cosmatesque doorway of 1269, and (r.) *Santi Vito e Modesto* (4C; restored in 1900), containing frescoes by Antoniazzo Romano. Near by is the *Arch of Gallienus,* the middle arch of a triple gate erected in the time of Augustus and dedicated in A.D. 262 in honour of Gallienus and his consort Salonina by the city prefect M. Aurelius Victor; it occupies the site of the Porta Esquilina of the Servian Wall. The street ends in the spacious tree-planted PIAZZA VITTORIO EMANU-ELE (Pl. 5; 6); surmounted by porticoes, it is the scene of Rome's most important food-market, particularly noted for fish.

In the garden of the square are the ruins of a fountain of the time of Alexander Severus, where the marble panoplies known as the 'Trophies of Marius', now on the balustrade of Piazza del Campidoglio, remained until the 16C. Near the fountain is the curious *Porta Magica,* with an alchemist's prescription for making gold. In the N. corner of the square is the church of **Sant'Eusebio,** founded in the 4C and rebuilt in 1711 and 1750. The ceiling painting, the Triumph of St Eusebius, is by *Raphael Mengs;* in the apse are fine, elaborately carved 16C stalls. In the Sacristy, in the r. aisle, is the carved top of the tomb of St Eusebius (15C) from the earlier church.

In Largo Leopardi, junction of Via Leopardi and Via Merulana (Pl. 5; 6, 8), is the so-called **Auditorium of Mæcenas** (adm. see p. 47). An Augustan apsidal building, this was in the gardens of Mæcenas, and may have been a nymphæum. The unusual apse has tiered seats in a semicircle. Traces of red landscape paintings can be seen in the apse and wall niches.—Adjoining is a portion of the Servian Wall.

Across Via Merulana (r.), is *Palazzo Brancaccio,* housing the *Istituto Italiano per il Medio ed Estremo Oriente.* On the second floor is the **Museo Nazionale di Arte Orientale** (adm. see p. 49), with a fine collection of Oriental art in eleven superbly arranged rooms.

ROOM I. Pre-Mohammedan Iran. Prehistoric ceramics, decorated with animal and geometric motifs, terracotta vases. Luristan bronzes, weapons, and horsebits.
RR. II and III. Mohammedan Iran. R. II. 9-15C glazed pottery, finely coloured. On the wall, a 16C gold-embroidered cope, with hunting motif.—R. III. 9-10C Orinetal-type vases (T'ang). 12-18C Mohammedan ceramics, including exquisite tiles. Indian and Siamese stelæ and images. 8C B.C. sculpture from Afghanistan, of the god Durga killing the demon buffalo.
R. IV. (G. Auriti donation). Chinese, Japanese, and Korean bronzes, ceramics and Buddhas.—R. V. (Exhibition room). Iranian art, including imitation T'ang ceramics.
RR. VI and VII. Architectural fragments and sculpture from Swat, in N.E. Pakistan.
R. IX. 18C paintings on decorated vellum from Tibet.—R. X. Paintings by Munchò (1362-1431) and Motonobu Kano (1477-1559). A 6C Buddha.
R. X. Chinese and Korean objects in silver, gold, and bronze. R. XI (to the left of R. I). Architectural fragments of 12-13C found in the Palace of Masud III in Ghazni. In the passage, collection of Oriental coins.

The Palazzo occupies part of the site of the Baths of Trajan; in the garden (no adm.) is a large vaulted building called *Le Sette Sale.* This building was a reservoir of Nero's Golden House adapted by Trajan for his baths.

Via Merulana returns to P.za Santa Maria Maggiore. Bus No. 70 from Piazza Santa Maria Maggiore returns to Piazza Venezia, or walkers may follow Via S. M. Maggiore from the w. side of the piazza into Via Panisperna (p. 175) and from there continue to Largo Magnan-ápoli.

## 15   FROM THE COLOSSEUM TO THE LATERAN AND PORTA MAGGIORE

On the E. side of the Colosseum, between Via Labicana and Via S. Giovanni in Laterano (Pl. 9; 1) are remains of the *Ludus Magnus,* the principal training school for gladiators constructed by Domitian, and excavated in 1960-61. Part of the curved wall of a miniature amphitheatre used for training can be seen. Via San Giovanni in Laterano continues past a new office block (beneath which were found remains of houses built before A.D. 64 with fine mosaics) to **\*San Clemente** (Pl. 9; 2), the best preserved of the medieval basilicas in Rome. It is dedicated to St Clement, the fourth pope. It consists of two churches superimposed, raised above a large early Imperial building owned possibly by the family of T. Flavius Clemens.

The *Lower Church,* mentioned by St Jerome in 392, was the scene of papal councils under St Zosimus in 417 and under St Symmachus in 499. Restored in the 8C and 9C, it was destroyed in 1084 during the sack of Rome by the soldiers of Robert Guiscard. Eight centuries later—in 1857—it was rediscovered by Father Mullooly, prior of the adjoining convent of Irish Dominicans, and was excavated in 1861.—The *Upper Church* was begun in 1108 by Paschal II, who used the decorative marbles from the ruins of the old church. In the 18C it was restored by Carlo Stefano Fontana at the instance of Clement XI (pope, 1700-21).

The **Upper Church,** perhaps the most complete example in existence of the Christian basilica, has its façade turned towards the E. A porch of four 12C Ionic columns leads into a quadriporticus surrounding a courtyard with a little fountain. At the end is the main door of the church (A; usually closed); there is another entrance by the side door in Via San Giovanni in Laterano (B).

The typically basilican interior has a nave and aisles separated by two rows of seven columns, and a cosmatesque pavement. In the NAVE, the Schola Cantorum (C), from the lower church, contains two ambones, candelabrum, and a reading-desk, all characteristic elements in the arrangement of a basilican interior. The \*Screen of the choir and sanctuary, with its transennae, marked with the monogram of John II (533-35), the choir raised above the confessio, the high altar with its tabernacle, the stalls of the clergy, and the bishop's throne, are also well preserved. In the PRESBYTERY is the baldacchino (D) borne by columns of pavonazzetto. The early 12C mosaics in the apse are especially fine; on the triumphal arch, Christ and the symbols of the Evangelists; on the right, SS. Peter and Clement, with the boat and oars, Jeremiah, and Jerusalem; on the left, SS. Paul and Laurence, Isaiah, and Bethlehem. In the apse-vault, Crucifixion with the Hand of God above, twelve doves (the Apostles), St Mary, and St John; from the foot of the Cross springs a vine, encircling figures of St John the Baptist, the Doctors of the Church, and other saints, while the rivers of Paradise flow forth from the Cross, quenching the thirst of the faithful (represented by stags) and watering the pastures of the Christian flock. Below are the Lamb of God and twelve companions. On the apse-wall, Christ, the Virgin, and the Apostles, a 14C fresco; to the right, is a beautiful wall-tabernacle, probably by *Arnolfo di Cambio.* The 18C ceiling of the nave has a Triumph of St Clement by *Gius. Chiari.*

In the RIGHT AISLE, at the side of the presbytery (E), tombs of Abp. Giov. Fr. Brusati, by *Luigi Capponi* (1485), and of *Card. Bart. Roverella, by *And. Bregno* and *Giov. Dalmata* (1476); Chap. at end (F), Statue of St John the Baptist, by *Sim. Ghini* (15C); in the chapel of St Cyril (K), Madonna, by *Sassoferrato* (one of several versions). In the chapel at the end by entrance door (L) are three paintings of scenes from the life of St Dominic, by *Seb. Conca.*—LEFT AISLE, 1st Chap. (G), Our Lady of the Rosary, by *Seb. Conca;* tomb of Card. Ant. Venier (d. 1479), incorporating columns from a 6C tabernacle. The chapel of St Cather-

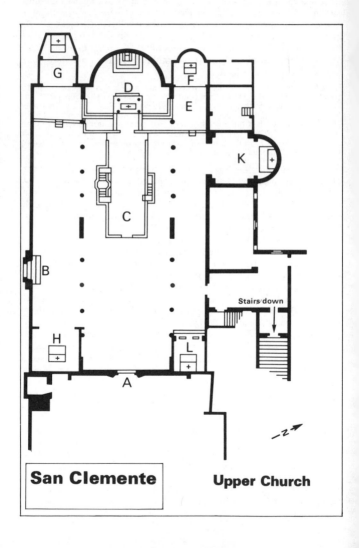

**San Clemente**          **Upper Church**

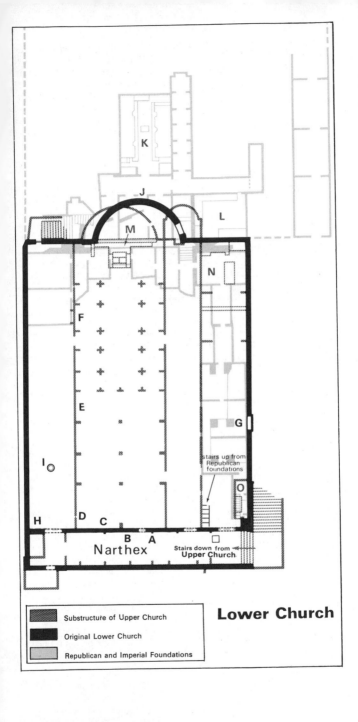

K

J

M

L

N

F

E

G

stairs up from
Republican
foundations

I

O

H    D    C

B    A

Narthex          Stairs down from
                 Upper Church.

Substructure of Upper Church

Original Lower Church

Republican and Imperial Foundations

**Lower Church**

ine (H) contains *Frescoes by *Masolino da Panicale,* probably with the help of his pupil, *Masaccio* (before 1430; restored 1956): on the left entrance pier, St Christopher; on the face of the arch, Annunciation; in the archivolt, the Apostles; in the vault, the Evangelists and Fathers of the Church; behind the altar, Crucifixion; right wall, Life of St Ambrose; left wall, Life of St Catherine of Alexandria. To the r. above, outside the chap., is a sinopia for the beheading of St Catherine (found during restoration) and, on the aisle wall, the sinopia for the Crucifixion.

Off the Right Aisle is the entrance to the **Lower Church** the apse of which was built above a Mithræum (3C). This formed part of a late-1C apartment house. Below this again are foundations of the Republican period. Adm. 9-12, 15.30-18; fest. 10-12, 15.30-18. The staircase, which has miscellaneous fragments of sculpture, descends to the frescoed NARTHEX.

At the foot of the steps a catacomb (comp. below) may be seen through a grate in the floor. On the right wall is a fresco of the the Legend of St Clement (A), who was banished to the Crimea and there executed by drowning in the Black Sea. Below are St Clement and the donor of the fresco. Farther on, to the right, Translation of St Cyril's body (B) from the Vatican to San Clemente (11C). An archway leads into the aisled church which has a wide NAVE obstructed by the foundation piers of the upper church, and is unequally divided by a supporting wall. Immediately to the left is a 9C fresco (C) of the Ascension, with the Virgin in the centre surrounded by the Apostles, St Vitus, and St Leo IV (with square nimbus). In the adjacent angle (D) the Crucifixion, the Marys at the Tomb, the Descent into Hell, and the Marriage at Cana. Farther along, on the l. wall of the nave is the Story of St Alexis (E; 11C): the saint returns home unrecognized and lives for 17 years beneath a staircase (comp. p. 90); before dying he sends the story of his life to the Pope, and is thus recognized by his wife and father. Above, lower part of a fresco of Christ amid angels and saints. Farther on, Story of Sisinius (F): the heathen Sisinius follows his Christian wife in secret, hoping thereby to capture the Pope, but he is smitten with a sudden blindness; below, Sisinius orders his servants to seize the Pope, but they, also struck blind, carry off a column instead (this fresco more probably depicts the building of the church, as is explained by the painted inscriptions, which are among the oldest examples of Italian writing). Above, St Clement enthroned by SS. Peter, Linus, and Anacletus, his predecessors on the pontifical throne (only the lower part of the fresco survives).—RIGHT AISLE. In a niche, Byzantine Madonna (G; 5C or 6C), which may have been originally a portrait of the Empress Theodora; female saints with the crown of martyrdom; and a beardless Christ. The frescoes, much damaged, probably depict the Council of Zosimus, the Story of Tobias, and the Martyrdom of St Catherine. At the end, a sarcophagus of the 1C A.D. with the story of Phaedra and Hippolytus, and a Byzantine figure of Christ (7C or 8C).—LEFT AISLE. Frescoes (H) of uncertain subjects. In the floor (I) is a circular recess, perhaps an early baptismal piscina. At the end, remains of a tomb perhaps that of St Cyril (869), the apostle of the Slavs.

From the end of the left aisle a 4C staircase descends to the 1C level with a 'palazzo', and a Mithraic temple of the late 2C or early 3C. Around the corner at the bottom (r.) is the pronaos of the temple (J), with stucco ceiling ornaments; opposite is the Triclinium (K) with benches on either side and an altar in the centre showing Mithras, in his Phrygian cap, sacrificing a bull to Apollo, and in the niche behind is a statue of Mithras; the vault imitates the roof of a cavern. At the far end of the corridor, to the r., is the presumed Mithraic School (L), where catechumens were instructed, with a mosaic floor and stuccoed vault.

From the pronaos, a door (l.) leads to the 1C 'palazzo', probably belonging to Flavius Clemens, which lies beneath the lower basilica. A long narrow passage (M) divides the temple area from the thick tufa wall of the building constructed after Nero's fire on Republican foundations. Only two sides of this building have been excavated. Immediately to the r., at the bottom of a short flight of steps, is a series of rooms; the last two are the best-preserved rooms of the Palazzo, showing the original brickwork. The 2nd side of the building is reached by returning to the opening from the corridor; beyond a room (N) with spring water which has been channelled away by tunnels, are seven more rooms, the last of which (O) has a small catacomb (probably 5C or 6C, as it is within the city walls). A staircase from here leads up to the Lower Church and exit.

Off Via dei Querceti, Via dei Santi Quattro (l.) leads steeply up to the church of **Santi Quattro Coronati** (Pl. 9; 2), a remarkable castellated building of the Middle Ages.

The original 4C or 5C foundation was destroyed by the Norman soldiery in 1084, and the present church was erected on a smaller scale in 1111 by Paschal II. It was restored in 1914 by Muñoz. Its dedication recalls the tradition of five Pannonian sculptors who refused to make a statue of Aesculapius, and of four soldiers (the Coronati; SS. Severus, Severinus, Carpophorus, and Victorinus) who refused to worship it when finished by other hands. The church is specially venerated by sculptors and marble masons.

The entrance passes beneath a squat campanile into a small court (the 5C atrium), then a portico, and then a second court, once part of the nave, whose columns have survived. On the right of the portico is the CHAPEL OF ST SYLVESTER (visitors ring for the key at the monastery of a closed order; 1st door on r.). It was restored in 1248, and contains delightful *Frescoes of the same date (and particularly well preserved), illustrating the legend of Constantine. The floor is Cosmatesque. The church proper lies at the back of the second court.

The aisled INTERIOR has a disproportionately wide apse and a matroneum, or women's gallery. The pavement is of 13C Cosmati work. On the w. wall and that of the s. aisle are 14C frescoes; and against the left pillar of the apse is a beautiful 15C tabernacle. The Baroque apse is effectively decorated with frescoes by *Giov. da San Giovanni* (1630), depicting the history of the Quattro Coronati and the glory of all saints. The tomb of the four martyrs is in the crypt.—From the N. aisle is the entrance to the delightful *Cloister (ring for adm.) of the early 13C, with a 12C fountain and lovely garden. It is one of the most secluded spots in Rome. On the l. is the 9C chapel of Santa Barbara interesting for its architecture and unusual corbels, and with remains of Medieval frescoes in the vault.

Via dei Santi Quattro leads to Piazza di San Giovanni in Laterano, round which and the adjoining Piazza di Porta San Giovanni are assembled some of the most important monuments in Christian history.

Near the centre is a red granite OBELISK, the oldest in Rome. It was erected by Thothmes IV in front of the Temple of Ammon at Thebes (15C B.C.), and brought to Rome by Constantius II (357) to adorn the Circus Maximus, where it was discovered in three pieces in 1587. It was set up on its present site by Dom. Fontana, in 1588. It is the largest obelisk in existence (31 m high, 47 m with the pedestal), though 1 m had to be sawn off during its reconstruction.—On the w. side of the square is the *Ospedale di San Giovanni,* the main hospital in Rome for emergencies ('pronto soccorso'; car accidents, etc.).

In the s.w. corner of the piazza is the *Baptistery of St John, or *San Giovanni in Fonte,* an octagonal building of the time of Constantine (324), though not, as legend states, the scene of his baptism as the first Christian emperor (337). It was the model for many subsequent baptisteries, and was restored by Sixtus III (432-40) and again by Adrian III in 884. The 17C decorations were added by Urban VIII (1623-44). The Baptistery is open daily, 8-12, 15-18.

The eight columns of porphyry within were erected by Sixtus III; they support eight others of white marble on which rests the cupola. In the centre is the green basalt *Font,* in which Rienzo bathed on 1 Aug 1347, before his public appearance as a knight outside the Lateran. The scenes from the life of St John the Baptist, on the drum of the cupola, are by *And. Sacchi.* The chapels are shown by the sacristan. To the right: CHAPEL OF ST JOHN THE BAPTIST. The bronze door, which resounds musically when opened, was the gift of the martyred pope, St Hilary (461-68).—THE CHAPEL OF SS. SECUNDA AND RUFINA (or SS. Cyprian and Justina) occupied the original narthex, altered to its present form in 1154. Over the door is a relief of the Crucifixion, after *And. Bregno* (1492); in the left-hand apse is a beautiful 5C *Mosaic of acanthus leaves on a brilliant blue ground. Over the door can be seen a fragment of the original decoration of the Baptistery (recently uncovered). Another door leads out into a courtyard from where can be seen the outer face of the original entrance to the Baptistery with a fine Roman architrave.—The CHAPEL OF ST VENANTIUS (640) contains 7C mosaics including views of Jerusalem and Bethlehem. Remains of a Roman building with a mosaic pavement may also be seen here. The structure of the original baptistery can be seen in the walls and beneath the apse.—The CHAPEL OF ST JOHN THE EVANGELIST, dedicated by St Hilary, with bronze doors of 1196, is decorated with a vault *Mosaic (5C) of the Lamb surrounded by symbolic birds and flowers. The altar is adorned with alabaster columns. On the left, *L. Capponi,* St Leo praying to St John.—In the courtyard is a statue of the Christian Workman, by *Ann. Monti* (1904).

The church of *St John Lateran (*San Giovanni in Laterano;* Pl. 10; 3) is the cathedral of Rome and of the world ('Omnium urbis et orbis Ecclesiarum Mater et Caput'). Until 1870 the popes were crowned here. Under the Lateran Treaty of 11 Feb 1929 (see p. 261), this basilica, with those of San Paolo fuori le Mura and Santa Maria Maggiore, was accorded the privilege of extraterritoriality. After the ratification of the treaty the pope, for the first time since 1870, left the seclusion of the Vatican. On 24 June 1929, Pius XI officiated at St John Lateran, and the annual ceremony of blessing the people from the loggia was later resumed. The Pope traditionally attends the Maundy Thursday celebrations in the Basilica.

This basilica derives its name from the rich patrician family of Plautius Lateranus, who, having been implicated in the conspiracy of Piso, was deprived of his property and put to death by Nero. The property afterwards became part of the marriage portion brought by Fausta to Constantine. The emperor presented it, together with land occupied by the Equites Singulares (excavated in 1934-38), to St Melchiades (pope 311-14), for the purpose of building a church for the see of Rome. The original five-aisled church was dedicated to the Redeemer and later to SS. John the Baptist and John the Evangelist. Partly ruined by the Vandals, it was restored by St Leo the Great (440-461) and Adrian I (772-795) and, after the earthquake of 896, by Sergius III (904-911). Nicholas IV (1288-1292) enlarged and beautified the building to such an extent that it was reckoned the wonder of the age; it was this church that Dante described with admiration on the occasion of the first Jubilee, or Holy Year, proclaimed on 22 Feb 1300 by Boniface VIII from the central loggia of the E. façade.

The church was destroyed by fire in 1308 and rebuilt by Clement V (1305-14) soon afterwards; it was decorated by Giotto. In 1360 it was burnt down again and its ruin was lamented by Petrarch. Under Urban V (1362-70) and Gregory XI (1370-78) it was entirely rebuilt by the Sienese Giovanni di Stefano. Martin V (1417-31), Eugenius IV (1431-47) and their successors added to its splendour (Sixtus V employing Dom. Fontana, and Clement VIII, Giac. della Porta). In 1646-49 Innocent X commissioned Borromini to rebuild the church yet again, and in 1734 Clement XII added the E. façade. The ancient apse was entirely reconstructed in 1875-85 and the mosaics reset after the original designs.—The basilica has been the seat of five General Councils: in 1123, 1139, 1179, 1215, and 1512.

**Exterior.** The principal or EAST FRONT, overlooking Piazza di Porta San Giovanni, is a plain and dignified composition by *Aless. Galilei* (1734-36). It consists of a two-storied portico surmounted by an attic with 16 statues of Christ with the Apostles and saints. On Maundy Thursday the pope gives his benediction from the central loggia (see above). Five doorways admit to the *Portico,* and five corresponding doors lead from there into the nave. The door on the extreme right is the *Porta Santa* which is opened only in Holy Years (see p. 262). The bronze central doors were first used for the Curia, and later the church of S. Adriano in the Forum. On the left (A) is a statue of Constantine, from his Baths on the Quirinal.—The NORTH FRONT, on Piazza di San Giovanni in Laterano, is likewise a portico of two tiers; it was built by *Dom. Fontana* in 1586. Beneath it, on the left, is a statue of Henry IV of France, by *Nicolas Cordier* (c. 1610), erected in gratitude for his gifts to the chapter. The two towers behind date from the time of Pius IV (1560).

**Interior.** The austere and dignified NAVE, with two aisles on either side, is well seen from the main entrance; but the effect is perhaps even more striking when it is approached through the wide N. transept, as the whole length of the church (130 m) is gradually unfolded.In the niches of the massive piers (with which Borromini encased the verde antico pillars), are colossal Baroque statues of Apostles, by pupils of *Bernini;* above them are stuccoes designed by *Algardi,* representing scenes from the Old Testament (l.) and New Testament (r.). Higher still are 18C paintings of prophets. The rich ceiling is perhaps by *Pirro Ligorio.* The marble pavement is of Cosmatesque design.—RIGHT AISLES (N.). On the nave piers: Boniface VIII proclaiming the Jubilee of 1300 (B), fresco attributed to *Giotto;* cenotaph of Sylvester II (d. 1003; C), by the Hungarian sculptor *William Fraknoi* (1909); beneath is a curious medieval memorial slab to the pope; tomb of Alexander III (D), the pope of the Lombard League; tomb of Sergius IV, with a medieval figure of a Pope (E); tomb of Card. Ranuccio Farnese (F), by *Vignola.* In the outer aisle: tomb of Paolo Mellini (1527), in the embrasure of the Porta Santa (G), with a damaged fresco; between 1st and 2nd chapels, tomb of Giulio Acquaviva (1574), made cardinal at the age of 20 by Pius V. The CAPPELLA TORLONIA (H), richly decorated by *Raimondi* (1850), is closed by a fine iron balustrade, and has a sculptured altarpiece (Descent from the Cross) by *Tenerani.* Over the window-screen outside the adjoining Cappella Massimo (closed) is a fragment of the original altar with a statuette of St James, ascribed to *And. Bregno;* towards the end of the aisle, tombs of Card. Casati (1287), by the *Cosmati,* and of Card. Ant. de Chaves (1447), attr. to *Isaia da Pisa.*—LEFT AISLES (S.). At the beginning of the outer aisle (K) is a sarcophagus with a recumbent figure of Card. Riccardo degli Annibaldi (1276), probably by *Arnolfo di Cambio.* The CAPPELLA CORSINI (L), a graceful 18C structure by *Aless. Galilei,* contains above its altar a mosaic copy of Guido Reni's painting of

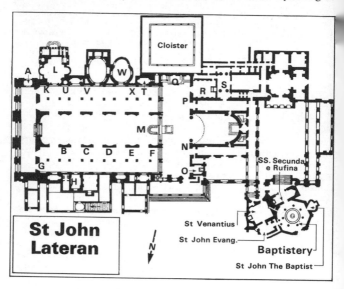

St Andrea Corsini; on the left, tomb of Clement XII (Lorenzo Corsini; d. 1740), a porphyry sarcophagus from the Pantheon, and in the vault below (apply to sacristan), a Pietà by *Ant. Montauti.* In the aisle, tombs of the Archpriest Gerardo da Parma (1061; U) and of Card. Bern. Caracciolo (c. 1300; V); at the end, beyond the pretty CAPPELLA LANCELLOTTI (W), by *Fr. da Volterra* (1585-90, rebuilt 1675), is the tomb of Card. Casanate (1707; X), founder of the libary that bears his name.

The TRANSEPTS were built under Clement VIII (1592-1605) by *Giac. della Porta,* with large manneristic frescoes of the conversion of Constantine, his gift to the pope, and the building of the Basilica. In the central space is the *Papal Altar,* reconstructed by Pius IX, containing many relics, including the heads of SS. Peter and Paul, and the greater part of St Peter's wooden altar-table; the rest of it is in the church of Santa Pudenziana (p. 204). Above is the Gothic *Baldacchino by *Giov. di Stefano* (1367), frescoed by *Barna da Siena.* In the enclosure in front of the confessio is the *Tomb-slab of Martin V (d. 1431), by *Sim. Ghini* (M).—In the right transept are the great organ (1598; by *Luca Blasi*), supported by two columns of giallo antico, and the tomb (N) of Innocent III (d. 1216), by *Gius. Lucchetti* (1891), erected when Leo XIII brought the ashes of his great predecessor from Perugia. In the corner, to the right in the little Cappella del Crocifisso (O), is a kneeling statue of Boniface IX (Cosmatesque; late 14C).—In the left transept is the tomb of Leo XIII (P), by *Giulio Tadolini* (1907). At the end is the Altar of the Holy Sacrament (Q), by *Pietro Paolo Olivieri* (temp. Clement VIII), flanked by four antique columns made of bronze taken from Etruscan tombs. On the right is the CAPPELLA DEL CORO (R), with fine stalls of c. 1625.

The APSE was reconstructed, at the expense of Leo XIII, by *Virginio* and *Fr. Vespignani* (1885). The fine *Mosaics are a resetting of the originals designed by *Iac. Torriti* and *Iac. da Camerino* (1288-94) from an antique model. Beneath the Head of Christ (the copy of a mosaic fabled to have appeared miraculously at the consecration of the church) the Dove descends upon the bejewelled Cross. From the hill on which it stands four rivers flow to quench the thirst of the faithful. On either side are (l.) the Virgin with Nicholas IV and SS. Peter and Paul, and (r.) SS. John the Baptist, John the Evangelist, and Andrew; the figures of St Francis of Assisi (l.) and St Anthony of Padua (r.) were added by Nicholas IV. At their feet flows the Jordan. Kneeling at the feet of the Apostles (in the frieze below) are the tiny figures of Torriti and Camerino.

The doorway beneath Leo XIII's tomb admits to the SACRISTY, reached by a corridor containing the tombs of And. Sacchi and the Cavalier d'Arpino, and (behind the apse) two fine statues of St Peter and St Paul by *Deodato di Cosma*. On the left is the OLD SACRISTY, with a beautiful Annunciation by *Marcello Venusti*, after Michelangelo.

In the left aisle (beyond T) is the entrance to the *CLOISTER (adm. 9-13, 15-18), the masterpiece of *Iac.* and *Pietro Vassalletto* (1215-32), a magnificent example of Cosmatesque art. The columns, some plain and some twisted, are adorned with mosaics and have fine capitals. The frieze is exquisite. Many interesting fragments from the ancient basilica are displayed around the cloister walls. From the left: Various pieces of Cosmati work, including (No. 38) Papal throne, an antique marble chair with Cosmati decorations; 89. Tomb of Card. Annibaldi, reconstructed from fragments, which include reliefs by Arnolfo di Cambio; 103. Roman sarcophagus, with four portraits; Various pavement tomb slabs, carved in relief; 208-24. Saints in niches (late 15C).

Adjoining the basilica on the right, and facing Piazza di Porta San Giovanni, is the **Lateran** (*Palazzo del Laterano;* Pl. 10; 3), the palace of the popes before the move to Avignon in 1309. The old palace, which is traced back to the time of Constantine, was almost destroyed in the fire of 1308 which devastated St John Lateran. On the return from Avignon in 1377 the Holy See was transferred to the Vatican. In 1586 Sixtus V demolished or displaced what the fire had left and ordered a complete reconstruction, though some remains of the old palace are preserved (see p. 213); he gave the work to Dom. Fontana. It was intended to make the new Lateran the summer palace of the popes, but the Quirinal was preferred (see p. 177). The interior (no adm.) was restored in 1838. Under the Lateran Treaty of 1929 (see p. 261), the palace was recognized as an integral part of the Vatican City. It is now the seat of the Rome Vicariate, the offices of the Rome diocese. The Lateran museums were moved to new quarters in the Vatican (p. 278) in 1963.

In Piazza di Porta San Giovanni are three survivals of the old Lateran Palace—the Scala Santa, the Chapel of St Laurence, and the Triclinium. A building (1589) by *Dom. Fontana,* architect of the new Lateran, opposite that palace, on the E. side of the piazza, houses the first two. The **Scala Santa** is supposed to be the staircase of Pilate's house which Christ descended after his condemnation. It is said to have been brought from Jerusalem to Rome by St Helena, mother of Constantine.

The 28 Tyrian marble steps are protected by boards and may be ascended only by worshippers on their knees. In the vestibule are two sculptures by *Ignazio*

*Iacometti* (1854), the Kiss of Judas and Ecce Homo. The Scala Santa and the side staircases, by which pilgrims descend, lead to the **Chapel of St Laurence**, or **Sancta Sanctorum**, the private chapel of the pope in the old palace. A Cosmatesque work of 1278, it contains a mosaic of Christ and, protected by a silver tabernacle presented by Innocent III, the relic which gives the chapel its peculiar sanctity. This is an ancient painting (6-7C) on wood of Christ, said to have been begun by St Luke and an angel: hence its name 'Acheiropoeton', or the picture made without hands. The Chapel is never open to the public, but it may be seen through the grating. The precious relics and their reliquaries, known as the Treasure of the Sancta Sanctorum are in the Museum of Christian Art in the Vatican.

To the E. of the Scala Santa is the **Tribune** erected by Fuga for Benedict XIV in 1743 and decorated with good copies of the mosaics from the *Triclinium of Leo III,* the banqueting hall of the old Lateran Palace. In the centre, Christ sending forth the Apostles to preach the Gospel; on the left, Christ giving the keys to St Sylvester and the labarum, or standard of the Cross, to Constantine; on the right, St Peter giving the papal stole to Leo III and the banner of Christianity to Charlemagne.— A fragment of the original mosaic is in the Museum of Christian Art in the Vatican.

**Porta San Giovanni** (Pl. 10; 3), built in 1574 by Giac. del Duca, superseded the ancient *Porta Asinaria,* on the site of the *Porta Coelimontana* of the Servian Wall. To the w. of the modern gateway, between two fine towers, may be seen the old gate with its vantage-court, excavated in 1954. Within the gate is a monument to St Francis by G. Tonnini (1927).

Outside Porta San Giovanni is *Piazzale Appio,* where several streets converge. The most important of these is **Via Appia Nuova** (now Highway 7), eventually joined by Via Appia Antica. It leads to Albano and Velletri (Rte 23c), past Ciampino Airport.—About 5 kilometres along this road Via Tuscolana diverges to the left for Frascati (Rte 23A).

From Piazza di Porta San Giovanni Viale Carlo Felice leads E. The first turning on the left is Via Conte Rosso, which runs N. to the *Villa Wolkonsky,* formerly the German embassy, and now the residence of the British ambassador. His Embassy has been transferred to its old site in Via Venti Settembre (p. 182). Viale Carlo Felice ends in Piazza Santa Croce in Gerusalemme, a busy traffic centre. Here is the church of **Santa Croce in Gerusalemme** (Pl. 10; 2), one of the 'Seven Churches' of Rome (p. 45), occupied by Cistercians since 1561. According to tradition, this church was founded by Constantine to enshrine the relics of the True Cross salved in Jerusalem by his mother St Helena. It was built within part of a large imperial palace, erected in the late 2C on the s.w. extremity of the city. The principal edifice was known as the *Sessorium,* and the church took the name of *Basilica Sessoriana.* It was rebuilt in 1144 by Lucius II, who added the campanile, and completely modernized by Benedict XIV in 1743-44, when the impressive theatrical façade and oval vestibule were added; the architects were Dom. Gregorini and Pietro Passalacqua.

The Baroque INTERIOR has the nave and aisles separated by granite columns, some of them boxed in pilasters. The pavement is Cosmatesque. Near the door is the epitaph of Benedict VII (d. 983), who is buried here. In the right aisle, at the second altar, St Bernard introducing Vittore IV to Innocent II, by *Carlo Maratta.* At the end of the left aisle in the CHAPEL OF THE RELICS, by Florestano Di Fausto (1930), are preserved the pieces of the True Cross together with other greatly venerated relics. The basalt tomb beneath the altar encloses the remains of SS. Cæsarius and Anastasius. The vault painting, Apparition of the Cross, is by *Corrado Giaquinto* (c. 1745). In the apse is a fresco of the Invention of the Cross, attrib. to *Antoniazzo Romano.* In the centre of the tribune, seen through a graceful 17C baldacchino, probably built to a design of Carlo Maderno, is the tomb of Card. Quiñones (d. 1540), by *Iac. Sansovino.*

A stairway at the end of the right aisle leads down to the CHAPEL OF ST HELENA. It contains a statue of the saint, originally a figure of Juno copied from the

Barberini statue in the Vatican. The altar is reserved for the pope and the titular cardinal of the basilica. The vault *Mosaic, the original design of which is probably by *Melozzo* (c. 1480), was restored by *Bald. Peruzzi* and later by *Fr. Zucchi.* It represents Christ and the Evangelists, SS. Peter and Paul, St Sylvester (who died here at Mass), St Helena, and Card. Carvajal. The fragments of 12C frescoes found here were detached in 1968. On the left is the GREGORIAN CHAPEL, built by Card. Carvajal in 1523, with an early 17C Roman bas-relief of the Pietà, flanked by statues of SS. Peter and Paul (French 14C).

To the N.E., in the adjoining garden of the *ex-Caserma dei Granatieri,* are the ruins of the Sessorium (see above). A fine *Museum of Musical Instruments* (adm. see p. 49) has been arranged here, formed largely from the Evangelista Gorga (1865-1957) collection. The exhibits include archaeological material, the 17C Barberini harp, and a pianoforte built by Bartolomeo Cristofori in 1722. To the E. excavations in 1959 revealed remains of the extensive *Circus Varianus,* well-preserved, and dating from the reign of Heliogabalus (218-22).—To the S. are the remains of the *Amphitheatrum Castrense* (Pl. 10; 2; no adm.), a small graceful edifice, built of brick by Heliogabalus or Alexander Severus for amusements of the Imperial court, incorporated with the Aurelian Wall by Honorius.

From Piazza Santa Croce Via Santa Croce leads N.W. to Via Conte Verde and Piazza Vittorio Emanuele. On the left it passes the end of the Villa Wolkonsky (see above). Via Statilia, skirting the N. side of the villa, runs parallel to a fine series of arches of the *Aqueduct of Nero,* an extension of the Aqua Claudia (see below), and built by Nero to provide water for his various constructions on the Palatine and Oppian hills.

Via Eleniana leads N. from Piazza Santa Croce to the large and busy Piazza di Porta Maggiore. On the W. side of this square is the beginning of Via Statilia, with some arches of the Aqua Claudia, restored to carry the Aqua Marcia (1923). On the E. side is the **Porta Maggiore,** or *Porta Prenestina* (Pl. 10; 2), formed by the archways carrying the Aqua Claudia and the Anio Novus over the Via Prenestina and the Via Casilina (see below). The Porta Prenestina was a gate in Aurelian's wall; it was restored by Honorius in 405.

The ancient Via Prenestina and Via Labicana (see below) can still be seen passing under the arches. Also here are foundations of a guard-house added by Honorius.

On the outside of the gate, is the curious **Tomb of the Baker** (M. Virgilius Eurysaces, a public contractor, and his wife Atistia), discovered in 1838. This somewhat pretentious monument, entirely of travertine, dates from the end of the Republic. The circular openings represent the mouths of a baker's oven; above is a frieze illustrating the stages of bread-making.

The **Aqua Claudia** and the **Anio Novus,** or *Acqua Aniene Nuova,* were two of the finest Roman aqueducts. Both were begun by Caligula in A.D. 38 and completed in 52. They were restored by Vespasian in 71 and by Titus in 81. The water of the Aqua Claudia was derived from two copious springs near Sublaqueum (Subiaco); its length was 68 kilometres. The Anio Novus was the longest of all the aqueducts (86 km.) and the loftiest; some of its arches were 33 m high.

Outside the Porta Maggiore are two main roads—VIA PRENESTINA on the left, leading to Palestrina (Præneste) and, on the right, VIA CASILINA, anciently Via Labicana, and now Highway 6. Via Casilina passes through Labico (Labicum), which gave it its original name. Both roads are described in Rte 24.

At No. 17 Via Prenestina, about 130 m from the gate, is the entrance to the *Basilica di Porta Maggiore (adm., see 49), unearthed in 1916. A modern staircase beneath the railway admits to this admirable building of the 1C A.D., in near perfect preservation. It has the rudimentary form of a cult building, with a central porch, an apse at the east end, a nave and two arched aisles with no clerestory. This became the basic plan of the Christian church. The ceiling and walls are covered with exquisite stuccoes representing landscapes, mythological subjects, scenes of child life, and the like; the principal design of the apse is thought to depict the Death of Sappho. The building may have been used by a mystical sect, perhaps the Pythagoreans.

From Piazza di Porta Maggiore Via Giovanni Giolitti, leading past the Stazione Termini to Piazza dei Cinquecento, passes on the right the so-called **Temple of Minerva Medica** (Pl. 6; 7). This is the picturesque ruin of a large ten-sided hall dating from the 4C, probably the nymphaeum of the *Gardens of Licinius*. The building owes its name to the discovery inside it of a statue of Minerva with a serpent, which probably occupied one of the nine niches round its walls. The cupola, which collapsed in 1828, served as a model for many classical buildings.

Beyond the temple Viale Manzoni leads left past the end of Via di Porta Maggiore. Near Via Luzzatti is the entrance to the **Hypogeum of the Aureli,** a series of tomb-chambers discovered in 1919. For admission, apply to the Pontificia Commissione di Archeologia Sacra, 1 Via Napoleone III. On the floor of the first room is a mosaic dedication showing that the vault belonged to freedmen of the Gens Aurelia. The well-preserved wall paintings (A.D. 200-250), include the Good Shepherd, the Christian symbol of the peacock, and some landscapes of obscure significance, suggesting a mixture of Christian and gnostic beliefs.

Via Giov. Giolitti continues to (r.) **Santa Bibiana** (Pl. 6; 5), a 5C church rebuilt by *Bernini* in 1625, interesting as his first architectural work. Within are eight columns from pagan temples, including (l. of entrance) that at which St Bibiana was flogged to death. On the architrave are frescoes by (r.) *Agost. Ciampelli* and (l.) *Pietro da Cortona.* The \*Statue of the saint, set in an ædicula above the altar, is a fine youthful work by *Bernini.*

Just beyond on the left is Piazza Guglielmo Pepe, in which are six arches of an ancient aqueduct.
Archi di Santa Bibiana leads under the railway to *Porta San Lorenzo* (Pl. 6; 5). Immediately N., in the Aurelian Wall, is *Porta Tiburtina,* built by Augustus and restored by Honorius in 403. The triple attic carried the waters of the Aquæ Marcia, Tepula, and Julia. Farther N., in Piazzale Sisto V, is an arch formed out of a section of the Aurelian Wall by Pius V and Sixtus V at the end of the 16C to carry the waters of the Acqua Felice.

The area to the N. and E. is described in Rte 13. Bus No. 70 returns to Piazza Venezia from Via Giov. Giolitti.

# 16   THE CAELIAN, THE BATHS OF CARACALLA, AND THE APPIAN WAY

The direct approach to the Appian Way from the centre of the city may be made from the Colosseum, by Bus No. 118. This runs by Via San Gregorio, Via delle Terme di Caracalla, Via di Porta San Sebastiano, Porta San Sebastiano and Via Appia Antica as far as the Osteria Belvedere (see below). The service is infrequent (every 20-40 mins.).—Bus No. 218, starting from St John Lateran joins Via Appia Antica at Piazza Cuma and then branches off beyond the church of Domine Quo Vadis? to the Fosse Ardeatine (p. 230).
The **Appian Way** is narrow and traffic ridden for the first few kilometres which makes this section of the road unpleasant to explore on foot. A recommended way of seeing it to best advantage is to walk from Piazzale Numa Pompilio (comp. p. 224) along Via di Porta S. Sebastiano as far as Porta San Sebastiano. From the gate Bus 118 may be picked up as far as the Catacombs of San Callisto or San Sebastiano. From San Sebastiano it is little more than a kilometre to the Osteria Belvedere where the bus diverges from the Appian Way. In the remaining four

kilometres as far as the Casal Rotondo (p. 234) the road becomes increasingly deserted (single visitors should take care) and at least part of the way should be explored as this is the most beautiful and characteristic section of the road. It now becomes one-way for cars leaving Rome. It is possible to diverge at the Casal Rotondo by a road to the left which leads to Via Appia Nuova. Opposite the point of junction with the main road is the tramway terminus of *Capannelle.* From the terminus back to Rome (Termini; Via Giovanni Amendola) is a journey of about 25 minutes.

The **Cælian** (51 m), next to the Aventine, is the southernmost of the Seven Hills of Rome and the most extensive after the Esquiline. Originally called *Mons Querquetulanus* from the oak forests that clothed its slopes, it received its name of Mons *Coelius* from Cælius (or Coelius) Vibenna, an Etruscan who is said to have helped Romulus in his war against the Sabine king Tatius, and to have settled here afterwards. Tullus Hostilius lived on the hill and transferred to it the Latin population of Alba Longa. It became an aristocratic quarter in Imperial times and did not escape the notice of Nero in his grandiose schemes of building. Devastated by Robert Guiscard in 1084, it remained almost uninhabited for centuries. Even today it is sparsely populated, but its ruins and churches are of the highest interest.

From the Arch of Constantine, in Piazza del Colosseo (Pl. 9; 1), the tree-lined Via di San Gregorio, on the line of the ancient *Via Triumphalis,* runs s., between the Parco del Celio (l.) and the verdant slopes of the Palatine (r.); on the other side of the Parco del Celio Via Claudia runs out of the s.e. corner of Piazza del Colosseo. On the right of Via Claudia are remains of the *Temple of Claudius* (p. 220), built by Nero's mother Agrippina, fourth wife of Claudius, to whom she dedicated the temple (A.D. 54). Nero converted it into a nymphæum for his Golden House (see p. 144), and Vespasian rebuilt it in A.D. 69. Via Claudia ends in Piazza della Navicella, into which also comes Via Celimontana, with the military *Ospedale del Celio* on its farther side. Just s. of the hospital, near a conspicuous survival of the Claudian aqueduct, a road leads left to **Santo Stefano Rotondo** (Pl. 9; 4), the largest circular church in the world and one of the oldest of its kind in Italy. It has been closed indefinitely for restoration.

It dates from the time of Pope St Simplicius (468-83). A Mithraeum (2-3C A.D.) was found beneath the floor in 1973. The original plan included three concentric rings, the largest 65 m in diameter, intersected by the four arms of a Greek Cross. The outer ring and two of the arms were pulled down by Nicholas V in 1450, so that the diameter was reduced to 40 m.

The entrance is at No. 7 Via di Santo Stefano Rotondo. The vestibule is formed by one of the two remaining arms of the Greek Cross. The throne to the left is said to be that of St Gregory the Great. The circular nave has a double ring of antique granite and marble columns, 34 in the outer and 22 in the inner series, while 2 Corinthian columns in the centre and 2 pillars support three arches. The walls are covered with frescoes by *Pomarancio* and *Tempesta,* depicting scenes of martyrdom in chronological order, and unpleasantly realistic detail. In the first chapel on the left (the other remaining arm of the cross) is a small 7C mosaic, showing Christ *above* the Cross, with SS. Primus and Felician; in the second chapel is a fine 16C tomb.

On the w. side of Piazza Navicella is the church of **Santa Maria in Domnica** (Pl. 9; 3, 4), or *della Navicella,* an ancient foundation and the senior diaconate of Rome; its title is a corruption of Dominica, i.e. Chief. The alternative name is derived from the Roman stone boat, which Leo X had made into a fountain in front of the church. The boat was probably a votive offering from the *Castra Peregrina,* a camp for non-Italian soldiers, situated between Via Santo Stefano and Via Navicella.

The present church, restored by St Paschal I (pope, 817-24), and practically rebuilt by Card. Giov. de' Medici (Leo X) in the 16C from the designs of Andr Sansovino, has a graceful portico. In the interior (if closed, ring at the door on the right) the nave contains 18 granite columns; over the windows is a frieze by *Perin del Vaga* from designs by *Giulio Romano.* On the triumphal arch, flanked by two porphyry columns, is a beautifully coloured 9C *Mosaic of Christ with two angels and the Apostles, and Moses and Elijah below; in the semi-dome, St Paschal kisses the foot of the Virgin surrounded by angels. In the nave are some interesting Roman sarcophagi.

On the left of the church is the main entrance of the **Villa Celimontana** or *Villa Mattei* (Pl. 9; 3), built for Ciriaco Mattei in 1582 and noted for its splendid gardens (now a public park, adm. free, 7-dusk). It houses the *Società Geografica Italiana.* In the grounds are ancient marbles found on the spot, and a granite obelisk, probably from the Temple of Isis Capitolina, presented by the Senate to Mattei. It formed a pair with that in Piazza della Rotonda (p. 97). The terrace of the casino and the belvedere at the end of an avenue command fine views. There is an exit from the park opposite the church of SS. Giovanni e Paolo (see below).

To the N. of Santa Maria in Domnica is the entrance to the former Trinitarian hospice of the church of *San Tomaso in Formis.* The doorway is surmounted by a mosaic (c. 1218) of Christ between two Christian slaves, one white, the other a Negro. In the hospice St John of Matha, founder of the Trinitarians, died in 1213. Beyond it is the *Arch of Dolabella and Silanus* (A.D. 10), a single archway that Nero afterwards used for his aqueduct to the Palatine. The archway leads into Via di San Paolo della Croce (beware of fast traffic), leading to the picturesque Piazza dei Santi Giovanni e Paolo.

Here, on the right, is the church of **Santi Giovanni e Paolo** (Pl. 9; 3; adm. 8-11 and 15-18). Its fine *Apse, visible in all its beauty from Clivo di Scauro (see below), is a rare example of Lombard work in Rome.

The church occupies a site traditionally connected with the house of John and Paul, two court dignitaries under Constantine II, who were martyred by Julian the Apostate. The original sanctuary, founded by the senator Byzantius and his son Pammachius, a friend of St Jerome, was demolished by Robert Guiscard in 1084. Rebuilding was begun by Paschal II (1099-1118) and continued by Adrian IV (Nicholas Breakspeare, the only English pope; 1154-59), who was responsible for the Ionic portico, with its eight antique columns, the doorway flanked by two lions, the apse and the beautiful *CAMPANILE, built on the foundations of the Temple of Claudius (clearly visible). Excavations carried out in 1949 on the initiative of Card. Spellman revealed the 5C entrance colonnade and other ancient constructions.

INTERIOR. The nave, with granite piers and columns, was restored in 1718 for Card. Paolucci by *Ant. Canevari;* Card. Cusani was responsible for the ceiling (1598); the floor, in opus alexandrinum, was restored in 1911. A tomb slab in the nave (protected by a railing) commemorates the burial-place of the three martyrs. Their relics are preserved in a porphyry urn under the high altar.—In the 3rd s. chapel (by *Fil. Martinucci,* 1857-80) is the altar-tomb of St Paul of the Cross (1694-1775), founder of the Passionists, whose convent adjoins the church.— The apse has frescoes by *Pomarancio.* In a store-room (unlocked by the sacristan) on the left of the high altar can be seen a remarkable 12C fresco originally over the altar of the church.

From the end of the r. aisle (apply to the Sacristan) steps lead down to the **House of SS. John and Paul** (open daily 8-12, 15.30-17.30; exc. fest. mornings), an interesting two-storied construction, with 20 rooms, originally part of three buildings: a Roman palace, a Christian house, and an oratory, decorated with frescoes of the 2C or the 3-4C. Near the foot of the stairs is a well-shaft. Behind it to the r. is a *Nymphum* with a striking fresco of Peleus and Thetis (or Proserpine) and a Nereid, and boats manned by Cupids. Beyond a foundation wall of the basilica are two rooms. Off the first (l.) is the *Triclinium* with pagan frescoes of peacocks and other birds and youths bearing garlands. A small adjoining room (reached by a flight of steps) has architectural frescoes.—The series of rooms to the left of the entrance have more frescoes, some with Christian subjects, including a large standing figure praying in the early Christian manner, with arms extended and eyes raised. The *Medieval Oratory* (near the road) has been closed during excavation work (and a fresco of the Passion has been removed for restoration). An iron staircase leads up to the *Confessio,* decorated with 4C frescoes the significance of which is not entirely clear. On the end wall is a praying figure, perhaps one of the martyrs, between drawn curtains, and at whose feet are two other figures. On the right, SS. Priscus, Priscillian, and Benedicta (who sought the remains of the martyrs and were themselves slain) awaiting execution with eyes bound—probably the oldest painting of a martyrdom.—Stairs lead down from a room N. of the Confessio to another series of rooms which were part of the *Baths* in a private house.

Outside the Passionist Convent in the piazza are some arches of Roman shops dating from the 3C.

From Piazza dei Santi Giovanni e Paolo the pretty Clivo di Scauro (the ancient *Clivus Scauri* probably opened in the 1C B.C.), descends beneath the medieval arches flanking the church. On the left are remains of Roman buildings of the Imperial era. The road affords a splendid view of the apse of SS. Giovanni e Paolo (comp. above). In Piazza di San Gregorio (l.) is the church of **San Gregorio Magno** (Pl. 9; 3), built originally by St Gregory the Great (590-604) on the site of his father's house, and dedicated to St Andrew. A new church on the site, dedicated to the founder, perhaps by Gregory II (715-731), was completely rebuilt in the 17C and 18C. The *EXTERIOR (staircase, façade, and atrium) are by *G. B. Soria* (1633) and are considered his masterpiece. The church is of special interest to English pilgrims, as it was here in 596 that St Augustine bade farewell to St Gregory and received his blessing before setting out, with forty other monks, on his mission to convert the English to Christianity.

In the ATRIUM are several tombs, including those of Sir Robert Peckham (d. 1659), a self-exiled English Catholic, and Sir Edward Carne (d. 1561), an envoy of Henry VIII and Mary I; and, beyond the gate leading to the chapels (see below), those of Canon Guidiccioni (1643) and the Brothers Bonsi (1481), the latter by *Luigi Capponi.*—The INTERIOR (if closed ring at the convent on r. of atrium) has 16 antique columns and a restored mosaic pavement; it was rebuilt in 1725-34 by *Fr. Ferrari.* At the end of the right aisle is the CHAPEL OF ST GREGORY, with a fine altar-frontal sculptured by *L. Capponi.* The predella is an early 16C painting, depicting St Michael smiting Lucifer, the Apostles with St Anthony Abbot, and St Sebastian. On the right is a small chamber containing the throne of St Gregory. In the left aisle is the SALVIATI CHAPEL (ring for the sacristan, in r. aisle), by *Fr. da Volterra* and *Carlo Maderna;* on the right is an ancient Madonna, which legend declares to have spoken to St Gregory; on the left, a fine tabernacle, of the school of *And. Bregno* (1469).

On the left of the church (reached through a gate in the atrium) are the remains of Roman walls and a pretty group of three chapels (open on Sun 8-12; or by request at the Convent in the atrium) surrounded by ancient cypresses. The frescoes inside have deteriorated and are in need of urgent repair. The chapel on the right is dedicated to **Santa Silvia,** mother of Gregory, and contains her statue by *Nicolas Cordier,* and an *Angel Choir, by *Guido Reni.* In the centre is the chapel of **Sant'Andrea,** with the *Flagellation of the saint (r.), by *Domenichino,* and the saint on the road to his Cross, by *Guido Reni;* the peasant-woman on the left repeats the well-known type of Beatrice Cenci. The third chapel, of **Sant Barbara,** or *Triclinium Pauperum,* contains a statue of St Gregory, and the table at which he served twelve paupers daily with his own hands, among whom an angel once appeared as a thirteenth. A fresco on the left, by *Ant. Viviani* (1602), depicts the famous incident of the fair-haired English children—'non Angli sed Angeli'—which culminated in the mission of St Augustine to England.

From Piazza di San Gregorio a flight of steps descends to Via di San Gregorio (comp. p. 219). The avenue ends at PIAZZA DI PORTA CAPENA (Pl. 9; 3), a spacious square adjoining the rounded end of the Circus Maximus and occupying the site of the *Porta Capena.* This was a gate in the Servian Wall (some remains survive) and the original starting-point of the Appian Way. Near the gateway was the *Fountain of Egeria,* where Numa Pompilius used to consult the nymph Egeria. After Aurelian had built his much more extensive wall (p. 18), the stretch of the road between Porta Capena and Porta Appia (now Porta San Sebastiano; see p. 226) became known as the URBAN SECTION OF THE APPIAN WAY. This section has now become Via delle Terme di Caracalla as far as Piazzale Numa Pompilio and, beyond that square, Via di Porta San Sebastiano. In Piazza di Porta Capena rises the *Stele of Axum,* brought from the ancient capital of Ethiopia in 1937. On the N.E. side of the square is *La Vignola,* a reconstruction (1911), with the original stones, of a charming little palazzo that stood near Via Santa Balbina (see below).

In the angle formed by Viale Aventino and Via delle Terme di Caracalla extends the PARCO DI PORTA CAPENA, formerly the *Passeggiata Archeologica,* planned by Guido Baccelli, Minister of Public Instruction, in 1887, and approved by the Italian Parliament in 1910 in honour of the 40th anniversary of Italian unity. On Viale Aventino is the modern building of the United Nations Food and Agriculture Organization. The park embraces the Baths of Caracalla and the church of Santa Balbina.

Viale Guido Baccelli leads s. to Via Santa Balbina, at the beginning of which is the church of **Santa Balbina** (Pl. 9; 5), which has been closed indefinitely for restoration. The 5C edifice was entirely rebuilt, and restored in 1930. In it are three fine works of art: a Cosmatesque episcopal chair, the *Tomb of Card. Stef. Sordi (1303) by *Giov. Cosmati,* and a *Bas-relief of the Crucifixion, by *Mino del Reame* (1460); also many fine old frescoes and fragments of 1C mosaics.

In Via delle Terme di Caracalla, just short of Piazza Numa Pompilio and opposite the church of Santi Nereo ed Achilleo (see below), is the entrance to the **\*Baths of Caracalla** (*Terme di Caracalla*), or *Thermoe Antoninianoe* (Pl. 9; 5; adm., see p. 48). The vast scale of these brick-built ruins makes an indelible first impression.

Begun by Antoninus Caracalla in 212, the Baths were opened in 217 and finished under Heliogabalus and Alexander Severus. After a restoration by Aurelian they remained in use until the 6C, when the invading Goths damaged the aqueducts. In luxury and splendour they surpassed all the other baths of Rome, and today the monumental ruins are perhaps the most striking in the city. In addition to affording accommodation for 1600 bathers, the buildings included public piscinæ, palæstrae, a stadium, Greek and Latin libraries, a picture gallery, and assembly rooms. In the 16-17C, the Belvedere Torso, the Farnese Hercules, the Farnese Flora, and many other statues were found among the ruins. From here also came the mosaics of athletes now in the Vatican (p. 282). Although these Thermæ have always been above ground, excavations in this century have greatly enlarged the area accessible to the public.—Shelley composed a large part of his 'Prometheus Unbound' amongst these ruins.—Opera performances are given here in summer; during the season the baths are transformed by the trappings of the set.

The excellence of the brickwork, the boldness of the architectural forms, and the modernity of the heating arrangements are astonishing. The impression of massive dignity, enhanced by the contrast of the sun-baked walls against the blue of the sky gives only a faint idea of the beauty and majesty of the monument when it was still intact, bright with coloured marble and precious metal, enlivened by fountains, adorned with statues, and animated by the bathers. Of the decoration only a few architectural fragments and some floor-mosaic remain, revealing the Baroque taste of the 3C in the introduction of divinities on the fine Composite capitals.

The main building of the Baths (220 m by 114) was surrounded by an enclosed garden, along whose boundary wall were exedræ and recreation rooms, the whole occupying an area 330 m square. Immediately in front of the entrance, facing N.E.,

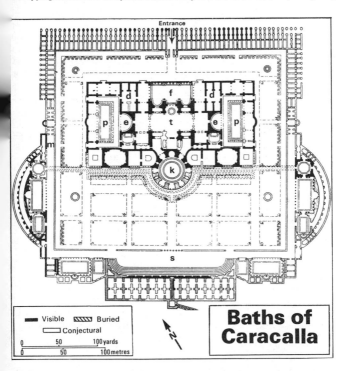

**Baths of Caracalla**

■ Visible   ▨ Buried
☐ Conjectural

is the rectangular *Frigidarium* (f), with a central piscina, and *Apodyteria* (d, d) or dressing-rooms, on either side. Beyond it is the *Tepidarium* (t), at each end of which is an exedra (e, e) facing the *Palaestroe* (p, p). At the back is the circular *Calidarium* (k), 35 m across. The smaller chambers are symmetrically disposed on each side. The boundary wall was lined with small chambers (booths and bathrooms) facing the garden; two broad and shallow apses opened out of the two side walls, and at the back was a large exedra for viewing the shows in the *Stadium* (s.). Outside the wall of the East Palaestra excavations (1974) revealed a house and triclinium of the time of Hadrian. Wall paintings discovered here are to be exhibited in a room of the Baths.—At the W. corner of the Baths older buildings may be seen below ground level, including a *Mithrum* (m) or subterranean sanctuary of the sun-worshippers.

Opposite the Baths, in Piazzale Numa Pompilio, is the church of **Santi Nereo ed Achilleo** (Pl. 9; 5; open daily exc. Fri 10-12, 16-19, ring for custodian), on the site of the Oratory of the Fasciola, so named in honour of a bandage which fell from the wounds of St Peter while he was fleeing from the Mamertine prison.

In 524 the oratory was enlarged into a church by John I, when he transported here the bodies of Nereus and Achilleus, the Christian servants of Flavia Domitilla (see p. 230), who had suffered martyrdom at Terracina. The church was enlarged by Leo III c. 800, and again by Sixtus IV (1471-84), and was rebuilt by Card Baronius in 1597.

The aisled INTERIOR has frescoes by *Pomarancio*. The ancient ambo and the 15C candelabrum come from other churches; the fine plutei and the high altar, which covers the body of St Domitilla, are of 13C Cosmati work. The mosaic on the choir-arch, of the time of Leo III, shows the Transfiguration, with a Madonna and an Annunciation at the sides. On the bishop's throne in the apse is carved a fragment of St Gregory's 28th homily, which he delivered from this throne when it stood in the first church dedicated to SS. Nereus and Achilleus in Via Ardeatina.

On the other side of the piazza is the rebuilt church of *San Sisto Vecchio,* with its convent, historically interesting as the residence in Rome of St Dominic (1170-1221). The campanile dates from the 13C.

From Piazzale Numa Pompilio roads lead to four of the gates in the Aurelian Wall: Via Druso N.N.E. to Porta Metronia, Via di Porta Latina S.E. to Porta Latina ('one way' from the gate), Via di Porta San Sebastiano S.S.E. to Porta San Sebastiano ('one way' to the gate), and the continuation of Via delle Terme di Caracalla S. to Porta Ardeatina, adjoining the Bastione del Sangallo (see p. 226).

Via di Porta San Sebastiano, on the line of the urban section of the Appian Way (see p. 226 and below), is a beautiful road running between high walls behind which are fine trees and gardens. On the right is the ancient church of **San Cesareo** (Pl. 9; 6) rebuilt at the end of the 16C, with a façade attributed to *Giacomo della Porta.* Inside is some fine *Cosmati work, including the high altar, the bishop's throne, the transennae, the candelabrum, the ambo, and the fronts of the side-altars. The two angels beneath the high altar are probably from a 15C tomb by *Paolo Romano.* The beautiful wooden ceiling, gilded on a blue ground bears the arms of the Aldobrandini Pope, Clement VIII. The apse mosaic of the Eternal Father was designed by the *Cavalier d' Arpino.* The baldacchino dates from the time of Clement VIII.

Below the church (reached by a stair to the l. of the entrance; apply to sacristan), is a large black-and-white *Mosaic of the 2C A.D. (suffering from humidity). The fantastical sea-monsters, animals, and figures may have decorated the floor of Roman baths. Two apses and the base of a large column, dividing the excavated area, suggest that the first part was later adapted as a church.

Beyond the church, on the right, at No. 8 is the **House of Cardinal Bessarion** (adm., see p. 47), the famous scholar (1389-1472), whose tomb is in the church of the SS. Apostoli. The delightful house and garden are a superb example of a 15C home. The loggia and several of the rooms are decorated with contemporary frescoes, which have recently been restored and the false additions removed. From the loggia with landscape scenes, is the entrance to the first large room which has wall-paintings of garlands and ribbons which cast painted shadows, and a fragment (in a niche) of a 15C fresco of the Coronation of the Virgin and two saints. The walls of the room on the right have an over-all pattern of acanthus leaves and pomegranates. The house is furnished in the Renaissance style. The rooms downstairs are used as reception rooms by the Commune of Rome.

About 500 metres farther along the road is (l.) the **Tomb of the Scipios** (adm., see p. 50; the ticket includes the Columbarium of Pomponius Hylas; see below), discovered in 1780. The excavated area is dominated by a three-storied house of the 3C which retains traces of paintings and mosaics. In front, is a Columbarium reached by a staircase below ground level, containing numerous niches with funerary urns. To the right of the house, a short passage leads to a small Christian catacomb, with a chapel attached. Store-rooms containing archæological material found during excavations, can be visited with special permission from the Commune.

The TOMB is reached from the left of the house. It was built for L. Cornelius Scipio Barbatus, consul in 298 B.C. and great-grandfather of Scipio Africanus. His sarcophagus is now in the Vatican. Many other members of the gens Cornelia were buried here also. It is uncertain whether Scipio Africanus was buried here or at Liternum (Patria, near Naples), where he died.

The cold dark interior contains a copy of the sarcophagus of Scipio Barbatus. The tombs include those of his son, Lucius Scipio (consul 259 B.C.), the conqueror of Corsica, of Cornelius Scipio Asiaticus, of Cn. Scipio Hispanus (prætor 139 B.C.) and Aula Cornelia his wife; also an inscription to Publius, perhaps the son of Scipio Africanus.

The caretaker conducts visitors through the pleasant Parco degli Scipioni to the **Columbarium of Pomponius Hylas,** which is one of the best preserved in existence. A steep staircase, with a small mosaic inscription, with the name of the founder and his wife Pomponia Vitalis, leads down to the 1C chamber decorated with stucco and paintings.

A gate leads out of the park into Via di Porta Latina, in which to the left is the church of *\*San Giovanni a Porta Latina, in a quiet cul-de-sac, with a large cedar and ancient well. It has a portico of four antique columns, and a beautiful 12C campanile. The 5C church was rebuilt by Hadrian I in 772, and several times restored, but the interior preserves a striking simplicity. The apse has three lovely windows of selenite, and 12C frescoes (restored 1940).

In the other direction Via di Porta Latina leads to the Gate, past the little octagonal chapel of **San Giovanni in Oleo** (restored in 1970), traditionally marking the spot where St John the Evangelist came forth unharmed from the cauldron of boiling oil. Rebuilt during the reign of Julius II, it has an interesting design, usually attributed to *Bramante* (or to Sangallo and his school). It was restored in 1658 by *Borromini,* who added the frieze.

Porta Latina is an opening in the Aurelian Wall with two towers built by Belisarius. Outside the gate Viale delle Mura Latine skirts the wall to Porta San Sebastiano, and Via di Porta Latina runs S.E. to Via Appia Nuova.

In Via di Porta San Sebastiano (comp. above), at No. 13 are other columbaria, of which the best is known as the *Ferro da Cavallo,* from its horseshoe shape, and consists of three vaulted galleries decorated with stuccoes and paintings; some of its marble urns are of beautiful workmanship. The largest of the columbaria here had room for 600 urns; the smallest dates from A.D. 10.

Near the end of the road is the so-called triumphal **Arch of Drusus** (Pl. 9; 8), in fact the arch that carried the aqueduct for the Baths of Caracalla over the Appian Way. Only the central of three openings survives; it is decorated with Composite columns of giallo antico. The **Porta San Sebastiano** (Pl. 9; 8), the *Porta Appia* of antiquity, is the most imposing gateway in the Aurelian Wall. It was rebuilt in the 5C by Honorius and restored in the 6C by Belisarius. The two medieval towers at the sides rest on basements of marble blocks.

It was at the Porta San Sebastiano that the senate and people of Rome received in state the last triumphal procession to enter the city by the Appian Way—that of Marcantonio Colonna II after the victory of Lépanto in 1571.

An interesting walk may be taken on the outside of the Aurelian Wall by Viale di Porta Ardeatina, from Porta San Sebastiano to Porta San Paolo. Beyond Porta Ardeatina the road passes the *Bastione del Sangallo,* a formidable structure built for Paul III (1534-49) by Ant. da Sangallo the Younger.—*Porta San Paolo,* see p. 91.

Outside Porta San Sebastiano, continuing the line of its urban section, is the beginning of the Appian Way. Nowadays a busy, but rather inconspicuous road (in its initial section), it falls away to the s. between two wide avenues skirting the Aurelian Wall which meet at the gate—Viale delle Mura Latine on the left and Viale di Porta Ardeatina on the right.

The *\*Appian Way (Via Appia)*, called by Statius the queen of roads (regina viarum), was the most important of the consular Roman roads. It was built by the censor Appius Claudius in 312 B.C. as far as Capua, and later extended to Beneventum (Benevento) and Brundusium (Brindisi). Paved throughout, it served for the first part of its course as a patrician cemetery, and was lined on either side by a series of family graves. The road is now called the *Via Appia Antica,* to distinguish it from the Via Appia Nuova, which starts at Porta San Giovanni (p. 216). The two roads converge at Frattocchie, 4 km. beyond the entrance to Ciampino Airport. The Via Appia Antica, in its initial stages, carries a good deal of noisy traffic, but the last 4 km. are more peaceful. The most interesting section of the road is that between Porta San Sebastiano and (8 km.) the Casal Rotondo. For the best way of exploring the road, see p. 218.

About 2 km. beyond tne Casal Rotondo the Appian Way is crossed by the **Circular Road** (Grande Raccordo Anulare; radius 11-16km.), linking all the consular highways that lead out of Rome. The first section was opened in 1951 and it has only recently been completed. Its total length is 68 km. It is already too narrow to carry the volume of traffic passing round Rome, and is always very busy.

At some points the ancient paving, of massive polygonal blocks of basaltic lava from the Alban Hills, is in good preservation, and at the sides are the *crepidines,* or sidewalks. In places the road is raised above the surrounding country, and good views are obtained; in other parts it is sunk below ground level. Few of the ruins have been identified with certainty and in many instances nothing is left but a concrete core, while only one milestone survives. The tombs vary greatly in form and size, but the predominating types are the tower and the tumulus. In the middle ages watch-towers and fortalices were frequently built on the solid bases of the tombs. There is a long-standing plan to make part of the area bordering the Appian Way into a National Park.

## THE CATACOMBS

ADMISSION. The Catacombs are usually open 8.30-12, and 14.30 or 15-dusk (fee). Those of St Calixtus are closed on Wed; of St Sebastian on Thurs; and of St Domitilla on Tues. These all have guided tours in several languages, and tend to be crowded with large tour groups which hamper the enjoyment of the single visitor. Routes often vary, and are shortened at the height of the tourist season. (The catacombs on Via Nomentana p. 184, and Via Salaria, p. 185 are less frequented). For permission to visit the others and for further information, apply to the Pontificia Commissione di Archeologia Sacra, 1 Via Napoleone III. See also p. 48.

It is difficult to imagine a greater contrast than that between the conspicuous patrician tombs that lined the Appian Way and the underground burial chambers of the early Christians in catacombs along the same road. It is also not clear whether the juxtaposition was deliberate or accidental. The most important of the Roman catacombs are those on the Appian Way, though similar burial-places are to be found in various other parts of the city. There is a series of them in the Nomentana Quarter (see pp. 183-84). The **Catacombs**, called *Coemeteria* up to the 15C, except for those of San Sebastiano (see p. 229), are subterranean tufa quarries used by the early Christians as a place for the burial of their dead outside the walls (burial within the walls was forbidden; the Roman custom was for cremation). After the official adoption of Christianity they were less necessary. The earliest of them date from the 1C, the latest from the end of the 4C. Later, burial near the churches became the custom and the catacombs, because they contained the remains of martyrs, became places of pilgrimage and were decorated with paintings. They were pillaged by the Goths (537) and the Lombards (755) and later thoroughly searched for precious objects and the bones of the martyrs, a large number of the latter being transferred to the Pantheon. In course of time the catacombs, except those of St Sebastian, were forgotten, and it was not until the 15C, that they were again visited and systematically explored. It was owing chiefly to G. B. De Rossi and Joseph Wilpert that public interest in them was revived.

The catacombs are a system of galleries of different sizes, often arranged in as many as five tiers. In the walls niches (*loculi*) were cut to receive the bodies, which were buried with all their ornaments. The apertures were then closed with slabs of marble or terracotta on which the names were inscribed (at first in Greek, later in Latin), sometimes with the words 'in pace' added. Larger spaces (*cubicula*) were cut to serve as family graves. The halls in which the galleries converged were used for feasts in honour of the dead. The tombs have now been almost entirely emptied in the hunt for treasure and for relics. The shallowest of the galleries are 7-8 m below the ground while the deepest lie 22 m down. Taking them all together, it is cautiously estimated that they extend for c. 250 km. The inscriptions and paintings have a great archæological interest. The oldest paintings, dating from the end of the 1C, show the adaptation of pagan forms to Christian ideas, and the later paintings mark the ensuing decadence in its various stages. They are almost always historical or symbolical in character, e.g. The Story of Jonah, Abraham's Sacrifice, Moses striking the Rock, Noah in the Ark, the Hebrew Children in the Fiery Furnace, Daniel in the Lion's Den, the Raising of Lazarus, the Good Shepherd, the Baptism, the Last Supper, and the Fish. This last-named symbol of Christianity is said to have been adopted (though this is now disputed) because the initial letters in the phrase, Ἰησοῦς Χριστός Θεοῦ Υἱὸς Σωτήρ (Jesus Christ Son of God, Redeemer) form the Greek word ΙΧΘΥΣ (fish).

The initial section of the Appian Way, the ancient *Clivus Martis,* gently descends. About 120 m from the gate, on the right, is the *First Milestone.* The road passes under the main Rome-Civitavecchia railway and crosses the brook *Almone* (or *Marrana della Caffarella*), where the priests of Cybele, the Magna Mater, used to perform the annual ceremony of washing the image of the goddess. Tombs appear here and there. On the left nearly 1 km. from the gate, is the little church of **Domine Quo Vadis?**

This church stands on the spot where, according to tradition, St Peter, fleeing from Rome to escape martyrdom, met an apparition of Jesus wending his way to the city. In reply to his question, "Domine quo vadis?" ("Lord, wither goest thou?")

he was told: "Venio iterum crucifigi" ("I go to be crucified anew"). Thereupon the saint returned to Rome and martyrdom. Sienkiewicz's famous novel has made the legend familiar. A reproduction of the imprint of Christ's feet is shown (original in San Sebastiano, p. 229).

By the church Via Ardeatina branches off to the right, followed by the bus (No. 218) to the Fosse Ardeatine (1 km. see p. 230).—At this fork is the entrance for cars to the catacombs of St Calixtus (see below). The drive is through the fields and farm of the monastery, and a beautiful cypress avenue.

About 100 metres from the church of Domine Quo Vadis? is a turning to the left, called Via della Caffarella. Less than a kilometre along this lane is a path (l.), leading to the so-called *Temple of the Deus Rediculus,* by a mill near the Almone brook. The 'temple' is really a sumptuous tomb of the 2C, possibly that of Annia Regilla, wife of Herodes Atticus (see below).

After making a short ascent (retrospective views of the walls of Rome; the Alban Hills to the left), the Appian Way passes the *Columbarium of the Freedmen of Augustus* (No. 87; l.). Beyond (No. 103) is the site of the *Second Milestone.* At No. 110, on the right, is the entrance to the *Catacombs of St Calixtus. Among the most important of the Roman catacombs, they were first investigated in 1850 by De Rossi and are not yet fully explored. They are named after St Calixtus (pope 217-22) and became the official burial-place of the bishops of Rome.

Visitors are conducted by an English-speaking priest to a small basilica with three apses, the *Oratory of SS. Sixtus and Cecilia,* where the dead were brought, before burial in the catacombs. Inside is a bust of G. B. De Rossi, father of modern Christian archaeology, who began his work in these catacombs. There are also inscriptions and sculptural fragments from the tombs. Before the central apse, *Tomb of Pope St Zephyrinus* (199-217).

Near by is the entrance to the dark and sinister catacombs, reached by an ancient staircase. The catacombs were excavated on five levels, but the tour usually remains on the second level, from which several staircases can be seen descending to other levels. The *PAPAL CRYPT preserves the tombs with original Greek inscriptions of the martyred popes, St Pontianus (230-35), St Anterus (236), St Fabian (236-50), St Lucius (253-54), and St Eutychianus (275-83). Here were probably also buried St Sixtus II (257-58), martyred under Valerian's persecution, St Stephen I (254-57), St Dionysius (259-69), and St Felix I (269-75). In honour of the martyred popes, Pope St Damasus (366-84) set up the metrical inscription seen at the end of the crypt.

In the adjoining crypt is the *Cubiculum of St Cecilia,* where the body of the saint was buried after her martyrdom at her house in Trastévere in 230. It is thought that it was moved by Paschal I in 820 to the church built on the site of her house. On the walls are 7-8C frescoes: Head of Christ; St Urban and other saints.—Beyond the crypt, a 3C passage leads down a short flight of stairs, with Christian symbols carved on stone slabs, to the *Cubicula of the Sacraments,* with symbolic frescoes. In the first cubicle are frescoes of the Raising of Lazarus, and opposite, the Miracle of the Loaves and Fishes. On the end wall, a fine double sarcophagus, with a lid in the form of a roof. The other cubicles have similar frescoes, several depicting the story of Jonah. Farther on is the *Crypt of St Eusebius,* martyred in 310. In the adjoining cubicles are the sepulchral inscriptions of Pope St Gaius (283-96) and two sarcophagi with mummified bodies. Next is the *Tomb of Pope St Cornelius* (251-53), with a contemporary Latin inscription containing the word 'martyr', and fine 6C Byzantine paintings. Adjoining is the *Crypt of Lucina,* the oldest part of the cemetery.

By the Catacombs of St Calixtus are further burial-places, including the Catacomb of the Holy Cross, discovered in 1953. Here are believed to have been the Tombs of SS. Marcus and Marcellianus and the *Hypogeum of St Damasus.*

Just beyond the Catacombs of St Calixtus a road branches off to the left. This is Via Appia Pignatelli, opened by Innocent XII (1691-1700) to link the Appian Way with the Via Appia Nuova. It is 4 km. long and joins the newer road near the tramway terminus of Capannelle, mentioned on p. 235.

Near the beginning of Via Appia Pignatelli, on the left, are the **Catacombs of Praetextatus** (adm. only with special permission). Above ground are pagan, below ground Christian sarcophagi. Here were buried several Christian martyrs. In the crypt is the *Spelunca Magna*, in which were buried the martyred companions of St Cecilia. In a cubicle excavated in 1850 are 2C paintings.—The next turning to the left, Vicolo S. Urbano (private road) leads to a villa gate. A path (l.) signed '*Per il tempio*', leads to the lonely church of **Sant'Urbano** in a classical landscape. This was orginally a temple forming part of the villa of the wealthy Herodes Atticus, patron of arts and man of letters of the time of the Antonines. The temple was converted into a church in the 9C or 10C and was restored in 1634, when four fluted columns from the pronaos were incorporated into the wall of the church. Inside (apply at villa for key) are remains of stucco ornamentation and interesting *Frescoes by a certain Bonizzo (1011). over the door, Crucifixion: on the end wall, Christ blessing, with saints and angels; on the other walls, Life of Jesus, and Lives of St Cecilia and her companions, and of St Urban.

Not far away, on a hill looking towards the Alban Hills, is the *Bosco Sacro* (Sacred Wood), erroneously identified as the place where Numa Pompilius used to consult the nymph Egeria. On the other side of the hill is the so-called *Grotto of Egeria*, watered by a branch of the Almone. The true Fountain of Egeria must be placed near the Porta Capena.

In the Appian Way, at No. 119A, is the entrance to the **Jewish Catacombs** (adm. see p. 48), excavated in 1857. The tombs, in the form of loculi or niches, are for the most part cut on end and date from the 3C to the 6C. Among the symbols are the cornucopia (Plenty), the palm-leaf (Victory), and the seven-branched candlestick. The epitaphs are mostly in Greek.

The road now descends to a small piazza in which, on the left, is a column of Pius IX (1852), and, on the right, the basilica of San Sebastiano. **San Sebastiano,** one of the seven pilgrimage churches of Rome, was originally dedicated to SS. Peter and Paul and called the *Basilica Apostolorum.* It was built in the first half of the 4C over the cemetery into which the bodies of the Apostles had been temporarily moved from their tombs in St Peter's and St Paul's-without-the Walls; this is said to have occurred in 258 during the persecution of Valerian. At a later date St Sebastian, who had suffered under Diocletian in 288, was buried here. After the 9C the association with the Apostles was forgotten and the church was named after St Sebastian. It originally had a nave and two aisles; the aisles were walled up in the 13C. In 1612 it was rebuilt for Card. Scipio Borghese by Flaminio Ponzio; the façade has a portico with six Ionic columns, taken from the preceding 15C portico.

INTERIOR (usually visited at the end of the tour of the Catacombs, see below). The ceiling is by Vasanzio. On the right is an apsidal chapel containing a stone with the imprint of Christ's feet, and other relics. On the r. of the chap. is a late-14C wooden crucifix (restored). Farther on, Tomb-chapel of the Albani family, built by C. Fontana for Clement XI. On the high altar, four columns of verde antico.—On the left, St Francis of Assisi, attrib. to *Girol. Muziano;* in a chapel near the entrance, recumbent *Statue of St Sebastian, by *Ant. Giorgetti,* from a design by Bernini. The adjoining staircase leads down to the Crypt of St Sebastian (see below). Still nearer the entrance is a stone from the catacombs with an inscription in honour of the martyr Eutychius, by Pope St Damasus.

The *Catacombs of San Sebastiano** (entrance to r. of church) have two special claims to fame: they are the only ones that have always been known, frequented, and therefore despoiled, and they were originally the only underground burial place to receive the name of Catacombs—*ad catacumbas*(literally, by the caves, or by the excavations). An explanatory film is shown in several languages before each conducted tour.

The descent to the CATACOMBS is by a stair with fragments of terracotta lids of sarcophagi with Imperial seals. The catacombs are excavated on four levels. The *Chapel of Symbols* has carved Christian symbols.—Beyond is an area (known as the *Piazzuola*) below the basilica (the walls of which can be seen), which has three tombs of the early 2C. The first, on the right, has a fresco above the tympanum of the Good Shepherd, Miracle of the Loaves and Fishes, and other scenes. The marble inscription names this the sepulchre of M. Clodius Hermes. The interior has a vault fresco with a Gorgon's head, and decorative frescoes on the walls, including a beautiful composition with a vase of fruit and flowers flanked by two birds. The floor preserves a mosaic. The centre tomb has a magnificent stucco vault, dating from the early 2C, terminating in a shell design decorated with lotus and acanthus leaves and a peacock. It is believed both pagan and Christian burials took place in this composite tomb on several levels. The Tomb to the left has a well-preserved stucco vault which descends to a lunette finely decorated with a grape and vine design. The cubicles here are also decorated with stucco.—From here ascends a steep staircase to the *Triclia,* a room reserved for the feast held in honour of a dead martyr or saint. There is a bench around the wall, and remains of red-painted decorations and fragments of pictures. The walls are inscribed with graffiti invoking the Apostles Peter and Paul. From the church (see above) stairs lead down to the *Crypt of St Sebastian* (restored). Here are a reproduction of the table altar, and a bust of St Sebastian, attrib. to Bernini.

Other parts of the catacombs are not usually shown. They include an ARCHAEO-LOGICAL MUSEUM (adm. by special permission only) opened in 1972 in the *Ambulatory* which forms an outer aisle of the church and runs round the apse. Here the construction of the 4C basilica can be seen clearly. The left wall is covered with epitaphs found in the course of excavations. In the centre, cases display objects found in the catacombs, and three models of the church and catacombs. To the left steps descend to the *Platonia,* once believed to be the temporary resting place of the Apostles, but now known to have been the tomb of St Quirinus. Also off the left side: the Chapel of Honorius III with 13C paintings, and an apsidal cubiculum with graffiti which indicate that this was the temporary grave of St Peter. Around the apse have been placed sarcophagi and fragments of sarcophagi.—In the vicinity of the basilica are numerous tombs and mausolea, some of them still visible. From the 3C to the 9C this was the most venerated area of subterranean Rome.

Just short of San Sebastiano Via delle Sette Chiese, on the right, leads to Via Ardeatina (600 m) and (250 m farther) the Catacombs of St Domitilla (see below). In Via Ardeatina (bus, see p. 218), a little to the left of its junction, is the **Mausoleo delle Fosse Ardeatine,** scene of one of the more horrifying occurrences of the Second World War. On 24 March 1944, by way of reprisal for the killing on the previous day of 32 German soldiers by the Resistance Movement in Via Rasella (p. 180), the Germans, then in occupation of Rome, shot 335 Italians, The victims, who had no connection with the killing of the Germans, included priests, officials, professional men, about a hundred Jews, a dozen foreigners, and a boy of 14. After the incident, the Germans buried the bodies under an avalanche of sand artificially caused by exploding mines. Local inhabitants who had taken note provided a medico-legal commission with the means of exhuming and identifying the bodies after the retreat of the Germans. The scene of the massacre, below a huge tufa cliff, now has cave chapels. The 335, reinterred after identification, are commemorated by a huge single concrete slab placed in 1949 over their mass grave, with a fine group of standing figures, in stone, by *F. Coccia* (1950).

Via Ardeatina goes on s. to (11 km. father) Castel di Leva (p. 235).

The **\*Catacombs of St Domitilla,** or *Catacombs of SS. Nereus and Achilleus,* farther along Via delle Sette Chiese, are among the most extensive in Rome and may be the most ancient Christian cemetery in existence. Here were buried St Flavia Domitilla (niece of Flavia Domitilla, sister of Domitian) and her two Christian servants, Nereus and Achilleus (p. 223), as well as St Petronilla, another Christian patrician, perhaps the adopted daughter of St Peter. The catacombs contain more than 900 inscriptions.

At the foot of the entrance stairway is the aisled *Basilica of SS. Nereus and Achilleus,* built in 390-95 over the tombs of the martyred saints. There are traces of a schola cantorum, and ancient columns probably from a pagan temple. The area below the floor level has sarcophagi and tombs. By the altar is a rare small column, with the scenes of the martydom of St Achilleus carved in relief. The adjoining chapel of St Petronilla (shown during the tour of the catacombs) with a fresco of the saint, contained the sarcophagus of the saint until the 8C, when it was removed to St Peter's.—A friar conducts groups from the Basilica to the catacombs, excavated on two levels. The *Cemetery of the Flavians* (the family of Domitilla) had a separate entrance on to the old *Via Ardeatina*. At this entrance, is a vaulted vestibule probably designed as a meeting-place for the service of Intercession for the Dead, with a bench along the wall, and a well for water. A long gallery slopes down from here, having niches on either side, with 2C frescoes of flowers and genii. From the original entrance a gallery leads to another *Hypogeum,* with four large niches decorated with 2C paintings (Daniel in the lions' den, etc.).—At the foot of a staircase is another ancient section; here is a cubicle with paintings of winged genii and the earliest representation of the Good Shepherd (2C).—On the upper level is the *Cubiculum of Ampliatus,* with paintings in classical style.—Other sections contain more paintings, including Seated Madonna and Child with four Magi; Christ and the Apostles; Cornmarket.

The Appian Way continues, leaving behind the area of the catacombs, and entering upon the finest section of the road. On the left, in a hollow, are the extensive remains of the **Circus of Maxentius** (No. adm.), built in 309 by the Emperor Maxentius in honour of his son Romulus (d. 307), and of the *Tomb-Temple of Romulus.*

The circus was a stadium for chariot-racing, measuring approximately 1630 Roman ft in length and 270 in breadth (513 by 91 m), and capable of holding 18,000 spectators. On the low wall (spina) which divided the arena longitudinally originally stood the obelisk of Domitian now in Piazza Navona. The chariots came in from the carceres near the entrance and the course was seven laps; the spina and the carceres were both somewhat obliquely disposed so as to equalize as far as possible the chances of all competitors. The remains of the circular tomb-temple are more immediately to the left.

A little farther on is the *****Tomb of Caecilia Metella** (Byron's "stern round tower of other days"), a massive circular tower of the Augustan period, 20 m in diameter, rising from a square base. It is usually open 9.30-12.30, 14-17; winter 9-15, Sun 9-13; closed Mon (informed custodian).

Much of the marble facing is still intact as is also part of the elegant frieze surrounding the upper part, in which were represented garlands of fruit and bucrania (hence the name *Capo di Bove* given to the adjacent ground). On the side nearest the road is the inscription to Caecilia, daughter of Quintus Metellus Creticus and wife of M. Licinius Crassus (elder son of the triumvir and one of Caesar's generals in Gaul). To the left is a statue of a soldier with Gallic bucklers. In the 13C the Caetani transformed the tomb into a crenellated tower to serve as the keep of their castle which bestrode the roadway and included a Gothic church, of which traces are still to be seen on the other side of the road. The interior of the tomb, constructed with small flat bricks, is particularly interesting; the room on the right contains a collection of inscriptions and fragments from tombs. The *Third Milestone* has been abandoned outside the enceinte of the castle, just to the left of the road.

A short distance farther on is the *Osteria Belvedere,* where the bus coming from the Colosseum diverges left from the Appia Antica along Via Cecilia Metella, which leads to Via Appia Pignatelli and Via Appia Nuova. The road, now mostly asphalted but retaining its ancient tombs, becomes more and more interesting and the view of the Campagna opens out. To the left is seen the imposing aqueduct of the Aqua Marcia and the Aqua Claudia. About 4 km. from Porta San Sebastiano the **Ancient Section of the Appian Way** is reached, excavated in 1850-59 between the 3rd and 11th milestones, the most picturesque and the least damaged part of the whole road. For ten Roman miles or more it was formerly bordered with tombs on both sides, and remains of these have been in many cases recovered while others have been reconstructed as far as possible. Some of the original sculptures have recently been

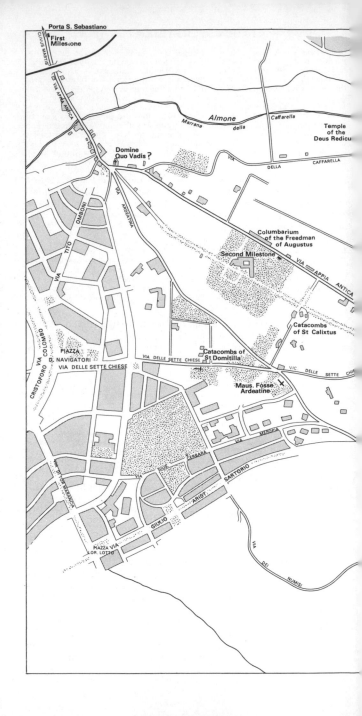

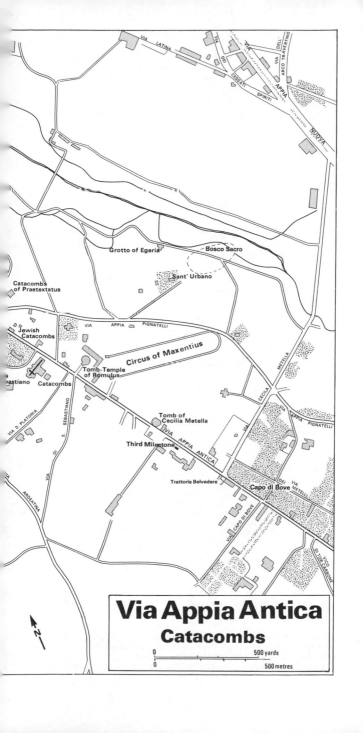

# Via Appia Antica
## Catacombs

removed to the Museo Nazionale Romano and replaced here by casts (easily identified by their yellow tint).—On a brick pilaster, on the left, opposite the site of the *Fourth Milestone,* are fragments of a tomb of a member of the Servilian gens. An inscription records that this was a gift made by Canova in 1808, who, contrary to the general practice of his time, felt that objects found during excavations should be left in situ. Beyond is the so-called *Tomb of Seneca* (l.; replaced by casts), immediately followed by the *Sepolcro Rotondo* (round tomb), a cella with four 'loculi', and the *Tomb of the Children of Sextus Pompeius Justus* (partly replaced by casts). Beyond this, set back from the road, is a so-called *Temple of Jupiter,* square with apsidal niches. On the right, in the Proprietà Lugari (near a clump of huge umbrella pines), is a superb monument in the form of a shrine (supposed to be that of St Urban), surrounded by the ruins of what was probably a villa. Then come, in the next 550 metres, the *Tombs of the Licinii,* of *Hilarius Fuscus* (the five busts replaced by casts), of the *Freedmen of the Claudian Gens,* and of *Q. Apuleius Pamphilius.* Beyond a sepulchre in the form of a temple is the *Tomb of the Rabirii* (the three busts replaced by casts). Beyond more tombs, one in peperino (decorated with festoons), and another with four busts (casts) the road crosses Via Erode Attico.—At a point marked by a group of gigantic pines, near the *Fifth Milestone,* the road makes a bend, probably to avoid some earlier tumuli, one of which (now surmounted by a tower) passes for the burial-place of one of the legendary *Curiatii,* while two others, surrounded by pines, about 350 m farther on (r.), represent those of the *Horatii.* In the field to the right of the first are the remains of an *Ustrinum* (cremation place). A gate on the left opens on a by-road leading to the estate of *Santa Maria Nuova,* built over ruins (see below), and, farther on, on the same side, is a great pyramidal tomb. Then, opposite the second of the graves of the Horatii, an inscription of the 1C B.C. marks the tomb of M. Cæcilius, in whose family grave (Eutropius tells us) was buried Pomponius Atticus, the friend of Cicero. Just beyond are the magnificent and picturesque ruins of the **\*Villa of the Quintilii,** now part of the property of Santa Maria Nuova (see above). The ruins sprawl across fields through which sheep are grazed.

These are so extensive as to suggest a town rather than a villa and in fact the name *Roma Vecchia* has been given to them. The villa, of which the principal mass dates from the time of Hadrian, belonged under Commodus to the wealthy brothers Quintilii, Maximus, and Condianus, consuls under Antoninus Pius (A.D. 151) and writers on agriculture, who were put to death by Commodus for the sake of their possessions, including the villa. This was kept in repair till the 4C. Near the road are the remains of a nymphæum (converted in the 15C into a castle), a hippodrome, and an aqueduct, and, a little in front of them, a cryptoporticus. But the greater portion of these ruins lies nearer the Via Appia Nuova, where there are high walls with windows and boldly-executed arcades, also the floor of a small amphitheatre of later date and traces of thermæ. Beyond the Via Appia Nuova is a fine monument, converted into a tower by the Saracens.

The road now becomes almost deserted.—8 km. The **Casal Rotondo,** a large round tomb on a square base, with a house and an olive garden on the summit.

This huge tomb, the largest on the Appian Way, dates from the Republic but was enlarged in early Imperial times. It is said to have been erected to the memory of the poet Messala Corvinus by his son Valerius Maximus Cotta. The stylobate is 120 Roman ft. (c. 36 m) in diameter, and the summit affords an extensive view.—

Attached to a wall close by are to be seen fragments of the tomb. Facing this monument is a smaller one attributed to the Aurelian gens.

Just beyond the Casal Rotondo are cross-roads, on the far side of which was the *Sixth Milestone.* Here also the Rome-Naples Direttissima railway passes diagonally below in a short tunnel. The road to the right is Via di Torricola, leading to Torricola and Via Ardeatina.

4½ km. from the intersection with the latter road is the **Santuario del Divino Amore,** at Castel di Leva. The sanctuary, visited by countless pilgrims on Whit Monday, was inaugurated in 1745 to enshrine a picture of the Virgin painted by an unknown 14C artist in the surviving tower of the *Castel di Leva,* a castle of the Orsini which passed to the Savelli before its destruction in the 15C. The painting, credited with miraculous powers of protection, is said to have saved the life of a pilgrim attacked here by mad dogs.

On the left Via di Casal Rotondo, bearing left after a short distance slopes down to the Via Appia Nuova and the tramway terminus of Capannelle (see p. 219). This is a convenient point at which to leave the Appian Way; otherwise it may be followed as far as Frattocchie.

Beyond the Casal Rotondo is a tomb with reliefs of griffons and a columbarium. Opposite another columbarium on the right of the road, is a tomb with four busts (casts). Some way farther on (about 1 km. from the Casal Rotondo) is the *Torre in Selce,* a pyramidal tumulus with a medieval tower, 107 m above sea-level, commanding a fine view. The remainder of the road is less interesting and finally becomes impracticable for wheeled traffic.

Beyond inscriptions of M. Julius Pietas Epelides and C. Atilius Eudos, a jeweller, the road swerves a little and begins to descend, and the arches of an aqueduct by which the water of a sulphur spring near Ciampino was formerly conveyed to the villa of the Quintilii, are prominent. Near this point the Appian Way is crossed by the Circular Road (see p. 226). The road then returns to its original direction and it passes in succession (l.) the stump of an apsidal monument; the *Torre Rossa* (a 12-13C structure on a Roman base); a restored tomb; the modern kennels of the Hunts Club; another core of concrete; a tall square monument; and, at about the end of the 8th Roman mile, a sepuchral chamber (or possibly a sanctuary of the mysteries), known as the 'Pillars of Hercules'.

Farther along Via Appia, beyond the *Torraccio del Palombaro* (a monument preserved through having been turned into a church in the 10C), is a path that leads on the right to *La Giostra,* a little hill upon which are the ruins of the very ancient Latin city of *Tellene.* Then come other tombs, more or less ruined (including one called the *Ruzzica d'Orlando*); and at the *Ninth Milestone* is what is left of the *Villa of Gallienus,* with a fine circular ruin that is regarded as the mausoleum of that emperor. Still passing traces of the past, the road crosses the Rome-Terracina railway and, a little beyond the *Twelfth Milestone,* the old and the new roads join.—16 km. *Frattocchie,* and from there (to 21 km.) *Albano Laziale,* see pp. 347.

# 17   TRASTÉVERE, THE JANICULUM, THE BORGO, AND CASTEL SANT'ANGELO

Castel Sant'Angelo may be reached directly from the centre of the city by the buses which cross bridges over the Tiber above or below it—No. 66 or No. 70 over Ponte Cavour, and No. 64 over Ponte Vittorio Emanuele. For details, see p. 41.
Ponte Garibaldi, starting-point of the following itinerary, is reached from Piazza Venezia by buses No. 56 or No. 60.

**Trastévere,** the quarter 'across the Tiber' (trans Tiberim), has been, since the middle ages, essentially the popular quarter of Rome, and its inhabitants most nearly preserve the characteristics of the original Roman people, an unconquerable pride and a strong love of liberty.

In earliest Republican days this bank of the Tiber was occupied by Lars Porsena in his endeavour to replace the Tarquins on the Roman throne; and here was the scene of the exploits of Horatius, Mutius Scævola, and Cloelia. Under the Empire, though built with aristocratic villas, it was still called the 'Ripa Veientana'. The unruly populace, in the middle ages, was held in subjection by families of even more turbulent barons; one of these, Titta Anguillara, it is recorded that he refused to uncover before the Emperor Charles V, gruffly alleging as excuse that he had "il cataro"—a cold in the head. Trastévere was the stronghold of independence during the Risorgimento; here Mazzini found support for his Republic of 1849, and here Giuditta Tavani Arquati, with her family made a gallant attempt to rouse the city on Garibaldi's behalf in 1867. In July, the gay festival of *'Noi Antri'* ('we others') takes place here.

The **Tiber,** or *Tévere* (418 km. long), is the most famous though not the longest of the rivers of Italy. It is said originally to have been called *Albula* and to have received the name of *Tiberis* from Tiberinus, king of Alba Longa, who was drowned in its waters.

It rises in the Tuscan Apennines, N.E. of Arezzo, and fed by numerous turbulent mountain streams, is liable to sudden flooding. Its swift waters are discoloured with yellow mud, even far from its source: hence the epithet *flavus* given to it by the Roman poets. The deposits brought down by the river have appreciably advanced the coastline; long ago the port of Ostia was rendered useless by silting up. The salt marshes near the river-mouth have been drained in a great scheme of reclamation.

*Ponte Garibaldi* (Pl. 7; 2), a modern bridge, with small obelisks, leads to *Piazza Gioacchino Belli,* named after the Roman dialect poet and containing a monument (1913) to him. On the left is the restored **Palazzetto degli Anguillara,** with its corner tower, the last of many which once guarded Trastévere.

The picturesque courtyard is largely a modern reconstruction of ancient material. The building is now the *Casa di Dante* (tablet), where readings from the 'Divine Comedy' are given by leading Italian men of letters. The library has a rich collection of works relating to Dante.

Immediately s. is *Piazza Sidney Sonnino,* in which, at the corner of Viale Trastévere (see below), is the church of **San Crisogono** (Pl. 7; 4), founded in the 5C, rebuilt by *G. B. Soria* in 1623 and restored in 1866. The campanile dates from John of Crema's rebuilding in 1122-24. Inside are 22 antique Ionic columns separating the nave from the aisles; the triumphal arch is supported by the two largest porphyry columns in Rome. The baldacchino rests on four columns of yellow alabaster. The church has a 13C Cosmatesque pavement. A mosaic in the apse by the school of *Pietro Cavallini,* depicts the Virgin and Child between SS. James and Chrysogonus.—Beneath the church (entered through the Sacristy in l. aisle) is an interesting 5C subterranean church, with 8-11C frescoes and sarcophagi.

The description below follows a somewhat circuitous route through old Trastévere to the church of Santa Cecilia (Pl. 8; 3); the direct route to this church is viâ Via dei Genovesi which runs left from Viale Trastévere.

Across the broad Viale Trastévere (which leads to the Stazione Trastévere) Via della Lungaretta leads E. The first turning on the right, in Piazza del Drago (Via di Monte Fiore) leads to the *Guardroom of the Seventh Cohort of Vigiles* (Roman firemen).

Remains can be seen from the street: the interior (entrance at No. 9, Via della VII Coorte) has been closed indefinitely. It contains interesting graffiti referring to reigning emperors, from Severus to Giordian III, and a bath or nymphaeum with a fine black-and-white mosaic. The barracks were built on the site of a 2C private house.

Via della Lungaretta continues to Piazza in Piscinula (Pl. 8; 3). In the far corner on the r. is the small church of *San Benedetto*, with a charming 11C roofed campanile. (If closed, ring at the door to the r. of the façade.)

On the left of the vestibule, a fine doorway leads into the cross-vaulted cell, in which St Benedict lived. To the l. of the entrance door is a detached 13C fresco of St Benedict (restored). Inside, eight antique columns with diverse capitals divide the nave from the aisles. The pavement is Cosmatesque. Above the altar is a 14C painting of St Benedict, and a damaged fresco of the Madonna and Child (attrib. to the early 16C Venetian school).

Opposite is the medieval *Casa dei Mattei* (restored), with a 15C loggia, and 14C cross-mullioned windows.

Via dell'Arco dei Tolomei leads out of the other side of the piazza through an arch, and Via dei Salumi diverges left. A short way along on the r., is Vicolo dell'Atleta (interesting house at No. 14), which leads to Via dei Genovesi, and its extension (l.), Via Augusto Jandolio. Immediately opposite is a house (Nos. 9, 10) with wooden eaves (characteristic of this area). To the left, at the end of the street, can be seen the restored church of Santa Maria in Cappella (No. 6), dating from 1090, with a contemporary campanile. From the charming garden courtyard (r.; now an old people's home) is a fine view of the Aventine hill. The lovely old Vicolo di S. Maria in Cappella leads to Piazza dei Mercanti (with fine houses, including one on the r. recently well-restored to its 15C appearance). The piazza now has several restaurants (not cheap).—To the right is Piazza di Santa Cecilia, in which is the church of **Santa Cecilia in Trastevere** (Pl. 8; 3). This church was founded perhaps by St Urban I (222-30) on the site of the house of St Valerian, husband and proselyte of St Cecilia. It was rebuilt by Paschal I (817-24) but was so much altered in the 16-19C that the work of 1899-1901 could do but little towards restoring its original form. The slightly leaning campanile dates from 1120.

St Cecilia, a patrician lady of the Gens Cornelia, was martyred in 230, during the reign of Alexander Severus. Refusing to sacrifice to idols, she was shut up in the calidarium of her own baths (see below), to be scalded to death. Emerging unscathed, she was beheaded in her own house, but the executioner was so maladroit that she lived for three days afterwards. She was buried in the Catacombs of St Calixtus, where her body remained until its reinterment in her church in 820 (see p. 228). As the inventor of the organ, she is the patron saint of music. On her day, 22 Nov, the churches hold musical services in her honour.

An atrium, with a fountain made from a large antique marble basin for ceremonial ablutions in a lovely garden of lilies, and a portico with four antique Ionic columns bearing a frieze of 12C mosaic medallions precede the Baroque façade. The INTERIOR, an aisled 18C hall whose piers (1823) enclose the original columns, contains several good monuments. On the left of the door, *Monument of Card. Nic. Forteguerri (d. 1473), the coadjutor of Pius II and Paul II in their suppression of the great feudal clans. The parts of this splendid work by *Mino da Fiesole* were dispersed about the church until the restoration of 1891, as were those of the tomb on the other side of the door, by *Paolo Romano*. This tomb, adorned with the arms of England, is that of Card. Adam Easton (d. 1397), a distinguished English churchman who was appointed cardinal in 1381, deposed by Urban VI (c. 1386), and reappointed by Boniface IX in 1389. In the 1st chap. on r., 15C fresco of the Crucifixion, and to the l., Madonna enthroned.

The corridor on the right, with landscapes (very ruined) by *Paul Brill* and a marble figure of St Sebastian by *Lorenzetto*, leads to the ancient CALIDARIUM, where St Cecilia was to be scalded to death by steam but was miraculously preserved. The steam conduits are still visible. On the altar is the Beheading of St Cecilia, and opposite, SS. Cecilia and Valerian, by *Guido Reni*. Next to the corridor opens the CAPPELLA DEI PONZIANI, with ceiling-frescoes of the school of *Pinturicchio* and, on the walls, SS. George, Catherine of Alexandria, Sebastian, and James, attrib. to *Ant. da Viterbo*. The last chap. on r. contains the theatrical 20C tomb of Card. Rampolla, who was responsible for the excavations beneath the church. In a small room to the l. is a tondo of the Madonna, by *Perugino* (kept locked).—In the chapel at the end of the aisle, Discovery of the Body of St Cecilia, 12-13C fresco (much damaged), detached from the portico.

In the SANCTUARY with a 9C gallery, is a fine tabernacle (1283), signed by *Arnolfo di Cambio*. Beneath the altar is the famous *Statue of St Cecilia, a work of much pathetic grace, by *Stef. Maderna*. The body of the saint is represented lying as it was found when her tomb was opened in 1599, on which occasion the sculptor was present.—The 9C mosaic in the APSE shows Christ blessing by the Greek rite, between (r.) SS. Peter, Valerian, and Cecilia, and (l.) SS. Paul, Agatha, and Paschal (the last with the square nimbus); below are the flock of the Faithful and the Holy Cities.—The LOWER CHURCH AND CRYPT are entered from the w. end of the N. aisle. The Roman structures include the pavement of a bath-house, a granary, and a lararium (which contains Republican columns), a relief of Minerva, mosaic pavements, and a number of Christian sarcophagi.—The CRYPT is a good interpretation (1899-1901) of the Byzantine by *Giovenale*, with luminous mosaics by *Bravi*. Through a grille may be seen the sarcophagi of St Cecilia, St Valerian and his brother St Tiburtius, St Maximus, and the Popes Lucius I and Urban I. The statue of St Cecilia is by *Aureli*.

Inside the CONVENT (adm. to l. of Portico, Tues and Thurs 10-11, Sun 11-12) is the *Last Judgment, by *Pietro Cavallini*, a masterpiece of medieval Roman fresco painting (c. 1293).

From the piazza Via di S. Cecilia leads left to reach Via dei Genovesi, which leads left again to the church of *San Giovanni Battista dei Genovesi* (1481; restored). The remarkable 15C *Cloister is entered along Via Anicia on the left (ring at No. 12). It has an arcaded lower gallery and a trabeated upper story, with a beautiful garden of orange trees. Via Anicia continues past (r.), the church of *Santa Maria dell'Orto*, with an unusual façade crowned with obelisks, and an ornate but not unpleasing interior.

Opposite the church, the road of the same name leads to the immense buildings, formerly occupied by the *Istituto Romano di San Michele*, founded in 1693 by Card. Odescalchi as a refuge and training centre for vagabond children. Beyond is the Tiber, crossed by Ponte Aventino (Sublicio; see p. 92). On the right, the *Porta Portese*, built by Urban VIII (1623-44) replaces the former *Porta Portuensis*, dating from the time of Honorius. The Porta Portese 'flea' market is farther s., near the Stazione Trastévere. Open only on Sunday mornings, it is the largest general open market in Rome, noted for clothes.

Via Anicia ends in Piazza San Francesco d'Assisi, in which is the church of **San Francesco a Ripa** (Pl. 7; 4), built in 1231 to replace the old hospice of San Biagio, where St Francis stayed in 1219. The last chap. on the left has a *Statue of Blessed Luisa Albertoni, a late work by *Bernini*, displayed effectively by concealed lighting. Above is an altarpiece by *Baciccio*. The CELL OF ST FRANCIS (apply at the sacristy), contains relics (displayed in an ingenious reliquary), and a 13C painting of the saint, in the style of Margaritone d'Arezzo.

Via Tavolacci rejoins Viale Trastévere, across which Via Morosini leads past the right side of the Ministero di Pubblica Istruzione. Via Roma Libera is the first road to the right, and here, at No. 76 is the old people's *Hospice of Regina Margherita* (formerly the convent of San Cosimato).

Visitors are admitted to see the beautiful 12C cloister with twin columns, and in a garden on the left, the church of SAN COSIMATO dating from the 10C, rebuilt in 1475. It has a good doorway, and contains (on the l. of the altar) a 15C fresco of the Virgin with Saints, and the tomb of Card. Alderamo Cybo (d. 1550), ascribed to Iac. Sansovino (this is now a second altar in a chapel to the left). The second cloister has 15C octagonal columns.

From Via Roma Libera the original narthex can be seen, and beyond is Piazza San Cosimato with a large market. Via di San Cosimato leads N. to Piazza San Calisto, in which is the 17C *Palazzo di San Calisto,* belonging to the Holy See; it was designed by Orazio Torriani. Just beyond is Piazza di Santa Maria in Trastévere (Pl. 7; 2, 4; closed to traffic), with a handsome fountain of Roman origin, restored by Carlo Fontana (1692). On the w. side is the church of **Santa Maria in Trastévere**, probably the first officially recognized Christian building in Rome and certainly the first church in Rome dedicated to the Virgin. It was built near a Taberna Meritoria, or hostel for veteran soldiers, either by St Calixtus (pope 217-22) or by St Julius I (337-52). It was rebuilt by Innocent II in 1140, and slightly modified later. The campanile is Romanesque.

The FAÇADE is adorned with a 12-13C mosaic of the Madonna surrounded by ten female figures with lamps, two of which are extinguished (once thought to represent the Wise and Foolish Virgins). In the portico added by Carlo Fontana in 1702 are a small lapidary collection, and 15C frescoes of the Annunciation (very worn).
In the aisled INTERIOR, the capitals of the 21 vast antique columns, some with fine bases, were decorated with figures of Egyptian deities, which Pius IX caused to be removed. The Cosmatesque pavement is made up of old material; the ceiling was designed by *Domenichino* (1617), who painted the central Assumption. The charming tabernacle at the beginning of the s. aisle is by *Mino del Reame.* In the N. aisle is the tomb of Innocent II (d. 1143), erected by Pius IX in 1869; and beyond that is the Avila chapel, with a fanciful dome and other intriguing Baroque decorations, by *Ant. Gherardi* (1680-86).
The CHOIR is preceded by a marble screen, on the right of which near a Paschal candlestick is the spot on which a fountain of oil flowed throughout a whole day in the year of Christ's Nativity. The tabernacle of the high altar is by *Vespignani.*—The *MOSAICS of the triumphal arch and apse (1140) are particularly fine; on the arch, the Cross with the symbolic Alpha and Omega between the seven candles-ticks and the evangelical emblems; at the sides, Isaiah and Jeremiah, with the rare and touching symbol of the caged bird (Christus Dominus captus est in peccatis nostris). In the semi-dome, Christ and the Virgin enthroned beneath the hand of God bearing a wreath and the monogram of Constantine. On the right, SS. Peter, Cornelius, Julius, and Calepodius; on the left, SS. Calixtus and Laurence, and Pope Innocent II with a model of the church. Lower are six 13C mosaics of the Life of Mary, by *Pietro Cavallini,* and, in the drum of the apse, SS. Peter and Paul presenting the donor, Bertoldo Stefaneschi, to the Madonna (1290).
To the right of the choir are the Armellini monument (1524) with sculptures by *Michelangelo Senese,* and the WINTER CHOIR, with decorations after *Domenichi-no's* designs. The chapel was restored by Henry of York in the 18C.—To the l. of the choir is the ALTEMPS CHAPEL, frescoed by *Pasquale Cati* (1588), with a scene of the Council of Trent. On the altar was a Madonna, traditionally attrib. to the 8C but now thought to date from the 13C, which will be returned to the chapel on the left after restoration (comp. p. 199). On the l. wall outside the chapel is the tomb of Card. Stefaneschi (d. 1417) by *'Magister Paulus'.*—The SACRISTY, approached by a passage decorated with antique mosaics of elegant birds, contains a Virgin with SS. Sebastian and Roch, of the *Umbrian School.*

Via della Paglia skirts the N. side of the church. To the right opens Piazza Sant'Egidio, where, at No. 1B a *Folklore Museum* was opened in 1978 (adm. see p. 48). On the first floor are exhibits relating to G. G. Belli, the popular romagnole poet, and a series of life-size tableaux of Roman scenes by Orazio Amato (1884-1952) based on paintings by

Penelli. On the floor above is material connected with another poet, 'Trilussa' (Carlo Alberto Salustri, 1871-1950). The building is used as a cultural centre.—Via della Scala leads out of the piazza past the ornate church of SANTA MARIA DELLA SCALA (1592), containing (over the 1st altar on r.), St John the Baptist by *Honthorst*. If closed, the church can be entered through the Carmelite Monastery (r.), which adjoins the *Pharmacy of S. Maria della Scala*, administered by the monks. The old pharmacy may be seen upstairs. Via della Scala ends at *Porta Settimiana*, incorporated in the Aurelian Wall and rebuilt by Alexander VI (1492-1503).

The street to the right, just before the gate, is Via Santa Dorotea. At No. 20 is the *Casa della Fornarina*, the supposed house of Raphael's mistress. At the end of this street Via di Ponte Sisto leads to **Ponte Sisto,** erected for Sixtus IV (1471-84), probably by Baccio Pontelli, to replace the ancient *Pons Janiculensis* (or the *Pons Antoninus*), built by Caracalla, the scene of many Christian martyrdoms.

The Porta Settimiana marks the beginning of Via della Lungara (Pl. 7; 2, 1), the longest of the 'rettifili' or straight-drawn streets built by the Renaissance popes. On the left is the building which housed the **Museo Torlonia.** For years closed "for restoration" the interior has recently been converted into flats and the works put in store. For further information apply to the Amministrazione Torlonia, 30 Via della Conciliazione.

The museum was founded by Gian Raimondo Torlonia (1754-1829) with sculptures from Roman collections, to which were added later the yields of excavations on the family estates at Cervéteri, Vulci, and Porto. There are about 600 pieces of sculpture, some over-restored, including a few Greek originals. The most important works include the *Giustiniani Hestia,* attr. to Kalamis (5C B.C.), and a bas-relief of *Herakles liberating Theseus and Peirithöos* (school of Pheidias; 4C B.C.; see p. 279). There are numerous Roman copies of works by Greek sculptors, notably Kephisodotos, Polykleitos, Praxiteles, and Lysippos. Of the Roman originals perhaps the most striking is a portrait statue of *Lucilla,* daughter of Marcus Aurelius. The Roman iconographic collection contains over one hundred busts of the Imperial era. The valuable Etruscan paintings (4C B.C.) are from Vulci.

At the end of Via Corsini (No. 24) is the *Orto Botanico* (adm. on application to the Director), occupying the former Corsini garden on the slopes of the Janiculum. It is noteworthy for its palms and yuccas.

In Via della Lungara, just beyond Via Corsini, on the left, is **Palazzo Corsini** (Pl. 7; 1, 2), built for Card. Dom. Riario in the 15C. It later became the residence of Queen Christina of Sweden, daughter of Gustavus Adolphus, who became a Roman Catholic; she died here in 1689. Nine years before, she had founded an academy for the discussion of literary and political topics, which later was developed into 'Arcadia' (see p. 243). After Christina's death the palace came into the possession of Card. Neri-Corsini, nephew of Clement XII, under whom it was rebuilt by *Ferd. Fuga* in 1732-36. In 1797 Gen. Duphot was killed near here in a skirmish between the French democratic party and the papal dragoons, and in 1800 Madame Letizia, mother of Napoleon, came to live in the palace. In 1883 it was bought by the Italian Government and became the seat of the Accademia dei Lincei. It is now part of the **Galleria Nazionale d'Arte Antica,** the nucleus of which was formed in the 18C by Cardinal Neri Corsini. Part of the collection was removed to Palazzo Barberini in 1952 (p. 79). Both collections are now in the course of rearrangement, and it is planned to move the 17-18C paintings to

Palazzo Barberini, so that only the original Corsini collection and the Flemish paintings will remain here.

On the first floor is a VESTIBULE: sculptures in neo-classical style by *John Gibson, Antonio Solà, Pietro Tenerani*, etc. ROOM I. Views and landscapes. *G. van Wittel (Vanvitelli)*, 1415. Castel S. Angelo, 1410. Palazzo del Quirinale, and other Roman views; 1473. *I. Caffi*, The Corso; 2349. *G. P. Pannini*, Porticus of Octavia; 1084. *P. Brill*, Cephalus and Procris.—RR. II and III. Foreign schools. Genre scenes by *Frans Francken II* (Nos. 1076, 1108, 1132, and 989) on either side of the door, and above, two landscapes by *Giovanni Momper* (Nos. 75 and 73). *Paul Moreel*, 218, 845. Portraits; 911. *J. van Ravesteyn*, Old Man; 190. *Lucas van Uden*, Snow scene; *Frans Snyders*, Boar Hunt; *David Koninck*, Animal paintings; *Cristiano Berentz*, Still-lifes. To the right is R. III, 885. *Willem Moreel*, Man in steeple hat; 900. *attrib. Rubens*, Madonna and Child; 1072. *Gerbrandt van den Eckhout*, Supper at Emmaus; 388. *Rubens*, St Sebastian (being restored); 973. *Pieter de Hooch*, Sentry; 111. *Van Dyck*, Madonna; *Jan Verspronck*. 884, 890. Portraits; 367. *Sustermans*, Young girl; 872. *Thos. de Keyser*, Portrait of a woman; 1528. *Jan Brueghel the Younger*, *Snow scene; 988. *Hondecoeter*, Landscape; *464. *Murillo*, Madonna and Child; *Sustermans*, 428. Vittoria della Rovere, 414. Cosimo III; 1526. *Pierre Mignard*, Madonna with boy dressed as Carthusian; landscapes by *Callot*, and (997) a monk by *Gort*.

R. IV. 17C Genoese school. (Starting at l. of the door): *Aless. Magnasco*, 1505. Witches, *1534. Hermits; *Baciccia*, Portrait of Clement IX, Sketches for the ceiling of the Gesù (Nos. 1668 and 1667), 1774. Madonna, 1470. Sketch for Sant'Agnese in Agone; *Bern. Carbone*, 894, 904. Portraits of noblemen; *Giov. And. De Ferrari*, 1694. Jacob; 1704. *And. Ansaldo*, Flight into Egypt; 1121. *Bened. Castiglione*, Faun in the Forest; *Baciccia*, 1451. Portrait of Bernini, 371. Portrait of a Cardinal; 1517. *Bern. Strozzi*, Charity of St Laurence; *Valerio Castello*, 1576. Rape of Proserpina; 1696. *Dom. Fiasella*, Hagar, *Aless. Magnasco*, 1506, 1516. Two landscapes.—R. V. 18C Venetian school. (In the centre): *G. B. Tiepolo*, *Old Faun and young satyr; *Canaletto*, 1005, 1033, 1037, 1061. Views of Venice.—R. VI (reached through R. IV). 17C Emilian and Tuscan schools. (Above the door), *Sassoferrato*, Madonna and Child; (r.) *Guercino*, 276. Adoration of the shepherds; (l.) *Guido Reni*, 191. Herodias; 211, 2246. *Lanfranco*, St Agatha healed by St Peter, Resurrection; 1498. *Sassoferrato*, Mgr. Ottaviano Prati; *Guido Reni*, 285. Ecce Homo, 1944. Young Girl; *Carlo Dolci*, 92. Madonna of the Veil, 178. Ecce Homo; 137. *Giovanni da S. Giovanni*, Group of Elders. On the screen, *Fr. Grimaldi*, 419. 420. Landscapes; *Guercino*, 1440. Death in Arcady, 279. Portrait of a boy; *Pier Fr. Cittadini*, 1382. Young girl.

R. VII (Queen Christina of Sweden died here in 1689). *Caravaggio*, *1569. Narcissus, *433. Young St John the Baptist, 107. (attrib.) Madonna and Child; 1276. *Orazio Gentileschi*, S. Francesco. Frescoes by *Zuccari*. Bust of Pope Alexander VII, attributed to Bernini.—R. VIII. Followers of Caravaggio. 1499. *Mattia Preti*, Raising of Lazarus; 1155. *Honthorst* (?), Portrait of a painter.—R. IX. 336, *Carlo Maratta*, Portrait of Maddalena Rospigliosi; *Pompeo Batoni*. 272. Nativity, 1025. Portrait of Clement XIII. 1045. Portrait of Count Soderini; 1753.

*Pietro da Cortona*, Guardian angel; (on screen) 512. *Fr. Trevisani*, Madonna Addolorata; (other side of screen) 986. *Dom. Fetti*, Jacob's dream; 223. *Carlo Maratta*, Virgin and Child; 192. *Pier. Fr. Molá*, Homer; 1493. *Girol. Ferrabosco*, Portrait of a young woman; (on screen) 1531. *Ignaz. Stern*, Card. Fr. Landi; 1548. *Raphael Mengs*, Portrait of a lady; 1533. *Ant. Cavalucci*, St Benoit Labre.

R. X. 17-18C Neapolitan school. *Luca Giordano*, 1881. Self-portrait, 394. Jesus in the temple; *Salvator Rosa*, 1571, 2353. Two portraits; 1535. *G. B. Caracciolo*, St Onuphrius; *Pietro Novelli*, 921, 879, 1483. Two portraits, and St Pellegrinus; 1536. *Fr. Solimena*, Expulsion of Heliodorus; (on screen) *Salvator Rosa*, 106, 110, 503, 1466. Four landscapes, 500. Battle scene; (other side of screen) 1487. *Gius. Bonito*, Portrait of a noblewoman; (2nd screen) 153. *Seb. Conca*, Adoration of the Magi; 1485. *Bern. Cavallino*, Departure of Tobias; 233. *Ribera* Death of Adonis.

R. XI. *And. Pozzo*, Sketch for the ceiling of St Ignatius; 220. *Carlo Maratta*, The artist's daughter; *G. M. Crespi*, 1237. Death of St Joseph, 1938. Young woman, 1538. St Hyacintha with the Virgin in glory; 1519. *Gaetano Gandolfi*, The plague (sketch for the cathedral at Foligno).—R. XII. Still life. 526. *Gius. Recco*, Still life (fish).

The **Accademia Nazionale dei Lincei**, founded by Prince Federico Cesi in 1603 for the promotion of learning, is said to be the oldest surviving institution of its kind. The administrative offices are in the Villa Farnesina (see below). With it are incorporated the *Biblioteca dell'Accademia* (1848), with 100,000 volumes and other publications, the *Biblioteca Corsiniana*, founded in 1754 by Mgr. Lorenzo Corsini, with a valuable collection of incunabula, manuscripts, and autographs, and the *Fondazione Caetani*, whose object is to promote scientific knowledge in the Muslim world. The library may be visited (9-13; entered from the ground floor to the right, up a spiral staircase). A series of rooms lead to a terrace overlooking the garden.

Immediately opposite Palazzo Corsini is the entrance to the graceful Renaissance \***Villa Farnesina** (Pl. 7; 2), built by *Bald. Peruzzi* (1508-11), as the suburban residence of Agostino Chigi, 'the Magnificent', the banker who controlled the markets of the East. Adm., see p. 50.

Here Agostino Chigi entertained with fabulous luxury Pope Leo X, cardinals, ambassadors, artists, and men of letters, and here he died on 10 April 1520, four days after Raphael. When he gave open-air banquets in a portico (now vanished) overlooking the Tiber, the silver plates and dishes were thrown into the river after every course; but prudence tempered ostentation, as a net was in position to recover them. In 1580 the villa passed to Card. Alessandro Farnese and in 1731 to the Bourbons of Naples. Since 1927 it has been the property of the State, and houses the administrative offices of the Accademia dei Lincei (see above).

From the garden is the entrance to a long glazed GALLERY, on whose ceiling is the famous Legend of Cupid and Psyche, as told by Apuleius, a series of \*Frescoes painted by *Raphael* with the aid of *Giulio Romano, Fr. Penni*, and *Giov. da Udine*. In a room on the left is the famous \*Galatea fresco by Raphael, a superb composition.

In the same room the ceiling is adorned with the Constellations, by *Bald. Peruzzi*. The Polyphemus and the scenes from Ovid's 'Metamorphoses' in the lunettes are by *Seb. del Piombo;* the colossal charcoal head in one of the lunettes is attributed to *Seb. del Piombo* or *Peruzzi*. On the upper floor is the DRAWING ROOM (being restored in 1978) with *trompe-l'oeil* views of Rome and mythological subjects, vigorous frescoes by *Peruzzi;* in the Bedroom are frescoes by *Sodoma* (1511-12), the best of which is on the wall opposite the windows, \*Wedding of Alexander and Roxana.

Wall-paintings and stuccoes found in a Roman house of the Augustan age in the grounds of the Villa are exhibited in the Museo Nazionale Romano (p. 196).

On the second floor of the Villa Farnesina is the **Gabinetto Nazionale delle Stampe**, with an exceptionally fine collection of prints and drawings housed in a series of beautiful rooms. Exhibitions are held here periodically.

Via della Lungara, running N.N.W. along the right bank of the Tiber, to Piazza della Rovere, passes the *Carcere Regina Coeli*, a prison named after a vanished church, and *Palazzo Salviati*, built in the 16C for Card. Salviati and now an international hostel for pilgrims.

From Porta Settimiana (comp. above) Via Garibaldi leads up towards the Janiculum. At the end of the first straight section of the road (before a sharp turn to the left) is the entrance to the convent of *Santa Maria dei Sette Dolori.*

The church was begun by Borromini in 1643, and its unfinished façade (1646) can be seen through the gate. The vestibule and interior of the church are entered through the convent; door to the r. of the façade. The church is oblong with rounded ends, with two apses in the middle of the long sides, and a continuous series of pillars connected by a heavy cornice. The disappointing interior decoration was added later in the 17C.

The **Janiculum** (82 m), not counted as one of the Seven Hills of Rome, is a ridge rising steeply from the Tiber and approximately parallel to its course for the whole of its length. On the W. side it slopes gently away towards the Campagna. Its highest point, at Porta San Pancrazio, is near the S. end; to the N. it reaches almost as far as Piazza San Pietro. Its upper surface is formed of yellow sand which gave the hill its ancient alternative name of *Mons Aureus;* this name is preserved in the title of the church of San Pietro in Montorio. The name of Janiculum (*Mons Janiculus;* in Italian, *Monte Gianicolo*) is derived from the old Italian deity Janus, who is said to have founded a city on the hill; his temple was in the Roman Forum. Numa Pompilius; the Sabine successor of Romulus, was buried on the Janiculum, and Ancus Marcius, the fourth king, built the Pons Sublicius over the Tiber to connect the Janiculum with the city of Rome.

The hill was the natural bulwark against the Etruscan invaders, but it does not appear to have been fortified until the time of the Republic. Part of it was included within the Aurelian Wall, and it was completely surrounded by Urban VIII when he built his wall in 1642. It was the scene of Garibaldi's stand against the French troops of Marshal Oudinot in 1849.—The *Views from the ridge are deservedly famous.

Above, on the right, is the former entrance gate to the *Bosco Parrasio,* where in 1725 was established the academy of **Arcadia,** founded in 1690 to carry on the work of the academy inaugurated by Queen Christina of Sweden ten years before (see p. 240).

The garden can be seen on request at No. 32 Via di Porta S. Pancrazio. Beyond a lovely circular dining-room with a dome (1725) is an amphitheatre, beyond which stairs wind down through a small wood, circling a giant Roman pine.

The object of Arcadia was to eliminate bad literary taste and to purify the Italian tongue of the turgid style and meretricious ornament prevalent at the end of the 17C. Although its members indulged in the fantasies associated with the name of Arcadia, especially in the matter of nomenclature, it exercised a profound influence on Italian literature during the 18C. Later its importance gradually waned and in 1926 it was absorbed into the Accademia Letteraria Italiana.

Via Garibaldi continues to mount, in sweeping curves (pedestrians can take a short cut viâ steps to the r. of the road), until it reaches a terrace. Here is the church of *San Pietro in Montorio,** built on a site wrongly presumed to have been the scene of St Peter's crucifixion (see p. 246). Mentioned in the 9C, the church was rebuilt in the late 15C at the expense of Ferdinand and Isabella of Spain. The apse and campanile, damaged in the siege of 1849, were restored in 1851. Raphael's Transfiguration (p. 285) adorned the apse for nearly 300 years—from 1523 to 1809.

INTERIOR (lights in each chapel). RIGHT SIDE: 1st chap., *Scourging of Christ, a superb work by *Seb. del Piombo* (1518) from designs by Michelangelo, and other frescoes by the same artist; 2nd chap. Madonna della Lettera, by *Pomarancio* (detached fresco fragment), and above, *Coronation of the Virgin, and four Virtues, by *Peruzzi;* 4th chap., Ceiling fresco, St Paul, by *Vasari,* and two tombs, with statues, by *Ammannati.* In front of the high altar are the tombstones of Hugh O'Neill of Tyrone and Roderick O'Donnell of Tyrconnel (1608), leaders in the Irish revolt against James I. Here also lies, without memorial, the body of Beatrice Cenci, beheaded as a parricide at St Angelo in 1599.—LEFT SIDE: 5th chap., Baptism of Jesus, by *Dan. da Volterra;* 4th chap. (perhaps by Carlo Maderna with stucco work by Giulio Mazzoni), Descent from the Cross and other frescoes, by *Dirk Baburen* (1617), a pupil of Caravaggio; 3rd chap., SS. Mary and Anne, after *Antoniazzo Romano;* 2nd chap. by *Bernini,* with sculptures by his pupil, *And. Bolgi;* 1st chap., St Francis receiving the Stigmata, by *Giov. de' Vecchi;* near the door, tomb of Card. Giul. da Volterra (d. 1510), by a follower of And. Bregno.

On the right of the church is the court of the famous *Tempietto* of *Bramante* (1499-1502), erected on the supposed exact site of St Peter's martyrdom. This jewel of the Renaissance, a small circular building with 16 Doric columns of granite, combines all the grace of the 15C, with the full splendour of the 16C. The Interior (including a crypt with pretty stuccoes by G. F. Rossi) may also be seen (ring at the convent).—To the right of the court is the *Spanish Academy.*

Via Garibaldi continues to the severe neo-classical *Monumento ai Caduti di 1849-70* (l.), by Giov. Iacobucci (1941), which commemorates the defenders and deliverers of Rome, incorporating the tomb of Goffredo Mameli. Farther on is the **Fontana Paola,** constructed for Paul V (as the handsome inscription states), by Giov. Fontana and Flaminio Ponzio (1612), using marble from the Roman Forum. The water, which flows abundantly from the subterranean Aqueduct of Trajan, falls into a large granite basin added by Carlo Fontana in 1690, beneath six columns (four of which are from the façade of Old St Peter's). On the right of the road is a subsidiary entrance to the Passeggiata del Gianicolo (see below).—At the top of the hill is the **Porta San Pancrazio,** built by Urban VIII, breached by Oudinot in 1849, and rebuilt by Vespignani in 1857.

This gate, once known as the *Porta Aurelia,* was the starting-point of the **Via Aurelia,** known in antiquity as the *Great Coast Road.* It followed the line of a still older road which linked Rome with the Etruscan towns on the Tyrrhenian littoral. It reached the coast at Alsium (Palo Laziale), a port of the Etruscan city of Caere (Cervéteri), and then followed the coastline to Pisa and Genoa. It ended in Gaul at *Forum Julii* (Fréjus, on the French Riviera). Today the *Via Aurelia Antica* branches to the right just w. of the gate, and skirts the N. side of the Villa Doria Pamphilj (see below). About 8 km. w. of Rome it joins the modern Via Aurelia, which starts from Largo di Porta Cavalleggeri, to the s. of St Peter's (see Rte 28).

From the gate Viale delle Mura Gianicolensi leads s. to the *Villa Sciarra,* an attractive public park (open 9-dusk). Beyond is the *Quartiere Monteverde.*

In front of Porta San Pancrazio Via di San Pancrazio leads s.w. to the ruins of the *Vascello,* a Baroque villa where Goffredo Mameli and Luciano Manara were killed in a last sally in 1849. Farther on is the entrance to the *Villa Doria Pamphilj** or *Belrespiro,* the largest park near Rome (9 km. round); it was laid out for Prince Camillo Pamphilj, nephew of Innocent X, by *Algardi* in 1650. The park has recently been acquired partly by the State and partly by the Commune of Rome and is open to the public (daily, sunrise to sunset). The grounds are crossed by Via Olimpica (p. 258).

Via di San Pancrazio passes the *Basilica of San Pancrazio,* occupying an enclave in the Villa Doria Pamphilj. This church dates from the 5C, but was rebuilt in the 16C and 19C. Near by are the *Catacombs of San Pancrazio* (adm., see p. 48).

Beyond Porta San Pancrazio is the beginning of the \*__Passeggiata del Gianicolo,__ a delightful promenade laid out in 1884 across the Villa Corsini. At Piazzale del Gianicolo the road is joined by that from the Fontana Paola (see above). Here stands the conspicuous equestrian \*__Statue of Garibaldi,__ by Emilio Gallori, erected in 1895 on the site of the hero's exploits of 1849. Around the base are four bronze groups: in front, Charge of Manara's Bersaglieri (Rome, 1849); behind, Battle of Calatafimi (1860); at the sides, Europe and America. The statue itself is 7 m high.

The Passeggiata now goes downhill. On the right is the former *Casino Lante* (16C); on the left, the bronze equestrian *Statue of Anita Garibaldi,* by Mario Rutelli, presented by the Brazilian Government in 1935 to honour her Brazilian origin. At the foot of the statue lies the body of Anita, transferred to this place from her grave at Nice. Farther on is a *Beacon,* presented by Italians in Argentina.

The \*View of Rome from this point is of the finest. On the extreme left is the dome of St Peter's, then Castel Sant'Angelo, San Giovanni dei Fiorentini, Pal. di Giustizia and the modern Prati Quarter, with the green slopes of the Villa Borghese, the Pincio, and the Villa Medici behind, among which the French Academy and the Trinità dei Monti can be distinguished. To the right is the façade of Montecitorio with its clock, behind which rise the Pinciano and Salario quarters. Below the hill is the prison of Regina Cœli, and beyond the river the spiral campanile of the Sapienza, the dome of the Pantheon, and the Quirinal. Farther to the right is Sant'Andrea, and, more distant, the tower and domes of Santa Maria Maggiore. Then come the Torre delle Milizie, the triple-arched loggia of the Pal. Farnese, the Victor Emmanuel Monument, the Torre Capitolina, and the dome of the Synagogue. Behind them are the white palazzo on the Viminal and the statues of St John Lateran. Among the trees of the Janiculum, on the extreme right, is the Fontana Paola. The whole is framed in the girdle of the Alban, Tiburtine, and Prænestine hills, which fall away gradually on the right into the smiling foothills of Latium.

The Passeggiata continues downhill. A stairway on the right, avoiding a sweep of the road, leads direct to *Tasso's Oak,* the dead battered trunk (now supported by iron girders) of the tree beneath which Tasso used to sit (tablet; 1898), and around which St Philip Neri played 'sapiently' with the Roman children ("si faceva co' fanciulli fanciullo sapientemente").

Near the end of the promenade a short flight of steps leads up to the little Piazzale di Sant'Onofrio, with ilex trees and a fountain. Here is the church of __Sant'Onofrio__ (Pl. 1; 8), founded by Blessed Nicolò da Forca Palena in 1419 and restored by Pius IX in 1857.

A graceful L-shaped Renaissance portico connects the church and monastery. In the lunettes beneath the portico are three scenes from the life of St Jerome (Baptism, Chastisement for reading Cicero, Temptation) all frescoes by *Domenichino,* and over the door, a Madonna by *Claudio Ridolfi.* By the convent entrance is the tomb of the founder.
The dark INTERIOR (if closed, ring bell in cloister to the right) is paved with innumerable tombstones. On the left, 1st chap., monument to Tasso, by *Gius. de Fabris,* an unworthy work of 1857; 3rd chap., tombstone of Card. Mezzofanti (d. 1849), who could speak 50 or 60 languages. In the pretty apse over the main altar are repainted frescoes by the school of Pinturicchio; above them, Scenes from the life of the Virgin. The fresco of St Anne teaching the Virgin to read, on the right, above the monument of Card. Giov. Sacco (1505), is of the 15C Umbrian school. In the 2nd chap. on the right, Madonna di Loreto, by *Ann. Carracci;* in the vault pendentives above the altar in the 1st chap., \*Annunciation, by *Antoniazzo Romano.*
The __Monastery__ has a charming 15C cloister, with frescoes of the life of St Onophrius, mainly by *Cavalier d'Arpino.* It is now an orphanage tended by American Friars of the Atonement. Torquato Tasso (1544-95), the epic poet, spent

his last days and died here. In the atrium is a monument to the 'Arcadian' poet Aless. Guidi (d. 1712). In the upper corridor, above a Della Robbia frieze, is a fresco of the Virgin with a donor, much repainted, attributed to *Boltraffio*. The Museo Tassiano (adm., see p. 50) occupies two rooms, containing the poet's death-mask, his armchair, crucifix, inkstand, mirror, etc.; and MSS., editions, and translations of his works.

The steep Salita di Sant'Onofrio leads down to Piazza della Rovere, the end also of Via della Lungara. A gentler descent is by the road to the left, which passes the buildings of the pontifical *North American College,* transferred from Via dell'Umiltà in 1953. On the right at the foot is *Ponte Principe Amedeo* (1942); on the left the road tunnel known as the *Traforo Principe Amedeo,* which leads under the Janiculum to Largo di Porta Cavalleggeri. In front is *Porta Santo Spirito,* an uncompleted gateway begun in 1540 by Ant. da Sangallo. It leads by Via dei Penitenzieri into the *Città Leonina,* or Rione of the Borgo.

The **Borgo,** the district on the right bank of the Tiber between the Janiculum in the s. and Monte Mario in the N., was known in antiquity as *Ager Vaticanus.* It was the stronghold of the papacy from 850, when Leo IV surrounded it with a line of walls, until 1586, when it was formally incorporated in the city of Rome.

The **Ager Vaticanus** was chosen by Caligula (A.D. 37-41) for his circus, which was enlarged by Nero (54-68). It then became known as the *Circus of Nero.* Its site has been verified by excavations begun in 1940 under St Peter's and it has been located just s. of the basilica. In the adjoining gardens many Christians were martyred under Nero in A.D. 65. St Peter suffered here and he was buried in a pagan cemetery near by. Over his grave the first church was built (c. A.D. 90) to commemorate his martyrdom (comp. p. 265). In 135 Hadrian built in the Ager Vaticanus his mausoleum, now the Castel Sant'Angelo.

Paganism retained its hold with great tenacity in this quarter until the late 4C, as is evinced by inscriptions on the temples of Cybele and Mithras. Despite this tendency, churches, chapels, and convents were built round the first church of St Peter and the district, attracting Saxon, Frank, and Lombard pilgrims, came to be called the *Borgo* (borough), a name of Germanic origin. In 850 Leo IV (847-55) surrounded the Borgo with walls 12 m high, fortified with circular towers, to protect it from the incursions of the Saracens: hence the name *Civitas Leonina* or *Città Leonina.* Remnants of Leo IV's wall survive to the w. of St Peter's. The Leonine city became the papal citadel: within its walls John VIII (872-82) was besieged in 878 by the Duke of Spoleto; in 896 Arnulph of Carinthia attacked it and Formosus crowned him emperor. Gregory VII (1073-85), having taken refuge in the Castel Sant'Angelo from the Emperor Henry IV, was rescued by Robert Guiscard in 1084. After the coronation in 1167 of Barbarossa in St Peter's, the Romans attacked the Leonine City, and it was again assailed by them twelve years later.

During the 'Babylonian captivity' (1309-78) the Borgo fell into ruin, but when the popes returned from Avignon to Rome and chose the Vatican as their residence in place of the Lateran, a new era of prosperity began. In the 15C Eugenius IV (1431-47) and Sixtus IV (1471-84), and early in the 16C Julius II (1503-13) and Leo X (1513-21) were active in developing and beautifying the Borgo as well as the Vatican. The original area of the Borgo was enlarged by the addition, on the N. of the Borgo Angelico, a name which survived in the Porta Angelica now demolished, and still survives in the name of a street.

After the sack of Rome in 1527 the district, deserted by the richer citizens, became one of the poorest and least populated quarters of Rome, and the papal court, neglecting the Borgo, confined its activity to the embellishment of the buildings and gardens of the Vatican. In 1586 Sixtus V (1585-90) relinquished the papal claim to the Borgo, which was thereupon united to the city of Rome. In 1870, when Rome was united to the kingdom of Italy, the Borgo remained unaffected by the extraterritoriality conceded to the Vatican and St Peter's.

Five (originally seven) streets in the Leonine City have the prefix Borgo. Borgo Sant'Angelo and Borgo Santo Spirito run respectively N. and s. of Via della Conciliazione (p. 263). In the construction of that street, the central Borghi Nuovo and Vecchio were eliminated. The remaining streets—the Borghi Angelico, Vittorio, and Pio—are to be found between the Castel Sant'Angelo and the Vatican.

Via dei Penitenzieri leads into Borgo Santo Spirito. At the junction is **Santa Spirito in Sassia** (Pl. 1; 6), a church founded in 726 for Saxon pilgrims (comp. above) by Ine, king of Wessex, who died in Rome in the same year.

The church was rebuilt in 1540 by *Antonio da Sangallo:* the design of the façade was probably his, but the work itself was done in 1585 by *Ottavio Mascherino.* The campanile, entirely Tuscan in character is one of the most graceful in Rome. It is ascribed to *Baccio Pontelli.*—It was from the ramparts of the Leonine City near here that Benvenuto Cellini, according to his own statement, shot the Constable de Bourbon in 1527; a tablet on the outer wall of the church, however, attributes the deed to Bern. Passeri, another goldsmith.—Adjoining are the buildings of the huge **Arcispedale di Santo Spirito,** founded by Innocent III c. 1198 and rebuilt for Sixtus IV by various architects (c. 1473-78). The first building, the Palazzo del Commendatore (i.e. the house of the director of the hospital), with a spacious courtyard, dates from c. 1567. The harmony of the proportions of the main building was spoilt by Alexander VIII, who added a story, and by Benedict XIV, who blocked up the arches of the portico. The portal is an effective example of the early Renaissance style. The chapel (adm. by special permission only) contains an altar with a baldacchino of the time of Clement VIII (1592-1605) and an altarpiece (Job) by *Carlo Maratta.* The river front, on the Lungotévere in Sassia, was rebuilt and extended in 1926 in harmony with the old style.

The hospital contains several institutions devoted to the history of medicine: the *Lancisiana Library* (founded 1711; in the Pal. del Commendatore), the *Historical Medical Academy,* and the *National Museum of the History of Medicine,* unique in Italy, Adm. see p. 49.

Borgo Santa Spirito ends in Lungotévere Vaticano. On the right is *Ponte Vittorio Emanuele* (1911), decorated with monumental groups (fine view upstream, especially at sunset). It marks the end of Corso Vittorio Emanuele (p. 74). On the left is the beginning of Via della Conciliazione (p. 263). A little farther on is the celebrated *****Ponte Sant'Angelo** (Pl. 2; 5), the ancient *Pons Aelius* or *Pons Adrianus,* built by Hadrian (P. Aelius Hadrianus) in 134 as a fitting approach to his mausoleum—the Castel Sant'Angelo, as it has been called since the middle ages.

In 1530 Clement VII erected the statues of St Peter (school of *Lorenzetto*) and of St Paul (school of *Paolo Taccone,* 1464) at the end towards the Castel Sant'Angelo. Ten statues of angels, by pupils of *Bernini* (1688; to his design) completed the decoration; two of the angels are copies of originals in the church of Sant'Andrea delle Fratte. The central three arches are part of the original structure; the end arches were restored and enlarged in 1892-94 during the construction of the Lungotévere embankments. The Tiber in flood may rise to the top of the arches.

Facing the bridge is the *****Castel Sant'Angelo** (Pl. 2; 5), originally the *Mausoleum of Hadrian,* an enormous circular structure begun by Hadrian c. A.D. 130 as a sepulchre for himself and his family. It was completed in 139, a year after his death, by his successor Antoninus Pius. It now contains the Museo Nazionale di Castel Sant'Angelo. Adm., see p. 48.

The mausoleum consisted of a base 89 m square, supporting a round tower 64 m in diameter, of peperino and travertine overlaid with marble. Above this was an earthen tumulus planted with cypress trees. At the top was an altar bearing a bronze quadriga driven by a charioteer representing Hadrian, as the Sun, ruler of the world. Inside the building was a spiral ramp (still in existence), which led to a straight passageway ending in the cella, in which was the imperial tomb. Hadrian and Sabina (his wife), and his adopted son L. Aelius Cæsar, were buried in the mausoleum; and succeeding emperors until Septimius Severus.

When Aurelian built his wall round Rome, he carried it on the left bank of the Tiber above the Porta Settimiana. He built the Porta Aurelia Nova on the city side of the Pons Aelius and made Hadrian's mausoleum into a bridgehead on the other side of the river. He surrounded his bridgehead with a wall strengthened with towers. In this wall a gate, later known as the Porta San Pietro, gave access in the middle ages to the Vatican by means of the *Covered Way* (see below), used as an escape route by Alexander VI in 1494 and by Clement VII in 1527.

In the early middle ages the tomb was surrounded with ramparts and became the citadel of Rome. Theodoric (474-526) used it as a prison and for a time it became known as the *Carcer Theodorici*. According to legend, St Gregory the Great, while crossing the Pons Aelius at the head of a procession to pray for the cessation of the plague of 590, saw on the top of the fortress an angel sheathing his sword. The

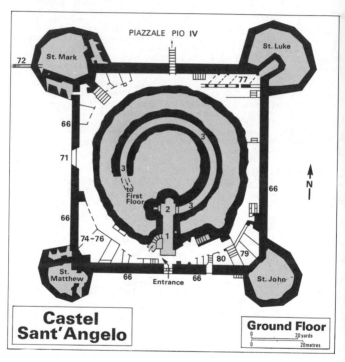

vision accurately presaged the end of the plague and thenceforth the castle bore its present name.

For centuries the Castel Sant'Angelo was a centre of strife between popes and antipopes, the imperial forces and the barons. In 1084 Gregory VII was rescued from Henry IV's siege by Robert Guiscard's timely advance. It was hence that Rienzo, at the end of his first period of dictatorship, fled to Bohemia on 15 Dec 1347. In 1378 the castle was severely damaged by the citizens of Rome, resentful of foreign domination. Shortly afterwards, in the reign of Boniface IX (1389-1404), it began to be rebuilt. The antipope John XXIII (1410-15) began the Covered Way to the Vatican; Alexander VI (1492-1503) completed it. He also completed the building of the four bastions of the square Inner Ward (see below) which had been begun by Nicholas V (1447-55). Julius II (1503-13) built the South Loggia, facing the river. When Clement VII took refuge here in 1527 from the troops of Charles V, the defence was materially assisted by Benvenuto Cellini, who tells in his 'Autobiography' about his prodigies of valour and marksmanship. Paul III (1534-49) built the North Loggia, to counterbalance the South Loggia of Julius II (see above). Under Paul III the interior was decorated with frescoes and a marble angel, by *Guglielmo della Porta,* was placed on the summit of the castle. The Outer Ward, with its defensive ditch, was the work of Pius IV (1559-65). Urban VIII (1623-44) provided the castle with cannon made of bronze taken from the ceiling of the Pantheon portico, and he employed *Bernini* to remodel the outworks. Benedict XIV (1740-58) replaced the marble angel with the bronze statue by *Verschaffelt* that is there today.—From 1849 to 1870 the castle was occupied by French troops. Under the Italian Government it was used as barracks and as a prison until 1901 when, thanks to the initiative of Gen. Mariano Borgatti, the work of restoration was begun. This was intensified in 1933-34, when the castle was adapted for use as a museum and the surrounding area was cleared of obstructions.

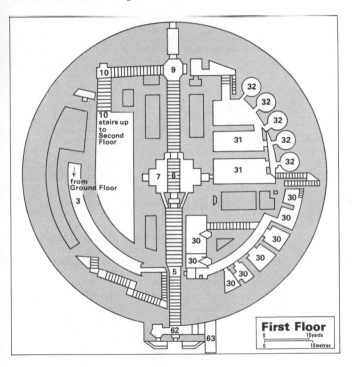

As it is today, the Castel Sant'Angelo rises from a square INNER WARD, with bastions named after the four Evangelists at each corner: N.W. St Mark, N.E. St Luke, S.W. St Matthew, S.E. St John.

Outside this enceinte is the OUTER WARD, pentagonal in shape. This had five bastions: from left to right, Santo Spirito (demolished by Pius IV to make room for Piazza Pia), San Pietro, San Paolo, Santa Maria, San Salvatore (eliminated during the construction of the Lungotévere). Between the two enceintes is the ditch, revealed during the excavations of 1933-34 after having been filled in for centuries. The area between the two enceintes has been laid out as a public garden, known as *Piazzale Pio IV.* The garden may be entered from the N. and W. sides. The *Covered Way* leads from the Bastion of St Mark across the garden on its way to the Vatican.

The *Museo Nazionale di Castel Sant'Angelo, inaugurated in 1925, is a military and artistic museum. It is arranged in 58 rooms of the castle. The military collections, giving, as they do, a comprehensive review of the appurtenances of war from the Stone Age to the present day, are probably unrivalled in their completeness. The art treasures have been enriched by the donations of benefactors, and the museum now has noteworthy collections of antique furniture, tapestries, and velvets. Some of the paintings are of great importance.

In its general plan, the castle follows the design of Hadrian's mausoleum. The curtain walls of the inner ward, between the medieval bastions, are original; so is the entrance, except that the Roman threshold was lower. The round tower is Hadrian's, without its marble facing and its statues. Above it are the Renaissance and later additions, such as the arcaded galleries. The place of the earthen tumulus is taken by the papal apartments. The central tower is the base of Hadrian's quadriga, now replaced by the bronze angel.

The various features of the interior are all numbered with arabic numerals, which correspond to the numbers given in the description below. Rooms are often closed for rearrangement. Refreshments available on the Gallery of Pius IV (60).

The entrance to the castle is by the bronze doors in the s. side between the bastions of St Matthew (l.) and of St John (r.). To the left of the *Cortile del Salvatore* is the *Antiquarium* (74-76), containing architectural and sculptural fragments found in the castle, many from Hadrian's original Mausoleum; vaults show the original construction of the base of the tomb. From the court steps descend to a spacious *Vestibule* (1), which leads into the interior. On the left is the shaft (2) of a lift built for the infirm Leo X and, in front, a niche for a statue of Hadrian.

In the centre are five models of Castel Sant'Angelo at different stages in its history, the second showing how much of the original structure remains today.

On the right begins the SPIRAL RAMP (3), 125½ m long, which rises gently to the sepulchral cella (see below). The ramp is in a wonderful state of preservation; the floor has remains of mosaic decoration. Along it are four ventilators, the last but one of which was converted into a prison, mentioned by Benvenuto Cellini.

At the end of the ramp the *Staircase of Alexander VI* (5), which cuts diametrically across the circular building, mounts to the left. By means of a bridge (6) built in 1822 by Valadier in place of a drawbridge the staircase passes above the SEPULCHRAL CELLA (7), of which only the travertine wall blocks survive, with some fragments of marble decoration. Here were kept the urns containing the imperial ashes. Hadrian's porphyry sarcophagus was annexed by Innocent II (1130-43) for use as his own tomb in the Lateran, where it was destroyed by the fire of 1360.

At a landing lit by a round window (9) the Staircase of Alexander VI originally turned to the right. Paul III closed this section and opened one to the left (10; by *Ant. da Sangallo the Younger*), to give access to the COURT OF HONOUR, or COURT OF THE ANGEL (11), as it is usually called. The alternative name is due to the *Angel* (13) of Gugl. della Porta, moved here from the top of the castle to make room for the bronze angel. This court has yet another name—*Cortile delle Palle,* from the marble and stone cannon balls collected here; they formed part of the castle's ammunition store. Here also are four 15C bombards.

At the end of the court are the *Staircase of Urban VIII* and the façade (by Michelangelo) of the *Medici Chapel,* built for Leo X (12). On the right is a series of rooms: the first (14) is a reconstruction of an ancient guard-room; the next nine (15, II-VII; on two levels) house a *Collection of Arms and Armour,* from the Stone Age to the 18C. R. II. Weapons from prehistoric times to the middle ages. R. III. 14-17C defensive arms. R. IV. Swords and pikes. R. V. Firearms from 15-18C. Stairs lead up to three rooms containing 19-20C arms from Western countries, and a last room (VII) with exotic arms from Africa, China, and other countries.

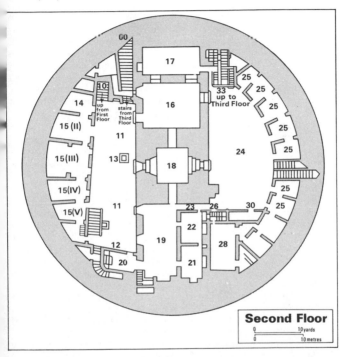

**Second Floor**

From the Court of the Angel there is access to the ROOMS OF CLEMENT VIII (16 and 17) which are usually open only for exhibitions.

The HALL OF JUSTICE (18; reached through Room 19) is so called because it was the seat of the tribunal of the 16-17C, and because of its fresco, Giustizia, by *Perin del Vaga.* It was built in Roman times above the sepulchral cella. It contains a collection of military equipment found in the excavations round the castle and in the Tiber.—The next room (19) is the HALL OF APOLLO, so called from the subject of the mythological grotesque decoration attributed to *Luzio Luzzi.* On the right is a trap-door covering a cellar 9 m deep; adjacent is the top of the lift-shaft seen from the spiral ramp (comp. above).

Leading out of this room (r.) is the CHAPEL OF LEO X (20; kept locked), restored by Prof. Riccardo Buttinelli. On the altar, 17C figure of St

Philip Neri praying; in a glass case are antique vestments. Near the door, wooden model of the Archangel Michael, after *Bernini*.—ROOMS OF CLEMENT VII (21, 22). In the first room is a frieze by *Guilio Romano*, and a coffered ceiling. The paintings include: *Taddeo Gaddi,* Triptych; two detached frescoes of the 15C Lombard School; *Fiorenzo di Loren- zo,* St Sebastian (fresco); *Tuscan 15C School,* Madonna enthroned; *Niccolò l'Alunno,* *St Sebastian and St John the Baptist; *Zavattari* brothers, Polyptych.—Room 22: *Martino Spanzotti,* Pietà; *Bart. Mon- tagna,* *Madonna and Child; *Luca Signorelli,* *Madonna and Saints; *Carlo Crivelli,* Two saints.

A passage (23) leads r. out of R. 19 into the large COURTYARD OF ALEXANDER VI (24). This court has three other names—*Court of the Well, of the Oil,* and *of the Theatre.* The names are derived from the fine marble well, from the oil formerly stored in the rooms below, and from the theatrical performances given here under Leo X and Pius IV.—A small staircase (26; not always open) leads to the BATHROOM OF CLEMENT VII (27) decorated with stuccoes and frescoes by *Giulio Romano.* This room communicates with a small dressing-room on the next floor (closed).

On the right side of the courtyard is a semicular two-storied building, the rooms of which (25) were formerly used as prison cells. In the second room from the right Benvenuto Cellini was imprisoned during the first period of his captivity.

Adjacent is the *Court of Leo X* (28) with a loggia; below it is a 15C casemate. Adjacent is a small triangular courtyard whence stairs lead to a chamber which had a stove for heating the bath water and the air which circulated between the hollow walls.

A small doorway (30) in the Courtyard of Alexander VI leads to the HISTORICAL PRISONS (also 30; closed in 1978). A sloping passage descends to a large underground room, at the end of which is a winding vestibule leading to a corridor on to which open the doors of some small cells. The numerous bones found under the floors indicate that the prisoners were buried where they had died. Despite tradition, there is no proof of the identity of any of those incarcerated here, though Benvenu- to Cellini is said to have passed the second period of his captivity in the last cell.—Beyond the prison cells are two large underground *Oil Stores* (31), containing 84 jars, with a capacity of c. 22,000 litres. The object of the stores was twofold: to feed the garrison and to discourage assailants by pouring boiling oil on them.—On the right of the oil stores are the *Grain Silos* (five chambers; 32), later used as prison cells.

Stairs lead back up to the Courtyard of Alexander VI, and from there a staircase (33) continues to the LOGGIA OF PAUL III (34; left), built by *Ant. Sangallo the Younger* and decorated with stuccoes and grotesques. From here and from the adjacent semicircular galleries there is a comprehensive *View of the pentagonal Outer Ward.—To the right of the Loggia of Paul III extends the semicircular GALLERY of PIUS IV (35), on the inner side of which is a series of small rooms used originally as quarters for the household of the papal court and later as political and military prison cells.

The first (36) is a reconstruction of a political prison in the first half of the 19C. In the rest (37; often closed) is an interesting muster of uniforms, decorations, and medals of the various Italian states before the Unification.

From the vestibule there is access to a terrace overlooking the Courtyard of Leo X. Beyond is the LOGGIA OF JULIUS II (38), built by *Bramante;* it faces s. and the Ponte Sant'Angelo.—A staircase leads from here to the **Papal Apartments** (39-49).

SALA PAOLINA OR DEL CONSIGLIO (39), adorned with *Stuccoes by *Girol. da Sermoneta* and *Baccio da Montelupo.* Walls decorated by *Perin del Vaga, Polidoro da Caravaggio, Giov. da Udine,* and others. On the right is an amusing trompe-l'œil fresco of a courtier entering the

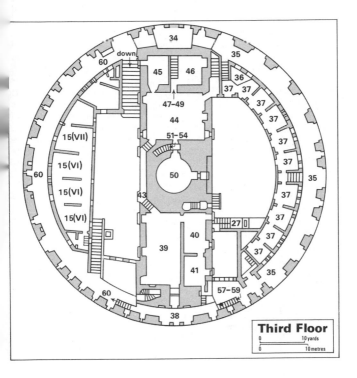

**Third Floor**

0           10 yards
0                10 metres

room through a painted door. In the floor, coat-of-arms of Innocent XIII, who restored the room.—CAMERA DEL PERSEO (40), so called from the subject of the frieze by *Perin del Vaga.* The wooden ceiling is intaglio work of the 16C. The tapestries come from State collections and the room is appropriately furnished. The contents are mainly from the Contini donation, as are those of RR. 44-49; the paintings are frequently changed around.—Two paintings of Christ carrying the Cross, one by *Paris Bordone,* and one by *Seb. del Piombo; Giac. Della Porta,* Bust of Paul III (cast); tapestry with an episode in the life of Julius Caesar.— CAMERA DI AMORE E PSICHE (41), called after the frieze by *Perin del Vaga,* illustrating the story of Cupid and Psyche in 17 episodes. Fine carved gilt 15C ceiling. Large 16C canopied bed, clavichord, and other furniture; Girl with a unicorn, by an unknown 16C artist; statuette attrib. to *Iac. della Quercia.*

From the Sala Paolina a frescoed corridor (43) leads to the HALL OF THE LIBRARY (44), with ceiling frescoes by *Luzzi* and stuccoes by *Sicciolante da Sermoneta* (16C). Marble chimney-piece by *Raff. da Montelupo.* The furniture includes four cassoni, a 15C wardrobe, chairs and candelabra.—ROOM OF THE MAUSOLEUM OF HADRIAN (45), so called from the frieze by *Luzzi* and his school. The paintings include: Three works representing Bacchanals by *Dosso Dossi, Giac. Jordeans,* and *Nic. Poussin* (a copy of a work by Giov. Bellini); and *Lor. Lotto,* *Madonna between SS. Roch and Sebastian. The adjoining rooms (46-49) have been closed for rearrangement. A small vestibule leads out of the Hall of the Library into the central ROOM OF THE SECRET ARCHIVES or of the TREASURE (50). The walnut cupboards in this room were used for the archives inaugurated by Paul III. In the middle are some large chests in which Julius II, Leo X, and Sixtus V kept the sacred treasure.

A Roman staircase ascends to the ROUND HALL (51), situated beneath the statue of the angel and above the last room. Formerly used as a political prison, it now contains flags, colours, and other military relics. In the middle of the room is the *Golden Book of the Dead,* containing the names of those who fell in Italy's wars.—A short staircase leads to the HALL OF THE COLUMNS which, with the two adjoining rooms (52-53), contains military souvenirs, documents, and drawings.

At the top of the staircase the TERRACE (54) is reached, familiar to play and opera-goers from the last act of 'Tosca', Verschaffelt's *Angel,* in the act of sheathing his sword, stands on a small higher terrace (inaccessible to the public), Near by is the *Campana della Misericordia,* the bell which used to announce the execution of capital sentences.

The *View from the terrace is unrivalled. On the left, in front, is the Palace of Justice, with the Trinità dei Monti behind it. Farther to the left, the Prati Quarter; at the back the verdure of the Villa Borghese and of the Pincio. Across the Tiber, the Ministry of Finance, with the Quirinal in front; then the Palazzo della Consulta, with Santa Maria Maggiore behind it. To the right, the Torre delle Milizie, with the cupola of the Pantheon in front. Next comes the Victor Emmanuel Monument, with St John Lateran behind it. In the background, the Castelli Romani. Continuing to the right, the Capitol; in front, the two cupolas of Sant'Andrea della Valle and San Carlo ai Catinari. Then is seen the Aventine, with San Paolo fuori le Mura in the background. Farther right, is Trastévere and the Janiculum; St Peter's and the Vatican; Monte Mario. Immediately below, Ponte Sant'Angelo and Ponte Vittorio Emanuele, with the Lungotévere.

The descent now begins viâ the Roman staircase. It is necessary to cross the Hall of the Library (44) diagonally, passing through a door left of the fireplace. The descent continues to the right, along the Gallery of Pius IV (35).

At the end a staircase leads to the APPARTAMENTO DEL CASTELLANO (59; usually closed). In the corridor (58) is a portrait by *Cav. d'Arpino* of Prospero Farinacci, the defender of the Cenci, a cast of the head of Verschaffelt's angel and its original sword. In the three rooms is a valuable collection of majolica paving-tiles, earthenware, iron and other utensils found in the excavations, secret ('insidious') weapons found on prisoners, and MSS. discovered in the castle.—On the upper floor (57) is a collection of prints and drawings of the castle at various stages of its existence, and the *Archivio dei Castelli d'Italia,* a similar collection with reference to the old castles of Italy.

The descent continues along the continuation of the Gallery of Pius IV (60; refreshments), opened by Alexander VII, and from there by Urban VIII's Staircase to the Court of the Angel (11). After this the route follows Paul III's staircase (10), and Alexander VI's staircase (5), at the foot of which is a small guard-room (62). From here a gateway leads on to a drawbridge (63.). An external staircase on the left from this point leads to the castle entrance.—To the right the *Bastion of St Matthew* may be reached by means of a walkway (66) between the Roman structure and the square inner ward, completely encircling the cylindrical centre, with several radial cells opening out of it. At the next corner steps lead down into the *Bastion of St Mark* (70). Here is the beginning of the *Passetto Vaticano,* or Covered Way (72; see p. 277). On the left are the *Mills* (Mole; 71), used from the time of Pius IV to grind the castle flour. Between the bastions of St Mark and St Luke is a passageway leading into the public garden (Piazzale Pio IV). By the *Bastion of St Luke* is the *Chapel of the Crucifix* or of *Clement XII* (77), in which condemned criminals had to attend before execution. The circuit continues past a reconstruction of the entrance gate to the castle which, built in 1556 by *Giov. Sallustio Peruzzi* for Paul IV, was adapted in 1628 for the use of barracks built by Urban VIII. It was demolished in 1892 when the Lungotévere was built. On the inner side of the *Bastion of St John* are further oil stores (79). Finally, beyond a radial cell (80) containing Byzantine and Roman marbles, the entrance gate is regained.

# 18   FROM PIAZZA CAVOUR TO MONTE MARIO AND PONTE MILVIO

Buses should be used on this route as distances are considerable.

**Piazza Cavour** may be reached from Piazza Venezia by bus No. 88. It is an important traffic centre served by trams and buses, many of which cross the Tiber by the neighbouring *Ponte Cavour* (p. 153). In the middle of the square is a statue of Cavour, by *Stef. Galletti* (1895). The square is dominated by the **Palace of Justice** (*Palazzo di Giustizia;* Pl. 2; 3), the main façade of which is on the Tiber. An ornate building in travertine, built between 1889 and 1910, it had to be evacuated in 1970 as it was in danger of collapse. The foundations are still being strengthened.

Over the main doorway is a group of Justice between Law and Force, by *Enrico Quattrini;* the façade and courtyard are decorated with colossal statues of eminent jurists; above is a colossal quadriga, by *Ettore Ximenes.* The frescoes in the Great Hall are by *Ces. Maccari.*

To the N. and N.W. are spread out the PRATI and TRIONFALE QUARTERS. From the piazza, Via Cicerone and its continuations run N.N.W. for over 2 km. direct to Piazzale Giardino (Pl. 15; 6: see below). Bus No. 28 follows the route. After 500 metres Via Pompeo Magno is crossed, in which (l.) is the church of *San Gioacchino,* erected by Raffaele Inganni in 1890 to commemorate the sacerdotal jubilee of Leo XIII (Gioacchino Pecci). The church has bronze capitals and an aluminium cupola painted inside to represent a star-strewn sky.

The next important cross-road is Viale Giulio Cesare. Beyond Viale delle Milizie lies *Piazza Giuseppe Mazzini,* centre of the Vittoria quarter. On the left, at No. 11 Via Andreoli, is the well-arranged **Museo Storico delle Poste e delle Telecomunicazioni** (Pl. 1; 2: adm. see p. 49).

The postal display begins with a casket of 1300 used by the Pontifical P.O. of Urbino and 17C letter-boxes, including a 'bocca di leone', and there is a fine copy of the Peutinger Table on tile. Later postal history (pioneer air-mail flights;

Ethiopian military cancellers, etc.) is well chosen. The history of telegraph and telephone is copiously illustrated by original appliances, including apparatus used by Marconi in his 1901 experiments between Cornwall and Newfoundland.

From here Viale Giuseppe Mazzini leads right to *Ponte del Risorgimento* (p. 258), past the church of *Cristo Re,* by Marc. Piacentini, while Via Oslavia continues straight on to PIAZZALE MARESCIALLO GIARDINO. On the right is the MUSEO DEL ARMA DEL GENIO (adm. see p. 49), illustrating Italian military transport, bridge building, and communications. It includes a military aircraft of 1909, and models of historical fortifications, and armoury from Roman times to the present day.

From the square Via di Villa Madama climbs the slopes of Monte Mario (see below) to *Villa Madama** (Pl. 15; 3; no adm.). This house, begun for Card. Giuliano de' Medici (Clement VII) by *Giulio Romano* from plans by Raphael, was altered by *Ant. da Sangallo the Younger.* Later it came into the possession of 'Madama' Margaret of Parma (p. 104) and was afterwards owned by the kings of Naples. Today it is used by the Italian Government for the accommodation of prominent visitors.—For permit to view, apply to the Foreign Office, Viale della Macchia della Farnesina.

The beautiful loggia, decorated with stucco reliefs by *Giov. da Udine* and paintings by *Giulio Romano* (1520-25) after Raphael's designs, rivals and even excels the famous Logge of the Vatican. In one of the rooms is a frieze of Cupids by Giulio Romano. A lovely *View of Rome is obtained from the balcony of the main façade. The attractive garden has served as a model for many Italian gardens.

**Monte Mario** (139 m) is the ancient *Clivus Cinnœ* and the medieval *Monte Malo.* Its present name is taken from the Villa Mario Mellini built on the summit.

It may be reached from Piazza Cavour by bus No. 47, which runs in a N.W. direction viâ Viale Giulio Cesare to *Largo Trionfale* (Pl. 1; 2), Piazzale degli Eroi, Via delle Medaglie d'Oro, and Parco Monte Mario. Pedestrians should alight at Largo Trionfale and take Via Trionfale and walk up the eastern side of the hill (the bus takes the western side).

Via Trionfale, ascending the S.E. slopes of the hill, passes the round *Church of the Rosary* (Pl. 15; 7, 5; 109 m; *View). Beyond the ditches of the Fort of Monte Mario, a road leads right to the summit at the *Villa Mario Mellini,* now incorporated in the **Astronomical and Meteorological Observatory** (Pl. 15; 5), with the Copernican Museum. Beyond the summit Via della Camilluccia descends right to Via Cassia and Ponte Milvio (p. 257). Via Trionfale, now called *Borgo Trionfale* (served by bus No. 47; see above), bears left to the Monte Mario station on the Rome-Viterbo railway. The road eventually joins the Via Cassia (p. 372).

At the foot of Monte Mario, extending along the river front, and reached from Piazzale Maresciallo Giardino (see above) by Lungotevere Maresciallo Cadorna, is the **Foro Italico** (Pl. 15; 4, 2), an ambitious sports centre built in 1931 by the former Accademia Fascista della Farnesina. Facing the entrance is the *Ponte Duca d'Aosta* (1939).

A marble monolith, 17 m high, inscribed 'Mussolini Dux', rises at the entrance in front of an imposing avenue paved with marble inlaid with mosaics, and ending in a piazza adorned with a fountain and with a huge marble sphere. On either side of the avenue are marble cubes, with inscriptions recording events in the history of Italy. At the end, beyond the piazza, is the *Stadio Olimpico,* finished for the Olympic Games in 1960, with accommodation for 100,000. To the right is the *Stadio dei Marmi,* capable of seating 20,000 spectators, adorned with 60 colossal statues of athletes. There are open-air and enclosed swimming-baths, the latter with good mosaics, lawn-tennis and basketball courts, running tracks, gymnasium and fencing halls, reading rooms and other facilities.

Lungotévere Maresciallo Diaz (as the riverside street is now called) skirts the right bank of the Tiber, passing the *Casa Internazionale dello Studente,* and behind it, the modern buildings of the *Italian Foreign Office.* Farther back is the *French Military Cemetery,* with the graves of 1500 French who fell in the Second World War.

The Lungotévere ends at Piazzale Milvio (Pl. 15, just beyond 2), where several roads converge. To the right, between Via Cassia (Highway 2 to Viterbo, Siena, and Florence) and Via Orti della Farnesina, is the church of *Madre di Dio,* rebuilt by Cesare Bazzani in 1933.

Ahead Via di Tor di Quinto continues along the river to the *Ponte Flaminio,* opened in 1951, a seven-arched entrance to the city from the north. Along it runs the new Corso di Francia, which passes above the *Villagio Olimpico,* built to accommodate athletes in 1960, and now a residential quarter.

**Ponte Milvio** or **Ponte Molle** (*Pons Milvius*), over the Tiber, was built by the censor M. Aemilius Scaurus in 109 B.C. Remodelled in the 15C, by Nicholas V, who added the watch-towers, it was restored in 1805 by Pius VII, who commissioned Valadier to erect the triumphal arch at the entrance. Blown up in 1849 by Garibaldi to arrest the advance of the French, it was again restored in 1850 by Pius IX.

It was at the Pons Milvius that Cicero captured the emissaries of the Allobroges in 63 B.C. on the occasion of the conspiracy of Catiline; and it was from the bridge that the Emperor Maxentius was thrown into the Tiber and drowned after his defeat by Constantine in 312 (see below).

Across Ponte Milvio is Piazza Cardinal Consalvi, with a shrine containing a statue by Paolo Taccone, erected by Pius II in 1462 on the spot where he had met Card. Bessarion (p. 224) returning from the Morea (Peloponnese) with the head of St Andrew (comp. p. 268).

The straight Via Flaminia returns from here to Piazza del Popolo and the centre of the city. Buses No. 202, 203, and 204 follow this route.

A short way along Via Flaminia which runs parallel with Viale Tiziano ('one way' going out of the city) is Piazza Apollodoro. To the left is the *Palazzetto dello Sport,* an adventurous and striking construction by Pier Luigi Nervi and Annibale Vitellozzi, designed for the Olympic Games in 1960. Beyond is the Villaggio Olimpico (see above). A little to the s. is the *Stadio Flaminio,* designed in reinforced concrete by Pier Luigi and Antonio Nervi in 1959 on the site of the old Stadio Nazionale. In addition to the football ground, which can accommodate 45,000 spectators, there are gymnastic halls, a fencing school, and a swimming-pool.

On the right of Piazza Apollodoro in Via Guido Reni, is the church of *Santa Croce,* built by Pius X in 1913 to commemorate the 16th centenary of the Edict of Milan (March 313), which conceded civil rights and toleration to Christians throughout the Roman Empire.

Farther s., on the left Viale Tiziano widens to form Piazzale Manila, from which Viale Maresciallo Pilsudski leads N.E. and then E. towards the Parioli Quarter (p. 185: Pl. 11; 2, 3).

On the right are the remains of the *Basilica of St Valentine,* built by St Julius I (pope 337-52) over the tomb of the saint; adjoining are the *Catacombs of St Valentine* (adm., see p. 48).—Farther on (l.) is the Corso di Francia (see above), and still farther the entrance to the *Parco di Villa Glori* (Pl. 11; 1). This park was converted in 1923-24 by Raff. De Vico into the **Parco della Rimembranza,** to commemorate the heroism of the Brothers Cairoli, who fell in 1867 (comp. p. 174). The park, planted with cypresses, oaks, elms, maples, horse-chestnuts and other

I

trees, has a column to the dead of 1867 and preserves the trunk of the almond tree beneath which Enrico Cairoli died. A clump of oak trees commemorates heroes of the First World War. There is a fine *View of the Tiber valley.

From Viale Maresciallo Pilsudski, may be reached a square called Piazza del Parco della Rimembranza, from where Viale dei Parioli winds s. to Piazza Ungheria and Viale Liegi (p. 185). From the square Via della Fonte dell' Acqua Acetosa leads to the mineral spring called *Acqua Acetosa;* the well-head was built by Bernini in 1661. From here Viale dell' Acqua Acetosa, on the N.E. side of the Villa Glori, follows the left bank of the Tiber to the Ponte Milvio (see above).

Via Flaminia continues to the graceful little circular church of *Sant' Andrea della Via Flaminia* by Vignola (1550-55), erected by Julius III to commemorate his deliverance from Charles V's soldiers while he was a cardinal. It is now between Via Flaminia and Viale Tiziano. Further s., on the left, is the beginning of Viale delle Belle Arti, which passes Villa Giulia (p. 163). On the right, beyond Piazzale delle Belle Arti, is *Ponte del Risorgimento,* a reinforced-concrete bridge with a single span of 100 m.

At the corner of Viale delle Belle Arti is the Palazzina of Pius IV (see p. 167), and where Via di Villa Giulia leads l. is a fountain of Julius III, beneath an imposing façade, originally of only one story, by Bart. Ammannati (1553); the second part was added by Ligorio in 1562. In Piazza della Marina is the vast *Ministry of Marine,* by Giulio Magni (1928), which has another façade on the Tiber. Via Domenico Alberto Azuni leads to Ponte Matteotti. Beyond the wooded grounds on the left of Villa Strohl Fern is Piazzale Flaminio (Pl. 2; 2), the starting-point of the Via Flaminia. On the E. side are the main entrance to the Villa Borghese (Rte 9), and the beginning of Viale del Muro Torto (p. 175), which runs outside the Aurelian Wall to Porta Pinciana.

Porta del Popolo opens into Piazza del Popolo (p. 153).

## 19   ESPOSIZIONE UNIVERSALE DI ROMA

**Approaches.** E.U.R. is easily reached in 12 min. from the Stazione Termini by the Metropolitana, on which it is the penultimate station. The line ends at Tre Fontane (Laurentino). It is also reached by the following buses: No. 93 from Stazione Termini, No. 97 from Piazza Sonnino, or No. 123 from San Paolo fuori le Mura.

For motorists the quickest route is by Via Cristoforo Colombo (c. 6 km), which starts at Porta Ardeatina (reached from the Colosseum by Via di San Gregorio and Viale di Caracalla). It passes through the arches of the Aurelian wall with its gallery, and a sepulchre to the left. It continues as a ten-lane highway, and passes straight through the middle of E.U.R.

Another route is viâ San Paolo. From Piazza Venezia to San Paolo, see Rte 3. From the front of the basilica Viale San Paolo and Via Levi Civita lead to Via Guglielmo Marconi, which continues left for 1½ km. before joining Via Cristoforo Colombo (see above).

Motorists returning towards the N. quarters of the city may take *Via Olimpica,* a road, 15 km. long, built for the Olympic Games of 1960. This links the two important sporting centres of E.U.R. and Foro Italico (p. 256), avoiding the centre of the city. Crossing the Tiber by *Ponte Marconi* it runs by way of the Circonvallazione Gianicolense, and passing across the Villa Doria Pamphilj reaches the Piazzale degli Eroi (p. 256). Beyond the Foro Italico it turns E. to recross the Tiber by the new *Ponte Tor di Quinto.* From here it passes the Centro Sportivo dell' Acqua Acetosa and joins the Via Salaria (p. 184).

**Esposizione Universale di Roma** (generally abbreviated to **E.U.R.**) was begun in 1938 to the designs of *Marcello Piacentini.* An ambitious project to symbolize the achievements of Fascism, it was to have been opened in 1942. Its buildings were only partly completed, however, and the site suffered some war damage. After 1952 the original buildings were restored, new ones were added, and Government offices and public institutions were moved to the site, which has also developed as a residential quarter but not as a social centre. The huge buildings are spaciously set out with wide avenues and parks. The roads are comparatively deserted.

Via Cristoforo Colombo passes over the Centro Sportivo delle Tre Fontane, before reaching Piazza delle Nazioni (Pl. 14; 1), with twin palaces whose façades form two hemicycles. Viale della Civiltà del Lavoro leads right to the *Palazzo E.U.R.* and, at the end, the *Palazzo della Civiltà del Lavoro* (Pl. 13; 2), popularly known as the 'square Colosseum', with statues symbolizing the arts beneath the lowest arches. At the opposite end of Viale della Civiltà is the *Palazzo dei Congressi.*

Beyond is the vast Piazza Marconi (Pl. 14; 3), in the centre of which is a Stele of Carrara marble (45 m) by *Arturo Dazzi* (1938-59), dedicated to Marconi. On the right are two edifices with symmetrical fronts (*Palazzi dell'Esposizioni*), while between them, farther back, is the *Grattacielo Italia,* with a cinema and hotel. On the left, joined by a huge colonnade, are two palazzi of similar design. The one to the left facing the colonnade contains the **Museo delle Arti e delle Tradizioni Popolari** (Pl. 14; 3; adm., see p. 47).

This museum, divided into ten sections, occupies the first floor of the building. It contains material collected by Lamberto Loria (1855-1913) for the Museo di Etnografia Italiana, founded in Florence in 1906, and illustrates with models, reconstructions, etc. the various aspects of Italian life. The sections are: 1. The cycle of the year; 2. The cycle of human life; 3. The home; 4. Agricultural and pastoral life; 5. Seafaring; 6. Town life; 7. Popular art; 8. Song, music, and dancing; 9. Costume; 10. Religion.

To the right of the colonnade is the *Palazzo delle Scienze* which contains the **Museo Preistorico ed Etnografico Luigi Pigorini** (Pl. 14; 3). For adm., see p. 48.

The museum, one of the most important of its kind in the world, is derived from the collection formed in the late 17C by Father Anastasius Kircher in the Collegio dei Gesuiti. From 1871 onwards it was greatly enlarged by the exertions of Luigi Pigorini and in 1876 it became the Museo Preistorico del Nuovo Regno d'Italia. Later it grew to such an extent that in 1913 some dispersal became necessary; protohistoric objects went to the Villa Giulia (p. 163), classical and Christian antiquities to the Museo Nazionale Romano (p. 192), and medieval exhibits to the Palazzo di Venezia (p. 72).

The MUSEO PREISTORICO is arranged geographically to indicate the way civilization developed regionally through the Stone, Bronze, and Iron Ages. Most of the exhibits are Italian, of the prehistoric period. They include specimens from all parts of the peninsula, so that a complete idea may be obtained of the growth of its civilization and of the commercial and artistic influences of the East and of the countries bordering on the Aegean. The descriptive labels, maps and diagrams are very informative.

Noteworthy in the collection are: material from cemeteries in the Lazio area; finds of the Italian School in Crete; curious Sardinian statuettes of priests and warriors in bronze; Tomb from Golasecca, representative of the western civilization of Northern Italy. The objects found in the cemeteries of Western and Southern Etruria (Vetulonia, Tarquinii, Vulci, Veii, etc.) are particularly interesting; among them are well-tombs (10-8C B.C.), with ossuaries resembling those of Villanova, closed with a flat lid or shaped like a house, and trench-tombs (8-7C B.C.) showing the influence of Greek commerce, especially on pottery.

The ETHNOGRAPHICAL COLLECTION includes material from Brazil, Argentina, and the Amazon region; Polynesia; Arctic circle, American Indian material from North America, Central and South America; New Guinea; Borneo; Oceanic islands; Solomon islands; Fiji; New Caledonia; Australia; Indonesia; North Africa, Ethiopia; Sudan, Nigeria, and Uganda; Belgian Congo and Tanganyika; East Africa; Rhodesia, South Africa; India, Burma, and Syria.

Farther along the colonnade, on the right, at Viale Lincoln, is the entrance to the **Museo dell'Alto Medio Evo,** which is on the first floor of the Palazzo delle Scienze. This contains seven rooms of Italian material from the fall of the Roman Empire to the 10C A.D. Adm. see p. 47.

R. I. Head of a Byzantine Emperor and Empress, gold fibula, all of the late 5C found on the Palatine.—R. II. Pottery, glass, and gold work (including beautiful jewellery) found in a 7C tomb at Nocera Umbra.—R. III. Contents of a 7C tomb at Castel Trosino, including more very fine jewellery (B, 115, 16), a blue glass rhyton (119), a gold dagger case (F), glass containers (37-45), and fragments of a shield (T).—RR. IV-V. Collection of 7-10C church reliefs and friezes (some of them formerly in the Museo Nazionale Romano).—R. V. Finds from the site of S. Cornelia, near Formello, excavated by the British School in 1963-65. Three distinct constructions were found: an early Roman house, a cult building of c. 780, and a monastic complex of 1100.—R. VI. 8-9C pottery from the Roman Forum.—R. VII. Fabrics (5-8C), etc.

Beyond the colonnade Viale della Civiltà Romana, leads to the piazza flanked by two symmetrical buildings again joined by a colonnade, the whole built at the charges of the Fiat organization. Here is the **Museo della Civiltà Romana** (Pl. 14; 4). Admission, see p. 48, but often closed.

The museum was formed from exhibits from the Archæological Exhibition of 1911 and from the Mostra Augustea della Romanità of 1937. They consist entirely of plaster-casts of famous statues and monuments, and reconstructions of buildings which illustrate the history of Rome and the influence of Roman civilization throughout the world. They are displayed in 59 rooms of monumental proportions. Among the most interesting are a reproduction of the pronaos of the temple of Augustus at Ancyra (R. IX; comp. p. 108; a model of Roman Bath in England (R. XXIX); a complete collection of casts from Trajan's Column (R. LI), and a reconstruction of part of the Column of M. Aurelius (R. LIX). In R. XXXVII is the celebrated * *Plastico di Roma,* a model of Rome as it was in the 4C.

Viale dell'Arte leads left; the second turning to the right is Viale Europa. Here are the ministries of Foreign Trade and Finance, built after the war. Viale Europa ends in steps which lead up to the massive church of *SS. Peter and Paul* (Pl. 13; 3), with a cupola almost as large as that of St Peter's. The first turning right at the foot of the steps leads to the *Piscina delle Rose* in Viale America and a large open-air theatre. Parallel to this road is the *Lake,* divided into three basins, the sides of which are planted with cherry-trees from Japan. This area is perhaps the most successfully planned within the E.U.R. complex. Bridges lead to the *PALAZZO DELLO SPORT (Pl. 13; 6), designed by Pier Luigi Nervi and Marcello Piacentini for the Olympic Games of 1960, and an outstanding work of modern architecture. Constructed of prefabricated concrete, it is covered by a fine rib-vaulted dome 100 metres in diameter, and seats 15,000 spectators. The *Velodromo Olimpico,* for cycling events, is about 500 m E.

About 1 km. E. of the point where Via Cristoforo Colombo crosses Via delle Tre Fontane, and reached by the latter and Via Laurentina, is the **Abbazia delle Tre Fontane** (Pl. 14; 2). This was built on the traditional site of the martyrdom of St Paul, whose severed head, rebounding three times, caused three fountains to spring up. St Bernard is believed to have stayed here on his visit to Rome in 1138-40. Three churches were built, but the locality was afterwards abandoned as malarial. In 1868 it was acquired by the Trappists, who drained the ground and planted large groves of eucalyptus. A eucalyptus liqueur is distilled in the community. This and chocolate made by the monks are on sale.

An ilex avenue leads to a medieval fortified gate, with a frescoed vault. A small garden contains classical fragments, and is filled with the sound of doves and a fountain. Ahead is the porch of *Santi Vincenzo ed Anastasio.** It was founded by Honorius I (625), rebuilt by Honorius III (1221), and has been restored by the Trappists. The spacious plain interior preserves its marble windows. In the nave are poorly restored frescoes of the Apostles (16C).

On the right on high ground, is **Santa Maria Scala Coeli,** an old church with an octagonal interior, rebuilt by *Giac. della Porta* (1582). The design can best be appreciated from the outside. It owes its name to the legend that St Bernard, while celebrating mass, saw in a vision the soul for which he was praying ascend by a ladder from purgatory to heaven. The Cosmatesque altar which was the scene of this miracle is still preserved in the crypt. The mosaics in the left-hand apse (Saints with Clement VIII and his nephew Aldobrandini) are by *Fr. Zucchi* from designs by *Giov. de' Vecchi.*

From the left of this church an avenue leads to **San Paolo alle Tre Fontane,** a 5C church, rebuilt by *Della Porta* in 1599, with a good façade. Inside to the right, is the pillar to which St Paul was bound; on the floor are two Roman mosaic pavements from Ostia.

# 20   THE VATICAN CITY. ST PETER'S AND THE VATICAN PALACE

The **VATICAN CITY,** or **Città del Vaticano,** lies on the right bank of the Tiber. By virtue of the LATERAN TREATY ('La Conciliazione'), signed in the Council Room of the Popes at the Lateran Palace on 11 Feb 1929, the Vatican City has the status of an independent sovereign state. Entirely surrounded by Italian territory, it is unhampered by frontier formalities. With an area of 43 hectares (less than half a square kilometre) and a population of about 500, it is, in size, the smallest independent state in existence (area of the States of the Church before the unification of Italy in 1870, 44,547 sq. kilometres), but its size bears no relation to its significance. As the residence of the head of the Roman Catholic Church and the home of its most important place of worship, it attracts pilgrims from all over the world. Moreover, the treasures of artistic and historical interest assembled in the Vatican Palace are unique in their scope, quality, and abundance.

The Lateran Treaty defined the limits of the Vatican State. They are (counterclockwise) St Peter's Colonnade, Via Porta Angelica, Piazza del Risorgimento, Via Leone IV, Viale Vaticano (which almost encircles the area), Via della Sagrestia, St Peter's Colonnade. The city is surrounded by a high wall, skirted by Viale Vaticano for the whole of its length. A walk round the confines takes about half an hour. On the N. side, Viale Vaticano rises fairly steeply, past (l.) the entrance to the Vatican Museums, to the top of the hill, known as *Monte Vaticano.* The city wall towers above the street the whole way. At the top Viale Vaticano bears left and after another left incline, still accompanied by the wall, descends towards St Peter's Colonnade.

The Lateran Treaty also accorded the privilege of extraterritoriality to the basilicas of St John Lateran (with the Lateran Palace), Santa Maria Maggiore and San Paolo fuori le Mura, and to certain other buildings, including the Palazzi della Cancelleria, di Propaganda Fide, del Sant'Uffizio, and dei Convertendi, and to the Pope's villa at Castel Gandolfo. Special clauses in the treaty provide for access to the basilica of St Peter and the art collections of the Vatican Palace. Under the treaty, Italy accepted canon law on marriage and divorce and made religious teaching compulsory in secondary as well as primary schools. She also agreed to pay 750 M lire in cash and the income from 1000 M lire in Italian State 5 per cent bonds, in final settlement of the claims by the Holy See for the loss of papal property taken over by the Italian Government. After the execution of the Lateran

Treaty the Pope, for the first time since 1870, emerged from the Vatican. On 24 June 1929, Pius XI visited St John Lateran.

By the Vatican City law of Pius XI, dated 7 June 1921, the Pope is head of the legislature, executive, and judiciary. He delegates the Cardinal Secretary of State to represent the Vatican in international relations, and nominates the General Council and the Governor of the Vatican. The State has its own postage-stamps, and its own currency which is legal tender in Italy, though rarely seen. Its newspaper, the *Osservatore Romano,* has a world-wide circulation. It owns a radio transmitting station (prominent in the Second World War) and has its own railway-station, now used only for merchandise.

**Security.** Within the Vatican City and in the buildings enjoying extraterritoriality, police duties are discharged by the *Swiss Guard,* a corps founded in 1506, which retains the picturesque uniform said to have been designed by Michelangelo. The Noble Guards and Palatine Guards established in the 19C, were disbanded by Pope Paul VI in 1970, and the Pontifical Gendarmes transformed into a private corps.

**The Hierarchy.** The Sovereign Pontiff is Bishop of Rome, successor to St Peter and, as such, the head of the Roman Catholic Church and the Vicar of Christ. He enjoys the *primatus jurisdictionis,* that is, the supreme jurisdictional power over the whole Church. He is assisted by the Sacred College of Cardinals and by the Roman Curia. The SACRED COLLEGE OF CARDINALS was limited by Sixtus V to 70, but after the consistory of March 1962 the number was increased to 87. John XXIII created 46 new cardinals, and laid down that they should all enjoy the episcopal dignity. At present there is no limit to the number of cardinals who can be appointed. The College consists of six Cardinal Bishops (whose dioceses are the suburbicarian sees of Ostia, Velletri, Porto and Santa Rufina, Albano, Frascati, and Palestrina), nearly 70 Cardinal Priests, and 14 Cardinal Deacons. The ROMAN CURIA comprises the 12 *Sacred Congregations,* which deal with the central administration of the Church, the three *Tribunals,* and the six *Offices:* among these last is that of the Segretario di Stato.

**Conclave** (Latin, a room that may be locked). On the death of a pope, the cardinals (only those under the age of 80) immure themselves in a chosen locality—usually the Sistine Chapel—to elect a new pope. The place chosen is locked both inside and outside and it includes rooms for the cardinals and their attendants. The internal guardian is the Camerlengo; the external guardian the Commander of the Swiss Guard. The cardinals meet twice daily and, having sworn to elect the individual who, under God, shall deserve the honour, proceed to the voting and the scrutiny of the votes. The result of their deliberation is indicated to the waiting world by the colour of the smoke which issues from a vent above the Sistine Chapel. If the smoke is black the election is still in doubt; if white, the new pope has been elected. The old practice whereby the voting papers (mixed with damp straw for the black) were burned to produce the smoke, was discontinued after the conclave of 1958 in favour of more modern methods. The final result is proclaimed from the central balcony of the façade of St Peter's, whence also the newly elected pope blesses the city and the world. Since the proceedings must take some time, there is always an interregnum (of 15-20 days) between the death of a pope and the election of his successor. Thus, John XXIII died on 3 June and Paul VI was elected on 21 June 1963; Paul VI died on 6 August and John Paul I was elected on 26 August 1978; John Paul I died on 29 Sept and John Paul II was elected on 16 Oct 1978.—When the Quirinal was used as the summer palace of the popes, conclaves were occasionally held there.

**Holy Year.** In adapting the Jewish idea of the jubilee, which was secular in content, the Roman Catholic Church gave it an exclusively religious meaning, and for the remission of debts substituted the remission of the temporal punishment due to sin. The first Holy Year was proclaimed from the balcony of St John Lateran on 22 Feb 1300, by Boniface VIII (see p. 213). The pope gave a plenary indulgence to those confessed communicants who, on the occasion of every centenary of the birth of Christ, should visit the four major basilicas—St Peter, St Paul, St John Lateran, and St Mary Major (Santa Maria Maggiore)—within a specified time. In 1343 Clement VI reduced the interval from 100 to 33 years and Paul II (1464-71) to 25 years. This quarter-century interval has been maintained, with few exceptions, ever since: i.e. in 1900, 1925, 1950, and 1975. In addition to the regular celebrations, a Jubilee may occasionally be proclaimed for a special reason, as in 1933, when Pius XI commemorated the 19th centenary of the Crucifixion. The Holy Year is inaugurated on the preceding Christmas Eve with the opening of the *Holy Doors* of the four major basilicas. The Holy Door of St Peter's (Porta Santa) is opened by the Pope; the other three are opened by their respective archpriests. At St Peter's, after preliminary prayers, the Pope leaves his throne and strikes the door with a silver hammer. The wall in front of the door having been previously cut round the edges, falls inwards. The Pope, bareheaded and bearing a torch, crosses the threshold, followed by his cardinals and attendants. At the end of the Holy Year the Holy Doors are reclosed by the Pope.

**Access to the Vatican City.** No formalities are required for visits to St Peter's and to the Vatican Museums and Sistine Chapel (adm., see p. 276). A ticket must be purchased in advance (comp. p. 314) to join the organized tours of the Vatican City and gardens. The entrances to the Vatican City are three. The famous BRONZE DOOR *(Portone di Bronzo)*, to the right and in front of St Peter's, is the main entrance; it is reserved for ecclesiastical and civil dignitaries and for those seeking audience of the Pope (see below); it was kept closed from 1870 to 1929. The *Arco delle Campane* (Arch of the Bells), to the left of St Peter's, is used by individuals armed with a permit (rarely granted) to visit the interior of the Vatican City, and by the organized tours of the gardens and City; it is also the means of access to the Necropolis below St Peter's. The *Cancello di Sant' Anna* (Gate of St Anne), in Via di Porta Angelica, to the right of St Peter's, admits to the Polyglot Printing Press and the offices of the *Osservatore Romano.*—The *Entrance to the Vatican Museums,* in the Viale Vaticano, gives access to the museums only, and not to the gardens outside them.—An *Information Office* (weekdays 8.30-18.30 or 19; March-Oct also on Sun, 8-13) is open in St Peter's Square.

**Audience of the Pope.** Application must be made to the Prefetto della Casa Pontificia (Prefect of the Pontifical Household) preferably 1-2 days before the Audience. Applicants enter by the Bronze Door (open 9-13.30). At the far end of the entrance hall (Corridore del Bernini) he sees the *Scala Regia,* the staircase leading to the Sala Regia. At a table just within the entrance he completes a form which he takes to the office of the Prefettura, situated on the first floor of the *Staircase of Pius IX* (Scala Pia), ascending to the right. Here he shows his credentials to the priest in attendance, after which he fills up a second form, stating the period within which the audience is requested (corresponding normally to the length of his stay in Rome), his nationality, his address in Rome, with telephone number. A few days later he will receive from the Prefettura a letter giving the date and hour at which he is to attend.

Audiences are now confined to General Audiences which normally take place at 11 o'clock on Wed mornings in the New Audience Hall (comp. p. 315), reached under the colonnade to the left of the façade of St Peter's. Newly-married couples may also attend audiences; a special section is set aside for them in the Audience Hall. They should furnish a certificate that the marriage has taken place with religious ceremony. No particular dress is prescribed for pilgrims attending audiences, although they are asked to dress in a sober manner.

When the Pope is in residence at Castel Gandolfo from mid July to mid-September, audiences are held there on Wed at 10 a.m. (comp. p. 347). It should be noted that the normal application procedure at the Prefecture in the Vatican must be followed, except for the audience on Sun (at 12 a.m.) which is open to anyone.

# A   St Peter's

The approach to St Peter's has been transformed by the building of **Via della Conciliazione** (Pl. 1; 6). This broad straight thoroughfare, completed in 1937, opens up the view of the basilica from Piazza Pia and Lungotévere Vaticano. In its construction two characteristic streets of the Città Leonina—the Borgo Nuovo and Borgo Vecchio (known as the Spina di Borgo)—and the buildings between them were erased, and one ancient palace suffered transplantation (see below). The colonnaded piazza in front of St Peter's was not originally designed to be seen from a distance; its impact is therefore lessened by this approach.

Via della Conciliazione first passes (r.) the Carmelite church of *Santa*

*Maria in Traspontina* (1566-87). Beyond is *PALAZZO TORLONIA (formerly *Giraud*), a delightful reproduction of the Palazzo della Cancelleria, built by *And. Bregno* in 1495-1504 for Card. Adriano da Corneto. Then comes *Palazzo dei Convertendi,* built in the second half of the 17C, and re-erected in its present position in 1937. It originally occupied the site of a house built by Bramante for Raphael, who died in it in 1520.—On the s. side of the street is PALAZZO DEI PENITENZIERI built (probably) by *Baccio Pontelli* for Card. Dom. della Rovere in 1480. It is now occupied by the Penitentiaries, whose office it is to hear confessions in St Peter's. Via della Conciliazione ends in *Piazza Pio XII,* separated only by the width of the side streets from Piazza San Pietro. The piazza opens out, framed in its semicircular colonnades; at the end, above a triple flight of steps, rises the basilica, with the buildings of the Vatican towering on the right.

The piazza is also reached, from the s.e., by Borgo Santo Spirito (p. 246), in which, on the right, a flight of steps leads up to the little church of *San Michele e Magno* (open on Sun morning), founded in the 8C and retaining a 13C campanile. Inside is the tomb of Raphael Mengs (d. 1779).

*Piazza San Pietro (Pl. 1; 6),** the masterpiece of *Bernini* (1656-67), is one of the most superb conceptions of its kind in civic architecture, and is a fitting approach to the world's greatest basilica. Partly enclosed by two semicircular colonnades, it has the form of an ellipse adjoining an almost rectangular quadrilateral. The diameter of the major axis is 240 m, that of the minor axis 195 m; the total length through the minor axis to the portico of St Peter's is 338 m. Each of the two colonnades has a quadruple row of Doric columns, forming three parallel covered walks. There are in all 284 columns and 88 pilasters. On the Ionic entablature are 96 statues of saints and martyrs. In the middle of the piazza is the *Obelisk of the Vatican* and on either side a fountain.

The **Obelisk**, devoid of hieroglyphics, is 25½ m high; it rests on a lofty plinth and is surmounted by a cross. The height from the ground to the top of the cross is 41 m. It was brought from Alexandria (where it had been set up by Augustus) in A.D. 37 and placed by Caligula possibly on the spina of his circus, later called the Circus of Nero. In 1586 Sixtus V ordered its removal from the s. of the basilica to its present site and put Dom. Fontana in charge of operations. No fewer than 900 men, 150 horses, and 47 cranes were required. The task was completed on 18 Sept 1586. It is said that Sixtus V forbade the spectators, under pain of death, to speak while the obelisk was being raised into position. A sailor, by name Bresca, seeing that the tension on the ropes had not been correctly assessed and that they were giving way under the strain, transgressed the order, shouted "Acqua alle funi" ("Wet the ropes") and so averted catastrophe. The Pope rewarded him by granting his family the privilege of supplying St Peter's with palms for Palm Sunday. The incident, now discredited as an 18C fabrication, is said to have been the origin of the industry, still flourishing at Bordighera, of exporting palm. Round the foot of the obelisk is a plan of the mariner's compass, giving the names of the winds. The globe which surmounted the obelisk until 1586, when it was replaced by a cross, is now in Palazzo dei Conservatori (p. 64).

The two *Fountains* are beautifully designed. The one on the right is by Carlo Maderna (1614), although a similar fountain had existed in the piazza since 1490. It was moved to its present site and slightly modified by Bernini in 1667, when the second fountain was begun. The two are remarkable for their abundance of water, supplied by the Acqua Paola. Between the obelisk and each fountain is a round porphyry slab from which the spectator obtains the illusion that each of the colonnades has but a single row of columns.

The quadrilateral beyond the colonnades widens from 98 m at the e. end to 119 m at the w. end. It is bordered by covered galleries, which unite the colonnades with the portico of St Peter's. The galleries are also adorned with statues (44 in all); the total number of statues is thus 140. The gallery on the right, known as the *Corridore del Bernini* and leading to the Scala Regia, is closed by the BRONZE DOOR (*Portone di Bronzo*), the main entrance to the Vatican. That on the left is skirted outside by Via della Sagrestia, one of the frontier streets of the Vatican city. The centre of the square is largely taken up by the great staircase, of three flights, leading up to the portico of the basilica. At the foot are colossal statues of St Peter, by *Gius. de Fabris,* and of St Paul, by *Adamo Tadolini,* set up here by Pius IX in place of two older statues now in the Vatican radio building (see below).

To the s. of St Peter's Colonnade, outside the Vatican City, but enjoying the privilege of extraterritoriality (p. 261), is **Palazzo del Sant'Uffizio.** The Holy Office, commonly known as the Inquisition, was established here in 1536 by Paul III to inquire into charges of heresy, unbelief, and other offences against religion. In Rome and the Papal States the Holy Office exercised a severe control over heresy and the suspicion of heresy but never, so far as is known, ordered the death of anyone found guilty, and the excessive rigours of the Spanish Inquisition were condemned by the Renaissance popes. The preparation of the Index of Prohibited Books was originally entrusted to the Congregation of the Holy Office. In 1571 Pius V established a special Congregation of the Index, which survived until its suppression by Benedict XV in 1917, when the duties were resumed by the Holy Office. The tribunal was formally abolished by the Roman Assembly in February 1849, but it was re-established by Pius IX a few months later. To the right the former *Palazzo del Museo Petriano* has been taken over by Vatican Radio.

To the s. of the Palazzo del Sant'Uffizio, at the w. end of the Traforo Principe Amedeo (p. 246), is the site of the *Porta Cavalleggeri,* named after a cavalry barracks in the vicinity. Close by is Largo di Porta Cavalleggeri, starting-point of the Via Aurelia.

**\*\*St Peter's,** or the **Basilica di San Pietro in Vaticano** (Pl. 1; 5, 6), is perhaps the most imposing church of Christendom. Though neither a cathedral nor the mother church of the Catholic faith, it is the composite work of some of the greatest artists of the 16C, and a masterpiece of the late Italian Renaissance. Orientated towards the west and approached through the monumental piazza, the church has its fitting culmination in Michelangelo's dome, outvying even Bramante's daring conception of "the Pantheon upon the Basilica of Constantine".

**History.** According to the Liber Pontificalis, Pope St Anacletus built an oratory (c. A.D. 90) over the tomb of St Peter, close to the Circus of Nero, near which he had suffered martyrdom (see p. 246). Modern research, however, points to a confusion of names and the likelihood that Pope St Anicetus (155-66) was responsible. On the site of this oratory Constantine, at the request of Pope St Sylvester I, began to build a basilica c. 324; it was consecrated on 18 Nov 326. The basilica was 120 m long and 65 m wide, about half the size of the present edifice. It was preceded by a great quadrangular colonnaded portico. The nave and double aisles were divided by 86 marble columns, some of which were said to have been taken from the Septizonium on the Palatine (if so, this was long before the demolition of that building by Sixtus V). Adorned with numerous monuments of popes, emperors, and others, and enlivened with frescoes and mosaics, it attracted pilgrims from all over Europe. Charlemagne was crowned here by Leo III in 800. Some of its relics are preserved (see below). Its façade is shown in the painting 'Incendio di Borgo' in Raphael's Stanza dell'Incendio in the Vatican (p. 288).

In the middle of the 15C the old basilica showed signs of collapse, and Nicholas V (1447-55) resolved to rebuild it, realizing its importance to the prestige of the Roman Catholic faith. He entrusted the work to *Bern. Rossellino, Leon Batt. Alberti,* and *Giuliano da Sangallo,* but on the death of Nicholas in 1455 it was virtually suspended for half a century. Julius II (1503-13) decided on a complete reconstruction. He employed *Bramante,* who started work in 1506. Bramante began by dismantling the greater part of the old church and destroying much that might have been preserved: so much so that he gained the nickname of 'Mastro

Ruinante'. His plan for the new basilica was a Greek cross surmounted by a gigantic central dome and flanked by four smaller cupolas. When he died in 1514, the four central piers and the arches of the dome had been completed.

From now on the history of St Peter's is one of conflicting plans, each architect (with few exceptions) reversing the policy of his predecessor. Bramante's Greek cross did not find favour with his successor, who planned a Latin cross. After that Greek and Latin alternated four times, Latin finally prevailing.

Leo X (1513-21), who succeeded Julius II, summoned *Raphael* to direct the work in collaboration with *Fra Giocondo* (d. 1515) and *Giul. da Sangallo* (d. 1516). Raphael's plan envisaged a Latin cross, but on his death in 1520 *Bald. Peruzzi* reverted to Bramante's design. Neither Adrian VI (1522-23), the austere theologian who regarded art as hostile to the Church, nor the hapless Clement VII (1523-34), overwhelmed by political disturbances brought about by the Reformation, and culminating in the sack of Rome (1527), was interested in the progress of the basilica. However, under Paul III (1534-49) the work received fresh impetus from *Ant. da Sangallo the Younger,* who adopted the Latin cross plan. At his death in 1546, *Michelangelo,* then seventy-two years old, was summoned by Paul III. He decided on the Greek cross originally planned by Bramante, and developed Bramante's idea with even greater audacity. Regarding the Pantheon as unambitious, he took Brunelleschi's Florentine cupola for his model, and substituted piers of tremendous strength for those of Bramante, though deriving from the Pantheon his plan for the façade. Confirmed in his appointment by Paul III's successors, he continued to direct the work until his death in 1564. His successors *Vignola* and *Pirro Ligorio* were followed by *Giac. della Porta* (assisted by *Carlo Fontana*), who completed the dome in 1590, and added the two smaller domes.

In 1605 Paul V demolished what had been left of the old basilica, pulled down the incomplete façade and directed *Carlo Maderna* to lengthen the nave towards the old Piazza San Pietro. The present façade and portico are Maderna's work. Thus, after many vicissitudes, the plan of the Latin cross has triumphed. On 18 Nov 1626, the 1300th anniversary of the original consecration, Urban VIII consecrated the new church. *Bernini,* who succeeded Maderna in 1629, and was charged with the decoration of the interior, wished to erect two campanili by the façade, but the one that he completed collapsed on its sinking foundations. Alexander VII kept Bernini as architect of St Peter's, and under him the piazza was begun in 1656. The Sacristy was built in the 18C.

In 1940 systematic excavations were begun beneath St Peter's. Beneath the Vatican Grottoes the excavators discovered the ancient cemetery in which St Peter was buried after his crucifixion. On 23 Dec 1950, the Pope announced that the tomb of St Peter had been identified (see p. 275).

**Dimensions.** The exterior length of the church, including the portico is 211½ m; the cross on the dome is 136½ m above the ground. The façade is 115 m long, and 45½ m high. Within, the church is 186 m long and 137 m wide across the transepts. The nave is 60 m across (including the aisles) and 44 m high; the diameter of the dome is 42 m or 1½ m less than that of the Pantheon. The total area is 49,737 sq. m (St Paul's in London 26,639 sq. m).

**Admission.** The basilica is open daily from 7-19 (18 in winter). Mass is held on Sun at 8, 9, and 10 (Sung Mass at 10.30), and frequently during the week. Holy Communion may be taken in the Cappella del Santissimo Sacramento throughout the day on Sunday.

Exterior. At the top of the triple flight of steps rises the long FAÇADE. Its great size impairs the view of the dome from the piazza. Eight columns and four pilasters support the entablature. A dedicatory inscription on the frieze records its erection in 1612, during the pontificate of Paul V. The attic, almost without ornament, is surmounted by a balustrade on which are statues of Christ, St John the Baptist, and eleven of the Apostles (St Peter's statue is inside), and two clocks, by *Valadier* (near the ends). Under the left-hand clock are the six bells of the basilica, electrically operated since 1931. The oldest bell dates from 1288; the largest (1786) is 7½ m round and weighs 9¾ tons.

The PORTICO is prolonged by vestibules at both ends connecting with the covered galleries of the piazza.

The pavement was designed by *Bernini*. The vault is magnificently decorated in stucco, by *Martino Ferrabosco;* in the lunettes below it are 32 statues of canonized popes. Of the five entrances to the church, that on the extreme right is the HOLY DOOR (*Porta Santa*), opened only in Holy Years. The central *Bronze Doors, from Old St Peter's, were decorated by *Ant. Filarete* in 1439-45 with reliefs of Christ, the Virgin, SS. Peter and Paul and their martyrdom, and events in the life of Pope Eugenius IV; the whole is enclosed in a frieze of classical and mythological subjects, animals, fruits, and portraits of emperors. Between the doors are three inscriptions. From the left, Commemorating the donation by Gregory II of certain olive trees to provide oil for the lamps over the tomb of St Peter; Latin epitaph of Adrian (772-95), attributed to Charlemagne; Bull of Boniface VIII proclaiming the first jubilee or Holy Year (1300). The other doors are modern: the one on the extreme right (the Porta Santa) is by *Vico Consorti* (1950), and the one to the r. of the main door, is by *Venanzio Crocetti* (1968); the door on the extreme left is by *Luciano Minguzzi* (1977), and the one to the l. of the main door by *Giac. Manzù* (1963), with good sculptures depicting the death of religious figures and abstract themes of death.—Above the doors and extending beyond them on either side is a row of nine large windows with balconies. The central balcony is that from which the senior cardinal-deacon proclaims the newly-elected pope and from which the Pope blesses the city and the world. The ceremony, discontinued in 1870, was revived by Pius XI after the concordat. Below the balcony is a relief, by *Ambr. Bonvicino*, of Christ handing the keys to St Peter.

In the tympanum, above the central entrance (that is, looking backwards, against the light) is the famous *NAVICELLA, a mosaic representing Christ walking upon the waters, executed by *Giotto* for the old basilica. Owing to frequent removals it has suffered from resetting and restoration.

The equestrian statue of Charlemagne (1), at the left end of the portico, is by *Cornacchini;* that on the right, of *Constantine (2) by *Bernini*, is beyond a door which gives access to the corridor leading to the Scala Regia. This is often open for visitors leaving the Sistine Chapel (comp. p. 296).

The immensity of the vast **Interior** is disguised by the symmetry of its proportions. The work of *Bernini* for this majestic church, which had begun with the Ponte Sant'Angelo and was continued in the piazza, culminates in the magnificent baldacchino and exedra in the tribune. As the shrine of St Peter, the whole has a ceremonial air, with temporary pews beneath the gilded coffered ceiling designed by *Bramante*. The coloured marble of the walls and pavement is the work of *Giac. della Porta* and *Bernini*.

NAVE. The first part of the nave, with its aisles and three side chapels, is Maderna's extension, which transformed the plan of the church from a Greek to a Latin cross. The round slab of porphyry let into the pavement in front of the central door is that on which the emperors used to kneel for their coronation in front of the altar of the old basilica. Farther on are metal lines indicating the lengths of the principal churches of Europe. The nave is separated from the aisles by colossal piers, each adorned with two fluted Corinthian pilasters, which support great arches. In the niches between the pilasters of the nave and transepts are statues of the founders of the religious orders. The aisles have sumptuous decorations by Bernini. Over the spaces between the piers are elliptical cupolas—three on either side—richly aodorned with mosaics. In addition to these six minor cupolas there are four circular domes over the corner chapels in the main body of the church, where the sessions of the second Vatican Council took place in 1962-65.

The *DOME is an architectural masterpiece. Simple and dignified, and flooded with light, it rises immediately above the site of St Peter's tomb.

Four pentagonal PIERS support the arches on which rests the drum of the cupola. The piers are adorned with balconies and niches designed by Bernini. Each balcony has two spiral columns taken from the old basilica (another of these columns is the Colonna Santa; see below). The niches are filled with colossal statues, which give each of the piers its name. Beginning from the right (N.E.) and going counter-clockwise, they are: *St Longinus (3), by *Bernini;* St Helena (4), by *And. Bolgi;* St Veronica (5), by *Fr. Mochi;* St Andrew (6), by *Fr. Duquesnoy.* The balconies are adorned with reliefs referring to the 'Reliquie Maggiori'; these relics, which are displayed in Holy Week, are preserved in the podium of the pier of St Veronica. They are the lance of St Longinus, the soldier who pierced the side of Christ on the Cross, presented to Innocent VIII; a piece of the True Cross, collected by St Helena; and the napkin of St Veronica, with the miraculous image of the Saviour. The head of St Andrew, presented to Pius II in 1462 by Thomas Palaiologos, despot of the Morea, was recently returned to the Greek Orthodox Church at Patras.

The Latin inscription on the frieze of the dome is a continuation of the Greek inscription in the tribune. In the pendentives of the dome are mosaics of the Evangelists; the scale of the decorations will be appreciated when it is realized that the pen of St Mark is 1½ m long. On the frieze below the drum is inscribed in letters nearly 2 m high: "Tu es Petrus et super hanc petram aedificabo ecclesiam meam et tibi dabo claves regni coelorum." The dome is divided into sixteeen compartments, corresponding to the windows of the drum, by ribs ornamented with stucco; in these compartments are six bands of mosaic by the *Cav. d'Arpino,* representing saints, angels, and the company of Heaven; in the lantern above is the Almighty.

Under a canopy against the pier of St Longinus, facing inwards, is the famous bronze *STATUE OF ST PETER (7), seated on a marble throne. It was believed to date from the 5C or 6C, but is now considered to be a transformation by *Arnolfo di Cambio,* or wholly his work. The extended foot of the statue has been worn away by the kisses of the faithful. The statue is robed on high festivals. Above is a portrait in mosaic of Pius IX (1871).

Over the high altar rises the renowned *BALDACCHINO (8), designed by *Bernini* and unveiled on 28 June 1633, by Urban VIII. This colossal Baroque structure, combining architecture and decorative sculpture, is cast of bronze taken from the Pantheon. Four gilt bronze spiral columns rise from their marble plinths, which are decorated with the Barberini bees. The columns resemble in design the Colonna Santa (see below) but are adorned with figures of genii and laurel branches. They support a canopy from which hang festoons and tassels and on which angels (by *Duquesnoy*) alternate with children. From the four corners of the canopy ascend ornamental scrolls, which support the globe and cross. Inside the top of the canopy is the Dove in an aureole.

The HIGH ALTAR, at which only the Pope may celebrate, is formed of a block of Greek marble found in the Forum of Nerva and consecrated by Clement VIII on 26 June 1594. It covers the altar of Calixtus II (d. 1123) which in turn encloses an altar of Gregory the Great (d. 604) who elaborated and built upon the shrine of Constantine (p. 265). It stands over the space which is recognized as the tomb of St Peter.

In front (9) is the CONFESSIONE, built by *Maderna* and encircled by perpetually burning lamps. Within is a *Statue of Pius VI in prayer, by *Canova* (1822).

When excavations began in 1940, it was discovered that the foundations of the Confessione were hollow. When they were opened, they led into the ancient Roman necropolis below the Vatican Grottoes. Here was found the Tropaion of Gaius (p. 275).

RIGHT AISLE. By the Porta Santa is a mosaic of St Peter (10), designed by *Ciro Ferri* (1675). The CAPPELLA DELLA PIETÀ (11) is named after *Michelangelo*'s exquisite *Pietà (1499; restored and protected by glass since its damage in 1972), executed in the artist's 25th year for the French ambassador, Card. Villiers de la Groslay. This is perhaps the most moving of all Michelangelo's sculptures and is the only one inscribed with his name (on the ribbon falling from the left shoulder of the Virgin). The mosaic decorations of the cupola, by *Pietro da Cortona* and *Ciro Ferri,* depict the Passion. The triumph of the Cross is by *Lanfranco.*— Under the first arch of the aisle are a monument to Queen Christina of Sweden (12), by *Carlo Fontana* (1689), and opposite, a statue of Leo XII (13), a heavy and uninteresting work by *De Fabris* (1836). Beneath it is the entrance to the small CAPPELLA DEL CROCIFISSO (14; usually closed), with a Crucifixion ascribed to *Pietro Cavallini.*

The CAPPELLA DI SAN SEBASTIANO (15) has an altar mosaic of the saint's martyrdom, after *Domenichino.* The monument to Pius XI (d. 1939; 16) is by *Fr. Nagni.* Opposite, a monument to Pius XII (d. 1958) by *Francesco Messina.* Under the next arch are the fine Baroque monument to Innocent XII (d. 1700; 17), by *Filippo Valle,* and one by *Bernini* (18) of the Countess Matilda of Tuscany (d. 1115), whose remains were moved from Mantua in 1635.—The iron grille of the *CAPPELLA DEL SANTISSIMO SACRAMENTO (19) was designed by *Borromini.* Over the altar is a gilt bronze ciborium by *Bernini,* modelled on Bramante's 'tempietto' at San Pietro in Montorio. The two angels also form part of this unfinished composition. Behind is the Trinity, by *Pietro da Cortona.* Over the altar on the right is a mosaic, Ecstasy of St Francis, after *Domenichino.*—Under the next arch are the monument (20) to Gregory XIII (d. 1585), the reformer of the calendar (by *Rusconi;* 1723), and the unfinished tomb (21) of Gregory XIV (D. 1591). Opposite, on the pier of St Longinus, is a *Mosaic of the Communion of St Jerome (22), after *Domenichino* (original in the Vatican; p. 286).

In the N.E. corner of the great rectangle which forms the main body of the church is the CAPPELLA GREGORIANA (23), built by Gregory XIII from designs by *Michelangelo,* with a cupola 42 m above the floor. The chapel is dedicated to the Madonna del Soccorso, an ancient painting on part of a marble column from the old basilica, placed here in 1578 (24). Beneath the altar is the tomb of St Gregory Nazianzen, and on the right is that of Gregory XVI (d. 1846), by *Luigi Amici* (1855; 25).—Under the next arch is the Altar of St Basil (26); over it is the Mass of St Basil, a mosaic after *Subleyras.* Opposite is the tomb of Benedict XIV (27), by *Bracci;* the statue of the Pope (d. 1758) shows him proclaiming the Holy Year of 1750.

The RIGHT TRANSEPT was used for the sessions of the Council in 1869-70. Its three altars are decorated with mosaics; St Wenceslas (28), after *Angelo Caroselli;* the Martyrdom of SS. Processus and Martinian, St Peter's gaolers, after *Valentin* (29); the Martyrdom of St Erasmus (30), after *Nic. Poussin* (1629; originals of the last two in the Vatican; p.

288).—In the arch beyond are the celebrated *Monument of Clement XIII (31), by *Canova,* and, against the pier of St Helena, the Altar of the Navicella (32), with a mosaic of Christ walking on the waters, after *Lanfranco;* the subject is the same as that of Giotto's mosaics in the portico.

The CAPPELLA DI SAN MICHELE (33) contains mosaics of St Michael (34), after *Guido Reni,* and of *St Petronilla (35), by *Cristofari* after *Guercino.* This chapel, in the N.W. corner of the basilica, has a round cupola, decorated with mosaics of angels, and pendentives with mosaics of the Doctors of the Church, after *Romanelli* and *Sacchi.*—To the left (36) is the monument of Clement X (d. 1676), by *De Rossi* and others; opposite, on the pier of St Helena, is a mosaic of St Peter raising Tabitha, after *Placido Costanzi* (37).

Two porphyry steps from the old basilica lead to the TRIBUNE, the most conspicuous object in which is the *CHAIR OF ST PETER (38), an ambitious and theatrical composition by *Bernini*(1665). This enormous gilt bronze throne is supported by statues of four Fathers of the Church: SS. Augustine and Ambrose, of the Latin Church (in mitres), and SS. Athanasius and John Chrysostom, of the Greek Church (bareheaded). It encloses an ancient wooden chair (comp. p. 273) inlaid with ivory, said to have been the episcopal chair of St Peter. A great halo of gilt stucco surrounds the Dove set in the window above the throne; outside the halo is a circle of flying angels.—On the right of St Peter's Chair is the fine *Monument to Urban VIII (d. 1644), also by *Bernini,* with statues of the pope and allegorical figures of Charity and Justice (39). The design of the tomb is clearly influenced by the Medici tombs in Florence by Michelangelo. The use of different materials in the sculpture give an effective colour to the monument. On the left is the Monument to Paul III (d. 1549; 40), *by Gugl. della Porta,* a less successful attempt at the same type of tomb sculpture and design.—Beyond the tribune, on the pier of St Veronica, is a mosaic of St Peter healing the paralytic, after *Fr. Mancini* (41); opposite is the monument to Alexander VIII (d. 1691; 42), by *Arrigo di San Martino;* the bronze statue of the pope is by *Gius. Bertosi,* and the other sculptures are by *Angelo De Rossi.*

LEFT AISLE. The CAPPELLA DELLA COLONNA (43), one of the corner chapels with round cupolas, was decorated in 1757 with figures of angels carrying garlands and with symbols of the Virgin. The lunettes have mosaics after *Fr. Romanelli.* In this chapel is the tomb of St Leo the Great (d. 461; 44); above is a noble *Relief by *Aless. Algardi* (1650), representing St Leo arresting the progress of Attila with the aid of SS. Peter and Paul. On the altar (l., 45) is an ancient and greatly venerated representation of the Virgin painted on a column from the old basilica. In the middle of the chapel is the tombstone of Leo XII (d. 1829).— Under the next arch is the monument of Alexander VII (d. 1667; 46), *Bernini's* last work in St Peter's. Although the design is original, the execution is not very careful. Opposite is a mosaic (47), Apparition of the Sacred Heart, after *Carlo Muccioli,* set here in 1922 by Benedict XV in place of an oil-painting on slate (Punishment of Simon Magus, by Fr. Vanni).

The LEFT TRANSEPT contains confessionals for foreigners, served by the Penitentiaries, who hear confessions in ten languages. The three altars are decorated with mosaics; St Thomas (48), after *Vinc. Camuc-*

*cini;* Crucifixion of St Peter (49), after *Guido Reni* (original in the Vatican; p. 286); and St Joseph (50). In front of the central altar is the tomb of Palestrina (1594).

Over the door to the Sacristy (see below) is the neo-classical monument to Pius VIII (d. 1830), by *Pietro Tenerani* (51); opposite, against the pier of St Andrew, Ananias, and Sapphira (52), a mosaic after *Pomarancio.*—The CAPPELLA CLEMENTINA (53) is the fourth of the corner chapels with round cupolas; the cupola is decorated with mosaics after *Pomarancio;* in the pendentives are four Doctors of the Church. The chapel is named after Clement VIII (d. 1605), who ordered *Giac. della Porta* to decorate it for the jubilee of 1600. It contains the tomb of St Gregory the Great (d. 604; 54), beneath the altar. Above it is a mosaic of a miracle of St Gregory, after *And. Sacchi.*—To the left of the altar is the monument to Pius VII (d. 1823), by *Thorvaldsen,* a classical work showing the influence of Canova (55).

On the E. side of the pier of St Andrew is a Mosaic of the Transfiguration (56), after *Raphael,* four times as large as the original in the Vatican (p. 285). Opposite, beneath the aisle arch, are the monuments of *Leo XI, who reigned for only 27 days (d. 1605; 57), by *Algardi,* and of Innocent XI (d. 1689; 58), by *Pierre Monnot* (the urn decorated with a relief of the liberation of Vienna by John Sobieski).—The CAPPELLA DEL CORO (59) is richly decorated in stucco by *G. B. Ricci* after designs by *Giacomo della Porta.* It is closed by a fine gate with the arms of Clement XIII. It is furnished with elegant classical stalls by *Bernini,* and two large organs. The altarpiece (60), after a painting by *Pietro Bianchi,* represents the Immaculate Conception. In the pavement is the simple tombstone of Clement XI (d. 1721).—Under the next arch is the bronze *Monument to Innocent VIII (d. 1492; 61), by *Antonio del Pollaiolo,* the only monument from the old basilica to be recreated in the new (see p. 265). The Pope is represented by two bronze statues: one recumbent on the urn, the other seated and holding in the left hand a spearhead, in allusion to his reception from the sultan Bajazet II of the spear that pierced the side of Christ. Opposite (62) is the monument to St Pius X (d. 1914), by *Pier Enrico Astorri.* The ceremony of the canonization of Pius X took place on 26 May 1954.

The CAPPELLA DELLA PRESENTAZIONE (63) is named after its altar-mosaic of the Presentation of the Virgin, after *Fr. Romanelli;* beneath the altar is the tomb of St Pius X. The cupola is decorated with a mosaic, after *Carlo Maratta,* exalting the glory of the Virgin. On the right is a monument to Pope John XXIII, by Emilio Greco. On the left is the monument to Benedict XV (d. 1922; 64), by *Pietro Canonica.*—Under the next arch are the Stuart monuments: above the door on the right (leading to the dome; see p. 274) is the monument (65) to Clementina Sobieska (d. 1735), wife of James Stuart, the Old Pretender (she is here called Queen of Great Britain, France, and Ireland), by *Barigioni;* on the left is the *Monument to the last Stuarts (66), by *Canova,* with busts of the Old and Young Pretenders (d. 1766 and 1788) and of Henry, Cardinal York (d. 1807). George IV contributed to the expense of this monument.

In the BAPTISTERY (67) the cover of a porphyry sarcophagus, placed upside-down, is used as the font. It formerly covered the tomb of the Emperor Otho II (973-83; in the Grottoes). According to a tradition (now discredited), the sarcophagus came from the sepulchral cella of Hadrian's mausoleum (Castel Sant' Angelo) and was the emperor's own. The present metal cover is by *Carlo Fontana.* The mosaics reproduce paintings of the Baptism of Christ, by *C. Maratta;* of St Peter baptizing the centurion Cornelius, by *And. Procaccini;* and of St Peter baptizing his gaolers SS. Processus and Martinian, by *Gius. Passeri.*—At the end of the nave can be seen the back of the doors by *Giac. Manzù* (p. 267), with a dedicatory inscription.

The **Treasury** is entered by the door under the monument to Pius VIII (51). It has recently been rearranged as the **Museo Storico Artistico di San Pietro** (adm. 9-

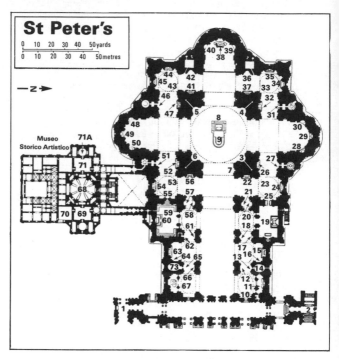

12.30, 15-16.30; 700 lire). In the VESTIBULE is a large stone slab with the names of the popes buried in the basilica, from St Peter to Pius XII. A corridor leads to the entrance of the Museum.

The Treasury was plundered by the Saracens in 846, and again during the sack of Rome in 1527, and was impoverished by the provisions of the Treaty of Tolentino (1797), which Pius VI was constrained to conclude with Napoleon. It still, however, contains objects of great value and interest, and the depredations of the past have, to a certain extent, been made good by the gifts and bequests of later years. The exhibits include vestments, missals, reliquaries, pyxes, patens, chalices, monstrances, crucifixes, and other sacred relics, as well as candelabra and ornaments.

ROOM I. The *Colonna Santa, a 4C Byzantine spiral column, one of twelve from the old basilica (eight decorate the balconies of the great piers of the dome in St Peter's; the remaining three are lost). The column is mistakenly venerated as that against which Christ leaned when speaking with the doctors in the Temple. The gilt

bronze Cock (9C) used to decorate the top of the campanile of the old basilica.—R.
II (SAGRESTIA DEI BENEFICIATI; 71). *Crux Vaticana, the most ancient possession
of the Treasury, dating from the 6C, the gift of the emperor Justinian II (685-711).
It is made of bronze and set with jewels. So-called *Dalmatic of Charlemagne, now
thought to date from the early 15C; Byzantine case with an enamelled Cross;
fragment of a Byzantine diptych in ivory; copy (1974) of the ancient Chair of St
Peter, now incorporated in Bernini's decoration in the Tribune of St Peter's (comp.
p. 272).—CAPPELLA DELLA SAGRESTIA DEI BENEFICIATI (71A). Here is the
celebrated *Ciborium of *Donatello* (c. 1432), from the old basilica. Inside is
preserved a painting of the Madonna della Febbre (the protectress of malaria)
attrib. to *Lippo Memmi*. Over the chapel altar is St Peter receiving the keys, by
*Girol. Muziano.*—ROOM III. *Monument of Sixtus IV, a masterpiece in bronze by
*Ant. Pollaiolo* (1493). It can be seen to advantage from above (from the raised

Vatican
Grottoes

platform).—In the passage leading to Room IV, is displayed a 13C Slavonic Icon
(with SS Peter and Paul) in a silver frame.—ROOM IV. Ceremonial ring of Sixtus
IV (1471-84); Cross in rock crystal (13C); Reliquary bust of St Luke the Evangelist
(13-14C); Reliquary of St Blaise (14C).

A passage containing illuminated manuscripts, including one from the Giulia
choir (1534) and a 17C ivory Crucifix leads to ROOM V. Here are displayed a Cross
and Candelabra by *Seb. Torrigiani;* a Crucifix and six candelabra (1581) made by
*Ant. Gentili* for Card. Aless. Farnese and by him presented to the basilica in 1582;
and two huge *Candelabra of the 16C, traditionally attrib. to *Cellini.*—R. VI.
Model of an Angel in clay by *Bernini* (1673) used for one of the angels flanking the
ciborium in the Cappella del Sacramento (comp. p. 269).—RR. VII-VIII. Gilt
bronze tiara (18C) for the statue of St Peter; on high festivals this statue is attired in
full pontificals. Gold Chalice set with diamonds (18C), bequeathed to the Vatican
by Henry Stuart, Cardinal York; Platinum Chalice, presented by Charles III of
Spain to Pius VI, noteworthy as the first recorded use of platinum for such a

purpose—R. IX. *Sarcophagus of Junius Bassus, prefect of Rome in 359.—Plaster-cast of *Michelangelo*'s Pietà (comp. p. 269).

From the entrance, to the museum a second corridor leads right, off which is the Sacristy (68; open only 7-12). Known as the *Sagrestia Comune* its construction was ordered by Pius VI in 1776; he gave the work to *Carlo Marchionni*, who completed it in 1784. It is an octagonal hall with a cupola supported by pilasters of yellow Siena marble and grey marble columns from Hadrian's Villa near Tivoli.

To the left is the SAGRESTIA DEI CANONICI (69; special permit required, but sometimes open in the morning), with a chapel containing a Madonna and Saints by *Fr. Penni,* and an early Madonna with St John by *Giulio Romano.*—The adjoining Chapter House (70) contains paintings of saints by *And. Sacchi.*

**Ascent of the Dome.** Adm. daily 8-17 or 18, exc. Christmas Day and Easter Day, and when the Pope is in the basilica (often on Wed morning); 600 l; incl. lift 700 l. The entrance is under the Sobieska monument next the baptistery (65). The dome was completed as far as the drum by *Michelangelo* (d. 1564), the vault and the lantern by *Giac. della Porta* in 1588-90. Clement VIII (1592-1605) covered the vault with strips of lead reinforced with bronze ribs.

The lift may be used or the easy spiral staircase (73), which is covered with inscriptions relating to Holy Year ceremonies and recording the visits of visiting crowned heads. On reaching the roof, there is a close view of the spring of the dome, whose cross is 92 m above. The two side cupolas, by *Vignola* are purely decorative and have no opening into the interior of the church. On the roof are buildings occupied by the *Sampietrini,* masons and others employed on the maintenance of the fabric. From the parapet there is an extensive *View of Piazza San Pietro and of the city. From this point of view the statues of the façade look somewhat rough-hewn.

Two stairways lead to a curving corridor from which is the entrance left into the *First Circular Gallery* (53 m above the ground and 67 m below the top of the dome). From there, there is an impressive, if vertiginous, view of the pavement far below and of the interior of the dome; its immensity may be gauged by the coarseness of the mosaic and the vast scale of the decorative details.—The higher Gallery and Loggia are at present closed to the public. Resuming the ascent, a narrow winding staircase continues and then a spiral staircase to the *Second Circular Gallery* (closed to the public), 73 m above the ground; from here there is another and still dizzier view. The *Loggia of the Lantern,* 537 steps above the pavement of the basilica, commands a magnificent *View of the whole city and of the Campagna from the Apennines and the Alban Hills to the sea. The *Cross* surmounting the copper *Ball* (2½ m in diameter; just large enough to hold 16 persons) is 132½ m above the ground.

The *Vatican Grottoes are open on weekdays 8-17, exc. when the Pope is in the basilica. The entrance is by the pier of St Andrew (6), and the exit on the outside of the church, to the right of the main door. In the space between the level of the existing basilica (30 m above sea-level) and that of the old one (27 m) the Renaissance architects formed the so-called *Sacred Grottoes* and placed in them various monuments and architectural fragments from the former church. They were used for the burial of numerous popes and other illustrious personages. In 1940 excavations were begun at the instance of Pius XII, below the level of the old basilica; they continued until 1957.

The Grottoes, which follow the outline of the basilica above them (except for their annexes), are in two adjoining sections. The OLD GROTTOES have the form of a nave with aisles (corresponding to Maderna's nave but extending beyond it); on either side are the annexes discovered during the excavations. The NEW GROTTOES are in the form of a horse-shoe, with extensions. The centre is immediately below the high altar of St Peter's. Four of the extensions reach to points below the four piers of St Longinus, St Helena, St Veronica, and St Andrew. A large part of this area has been closed indefinitely, and the route described below has been imposed for several years.

Stairs lead down from the church (6) to the **New Grottoes,** where visitors are directed left (1). On the left (2) is the 14C chapel of the Madonna della Bocciata, and beyond (3), the 15C chapel of the Madonna delle Febbri. The horse-shoe passage continues to the Clementine Chapel (4), which is immediately beneath the centre of the church above. Here the rear wall was breached during the excavations for St Peter's tomb. Behind is the foundation of the altar of Calixtus II enclosing that of Gregory I (p. 268). The Tropaion of Gaius (see below) is therefore beneath (5). Openings to the left and right show the structure of the foundations more clearly (visible only when the grille is opened on a guided tour of the Necropolis—see below). Opposite the chapel is (6) the tomb of Pius XII (d. 1958).—The passage continues, lined with fine reliefs attrib. to *Matteo del Pollaiolo* of the life of St Peter which decorated the tabernacle over the high altar of the old basilica. At the end on the left (7; sometimes unlit) is the unfinished tomb of Paul II (d. 1471) by *Mino da Fiesole, Giov. Dalmata,* and others.

The area of the **Old Grottoes** lies at the w. end of the right aisle. Immediately to the right is a chapel (8) with a 15C altar of the Virgin, and the tomb (9) of Pius VI (d. 1799) in an early Christian sarcophagus. At the w. end of the nave (seen across the barrier) is the 15C *Altar of Christ in majesty with the Evangelists (10), by Giov. Dalmata.* Continuing down the aisle, the route passes the tomb of Pope John XXIII (11). Beyond on the left (12) is the tomb of Christina of Sweden (d. 1689), and opposite (13), the tomb of Queen Charlotte of Cyprus (d. 1487). After a short flight of steps are more tombs: on the l. (14) Innocent IX (d. 1591), and r. (15) Benedict XV (d. 1922), followed by (16) Marcellus II (d. 1555). The chapel (17) beyond has a relief of the Madonna attrib. to Isaia da Pisa. Here is the plain tomb slab of Paul VI (d. 1978).—A turning left leads away from the Old Grottoes, passing l. (18) the tomb of Julius III (d. 1555) into the N. ANNEXE, a series of four rooms (19-22) containing interesting inscriptions and fragments from the old basilica. In the two rooms to the left (19 and 20; sometimes unlit) is the sarcophagus of Anicius Probus, Prefect of Rome in 395.—From here the Corridor of Clement VIII (23) leads out towards Via delle Fondamenta, N. of St Peter's, from where it is possible to regain the portico of the church.

**\*Necropolis and St Peter's Tomb.** (Application may be made in writing or in person to the Ufficio Scavi (left of the Basilica) for permission to join the group of 15 which is conducted on most days at 3 p.m. (1500 l.). Details of name, number of persons, and language should be sent together with length of stay, address and Tel. no. in Rome.) A double row of mausoleums, dating from the 1C A.D., running from E. to W. were discovered below the level of the old basilica. The extreme w. series of these is on higher ground and adjoins a graveyard which is immediately beneath the high altar of the present church. Constantine significantly chose to erect his basilica above this necropolis, a most difficult undertaking because of the slope of the hill. He had to level the terrain and make use of supporting foundation walls. A baldacchino in the presbytery covered the *Tropaion of Gaius,* a funerary monument referred to c. 200, and probably built by Pope Anicetus (p. 265).

Excavations have discovered this monument, which backs on to a supporting wall plastered with red, dating from the same period. An empty space beneath it is believed to be St Peter's Tomb—what was probably a mound of earth covered by brick slabs, and showing signs of the interference which history records. That this was a most revered grave is evident from the number of other graves which crowd in upon one another, without cutting across or lying upon it, seemingly in an effort to be near it. In front of the supporting red wall, on which a Greek inscription is taken to name the saint, is a later wall, scratched with the names of pilgrims invoking the aid of Peter. Bones, obviously displaced, of an elderly and powerfully built man, were found beneath the red wall, and declared by Paul VI to be those of St Peter.

The site of the Circus of Nero, the most likely place of St Peter's martyrdom, lay along the s. flank of the basilica, and extended as far as Via Sant'Uffizio.

Visitors meet inside the Vatican City, entered through the Arco delle Campane (p. 263), which is protected by a member of the Swiss Guard, and cross Piazza dei Protomartiri Romani. The visit usually commences at the S. ANNEXE (24) of the Old Grottoes, through two rooms (25 and 26) with 14-15C tomb slabs and sarcophagi. A third room (27) has transennæ and architectural fragments of the 4-9C, and part of the nave foundation wall of the old basilica; from here stairs lead down to the Necropolis. (If, however, work on the excavations prevents this route being used, visitors are conducted into St Peter's and through the new Grottoes (5), from which these stairs can also be reached.)

The necropolis is well-preserved and was in use until Constantine's reign. Among the 18 loculi cleared the one purely Christian mausoleum provides the most ancient mosaics yet discovered on a Christian subject. Here, on the vault richly decorated with a vine pattern, Christ is depicted as Helios, the sun-god. On the walls the sinopie remain of mosaics which have become detached from the surface (on the left, Jonah, and ahead, Fishermen). In the other mausoleums Oriental cults and those of Greece and Rome are combined. Christians were also buried in the mausoleum of the Cætenii, where is the grave of Aemilia Gorgonia; in the magnificent stuccoed mausoleum of the Valerii, with reliefs in niches, where the inscription of Valerinus Vastulus, despite the pagan sarcophagus (3C), specifies his Christian burial; and in the so-called Egyptian chamber. The paintings of peacocks in the mausoleum of the family of P. Aelius Tyrannus, the marble bust of the woman in that of the Valerii, and the remarkable sarcophagus of Q. Marcius Hermes and his wife mirror the tastes and wealth of the families of freedmen to whom the loculi belonged. Among the many sarcophagi one for a child, with figures of the mourning parents, should be noted.

# B   The Vatican Palace

**Admission.** The Vatican Museums and Galleries are open Mon-Sat from 9 to 14; in July, Aug, and Sept, and during the Easter period they are open from 9-17. They are also open free on the last Sun of the month, unless it is a feast day. The museums and galleries covered by the ticket (1500 l.; 500 l. for students)—for one single visit—are the Gregorian Museum of Pagan Antiquities and the Pio Christian Museum (both formerly in the Lateran), the Picture Gallery, the Museo Pio-Clementino (sculpture), the Museo Chiaramonti (sculpture), the Egyptian Museum, the Etruscan Museum, the Museum of Pagan Antiquities, the Exhibition Rooms of the Library, the Museum of Christian Art, the Borgia Rooms and the Gallery of Modern Religious Art, the Raphael Rooms, the Loggia of Raphael, the Sistine Chapel, the Chapels of Nicholas V and of Urban VIII, the Room of the Chiaroscuri, the Hall of the Immaculate Conception, the Gallery of Maps, the Gallery of Tapestries, the Ethnological Missionary Museum and the Historical Museum.—An official Guide in English is available.

The Vatican collections are closed on Sundays (exc. the last in the month) and on the following days: 6 Jan, 11 Feb (Anniversary of the founding of the Vatican City State), Easter Monday, 1 May, Ascension Day, Corpus Christi, 29 June, 15 Aug, 1 Nov, 8 Dec, 25 Dec, and whenever special reasons make it necessary.

A **Bus Service** runs every half hour (between 9 and 12.30) from the Arco delle Campane (left of the façade of the basilica, comp. p. 265) through the Vatican gardens to a side entrance to the Museums (5 min.; 250 l.). This is recommended not only as the most convenient way of reaching the museums from St Peter's, but also it provides the opportunity of seeing part of the Vatican city and gardens, which can otherwise be seen only on an organized tour (comp. p. 314).

The \*\***Vatican Palace** occupies a special position in the realm of art; some of the world's greatest treasures are to be found within its walls. Its extent is stupefying. The buildings, without the gardens, cover an area of 5½ hetares, of which 2½ hectares are occupied by the interior courts. The halls, rooms, galleries, and chapels number some 1400; most of them are open to the public, as the apartments reserved for the Pope and the papal court form a relatively small part of the whole. The gardens are not accessible from the museums; for the organized tour of the gardens and city, see p. 314.

**History.** In the days of Pope St Symmachus (498-514) a house was built beside the first basilica of St Peter. This house was not the residence of the popes as, until the migration to Avignon in 1309, they lived in the Lateran Palace; but it was used for state occasions and for the accommodation of foreign sovereigns. In it Charlemagne stayed in 800 and Otho II in 980. By the 12C it had fallen into decay. Eugenius III (1145-53) was the first of numerous popes to restore and enlarge it. When Gregory XI returned from Avignon in 1378 he found the Lateran uninhabitable and he transferred his residence to the Vatican. On his death in the same year, the first Conclave was held in the Vatican. To safeguard the security of the occupants, the antipope John XXIII began in 1410 to build the Covered Way to the Castel Sant'Angelo.

Nicholas V (1447-55) transformed the house into a palace, built round a courtyard—the Cortile dei Pappagalli. In 1473 Sixtus IV added the Sistine Chapel. Innocent VIII (1484-92) built on the N. summit of the Vatican Hill the Belvedere Pavilion; the architect was Giac. da Pietrasanta. Alexander VI (1492-1503) decorated a suite of rooms on the first floor of the palace of Nicholas V and they became known, after his family name, as the Appartamento Borgia; he added the Borgia Tower. Julius II (1503-13) began to form the famous collection of classical sculpture, which he placed in the courtyard of the Belvedere Pavilion. He also commissioned Bramante to unite this pavilion with the palace of Nicholas V by means of long corridors, thus creating the great Courtyard of the Belvedere.

Leo X (1513-21) adorned the E. side of the palace with open galleries looking on to the Courtyard of St Damasus, one of which became known as the Loggia of Raphael. Paul III (1534-49) employed Ant. da Sangallo the Younger to build the Cappella Paolina and the Sala Regia. Under Pius IV and Gregory XIII various additions were made by Pirro Ligorio. Sixtus V (1585-90) assigned to Dom. Fontana the construction of the block overlooking Piazza San Pietro and of the great Library, which was formed at right angles to the long corridors and thus divided the Courtyard of the Belvedere in two. The Scala Regia of Bernini was begun under Urban VIII and completed under Alexander VII (1655-67). The Museum of Pagan Antiquities was founded by Clement XIII (1758-69).

Clement XIV (1769-74) converted the Belvedere Pavilion into a museum which Pius VI (1775-99) enlarged; whence its name 'Pio-Clementino'. The architect was M. Simonetti, who altered the courtyard and added several rooms. Pius VI was also the founder of the Picture Gallery. Pius VII (Chiaramonti; 1800-23) founded the Sculpture Gallery which bears his name and added the New Wing (by Raff. Stern), which paralleled the Library. Its construction divided the Courtyard of the Belvedere into three. From now on the sections became known as the Courtyard of the Belvedere (retaining the old name; nearest the pontifical palace), the relatively small Courtyard of the Library and the Courtyard of the Fir Cone (Pigna; after a bronze fir cone placed in it by Paul V; 1605-21; nearest to the Belvedere Pavilion). Gregory XVI (1831-46) was responsible for the Etruscan and Egyptian Museums. Pius IX (1846-78) closed the fourth side of the Courtyard of St Damasus and built the Scala Pia. Leo XIII (1878-1903) restored the Borgia Rooms and reopened them to the public. Under Pius XI (1914-39) were built the new Picture Gallery and the new entrance to the Vatican Museums in the Viale Vaticano, both of them dating from 1932. A new building was opened in 1970 by Paul VI to house the former Lateran museums (the Gregorian Museum of Pagan Antiquities and the Pio Christian Museum); in 1973 the Ethnological Missionary Museum was opened beneath, and a Historical Musum was built under the gardens. An extensive series of galleries in and around the Borgia apartments were opened in 1973 as a Museum of Modern Religious Art.

The entrance to the Vatican Museums is reached on foot along Via di Porta Angelica (Pl 1; 4) to the right (N.) of Bernini's colonnade in Piazza San Pietro (or by bus through the Vatican gardens, see p. 276). At the beginning of the street is the battlemented Covered Way to Castel Sant'Angelo. Porta Angelica which gave the street its name is no more; its site was at the N. end, by the modern Piazza del Risorgimento. On the left is the Cancello di Sant'Anna, one of the entrances to Vatican City. The road skirts the city wall, and turns left out of Piazza del Risorgimento. Continuing along the wall Viale Vaticano (p. 261), leads left to the ENTRANCE TO THE VATICAN MUSEUMS (Pl. 1; 3, 4). This consists of an entrance hall (with a ticket office for tour groups, and an Information Office), leading to a monumental *Double Staircase, by *G. Momo*, with independent ascending and descending spirals, carved out of the hill, to connect the street level with that of the museums. The bronze balustrade is by *A. Maraini*. There is also a lift, but the staircase deserves close inspection.

The *Ambulatory* at the top of the staircase is decorated with mosaics and busts. Here is the ticket office for individual visitors, and a post office where postcards and Vatican stamps are sold.—Beyond the ticket gates a short flight of steps mounts to the *Vestibule* decorated with three mosaics from Hadrian's Villa. On the right is the entrance to the new building which houses the Gregorian Museum of Pagan Antiquities and the Pio Christian Museum. Beyond is an open court. On the left is the entrance known as the *Quattro Cancelli* (Four Gates), which gives access to the Sculpture Galleries, to the Museum of Pagan Antiquities and, beyond these, to the rest of the Vatican Museums. In front a passageway leads to the Picture Gallery.

The collections are so extensive and their layout is so complicated that is is not practicable to see them all in a single day, let alone in a single tour. To add to the complication, the exhibits are arranged on different floors, and, in the case of the Sculpture Galleries, on two floors. However the visit is planned a certain amount of duplication cannot be avoided. Refreshments may now be obtained in the Cortile della Pinacoteca.

Four one-way itineraries have recently been imposed by the Vatican authorities and visitors are expected to chose one of the four 'tours' depending on the time at their disposal. This is primarily to regulate the flow of people to the Sistine Chapel and tour groups have to take the signposted routes. However, with some persuasion, these may be disregarded to some extent, especially if the visitor is alone. Travellers wishing to see one particular collection only, and especially those who already know the Museums will not be helped by the one-way systems, since, in some cases, access from one part of the museums to another is no longer possible. The number of people and tours in the Vatican can seriously impede the visitor's enjoyment of the museum. Those with time may do well to proceed straight to the Sistine Chapel at opening time in order to enjoy it in comparative peace, and then return to the Quattro Cancelli to begin the detailed tours described below. It should be noted that visitors are now often able to leave the museums through the Sistine Chapel by the Scala Regia which descends directly to the portico of St Peter's. A new staircase is being built which will descend directly from the sacristy of the chapel to the atrium of St Peter's.

The four separate tours suggested below can be made taking into account the new one-way systems.

1. Vestibule—Gregorian Museum of Pagan Antiquities—Pio Christian Museum—Ethnological Missionary Museum—Historical Museum—Vestibule.

2. Quattro Cancelli—Vatican Picture Gallery—Quattro Cancelli.

3. A very long and tiring route which should, if time permits, be taken in two stages. Quattro Cancelli—upstairs to the Gallery of the Candelabra—Gallery of Tapestries and Gallery of Maps—Hall of the Immaculate Conception—Raphael Rooms—Loggia of Raphael—Room of the Chiaroscuri—Chapel of Nicholas V—Chapel of Urban VIII—Borgia Rooms and Gallery of Modern Religious Art—Sistine Chapel—Museum of Christian Art—Sistine Hall and Library—New Wing of the Museo Chiaramonti—Museum of Pagan Antiquities—Quattro Cancelli.

4. Quattro Cancelli—Simonetti staircase—Egyptian Museum—Museo Chiaramonti—Museo Pio Clementino—upstairs to the Room of the Biga—Etruscan Museum—return to the Quattro Cancelli.

The itineraries described below follow the above scheme.

## 1.   THE GREGORIAN MUSEUM OF PAGAN ANTIQUITIES

This striking building in the modern idiom was designed by a group of Italian architects headed by the Passarelli brothers, and opened in 1970. Using the latest methods of display, it contains the collections that were in the Lateran, comprising the **Museo Gregoriano Profano** (*Gregorian Museum of Pagan Antiquities*), consisting entirely of Roman and neo-Attic sculpture, the **Pio Christian Museum,** and the **Ethnological Missionary Museum,** as well as additional material.

The arrangement is still not complete, and the section containing the Pagan Inscriptions has not yet opened. The exhibits are not fully labelled. The design of the building precludes divisions between the various sections, but the visitor is directed by arrows.

The Museo Profano was founded by Gregory XVI (1831-46) to house the overflow of the Vatican Museums and the yields of excavations during his pontificate at Rome, Ostia, Veii, and Cære (Cerveteri). It was enriched by further excavations up to 1870, and at the end of the 19C by a collection of pagan inscriptions. John XXIII was responsible for its removal to the Vatican.

Near the entrance are Roman copies of original Greek sculpture (torsoes, statuettes, and heads), including MARSYAS (1), a marble copy of a bronze by Myron which formed part of a group placed at the entrance to the Acropolis in Athens in the mid-5C B.C. Marsyas is attracted by the sound of the double flute, which Athena had invented and just thrown away. He tries to pick up the instrument, but is foiled by Athena's commanding gesture (only her head remains).

Behind is SOPHOCLES (2), a marble statue from Terracina, with admirable drapery, copy of a 4C work.—Stairs (3) lead up to an area which will eventually contain the Lateran collection of PAGAN INSCRIPTIONS.—There follow a series of HERMS (4), and, on the floor, the *HERACLITUS MOSAIC (5) of an unswept floor from the triclinium of a house on the Aventine, showing the remains of a banquet. It is signed 'Heraclitus', and may be a copy of a celebrated work by Sosus of Pergamon. Other works in this section include: Round altar, with a faun playing for two dancing women; Triangular tripod base, with reliefs of dancing figures taking part in Dionysiac rites, a neo-Attic work in Pentelic marble of the 1C B.C., after a 4C original; Copy of the Resting Satyr of Praxiteles (others in the Museo Pio-Clementino and the Capitoline Museum); Colossal statue of Poseidon (Neptune), after a bronze original by Lysippos (with several restorations).

Beyond is a relief of Medea and the daughters of Pelias whom she is inducing to kill their father, neo-Attic copy of a late 5C B.C. original. It is one of a series of four relating to the dramatic competitions in Athens. The best copy of the second (Orpheus and Eurydice) is in the Naples Museum, a third (Herakles, Theseus, and Peirithöos) is in the Museo Torlonia.

Beyond a colossal statue of Zeus are the remains of the large circular VICOVARO MONUMENT (6), dating from the early 1C A.D.—In the next recess is the CHIARAMONTI NIOBID (7), a fine Roman copy of an original by Leochares of the 4C B.C.; head of a Muse, crowned with ivy, in the manner of Praxiteles (good copy of a 4C B.C. original); Torso of a statue of Diana; the motion expressed in the drapery is particularly fine in this Roman copy of a Greek original of the 4C B.C.; two Roman orators in togas (1C A.D.); fine Roman portrait heads (the last two perhaps portraits of Virgil).

The following sections contain Roman sculpture in chronological order, beginning with the late Republican era:

Opposite two statues of the sleeping Silenus (copies of Hellenistic works), found in the Roman Theatre at Cære (see below), are a series of funerary reliefs: the first with portraits of parents and a young son, and the second with five busts of members of the Furia family. In the centre, circular altar dedicated to Piety, from Veii, adorned with garlands, citharæ, and the attributes of Vulcan (1C A.D.).

Around to the left are a group of STATUES FROM THE ROMAN THEATRE AT CAERE (8), mainly of the Julio-Claudian family: Agrippina, mother of

Nero and wife of Claudius, as a goddess; Colossal seated statue of Claudius as Jupiter; Relief with figures symbolizing three Etruscan cities—Vetulonia, Vulci, and Tarquinia—found with the statue and believed to have been part of his throne; Colossal head, probably of Augustus; Colossal seated statue of Tiberius idealized as Jupiter; Series of inscriptions found with the statues, explaining their identity; Drusus and elder, with a cuirass decorated with bas-reliefs of two griffins and above, a gorgon; Altar dedicated to C. Manlius, a censor of Caere, by his clients (1C A.D.); Statue of an Emperor in a cuirass, decorated with reliefs.

Next comes the so-called ALTAR OF VICOMAGISTRI (9), 1C A.D., found near the Cancelleria. The relief is of a sacrificial procession, followed by four figures carrying statuettes of lares and by priestly officials known as Vicomagistri.—Two Statues of young boys wearing togas, belonging to the Julio-Claudian family (one with a 3C head); more Roman portrait busts and heads.

To the left is an area with CINERARY URNS (10), among which are: Urn with finely carved reliefs, with the head of Medusa in the centre, and below a cock-fight. At the sides festoons, with eagles and genii; Covered urn with good reliefs and an inscription relating to Quinto Volusio Antigono.—The next section has architectural fragments, and some exquisite decorative reliefs with small Bacchic scenes and vine leaves (1C A.D.).—The area is dominated by two large CANCELLERIA RELIEFS (11), dating from the Flavian period (A.D. 70-96).

The frieze on the left (damaged) represents the return to Rome of Vespasian (who appears on the extreme right of the 3rd panel). Surrounding the Emperor, are Vestals, the Roman Senate and people, and the seated figure of Rome. The frieze on the right represents the departure from Rome of Domitian who appears (restored as Nerva), in the second panel from the left, surrounded by (l.) Minerva, Mars, and Victory, and (r.) Rome with soldiers.

Beyond more portrait busts is the sculpture from the TOMB OF THE HATERII (12), near Centocelle: Two similar niches with well-modelled portrait busts of a man and woman; three Reliefs of ceremonies of a woman's funeral: Body lying in state, surrounded by relatives and mourners in the atrium of a house; Funeral procession, passing buildings on the Via Sacra; Sepulchral monument of the Haterii, with a view of the inside and the apparatus used in its construction. Above, High relief with three busts of gods of the underworld; triangular pillar, beautifully carved, with candelabrum, rose branches, and birds.—Relief of a procession of Roman magistrates before a temple (1C A.D.). A head has been restored (erroneously) by Thorvaldsen to represent Trajan.

Towards the windows, large Funerary relief of a woman (the head is a portrait) lying on a bed with a small dog; Sepulchral relief of a chariot race, a side view of the circus seen from above. The organizers of the games in whose memory the relief was made appear on the left (early 2C A.D.); two Columns, carved with a papyrus motif and lotus leaves around the base.

To the right, colossal STATUE OF A DACIAN (13), of the time of Trajan, found in 1841 in Via dei Coronari, on the site of a sculptor's studio of the Imperial era.

A series of capitals and antifixes follow, with two fragments of an architectural frieze from the forum of Trajan, with cupids and griffins and a neo-Attic amphora.

The next sections contain *PAGAN SARCOPHAGI (14), with mythological scenes. Among them, several depicting the story of Adonis, of Hippolytus and Phædra (with scenes of the wild boar hunt), of Orestes, and of the slaughter of the family of Niobe. Farther on, the

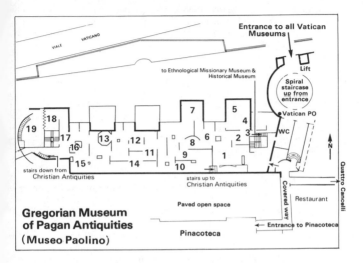

**Gregorian Museum
of Pagan Antiquities
(Museo Paolino)**

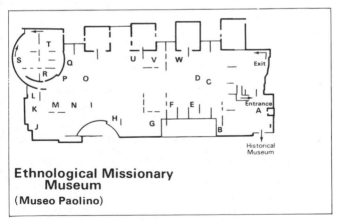

**Ethnological Missionary
Museum
(Museo Paolino)**

triumph of Dionysos (Bacchus). He is represented as a victor on his return from India in a triumphal car drawn by two elephants, and being crowned by Nike (Victory)—fine workmanship of the 3C A.D.

Beyond is a colossal statue of Antinöus as the god Vertumnus (with finely modelled drapery; the head is modern); fragment of a relief with two boxers, presumably part of a large monument (2C A.D.).

Fragment of the large oval PLOTINUS SARCOPHAGUS (15), with figures in relief in philosophical discussion (?), and part of a lion hunt; on the wall behind, Sepulchral relief with the deceased man reading from a large scroll, surrounded by his family and pupils (3C A.D.); on the right, Funerary monument in high relief of a warrior saluting his wife who is seated; a horse stands ready, and a snake is depicted in the tree above. Fragments of draped IMPERIAL PORPHYRY STATUES (16).—Towards the windows, Relief of a nymph feeding an infant satyr from a large horn-shaped vessel, while in a grotto near by a young Pan plays the syrinx. Known as the Amaltheia relief, this was originally part of a fountain.— To the right is the STATUE OF DOGMAZIO (17). Another area (18) contains Roman religious sculpture, including statues of Mithras and the bull (3C A.D.), Diana of the Ephesians, and Asklepios.

To the right of the stairs are fragments of a group with a boy riding a horse, and a naiad on a sea centaur. Upstairs a walkway passes above a MOSAIC OF ATHLETES FROM THE BATHS OF CARACALLA (19) and a black marble statue of a stag (Roman copy of a 4C Greek original). Beyond a double row of laughing silene busts and some exquisite bas-reliefs (including a tondo of Hercules and the Lion), a balcony overlooks a second fine mosaic from the Baths of Caracalla.

The rest of the upper floor is occupied by the **Pio Christian Museum of Antiquities,** founded by Pius IX in 1854 with objects found mainly in the catacombs, and displayed by subject matter. The display begins at the other end of the mezzanine floor, at the entrance to the building (comp. p. 279). The first section is devoted to the valuable collection of Christian sarcophagi of the 2-5C, of the highest importance to students of early Christian iconography; some famous sarcophagi owned by the Vatican but not on view here are represented by casts (numbered with Roman numerals). At the beginning, on the l. wall, are fragments of sarcophagi representing the Nativity and Epiphany (124, 190.) of the 4C A.D. Farther on (r.) is a sarcophagus showing the Crossing of the Red Sea.—Three steps lead up to the next section: in the middle, cast of the Sarcophagus of Junius Bassus (the original is in the Museo Storico Artistico in St Peter's, comp. p. 274). Round the corner to the left is a sarcophagus (164.) with five niches showing Christ triumphant over death, Cain and Abel, Peter taken prisoner, the Martyrdom of Paul, and Job.—Another short flight of steps ascends past (r.) 152. Sarcophagus of the husband and wife Crescentianus and Agapene, found in the Vatican necropolis. At the top of the stairs (left) is a large sarcophagus (104.) with episodes from the Bible. To the r.: panels (184, 189, 178, 175, 183A) with scenes from the Old and New Testaments; cast of the Sarcophagus from Sant'Ambrogio in Milan.—The next part of the gallery contains more sarcophagi (including one from St Calixtus) and some mosaic fragments.—Three steps lead up to the last section of the Museum. On the l. is a well-preserved sarcophagus (150.) with traces of the original polychrome decoration. At the end, 191A. Sarcophagus illustrating the Good Shepherd. On the right wall begins the collection of tablets from the MUSEUM OF CHRISTIAN INSCRIPTIONS, the largest and most important collection of Christian inscriptions in existence. The whole collection was arranged and classified by G. B. De Rossi (1822-94) in four series.

FIRST SERIES. Inscriptions from public monuments connected with Christian worship. The exhibits include a fragment of the sepulchral inscription of Publius Sulpicius Quirinus (Cyrenius), Governor of Syria, who took the census at the time of the birth of Christ; inscriptions of Pope St Damasus (366-84).—SECOND SERIES. Dated sepulchral inscriptions. Dogmatic inscriptions, including the *IXΘYΣ*(fish) acrostic.—Inscriptions relating to the ecclesiastical hierarchy, virgins, catechumens, senators, soldiers, officials, and workers, etc.

THIRD SERIES. Chi-Rho and other symbols and representations of Christian dogma.—FOURTH SERIES. Topographical. Inscriptions from the cemetery of Priscilla, the cemetery of Prætextatus on the Appian Way, Sant'Agnese fuori le Mura, Ostia, tombs near the Vatican, San Lorenzo fuori le Mura, San Pancrazio, Monte Mario. These inscriptions range from 2C-6C.

The statue of the Good Shepherd is a fine work dating from the late 3C. A passage continues past (177.) a sarcophagus from San Lorenzo fuori le Mura, and the cast of a seated statue of the martyred doctor St Hippolytus. On the left of his chair is a list in Greek of the saint's works, and on the right a paschal calendar for the years 222-334. The original was moved by Pope John XXIII to the entrance of the Biblioteca Vaticana, in the Belvedere Court (see below).—On the balcony overlooking a mosaic from the Baths of Caracalla (comp. above) is a fragment of the tombstone of Abercius, bishop of Hierapolis (Phrygia), who lived in the reign of Marcus Aurelius (161-180), discovered by Sir William Ramsay and presented to Leo XIII. The Greek text is in three parts: in the first part Abercius says that he is a disciple of Christ the Good Shepherd, in the second he mentions his journey to Rome and the East, in the third he asks the faithful to pray for him and threatens defilers of his grave.

The *Ethnological Missionary Museum* occupies the whole of the area below ground level. It was established by Pius XI in 1927 as a development of the Vatican Missionary Exhibition of 1924-26. The primitive and more recent cultures of each country have been arranged according to subject matter; labelling is kept to a minimum. The countries are indicated by a letter (comp. the plan), and the visitor is directed by arrows. The exhibits illustrate the ways of life and religious customs in: *China* (A), with fine Buddhist sculpture and religious figures of the Ming and T'ang dynasties; *Japan* (B), with ceremonial masks and paintings of martyrs; *Korea* (C); *Tibet, Mongolia* (D); *Indochina* (E), where examples of local art and manufacture show the adaptation of European sacred art to the local genius; *Indian sub-continent* (F), illustrating Shivaism and Vishnuism; *Indonesia, Philippines* (G); *Polynesia* (H); *Melanesia* (I), with protective spirits, ceremonial masks and costumes, and the reconstruction of a hut of the spirits from New Guinea; *Australia* (J); *North Africa* (K); *Ethiopia* (L); *Madagascar* (M); *West Africa* (N), with statuettes of tribal gods; *Central Africa* (O); *East Africa* (P); *Southern Africa* (Q); *Christian Africa* (R); *South America* (S), including ancient wood sculpture from Columbia; *Central America* (T); *North America* (U); *Persia* (V); *Middle East* (W); and Christian art from countries penetrated by the missions. A mezzanine floor contains study collections open to students.

The *Historical Museum*, at present entered from the Ethnological Museum (comp. plan p. 281), was established by Paul VI in 1973. It is arranged in a huge gallery beneath the Vatican gardens. The magnificent collection of carriages used by Popes and Cardinals include a landau in which the Pope was carried daily until the time of Pius XI, and a coach made for Leo XII by Gaetano Peroni. The second section contains uniforms and relics of the Papal armed forces disbanded in 1970, and a collection of arms and armour.

## II  THE VATICAN PICTURE GALLERY

The *Vatican Picture Gallery*, or *Pinacoteca Vaticana*, is reached by the passageway from the open court to the right of the Quattro Cancelli.

The gallery owes its origin to Pius VI (1775-99), who formed a collection of pictures from the museums and library. Under the Treaty of Tolentino (1797), which he was forced to conclude with Napoleon, he had to surrender the best works to France. Of these, 77 were recovered in 1815. The gallery has had various homes. The present building, of 15 public rooms, in the Lombardic Renaissance style, by *Luca Beltrami* (1854-1933), was opened in 1932.

ROOM I. BYZANTINE SCHOOL AND ITALIAN PRIMITIVES. *Ant. Veneziano,* 16. St James, 19. Mary Magdalene; 18. *Jacopo da Bologna,* Death of St Francis; 17. *Vitale da Bologna,* Madonna and Child; 20. *12C Roman School,* Christ in judgement; 23. *Giunta Pisano,* St Francis, and panels illustrating his life; *526. *Giovanni* and *Niccolò* (Rome; late 11C), Last Judgement, the oldest picture in the gallery; 2. *Margaritone d'Arezzo,* St Francis of Assisi; (window wall) 14. *Giov. del Biondo,* Madonna and Child with saints; 169. *Taddeo di Bartolo,* Death of the Virgin; 9. *Giov. Bonsi,* Madonna and saints, signed and dated 1371; *146-150, 158-161. *Bern. Daddi,* Legend of St Stephen. Also works by *Niccolò di Pietro Gerini,* and the Florentine School.

ROOM II. In the centre, *120. The STEFANESCHI TRIPTYCH, by *Giotto* and assistants. This altarpiece for the Confessio of Old St Peter's painted on both sides (recently restored), represents Christ enthroned, the martyrdom of SS. Peter and Paul (at the foot of the throne is the donor, Card. Stefaneschi); on the back, St Peter accepting the triptych from the Pope; at the sides, four Apostles; on the predella, other Apostles.— Around the walls is an exquisite series of small paintings: 168, 166, 163, 170. *Pietro Lorenzetti,* Christ before Pilate, St John the Baptist, St Peter, the Virgin; 165. *Simone Martini,* Redeemer; *174. *Bern. Daddi,* Madonna of the Magnificat; 102, 97, 101. *Mariotto di Nardo,* Nativity, St Nicholas freeing three knights, Annunciation; works (136, 138) by *Sano di Pietro;* 132. *Giovanni di Paolo,* Nativity; 234. *Sassetta,* Vision of St Thomas Aquinas; 193. *Lorenzo Monaco,* Stories from the life of St Benedict; 247-50. *Gentile da Fabriano,* Stories from the life of St Nicholas of Bari; 2139. *Sassetta,* Madonna and Child; (window wall) 263. *Fr. di Gentile,* Madonna and Child.

R. III. FRA ANGELICO AND OTHERS. *Masolino da Panicale,* 260. Crucifixion, 245. Transition of the Virgin; *Fra Angelico,* *251, 252. Scenes from the life of St Nicholas of Bari, 253. Madonna and Child with saints; 243. *Filippo Lippi,* Coronation of the Virgin, a triptych; 262. *Benozzo Gozzoli,* St Thomas receiving the Virgin's girdle.

R. IV. MELOZZO AND PALMEZZANO. 269. Remaining fragments of the *Fresco by *Melozzo da Forlì* formerly in the church of the Santi Apostoli; another portion is in the Quirinal (p. 177). The fragments in this room represent the Ascension; note the eight *Angel Musicians. *270. *Melozzo,* Sixtus IV conferring on the humanist Platina the librarianship of the Vatican in the presence of Giuliano Della Rovere (afterwards Julius II), his brother Giovanni, and Girolamo and Raffaele Riario, an admirable fresco transferred to canvas.—On the right wall, *80. Tapestry of the Last Supper (16C Flemish, from Leonardo's fresco in Milan); *Marco Palmezzano,* 619, 273. Madonna and saints.

R. V. 15C ARTISTS. 286. *Fr. del Cossa,* Predella with Miracles of St Vincent Ferrer; 275. *Lucas Cranach,* Pietà; 294. *Giov. Battista Utili,* Madonna and Child.

R. VI. POLYPTYCHS. *Carlo Crivelli,* 297. Madonna (dated 1482), 300. Pietà. *Vitt. Crivelli,* Madonna with saints (dated 1481); *Niccolò l'Alunno,* 299. Crucifixion, 307. Polyptych of Montelparo; *Ant. Viviani,* St Anthony Abbot (in relief) and other saints (signed and dated 1469).

R. VII. UMBRIAN SCHOOL. 312. *Pinturicchio,* Coronation of the Virgin; 313. *Umbrian 15C school,* Madonna with St John; 316. *Lo Spagna,* Adoration of the Magi ('Madonna della Spineta'); *Perugino,* *317. Madonna enthroned with saints (318. Resurrection), 319-321. Part of predella with SS. Benedict, Flavia, and Placidus; 326. *Giov. Santi* (father of Raphael), St Jerome.

R. VIII, the largest room in the gallery, is devoted to the works of RAPHAEL. It contains three of his most famous paintings, two predellas, and 10 tapestries executed after his original cartoons. *334. Coronation of the Virgin, belonging to Raphael's first Perugian period and his first large composition, painted in 1503, when he was 20 years old; (in a table case) 335. Predella to the above, The Mysteries, i.e. Annunciation, Adoration of the Magi, and Presentation in the Temple. **329. The MADONNA OF FOLIGNO, a mature work painted about 1512-13. It was a votive offering by Sigismondo Conti in gratitude for his escape when a cannon-ball fell on his house during the siege of Foligno. From 1565 until carried off by Napoleon in 1797, it was in the Convent of Sant'Anna in that city.

The Madonna with the Child is seated on clouds above a sphere surrounded by cherubs; beneath, on the left, SS. John the Baptist and Francis; on the right St Jerome presenting Conti to the Virgin; in the middle an angel. In the distance are Foligno with the descending bomb and a rainbow signifying peace. The dignity, grace, and colour of this picture make it one of the painter's most sublime achievements. The predella, depicting the Three Theological Virtues, is of an earlier period and belongs to Raphael's Descent from the Cross now in the Borghese Gallery.

*333. The TRANSFIGURATION, Raphael's last work. From 1523 to 1809 it was in the church of San Pietro in Montorio. It was restored in 1972-77.

On the summit of Mount Tabor the Apostles Peter, James, and John see, through a veil of dazzling light, Christ rising towards heaven, with Elijah and Moses in attitudes of adoration. At the foot of the mountain are the other Apostles and the crowd with the young man possessed of a devil. The composition and the upper part of the picture are by Raphael; the lower part was probably completed by *Guilio Romano* and *Francesco Penni.* A mosaic reproducing this painting, four times the original size, is in St Peter's.

In the cases are the ten celebrated *TAPESTRIES representing scenes from the Acts of the Apostles. Intended for the adornment of the Sistine Chapel (p. 294), they were ordered by Leo X and woven in Brussels by *Pieter van Aelst* from cartoons drawn by Raphael in 1515-16.

Seven of the cartoons (three of them having been lost) are in the Victoria and Albert Museum, London, though some authorities state that these seven, which were bought in 1630 by Charles I of England, are 17C copies and that all the originals have been lost. Other tapestries from the same cartoons, but of inferior quality, are in Hampton Court Palace near London, in the Palazzo Ducale at Mantua, and in the Palazzo Apostolico at Loreto. The tapestries were first exhibited in 1519, in the Sistine Chapel. They have borders of grotesque ornamentation and broad bases decorated with bronze-coloured designs; most of this work is by *Giov. da Udine.* The subjects are: A. Blinding of Elymas (this tapestry was cut in halves during the sack of Rome in 1527), B. Conversion of St Paul, C. Stoning of St Stephen, D. St Peter healing the paralytic, E. Death of Ananias, F. St Peter receiving the keys, G. The miraculous draught of fishes, H. St Paul preaching in Athens, I. Inhabitants of Lystra desiring to sacrifice to SS. Paul and Barnabas, L. St Paul in prison at Philippi.—These tapestries belong to the so-called 'Old School' series. Ten of the 'New School' series are in the Gallery of Tapestries (p. 291).

R. IX. LEONARDO DA VINCI AND OTHER 15-16C MASTERS. *337. *Leonardo da Vinci*, St Jerome; 340. *Lor. di Credi*, Madonna; 339. *16C Lombard School*, Christ at the Column, Portrait of Bramante (?); *290. *Giov. Bellini*, Pietà.

R. X. TITIAN, VERONESE, FRA BARTOLOMEO. 347. *Girol. Genga*, Madonna and saints; 346. *Veronese*, Allegory; 349. *Moretto*, Madonna and Child enthroned with saints; 351. *Titian*, Madonna of San Niccolò de' Frari; 352. *Veronese*, St Helena; 354. *Paris Bordone*, St George and the Dragon; 355. *Garófalo*, Apparition of the Virgin to Augustus and the Sibyl; *359. *Giulio Romano* and *Fr. Penni*, 'Madonna of Monteluce'; 336. *Lombard 16C School*, 'Madonna della Cintura'.

R. XI. BAROCCI and others. 363. *Vasari*, Stoning of St Stephen; 365. *Cav. d Arpino*, Annunciation; 368. *Muziano*, Raising of Lazarus; 372. *Cola dell Amatrice*, Assumption of the Virgin; *Barocci*, 375. Head of the Virgin; 376. Annunciation, 377. 'Madonna of the Cherries', 378. The Blessed Michaelina, 380. St Francis receiving the stigmata.

R. XII. 17C MASTERS. There is a fine view of the cupola of St Peter's from the window. 381. *Valentin*, Martyrdom of SS. Processus and Martinian (mosaic in St Peter's); *382. *Sacchi*, Vision of St Romauld; 383. *Guercino*, Incredulity of St Thomas; *384. *Domenichino*, Communion of St Jerome (mosaic in St Peter's); 385. after *Caravaggio*, Denial of St Peter; *386. *Caravaggio*, Descent from the Cross (copy in St Peter's Sacristy); *Guido Reni*, 387. Crucifixion of St Peter (mosaic in St Peter's). *389. The Virgin in glory with saints; 388. *G. M. Crespi*, Holy Family; 391. *Guercino*, Mary Magdalene, 392. St Margaret of Cortona; 394. *Nic. Poussin*, Martyrdom of St Erasmus; *395. *Guido Reni*, St Matthew. St Matthew.

R. XIII. MARATTA, RIBERA, VAN DYCK, and others. *396. *Sassoferrato*, Madonna and Child; 1059. *Orazio Gentileschi*, Judith; *775. *Van Dyck*, St Francis Xavier; 1931. *P. F. Mola*, Vision of St Bruno; 405. *Pietro da Cortona*, Appearance of the Virgin to St Francis; 408. *Ribera* (or his pupil *Henry Somer*), Martyrdom of St Laurence; 410. *Pietro da Cortona*, David and a lion; 415. *Pompeo Batoni*, Appearance of the Virgin to St John Nepomuc.

R. XIV. FLEMISH, DUTCH, GERMAN, FRENCH, and ITALIAN PAINTERS (17-18C). *Daniel Seghers*, 416, 418. Small religious pictures with flower borders; 421. *Rosa da Tivoli*, Hunter; 419. *Matthias Stomer*, Orpheus, Pluto, and Proserpina; 784. *Rubens*, Triumph of Mars, mainly executed by his pupils; 432-439. *Donato Creti*, Astronomical Observations; 815. *Nic. Poussin*, Gideon; 423. *Van Bloeman*, Horses.

R. XV. PORTRAITS. *445. *Titian*, Doge Niccolò Marcello; 446. *Bernardino Conti*, Fr. Sforza, 447. *P. Meert*, Philosopher; 448. *Sir Thomas Lawrence*, George IV of England; 451. *David Teniers the Younger*, Old man; 1210. *Muziano*, Idealized portrait of Gregory XII, who abdicated in 1415; 455. *Pompeo Batoni*, Pius VI; 457. *Scipione Pulzone*, Card. Guglielmo Sirleto; 458. *G. M. Crespi*, Benedict XIV, painted while still a cardinal (papal robes added afterwards); *460. *Carlo Maratta*, Clement IX.—The Vestibule contains modern works.

III GALLERY OF TAPESTRIES, RAPHAEL ROOMS AND LOGGIA, BORGIA ROOMS AND GALLERY OF MODERN RELIGIOUS ART, SISTINE CHAPEL, MUSEUM OF CHRISTIAN ART, SISTINE HALL AND LIBRARY, MUSEUM OF PAGAN ANTIQUITIES

From the Quattro Cancelli the Scala Simonetti leads up two flights of stairs to the landing outside the Room of the Biga. Here is the beginning of Bramante's long West Gallery with the Gallery of the Candelabra, the Gallery of Tapestries, and the Gallery of Maps.

The **Gallery of the Candelabra** (80 m long) is named after the pairs of marble candelabra, of the Roman Imperial period, placed on either side of the arches which divide it into six sections. The ceiling has frescoes (restored in 1974) by *D. Torti* and *L. Seitz* illustrating events in the pontificate of Leo XIII. In the pavement are inserted marbles from the Emporia, the warehouses of ancient Rome.

SECTION I. 20. Sarcophagus of a child, Roman, 3C A.D.; 32, 39. Pair of candelabra from Otricoli, with reliefs of Bacchic rites and of Apollo and Marsyas, Roman, 2C B.C.—SECT II. 10. Pan extracting a thorn from a satyr's foot, copy of a 2C Hellenistic original; 22. Diana of the Ephesians, 3C A.D.; 28. Sarcophagus with the legend of Orestes, 2C A.D.; 44, 51. Candelabra of the 2C A.D. from a Roman villa later used in the churches of Sant'Agnese fuori le Mura and Santa Costanza; 72. Sarcophagus with the story of Protesilaos and Laodamia; 83. Ganymede carried off by the eagle, after a bronze original by Leochares.

SECT III. On the walls, Fragments of frescoes from a Roman villa at Tor Marancia (near the Catacombs of Domitilla), with flying figures, 2C A.D.; 12. Mosaic of fish, fruit, etc.; 18. Apollo from an archaic Greek type; 40. Satyr with young Dionysos on his shoulders (1C A.D.).

SECT. IV. 19. Statuette of Maritime Victory, from a Hellenistic original (the head is from another figure); 20. Portrait statue of a woman (with substituted head), 1C A.D.; *30. Sarcophagus with Dionysos and Ariadne and Dionysiac scenes, 2C A.D.; *38. Fisherman, a realistic work of the school of Pergamon (3C B.C.); 48. Upper part of a statue of Cronos (Saturn), copy of a 4C original; *49. Tyche (Fortune) of Antioch, from a bronze by Eutychides, a pupil of Lysippos; *66. Boy with goose, from a bronze by Boethus of Chalcedon, 3C B.C.; *85. Sarcophagus with the slaughter of the Niobids, an admirable work of the 2C A.D.; 93. Boy of the Julio-Claudian family, 1C A.D.

SECT. V. *5. Girl running in a race during a Peloponnesian religious festival, Roman copy of a Greek bronze original of the 5C B.C.; 25. Young satyr playing the flute.—SECT. VI. 1. Artemis, from a Praxitelean original; the head (which does not belong) is a copy of a 5C bronze; 5. Statuette of a woman wearing a cloak, copy of a Hellenistic original of the 4C or 3C B.C.; 8. Sarcophagus with Diana and Endymion; 20. Youth wearing the Phrygian cap, in the manner of Praxiteles; 24. Niobid, copy of a Hellenistic original of the 4C or 3C B.C.; *32. Fighting Persian, statuette after an original bronze belonging to the series of statues given by Attalos I of Pergamon to the Athenians which were placed on the Acropolis in Athens; 35. Sarcophagus with the rape of the daughters of Leukippos.

The **Gallery of Tapestries** is divided into three rooms, and contains the so-called 'New School' series of tapestries executed after Raphael's death from cartoons by his pupils, some of which were copied from drawings he had left. Also displayed here are Roman and Flemish tapestries. ROOM 1. Raphael 'New School' tapestries, woven in Brussels in the 16C: *149. Adoration of the Shepherds; *151. Adoration of the Magi; 148. Presentation at the temple.—209, 210, 211. Tapestries illustrating the life of Urban VIII, manufactured in Rome in the 17C.—ROOM 2. Raphael 'New School' tapestries: *152. Resurrection of Christ; 156-154. (156 in restoration in 1978). Massacre of the Innocents (from a cartoon attrib. to *Tomaso Vincidor*); 146. Christ appearing to Mary Magdalene; 147. Supper at Emmaus.—215, 213, and 212. Further tapestries illustrating the life of Urban VIII, manufactured in Rome in the 17C.—ROOM 3. 79. Death of Julius Cæsar, Flemish (1594).

The **Gallery of Maps** (*Galleria delle Carte Geografiche*) was decorated in the time of Gregory XIII, the reformer of the calendar. On the walls are maps and plans painted in 1580-83 by the Dominican cosmographer, architect, and painter, *Ignazio Danti* of Perugia. They represent ancient and modern Italy; various regions of Italy and the neighbouring islands; and the papal territory of Avignon. There are also several town plans and views of seaports, including one (on the end wall) of *Venice.—The ceiling was decorated with stuccoes and frescoes by a group of painters under the direction of *Girolamo Muziano*. Along the walls are herms of Socrates, Plato, and others.

Beyond the Gallery of Maps is the **Gallery of Pius V** in which are more tapestries of the late 15C: 33. Scenes of the Passion; *34. The Creed. On the r., 157. Religion, Grace, and Charity, woven in 1525 in Brussels; 143. Coronation of the Virgin, woven in Brussels in the 16C from a cartoon of the 'New School' of Raphael. To the right is the **Ladies' Audience Room** (*Sala delle Dame;* closed indefinitely), added by Paul V (1605-21). This room was formerly used as a private audience chamber for ladies, who were not admitted into the pontifical apartments. The frescoes, by *Guido Reni,* represent the Transfiguration, Ascension, and Pentecost.—At the end of the gallery is the *Chapel of St Pius V,* one of three superimposed; to the left is the SOBIESKI ROOM, where the floor is inlaid with mosaics from Ostia. The room is named from a painting by *J. Matejko,* Relief of Vienna by John Sobieski on 12 Sept 1683.

Beyond is the **Hall of the Immaculate Conception,** a room decorated with frescoes by *Fr. Podesti* which illustrate the definition and proclamation of the dogma of the Immaculate Conception pronounced by Pius IX on 8 Dec 1854. On the ceiling are the arms of Pius IX; the floor has 2C mosaics from Ostia. In the centre is a wooden model of the dome of St Peter's, made from the design by Michelangelo (1558-61).—Beyond are the Raphael Rooms.

## Stanze and Loggia of Raphael

The series of rooms was built by Nicholas V, and the walls were originally painted by Andrea del Castagno, Piero della Francesca, and Bened. Bonfigli. Julius II employed a group of great artists to continue the decoration, including Luca Signorelli, Perugino, Sodoma, Bramantino, Bald. Peruzzi, Lor. Lotto, and the Flemish painter Jan Ruysch. Bramante, the Urbinese architect of St Peter's, recommended his fellow-citizen, Raffaelo Sanzio, and the Pope forthwith sent for him, and set him to a trial work immediately on his arrival in Rome in 1508. The result proved so satisfactory that Julius dismissed all the other painters, ordered their works to be destroyed, and commissioned Raphael to decorate the whole of this part of the Vatican. The Stanze are the painter's master-work; they are a measure of his genius and of the development which took place in his art during the years between his coming and his early death in 1520.

When Raphael arrived, the court of Julius II was an intellectual centre of the first rank; the College of Cardinals and the Curia included among their members many celebrated savants, humanists, and men of letters; and a crowd of artists, chief among whom were Bramante and Michelangelo, added lustre to the city. In this highly cultured environment Raphael, who had great powers of assimilation, acquired an entirely new manner of painting. But though he sought guidance in the composition and treatment of these frescoes, especially the Disputa and the School of Athens, he was great and original enough to transform and vivify the ideas of his advisers in accordance with his own genius, which dominates the conceptions in every case.—The chronological order of the paintings is as follows: the Astronomy, Apollo, Adam and Eve, and Judgment of Solomon, in the Stanza della Segnatura (II), which were probably his trial works; next come the other frescoes in this room, then successively, the Stanza d'Eliodoro (III), Stanza dell'Incendio (I), and Stanza di Costantino (IV). The description below follows the topographical order of the rooms. The frescoes have recently been well restored.

I. **Stanza dell'Incendio.** On the ceiling is the Glorification of the Holy Trinity by *Perugino,* Raphael's master (the only work not destroyed when Raphael took over the decoration of the Stanze, comp. above). The walls were painted in 1517 by Raphael's pupils (*Giulio Romano, Francesco Penni,* and perhaps *Perin del Vaga*) from his own designs. The subjects chosen were events of the times of Leo III (795-816) and Leo IV (847-55), most of which, however, allude to episodes in the history of Leo X.

Facing the window is the *INCENDIO DI BORGO, illustrating the fire that broke out in Rome in 847, and was miraculously extinguished when Leo IV made the sign of the Cross from the loggia of St Peter's.

It was probably intended as an allusion to the achievement of Leo X in restoring peace to Italy. In the background the flames are seen threatening the old church of St Peter, the façade of which is shown; on the right, the Pope is seen issuing from the Vatican. In the foregound surges a distracted supplicating crowd, part paralysed by fear and part running frantically with water to put out the fire. On the left a classic reminiscence is introduced in the form of the Burning of Troy, with naked figures scaling the walls and Aeneas carrying his father Anchises on his back, followed by his wife Creusa and their son Ascanius.

On the right wall is the CORONATION OF CHARLEMAGNE BY LEO III in 800, an obvious reference to the meeting of Leo X and Francis I at Bologna in 1516 (comp. p. 76), for Leo and Charlemagne have the features of the later pope and king.—On the left wall the subject is the VICTORY OF LEO IV OVER THE SARACENS AT OSTIA (849), in allusion to the Crusade against the Turks proclaimed by Leo X, who is again represented in the figure of Leo IV, the two cardinals behind him being portraits of Cardinal Bibbiena and Giulio de' Medici.—On the window wall (being restored in 1978) is the *Oath of Leo III*, with which that pope cleared himself in St Peter's, on 23 Dec 800, of charges that had been brought against him. The allusion is to the Lateran Council held by Leo X.

The monochrome figures below the paintings represent Godfrey de Bouillon, Ethelwulf of England (called Astolfo), Charlemagne, Lothair I and Ferdinand of Castile.

II. **Stanza della Segnatura,** where the pope signed bulls and briefs. It was painted entirely by *Raphael* (1508-11), except the small central octagon in the ceiling, which is by *Bramantino*. On the ceiling, above the Disputa, Theology (Divinarum rerum notitia); above the Parnassus, Poetry (Numine afflatus); above the School of Athens, Philosophy (Causarum cognitio); and above the window wall Justice (Jus suum unicuique tribuit). In the pendentives, Adam and Eve, reminiscent of works by Masaccio and Michelangelo; Apollo and Marsyas, recalling the manner of Leonardo; Astronomy, a gracious figure in the Umbrian-Florentine style; and the Judgment of Solomon, in part derived from drawings by Leonardo.—The floor, in opus alexandrinum, shows the arms of Nicholas V and Leo X, and the name of Julius II.

On the right of the entrance is the famous *DISPUTA or DISPUTATION ON THE HOLY SACRAMENT*, representing a discussion on the Eucharist but essentially intended as a Glorification of Catholicism. Given an extremely difficult subject, the art of the painter has made the relatively limited space occupied by the composition, which is divided into two zones, appear far larger than it is. In the celestial portion Christ appears between the Virgin and St John the Baptist; above is God the Father surrounded by angels; beneath, the Holy Dove between the four angels holding the book of the Gospels; on the left are St Peter, Adam, St John the Evangelist, David, St Lawrence, and Jeremiah (?); on the right, St Paul, Abraham, St James, Moses, St Stephen and Judas Maccabæus. In the middle of the terrestrial portion stands an altar on which is a monstrance with the Host; on the right are SS. Augustine and Ambrose, on the left SS. Gregory and Jerome; around, an assembly of doctors, popes, cardinals, dignitaries, and the faithful. Certain figures are pointed out as portraits of Duns Scotus, SS. Dominic, Francis, Thomas Aquinas, and Nicholas of Bari; the man pointing upward with his right hand is said to be Pietro Lombardo; on the right is seen the head of Dante crowned with laurel, and, beyond him (in a black hat), Savonarola; on the extreme left is Fra Angelico in the black Dominican habit and, in the foreground, Bramante.

Beneath the picture are three monochrome paintings by *Perin del Vaga:* Pagan Sacrifice, St Augustine and the child on the seashore, and the Cumaean Sibyl showing the Virgin to Augustus.

On the wall nearest the Courtyard of the Belvedere is the PARNASSUS. On a hill from which a stream gushes out Apollo is playing the violin in the shade of laurels. Around him are grouped the nine Muses and the great poets: Calliope is seated on the left, near the heavenly musician, and behind her are Melpomene, Terpsichore, and Polyhymnia; on the right, also seated, is Erato, and behind her are Clio, Thalia, Euterpe, and Urania. In the group of poets on the left appears the noble figure of the

K

blind Homer, between Dante and Virgil; lower are Alcæus, Corinna, Petrarch, and Anacreon, with the voluptuous form of Sappho seated beside them. In the group on the right are Ariosto (?), Ovid, Tibullus, and Propertius, and, lower, Sannazaro, Horace, and Pindar, seated. The whole design shows a marvellous ease and clarity and a rare freshness of inspiration.

Below the picture are two monochrome subjects: on the left, Alexander placing Homer's poems in the tomb of Achilles (or, possibly, the discovery of a sarcophagus containing Greek and Latin MSS. on the Janiculum in 181 B.C.); on the right, Augustus preventing Virgil's friends from burning the Aeneid (or else the consuls causing Greek works to be burned as harmful to the Roman religion). Below these again is some very fine painted intarsia-work by Fra Giovanni da Verona.

On the wall facing the Disputa is the SCHOOL OF ATHENS, which represents the triumph of Philosophy, forming a pendant to the triumph of Theology opposite. The scene is a portico, at the sides of which are statues of Apollo and Minerva, with steps ascending to the façade of the palace of Science, a magnificent example of Renaissance design for which Raphael was indebted to Bramante. The magnificent vaulting, well depicted in light and shade, is clearly inspired by the Baths of Caracalla.

In this stately framing the greatest philosophers and scholars of all the ages are gathered round the two supreme masters, Plato and Aristotle. Plato (thought to be intended as a portrait of Leonardo da Vinci) points heavenward, thus symbolizing his system of speculative philosophy, while Aristotle's calm gesture indicates the vast field of nature as the realm of scientific research. The other philosophers are grouped about one or other of these two. At the top of the steps, on Plato's side, we recognize the bald head and characteristic profile of Socrates: Aeschines, Alcibiades (represented as a young warrior), Xenophon, and others are conversing near him; the beckoning figure next to Xenophon is evidently Chrysippus. At the foot of the steps on the left is Zeno, an old man with a beard, seen in profile; near him Epicurus, crowned with vine leaves, is reading a book; in the foreground Pythagoras is writing out his harmonic tables, with Averroes, in a turban, and Empedocles looking over. The young man sitting down is Federigo Gonzaga, who was included by order of Julius II; the handsome youth standing up is Francesco Maria della Rovere; beside him, his foot resting on a block of marble, is Anaxagoras or Xenocrates, or, according to some, Aristoxenus. The seated figure of Heracleitus, isolated in the centre foreground, was not part of the original composition; obviously inspired by Michelangelo's work in the Sistine chapel, it has also recently been suggested that it was intended as a portrait of him. On the right, around Aristotle, are the students of the exact sciences; at the foot of the steps is Ptolemy, with his back to the spectator, and, owing to a confusion with the Egyptian kings of the same name, wearing a crown. Opposite him is Zoroaster, holding a sphere, and near by, in the right-hand corner, Raphael has introduced portraits of himself and Sodoma. To the left is Archimedes or Euclid (with the features of Bramante), surrounded by his disciples and bending over a blackboard on which he is tracing figures with a compass. The solitary figure on the steps is Diogenes.

The monochromes beneath the picture are by *Perin del Vaga,* and represent Philosophy, Astrologers in conference, and the Siege of Syracuse with the Death of Archimedes.

On the fourth wall, above the window, are the three CARDINAL VIRTUES, Fortitude, Temperance, and Prudence. On the left of the window, Justinian publishing the Pandects, representing CIVIL LAW, and beneath, Solon haranguing the Athenians, by *Perin del Vaga*. On the right, Gregory IX (in the likeness of Julius II) handing the Decretals to a jurist (1227), to represent CANON LAW. The prelates around the Pope are portraits of Raphael's contemporaries; on the left, in front, is Giov. de' Medici, afterwards Leo X, then Cardinal Antonio Del Monte, Alessandro Farnese (Paul III), etc.

Beneath is Moses bringing the Israelites the Tables of Stone, by *Perin del Vaga*.

III. *Stanza d'Eliodoro, painted by *Raphael* in 1512-14, the subjects being nearly all chosen by Julius II. On the principal wall is the EXPULSION OF HELIODORUS FROM THE TEMPLE at Jerusalem, alluding to Julius II's success in freeing the States of the Church from foreign powers. The picture illustrates a story in the Apocrypha (Macc. II, 3), which tells how King Seleucus sent his treasurer Heliodorus to Jerusalem to seize the Temple treasure, and how the crime was avenged by a celestial messenger on a fiery steed assisted by two angels with whips. As pictured by Raphael, the incident takes place in the vestibule of the temple, which is seen at the back. On the right are Heliodorus and his men struggling with the divine emissaries, a group remarkable for vigour and movement; on the left are the widows and orphans who were to have received the money and naturally exhibit great interest in the proceedings. In the middle of this crowd appears the figure of Julius II, carried on the sedia gestatoria, the foremost of the bearers being the celebrated engraver Marcantonio Raimondi. In the centre of the composition, under the vault of the temple, the high priest Onias renders thanks to God before the Ark of the Covenant.

On the right is the MASS OF BOLSENA, a representation of a famous miracle which took place in 1263. A priest, who had doubts regarding the doctrine of Transubstantiation, saw blood issue from the Host at the moment of the sacrifice, and became convinced. (The stained corporal is preserved in the cathedral at Orvieto.) The allusion is to the vow made by Julius II when, on his first expedition against Bologna in 1506, he stopped at Orvieto to pay honour to the corporal. The scene is the interior of a church; the officiating priest, who appears stunned by the phenomenon, is shown under the arch of an exedra of wood; opposite him kneels Julius II, represented as assisting at the mass in the place of Urban IV, the contemporary pope; on the right are cardinals and guards, on the left the marvelling populace. Some admirable portraits are included. The warm colouring and, especially, the harmony of reds are new and surprising in Raphael's art, and may be ascribed to the influence of Seb. del Piombo, who had just revealed to Rome the glories of Venetian colouring.

On the next wall is LEO I REPULSING ATTILA, a subject originally selected by Julius II and taken up again at the instance of Leo X, considerable changes then being made in the design. The scene representing the banks of the Mincio, where the event took place, was replaced by the environs of Rome, and the figure of the Pope was brought from the back of the picture into the foreground in order to accentuate the allusion to the battle of Ravenna (11 Apr 1512), at which Leo X, then a cardinal, was present, and which resulted in the expulsion of the French from Italy. Attila, on a horse recalling that of the Marcus Aurelius statue at the Capitol, is struck with terror on seeing St Peter and St Paul descend, fully armed, from heaven; behind him is the camp of his affrighted Huns; and to the left the Pope, in the likeness of Leo X, advances on a white mule followed by two cardinals. Rome is seen in the distance.

On the fourth wall is the DELIVERANCE OF ST PETER, alluding to the captivity of Leo X after the battle of Ravenna. The picture is in three parts: in the middle, the interior of the prison is seen through a high window, with St Peter awaking as the Angel frees him from his chains; the left portion shows the guards outside the prison; and the right, St Peter escaping with the Angel. This fresco is much admired for its contrasting effects of light: the glow of the torch, the pale moonlight, and the golden radiance of the angel.

Beneath are caryatids and four herms. The ceiling paintings, by *Peruzzi*, represent God appearing to Noah, Jacob's dream, the Burning Bush, and Abraham's Sacrifice.

IV. **Sala di Constantino,** painted almost entirely in the time of Clement VII (1523-34), after Raphael's death, by *Giulio Romano* with the assistance of *Francesco Penni* and *Raff. del Colle.* On the wall facing the window is the VICTORY OF CONSTANTINE OVER MAXENTIUS near the Pons Milvius (p. 257), for which Raphael had made some sketches.

The composition is full of life and movement; in the middle Constantine is seen on horseback, in the thick of the fight, followed by the standards and crosses; on the right Maxentius is being carried away by the current of the river; in the sky appear triumphant angels. The reddish tint which suffuses the whole is characteristic of Giulio Romano. To the right of the picture are figures of St Urban, Justice, and Charity; to the left, St Sylvester, Faith, and Religion.

On the wall opposite the entrance: CONSTANTINE ADDRESSING HIS SOLDIERS AND THE VISION OF THE CROSS, by *Giulio Romano,* perhaps from Raphael's design; to the right of this, St Clement, Temperance, and Meekness; to the left, St Peter, the Church, and Eternity.—On the entrance wall: The BAPTISM OF CONSTANTINE by St Sylvester (a portrait of Clement VII), by *Fr. Penni,* and at the sides (r.) St Leo, Innocence, and Truth, and (l.) St Damasus, Prudence, and Peace.—On the window wall: CONSTANTINE'S DONATION OF ROME TO SYLVESTER, by *Raff. del Colle.* At the sides: (r.) Gregory VII (?) and Fortitude; (l.) St Sylvester and Courage. Below are other scenes from the life of Constantine. On the ceiling, the Triumph of Christianity, by *Tomaso Laureti.* In the floor is a 2C Roman mosaic with the Seasons.

From the Sala di Costantino, a door leads into the \*Loggia of **Raphael,** a long gallery of 13 bays, overlooking the Courtyard of St Damasus with a fine view of Rome beyond. Situated on the second floor, of the palace, it was begun by Bramante about 1513 and completed after Bramante's death by Raphael and his pupils. The vault of each bay has four little paintings, so that there are 52 in all. The grotteschi of the borders are considered to have been inspired by those in the Domus Aurea of Nero, which were discovered in 15C and known to Raphael. The designs were carried out by *Giulio Romano, Giov. da Udine, Fr. Penni, Perin del Vaga, Polidoro da Caravaggio,* and others. Controversial restoration work is being carried out on the paintings in 1978.

The subjects of the paintings in the vaults are (beginning at the other end of the Loggia): I. Separaration of light from darkness; Separation of land and water; Creation of sun and moon; Creation of the animals.—II. Creation of Eve; the Fall;

Expulsion from Paradise; Adam and Eve labouring.—III. Building the Ark; the Deluge; Coming out of the Ark; Noah's Sacrifice.—IV. Abraham and Melchisedek; God's covenant with Abraham; Abraham and the three angels; Flight of Lot.—V. God appearing to Isaac; Abimelech spying upon Isaac and Rebecca; Isaac blessing Jacob; Jacob and Esau.—VI. Jacob's dream; Jacob and Rachel at the well; Jacob reproaching Laban; Jacob's journey.—VII. Joseph telling his dream to his brethren; Joseph sold by his brethren; Joseph and Potiphar's wife; Joseph interpreting Pharaoh's dream.—VIII. Moses in the bulrushes; the Burning Bush; Pharaoh drowned in the Red Sea; Moses striking the rock.—IX. Moses receiving the Tables of the Law; Worship of the Golden Calf; Moses and the pillar of fire; Moses showing the Tables of the Law to the people.— X. Crossing of Jordan; Fall of Jericho; Joshua making the sun stand still; Joshua and Eleazar dividing Palestine among the twelve tribes.—XI. Samuel anointing David; David and Goliath; Triumph of David; David and Bathsheba.—XII. Crowning of Solomon; Judgment of Solomon; Queen of Sheba; Building of the Temple.—XIII. Nativity; the Magi; Baptism of Christ; Last Supper.

A door off the loggia leads into the **Room of the Chiaroscuri** or the *Room of the Grooms (Sala dei Palafrenieri)*. This room has a magnificent carved and gilded \*Ceiling, with the Medici arms, but the frescoes by Raphael were obliterated under Pius IV, and the existing monochrome frescoes were added under Gregory XIII.—The adjoining **Chapel of Nicholas V** has \*Frescoes by *Fra Angelico,* painted between 1448 and 1450. These represent scenes from the lives of the deacon saints Stephen (upper section) and Laurence (lower section); especially noteworthy is the painting of St Stephen preaching. On the ceiling are the four Evangelists and on the pilasters the Doctors of the Church.

From the Room of the Chiaroscuri, a door leads back to the Stanza d'Eliodoro; from here it is necessary to return to the first Raphael Room, off which is the **Chapel of Urban VIII,** richly decorated with frescoes and stuccoes by *Pietro da Cortona.*

Outside the chapel a stairway leads down (r.) to the Borgia Rooms and the new Museum of Modern Religious Art. It is possible at this point to proceed direct (l.) to the Sistine chapel instead of approaching it through the Borgia Rooms and the Museum of Modern Religious Art. However the first six frescoed Borgia Rooms should not be missed even if it is not intended to continue through the 50 subsequent galleries of the Museum of Modern Art.

## The Borgia Rooms and Gallery of Modern Religious Art

The **Borgia Rooms** (*Appartamento Borgia*) are named after Alexander VI (Borgia; 1492-1503), who adapted for his personal use a suite in the palace of Nicholas V and had it decorated by Pinturicchio. There are six rooms in the suite. The first two are under a quadrilateral tower—the Borgia Tower—built by Alexander VI; the last was originally part of the house that preceded the palace of Nicholas V.

After the death of Alexander VI, the Borgia Rooms continued to be occupied as papal apartments until Julius II abandoned them in 1507. Leo XIII had them restored by Lod. Seitz in 1889-97 and opened them to the public. The first two rooms (under the Borgia Tower) are immediately beneath the Hall of the Immaculate Conception; the other rooms are beneath the Raphael Rooms. The \*Frescoes were executed by *Pinturicchio* and his school in 1492-95.

R. I, OF THE SIBYLS, is square and has 12 lunettes each with a sibyl accompanied by a prophet. The juxtaposition of sibyls and prophets illustrates an ancient belief that the sibyls foretold the coming of the Messiah to the heathen (comp. p. 70; legend of Santa Maria in Aracoeli). Here Caesar Borgia was imprisoned by Julius

II in 1503, in the very room where he had caused his cousin Alfonso of Aragon to be murdered in 1500.—R. II (left) contains copies designed by *Matisse*.

R. III, OF THE CREED, is named after the scrolls on which are written the sentences of the Creed, held by the twelve Apostles depicted in the lunettes. Each Apostle is accompanied by a prophet holding an appropriate inscription. These frescoes are attributed to *Pier Matteo d' Amelia,* a successor of Pinturicchio.

R. IV, OF THE LIBERAL ARTS, symbolises the seven liberal arts: the *Trivium* (grammar, dialectic, rhetoric) and the *Quadrivium* (geometry, arithmetic, astronomy, music) which were the basis of medieval learning. The paintings are attributed to *Ant. da Viterbo,* a pupil of Pinturicchio. The Arch of Justice, in the middle, is named after its subject: the treatment is of the 16C. The ceiling is decorated with squares and grotesques alternating with the Borgia bull. The fine chimney-piece is by or after Sansovino. In this room was found the hidden treasure of Alexander VI.

R. V, OF THE SAINTS. The walls and the vault are covered with *Frescoes by *Pinturicchio,* regarded as his greatest achievement. The room is divided by an arch into two cross-vaulted areas forming six lunettes. On the ceiling, Legend of Isis; Osiris and the bull Apis (in reference to the Borgia arms; comp. above), with reliefs in gilded stucco. Above the door, Madonna and Child with saints (medallion), not portraying Giulia Farnese. Entrance wall, the Visitation; SS. Paul the Hermit and Anthony Abbot in the desert (r.); End wall, *Disputation between St Catherine of Alexandria and the emperor Maximian; the saint's head has been wrongly thought to be a portrait of Lucrezia Borgia or Giulia Farnese; Pinturicchio's self-portrait is seen behind the throne; in the background is the Arch of Constantine. Window wall, Martyrdom of St Sebastian, with a view of the Colosseum. On the exit wall, Susanna and the Elders; Legend of St Barbara.

R. VI, OF THE MYSTERIES OF THE FAITH. The frescoes, partly by *Pinturicchio,* represent the Annunciation, Nativity, Adoration of the Magi, *Resurrection (the kneeling pontiff is Alexander VI), Ascension, Pentecost, and Assumption of the Virgin. The last fresco includes a portrait of the donor, perhaps Francesco Borgia. In the ceiling are stuccoes and paintings of prophets.

R. VII, OF THE POPES. The frescoes and stucco ornamentation of the splendid vaulted ceiling are by *Perin del Vaga* and *Giov. da Udine,* who carried out the work at the order of Leo X (1513-21). The room is named after portraits of the popes which have disappeared.

The **Gallery of Modern Religious Art** was arranged in 1973 in the Borgia Apartments, and in 50 or so rooms (previously closed to the public), lavishly renovated. It is an exhibition of works presented to the Pope by invited artists from all over the world. They include: Pietro Annigoni, Francis Bacon, Giac. Balla, Bernard Buffet, Carlo Carrà, Marc Chagall, Salvador Dali, Giorgio De Chirico, Fil. de Pisis, Max Ernst, Paul Gauguin, Renato Guttuso, Wassily Kandinsky, Paul Klee, Oskar Kokoschka, Fernand Leger, Carlo Levi, Giac. Manzù, Marino Marini, Arturo Martini, Henry Matisse, Henry Moore, Giorgio Morandi, Edvard Munch, Ben Nicholson, José Clemente Orozco, Pablo Picasso, Auguste Rodin, Georges Rouault, David Alfaro Siqueiros, Mario Sironi, Ardengo Soffici, Graham Sutherland, Maurice Utrillo, Maurice de Vlaminck, and numerous others. The works are arranged in no particular order, but they are fully labelled, and a hand list (150 l.) is available at the door.

Stairs lead up from the last gallery to the Sistine Chapel.

# *The Sistine Chapel

The Sistine Chapel is entered in the w. wall, to the r. of the altar.

The chapel was built for Sixtus IV by *Giov. de' Dolci* in 1473-81. It is a rectangle 41 m long and 13 m wide, lit on either side by six windows, placed rather high up. It is the official private chapel of the popes and in it are usually held the conclaves for the election of the popes. The frescoes for which the chapel is famous are best seen by morning light. The celebrated tapestries of Raphael, now in the Vatican Picture Gallery, were first exhibited here in 1519.

A graceful marble screen by *Mino da Fiesole, Giov. Dalmata,* and *And. Bregno* divides the chapel into two unequal parts, a larger choir and a small nave. The same artists were responsible for the cantoria. The 15C mosaic pavement is a fine example of opus alexandrinum.

The \*Frescoes (1481-83) on the long walls depict parallel events in the lives of Moses (l.) and of Christ (r.). There are six (originally seven) on either side; the two nearest the altar were eliminated to make room for Michelangelo's Last Judgment.

Left (South) Wall, beginning from the altar: *Pinturicchio,* Moses and Zipporah his wife in Egypt and the Circumcision of their son; *Botticelli,* \*The Burning Bush, with Moses slaying the Egyptian and driving the Midianites from the well; *School of Ghirlandaio,* Passage of the Red Sea; *Cosimo Rosselli,* Moses on Mount Sinai and the Worship of the Golden Calf; *Botticelli,* \*Punishment of Korah, Dathan, and Abiram (in the background are the Arch of Constantine and the Septizonium); *Luca Signorelli* and *Bart. della Gatta,* Moses giving his rod to Joshua and Mourning for the death of Moses.—Right (North) Wall, beginning from the altar: *Perugino* (?) and *Pinturicchio,* Baptism of Christ; *Botticelli,* Cleansing of the Leper and the Temptation in the Wilderness (in the background, the hospital of Santo Spirito); *Dom. Ghirlandaio,* \*Calling of Peter and Andrew; *Cosimo Rosselli* and *Piero di Cosimo,* Sermon on the Mount and Healing the Leper; *Perugino,* \*Christ giving the keys to St Peter; *Cosimo Rosselli,* Last Supper.—On the East Wall are two frescoes overpainted at the end of the 16C by Arrigo Fiammingo and Matteo da Lecce; they were *Dom. Ghirlandaio,* Resurrection, and *Salviati,* St Michael defending the body of Moses.—In the niches between the windows are 28 portraits of the first popes, by Fra Diamante, Dom. Ghirlandaio, Botticelli, and Cosimo Rosselli.

**Ceiling Frescoes.** The barrel-vaulted ceiling is entirely covered by the famous \*\*FRESCOES OF MICHELANGELO, which were painted between 1508 and 1512. They depict a series of episodes from Genesis, beginning with the creation of the world and ending with events in the life of Noah. The decoration of the ceiling was ordered by Julius II, who was a nephew of Sixtus IV, and, according to Biagetti, appears, in some details, to have been executed by the master's assistants.

The general design is architectural, the figures and groups, with an effect of high relief and rich yet sober colour, being set among the columns, arches, and mouldings in warm grisaille. Along the sides and at the ends are large figures of prophets and sibyls, recalling a similar association in the Borgia Room of the Sibyls. Nearest the altar, in front of the Last Judgment, is Jonah issuing from the whale. Michelangelo's marvellous skill in foreshortening is well illustrated by the manner in which Jonah's legs appear to project forward, although, because of the curve of the vault, they are in reality the part farthest from the spectator.—Five alternating prophets and sibyls are along the left wall and a similar series along the right wall. Left Wall, from the altar end. Jeremiah; the Persian Sibyl; Ezekiel, with a scroll; the Enythnaean Sibyl; Joel. Right Wall, from the altar end. The Libyan Sibyl; Daniel, writing; the Cumaean Sibyl; Isaiah, in deep meditation; the Delphic Sibyl.—At the E. end is Zechariah.

In the lunettes over the windows are figures representing the forerunners of Christ, expectant of His appearance. In the spaces on either side of the prophet-sibyl sequence are: over the altar, the Brazen Serpent (r.) and Ahasuerus, Esther, and Haman (l.); at the other end, Judith and Holofernes (r.) and David and Goliath (l.)—The central part of the ceiling is divided into nine rectangles, alternately large and small, illustrating scenes from the Old Testament, and bordered with arcades on which are nude figures. From the altar end: Separation of light from darkness; Creation of the sun, moon, and planets; Separation of land and sea and Creation of fishes and birds; *Creation of Adam; Creation of Eve; Fall of man and the expulsion from Paradise; Noah's sacrifice; the Flood; Drunkeness of Noah.

More than twenty years later, in 1534-41, Michelangelo painted his great fresco of the *LAST JUDGMENT on the altar wall. This involved the walling-up of two windows and the destruction of two frescoes (both by Perugino) on the side walls. The size of the great altarpiece is 20 m by 10 m. The conception is extraordinarily fine and, despite the deterioration of the surface, which has been blackened by incense and stained with damp, the effect is undeniably impressive. In the upper centre stands a beardless Christ, who appears as a stern and threatening judge. Near him are the Madonna, St John the Baptist, and St Andrew with his back turned. On the other side are St Peter with the keys, and St Paul. At Christ's feet are St Laurence and St Bartholomew bearing his flayed skin; the caricature of a face seen in the folds of the skin is held to be a portrait of Michelangelo. Above the figure of Christ are two groups of angels bearing the instruments of the Passion. Beneath, in the central zone, on the left, are the elect ascending to heaven with the help of angels; in the centre is a group of angels with trumpets; on the right the damned are being hauled into hell and their resistance is being overcome by other angels. Especially noteworthy is the figure of the Soul in Despair (Disperato) looking down into the abyss. In the lowest zone, on the left, is represented the Resurrection of the Body; in the middle is a cave full of devils; on the right is the entrance to hell, with the boat of Charon (as in Dante's description) and Minos, the guide to the infernal regions. Minos has the features of Biagio da Cesena (with ass's ears); he was Master of Ceremonies to Paul III and he had objected to the nudity of the figures. On the same ground Pius IV at one time intended to destroy the fresco but he contented hinself with ordering Daniele da Volterra to paint garments on some of the figures. This earned for the artist the nickname of Il Braghettone (the 'breeches maker').

Through the main door of the Sistine Chapel the sumptuous **Sala Regia** (no adm.) can usually be seen. It was begun by Ant. da Sangallo the Younger in 1540, but not completed until 1573, and originally intended for the reception of ambassadors. The rich stucco decorations of the ceiling are by *Perin del Vaga;* those of the walls by *Dan. da Volterra.* The large frescoes are by *Vasari, Salviati,* and the *Zuccari.* They depict Gregory VII releasing the emperor Henry IV from excommunication; Charles V at the battle of Tunis; Return of Gregory XI from Avignon; Reconciliation of Alexander III and Barbarossa; Battle of Lépanto; Massacre of St Bartholomew. Here the first official meeting since the Reformation took place between the Pope and the Abp. of Canterbury in 1966.—Adjoining is the vast AULA DELLE BENEDIZIONI, situated above the portico of St Peter's. From the central window of this hall the Pope blesses 'Urbi et Orbi'.

Visitors not wishing to continue the tour of the museums are able to leave the chapel by the *Scala Regia* (when open), an imposing staircase built by Bernini which descends past a statue of Constantine (comp. 267) to the portico of St Peter's. A new staircase is to be opened which will descend from the sacristy direct to the portico of St Peter's.

A special permit must be obtained from the Governor of the Vatican City to visit the Sala Regia (when closed), the Aula delle Benedizioni, the **Sala Ducale** of Bernini, and the **Cappella Paolina**, by *Ant. da Sangallo the Younger*. The Sala Ducale is decorated with landscapes by *Paul Brill*, and the Cappella Paolina with two *Frescoes by *Michelangelo* (Conversion of St Paul and Crucifixion of St Peter), painted in 1542-45 and 1546-50.

The Chapel is left by a small door in the N. wall of the nave, which leads to the Museum of Christian Art.

## Museum of Christian Art

In order to view the rooms of this museum in the correct order, it is necessary to proceed to Room I, through the Chapel of Pius V (l.) and two rooms beyond the Room of the Aldobrandini Marriage which is passed on the left.

The Museum (*Museo Sacro*) was founded by Benedict XIV in 1756 and was enlarged in the 19C, partly by the acquisitions of Pius IX but chiefly by the yields of excavations carried out in the catacombs by De Rossi and his successors. In 1934 more rooms were added, and the museum was rearranged to illustrate the historic development of the Christian minor arts.

ROOM I. Early Christian Antiquities from the Catacombs of St Calixtus, Domitilla, St Sebastian, and other cemeteries. Wall case I. Collection of glass, some of the finer specimens gilded.—Table 1. Monogram of Christ; Christian, gnostic, and pagan objects in bone, ivory, and glass.—Case II. Engraved 4C Christian glass from Ostia; multicoloured glasses known as *millefiori* (2-3C).—Table 2. Christian and pagan lamps (1-4C), some with symbolic representations, such as the Good Shepherd, the fish, the peacock, the monogram of Christ.—Case III. Flagon (7-8C) from a church of St Laurence; Situla with representation of Christ and the Apostles (5C). Inlaid enamel *Reliquary (9C), from the church of the Santi Quattro Coronati; 3C pyx from Africa. Bronze lamps (3-5C).—Table 3, Objects in gold and bronze: Byzantine weights, amulets, and crosses.—Table 4. Objects from the East in soap-stone, semi-precious stones, and metal; 11-12C, Italian triptych; Byzantine mosaic with representation of St Theodore (12C); 12C Byzantine wax cast.—Case IV. 11-13C Church embroideries.—Table 5. Christian and pagan lamps.—Case V. Pottery.—Table 6. Earthenware lamps.

ROOM II, OF THE PAPYRI, was originally intended for the reception of the 6-9C papyri from Ravenna. It dates from 1774, the last year of Clement XIV, and has frescoes by *Raff. Mengs* and his assistant *Christopher Unterberger*. It contains two cases of gilt-engraved glass of the 3-5C from Roman catacombs.

ROOM III, OF THE ADDRESSES (*degli Indirizzi*), was so called because in the time of Pius XI, the address or congratulatory documents sent to Leo XIII and Pius X were kept here. In the cases is a splendid collection of church furniture in metal, ivory, enamel, majolica, etc. Case 1. Italian silver sacramental objects, mainly 18C.—Case 2. 18-20C missals.—Case 3. 14-16C crucifixes in silver and gold.— Case 4. 18C Roman and Neapolitan silver vessels; Gold roses of the type blessed by the pope in Lent and presented to Catholic sovereigns (originally the traditional papal gift to the prefects of Rome).—Case 5. Papal rings, with imitation stones (14-16C).—Case 7 and 8. Limoges and other enamels.—Case 9. Early crucifixes.— Cases 10-14. Carved ivories. Case 12. Diptychs and triptychs (9-15C): *Ramboyna Diptych (c. 900), Christian scenes with representation of the Roman wolf in the bottom of the left-hand panel; *Five-pannelled wooden tablet with Christ blessing, part of the cover of the New Testament; the other half is in the Victoria and Albert Museum, London; *Book Cover with the Nativity, from the Convent of St Gall, Switzerland. On exit wall, fragment of mosaic of the head of an Apostle from the Lateran Triclinium (c. 800); fresco of Charlemagne from the Pincio.—In the table case, glass and precious stone objects.—Cases 16-19. Late 16C silverwork from Germany, Rome, France, and Genoa (early 17C). In the table case, seals, cameos, and crosses.

The **Room of the Aldobrandini Marriage** (r.) was built by Paul V in 1611 and restored by Pius VII in 1817. In 1838 Gregory XVI placed the wall-painting here that gives the room its name. The ceiling frescoes are by *Guido Reni*. In the pavement is a 2C geometric mosaic; in the centre, within an octagon, is Achilles dragging the body of Hector. On the upper part of the walls are *Frescoes of the 1C B.C., with scenes from the Odyssey, found on the Esquiline in 1848. Lower down are paintings of famous women of antiquity, five of them from Tor Marancia (p. 287), and paintings of children, from Ostia (1C A.D.).

On the centre wall is the *ALDOBRANDINI MARRIAGE (*Nozze Aldobrandine*), a masterpiece of Augustan art inspired by a Greek model of the 4C or 3C B.C., found on the Esquiline in 1605 and kept in one of the garden pavilions of the Villa Aldobrandini (p. 188) until its removal to this room. The painting, of a marriage scene, combines realism and symbolism.

At the end of the corridor is the **Chapel of St Pius V**, decorated by *Giac. Zucchi* after the designs of *Vasari*. The portrait of St Pius V is on the right in the apse. In the wall case is part of the *Treasure of the Sancta Sanctorum,** the pope's private chapel in the old Lateran Palace. The relics were contained in precious reliquaries inside a case made of cypress wood at the command of Leo III (795-816). Here can be seen objects from 9C-12C, including a large enamelled *Cross presented by St Paschal I (817-24), containing five pieces of the True Cross; large Greek Cross of gold filigree work containing a small piece of the True Cross, decorated with precious stones and still partly covered with the balsams with which it was anointed every year by the Pope.

From the first room of the Museum of Christian Art there is access to the first of the exhibition rooms of the Vatican Library.

## The Vatican Library

The **Vatican Library** (*Biblioteca Apostolica Vaticana*) was founded by Nicholas V with a nucleus of some 350 volumes, which he increased to 1200. Sixtus IV brought the total to 3650. The Library suffered loss in the sack of 1527, but soon afterwards resumed its growth, and the problem of accommodation became increasingly acute. Before the end of the 16C Sixtus V commissioned Dom. Fontana to build the great Sistine Hall. Later popes adapted numerous rooms in Bramante's W. corridor to house the ever-increasing gifts, bequests, and purchases. Among the notable acquisitions are the Biblioteca Palatina of Heidelberg (1623), the Biblioteca Urbinas (1657), founded by Federico, duke of Urbino, Queen Christina of Sweden's library (1690), the Biblioteca Ottoboniana bought in 1748 (formerly the property of Alexander VIII Ottoboni), the Jesuit Library (1922), the Biblioteca Chigiana (1923), and the Biblioteca Ferraioli (1929). There are now about 60,000 MSS., 7000 incunabula, and 1,000,000 other printed books. Leo XIII added a reference library; Pius X reorganized the manuscripts and provided a room for their study; and Pius XI carried out further reorganization. A disastrous collapse in December 1931 of part of the ceiling of the Sistine Hall was made good two years later. The Library may be visited by students, by introduction, on week-days between 8 and 13.30. The *Vatican Archives* are available on week-days 8-13.30 to students who have obtained a permit from the Prefecture.

The exhibition rooms of the Library are the Museum of Pagan Antiquities, the Clementine Gallery, the Alexandrine Room, the Pauline Rooms, the Sistine Hall, the Sistine Rooms, and the Gallery of Urban VIII. All the rooms, except the Sistine

Hall, are in Bramante's w. corridor. The literary contents are not normally visible, as they are kept in cupboards; but in the Sistine Hall there is usually an exhibition (changed annually) of valuable MSS. and printed books.

The first room is the **Gallery of Urban VIII.** By the entrance wall are two statues, 1. the sophist Aelius Aristides (A.D. 129-189) dating from the 3C; on r. the Greek orator Lysias, dating from the 2C. Here are shown astronomical instruments, sailing directions dating from the early 16C, and the Farnese Planisphere (1725), given to Leo XIII by the Count of Caserta.

Beyond are the two **Sistine Rooms,** part of the Library of Sixtus V (see below). In the first, paintings of St Peter's as planned by Michelangelo, and of the erection of the obelisk in Piazza San Pietro. Over the doors of the second room, Sixtus V proclaiming St Bonaventura Doctor of the Church in the church of the Santi Apostoli (Melozzo's frescoes are seen in their original place on the wall of the apse; see p. 169); Canonization of St Diego in Old St Peter's. Here also is a press designed by Bramante for sealing papal bulls.

The **\*Sistine Hall,** named after its founder Sixtus V, was built in 1587-89 by *Dom. Fontana* athwart the great Courtyard of the Belvedere, cutting it into two. It was later paralleled by the New Wing, the construction of which created a small central courtyard, known thenceforth as the Courtyard of the Library. The Sistine Hall is 71 m long, 15 m wide, and 9 m high; it is divided into two vaulted aisles by seven columns. The decorations of the hall embody two main themes— the glorification of literature and of the pontificate of Sixtus V. At the ends of the aisles and in the lunettes over the windows are paintings, most of them views of Rome in the time of the pope and some of them illustrating events of his reign, such as his coronation on the steps of St Peter's, and the papal processions to the Lateran and to Santa Maria Maggiore, the latter for the inauguration of the special Holy Year of 1585. \*Exhibitions here of the precious possessions of the Library are changed annually.

Under the arches of the hall are displayed some of the gifts (vases, etc.) made to the popes by various foreign rulers.

In the VESTIBULE (l.), which is divided into two small rooms, is a pair of colossal enamel and gilt candelabra used at Napoleon I's coronation and presented by him to Pius VII. Above the doors are paintings of the Lateran Palace before and after its reconstruction by *Dom. Fontana.* Here are displayed the largest and smallest MSS. in the Vatican Library, namely the Hebrew Bible of Urbino (1295) and the Masses of SS. Francis and Anne, decorated with 16C miniatures. Also, the medal taken on the first Apollo flight to the moon in 1968.

Beyond the two PAULINE ROOMS, added by Paul V, and decorated in the Mannerist style of 1610-11, is the ALEXANDRINE ROOM, adapted in 1690 by Alexander VIII, and decorated with scenes in the life of Pius VII by *De Angelis.* It contains a bozzetto by *Bernini,* and an early embroidered cope and altar cloth (11-12C).

The new one-way systems recently imposed by the Vatican authorities make it obligatory at this stage to visit the **New Wing,** or **Braccio Nuovo** of the Chiaramonti sculpture gallery (comp. p. 303) from the Alexandrine Room since access to it from the Chiaramonti Gallery is now closed.

Its construction (1817-22; by Stern) is due to Pius VII, and it forms an extension of his Chiaramonti Gallery. The New Wing, which contains some of the most valuable sculptures in the Vatican, is a noble hall, 70 m long and 8 m wide, with a vaulted coffered ceiling and an apse in the middle of the s. side, facing the Courtyard of the Library. The floor is inlaid with mosaics of the 2C A.D. from a Roman villa at Tor Marancia (comp. p. 287).

The collection, arranged to be seen from the Chiaramonti Gallery, begins at the farthest end of the hall —5. Caryatid, copy of one of the Caryatids of the Erechtheion on the Acropolis of Athens (5C B.C.); 9. Head of a Dacian, from the Forum of Trajan (2C A.D.); 11 Silenus carrying the infant Dionysos, copy of an original ascribed to Lysippos; *14 The AUGUSTUS OF PRIMA PORTA, one of the most famous portraits of the emperor, found in Livia's villa at Prima Porta.

The emperor, who appears to be about 40 years old, is wearing a cuirass over his toga; he holds a sceptre in his left hand; his raised right hand shows that he is about to make a speech. The head is full of character and the majestic pose suggests the influence of Polykleitos. The cuirass, a remarkably delicate piece of work, is decorated with scenes that date the statue. The central scene depicts the restoration by the Parthians in 20 B.C. of the eagles lost by Crassus at Carrhæ in 53 B.C. The small cupid riding a dolphin, placed as a support for the right leg, may be a portrait of Gaius Cæsar, grandson of Augustus.

*23. Modesty, so called, probably Mnemosyne, copy of a Greek original of the 3C B.C.; 26. Statue of Titus.

In the rectangular recess opposite the apse, 32. Priestess of Isis. In the centre, *Bust of Julius Cæsar; above is an alabaster cinerary urn said to be that of Livilla, daughter of Germanicus. At the sides are six tombstones found near the Mausoleum of Augustus; five of them belong to the Julian family and the sixth to Vespasian's.—37. Wounded Amazon (comp. below); 41. Bust of Trajan; 43. Selene (the Moon) approaching the sleeping Endymion, copy of a Hellenistic original of the 4C-3C B.C.; 46. Statue of a tragic poet (the head of Euripides does not belong), copy of a 4C original (? Aeschylus); *53. Portrait bust of a Roman (1C A.D.)

Returning down the other side: *64. DEMOSTHENES.

This is a replica of the original statue by Polyeuctos of Athens, set up in Athens in 280 B.C. to the memory of Demosthenes. It expresses with great vigour the character of the orator and statesman. The hands were originally joined, with the fingers crossed. The mouth plainly suggests the stutter from which the great Athenian suffered.

65. Portrait bust of Ptolemy of Numidia (1C A.D.); *67. Wounded Amazon, a replica of one of the statues from the Temple of Diana at Ephesos, by Polykleitos. According to the Elder Pliny, this statue won the prize in a competition in which Polykleitos, Pheidias, Kresilas, and Phradmon entered. The arms and feet were restored by Thorvaldsen; 74. Bust of Hadrian wearing armour; 76. Statue of Hera, copy of a 5C Greek original (attributed to Alkamenes); 79. Fortune, copy of a 4C Greek statue (the head, though antique, is from another figure; the oar and globe are Roman additions); 80. Portrait bust of an unknown Roman of the 2C A.D.; 82. Statue of a man, a Greek portrait of the 4C B.C.; *85. Statue of Artemis, from a 4C original.

In the apse. *89. Bust of a man of the late Republican era, possibly Mark Antony; 94. Bust of Marcus Aurelius as a young man; statuettes of athletes; 105. Statue of Diana; in the floor, mosaic of Diana of the Ephesians; *106. THE NILE, an admirable Hellenistic work, found, in 1513, with a statue of the Tiber (now in the Louvre), near the Temple of Isis.

The river-god, who reclines near a sphinx and holds a horn of plenty, has the calm benevolent mien of a benefactor who enjoys his munificence. The sixteen children who frolic over him are supposed to symbolize the sixteen cubits which the Nile rises when in flood. The plinth is decorated with characteristic scenes of life on the banks of the Nile.

108. Statue of Julia, daughter of Titus; *111. The GIUSTINIANI ATHENA, after a Greek original of the 4C B.C.; this is the best existing copy of an original in bronze attributed to Kephisodotus or to Euphranor; it happily portrays the goddess's twofold function as the divinity of the intellect and of arms. 112. Portrait bust of an unknown Roman of the 1C A.D., possibly Cn. Domitius Ahenobarbus; 114. Statue of a man wearing a toga, with the head of Claudius; *117. RESTING SATYR, copy of the famous statue by Praxiteles (replica in the Gallery of Statues; others in the Museo Gregoriano Profano and in the Capitoline Museum); 118. Bust of Commodus (180-92); 120. Statue of an athlete with the head of Lucius Verus; the body is a copy of a 5C Greek original; 121. Bust of the emperor Philip the Arabian (244-49); *123. DORYPHOROS OF POLYKLEITOS, copy of the famous bronze statue.

Polykleitos, chief of the school of Argos and Sikyon, devoted himself especially to the study of the proportions of the human body, and embodied in this figure of the spear-bearer, known as the 'canon', the results of his researches into the problem of the most perfect conception of the youthful male form (comp. p. 305). Innumerable copies were made of the Doryphoros, which is vigorous in construction, with a head of the dolichocephalic type, and is admirably harmonius in line and proportions.

124. Head of a Dacian, from Trajan's Forum (comp. No. 9 above); *126. Statue of Domitian, wearing a cuirass.

It is now necessary to return to Bramante's w. corridor. From the Alexandrine Room a door leads into the Clementine Gallery.

The **Clementine Gallery**, in five sections, was added to the Library by Clement XII in 1732; in 1818, under Pius VII, it was decorated by *De Angelis* with paintings of scenes in the life of that pope. The first two rooms contain a collection of plans of Rome, including one by *Ant. Tempesta* (1606), and valuable 16-17C Italian and German bookbindings, and bozzetti by Bernini. The last room has a 4C Greek relief of a horseman presented to Pius IX by Ferdinand II of the Two Sicilies, a bronze head of a Muse (Roman copy of a Hellenistic original), and two bronze hippogriffs of the Imperial period. On either side of the entrance are two Mithraic divinities.

Beyond is the main hall of the **Museum of Pagan Antiquities** (*Museo Profano della Biblioteca*), a museum and coin collection of the 18C, with additions from the excavations of 1809-15. It was begun under Clement XIII in 1767 and completed in the time of Pius VI, when it was furnished by Valadier. The ceiling paintings symbolize Time.

In the cupboards on the r. wall; carved Roman ivory, busts in semi-precious stones, a miniature torso, and a mosaic from Hadrian's Villa at Tivoli. Beyond, Roman bronze statuettes (1-3C A.D.) and Plaques with inscriptions.—In the cupboards on the l. wall: head and arm of a chryselephantine statue of Minerva, claimed to be a 5C Greek original; Etruscan bronzes and carved Roman ivory. Beyond, Etruscan and Roman objects found in Rome and the Pontine Marshes. On the end wall in a niche to the l., *Bronze head of Augustus, on r., bronze head of Nero.

IV   THE MUSEUMS OF ANTIQUITIES

The Vatican Palace houses the largest collections of antique sculpture in the world. These collections owe their origin to the Renaissance popes in particular to Julius II. Many of the exhibits were, however, afterwards dispersed, Pius V (1566-72) being largely responsible, with his gifts to the city of Rome and to private individuals. This trend was reversed by the popes of the late 18C and early 19C, who reassembled the old collections and formed new ones.

The museums about to be described are the *Egyptian Museum;* the *Chiaramonti Sculpture Gallery;* the *Pio Clementino Museum;* and the *Etruscan Museum.* The *Gregorian Museum of Pagan Antiquities* (p. 278), and the *New Wing* (p. 299) of the Chiaramonti Gallery, have already been described.

The contents of the sculpture galleries are mainly Greek originals, Roman originals, or Roman copies of Greek originals executed in the 1C and 2C A.D. In some instances the Roman sculptor when copying a Greek model has placed a contemporary portrait head on his copy; modern restorers have often made additions in marble, stone, or plaster and have also, on occasion, put heads on statues to which they do not belong. In addition, all the male sculpture has been ludicrously disfigured by prudish plaster additions, and there are few undraped female statue (this does not apply to the Gregorian Museum of Pagan Antiquities).

The Inventory numbers (given in the following description) are sometimes difficult to decipher.

The one-way systems (comp. p. 278) make it, at present, obligatory to approach the sculpture galleries through the Egyptian Museum.

## The Egyptian Museum

The Egyptian Museum occupies rooms in the lower floor of the Belvedere Pavilion adjoining the Museo Pio-Clementino. The entrance is at the top of the first flight of the Simonetti Staircase outside the Hall of the Greek Cross (p. 310). The museum was founded by Gregory XVI in 1839 and was arranged by Father Luigi Maria Ungarelli, one of the first Italian Egyptologists to continue the scientific research of G. G. Champollion. The rooms were decorated in the Egyptian style by G. De Fabris.

ROOM I. Statues in black granite of the lion-headed goddess Sekhmet (XVIIIth Dyn.); two crouching lions, once part of a monument to Nectanebo I (XXXth Dyn.); they were removed by Gregory XVI from the Fontana dell'Acqua Felice in Piazza San Bernardo (comp. p. 181); funerary stelæ.—ROOM II reproduces an underground tomb chamber in the Valley of the Kings. Here are displayed three lidless sarcophagi in black basalt, with Hieroglyphic inscriptions, of the Saitic period (6C B.C.) and mummies and canopic jars. The papyrus of the Book of the Dead, which belonged to a priest of the Saitic period, is being restored; a photocopy is displayed.—R. III contains works by Roman artists of the 2C and 3C in imitation of Egyptian art. Most of them come from Hadrian's Villa at Tivoli, others from the Temple of Isis, in the Campus Martius. Statue of Antinous in white marble; colossal bust of the goddess Isis; Grey marble statue personifying the Nile.—R. IV. Basalt statuette of Psammeteksenb, a priest-physician of the XXVIth Dyn., depicted as a naophoros, i.e. carrying a small temple; basalt statuette of the naophorus Udjeharresnet who was present when the city of Sais was taken by the Persians under Cambyses in 525 B.C.

ROOM V, THE HEMICYCLE, conforms in shape to the Niche of the Bronze Fir Cone. Here are displayed part of the throne of a seated statue of Rameses II (XIX Dyn.); *Colossal statue of Queen Tuaa, mother of Rameses II; *Sandstone Head of Mentuhotep IV (XIth Dyn.), the oldest portrait statue in the museum; Colossal granite statue of Ptolemy Philadelphos (285-247 B.C.) and his wife Arsinoe, and of a Princess of the Ptolemy family.—R. VI. Mummies or mummy-cases of sacred animals; scarabs.—R. VII. Funerary statuettes; R. VIII-IX. Mummies and mummy-cases. R. X. Objects from the Grassi collection.

The **Niche of the Bronze Fir Cone** (*Nicchione della Pigna*), reached from a door in the Hemicycle (see above; apply to the custodian), is the apse at the N. end of the extensive COURTYARD OF THE FIR CONE (*Cortile della Pigna*), one of the three sections into which Bramante's Courtyard of the Belvedere was eventually divided. Here stands the colossal bronze FIR CONE, placed here by Paul V (1605-21). The cone was found near the Thermæ of Agrippa and formed the centrepiece of a fountain beside the Temple of Isis; this is inferred from the holes in the top of the scales. It was made by a certain P. Cincius Salvius, in the 1C A.D. In the middle ages it was in the portico of Old St Peter's, together with the two bronze-gilt peacocks on either side of it; these came from Hadrian's Mausoleum and probably stood at one of its entrance gates. The fir cone was seen by Dante ('Inferno', xxxi, 53) and gave its name to a district, the Quartiere della Pigna. Near by is the *Base of the Column of Antoninus Pius* (A.D. 138-61); it originally stood in what is now Via della Missione, near the Chamber of Deputies. On it is depicted the Apotheosis of Antoninus and his wife Faustina, who are being conducted to heaven by a winged genius personifying Rome. In the middle of the courtyard is the bronze statue of St Peter which was erected in 1886 in commemoration of the Council of 1869-70.

From the landing outside R. X of the Egyptian Museum stairs lead down to the Chiaramonti Sculpture Gallery.

## The Chiaramonti Gallery

The **Chiaramonti Sculpture Gallery** is reached by stairs leading down from the landing outside the Egyptian Museum and near the Round Vestibule (p. 304). This gallery is named after its founder Pius VII (Chiaramonti). With it are associated the New Wing (p. 299) and the Gallery of Inscriptions (Galleria Lapidaria). The gallery occupies a considerable section of Bramante's E. corridor and is 300 metres long. It flanks and overlaps the Courtyard of the Fir Cone. The exhibits are divided into 59 Sections, numbered with roman numerals (odd numbers on left, even numbers on right).

*Section I.* 3. Sarcophagus of C. Junius Euhodus and his wife Metilia Acte, sometime a priestess of the Magna Mater at Ostia, with relief of the story of Alcestis; the faces of Alcestis and her husband Admetus are portraits of the Roman couple (2C A.D.).—*II.* 15. Herm of Hephaistos (Vulcan); the head may be derived from a statue by Alkamenes; Roman copy of a 5C Greek original.—*IV.* 4. Statue of Hygieia, part of a group of Hygieia and Asklepios, Roman copy of a 4C original by the sons of Praxiteles in the Asklepieion on the island of Kos.—*V.* 3. Antoninus Pius, wearing armour.—*IX.* 3. Herakles with his son Telephos; the statue of Herakles is after a 4C original, that of Telephos after a 3C original; the group is a Roman synthesis.—*X.* 26. Sepulchral monument of P. Nonnius Zethus and his family (1C A.D.), a square marble block with eight conical cavities for the various members of the family. The reliefs—of a mill being turned by a donkey and of baking implements—probably indicated the man's trade.—*XI.* 15. Portrait bust of Cicero; 21. Sarcophagus lid.—*XII.* 3. Relief from a 3C sarcophagus, with a mule in blinkers turning a wine-press.—*XIII.* I. Hermes, from an original of the 5C B.C.; 4. Ganymede and the eagle, copy of a 3C Hellenistic original—*XV.* 14. Portrait bust of Pompey.

*XVI.* *3. Head of Athena, copy of a Greek original of the 5C B.C.; the eyes are restorations but they indicate the skill with which Greek artists caught the expression of the human eye. The whites of the eyes were probably of ivory, the pupils of semi-precious stone, and the lashes and brows of bronze (comp. head of Athena on p. 313).—*XVII.* 3. Silenus with a panther, copy of a 3C Hellenistic original.—*XIX.* 12. Portrait-head of a priest of Isis (1C B.C.); 13. Head of a Roman of the late Republican period.—*XX.* 5. Athena, from a Greek original of the 5C B.C.—*XXI.* 1. Eros bending his bow, probably a copy of a bronze original by Lysippos; *4. Statue of a boy.—*XXIII.* *16. Fragment of a relief of Penelope in her characteristic attitude: sitting on a chair and resting her head on her right hand; from a Greek original of the 5C B.C.—*XXVI.* 15. Head of the Discobolos of

Myron, Roman copy of the 5C Greek original (comp. copies on p. 310); *21. Head from a Palmyran sepulchral relief, in the limestones typical of Palmyran sculpture, which was a fusion of Syrian and Hellenistic-Roman styles; 2C A.D.

*XXIX.* 2. Colossal head of Augustus; 4. Statue of Tiberius; 5. Head of Tiberius.—*XXXI.* 2. Relief of 3 Women, Archaic period,—*XXXII.* 3. Dacian prisoner of high rank, Roman art of the 2C A.D.—*XXXV.* 18. Roman pontiff in the act of sacrifice (1C B.C.).—*XXXVI.* 3. Resting athlete, Roman copy of a 4C Greek original.—*XXXVII.* 3. Statue of Herakles; from a Greek original of the 4C B.C.—*XL.* 1. Statue of the Muse Polyhymnia, Roman copy of a Hellenistic original of the 3C or 2C B.C.; 3. Statue of Artemis (Diana), Roman copy of a 4C Greek original.—*XLIII.* *19. Statuette of Ulysses, part of a group of Ulysses offering wine to Polyphemus, Roman copy of a 3C Greek original.—*XLIV.* 4. Sarcophagus; 1. Statue of tripod group.—*XLV.* 3. Colossal head of Trajan.—*XLVII.* 15. Portrait bust of a lady of the Julio-Claudian gens; the hair is typical of the fashion of the age of Augustus (1C A.D.); 17. Portrait statue of a Roman thought to be Sulla (1C B.C.)—*LVIII.* 8. Personification of Winter; the female figure is wrapped in a cloak and holds a pine branch in her left hand; she is reclining near a stream where cupids are catching waterfowl and fishes; a Hellenistic-Roman work of the 2C A.D.; 9. Sepulchral relief of a Roman family (1C B.C.).—*LIX.* 7. Personification of Autumn, a companion piece to Winter (above); the female figure is surrounded by cupids gathering grapes; 8. Sepulchral relief of a Roman family (1C B.C.).

At the ened of the Chiaramonti Gallery is a gate (closed), beyond which is the **Gallery of Inscriptions** (*Galleria Lapidaria*), open only to scholars armed with a permit from the Director-General. It occupies the remaining part of Bramante's E. corridor. The gallery was founded by Clement XIV and reorganized and classified by the celebrated epigraphist Monsignor Gaet. Marini (1742-1817). It contains over 5000 pagan and Christian inscriptions from cemeteries and catacombs.

The Braccio Nuovo (New Wing) of the Chiaramonti Gallery can only, at present, be seen from Bramante's W. corridor (comp. p. 299).

It is now necessary to return through the Chiaramonti Gallery to the landing outside the exit from the Egyptian Museum. Ahead is the present entrance to the Museo Pio Clementino.

## Museo Pio-Clementino

This sculpture gallery occupies two floors of the Belvedere Pavilion, which was adapted by M. Simonetti for the purposes of a museum. The present entrance is from the landing outside the exit from the Egyptian Museum.

In the first vestibule is the *Sarcophagus, in peperino, of L. Cornelius Scipio Barbatus, from the Tomb of the Scipios (p. 225); the sarcophagus is in the form of a Doric altar but the general character is Etruscan. The archaic inscription, in Saturnine verse, is said to be by Ennius. Above are two inscriptions, also from the Tomb of the Scipios, to the son of Scipio Barbatus, who conquered Corsica in 259 B.C.—On the right: 44. So-called Casali Altar, Roman, 2C A.D., with reliefs on all four sides.

Ahead is the **Round Vestibule** (*Vestibolo Rotondo*). Here are a large bowl of pavonazzetto and sculptural fragments.—Beyond is the **Gabinetto dell'Apoxyomenos**. *67. APOXYOMENOS ('The Scraper'), a finely built athlete scraping the oil from his body with a strigil, from a bronze original by Lysippos; this was the masterpiece of the sculptor's maturity (c. 330 B.C.) and illustrated his canon of proportions.—Above, Archaic Latin inscriptions from the Tomb of the Scipios; to the right, Inscriptions, among them that of L. Mummius Achaicus, the conqueror of Greece (146 B.C.).—Annexe (unlit), 122. Relief of a Roman galley; above, amusing mosaic panels.

From the Round Vestibule is the entrance to the **Octagonal Court-yard** of the Belvedere (not to be confused with the larger courtyard of the Belvedere, to the s.; p. 308), where Julius II placed the first classical sculptures to form the nucleus of the great collections now in the Vatican. When Pius VI had the museum enlarged in 1775, Simonetti made the courtyard into an octagon by forming the recesses (gabinetti) in the four corners.

To the left is the **Gabinetto dell'Appollo.** *92. APOLLO BELVEDERE, from a bronze original, probably of the 4C B.C., which experts now consider to have been the work of Leochares.

The god is stepping forward to see the effect of the arrow that he has just shot. The slender elegance and smooth modelling of the youthful body, the keen lifelike gaze, have caused this to be one of the most generally admired of ancient masterpieces.

Under the adjoining colonnade is a plaster-cast of the Laocoön (comp. below); and *81. Relief of a procession, from the Ara Pacis Augustae, an original fragment not returned to the altar on its reconstitution in 1937-38; nearly all the heads are restorations.

The **Gabinetto del Laocoonte** contains the famous group of *LAOCOÖN and his two sons in the coils of the serpents of Apollo, a vivid and striking illustration of the story related by Virgil in the Aeneid.

Laocoön, priest of Apollo, warned his fellow Trojans against the trickery of the Greeks and adjured them not to admit the wooden horse into the city, whereon the angry god sent the serpents to crush him and his young sons to death in their coils. This group, of Greek marble, was found in Nero's Golden House, in 1506, and was at once recognized as that described by Pliny, though it is not carved from a single block, as he states, but from at least three pieces. It is ascribed to the Rhodian sculptors Agesander, Polydoros, and Athenodoros (c. 50 B.C.), and thus belongs to the end of the Hellenistic period, as might be inferred from the violent realism of the conception as well as from the extreme skill and accurate detail with which the agonized contortions of the bodies are rendered. The group acquired its present appearance in a recent reconstruction. Its more familiar appearance as restored by Montorsoli on the opinion of Michelangelo is preserved in a plaster-cast under the adjoining colonnade.

The group has become classic from the eminence of the authors who have written about it; Byron, in 'Childe Harold' vividly describes 'Laocoön's torture dignifying pain.'—Many fragments of a larger group and a base inscribed with the same three sculptors' names were found in 1957 in a cave at Sperlonga (Lazio). This is now known not to be an earlier version of the same subject.

Flanking the doorway beyond are two *Molossian Hounds of the school of Pergamon.

**Gabinetto dell'Hermes.** *53. Hermes (not Antinoüs, as was formerly thought), perhaps Hermes Psychopompos, the conductor of souls to the underworld, copy of an original by Praxiteles. The head is reminiscent of that of his famous Hermes at Olympia.

In the portico beyond (niche), Venus Felix and Cupid: the body is copied from the Venus of Knidos in the Mask Room; the inscription on the plinth states that the group was dedicated to Venus Felix by Sallustia and Helpis. It has stood in the courtyard since Julius II began the collection here.—959. Small marble funerary urn in the shape of a house or shrine, and beyond, Sarcophagus with a battle of the Amazons, Achilles, and Penthesileia grouped in the centre, 3C A.D.

The **Gabinetto del Canova** contains three statues by *Antonio Canova* placed here when most of the classical masterpieces were taken to Paris by Napoleon in 1800, after the Treaty of Tolentino. 32. Perseus, a pure but cold creation, inspired by the Apollo Belvedere; 33, 33A. Creugas and Damoxenes, boxers, figures of considerable nobility but showing the weakness of an imitative style.

Beneath the following portico, 30. Sarcophagus of Sextus Varius Marcellus, father of Heliogabalus; 28. Sarcophagus with curved ends and a relief of a Bacchic procession.

Beneath the porticoes are six granite basins, the four smaller ones being from the Baths of Caracalla.

The door flanked by the two Hounds leads out of the Courtyard and into the **Animal Room** (*Sala degli Animali*). Most of the animal statues are by *F. A. Franzoni* (1734-1818), who made them for this room at the behest of Pius VI. Some are entirely Franzoni's work; others were made up by him from ancient fragments. The antiques include: (in the room on the left), 10. Sow with litter of twelve, perhaps of the Augustan period; (under the far window) 25. Colossal head of a camel (fountain head), copy of a Hellenistic original of the 2C B.C.; *40. Meleager with his dog and the head of a boar, copy of a 4C original by Skopas; 62. Triton and nereid, with cupids, perhaps a Hellenistic original of the 2C B.C.; 68. Head of a minotaur, copy of a 5C Greek original. In the room on the right, 150. Mithras slaying the bull (2C A.D.); (on the wall behind), *138, 152. Mosaics with animals, from Hadrian's Villa at Tivoli (2C A.D.).—In the pavement of each room, Mosaics, with animals and plants (2C A.D.).

The **Gallery of Statues** (r.) is part of the original Belvedere Pavilion built by Innocent VIII. Remains of paintings by Pinturicchio may still be seen on the walls.—*250. Eros of Centocelle, also called the Genius of the Vatican, probably a statue of Thanatos, the god of death, from an original attributed to Kephisodotos; 253. Triton, copy of a Hellenistic original of the 2C B.C.; 255. Judgment of Paris, possibly a copy of an original by Euphranor (4C B.C.); 259. Apollo Kitharoidos, restored as Minerva, late 5C; 261. Penelope (so called; with a head from another antique statue); *264. APOLLO SAUROCTONOS, representing the god watching a lizard that he is about to kill, an attractive composition, copy of the famous bronze original by Praxiteles; 265. So-called Mattei Amazon, from an original attributed to Kresilas (head from another statue; comp. No. 67, p. 300); 267. Satyr; 270. Muse, restored as Urania, belonging to the series found at Tivoli (see above); 271.Poseidippos, 390. Menander (?), the comic poets, copies of Hellenistic originals, forming a pair; 393. Suppliant; 395. Apollo Kitharoidos, copy of an archaistic Greek original of the 5C B.C.; 396. Narcissus, a Roman work of Alexandrian type; 398. The emperor Macrinus (A.D. 217-18); 399. Aesculapius and Hygieia, of Alexandrian type; 401. Two children of Niobe, fragment of the well-known Florentine group; 405. Danaid; *406. RESTING SATYR, one of several known replicas of the famous statue of Praxiteles; *412, 413. The BARBERINI CANDELABRA, a famous pair, with representations of divinities, from Hadrian's Villa at Tivoli, Roman work in neo-Attic style (2C A.D.); *414. Sleeping Ariadne, copy of a Hellenistic original of the 3C or 2C B.C.; below, 414A. Sarcophagus with a gigantomachia, 2C A.D. after a Hellenistic original of the 2C B.C.; 416. Bacchus and Ariadne, from Hadrian's Villa; 417. Hermes, copy of a 5C Greek original (school of Myron); 420. Male statue of the 1C A.D. with the head of Lucius Verus (A.D. 161-69). On the bases of several of the statues are inscriptions relating to the gens Julia-Claudia found near the Mausoleum of Augustus.

At the end is the **Gallery of Busts** divided by arches into four little rooms. ROOM I. To the r. (above) 292. Caracalla; 285. Marcus Aurelius; 284. Antoninus Pius; (below) 282. Trajan; 277. Nero idealized as Apollo; 275. Old man wearing a crown of vine-leaves, possibly a priest of Dionysos, Hellenistic, 2C B.C.; 274. Head of Augustus as one of the Fratres Arvales, and as a boy (273); 3. Julius Cæsar, 389. Column with three dancing Hours, found near the Ara Pacis; 383. Porphyry bust of a youth perhaps Philip the Arabian, emperor in 244-49; *388. Portrait group, Cato and Porcia, probably from a tomb, Roman, 1C B.C.—R. II. 303. Apollo; 307. Saturn, after an original of the 5C or 4C B.C.; (above) 298. Colossal bust of Serapis; 308. Isis; 311. Head of Menelaus, from a group of Menelaus with the body of Patroclus (comp. Pasquino; p. 101). In the middle of the room, Base in the form of a rectangular chest standing on legs of winged lions, the lid decorated with flowers and foliage; on the sides, reliefs of uncertain significance.—R. IV (the recess to the left). 348. Mask of Jupiter Ammon, copy of a 4C original; 352. Woman in the attitude of prayer, Augustan after a 5C original *357. Bust of Antinoüs, an exquisite portrait; 363. Head of Juno, after a Greek original of the 5C B.C.—R. III. *326. Seated statue of Zeus (Jupiter Verospi), copy of a Hellenistic original (the lower part is a restoration); 341. Celestial globe; 338. Head of one of the Diadochoi wearing the regal fillet; 327. Augur; 329. Mithras in Phrygian cap; 316. Pan.

The so-called **Open Loggia** (*Loggia Scoperta*), not always open to the public, skirts the N. side of the Belvedere Pavilion as far as the Mask Room. 10. Fragment of relief depicting a youth taking part in a Bacchic procession, 3C A.D.; 15. Frieze, in two sections, with scenes of farm activities and of the sale of bread in a baker's shop, 3C A.D.; over the door to the Mask Room, Sepulchral relief of Galatea, a priestess of Isis, with her husband, 2C A.D.

The **Mask Room** (*Gabinetto delle Maschere;* usually locked), entered also from the Gallery of Statues, derives its name from four *Mosaics of theatrical masks in the pavement. They came from Hadrian's Villa and date from the 2C A.D. The border is of the time of Pius VI and bears his coat of arms. Opposite the entrance, *474. VENUS OF KNIDOS, a fine copy of the famous statue of Praxiteles. The head belongs to another copy of the statue; the limbs are mainly restorations. The goddess is about to bathe; she has a towel and, near by, a pitcher (hydria).—On the left, 433. The Graces, from an original perhaps of the 2C B.C. In the niche opposite, 432. Satyr, in rosso antico, from a bronze original (Hellenistic, 2C B.C.). On the wall between the doors, 427. Venus at her bath, copy of a larger original by Doidalsas, a Bithynian sculptor of the 3C B.C.

From the Animal Room (comp. above) is the entrance to the **Hall of the Muses** (*Sala delle Muse*) with paintings by Conca; it comprises an octagon, with a vestibule at either end. FIRST VESTIBULE. Herms: 492. Sophocles; 490. Diogenes (?). Reliefs (above): 489. Pyrrhic dance, a 4C Attic work; 493. Birth of Bacchus.—OCTAGON, a magnificent hall with 16 columns of Carrara marble. Seven of the statues of the Nine Muses in this room were found, along with that of Apollo, in a villa near Tivoli, and are generally held to be copies of originals, apparently of bronze, by Praxiteles or his school, but possibly they do not all belong to the same group. 511. Erato; 515. Calliope; 516. Apollo Kitharoidos, an expressive figure; 517. Terpsichore. Nos. 520 and 504 (Euterpe and Urania) were not found with the rest and were not, in fact, originally intended for muses. 499. Melpomene; 503. Thalia; 505. Clio; 508. Polyhymnia. The statues alternate with hermae: 509. Metrodorus; 510. So-called Alcibiades; 512. Homer; 514. Socrates; 518. Strategos (Alcibaides?); 519. Plato (not Zeno); 521. Euripides; 498. Epicurus; 500. So-called Zeno; 502. Aeschines; 506. Demosthenes; 507. Antisthenes. In the centre, *3. BELVEDERE TORSO, found in the Campo dei Fiori at the time of Julius II, and bearing the signature of Apollonios, an Athenian

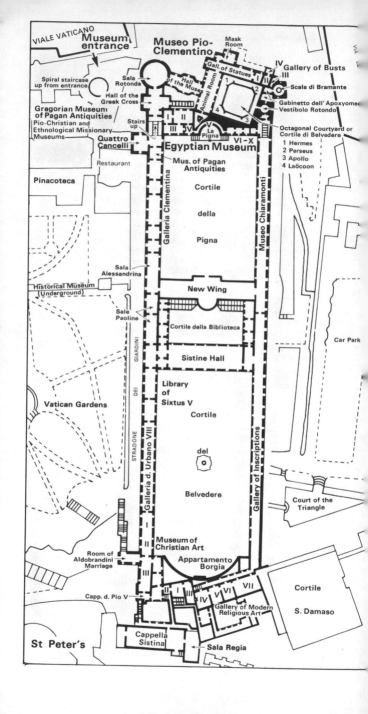

VIALE VATICANO

**Museum entrance**

**Museo Pio-Clementino**

Mask Room

Gall. of Statues

IV

**Gallery of Busts**

III

Spiral staircase up from entrance

Sala Rotonda

Hall of the Muses

Scala di Bramante

Hall of the Greek Cross

**Gregorian Museum of Pagan Antiquities**

Pio-Christian and Ethnological Missionary Museums

Gabinetto dell' Apoxyomenos

Vestibolo Rotondo

Stairs up

La Pigna

Octagonal Courtyard or Cortile di Belvedere

Animal Room

**Quattro Cancelli**

**Egyptian Museum**

VI-X

1 Hermes
2 Perseus
3 Apollo
4 Laöcoon

Restaurant

Mus. of Pagan Antiquities

**Pinacoteca**

Cortile

della

Pigna

**Galleria Clementina**

**Museo Chiaramonti**

Sala Alessandrina

**Historical Museum (Underground)**

Sale Paoline

**New Wing**

Cortile della Biblioteca

**Sistine Hall**

GIARDINI

DEI

**Library of Sixtus V**

Cortile

del

Belvedere

Car Park

**Vatican Gardens**

STRADONE

Gallery of Inscriptions

Court of the Triangle

**Galleria d. Urbano VIII**

II

Room of Aldobrandini Marriage

III

**Museum of Christian Art**

**Appartamento Borgia**

Capp. d. Pio V

I

IV

V VI VII

**Gallery of Modern Religious Art**

**Cortile S. Damaso**

**Cappella Sistina**

**Sala Regia**

**St Peter's**

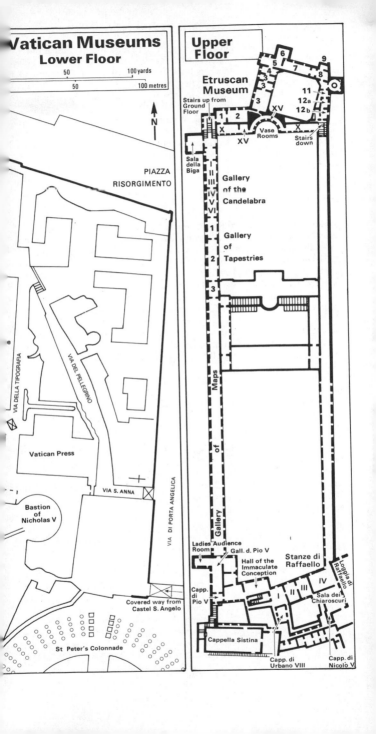

# Vatican Museums
## Lower Floor

50    100 yards
50    100 metres

N

PIAZZA
RISORGIMENTO

VIA DELLA TIPOGRAFIA

VIA DEL PELLEGRINO

Vatican Press

VIA S. ANNA

VIA DI PORTA ANGELICA

Bastion
of
Nicholas V

Covered way from
Castel S. Angelo

St Peter's Colonnade

## Upper Floor

Etruscan Museum

Stairs up from
Ground Floor

6
5
7
9
4
8
3
3
11
3
12a
1   2   XV   12b
X
XV
X
Vase
Rooms    Stairs
down

Sala
della
Biga

I
II
III
IV
V
VI

Gallery
of the
Candelabra

1

2

Gallery
of
Tapestries

3

Maps

Gallery    of

Ladies Audience
Room    Gall. d. Pio V

Hall of the
Immaculate
Conception

Stanze di
Raffaello

Loggia di Raffaello

Capp.
di
Pio V

I    II    III    IV

Sala dei
Chiaroscuri

Cappella Sistina

Capp. di
Urbano VIII

Capp. di
Nicolò V

sculptor of the 1C B.C. The figure is sitting on a hide laid over the ground. Greatly admired by Michelangelo, Raphael, and other Renaissance artists, its subject is uncertain: Hercules, Polyphemus, Prometheus, Sciron, Marsyas, and Philoctetes, are among the guesses.—SECOND VESTIBULE. Herm of Pericles, copy of a 5C original by Kresilas; herms of Bias and Periander.

**Circular Hall** (*Sala Rotonda*) designed on the model of the Pantheon. In the pavement, Mosaic of Otrícoli, representing a battle between Greeks and Centaurs, Tritons, and Nereids; in the centre of the room, a huge monolithic porphyry vase found in the Domus Aurea; *539. Jupiter of Otricoli, a colossal head of majestic beauty, attributed to Bryaxis (4C B.C.); 540. Antinoüs (d. A.D. 130) as Bacchus, from a Greek prototype of the 4C B.C. (the drapery, which was originally of bronze, was restored by Thorvaldsen); 541. Faustina the Elder (d. 141), wife of Antoninus Pius; *542. Female divinity, perhaps Demeter, wearing the peplos, after a Greek original of the late 5C B.C. 543. Head of Hadrian, from his mausoleum; 544. Hercules, colossal statue in gilded bronze, an early Imperial copy of a work of the school of Skopas; 545. Bust of Antinoüs, 546. Juno (the Barberini Hera), a Roman copy of a cult-image in the manner of the late 5C; 547. Marine divinity (from Pozzuoli), believed to personify the Gulf of Baiæ, an interesting example of the fusion of marine elements and human features; *548. Nerva (or Galba), after a statue representing Jupiter; 549. Bust of Serapis, after a work by Bryaxis; 550. Claudius as Jupiter; 551. Head of Claudius; 552. Juno Sospita from Lanuvium, dating from the Antonine period; 553. Head of Plotina (d. 129), wife of Trajan; 556. Head of Pertinax (?); 555. Genius of Augustus; 554. Head of Julia Domna (d. 217), wife of Septimius Severus.

**Hall of the Greek Cross** (*Sala a Croce Greca*). To the l. of the doorway, 597. C. Caesar, nephew of Augustus, sacrificing. *589. Sarcophagus in porphyry of St Helena, mother of Constantine, decorated with Roman horsemen, barbarian prisoners, and fallen soldiers; *566, Sarcophagus of Constantia, daughter of Constantine, in porphyry, decorated with vine-branches and children bearing grapes, peacocks, and a ram (Christian symbols); this sarcophagus was once in the church of Santa Costanza, in Via Nomentana, built by Constantine as a mausoleum for his daughter. 578, 579. Two granite sphinxes; and, in the pavement, Mosaics: *Basket of flowers, Shield with the head of Minerva and the phases of the moon. At the exit, Bust of Pius VI, who enlarged the museum founded by his predecessor Clement XIV.

Ahead is the landing of the Simonetti Staircase. It ascends to a second landing outside the Gallery of the Candelabra (p. 286) and the Room of the Biga (r.).

The **Sala della Biga** is a circular domed hall by *Camporese*. *623. BIGA, or two-horsed chariot, a reconstruction in 1788 by *F. A. Franzoni* from ancient fragments; only the body of the chariot and part of the offside horse are original. The body was used as an episcopal throne in the church of San Marco during the Middle Ages. The bas-reliefs suggest that the Biga was a votive chariot dedicated to Ceres and that it dates from the 1C A.D.—Along the wall, from the left, 619. Charioteer; with the head from another statue; *618. Discobolos, a copy of Myron's work with the head wrongly restored; 616. Hermes (so-called Phokion), from a 5C original (head a copy of a head of a 4C strategos); *615. Discobolos, from a bronze original by Naucides, nephew and pupil of Polykleitos, a fine example of Peloponnesian sculpture of the 5C B.C.; *612. Roman in the act of sacrifice (early Empire), with voluminous draperies admirably rendered; *608. Bearded Dionysos, called Sardanapalus, at once majestic and benevolent in expression, a work of the early 4C B.C., attributed to Kephisodotos.—609, 613, 617, 621. Sarcophagi of children (3C A.D.); the first three are adorned with circus scenes, with cupids as competitors; the fourth represents the chariot race between Oinomaos and Pelops.

The Simonetti Staircase continues up to the Etruscan Museum.

## The Etruscan Museum

The *Etruscan Museum, reached by a staircase from the landing outside the Room of the Biga, was founded in 1837 by Gregory XVI and its official name is *Museo Gregoriano Etrusco*. One of the most important collections of its kind in existence, it has been undergoing a complete reorganization since the time of Pio XII; this has recently been completed. Most of the contents come from Southern Etruria, but there are also outstanding examples of Greek and Roman art, the collection of Greek vases being especially notable.

R.I, OF THE SARCOPHAGI. Sarcophagi from Tuscania, with the slaughter of the Niobids, and from Tarquinia, with mythological scenes (1C B.C.); Sarcophagi with scene of procession (3C), and a wedding (?) procession from Caere (Cerveteri; 5C); Cippus from Todi, with bilingual inscription in Latin and Celtic.

R. II, OF THE REGOLINI-GALASSI TOMB. The interesting frescoes are by *Barocci* and *F. Zuccari*. The room contains objects found in 1836 in an Etruscan necropolis s. of Caere where a small group of tumulus chamber-tombs have been unearthed; the most important is the *REGOLINI-GALASSI TOMB, named after its discoverers. The funeral equipment of at least two individuals is involved; they were buried around the middle of the 7C. The contents are arranged in a large wall case according to the position in which the objects were found (as illustrated). They include: *Gold clasp, with repoussé decoration; gold necklaces; bracelets. Ivories, cups, plates, and silver ornaments, of Greco-Oriental provenance. Lebes, or libation bowl, with six handles in the forms of animals: reconstructed chair.—Equipment of a man, who was probably a lucumo or priest-king. *Vase, where ashes were found (possibly a cremation urn); series of fictile statuettes; equipment of a buried man, who was doubtless a warrior of high rank. Bronze incense-burner in the shape of a wagon. Bronze stand with repoussé figures; two five-handled lebetes. Silver drinking cup; small dishes of Eastern origin. In the middle of the room, the reconstructed Biga, funeral chariot and bronze bed.—The two cases on the window wall contain the equipment of tombs in the immediate vicinity of the Regolini-Galassi Tomb, including Bucchero Vases in relief, and ceramics from another tomb in the necropolis.

ROOM III, OF THE BRONZES. The frescoes were painted under Pius IV by *Nic. Pomarancio* and *Santi di Tito*. It contains a rich collection of objects in common use.—In glass cases: incense-burner, tripod, buckles,

jars, small throne, etc. Two statuettes of children wearing the bulla.—
*Mars of Todi, wearing armour, a bronze statue dating from the beginning of the 4C, but inspired by Greek art of the 5C. In glass cases to left, Mirrors and Candelabra; to the right, Mirrors, cistae, paterae, sheet bronze, vases, etc. Among them note the *Mirror engraved with Herakles and Atlas, and another with Chalchas, the soothsayer, transformed into a haruspex, both designs derived from Greek models of 5-4C B.C.; oval *CISTA, with a battle between Greeks and Amazons, the handle formed by a satyr and a nymph riding on swans (from Vulci). Most of these cistae, which were used to hold toilet implements, came from Praeneste (see p. 353). Patera with the figure of Eos (Aurora) carrying away Kephalos.—R. IV, OF THE URNS. Cinerary urns of marble, travertine, and alabaster. They are of the type from Chiusi and Volterra. Notable is the *Alabaster urn, with relief of the chariot-race between Pelops and Oinomaos (2C B.C.).

A short flight of stairs leads up to the next series of rooms, all with extensive views over Rome, towards Monte Mario.—R. V. THE GUGLIELMI ROOM, named after Benedetto Guglielmi of Vulci, was opened in 1937 to mark the centenary of the museum. All the exhibits are from Vulci. Of particular interest are: Bronze incense-burner supported by the figure of a youth (in the wall-case to the l., with no number); Bucchero jar with incised decoration and a 6C inscription (in the wall-case to the r., on the extreme left with no number); *Red-figured hydria, perhaps by the Athenian Euthymides c. 520 (opposite, in Case K). Other glass cases contain bronzes, Greek red- and black-figured vases, Etruscan vases, and gold objects.—R. VI (to the l.) is opened on request. It contains a collection of jewellery, mostly from Vulci. Interesting are: Necklace with pomegranate drops; coronets and diadems used as funerary wreaths; bulla in gold, on a chain, found at Ostia; silver and bronze clasp in the Daedalic style (7C B.C.).—R. VII, OF THE TERRACOTTAS, contains cinerary urns in cases, Bucchero vases, antefixes, statues, votive objects, etc. Etruscan portrait heads of both sexes and all ages date from the Archaic period to the 1C A.D. They were probably ex-votos, as were the models of legs, feet, etc. The animated expression of the heads is heightened by the colouring. Some of the urns bear traces of their original colour. The fronts are decorated with reliefs of funeral or mythological scenes after Greek models, or scenes of combat, abduction, or the chase. In Case M is a lifelike figure of a young man. There are also lids of sarcophagi in the shape of beds on which the deceased are lying. On the end wall is a group of terracotta statues from a temple in Tivoli, including part of a frieze with male and female heads flanked by figures of children.

R. VIII. ANTIQUARIUM ROMANUM. This room is in three sections. Section 1. On the right wall, cases A and E: Three reliefs showing Hercules fighting the lion, the hydra, and the bull; Roman scales; bronze weight in the shape of a crouching pig, marked C (i.e. 100 Roman pounds); armour in bronze and iron; rings, pins, keys, etc. In the other wall cases (B, C, F, and G) are antefixes and friezes in terracotta, and architectonic fragments. In the centre (D), ivory and bone objects, including a doll with movable limbs (4C A.D.), also bronze statuettes.— Section 2. To the right, fragmentary bronze male torso.—Cases I and K: Ceramics from Arezzo, finely decorated; Roman lamps. Case M:

Roman glass vases, some of which still have their lids. Other cases contain terracotta wall reliefs, alabaster phials of Greek and Eastern origin found in Etruscan tombs, and ivory work.—Section 3. Bronze head of a woman (1–2C A.D.); portrait of a Roman wearing a laurel crown (3C A.D.); fragment of a bronze portrait-statue of a Roman (1C B.C.). From the second section of the Antiquarium there is access to R. IX (the FALCIONI collection), containing bronze, gold, and terracotta objects coming from the neighbourhood of Viterbo.

Just before R. XI, is the *STAIRCASE OF BRAMANTE which descends to the Museo Pio-Clementino. Although the staircase is not usually open, part of it can be seen here through glass doors. The design is masterly; it has recently been discovered that each pillar varies slightly in length creating a perfect spiral.

R. 12a and b. *GREEK ORIGINALS. 12a. Head of Athena, a 5C Greek original, from an acrolith; on the head was a helmet, probably of bronze; the eyes are made of polished grey stone in which were set glass pupils: the eyebrows and eyelashes were made of thin strips of bronze, and the ears had gold earrings. Two *Relief fragments of horsemen, perhaps part of a frieze. Greek originals of the 5C, in style they resemble the Parthenon frieze.—12b. (left). Two heads, fragments from one of the metopes and from the N. frieze of the Parthenon; and fragment of a horse's head from the W. pediment of the Parthenon, probably one of Athena's horses. Among the fine reliefs displayed here is one of dancing nymphs, an Attic work of the 4C. To the right, superb *SEPULCHRAL STELE, showing a young man with his small slave handing him a strigil and a flask of oil (5C B.C.).

A corridor, with objects from the Antiquarium Romanum, bends to the left, and ends on a landing at the top of the *Staircase of Assyrian Reliefs,* with reliefs and inscriptions of the 9–7C B.C.; also some Cufic sepulchral inscriptions of the 11–12C A.D. The staircase goes down to the landing near the Round Vestibule (p. 304).

RR. XIV–XVIII. The **Vase Rooms** include two floors of the hemicycle (RR. XVI, XVII) which looks out on the Cortile della Pigna. They contain a valuable *COLLECTION OF GREEK, ITALIC, AND ETRUSCAN VASES. Most of them come from the Etruscan tombs of S. Etruria, where they were discovered in the course of the excavations of the first half of last century. At the time of their discovery, when the science of archæology had scarcely developed, the vases were all indiscriminately called Etruscan. It was only later that the Greek origin of many of them was realized and, with this realization, was appreciated the importance of the commercial relations between Greece and Etruria. From the end of the 7C to the later 5C many Greek vases were imported. By the middle of the 4C the Greek imports were largely replaced by the products of Magna Græcia, Lucania, and Campania.

R. XVIII. ITALIOT VASES. Here are interesting examples of the products of Magna Græcia. During the 4C the centres of ceramic activity shifted from Attica to the Greek colonies in Southern Italy. Conspicuous among these Italiot vases were the products of the potteries of Tarentum. Among them is a vase with elaborate handles, illustrating the myth of Triptolemos, the inventor of agriculture. Another (4C B.C.) has a caricature of a classical myth.—R. XVI (hemicycle), with frescoes of the time of Pius VI, depicting Rome, the Vatican, and scenes in the Papal States. There is a view of St Peter's Sacristy, then recently built. (In the courtyard an earth-moving operation is underway to construct a building 12 metres below ground level to house the Secret Archives of the Vatican Library).

Here are displayed ATTIC VASES. Among the BLACK-FIGURED type is an *Amphora signed by Exekias, who flourished in the second half of the 6C. One side shows Achilles and Ajax playing with dice; on the other side Castor and Pollux are being welcomed on their return home by their parents, Tyndareus and Leda. Another amphora shows Eos grieving over the dead body of her son Memnon. There are also Panathenaic amphorae, with the figure of Athena Promachos, of the type given to winners at the great Athenian festivals. Until the end of the 6C figures had been painted in black on the red background; colours were often added to the black; white to indicate flesh and red or violet for draperies. Now the process was reversed. The figures were surrounded with black and appeared in the natural red colour of the vase. This technique survived until the Hellenistic period to the exclusion of that of the black figures, except for the Panathenaic vases (see above) which retained the old style. A kylix with a black figure of a running youth inside and red figures outside is an interesting example of the transition. Another kylix with a similar subject has all the figures in red. Both are of the 6C. *Kylix by the famous 5C vase painter Duris, with Oedipus trying to solve the riddle of the Sphinx.—In the upper hemicycle (R. XVII) the display includes: *Hydria, with Apollo flying over the sea; Amphora, with figures of Achilles and Briseis (5C); *Krater with a white background, depicting Hermes carrying the infant Dionysus to the nymphs of Mount Nysa, who are to bring him up; *Oinochoë (wine jug), with two youths about to set on their fighting cocks (5C B.C.).

R. XV, frescoed by Pomarancio, contains the private collection left to the Museum in 1967 by Astarita of Naples. It includes a large Krater of the late Corinthian period showing Ulysses and Menaleus asking for the return of Helen.—R. XIV contains specimens of EARLIER PERIODS. Among them are examples of the Geometric style, which reached its peak of development in the 8C, and of the orientalizing style, which appeared in the 7C. As its name implies, the Geometric style relied on geometric designs and excluded floral and animal motifs. In the later style representations of animals and mythological figures began to appear. The most important vases in this new style were made in Corinth, and the first examples were called Protocorinthian.

Decorated with geometric designs and made by hand are Cinerary urns of the Villanova period (1st Iron Age; 9-8C), so called after Villanova, near Bologna, where an important necropolis was discovered. There are also Protocorinthian aryballoi (oil jars used by athletes); the human figures show the orientalizing style (7C). Note also Corinthian dinos (wine-cooler); Caeretan hydria, so called because the type came from Caere (Italic, showing the influence of Ionia, 6C); Laconian kylix, from Sparta, with figures of Tityos and Sisyphos (6C).

The Simonetti staircase leads back down to the Quattro Cancelli and the exit from the Museums.

## V   VISIT TO THE VATICAN CITY AND GARDENS

Tours of part of the Vatican city and gardens are organized (March-Oct) at the Information Bureau to the left of St Peter's façade. Tickets (4000 l., including the Sistine Chapel; 2500 l., including St Peter's, and 2000 l. for the gardens only) should be obtained at least one day in advance. The tours, partly by bus and partly on foot (c. 3 hrs) depart at 10 on Mon, & Fri for Vatican city, gardens, and St Peter's; and at 10 on Tues, Thurs, & Sat for the gardens, & Sistine chapel, and at 10 on Sun for gardens only. Individual visitors are not admitted to the city or gardens (exc. with a special permit).

The **Vatican Gardens** cover the N. and W. slopes of the Vatican Hill. Although somewhat diminished in extent by intrusive constructions such as the new building of the Museo Gregoriano Profano, the Seminario Etiopico, and the Vatican Radio Station, they retain the charm and elegance of the 16C.

The *Arco delle Campane* is protected by a sentry of the Swiss Guard, armed with a rifle instead of the halberd carried by the guard at the Bronze Door. The square beyond is Piazza dei Protomartiri Romani, the site of the martyrdom of the early Christians near the Circus of Nero.

On the left is the *Camposanto Teutonico,* dating from 779, and probably the oldest of medieval cemeteries; it is still reserved for Germans and Dutch. In the adjacent *Collegio Teutonico* are a small museum and a library. Beyond, against the wall of the city, is the new *Audience Hall* (1971), by Pier Luigi Nervi. Designed in the shape of a shell it has seating for 8000 people.

In the pavement in front of the first arch of the passage beneath the Sacristy of St Peter's a slab marks the former emplacement of the obelisk in Piazza San Pietro. A road leads beneath the Sacristy to emerge into Piazza Santa Marta. Here, on the right, is a fine view of the left transept of St Peter's in all its grandeur; on the left is the *Palazzo dell' Arciprete di San Pietro.* At the w. end of the square is the *Palazzo di Giustizia.*

Opposite the majestic w. end of St Peter's is the little church of *Santo Stefano degli Abissini,* built by Leo III as Santo Stefano Maggiore. In 1479 Sixtus IV conveyed it to Coptic monks; it was rebuilt by Clement XI.

A road ascends past the *Studio del Mosaico,* with an exhibition room, and (r.) the modern Governor's Palace *(Palazzo del Governatorato),* seat of the civic administration of the Vatican City. To the s. is the little-used *Vatican Railway Station.* Viale dell'Osservatorio continues through the gardens past the *Seminario Etiopico.* At the w. extremity of the city are a reproduction of the Grotto of Lourdes, presented by the French Catholics to Leo XIII, and a stretch of the wall built by Nicholas V on the site of the ancient walls put up by Leo IV. Here the *Tower of St John,* once an observatory, is now used as a guest-house. Below is the first building used by the Vatican Radio Station, designed by Marconi and inaugurated in 1931. On the westernmost bastion of the city walls is the *Heliport.*

The descent is through exotic vegetation past the new *Vatican Radio Station* and the *Fontana dell' Aquilone* (1612; by Jan van Santen), with a triton by Stefano Maderno. Nearer the huge Museum buildings is the **\*Casina of Pius IV.** A little masterpiece of Baroque architecture it was built in 1558-62 by Pirro Ligorio. In the villa, now the seat of the *Pontifical Academy of Sciences,* Pius IV held the meetings which received the name of *Notti Vaticane;* at them were held learned discusions on poetry, philosophy, and sacred subjects. Pius VIII and Gregory XVI used to give their audiences here.

Towards St Peter's a group of buildings include the *Floreria,* formerly the *Mint* (Zecca), founded by Eugenius IV. The *Stradone dei Giardini,* an avenue which skirts Bramante's w. corridor, ends at the Quattro Cancelli (p. 278); it is necessary to return through Piazza del Forno (overlooked by the Sistine Chapel) around St Peter's to leave the city by the Arco delle Campane.

The northern part of the city, normally closed to visitors, is entered through the *Arco della Sentinella.* On the left is the Borgia Tower (p. 277). Beyond this are two more courtyards, in the heart of the Vatican Palace. The first is the *Cortile Borgia,* the second the *Cortile dei Pappagalli* (p. 277), so called from its frieze of parrots, now almost obliterated. A subway leads to a fourth courtyard, *Cortile di San Damaso,* overlooked by the Loggia of Raphael.

From the Cortile della Sentinella there is access viâ the *Grottone* into the vast *Courtyard of the Belvedere* which, before the construction of the Sala Sistina was far more extensive. It acquired its present dimensions when the New Wing was built. In the middle of the courtyard is a fountain with a large basin.—A subway leads out into Via del Belvedere. In this street are the *Pontifical Polyglot Printing Press* and the *Vatican Post Office*. On the right are the barracks of the Swiss Guard.

In 1956 a Pagan Necropolis (tombs of 1-4C) was discovered beneath the car park. The cemetery was alongside Via Triumphalis, the line of which is now followed by Via del Pellegrino. It may be visited with special permission.

Beyond the Post Office the animated Via del Pellegrino leads to the left. On the left of this street is the building of the *Annona* (victualling board); on the right are the *Casa Parrochiale;* the workshop where Vatican tapestries are repaired; the restored church of *San Pellegrino;* the offices of the *Osservatore Romano;* and other offices.

From Via del Belvedere, on the left can be seen the church of *Santa Anna dei Palafrenieri,* the parish church of the Vatican City, built in 1573 by the Papal Grooms (Palafrenieri della Corte Papale) to the designs of *Vignola.* Immediately beyond the church is the *Cancello di Sant' Anna* (p. 277), which leads out into Via di Porta Angelica.

# ENVIRONS OF ROME

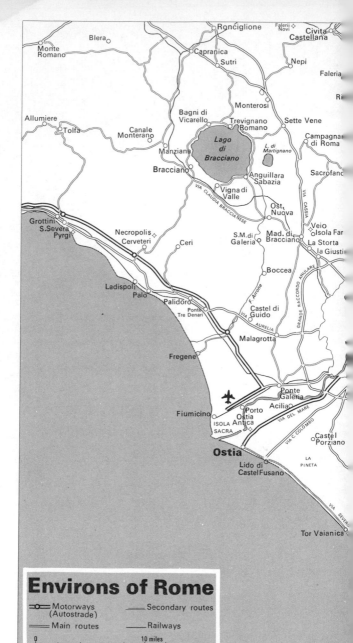

# Environs of Rome

- ○=○ Motorways (Autostrade)
- === Main routes
- ——— Secondary routes
- ——— Railways

```
0                    10 miles
0        10        20 kilometres
```

Ronciglione  
Falerii Novi  
Civita Castellana  
Blera  
Capranica  
Sutri  
Nepi  
Monte Romano  
Faleria  
Monterosi  
Allumiere  
Tolfa  
Canale Monterano  
Bagni di Vicarello  
Trevignano Romano  
Sette Vene  
Campagnano di Roma  
Lago di Bracciano  
L. di Martignano  
Manziana  
Anguillara Sabazia  
Sacrofano  
Bracciano  
VIA CLAUDIA BRACCIANESE  
Vigna di Valle  
Ost. Nuova  
VIA CASSIA  
Grottini S.Severa Pyrgi  
Necropolis Cerveteri  
Ceri  
S.M. di Galeria  
Mad. di Bracciano  
Veio Isola Far  
La Storta  
la Giusti  
Boccea  
GRANDE RACCORDO ANULARE  
Ladispoli  
Palo  
Palidoro  
Ponte Tre Denari  
F. Arrone  
Castel di Guido  
VIA AURELIA  
Malagrotta  
Fregene  
Ponte Galeria  
Acilia  
Fiumicino  
Porto  
Ostia Antica  
ISOLA SACRA  
VIA DEL MARE  
VIA C. COLOMBO  
Castel Porziano  
Ostia  
LA PINETA  
Lido di Castel Fusano  
VIA SEVERI  
Tor Vaianica

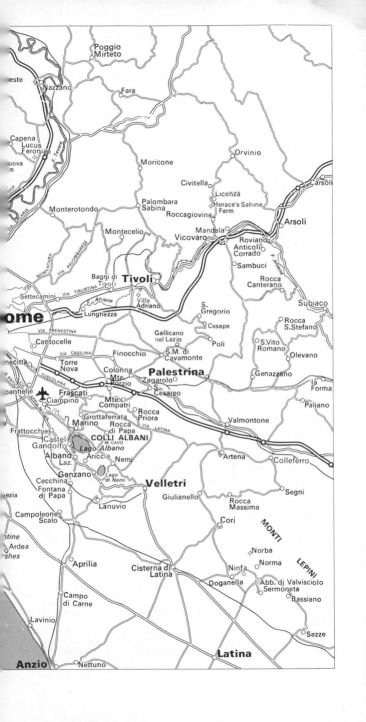

# ENVIRONS OF ROME

The **Roman Campagna** (40-70 m), the country surrounding Rome, is an undulating plain, with indeterminate limits, extending from the Tyrrhenian Sea to a semicircle of hills some distance inland. These are the Monti della Tolfa and Monti Sabatini, to the N.W. of Rome, the Monti Tiburtini and Monti Prenestini, to the E., and the Monti Lepini and Monti Ausoni, to the S.E. The area is traversed by the Tiber, into which flow the Aniene and other tributaries. In the Tertiary Age the plain was occupied by a gulf of the sea, which went even beyond its limits. In this gulf volcanic eruptions formed numerous islands. In the centre the islands became the Alban Hills. In the N.W. they formed a series of ranges, one behind the other, having craters now filled up by lakes, namely the Monti Sabatini, with the Lago di Bracciano, the Monti Cimini, with the Lago di Vico, and the Monti Volsini, with the Lago di Bolsena. The lava from the eruptions spread as far as the hills where Rome later was built.

The name of *Campania Romana,* dating from the time of Constantine and replacing that of *Latium,* was used to distinguish the area from that of the Campania Felix, which surrounds Naples. In the widest sense of the term, the Roman Campagna includes the *Agro Pontino,* formerly the Pontine Marshes, described on p. 335. In a more restricted connotation it is held to comprise the area between the sea, the Monti Sabatini, and the Alban Hills, thus corresponding roughly to that of the *Agro Romano,* or administrative division of the Commune of Rome, with an area of 2074 sq. kilometres and forming a considerable part of the Province of Rome.

The *Province of Rome* (8438 sq. km.) is one of four that make up the modern region of *Lazio;* the others are Frosinone (3064 sq. km.), Rieti (2737 sq. km.), and Viterbo (2934 sq. km.). The area of Lazio is thus 17,174 sq. km.

The Campagna was the focus of almost all the people who were to form the Italic race. Here, in prehistoric times, originated the legends of the earliest struggles of the Romans, and here was displayed the nascent power of the city that was to dominate the world. The land was fertile in Roman times, although even then malaria was prevalent in certain districts. Later, when the work of drainage was abandoned and the waters were allowed to stagnate, the disease raged unchecked, impoverishing and sterilizing the whole region. Today, thanks to unremitting effort, the ancient fertility has returned.

RECLAMATION. In the early days of Rome the growing of corn was the main activity of the Campagna. After their Mediterranean conquests the Romans were able to import cereals and they gave their attention to the planting of gardens and orchards, which they sustained by irrigation. The ruins of the villas, aqueducts and cisterns found in every part of the Agro Romano testify to the productivity of the farms that once surrounded the city. In the early days of the Empire the farms began to be displaced by the large landed estates (*latifundia*), fertility declined, and the population dwindled. The decadence was accelerated by the invasions of the barbarians and by the scourge of malaria. As time went on, some of the popes tried in vain to arrest the decay with schemes of repopulation and the setting up of agricultural centres for the feeding of the city.

United Italy found the Agro Romano one vast malarial desert. The first efforts of the Government (1878) were directed to the drainage of the marshes and stagnant waters and to the reclamation of a belt extending to 10 kilometres from the centre of the city. At the same time the Government divided up the estates of the suppressed religious organizations. In 1883 it established the principle of compulsory cultivation on pain of expropriation. Further measures culminated in the law of 23 Jan 1921, which extended the principle of compulsion to the whole of the Agro Romano. The first effect of these laws was the recuperation of the unhealthy marshy districts, involving the construction of watercourses, drainage canals, and other works, with a view to the re-establishment of agriculture. In the years following the First World War, farms, orchards, and gardens made their appearance and scientific methods were applied to agriculture. New villages were built, replacing the characteristic *capanna,* or hovel, in which, for centuries, the nomadic shepherd had found shelter. Today the Agro Romano is enlivened with cornfields, pasture-land, gardens, orchards, vineyards, and olive groves. Parts of the territory have been left in their natural state.

The environs of Rome are still reached on the line of the ancient Roman roads, with comparative ease and speed from the centre of the capital. They are well served by public transport, but are most conveniently reached by car. The routes given are each intended as a day's excursion from Rome; the more hurried visitor may sometimes combine two routes in a day. The country looks its best in the spring, when the Campagna is in flower, and in autumn, when the hills are ablaze with colour.

# 21   OSTIA

The excavations at Ostia Antica should not be left unvisited.

The Lido di Ostia, now often more appropriately called the Lido di Roma, is the over-crowded seaside resort of Rome. The visitor with his own transport would be well advised to seek more pleasant bathing beaches to the s. (Tor Vaiánica) or n. towards Fregene.

## A   Ostia Antica and the Isola Sacra

ROAD to Ostia Antica, 23 km. VIA DEL MARE (N. 8) from Viale Marconi (p. 95). This two-lane highway reaching the coast (28 km.) at the w. end of the Lido di Ostia (see Rte 21B), was opened in 1928. It runs parallel to the old Via Ostiense for the whole of its length. The *Via Ostiensis,* one of the earliest consular roads, dates from the victorious campaign of the Romans against the inhabitants of Veii to secure their salt supply (5C B.C.). It ran to Ostia from where, under the name of *Via Severiana,* it followed the coast to Laurentum (near Castel Fusano), Antium (Anzio), and Terracina, where it joined the Via Appia.

RAILWAY. *Metropolitana* trains from Termini run c. every 20 min. for Ostia Antica and Ostia Lido. Limited stop trains from Porta S. Paolo call at Tor di Valle—Vitinia—Acilia—Ostia Antica—Lido Centro—Stella Polare—Castel Fusano—Lido Cristoforo Colombo.

Outside Porta San Paolo (Pl. 8; 7) Via Ostiense leads s. After 1½ kilometres, just before the Basilica of San Paolo, Lungotevere San Paolo branches right. This joins Viale Marconi, and off this (r.) begins Via del Mare proper.

The road runs parallel to Via Ostiense, which is on the left. Farther to the left many prominent buildings of E.U.R. (p. 258) are conspicuous. To the right is a road to the racecourse of Tor di Valle.—12 km. Crossing of the Grande Raccordo Anulare (Rome Circular Road).—13 km. *Mezzocammino;* on a hill are the remains of a Roman villa and between

the two roads is the tomb of a Roman knight. The road runs close to the
Tiber for a very short period.—18 km. *Acilia.* Here excavations were
begun in 1976 of *Ficana.* From here three parallel roads continue to the
sea.—23 km. Ostia excavations (turning r.; *Scavi di Ostia Antica*).

From the railway station of Ostia Antica Via Ostiense and Via del
Mare are crossed by a footbridge; straight ahead is the entrance of the
excavations.

At least half a day should be devoted to the *Excavations of Ostia
which are open daily, except Mondays, from 9 to one hour before
sunset. In 1978 the Museum was only open on Thurs (9–13). Cars may be
left at the ticket entrance or (more conveniently) in the car park near the
Museum. Refreshments, see below.

**Ostia,** or *Ostia Antica,* is named after the ostium, or mouth of the Tiber. In
antiquity the river flowed past the city on the N. in a channel, the *Fiume Morto,* dry
since a great flood in 1557. According to legend, Ostia was founded by Ancus
Marcius, fourth king of Rome, to guard the mouth of the river Tiber. The surviving
remains are not, however, older than the 4C B.C., and the city, which was probably
the first colony of Rome, may have been founded about 335 B.C. It was originally a
fortified city (*Castrum*), whose walls survive in part; later it became a much larger
commercial city (*Urbs*), also surrounded with walls. Its first industry was the
extraction of salt from the surrounding marshes, but it soon developed into the
commercial port of Rome and, shortly before the outbreak of the First Punic War
(264 B.C.), it became also a naval base. The link between the port and the capital
was the *Via Ostiensis,* which, carrying as it did all Rome's overseas imports and
exports until the construction of the Via Portuensis, must have been one of the
busiest roads in the ancient world.

The commerce passing through Ostia was vital to the prosperity and even the
existence of Rome. One of its most important functions was the organization of the
*Annona,* for the supply of produce, mainly corn, to the capital. At the head of the
Annona was originally the *Quoestor Ostiensis,* who had to live at Ostia. He was
appointed by lot and his office, according to Cicero, was burdensome and
unpopular. By 44 B.C. the Quoestor was replaced by the *Procuratores Annonoe,*
answerable to the Praefectus Annonæ in Rome. The organization involved the
creation of a large number of commercial associations or guilds covering every
aspect of trade and industry. Numerous inscriptions referring to these associations
have been found in the Piazzale delle Corporazioni. Ostia suffered a temporary
setback in 87 B.C., when it was sacked by Marius, but Sulla rebuilt it soon
afterwards and gave it new walls.

As the city continued to thrive, it outgrew its harbour and the construction of
another port became, by the 1C A.D., an imperative necessity. Augustus planned,
Claudius and Nero built, to the N.W. of Ostia, the new Portus Augusti, which
Trajan enlarged (Porto; see p. 334). For a time Ostia remained the centre of the vast
organization for the supply of food to the capital. It added to its temples, public
buildings, shops and houses, and it received especial marks of favour from the
emperors.

The decadence of Ostia began in the time of Constantine, who favoured Porto.
The titles conferred by the emperor on the newer seaport must have been
particularly galling to the inhabitants of Ostia. But even in the 4C, though it had
become a residential town instead of a commercial port, it was still used by notable
persons travelling abroad. In 387 St Augustine was about to embark for Africa
with his mother, St Monica, when she was taken ill and died in a hotel in the city. In
the following centuries Ostia's decay was accelerated by loss of trade and by the
scourge of malaria. Its streets and temples were neglected and despoiled. Columns,
sarcophagi and statues stolen from the ruins have been found as far afield as Pisa,
Amalfi, Orvieto, and Salerno. An attempt to revive the city was made by Gregory
IV, when he founded the present village of Ostia, but all in vain. In 1756 the city,
which at the height of its prosperity boasted a population of some 80,000 had 156
inhabitants; half a century later there were only a few convicts of the papal
Government; Augustus Hare, writing in 1878, speaks of one human habitation
breaking the utter solitude.

Excavations of the site began on a small scale at the beginning of the 19C, under
Pius VII. Further work was instituted in 1854 under Pius IX, but systematic
excavations did not begin till 1907. They have been continued with few interrup-

tions, until the present day. The work carried out in 1938-42 by Guido Calza and others has been brought to light many monuments of great interest. The excavated area has been doubled and is now c. 33 hectares, or half the area of the city at its greatest extent, and the remains are as important for the study of Roman urban life as those of Pompeii and Herculaneum. The site is attractively planted with umbrella pines and cypresses.

DWELLING HOUSES. One result of research has been the great increase in knowledge of the various types of house occupied by Romans of the middle and lower classes. Since it is not likely that the domestic architecture of Ostia differed radically from that of the capital, the examples that have been unearthed of the lower-grade house at Ostia may be taken as typical of such dwellings in Rome itself. The middle- and lower-class house at Ostia (*Insula*) was in sharp contrast to the typical Pompeian residence (*Domus*), with its atrium and peristyle, its few windows and its low elevation. This occurs only rarely at Ostia.

The ordinary Ostia house usually had four stories and reached a height of 15 metres the maximum permitted by Roman law. It was built of brick, probably not covered with stucco, and has little in the way of adornment. Sometimes bricks of contrasting colours were used. The entrance doors had pilasters or engaged columns supporting a simple pediment. There were numerous rooms, each with its own window. The arches over the windows were often painted in vermilion. Mica or selenite was used instead of glass for the windows. The façades were of three types: living-rooms with windows on all floors; arcaded ground floor with shops, living-rooms above; and ground floor with shops opening on the street, living-rooms above. Many of the houses had balconies, which were of varying designs. The apartment houses contained numerous flats or sets of rooms designated by numbers on the stairs leading to them. They too, were of different types; some were of simple design and others were built round a courtyard.—The rare *Domus*, built for the richer inhabitants, were usually on one floor only and date mostly from the 3C and 4C. They were adorned with apses, nymphaea, and mosaic floors. The rooms often had columns and loggias.

RELIGION. In Ostia, as elsewhere in the Roman world, different religious cults flourished without disharmony. As well as temples dedicated to the traditional deities such as Vulcan, Venus, Ceres, and Fortuna, there was a vigorous cult of the emperors and a surprisingly large number of eastern cults, such as the Magna Mater, Egyptian and Syrian deities, and especially Mithras. Singularly few Christian places of worship have been found.

The city of Ostia appears to have been divided into at least five *Regiones,* the precise limits of which are not yet determined. It has, however, been found convenient to classify the various monuments according to the region to which they are believed to belong. The streets and buildings are thus marked with signs indicating (*a*) the number of the region, (*b*) the number of the block (*c*) the type of construction, such as temple, warehouse, dwelling-house (insula), residence (domus), etc., (*d*) the traditional name of the street or building.—Some of the *Mosaics discovered in the ruins are occasionally covered with wind-blown sand.

The entrance to the excavations (at the ticket office) leads into *Via Ostiense,* outside the walls (since the description of the site begins here, those using the car park near the Museum, comp. above, should return to the ticket office entrance, see the plan p. 331). Parallel on the s. is Via delle Tombe. This street is also outside the walls, in conformity with Roman law, which prohibited intramural burials. In it are a few terracotta sarcophagi and sealed graves, as well as columbaria for the urns holding the ashes from cremations.

The entrance to the city is by the *Porta Romana,* with remains of the gate of the Republican period; some fragments of a marble facing of the Imperial era have been found and placed on the inner walls of the gate.— The PIAZZALE DELLA VITTORIA is dominated by a colossal **Statue of Minerva Victoria,** dating from the reign of Domitian and inspired by a

Hellenistic original. The statue may once have adorned the gate.—On the right of the square are the remains of *Horrea* (warehouses), later converted into baths. In the *Thermoe of the Cisiarii* on the far side of the warehouses are several mosaics, one with scenes of life in Ostia.

Here begins the **Decumanus Maximus,** the main street of Ostia. It runs right through the city and is c. 1200 metres long. A little way along this street, on the right, is a flight of steps leading to a platform, on the second story of the BATHS OF NEPTUNE. From the platform can be seen the tepidarium and calidarium, remains of columns, and the floor of the large entrance hall with a *Mosaic of Neptune driving four sea-horses and surrounded by tritons, nereids, dolphins, etc. In an adjoining room is another mosaic: Amphitrite escorted by Hymen. The platform commands a fine view of the excavations and of the country from the Alban Hills to the mouth of the Tiber.—Adjoining is the *Paloestra* (Gymnasium) a large colonnaded courtyard surrounded by rooms.

Just short of the Baths of Neptune is *Via dei Vigili* (Street of the Firemen), the construction of which involved the demolition of some earlier buildings, to which belonged a mosaic (displayed nearby) representing the Four Winds and Four Provinces (Sicily, Egypt, Africa, Spain). The street leads to the *Caserma dei Vigili* (Firemen's Barracks), built in the 2C A.D. It has an arcaded courtyard, a shrine dedicated to Fortuna Santa, and an *Augusteum,* or shrine for the cult of the emperors.

An archway leads into *Via della Fontana,* one of the best-preserved streets in Ostia. Here is a typical apartment house, with shops and living-rooms over them.

To the right the street joins *Via della Fullonica,* named from its well-equipped fullers' establishment, complete with courtyard for cloth-drying.

The street rejoins the Decumanus Maximus at the *Tavern of Fortunatus* in which is a mosaic pavement with the broken inscription: 'Dicit Fortunatus: vinum cratera quod sitis bibe' ('Fortunatus says: drink wine from the bowl to quench your thirst'). The next street to the right (W.) is *Via delle Corporazioni;* in it is a well-preserved apartment house, with paintings on the walls and ceilings. On the other side of the street is the *Theatre,* built by Agrippa, enlarged by Septimius Severus in the 2C.

The theatre is a semicircular building of the usual Roman type. It has two tiers of seats (originally three), divided by stairways into five sections or *Cunei.* It could accommodate 2700 persons. Of the *Stage* there survive a tufa wall with some marble fragments and three marble masks. Behind the stage have been set up some cipollino columns that once decorated the third tier of the auditorium. In the main façade, towards the Decumanus Maximus, is a series of covered arcades with shops, one appropriately used as a **Refreshment Bar.** Between the arcades and the street are areas paved with travertine and adorned at either end with a fountain. Into the fountain on the E. side was built a *Christian Oratory* in honour of St Cyriacus and his fellow-martyrs of Ostia.

Behind the theatre extends the spacious *PIAZZALE DELLE CORPORAZIONI (Square of the Guilds). In this square were 70 offices of commercial associations ranging from workers' guilds to corporations of foreign representatives from all over the ancient world. Their trade-marks are preserved in the mosaic floors of the brick-built arcade running round the square. The trade-marks of the foreign representatives are historically valuable, as they tell from where the merchants came (e.g. Carthage, Alexandria, Narbonne, etc.) and what was their trade. Equally informative are the inscriptions relating to the citizens, some of whom were employed in ship repair and construction, in the maintenance of docks, warehouses, and embankments, as dockers, salvage crews, and customs and excise officials.—In the middle of the square are the stylobate and two columns of a small temple in antis known as the *Temple of Ceres,* and the bases of statues erected to the leading citizens of Ostia.

Beyond the square is a handsome house of the Pompeian type, rare at Ostia, with an atrium and rooms decorated with mosaics. It is called the *House of Apuleius.* Beside it is a *Mithræum,* one of the best-preserved of the many temples dedicated to Mithras in the city. It has two galleries for the initiated, on the walls of which are mosaics illustrating the cult of the god. There are also casts of the marble relief of Mithras which was found here, with several inscriptions.

In front are four small tetrastyle *Temples,* erected in the 2C b.c. upon a single foundation of tufa. They are supposed to have been dedicated to Venus, Fortuna, Ceres, and Hope. In the square in front of the temples are the remains of a *Nymphæum* and of a *Sanctuary of Jupiter.*

From the Decumanus Maximus can be seen, on the right, large *Warehouses (Horrea)* for the storage of corn. They have over 60 small rooms, some of them arranged round a central colonnaded courtyard. At the corner of the next street on the right—*Via dei Molini,* so called after a building in it containing millstones—are the remains of a *Republican Temple.* Here is the *Porta Orientale,* the East Gate of the original fortified city, or Castrum; to the left are the original tufa walls. At this point the Decumanus Maximus has been excavated down to the level of the ancient city and is liable to flooding in bad weather.

A street on the w. side of Via dei Molini—*Via di Diana*—takes its name from a house called the *CASA DI DIANA.* The façade is characteristic: shops on the ground floor, rooms with windows on the first floor, and a projecting balcony on the second floor. The house is entered through a vaulted corridor. On the ground floor is a room (l.) whose ceiling and walls have been restored with fragments of frescoes. The small interior courtyard has a fountain and a relief of Diana. At the back of the premises are two rooms converted into a Mithræum. Opposite the entrance to the Casa di Diana Via dei Lari opens into *Piazzetta dei Lari,* with a round marble altar dedicated to the Lares of the Quarter.

In Via di Diana beyond the Casa di Diana, is (l.) the *Thermopolium,* which bears a striking resemblance to a modern Italian bar. Just outside the entrance, under the balcony, are two small seats. On the threshold is a marble counter, on which is a small stone basin. Inside the shop is another counter for the display of food dishes; above are wall-paintings of fruit and vegetables. On the rear wall is a marble slab with hooks for hats and coats. Beyond is a delightful court and fountain.

At the end of Via di Diana (r.) is an apartment house, originally of four stories, called the CASA DEI DIPINTI. A staircase leads up to the top floor from which there is a fine view of the excavations. The ground floor (entered around the corner from Via dei Dipinti) has been closed: the corner room has a mosaic floor and 'architectural' wall-paintings; beyond is a fine *Hall painted with mythological scenes, human figures, and landscapes. In the garden of the house are numerous *Dolii,* large terracotta jars for the storage of corn and oil.—At the end of the street is the Museum, which contains the principal finds from the excavations.

The *Museo Ostiense* is housed in a building dating from 1500 and originally used by the authorities concerned with the extraction of salt; it was given its neo-classical façade in 1864. The exhibits have been recently well rearranged.

Room I (left). *Bas reliefs showing scenes of everyday life (including various arts and crafts, the scene of a birth, a surgical operation, etc.); by the window, two bas-reliefs with the plan of a temple and the topographical plan of a city.—Room II. Architectural and decorative terracotta fragments; Statue of Fortune (2C A.D.).— Off the Atrium (with a statue of Apollo Kitharoidos of 2C A.D.) are (l.) RR. III and IV with works relating to Eastern cults. R. III. In the niche at one end, *Mithras slaying the bull, from the Baths of Mithras, signed by Kritios of Athens (first half of the 2C B.C.); in the niche to the r., group of 18 cult statues found in the Sanctuary of Attis (140–170 A.D.); circular *Altar with reliefs of the Twelve Gods, a neo-Attic work of the 1C B.C.—R. IV. Recumbent figure of a priest of Cybele (second half of 3C A.D.); Egyptian-Roman relief in black basalt of Asklepios; Stele with a boy initiated in the cult of Isis (early 4C A.D.).

Steps descend from the Atrium into Room VI. To the left is R. V with sculpture inspired by Greek art of 5C B.C.: inscribed Bases testifying to the presence of Greek artists; Head of Hermes; Votive relief (an original Greek-Italiot work of the first half of 5C B.C.); three heads of Athena, from originals of the Phidias type, the Kressilas type, and the Kephisodotos type (first half of 4C B.C.); upper part of a herm of Themistocles, copy of an original of the 5C; Omphalos Apollo, from the 5C original; Head of an unknown man.—R. VI contains sculpture inspired by Greek art of the 4C and 3C B.C.: two copies of Eros drawing his bow (one a replica of an original by Lysippos); cult statue of Asklepios (?); two herms of Hermes (of the Alcamene type); Dionysos (with elements inspired by Praxiteles). In the centre, fragment of a group of Wrestlers dating from the Trajan era on a Hellenistic model.—R. VII. Sculpture inspired by Hellenistic works. Head of a satyr and of a barbarian of the Pergamene type (2C B.C.); two heads of Korai; Head of Victory (Giulio-Claudian era); Perseus with the head of Medusa; Cupid and Psyche from the House of Cupid and Psyche; replica of the crouching Venus of Doidalsas (3C B.C.; comp. p. 194); Statue of the Three Graces.

The glass cases between R. VI and R. VIII contain Attic pottery (including a fragment of a red-figure cup showing Orpheus dating from the second half of 5C B.C.), Aretine vases, and 'terra sigillata' ware.—R. VIII (Sala Guido Calza). Roman sculpture from the 1C B.C. to the mid-2C A.D. *Headless male statue, nude except for the drapery over the left arm, signed with the name of the donor C. Cartilius Poplicola, whose sarcophagus is near Porta Marina. This statue is regarded as the best extant copy of the type known as the Hero in Repose; Portraits of Augustus, Trajan (including a statue of him wearing a cuirass), Hadrian, Sabina, wife of Hadrian, and a group of portraits of members of the family of Marcus Aurelius. Herm of Hippocrates (from an original of 3C B.C.); funerary statue of Giulia Procula; relief (fragment of an architectural frieze) showing the sacred geese in front of the Temple of Juno Moneta on the Capitoline (comp. p. 56).—The small cases between R. VIII and R. X contain kitchen pottery, terracotta statuettes, and oil lamps.

Room IX (left of R. X). Roman sarcophagi of the 2–3C A.D., including the *Sarcophagus of a boy, from the Isola Sacra Necropolis, a magnificent example of the Attic type, dating from the 2C A.D.; on the lid is the figure of a boy lying on a couch decorated with bas-reliefs; while three sides have reliefs of Dionysiac rites with a charming freize of putti (illustrating the direct influence sarcophagi of this type had on artists of the Renaissance). On the back is the scene of a wrestling match which was left in a rough, unfinished state. Also displayed here, Sarcophagus with a scene of Lapiths and Centaurs.—R. X. Roman sculpture (end of 2C to 4C A.D.). Maxentius (?) as Pontifex Maximus, found in the Edificio degli Augustali; Statue of Fausta, sister of Maxentius (310–312 A.D.); Giulia Domna, in the semblance of Ceres, and a bust of Septimius Severus, her husband.—R. XI. Roman art of the 4-5C A.D. Magnificent *Opus sectile panels found in an edifice near Porta Marina. The design includes various portraits, and a head thought to be that of Christ (with a halo), and two scenes of a lion attacking a horse. Relief showing scribes recording an orator's speech (thought to have a Christian significance).—Between R. IX and R. XII cases display Roman glass (including a cup engraved with the figure of Christ, the Cross, and the Monogram, 4-5C), and objects in bone, ivory, bronze, and lead.—R. XII. Imperial wall paintings and mosaic fragments.

Parallel with Via dei Dipinti, on the w. is the wide CARDO MAXIMUS with arcaded shops, which runs from the Tiber to the Forum and from there to the Porta Laurentina. To the w. of this street and also parallel is the narrow *Via Tecta,* on the brick walls of which have been affixed many of the best preserved inscriptions found in the ruins. Via Tecta runs beside a grain warehouse called the *Piccolo Mercato;* some of its rooms form the Antiquarium Ostiense housing archæological material (no adm.). In the s. wall have been incoporated several layers of the tufa blocks of the primitive city walls.—The Cardo Maximus runs s. to the **Forum,** which is traversed from E. to W. by the Decumanus Maximus. At the N. end of the Forum is the **\*Capitolium,** the city's most important temple, dedicated to Jupiter, Juno, and Minerva. This prostyle hexastyle building, dating from the first half of the 2C had six fluted white marble columns. The pronaos is reached by a wide flight of steps, before which is an altar (reconstituted). In the cella are niches and a plinth for statues of the deities.

During the invasion of the barbarians the temple was stripped of nearly all its marble facing, but a magnificent slab of African marble is still in place on the threshold and a few surviving marble fragments have been placed to the E. of the building under a colonnade, which defined the sacred area.

Opposite the Capitolium, on the s. side of the Forum, are the remains of the 1C TEMPLE OF ROME AND AUGUSTUS. Like the Capitolium it had six fluted marble columns across the front, but with two side staircases. Fragments of the pediment have been placed on a modern wall to the E.; the cult statue of Rome as Victory, dressed as an Amazon, has been placed inside the temple on a plinth, and a headless statue of Victory near the rearranged pediment fragments.

On the E. side of the Forum are the BATHS OF THE FORUM, built in the 2C and restored in the 4C. When restored the baths were adorned with mosaics and cipollino columns; some of the columns have been re-erected. The *Frigidarium* survives, together with a series of rooms warmed by hot air. Off the N. side is the town *Forica,* with its 20 seats all but completely preserved.—Also on the E. side, at the corner where the Decumanus Maximus enters the Forum, is the *Casa dei Triclini,* so called from the couches to be found in each of the three rooms on the right wing of the central courtyard. Behind the courtyard is a room with a high podium decorated with coloured marbles.

Opposite, on the w. side of the Forum, is the BASILICA, or law courts and place of assembly. The façade towards the Forum had a portico of marble arches with a decorated frieze. Fragments of this decoration and of the columns have been preserved. To the s. of the Basilica is the *Tempio Rotondo,* dating from the 3C and probably an *Augusteum,* or temple erected to the worship of the emperors. The peristyle was paved with mosaics and surrounded by marble-faced niches. It was reached by a flight of steps (preserved), which led to the pronaos; this comprised a portico with brick piers faced with marble and with cipollino columns. In the cella are seven niches, three rectangular and four circular. Between the niches are column bases; to the right are the remains of a spiral staircase that led to the dome.

Also on the w. side, N. of the Decumanus Maximus, is the *Curia,* or senate house. The inscriptions on the walls are lists of *Augustales,* citizens of Ostia belonging to the cult of the emperors.—Beside the Curia is the *Casa del Larario,* or House of the Shrine of the Lares, a combination of a house and shopping centre.

Leaving the Forum the Decumanus Maximus continues to the *Porta Occidentale,* the West Gate of the original Castrum; the ancient walls are well seen in Via degli Horrea Epagathiana, a turning on the right. In this street are the *HORREA EPAGATHIANA ET EPAPHRODITIANA, warehouses in a remarkable state of preservation, and used as a sherd store (no adm.).

These warehouses were built by two Eastern freedmen, Epagathus and Epaphroditus, whose names are preserved on a marble plaque above the entrance; this is a brick portal with two engaged columns supporting a pediment. The inner courtyard was surrounded by an arcade of brick piers, repeated on the upper floor. On the walls of the vestibule and courtyard are four intact aediculae. In a large vaulted room at the rear of the Horrea are further remains of the primitive town wall.

The region to the w. of the Decumanus Maximus is that excavated in 1938-42. The Decumanus Maximus now forks. The right fork is *Via della Foce* (Street of the River Mouth); it has been excavated for c. 270 m. The left fork is the continuation of the Decumanus Maximus (see p. 324) and runs s.w. to the Porta Marina, or Sea Gate.

In Via della Foce, on the left, a long passageway leads to the *Mitreo delle Pareti Dipinte,* built in the 2C into a house of the Republican period. The Mithraeum is divided into two parts by partly projecting walls with ritual niches. The two stucco-faced galleries of the inner section also have niches. In the rear wall is the brick-built altar, with a marble cippus on which is a bust of Mithras. On the N. wall are paintings of initiation rites.

A short street to the right leads to the *Sacred Area of Three Republican Temples.* The central and largest is the prostyle hexastyle *Temple of Hercules Invictus.* The pronaos, paved with mosaics, is reached by a flight of nine steps as wide as the façade. Inside the cella was a small marble column carved to represent the club of Hercules with the lion skin thrown over it. The temple, which may date from the time of Sulla, was given an altar in the 4C A.D. by Hostilius Antipater, Praefectus Annonae (comp. p. 322).—On the N. side of the Sacred Area is a *Tetrastyle Temple* (dedication unknown) of the same date as the first.—Between the Temple of Hercules and Via della Foce is the *Temple of the Amorini,* named after a round marble altar with winged cupids found there. It was built in the early republican and rebuilt in the Imperial period. Its final form was distyle in antis.

Behind the temple is a street leading to the *House of Cupid and Psyche,* a Domus dating from the end of the 3C. It is named after a marble group found in it and now in the Museum. On the w. side of the central atrium are four rooms, one with a pavement of coloured marbles (and a copy of the statue); on the E. is an attractive nymphaeum in a courtyard with columns and brick arches. At the N. end of the Atrium is a large room paved with opus sectile, and preserving some marble mural facing.—Farther along Via della Foce, is *Via delle Terme di Mitra* (r.). The BATHS OF MITHRAS date from Trajan and were rebuilt in the 2C. They had elaborate arrangements of heating and for pumping the water. In the basement is a Mithraeum, in which was found the group of Mithras and the Bull, now in the Museum.

On the left side of the main street are three blocks of small apartment houses; then follows a complex of two apartment blocks with baths between them. The *Insula di Serapide* is named after a figure of Serapis in an aedicula which adorns the courtyard.—The *Terme dei Sette Sapienti* were so called from a satirical painting of the Seven Sages found in one of the rooms. The Sages are distinguished by name (in Greek); to each of them is attached a frank inscription on the subject of rude health. The baths have a round central hall (once domed), paved with a beautiful *Mosaic with five concentric rows of hunting scenes, including what appears to be a tiger. In a room next to a marble plunge pool is a painting of Venus Anadyomene.—A passage leads to the extensive *Insula degli Aurighi,* an apartment block with large central courtyard. Two small paintings of charioteers belonging to opposing factions in the E. wall of the arcade give the house its name. Off the N. walk is a flat of six rooms with interesting paintings. Beyond the E. side of the courtyard is a shrine presumably of Mithras.

Farther along Via della Foce, on the left, is a group of buildings of Hadrian's time. The *Baths of Trinacria* preserve good mosaics, and interesting installations for heating and conducting the water. On the other side of Via Serapeo is the *House of Bacchus and Ariadne,* with rich floral mosaics. The *Serapeum,* behind, was dedicated in A.D. 127, and included a temple, with courtyard flanked by porticoes and cult rooms. To the W., originally connected with the Serapeum, is an admirable domus, with more mosaics.

Beyond the Insula degli Aurighi is *Via degli Aurighi,* which runs E. to join the extension of the Decumanus Maximus. In this street are the *Insula delle Celle* (l.), a type of warehouse with small rooms, and, opposite, a modest hotel with a stable called *Albergo con Stalla.* This inn also faces a street named after the *Insula delle Volte Dipinte* (no adm.), with painted ceilings. Across the street is the *Casa delle Muse* (temporarily closed), dating from the time of Hadrian. This house has a central courtyard with a covered arcade. The restored wooden roof of the arcade rests on the ancient brick cornice. In a room to the E. are paintings of Apollo and the Muses; in one to the N. are panel paintings of divinities and satyrs. On a wall of the arcade are some graffiti, one of them representing the lighthouse of Ostia.

To the right is the *Casa a Pareti Gialle,* or House with the Yellow Walls. This looks on to a vast square of four large apartment houses built round a garden and known as the *Case a Giardino.* The scale of construction, the provision of a private garden, and the absence of shops all indicate that the flats in these buildings were intended for the wealthier inhabitants of Ostia.

The Decumanus Maximus and its extension from the fork outside the West Gate, continues s.w. and runs for 350 m to the Porta Marina and, beyond it, to the sea-coast. The *Porta Marina,* or Sea Gate, was an opening in the walls built by Sulla, remains of which may be seen. Just inside the gate is a wine-shop the *Caupona di Alexander,* and, outside, a large square. The extension of the Decumanus Maximus beyond the gate, built in the time of Augustus, ran through an earlier cemetery (comp. below). On this section is the *Santuario della Bona Dea,* a small prostyle tetrastyle temple, whose four column bases survive. Farther towards the sea is the *Domus Fulminata,* with a small monument recording the fact that the house had been struck by lightning.— Opposite, Via di Cartilio Poplicola leads to the *Baths of Porta Marina* past the *Tomb of L. Cartilius Poplicola,* a prominent citizen. The surviving fragment of its decorative frieze shows a trireme adorned with

the helmeted head of a goddess. This and another tomb close by attest to
the existence of a cemetery in the Republican era.

On the outskirts of the town towards the shore; between the sea and the ancient
Via Severiana (on the s.w. side of this street) has been excavated (1961-63) the most
ancient Jewish *Synagogue* known from monumental remains. It was in continuous
use from the 1C to the 5C A.D. Ritual carvings and poorly preserved mosaics have
been found; several Ionic columns have been re-erected. It was discovered while
the new road to Fiumicino airport was being laid out.

The Decumanus Maximus returns past the charming *Fontana a
Lucerna.* In a street to the s. beyond the junction with Via degli Aurighi
is a block of shops with windows beside their doors. Close by is the
SCHOLA DI TRAIANO, seat of an Ostian corporation named after a statue
of Trajan found in it. In the courtyard, which has stuccoed brick
columns, is a long basin provided with niches. The central room has a
headless statue of Fortuna and a mosaic pavement. The school overlay
earlier constructions, among them a 1C Domus; its nymphæum has
been partly restored.—On the opposite side of the main street is the
*School of the Naval Smiths,* with a temple. The arcade of the courtyard
in front of the temple was evidently a marble store: unused and partly
finished columns, bases and capitals have been found in it. The store
appears to have belonged to Volusianus, a senator of the 4C, as his name
is carved on some of the column shafts. Adjoining is the *Christian
Basilica,* an unpretending structure with two aisles divided by columns
and ending in apses.

Vico del Dionisio leads s. to the *Cortile di Dionisio,* surrounded by several
houses, and to the *Mitreo delle Sette Porte,* a Mithræum which displays in seven
arches the seven grades of the Mithraic cult.

The Decumanus Maximus continues to (r.) the *Macellum,* or Market,
which occupies the area between the Decumanus and a street running s.,
*Via Occidentale del Pomerio.* The market has numerous shops; two fish-
shops open on to the Decumanus. Behind them is the market-place.—
Via Occidentale del Pomerio and Via del Tempio Rotondo behind the
Tempio Rotondo at the s. end of the Forum lead to the s. continuation of
the Cardo Maximus. On the right here is the *Domus di Giove
Fulminatore,* a house of the Republican period remodelled in the 4C,
with a striking phallic 'doormat' mosaic. Beside it is the *Domus della
Nicchia a Mosaico,* another Republican house, twice rebuilt. It is named
after a semicircular niche faced with polychrome mosaic in the
tablinum. Adjoining is the *Ninfeo degli Eroti,* with well-preserved
marble floor and walls and niches in which were found two copies of the
Eros of Lysippos. The next building is the DOMUS DELLE COLONNE, a
large corner house, with façades on the Cardo Maximus and on Via
della Caupona del Pavone (r.) In the centre of the courtyard is a stone
basin with a double apse and short white marble columns; beyond is the
large tablinum with its entrance between two columns.

In the side street is an ancient wine-shop, the 3C *Caupone del Pavone.* One of its
rooms is decorated with paintings of flying bacchanals and muses; beyond is the
bar, with a counter and small basins.—On the opposite side of the street is the
*Domus dei Pesci,* evidently a Christian house. A vestibule has a mosaic with a
chalice and fishes. A large room on the s. side, with two marble columns, has a fine
*Mosaic Floor.

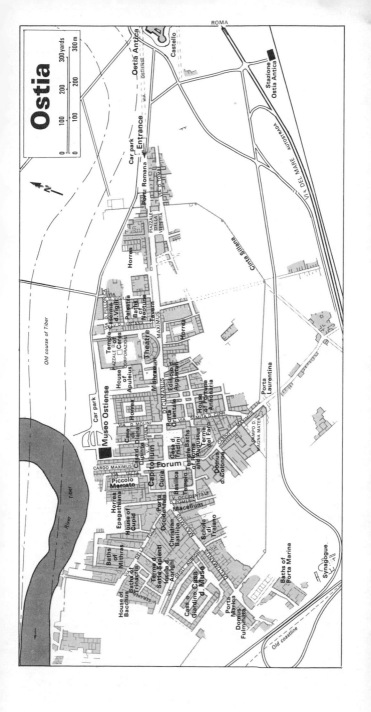

# Ostia

0   100   200   300 m
0   100   200   300 yards

ROMA

Ostia Antica
VIA OSTIENSE
Castello

Stazione
Ostia Antica

VIA DEL MARE   AUTOSTRADA

Cinta Sillana

VIA DELLA VITTORIA

Old course of Tiber

River Tiber

Old coastline

Car park
Entrance
Porta Romana

PIAZZALE
DELLA
VITTORIA

Horrea

VIA DELLA
FOCE

VIA DELLA
CASERMA
D. VIGILI

Temple of Ceres
Caserma
d. Vigili
Palestra
Baths of
Neptune
Tavern

House
of
Apuleius

PIAZZALE
CORPORAZIONI

VIA DEGLI
HORREA

Theatre

Mithraeum

DECUMANUS
MAXIMUS

Horrea

Museo Ostiense

Car park

Casa d. Temo
Casa di Diana
Caseggiato
d. Molini

VIA D. MOLINI
VIA DIANA

Edificio di
Augustana

House of
Fortuna
Annonaria

VIA SEMITA D. CIPPI

Porta
Laurentina

CAMPO D.
MAGNA MATER

CARDO MAXIMUS

Piccolo
Mercato

Horrea
Epagathiana

House of
Cupid

Baths
of
Mithras

Capitolium

Forum

Casa d.
Triclini

Temple Baths
of Rome
and Augustus

Domus
d. Colonne

CARDO
MAXIMUS

Curia

Basilica

Tempio
Rotondo

VIA OCCIDENTALE

Porta
Occidentale

Macellum

Christian
Basilica

VIA D. POMPIERI

Schola
di Traiano

DECUMANUS MAXIMUS

Baths of
Trinacria

Baths of
Porta Marina

Terme d.
Sette Sapienti

VIA DELLE SEBASTE

Casa d.
Aurighi

VIA DEGLI AURIGHI

House of
Bacchus

Casa a.
giardini

Casa
d. Muse

Porta
Marina

Domus
Fulminata

Synagogue

Old coastline

The Cardo Maximus passes on the right the *Portico dell'Ercole;* opposite is a fulling mill. Adjoining are the TERME DEL FARO. In a floor of the Frigidarium of the baths is a mosaic with fishes, sea monsters, and a lighthouse (pharos), after which the baths were named. One of the rooms has a white marble pool and frescoed walls in the 3C style.—A ramp leads from the Cardo to the triangular CAMPO DELLA MAGNA MATER, one of the best preserved sacred areas of the Roman world. At the W. corner is the prostyle hexastyle *Temple of Cybele.* At the E. corner the *Sanctuary of Attis* has an apse flanked by telamones in the shape of fauns. On the same side is the *Temple of Bellona,* dating from the time of Marcus Aurelius, and, opposite, the *Schola degli Hastiferes,* seat of an association connected with the cult of Bellona.—The sanctuary is close to the *Porta Laurentina,* which retains the tufa blocks of Sulla's circumvallation (c. 80 B.C.).

To the S. of the Porta Laurentina, along the line of the ancient Via Laurentina, is (½ km.) the *Cemetery of the Porta Laurentina,* first excavated in 1865 and systematically explored in 1934-35. Many of the inscriptions relate to freedmen. Beyond the motorway, in the locality called Pianabella, excavations are in progress of a necropolis and Christian church.

A short distance back along the Cardo Maximus, the *Semita dei Cippi* leads to the right (N.). This street is flanked by two cippi and contains a 3C Domus (*Casa del Protiro*), its reconstituted portal prettily flanked by cypresses. To the N. a right turn leads into a street named after the *House of Fortuna Annonaria,* which has a garden in its peristyle. On the W. side of the peristyle is a large room with three arches, columns, and a nymphæum.

At the end of the street, on the right, is another temple of Bona Dea, with a mithræum next door, notable for its mosaic pavement.

Also in the street is the *Domus Republicana,* with four Doric columns; it is adjoined by the *Edificio degli Augustali,* the headquarters of the Augustales (p. 328). This building has another entrance in Via degli Augustali, which leads to the Decumanus Maximus, and the main entrance.

Near the entrance to the excavations lies **Ostia,** a fortified village whose walls are still standing, founded by Gregory IV in 830 and given the name of *Gregoriopolis.* Today Ostia (3000 inhab.) is a collection of picturesque old houses, most of them restored, within the walls, and some modern houses outside. Its dominant feature is the *CASTELLO (open 9-12 exc. Mon), built in 1483-86 by Baccio Pontelli for Julius II while still a cardinal. It contains archæological collections of minor importance from the excavations. The church of *Santa Aurea,* by Baccio Pontelli or Meo del Caprina, contains the body of the martyred St Aurea (d. 268) and, in a side chapel, a fragment of a gravestone which is most probably that of St Monica (d. 387), mother of St Augustine; the Episcopal Palace is the residence of the Bishop of Ostia, holder of one of the six suburbicarian sees allotted to the cardinal bishops.

Via del Mare continues to the coast and (4 km.) *Lido di Ostia* (Rte 21B). A branch road skirts the excavations, curving right (signposted to Fiumicino) on a spur from Via del Mare. It crosses the Tiber to the **Isola Sacra,** a tract of land made into an island by the cutting of Trajan's canal, the Fossa Traiana, from Porto to the sea (see Rte 21C). It derives its name from the necropolis of the ancient seaport. Its area has been considerably increased by silt deposits.

The region, once a flourishing horticultural centre, was abandoned after the fall of the Western Empire and degenerated into an uninhabited malarial marsh. So it remained until in 1920 it was taken over by the Opera Nazionale Combattenti; and now it has been completely reclaimed. Swamps have been drained, roads ballasted, canals dug, and houses, schools, farms, and silos built.

About 1 km. farther on is a small signpost (r.) for the **Necropolis of Portus Romæ,** or the *Sepolcreto dell'Isola Sacra* (open 9-12.30, 15.30-16 or 17.30, exc. Mon). A track leads to the delightfully planted site. This was the cemetery of Trajan's seaport, later known as Portus Romæ and still later as Porto. It was not used for burials from the earlier Portus Augusti (see p. 334).It was in use for c. 250 years, from the 2C to the 4C. Only part has been excavated as much of it is under cultivation.

Since the necropolis was the burial-place of the middle- and lower-class inhabitants of Porto such as merchants, artisans, craftsmen, sailors, and the like, there are no elaborate mausolea. The tombs, which have been preserved by the sand that covered them for centuries, are arranged in groups. They have or had barrel vaults of brick and masonry faced with stucco; some of them had gable roofs. Internally they are decorated with stuccoes, paintings, and mosaics. Sarcophagi and urns in columbaria have been found, often in the same tomb— evidence of the simultaneous practice of burial and cremation. Many of the sarcophagi are adorned with mythological reliefs; terracotta reliefs are found with representations of arts and crafts, indicating the trade of the deceased. Nearly every tomb has a name inscribed over the door. The tombs of the wealthier citizens have sepulchral chambers, with fanlights. Outside, by the door, are couches for funeral feasts.

Some of the tombs are like old-fashioned round-topped travelling trunks, and recall similar examples in North Africa. The poorest citizens, who could not afford the cost of a monument buried their dead in the ground and marked the place with amphoræ through which they poured libations; or they set up large tiles to form a peaked roof over the remains.

The road through the cemetery—the Via Flavia—is a section of the ancient road from Ostia to Porto. Of particular interest are a *Chamber Tomb* (11), with a marble sarcophagus with a scene of a funeral feast, and two other sarcophagi; the *Tomb of the Children* (16), with mosaics, an entrance adorned with Nile, and a beautiful sarcophagus now in the Museo Ostiense; the *Tomb of the Smith* (29), with a façade divided by three pilasters and terracotta reliefs indicating the man's trade; the *Tomb of Telesphorus and Julia Eunia* (39), with the Christian symbols of the lamb, dove, and anchor, apparently unique in this cemetery; a two-storied tomb (41); a tomb with a ship mosaic with the Pharos of Porto (43). In the row behind are two tombs (55 and 56), the first pedimental, the second with a square-corniced façade, both preserving their inscriptions. Close by are a series of *Four Chamber Tombs* (77-80), with pedimental façades with reliefs (the paintings from these tombs are in the Ostia Antiquarium).

The road continues to Fiumicino and the Airport (Rte 21c).

## B    Lido di Ostia

Road. The fastest route is Via Cristoforo Colombo (27 km.).

Railway. Trains from Porta S. Paolo and the Metropolitana from Termini run c. every 20 min. to Lido Centro—Stella Polare—Castel Fusano—Lido Cristoforo Colombo, viâ Ostia Antica.

Buses from Piazzale Ostiense viâ E.U.R. to Castel Fusano. The sea-front from Castel Fusano to Fiumicino is served by frequent bus services.

Via Cristoforo Colombo is a straight four-lane highway, which is a continuation of the road running through the centre of E.U.R. (Rte 19). It reaches the coast at **Castel Fusano** and the beautiful pine forest of

Rome (*La Pineta*). This spreads over 4 km. and has convenient interior roads.

The first pines were planted c. 1710. In 1755 the property was acquired by the Chigi family and was afterwards let as a royal chase. In 1932 it was bought by the Commune of Rome and in 1933 part of it was opened as a public park.

**Lido di Ostia** itself extends for several kilometres to the w. It has been the capital's seaside resort since the First World War. New hotels, bathing establishments, villas and blocks of flats continue to be built in this overcrowded summer town, all but deserted in winter. On the E., Via del Mare from Rome (Rte 21A) terminates, and farther along the esplanade a road leads to the *Idroscalo*, the former seaplane station near the mouth of the Tiber.

# C   Porto and Fiumicino

MOTORWAY. Air passengers for Fiumicino (main airport of Rome) take Autostrada A16 from Stazione Trastévere. At 21 km. it diverges to the right for Civitavecchia, but an extension continues to the airport.

VIA PORTUENSE runs viâ Porto to Fiumicino. Beyond Stazione Trastévere, at the end of the broad Viale Trastévere, Via Portuense diverges right. This follows the ancient *Via Portuensis* which ran on the right bank of the Tiber to Portus Augusti, later Portus Traiani, and now the modern village of Porto.

24 km. **Porto,** now 5 km. inland, was once a seaport of greater significance than Ostia. To the w. of the village, on the right of the road, is a hexagonal basin built by Trajan, now called the *Lago Traiano* (in a private villa; no adm.).

When the harbour of Ostia, already inadequate for its trade, began to silt up with the action of the Tiber, Augustus planned the creation of a larger port in the vicinity. In A.D. 42 Claudius began operations. His harbour, of which scarcely any traces remain, was sited about 1 km. w. of the basin which Trajan built later. It was connected to the Tiber by a canal. The work was completed in 54 by Nero, who issued commemorative coins stamped *Portus Augusti.* Even this harbour proved insufficient and in 103 Trajan constructed a new basin, the *Portus Traiani,* hexagonal in shape (650 m across), surrounded by warehouses, and forming the nucleaus of a city. It is today merely a picturesque little lake (Lago Traiano), but shows up excellently from the air when landing at Fiumicino. Recent excavations have unearthed the remains of granaries, porticoes, and baths. Trajan as well as Claudius, dug canals in connection with the seaport. The *Fossa Traiana* survives as a navigable canal between the Tiber and the sea, forming the Isola Sacra (p. 333). In this island was the city's cemetery.—Porto was favoured by Constantine at the expense of Ostia; in 314 it had its own bishop and became known as *Portus Romoe* or *Civitas Constantina.* In the village are the church of *Santa Rufina* (10C, rebuilt), an old episcopal palace, and the Villa Torlonia (with a safari-park). The suburbicarian see of Porto and Santa Rufina is one of the six held by the cardinal bishops.

To the right are the graceful cantilevered buildings of *Leonardo da Vinci Airport,* still usually called 'Fiumicino', officially brought into operation early in 1961.

28 km. **Fiumicino** is a small seaside resort, which was heavily bombed in the Second World War.—From Fiumicino by road to Ostia and Lido di Ostia across the Isola Sacra, see Rte 21A and 21B.

## 22  ANZIO AND NETTUNO

ROAD (Via Pontina), 60 km. Buses from Rome (Viale Carlo Felice) to *Anzio* and *Nettuno* hourly viâ Pavona and Aprília in 1 hr., or viâ Albano and Aprília in 1½ hrs.

RAILWAY. From Rome (Termini) to *Anzio* (57 km.) in c. 1 hr; to *Nettuno,* (60 km.) in 3 min. more.

Both road and railway cross the AGRO PONTINO, a tract of land with an area of c. 750 sq. km. formerly known as the *Pontine* or *Pomptine Marshes* and regarded as a part of the Roman campagna in the widest sense of that term. The Agro Pontino is a plain extending s.w. to the coast of Latium from the Via Appia (Highway 7) between Cisterna di Latina and Terracina. As its former name implies, the plain, even in Roman times, was marshy, though, when the Appian Way was built in 213 B.C., the marshes must have covered a relatively small part of the whole, which is said to have supported 23 towns. One of these towns was the long-vanished *Pontia,* which gave its name to the district. The marshes were mainly formed by numerous small streams which could not find their way to the sea and therefore stagnated. When the marshes spread the whole area became pestilential and the inhabitants, attacked by malaria, died off or moved elsewhere if they could. Until recent years it was sparsely populated and it had a sinister reputation.

Julius Cæsar planned to drain the marshes but his assassination wrecked the project. In the time of Augustus a navigable canal, which partly drained off the waters, ran alongside the Appian Way. Horace used this canal in the course of his journey from Rome to Brundusium in 37 B.C. (*Satires,* I, 5); he embarked on the canal barge at Appii Forum (at the 43rd milestone on the Appian Way) and left it at Anxur (Terracina). No further work of importance was undertaken until the 16C, when Leo X (1513-21) cut the *Canale Portatore* to run from the Appian Way into the sea at Porto Badino, w. of Terracina. Sixtus V (1585-90) built a more ambitious canal, the *Fossa Sisto,* which runs parallel to the Appian Way on its s.w. side and reaches the sea to the w. of Leo X's canal. Pius VI (1775-99) enlarged the Canale Portatore and built the *Canale Linea Pio,* which accompanies the Appian Way for 30 kilometres.

Not until 1928 did reclamation of the marshes begin in earnest. In that year the Agro Pontino was divided into two reclamation areas, the Bonifica di Piscinara and the Bonifica Pontina, one on each side of the Fossa Sisto. More canals were built, as well as roads and other works. In 1931 the Opera Nazionale Combattenti undertook the task of colonization, leaving the land reclamation to the earlier organizations. New towns began to arise. The year 1932 saw the foundation of Littoria, now Latina, in the centre of the Agro Pontino. There followed in 1934 Sabaudia, on the coast near Monte Circeo; in 1935 Pontinia, s.E. of Latina; in 1937 Aprilia, to the N.W.; and in 1939 Pomezia, N.W. of Aprilia. The Agro Pontino was completely reclaimed, as well as a considerable area outside its confines. There were five main canals, including a deep collecting-canal which became the right flank of the Anzio bridgehead, and a network of secondary canals, 1300 km. of roads and some 4000 settlers' houses. Many of these houses were grouped in villages called Borghi.

The Second World War caused immense damage, due largely to the repercussions of the bridge-head landings at Anzio (see below). Nearly 800 houses were destroyed or damaged. Livestock decreased from 30,000 to 4000; 80 sq. kilometres were mined and an almost equally large area flooded. The work of reconstruction was begun immediately after the end of the war. Today the state of the Agro Pontino is equal and in some ways superior to that prevailing before the war.

Via Cristoforo Colombo leaves Rome and passes through E.U.R., see Rte 19.

Via Laurentina, diverging to the left and skirting E.U.R., runs s. to join N 148 at (32 km.) *Santa Prócula Maggiore* (see below).

The road passes under the Rome Circular Road. At (16 km.) *Osteria del Malpasso* is an entrance to *Castel Porziano*, once a royal chase and now a holding of the President of the Republic.—28½ km. *Pomezia,* the westernmost and latest (1939) of the new towns of the Agro Pontino (comp. above), stands at cross-roads. A road (r.) leads to (2 km.) *Prática di Mare,* where a medieval castle occupies the site of *Lavinium,* the town supposedly founded by Aeneas in honour of his wife Lavinia. Thirteen archaic altars (6C B.C.) have been found here, and a tomb sanctuary of Aeneas. Lavinium remained the official centre of Roman religion. Excavations are still in progress.

Farther along Highway 148, to the right, is a German military cemetery, and beyond (33½ km.) *Santa Prócula Maggiore,* the cross-roads where Via Laurentina comes in.—*Ardea,* 4½ km. to the right, the capital of Turnus, king of the Rutuli, is now a village with some antique remains. It is the birthplace of the Italian sculptor Giacomo Manzù, and there is a museum (open Mon-Fri 10-13, 15-18) of his work just outside the village.—A crossing is soon made into the province of Latina, and Via Pontina runs through the middle of the area of land reclamation (comp. above).—44 km. **Aprília** (33,300 inhab.), the fourth of the new towns of the Agro Pontino, was founded in 1937. It lies to the left of the road on a spur of the Alban Hills, 80 m above sea-level.

Aprília was in the centre of a salient formed in the British sector soon after the landings of 22 Jan 1944, at Anzio and Nettuno; the peak was just s. of Campo Leone station. The salient was reduced by the Germans in bitter counter-attacks. The town, fought over, bombed, and shelled, was destroyed in four months of fighting. Retaken by the British on 28 May 1944, in the break-out operations, it has been completely rebuilt. The main buildings are grouped round Piazza Roma, with the church of *San Michele Arcangelo.*

Via Nettuense (N 207) leads s. Beyond (48 km.) *Campo di Carne* the road traverses an extensive oak wood called the Bosco di Padiglione.—59½ km. *Anzio (Beach Head) Cemetery,* with the graves of 2312 members of the British forces who lost their lives in the beach-head operations.

Farther on, the trees of the Villa Aldobrandini are seen on the left. A few metres N. of the railway, which is recrossed, is the smaller *Anzio Military Cemetery,* with 1056 British graves. On rising ground near by is the Carmelite *Santuario di Santa Teresa del Bambino Gesù* (1939), in the Romanesque style. Beyond the railway the road descends.

60 km. **ANZIO** (25,500 inhab.), the *Antium* of antiquity, has been known to history from the 5C B.C. It became prominent anew in the landings of Jan 1944, and suffered great damage in the ensuing fighting. Now largely rebuilt, it is again a favourite seaside resort of the Romans, second only in popularity to the Lido di Ostia. Anzio has another claim to celebrity, for it was here that some of the world's greatest works of art were discovered (see p. 337).

**History.** Antium was one of the chief cities of the Volsci, an ancient people constantly at war with the growing might of Rome. The city was a centre of commerce and its ship captains were notorious pirates. When Coriolanus was banished from Rome in 491 B.C. he went over to the enemy against whom he had won fame in battle, and sought refuge at Antium, and it was to Antium two years later, in response to the entreaties of his wife and mother, that he withdrew from the gates of Rome. In 468 B.C. Antium was captured by the Romans, who planted a colony there. Revolting soon afterwards, it long maintained its independence, but was finally subdued in 338 B.C. when all its ships were seized and their beaks sent to adorn the Rostra in the Roman Forum. In the late Republic and early Empire it was a favourite summer resort of the wealthier Romans. Cicero describes his villa at Antium in his letters to Atticus, and Horace, in his Ode to Fortune, refers to her temple at 'loved Antium'. Caligula and Nero, both natives of the town, embellished it. Nero built a magnificent villa, traces of which survive, and the original harbour. The ancient city was situated somewhat to the N.E. of present-day Anzio on high ground above the Villa Aldobrandini and the Villa Borghese. In the middle ages the inevitable decay set in. The Saracens destroyed the harbour. A new harbour was built in 1698 by Innocent XII, to the E. of the old one, and round it grew the modern town.

The landings during the Second World War, far in advance of the main battle line, and timed to follow an Allied attack on it, were devised to cut the German line of communications, to link up with the main Allied forces advancing from the s., and to seize the Alban Hills. The principal objective was to draw off and contain German forces from N.W. Europe, with the subsidiary hope of capturing Rome. Though the landing operations were completely successful, the initial surprise was not exploited. The reactions of the Germans were violent and four months of bitter fighting ensued.

The tree-lined Piazza Pia is the centre of Anzio. From the railway station it is reached by the wide Viale Mencacci, Via Claudio Paolini, Piazza Cesare Battisti, in which is the *Municipio,* and Via dei Fabbri. In Piazza Pia is the church of *San Pio,* with a neo-classical portico. The bus terminus for Nettuno is near by. From the square Via Venti Settembre leads to the Riviera Mallozzi, a broad thoroughfare following the coastline to the w., with villas and bathing establishments. It passes the ancient harbour built by Nero. At the end of the avenue, high up, are the so-called *Grottoes of Nero,* a complex of rectangular chambers. A little farther, near the promontory of *Arco Muto,* are the ruins of **Nero's Villa,** built of opus reticulatum.

Here were found the Apollo Belvedere, now in the Vatican, during the pontificate of Julius II (1503-13), the Borghese Gladiator, now in the Louvre in Paris, and (in 1878) the Maiden of Anzio, now in the Museo Nazionale Romano. Arco Muto is the possible site of the Temple of Fortune once visited by countless pilgrims and mentioned by Horace in his Ode to Fortune. Near the lighthouse some ancient sculptures have been discovered.

On the way back along the shore, the harbour built by Innocent XII is passed on the right. On the right is the breakwater, with a splendid view towards the E.: it takes in Villa Aldobrandini and part of Villa Borghese on the left of the town and the wooded coast-line as far as Torre Astura, with Monte Circeo in the distance. Via Porto Innocenziano runs along the harbour.—From the station Viale Mencacci to the right leads to the railway bridge. *Villa Spigarelli* (adm. on request), reached by Viale Oleandri (l.), has some well-preserved ancient tombs. On the high ground above is the site of the ancient city of *Antium;* the remains include an Odeum of the Imperial era.

From Piazza Pia, Riviera di Levante, close to the shore, or the parallel Via Gramsci lead out of the town. On the latter road is the *Villa Borghese* (l.; adm. on application to the owner) with its fine *Park. The coast-line between Anzio and (63½ km.) Nettuno is almost completely built up.

**Nettuno** (27,300 inhab.), comprises a medieval walled town and a modern quarter in process of rapid development.

The well-preserved CASTLE (*Forte*) was built for Alexander VI by Ant. Sangallo the Elder or Baccio Pontelli. Rectangular in plan, with corner bastions and a portcullis, it is surrounded by a moat.—Piazza Mazzini is the centre of the modern town. To the right is the medieval Borgo, with its narrow winding alleys and its partly-surviving walls. Near Piazza Vittorio Emanuele is the medieval *Palazzo Colonna.*—Beyond Piazza Mazzini the *Belvedere* commands an extensive view of the bay.

About 1 km. N. of the town, off Via Santa Maria, is the *American Military Cemetery,* the larger of the two remaining in Italy, with 7862 graves of Americans who lost their lives in the beach-head operations.—For *Torre Astura,* 13 km. s., see the 'Blue Guide to Southern Italy'.

The return to Rome (71½ km. may be made viâ Ostia on the coast road, Via Severiana. This passes through an almost continuous line of unattractive resorts, and can be very crowded in summer. Beyond *Tor Vaianica* (28½ km.), building is restricted and the President's game reserve stretches on either side of the road (see p. 336).—44½ km. *Ostia* (Lido di Castel Fusano), and from there to Rome, see Rte 21B.

# 23   THE ALBAN HILLS

The *Alban Hills* are an isolated volcanic group over 60 km. in circumference rising from the Roman Campagna, with foothills reaching to within twelve kilometres of Rome. They comprise a vast crater in the form of a horseshoe, with its open end on the Via Appia. The numerous summits on the rim of the crater include Monte Salomone (773 m), Monte Ceraso (766 m), Maschio di Lariano (891 m), Monte Peschio (939 m) and Maschio d'Artemisio (812 m), highest peak of the Artemisio range. Near the open end of the horseshoe are smaller craters, two of them filled with water and forming the lakes of Albano and Nemi, and a third, now dry, comprising the Valle Aríccia. In the centre of the complex is a secondary crater, from which rise the peaks of Monte Cavo (949 m) overshadowing Rocca di Papa, and Maschio di Faete, the highest of all (956 m) as well as others, including Colle Iano (938 m) and La Forcella (807 m).

The outer slopes of the Alban Hills are planted with vineyards producing the renowned *Vini dei Castelli,* and with olive groves; the interior is pasture and woodland, with chestnut trees predominating. Distributed over the area are the picturesque towns known as the **Castelli Romani,** some of them of great antiquity but most of them owing their origin to the initiative of the popes and the patrician Roman families. There are in all thirteen Castelli, properly so called, some of them world-famous, others scarcely known outside Lazio. In the N. are Frascati, Monte Porzio Catone, Monte Cómpatri, Rocca Priora, and Colonna; in the centre Rocca di Papa; in the w. and s.w. Grottaferrata, Marino, Castel Gandolfo, Albano Laziale, Artíccia, Genzano, and Nemi.

All the Castelli suffered in the Second World War, particularly during the period between the end of January 1944, after the landings at Anzio, and the beginning of June in the same year, when the Allies, having overrun the German Alban Hills defences, entered the city of Rome. The damage has been largely repaired, though many works of art have been irremediably lost.

The Alban Hills look their best in spring and autumn, but they are always enchanting, with their attractively sited little towns and their varied scenery. Even the most hurried visitor to Rome should devote a day to the area, though at least two or three days are needed to do it justice. To those who can spare only one day the following rather strenuous itinerary is recommended. Morning: Frascati; from there viâ Grottaferrata, and Castel Gandolfo to Albano. Afternoon: Lake Albano, Aríccia, and Genzano, with a visit to Lake Nemi.

ROAD. **A.** VIA TUSCOLANA. 21 km. *Frascati.*—24 km. *Grottaferrata.*—**B.** VIA DEI LAGHI, skirting Lake Albano and Lake Nemi, beautifully landscaped and well provided with parking places and viewpoints. 22 km. *Marino* (l.).—27 km. By-road

l. for *Rocca di Papa.*—31 km. By-road r. for *Nemi*(1 km.).—C. VIA APPIA NUOVA. 21 km. *Castel Gandolfo.*—24 km. *Albano Laziale.*—26½ km. *Aríccia.*—29½ km. *Genzano.*—39 km. *Velletri.*

RAILWAY. Routes from Rome (*Termini*) diverge at Ciampino Station for Frascati, Velletri, and Albano Laziale (viâ Marino and Castel Gandolfo).

BUSES. A.CO.TRA.L. line from Viale Carlo Felice (S. Giovanni) run c. every 30 min to Frascati, Rocca di Papa, Grottaferrata, Marino, Castel Gandolfo, Albano, Ariccia, Genzano, Nemi, and Velletri.

CIRCULAR COACH TOURS (*Gran Turismo*) are arranged by various companies. A typical half-day excursion includes Frascati, Grottaferrata, Via dei Laghi, and Castel Gandolfo. Tours of this nature, while admirable from the scenic point of view, do not give the traveller time to explore any of the localities visited.

## A    Rome to Frascati and Grottaferrata

The direct road to Frascati (21 km.) is the VIA TUSCOLANA. Rome is left by Porta S. Giovanni (Pl. 10; 3); Via Appia Nuova continues for a short distance to Piazza Sulmona where (l.) Via Tuscolana (N 215) begins.

The *Via Tuscolana* was a short branch of the Via Latina and ran to Tusculum, to the E. of present-day Frascati. The VIA LATINA, issuing from the Porta Capena (p. 222) passed through Ferentinum (Ferentino), Frusino (Frosinone), Aquinum (Aquino), Casinum (Cassino), and Venafrum (Venafro) to Beneventum (Benevento) where it joined the Appian Way. At *Ad Bivium,* c. 145 km. E.S.E. of Rome, it was joined by the *Via Labicana,* now Via Casilina or Highway 6 (see p. 352).

The road follows the tram-line which once had services to several points in the Alban Hills, It now operates only as far as Cinecittà (see below).—7½ km. *Porta Furba* incorporates an arch of the Acqua Felice, with a fountain built by Clement XII (1730-40); near by are picturesque remains of the Aqua Claudia (see p. 217). Farther on, beyond the railway, to the right is seen *Monte del Grano,* whence came the reputed sarcophagus of Alexander Severus (p. 59).—10 km. *Cinecittà,* centre of the Italian film industry, built in 1937, was damaged in the Second World War but rebuilt. Now increasingly used by foreign companies, it preserves some of the largest sets ever constructed. On the right, beyond an avenue of pine-trees, are seen the scattered ruins of the Villa of Quintilii (p. 234). On the left is the 13C *Tor Fiscale.*—At (11½ km.) *Cantoniera* Via Anagnina forks to the right (p. 342); while this road crosses the Ring Road.

On the right is the medieval *Torre di Mezzavia* (76 m), marking the half-way point between Rome and Frascati. A little farther is (l.) the battlemented *Torre dei Santi Quattro.*—17 km. *Osteria del Vermicino,* with a fountain dating from the time of Clement XII. The road crosses the old Rome-Naples railway and the Frascati railway (retrospective views of Rome), and soon passes on the right the *Villa Sora,* once a residence of Gregory XIII (1572-85) and now the College of the Salesians.—21 km. *Frascati.*

**Frascati** (18,700 inhab.) delightfully situated on the N.W. slopes of the Alban Hills, was, until its partial destruction in 1943-44, when it was the Army Headquarters of Field-Marshal Kesselring, the most elegant and prosperous of the Castelli Romani. It has again become a holiday resort in spring, summer, and autumn. It is noted for its once-sumptuous villas and for its white wine. The suburbicarian see of Frascati is one of the six held by cardinal bishops.

**History.** Frascati was overshadowed by Tusculum in Roman days. A small village in the middle ages, it expanded in 1191, when the inhabitants of Tusculum, after the destruction of their city, sought refuge there around the ancient churches of Santa Maria and San Sebastiano in Frascata. Later it was a feudal holding and at the beginning of the 16C, it passed into the possession of the Holy See. Henry, Cardinal York, was Bishop of Frascati and died there in 1807; the body of his brother, the Young Pretender (d. 1788) was at first buried in the Duomo at Frascati; it is now in the Vatican Grottoes. As German Army Headquarters in 1943-44, Frascati suffered a severe attack from Allied bombers early in Sept 1943, just before the landings at Salerno. Between then and the following June over 80 per cent of the buildings were destroyed or damaged, including all the churches to a greater or less extent and the principal villas. The churches and other public buildings have been restored wherever possible, as well as some of the villas.

Information about visits to the villas should be obtained from the Azienda Autonoma di Soggiorno e Turismo, Piazza G. Marconi.

The vast tree-planted Piazza G. Marconi is the town centre and bus-terminus. In the middle is a Monument to the Dead of the First World War, by *Cesare Bazzani.* The balustrade on the N.W. side of the square overlooks the railway station, to which it is connected by a long flight of steps. On the opposite (S.E.) side is the monumental entrance with a magnificent hedge forming an avenue to \*Villa Aldobrandini, or *Belvedere,* the finest of the villas at Frascati. Visitors enter from the Via Card. Massaia, a continuation of Corso Italia from the Piazza San Pietro (permission to visit the villa must be obtained from the Azienda Autonoma di Soggiorno e Turismo, see above). Concerts are held here in summer.

Villa Aldobrandini was built by Giac. delle Porta in 1598-1603 for Card. Pietro Aldobrandini. The rooms are decorated with paintings by the Zuccari, the Cavalier d'Arpino, and of the school of Domenichino. The superb \*Park, with its verdure, statuary, grottoes, and fountains was badly damaged in the war, but all has now been made good. A magnificent view is obtained from the front, extending to Rome and, in clear weather, to the hills behind the city.

Via Massaia continues to the *Capuchin Church* (300 m.; l.). It contains a replica of an altarpiece by Giulio Romano, and other paintings by Girol. Muziano, and Paul Brill, and the tomb of Card. Massaia (d. 1889), missionary to Abyssinia. There is also an Ethiopian Museum (adm. 9-12, 16-18).

The *Municipio,* on the N.E. side of Piazza Marconi, escaped serious damage; it contains a collection of local antiquities and a statue of Canova, by Giov. Ceccarini.—On the S.W. side of the square is the beautiful park (open to the public) of *Villa Torlonia,* which formerly belonged to Annibal Caro (1563-66). It is remarkable also for its fountains (Teatro delle Acque, by Carlo Maderna), and for its views. There is a swimming-pool open in summer.

To the N. of Piazza Marconi, beyond Piazza Roma and Via Battisti, lies Piazza San Pietro, rebuilt after tragic devastation. The fountain, by Girol. Fontana has been restored. The *Duomo,* on the right, has preserved most of its façade, also by Girol. Fontana, as well as the unattractive campanili of later date.

The INTERIOR has an interesting plan by Mascherino (1598). It contains a Madonna of the Rosary after Domenichino (3rd chap. on r.) and a relief by Pompeo Ferrucci over the high altar. To the left of the main door is the cenotaph of Prince Charles Edward (see above).

In Piazza del Gesù, beyond the fountain, is the church of *Gesù,* by Pietro da Cortona, restored after war damage. It contains remarkable and daring perspective paintings by Pozzi. Via Cairoli, to the left of the church, leads to Piazza Paolo III, in which is the *Castle*, built with three towers; it is now the bishop's palace. Beyond it is the rebuilt church of *Santa Maria del Vicario*, or *San Rocco*, with a fine Romanesque campanile.

From Piazza Marconi, to the left of Villa Aldobrandini, the curving road for Tusculum (see below) leads to *Villa Lancellotti* (formerly Villa Piccolomini; no adm.) with a graceful nymphæum and an ancient mosaic found at Tusculum in 1863. The road continues between park walls (passing a splendid gate-way by Borromini, with a tree growing through it) to *Villa Falconieri*, built in 1545-48 for Bp Aless. Ruffini and enlarged by Borromini. It was occupied before 1914 by Wilhelm II of Germany, was presented by the State to Gabriele d'Annunzio in 1925, and is now a European Centre for Education where courses are held by the Italian Ministry of Education (no adm.).—About 2km. E. is the Camaldoli Convent (see below).

About 1½ km. E. of Frascati is *Villa Mondragone*, now a Jesuit seminary (apply to the Father Rector). It is reached by Via Matteotti, to the right of the fountain in Piazza San Pietro, and then Via di Villa Borghese to the right. This road leads to *Villa Parisi* (formerly Villa Borghese) and, just beyond this villa, to the gates of Villa Mondragone. This was built in 1573-75 for Card. Altemps mainly by Martino Longhi the Elder. In 1613 it was bought by Card. Scipio Borghese, who enlarged it. The so-called *Portico* of Vignola is by Vasanzio. The terrace commands a good view of Rome.

Below it two roads nite in a cypress avenue which ascends to the monumental entrance of the villa on the San Cesareo road. On 24 Feb 1582, Gregory XIII here issued his famous bull for the reform of the calendar.

## EXCURSIONS FROM FRASCATI

1. To TUSCULUM. ROAD 5km. The road to the left of Villa Aldobrandini, leads out of Frascati through wooded country, near the beautiful 16C *Villa Rufinella*, or *Villa Tuscolana*, with its expanse of gardens, fountains and woods (adm. on request). The villa, injured by bombing, has had several owners, including Lucien Bonaparte, Queen Maria Christina of Sardinia, and Victor Emmanuel II, passing c. 1874 to the princely family of Lancellotti. From the villa a steep path leads up to the ancient paved road leading to the amphitheatre and city of Tusculum.

**Tusculum** (610 m) said to have been founded by Telegonus, son of Ulysses and Circe, is certainly Etruscan in origin. It was the birthplace of Cato the Censor (234-149 B.C.). On the surrounding hills were villas, of which no fewer than 43 are mentioned in classical literature. The most famous of these was the *Tusculanum*, or Cicero's Villa, where the Tusculan Disputations were supposed to have been held. The exact site of the villa is doubtful. In 1191 the Romans destroyed Tusculum in revenge for their defeat at Monte Porzio Catone in 1167 (see below), and the inhabitants sought refuge at Frascati.

The ascent passes the scanty remains of the *Amphitheatre* (70 by 60 m; arena 48 by 29 m), with room for 3000 spectators. It has been given the name of *School of Cicero*.—After ¼ hr more uphill is the so-called *Villa of Cicero*. Continuing to the left are the ruins of the *Forum*, more probably a quadrilateral annexe to the *Theatre*, which is just beyond. This elegant little building, excavated in 1839, is well preserved. Its cavea was hewn out of the hillside. On the summit of the hill, marked with a cross (760 m), are traces of the citadel or *Arx*. The *View is incomparable: it takes in the Castelli, with the Monti Sabatini, Soratte, and Cimini on the right, the mountains of Lazio on the left, and the city of Rome in the distance.—On the way back a fork right leads to the *Convent of Camaldoli*, on a hill and dating from 1611, once a favourite resort of James Stuart, the Old Pretender.

2. To MONTE PORZIO CATONE, MONTE CÓMPATRI, AND SAN CESAREO. ROAD, 16 km.; bus in 45 min. The road leaves Frascati to the N.E., and at a road fork bears right (the left fork is Via Colonna, leading to Via Casilina at Colonna; p. 353).—It passes on the right the entrance to Villa Borghese and the monumental entrance to Villa Mondragone.—Near (2 km.) *Le Cappellette* are the ruins of a Roman villa said without justification to be that of Cato.—3½ km. **Monte Porzio Catone** (451 m), is one of the 13 Castelli, with 4400 inhabitants. It takes its name from the family of the Catos. Both Cato the Censor and Cato of Utica (95-46 B.C.) may have had villas here, though the place is first mentioned in history in the 11C. Here the Tusculans, aided by Frederick Barbarossa, gained a victory over the Romans in 1167; for the sequel, see above.—6½ km. **Monte Cómpatri** (583 m), is another of the Castelli, with 6000 inhabitants. It is charmingly situated on a height. Successor to the ancient *Labicum,* it was owned by the Annibaldi, the Colonna, and other families in turn. Its large 17C parish church was enlarged in the 19C.—A short distance s.w. of the town is the ancient *Convent s an Silvestro,* with a fine view.

Outside the town the road forks; the right branch leads in 3½ km. to Rocca Priora (see below). This route follows the left branch and, traversing the Piano della Faeta and the Campo Gillaro, reaches Via Casilina 1 km. before the village of San Cesareo.—16 km. *San Cesareo,* see p. 353.

3. To ROCCA PRIORA. TWO ROADS: (*a*) viâ Monte Cómpatri, 11 km.; bus in ½ hr, (*b*) by the Via Anagnina, 9½ km; bus c. 5 times daily.

For the route viâ (6½ km.) *Monte Cómpatri,* see above.—The alternative route (*b*) is followed by the main Marino-Albano road to the s., and after 3 km. turns left into Via Anagnina. The road climbs past two wooded hills on the right; on the first is the little church of the *Madonna della Molara;* on the second the ruins of the Greek monastery of *Sant'Agata.* On the left are the ruins of Tusculum; a by-road on the right leads to Rocca di Papa. The road passes through a cutting and then emerges in a spacious upland valley, with meadows and cornfields, corresponding to the *Albana Vallis* of Livy.—Farther on this road bends sharply to the left and ascends; the ancient Via Latina keeps straight on. On the right a short cut leads to the *Oratory of St Sebastian,* which the road passes later on, shortly before joining the road from Monte Cómpatri.

9½ km. **Rocca Priora** (768 m), another of the Castelli, with 5200 inhab. is situated on the N. side of the great crater of the Alban Hills, overlooking the ancient Valle Latina. It is said to have been built over the ancient town of *Corbio,* long in dispute between the Romans and the Aequi, and is believed to have been the first town built in the neighbourhood after the destruction of Tusculum. In the 14C it belonged to the Savelli, after which it passes into the possession of the Holy See.

From Piazza Marconi Viale Vitt. Veneto runs below Villa Torlonia, and branches left for Grottaferrata (3 km.).

**Grottaferrata** (329 m; 13,000 inhab.), is situated amid vineyards producing some of the finest Castelli wines. The lively little town, which escaped major war damage, is famous for its monastery.

From the bus station Corso del Popolo leads r. to reach the *Abbazia di Grottaferrata,** which has the appearance of a castle, with its walls, bastions, and defensive ditches.

The Abbazia is a monastery of Basilian monks, who celebrate according to the Greek office. Founded by St Nilus, a Calabrian abbot, who died there in 1004, and built by his disciple St Bartholomew of Rossano (d. 1064), it enjoyed the favour of Gregory IX (1227-41) and other pontiffs, and it was enclosed in a defensible enciente by Card. Giul. della Rovere, afterwards Julius II (1503-13).

Across the defensive ditch is the entrance to the CASTLE COURTYARD, with a statue of St Nilus, by Raff. Zaccagni (1904). Beyond an anteroom (ring if closed) is the FIRST COURT, at the back of which is the **Monastery** (adm. 9-12.30, 16-19).

Visitors ring at the door of the monastery and are accompanied by a monk (offering expected). It contains a rich library with precious codices, and a museum of classical and medieval sculptures, including a fine Attic *Stele of the 5C B.C. There are also icons, vestments, and detached frescoes from the church.

From the castle courtyard there is access to the SECOND COURT, a smaller enclosure on the right of the anteroom. Here is the church of **Santa Maria,** consecrated by John XIX in 1025, redesigned internally in 1754 and restored in 1902-30. The pronaos is ancient, and the fine campanile dates from the 12C. In the beautifully carved Romanesque portal of marble is a door of carved wood (11C), surmounted by a *Mosaic of Christ between the Virgin and John the Baptist. The font is an antique marble urn, decorated with swimming cupids.

INTERIOR. Nearly all the inscriptions are in Greek. The roof of the nave dates from 1595; the Byzantine mosaic of the Apostles on the triumphal arch and the damaged fresco above date from the 13C. Frescoes from the clerestory walls have been detached and are now in the Museum (see above). Off the right aisle opens the **Chapel of St Nilus,** the frescoes in which, depicting the lives of St Nilus and St Bartholomew, are masterpieces by *Domenichino* (restored by Camuccini in 1819). To the right of the entrance, St Nilus before the Crucifix, and St Nilus averting a tempest by his prayers. Inside the chapel, to the left: St Nilus and the Emperor Otho III (the page holding the emperor's horse is Domenichino, and the figures on the right of the horse are Guido Reni and Guercino). On the r., St Bartholomew averting the fall of a pillar during the building of the convent; on the end wall (left of the altar), Exorcism of a devil and (r.) the Virgin presenting a golden apple to SS. Nilus and Bartholomew; in the lunette, Death of St Nilus; in the triumphal arch, Annunciation. At the altar is a Virgin, by *Ann. Carracci.*—A door from here leads into the sacristy, off which are two small rooms, dating from Roman times with iron grille windows. Known as the 'crypta ferrata', these were transformed in medieval times into a Christian chapel. It is thought that here the name of the monastery, and later the town, originated.

The return to Rome may be made by Via Anagnina (21 km.). The road partly follows the line of the ancient Via Latina.—3 km. The *Borghetto,* or *Castel Savelli* (325 m), a ruined 13C castle with 13 towers, built on Roman foundations, passed from the counts of Tusculum to the Savelli, and later to Julius II, who converted it into an outwork of the Abbey of Grottaferrata.—The road passes over the old Rome-Naples railway, near (5 km.) *Villa Senni,* where some 4C catacombs have been discovered, and the Frascati railway.—At (11 km.) *Cantoniera,* this route rejoins Via Tuscolana (p. 339) to return to (21 km.) Rome.

# B    Via dei Laghi

VIA APPIA NUOVA (N 7) starts from Porta San Giovanni (Pl. 10; 3, 6). Tramway services along this route used to continue to Albano, etc., but now terminate at Capannelle (see below). Extensive works are in progress under the initial section of the Appia Nuova for the projected line of the Metropolitana from Termini to Osteria del Curato (beyond Cinecittà, p. 339). This has necessitated the demolition of houses, and the date of completion is uncertain.—7½ km. Intersection of the Via Latina, issuing from the Porta Latina (p. 225). The Via Latina is no longer a continuous street.

Via Latina leads to the left (guide-post marked 'Tombe della Via Latina'), crosses the Albano railway and reaches in 5 min. a group of *Tombs dating from the 1C and 2C. Most of them are square and brick-built, with recesses on the outside and interior chambers with interesting stucco ornamentation. Two of the best-preserved may be visited (caretaker near the railway line). On the right is the *Tomb of the Valerii* (A.D. 160), a subterranean chamber decorated with fine reliefs, in stucco on a white ground, of nymphs, sea-monsters, and nereids. On the left is the 2C *Tomb of the Pancratii,* with landscape paintings, coloured stuccoes, and four bas-reliefs: Judgment of Paris, Admetus and Alcestis, Priam and Achilles, and Hercules playing a lyre with Bacchus and Minerva.—Behind the tomb are the ruins of the 5C *Basilica of St Stephen.*

Farther on the ancient Appian Way, with its tombs and other buildings, becomes conspicuous on the right. On the left is the long line of arches of the Aqua Claudia.—The road crosses the Rome-Naples Direttissima near (11½ km.) *Capannelle,* noted for its racecourse. On the right, near the tramway terminus, can be seen the road to the Casal Rotondo on the Appian Way.—The road passes under the Rome Circular road near (13½ km.) *Barbula,* and soon passes (15 km.) the entrance (l.) to Ciampino Airport. Just beyond the airport, **Via dei Laghi** (N 217) diverges to the left. The road leads E. and S.E. towards the Alban Hills climbing steadily as it nears (22 km.) Marino.

**Marino,** situated at the N. end of Lake Albano, can be seen from the road which by-passes it to the s. The town, with 28,000 inhab., is less of a tourist centre than some of the other Castelli, but is celebrated for its wines. It suffered much damage during the Second World War.

Marino lies near the ancient *Castrimoenium,* colonized under Sulla and long since vanished. The modern name appears in the 11C. In the 13C Marino was a stronghold of the Orsini; in 1347 Giordano Orsini, who had been driven out of Rome by Rienzo, was here besieged in vain by the tribune. In 1419 the town passed to the Colonna. Many of its inhabitants took part in the battle of Lépanto (1571). Vittoria Colonna (1490-1548) and the musician Giacomo Carissimi (1604-74) were born at Marino. Annually on the first Sun in Oct the town celebrates the *Sagra dell' Uva* when the fountains of the central piazza flow with wine.

In Piazza San Barnaba is the restored 17C church of *San Barnaba.* It contains a Martyrdom of St Barnabas by Benedetto Gennari, and a Turkish shield taken at the battle of Lépanto. In the neighbouring Piazza Lépanto is the bomb-damaged *Fountain of the Four Moors,* by Pompeo Castiglia da Marino (1642), commemorating the battle of Lépanto. Damage to the 16C **Palazzo Colonna** has been made good. It is now the Town Hall, and contains an antiquarium.

In the church of the *Trinità* is a painting attributed to Guido Reni, and in the church of *Santa Maria delle Grazie* a St Roch, of the Emilian school. Attached to the Dominican convent is the church of *Madonna del Rosario,* with an elegant Rococo interior.—Near the station is a *Mithræum,* with interesting frescoes discovered in 1963.

Via dei Laghi continues to climb, with magnificent views, skirting *Lake Albano.

This charmingly situated sheet of water, elliptical in shape, occupies one of the smaller craters of the volcanic Alban Hills. It is 10 km. round and has an area of 2 sq. m.; its extreme depth is 170 m. It is fed by underground sources and by the drainage of the surrounding crater. Teeming with trout and other fish, it is much favoured by anglers. It is the *Lacus Albanus* of antiquity, and in the Imperial era its banks were adorned with villas and its waters used for mock sea-fights (naumachiæ; comp. p. 89). Regattas are held on them today.—It is possible to walk round the lake in 2 hrs by a track.

27 km. *Ponte di Nemi.* Road left for Rocca di Papa (3 km.), with good views of the country from Lake Albano to Grottaferrata.

**Rocca di Papa** (681 m; 8400 inhab.), built up in picturesque terraces on the flank of Monte Cavo, is the highest of the Castelli Romani. The lower part of the town is modern, the upper part medieval. Charmingly situated amid chestnut woods, it is a favourite resort during the summer season.

**History.** Rocca di Papa, originally *Rocca di Monte Cavo*, is said to occupy the site of the ancient Latin town of *Cabum*. It appears under its present name for the first time in the 12C, the name being derived from a castle built here by the popes. From them it passed in turn to several owners, among them the Annibaldi and the Colonna. The artist and statesman Massimo d'Azeglio lived here in 1821.

From Piazza della Repubblica there is an excellent view of the medieval town, with the observatory at its top, and of Monte Cavo. Relics of the *Castle* are still to be seen at the highest point of the town, from which there are views of the Campagna and of the lakes of Albano and Nemi.

SHORT EXCURSIONS may be made S.E. to (½ hr) *Campi d'Annibale* and S.W. to (½ hr) the *Sanctuary of the Madonna del Tufo* (see below).

ASCENT OF MONTE CAVO. BY ROAD, 5½ km. The road runs s. from Rocca di Papa (leading back to Via dei Laghi).—1 km. *Sanctuary of the Madonna del Tufo,* built over a block of tufa whose fall on to a passer-by was miraculously arrested by the Virgin. Just beyond, a good private road (toll) diverges left to wind up to the summit. A short way up, a sign indicates the ancient *VIA SACRA, called *Via Triumphalis* which climbs up the hill-side to the left. Perfectly preserved, it can be followed on foot for a considerable way, through beautiful woods. It was built to reach the Temple of Jupiter Latialis on the summit of Monte Cavo (see below), and for triumphal processions by generals whose feats of arms were not considered important enough for a triumphal procession along the Via Sacra in Rome.

BY MULE TRACK. Steep and narrow streets lead up through the town, past the remains of its castle at the top, to the edge of the Monte Cavo crater, where a mule track leads to the right. On the left, in the crater, is a flat floor called the *Campi d'Annibale,* the traditional halting-place of Hannibal in his march on Tusculum and Rome in 211 B.C., though it is more probable that it was the Romans who had a force here to command the Appian Way and the Latin Way. The ascent, which commands splendid views, follows for some time along the Via Triumphalis (see above).

**Monte Cavo** (949 m), the second highest summit of the Alban Hills (*Maschio di Faete,* 956 m), is the *Mons Albanus* of antiquity, the sacred mountain of the Latins. On its slopes was Alba Longa, the most ancient town in Latium. The name Monte Cavo is supposed by some to be derived from the ancient town of Cabum (see above), and by others from the word 'caput'. On its summit stood the *Temple of Jupiter Latialis,* the sanctuary of the Latin League, said to have been built by Tarquinius Superbus. Here the league's religious festivals, the *Feriae Latinoe,* were celebrated in spring and autumn by the 47 towns of the confederation. Excavations have failed to find any trace of the temple and it may be that no building existed, but merely a sacred area with an altar. On the presumed site of the temple Henry, Cardinal York, built a Passionist Convent in 1783; this later became an observatory, founded by Father Angelo Secchi in 1876; today it is a hotel-restaurant. The walls of the convent garden are built partly with blocks from ancient buildings. Here is also a television station.

The *View, which is of remarkable beauty at dawn and sunset and of singular transparency after rain, embraces the full circle: the coast from Monte Circeo to Civitavecchia, the Tolfa and Cimini ranges, the Sabine, Tiburtine and Prænestine Hills, and the Monte Lepini.—The descent may be made through the woods to Nemi (about 4 km.) and the walk continued from there to Genzano (p. 351).

Via dei Laghi continues to (31 km.) the turning (r.) for Nemi and its lake. The road skirts the E. and S. sides of the lake, while a turning to the r. after 1 km. leads to the village of **Nemi** (521 m; 1500 inhab.) picturesquely situated above the lake. It has an impressive castle which belonged in the 9C to the counts of Tusculum, later to Cistercian monks, and in 1428 to the Colonna. It later passed into the hands of the Orsini, and is now the property of the Ruspoli. It is well-preserved, and the road out of the village passes under the entrance bridge.

A festival of wild strawberries (*Sagra delle Fragole*) is held here every June. A narrow, poorly surfaced road descends to the lake-side and the ship Museum (better reached from the other side of the lake, see below), passing the so-called Giardino, in which are the ruins of the *Temple of Diana Nemorensis,* excavated in 1885; some of the finds are in the Museo di Villa Giulia in Rome. Further excavations in 1924-28, revealed a theatre.

The lake road continues above the E. and S. side through enchanting stretches of ilex and manna-ash woods (branch roads lead down to the lake side).

*Lake Nemi (Lago di Nemi;* 316 m) is the pearl of the Alban Hills. Almost circular in shape, it is 5½ km. round, with an area of 189 hectares and a maximum depth of 34 m. Its vivid blue waters, encircled by solitary wooded hills, produce an impressive, almost mysterious effect, admirably captured in Turner's well-known painting. The lake is the ancient *Lacus Nemorensis,* called also the Mirror of Diana, to whom were consecrated the grove and the temple on its N.E. side. Both lake and grove were sometimes called the lake and grove of Aricia.

Diana was worshipped here with barbarous rites: her priest, called *Rex Nemorensis,* was a killer and became a victim. The office could be held only by a run-away slave who had qualified by breaking off a branch (the golden bough) from a certain tree in the grove. Success in the attempt entitled him to fight the reigning priest in single combat; if he slew him he became the next Rex Nemorensis. The new priest-king, in his turn, was liable at any time to be challenged by a further aspirant. So it went on without end. It was the investigation of this sinister rule of succession to the priesthood of Diana that led Sir James Frazer to write *The Golden Bough.*

Before the approach to Genzano (see below), the road bears right round the lake-side to reach the **Nemi Museum of Roman Ships** (closed indefinitely; information from the Sovrintendenza alle Antichità di Roma, P.za delle Finanze) replacing the one which, in 1932-44, housed the two ancient ships said to have been built by Caligula to convey visitors across the lake for the festival of Diana. The ships were sunk at the time of Claudius, and they were located at the bottom of the lake in 1446 by Leon Battista Alberti, but nothing important was done for 400 years. In 1895 Eliseo Borghi recovered some fine bronzes; in 1928-31 the lake was partly drained and in 1932 the ships, of remarkable size, were taken out and placed in the museum. The larger was 71 m long and had a beam of 24 m; the other was 67 m by 20 m. On 1 June 1944, they were burned, with the museum, by German soldiers.

In the *Salone* are models of the ships, on a scale of one-fifth. The *BRONZES* escaped the fate of the ships. Among them are: Head of Medusa; Open hands—charms against the evil eye—found in the sterns; 4 Heads of a wolf, 3 of a lion, and one of a panther which covered the beams at the ships' side; ring from a rudder with a lion's head; small double-sided Herm with heads of Silenus and a satyr; another with two mænads (fragments of a balustrade).—In the *Galleria Centrale* is an iron anchor resembling in design the Admiralty anchor badge adopted by Great Britain in 1852. Glass cases contain gilded bronze plates, bronze and iron nails, cups, lamps, and other fittings from the ships.—The upper floor displays casts of monuments connected with naval engineering.

From here it is possible to return to Via dei Laghi (turning right for *Velletri,* 7½ km., described in Rte 23C, or left to return to Rome) or take the road which climbs the hill-side to Genzano, passing a path (l.) which leads to the *Outlet* of the lake, comprising two superimposed tunnels 1650 m long, used when necessary to drain the lake (see above). *Genzano* (Rte 23C) is entered at Piazza Dante; from the centre Via Appia Nuova leads back to Rome (29 km.).

## C   Castel Gandolfo, Albano, Genzano, and Velletri

Via Appia Nuova leads out of Rome. To (15½ km.) the junction with Via dei Laghi, see Rte 23B. The road continues, crossing the Terracina railway 1 km. before (20 km.) *Frattócchie,* where this route is joined by Via Appia Antica (p. 235). Here was the 12th (Roman) milestone. Highway 7 is now known simply as Via Appia. Via Nettunense branches off to the right for Anzío and Nettuno (Rte 22); on the left is the *Palazzetto della Sirene,* built by Card. Girol. Colonna and now a Trappist monastery. The road passes the ruins of tombs and other buildings that lined the Appian Way. Four imposing stumps of towers make their appearance, the first of them cylindrical and called the *Torraccio* (l.), the others square. A track to the right leads to the ruins of the ancient Latin town of *Bovilloe;* these include a circus, a cistern, and numerous tombs.

21 km. Turning left for **Castel Gandolfo.** A good road climbs to this gay little town in 3½ km. With 5400 inhab. it is situated on the lip of the Lake Albano crater at a height of 426 m above the sea. Here the Pope spends the summer.

The town occupies the site of the citadel of *Alba Longa,* founded, according to legend, by Ascanius, son of Aeneas. It was so called because it extended in a long line up the slopes of Mons Albanus. Head of the Latin League, Alba was the mother city of many of the Latin towns, and of Rome itself. Its war with Rome in the time of Tullus Hostilius, decided by the single combats of the three Roman Horatii and the three Latin Curiatii, the treachery of its dictator Mettius Fufetius, and its destruction by the Romans are famous episodes in the legendary history of Rome. The town was never rebuilt though its temples were respected and were still standing in the days of Augustus. Domitian built a villa here, ruins of which are visible (see below). Of the ancient town there is not a trace, but to the w. of Castel Gandolfo there is an extensive necropolis of the early Iron Age (9-7C B.C.), discoveries from which are in the Prehistoric Museum at E.U.R.

Castel Gandolfo derives its name from a castle of the Gandolfi, a Genoese family of the 12C. The castle passed to the Savelli and, in 1596, to the Camera Apostolica. In 1604 it was declared an inalienable domain of the Holy See. After the papal palace was built (see below), it became the summer residence of the popes and it has been used as such ever since, except for the period from 1870 to 1929 (see p. 261). Many distinguished people have lived at Castel Gandolfo: among them Goethe, Winckelmann, Angelica Kauffmann, and Massimo d'Azeglio. The town was little damaged in the Second World War.

A bus service (3 times daily) connects Castel Gandolfo with *Lake Albano* (p. 344).

At the N. entrance of the town, 133 m above the lake, extends the vast **Papal Palace,** built on the ruins of the castle and retaining some of its towers and walls. It was erected in 1624 by Carlo Maderna at the instance of Urban VIII and enlarged by Alexander VII, Clement XIII, and Pius IX. The palace, with its gardens and the former Villa Barberini, enjoys the privilege of extraterritoriality.

A special permit is necessary from the Director to visit the palace. The chapel has frescoes of the school of the Zuccari. In the neighbouring gardens of the Villa Cybo is a spacious hall (1959) for general audiences held when the Pope is in residence here from mid-July to mid-September (adm., see p. 263). At mid-day on Sun during this summer period, the Pope gives an audience in the courtyard of the palace. No formalities are required for those wishing to attend.

Since 1936 the villa has housed the **Vatican Observatory,** one of the most important in Europe. It was founded by Gregory XIII and from 1908 to 1936 occupied the Casina of Leo XIII in the Vatican Gardens. The observatory specializes in the study of variable stars; it contains a laboratory of astrophysics.

A short alley to the right of the palace leads to a terrace commanding a fine view. In the piazza are an elegant fountain and the church of *San Tomaso da Villanova* (1661, with a noteworthy cupola), both by Bernini. Inside are a painting of St Thomas of Villanova, by Pietro da Cortona, and an Assumption by Maratta.

At the S. end of the town is the sumptuous *Villa Barberini* (no adm.). With its fine gardens, now added to those of the palace, it occupies the greater part of a site once covered by the Villa of Domitian. Traces of nymphæa, of a small theatre, and of the royal mansion are still visible.— At the beginning of the road to Ercolano is the *Villa Torlonia,* with sculptures by Thorvaldsen and modern paintings, and a fine park.

The **Emissarium** or outlet of Lake Albano is reached in ½ hr from Castel Gandolfo. It is reached by the road to the railway station, and, beyond the line, by a track going downhill. At a gate a path leads right, at the end of which is another gate. It is necessary to descend toward the lake as far as a cave, occupied by the custodian (gratuity). The Emissarium, which maintains the water of the lake at a constant level, is a tunnel cut through the solid rock by the Romans in 397 B.C. (according to legend, though probably later) because an oracle had declared that Veii would not fall until the lake was drained. The tunnel is 1425 m long, 1 m wide, and 1½ m high; it pierces the rim of the crater and emerges at *Le Mole,* to the s.w.

The two celebrated ilex-bordered roads which lead from Castel Gandolfo to Albano Laziale were both opened by Urban VIII. They are known as the *Galleria di Sopra* and the *Galleria di Sotto* because the branches of the trees interlace above the roadways, forming arboreal tunnels. The less attractive lower road is used by the buses.—The Galleria di Sopra, that to the left of the exit of Castel Gandolfo, follows the lip of the crater and affords magnificent *Views of Lake Albano, the Campagna, and the neighbouring towns. Half-way along it is the summer convent of the *Collegio di Propaganda Fide.* Near the end of the road, close to the Capuchin Convent, there is a bifurcation. The left fork leads to Ariccia; the right fork to Albano Laziale, past the church of San Paolo. A path to the left of the convent leads to Palazzolo.

The lower road reaches Albano in under 3 km., passing on the right near the junction with the Appian Way, the so-called Tomb of Pompey.

**Albano Laziale** (378 m; 26,600 inhab.) officially so called, is generally referred to simply as Albano. Important among the Castelli, it is a good centre for excursions. The town rises in the form of a triangle from the Via Appia towards the top of the crater of Lake Albano; the crater cuts off the view of the lake from the town. Albano was badly damaged in the Second World War, nearly two-thirds of its buildings having been destroyed or damaged. It has been completely restored.

**History.** The name of Albano is derived from Alba Longa, but the town owes its origin to Septimius Severus, who established here (c. A.D. 195) the *Castra Albana* for the 2nd Legion (Parthica), with a view to the protection (among other duties) of the Appian Way. The camp occupied virtually the whole of what is now the town of Albano. Adjoining the camp was a small settlement that gradually developed and eventually overran the military area. Albano became a bishopric in 460; the see was held by Nicholas Breakspeare before he became the only English pope as Adrian IV (1154-59). Albano is today one of the six suburbicarian sees held by cardinal bishops. Devastated by the barbarian invasions and in the struggles of the papacy and empire, the town passed in the 13C to the Savelli, whose castle survives (to the w. of Albano; p. 351). In 1697 it was acquired by the Camera Apostolica. The eccentric Earl of bristol, bishop of Derry, died here in 1803.

The town centre is the spacious PIAZZA GIUSEPPE MAZZINI, a widening of the Via Appia and a busy traffic centre. On the right, coming from Rome, are the *Belvedere* and the *Villa Comunale,* a public park shaded by lofty pines and occupying the site of a villa of Pompey. Some ruins of this villa are visible. There is a good view from the Belvedere, extending to Rome.

From Piazza Mazzini Via Cairoli leads to Piazza Sabatini, in which is the *Duomo* (*San Pancrazio*), built and rebuilt on a temple dating from the time of Constantine. The temple columns may be seen incorporated in the walls.

Corso Matteotti leads out of Piazza Mazzini. Here is *Palazzo del Comune,* formerly the Palazzo Savelli. In the square opposite is the church of SAN PIETRO, built in the 6C over the remains of the thermae of the Roman camp. The right flank of the church incorporates masonry blocks from the baths; the jambs of a door on the left side are made up of fragments of an ancient architrave. There is an attractive Romanesque campanile. The spacious interior is refreshingly plain. An acanthus cornice supports the modern altar rails. The altar furniture and Stations of the Cross are modern.

Via Aurelio Saffi climbs to the upper part of the town. A turning to the left—Via Don Minzoni—leads to the ruins of the PORTA PRAETORIA OF THE CASTRA ALBANA, revealed by bombing in Feb 1944. This front gate of the camp, opening from its short s. side and facing the Appian Way, had three openings and was flanked by two towers. It was constructed of blocks of peperino. Its frontage was 36 m and its height 13 m. Only the E. opening survived the bombing; of the main central entrance only the lower part is extant.

Via della Rotonda leads left out of Via Saffi to *Santa Maria della Rotonda,* restored in 1937. This medieval circular church, once a nymphaeum belonging to the Villa of Domitian, has a Cosmatesque pulpit supported on a Roman capital. Near by are remains of the walls of the Roman camp. Continuing its ascent, Via Aurelio Saffi leads into the charming Piazza San Paolo, in which is the church of *San Paolo,* built in 1282 and remodelled in 1769. It stands at the apex of the triangle formed by the town. In the wall of the neighbouring *College of the Most Precious Blood* are incorporated further remains of the camp walls. At the top of the hill, beyond the cemetery, Lake Albano can be seen far below on the other side. At No. 100 Via Aurelio Saffi is the entrance to the *Cisternone,* a reservoir hewn out of rock for the use (probably) of the legionaries of the camp. It is still in use today.

The Cisternone is a quadrangular underground construction 46 m by 30 m, reached by 31 steps. It is divided into five compartments, each furnished with rows of columns. The ceilings, 12 m high, are perfectly preserved. The floor slopes gently towards the W. corner, where there is an underground outlet.

Near the civil hospital, off Via San Francesco, are a rectangular tower and the *Porta Principalis Sinistra,* or E. gate of the camp, now walled up.

Via San Francesco leads to the ruins of the AMPHITHEATRE, situated between the church of San Paolo and the Capuchin Convent; it dates from the second half of the 3C and could accommodate 15,000 spectators. On the hill above is the *Capuchin Convent* (1619), surrounded by a turreted wall (only men admitted). On the hill-side extends the *Bosco dei Cappuccini,* a public walk with fine views.—The parallel street to the S.E., in which are long tracts of wall returns to the centre of the town.

Just outside Albano, on the right of the road to Ariccia, is a majestic tomb in the Etruscan style, popularly known as the **Tomb of the Horatii and Curiatii** (see p. 347), or as the *Tomb of Aruns* (son of Tarquinius Superbus). It has a base, 15 m square made of peperino blocks, surmounted by two (originally five) truncated cones. The tomb is thought in fact to date from the Republican era.

WALKS may be taken from Albano, N. to (¾ hr) *Castel Gandolfo* by the Galleria di Sopra (reached from the church of San Paolo); N.E. to (1½ hr) *Palazzolo;* and w. to (½ hr) *Castel Savelli.* The castle (325 m) is reached by a road under the railway and by a path to the right at a road fork. This 13C stronghold of the Savelli was last restored in 1660. For the other Castel Savelli, see p. 343.

Beyond Albano the line of the Via Appia follows a course laid out during the pontificates of Gregory XVI (1831-46) and Pius IX (1846-78); the rectification involved the building of four viaducts over the Valle Ariccia, one of the smaller craters of the Alban Hills.

As the road leaves Albano, the so-called Tomb of the Horatii and Curiatii (see above) can be seen below on the right. This route bears to the left off the ancient Appian Way.

The ancient road descends to the right, passing near the church of *Santa Maria della Stella* (below which are the Catacombs of San Senatore, probably reserved for Christian soldiers of the 2nd Legion), and then crosses the valley by an imposing viaduct still partly surviving. It rejoins the modern road near the Sanctuary of Santa Maria di Galloro, only to part again soon afterwards before reuniting near Velletri.

The modern road crosses the valley higher up by the viaduct known as the PONTE DI ARÍCCIA, built by Ireneo Aleandri in 1847-54, partly blown up by the Germans in 1944 and rebuilt in 1947. The viaduct is 312 m long, 9 m wide, and 59 m above the valley floor. It is made up of a series of three superimposed arches (six below, twelve in the middle, and eighteen above). Three people were killed in 1967 when two central arches collapsed without warning.

Just short of the viaduct, on the right in a square, is a monument to Menotti Garibaldi, by Ernesto Biondi. Beyond the bridge, on the left, extends the luxuriant park of the Palazzo Chigi (see below); on the right there is an extensive view over the valley.

26½ km. **Aríccia** (412 m; 12,700 inhab.) is charmingly situated in wooded country, with numerous villas. It did not escape damage in 1943-44.

The ancient Latin city of *Aríccia,* mentioned in the legends of the kings, took a leading part in the wars with Rome until the dissolution of the Latin League in 338 B.C. With three other Latin towns it then lost its independence and received full Roman citizenship. In Cicero's time it was a flourishing municipium. It was the first stage in Horace's journey to Brundusium. In the middle ages the town was owned by the counts of Tusculum and later passed to the Savelli; in 1661 it was sold to the Chigi.—Henrik Ibsen 'disillusioned with the theatre' settled at Aríccia with wife and child in 1864 and here wrote 'Brand'. Here in 1826 Massimo d'Azeglio, statesman and artist, entertained Severn, the artist and friend of Keats.

On the N. (l.) side of the town is the *Palazzo Chigi,* in the form of a medieval castle with four towers, restored by Bernini and later enlarged. It has a delightful and extensive *Park (admission rarely conceded). On the right is the round church of *Santa Maria dell'Assunzione,* built by Bernini in 1664; it has a large dome and two campanili; within is a fresco of the Assumption, by Borgognone.

On leaving Aríccia the road crosses over a second viaduct; then bends round the head of the valley over a third viaduct. Here the road is lined with ilex and manna-ash trees. On the right, on the N.E. edge of the Valle Aríccia, is the pilgrim *Sanctuary of Santa Maria di Galloro* (429 m) by Bernini, with a venerated painting of the Madonna.—The road ascends gradually amid woods and crosses yet a fourth viaduct. From the top of the rise there is a gentle descent.

29½ km. **Genzano,** officially *Genzano di Roma* (435 m), famous for its *Infiorata,* a festival held on the Sunday after Corpus Domini, when the main street is carpeted with flowers, is a place of 16,400 inhabitants built in terraces on the outer slope of the crater of Lake Nemi. The town grew up round a castle built in 1235 facing the lake, rebuilt in 1621 by Prince Giuliano Cesarini to face the Via Appia.

The town centre is Piazza Tommaso Frasconi, with a terrace on the right. On the left, beyond an interesting fountain, are three streets—Via Garibaldi, Bruno Buozzi, and Italo Belardi—all going uphill fanwise from the square. The last-named street, scene of the Infiorata, climbs past the Municipio to the church of *Santa Maria della Cima.* Via Bruno Buozzi leads to the modern *Palazzo Cesarini,* which overlooks the lake, 90 m below. Via Garibaldi leads to Piazza Dante, where there is a road down to the lake (see pp. 346-347).

Beyond Genzano the road passes between (l.) Lake Nemi, glimpses of which may be obtained, and (r.) the *Monte Due Torri* (415 m), with its remaining squat medieval tower.—32½ km. Turning (r.) for Lanúvio (3 km.). This road turns E. and the scenery becomes more and more attractive. The hill-sides are covered with vineyards and chestnut woods. On the left are the wooded slopes and crest of the Maschio d'Artemisio (812 m).—Approaching Velletri, the road curves round the head of a valley.—38½ km. At the beginning of the tree-lined Viale Roma this route is joined by Via dei Laghi from Marino (Rte 23B).—(39 km.) Velletri is entered by *Porta Romana.*

**Velletri** (332 metres; 40,300 inhabitants) is picturesquely situated on a spur of the Artemisio range. It has been reconstructed after grave war damage.

Velletri is the Volscian *Velester,* subjugated by Rome in 338 B.C. and called Velitrae. It was the home of the Gens Octavia, of which Augustus was a member. It was an independent commune from c. 1000 to 1549, when it was absorbed in the States of the Church. From a window in the Palazzo Ginnetti Charles of Bourbon escaped in Aug 1744 from the Irish Gen. U. M. Brown's Austrian troops, later decisively defeating the Austrians in the same engagement. Velletri is one of the six suburbicarian sees; its bishop is Dean of the Sacred College of Cardinals.

VIA VITTORIO EMANUELE runs right through the town from N. to S. following the contour of the hill from Piazza Garibaldi, site of the Porta Romana, to Porta Napoli. About one-third of the way along opens Piazza Cairoli, the town centre, almost completely rebuilt except for the *Torre del Trivio* (c. 50 m), a striking Romanesque campanile, dating from 1353, of alternate black-and-white courses, with single and double window-arches; it has been cleverly restored after bomb damage.

To the right Via del Comune leads up to the piazza of the same name, the highest part of the town. Here is *Palazzo di Giustizia* (1835); in front are the little church of *San Michele* (1837) and the octagonal oratory of *Santa Maria del Sangue,* by Aless. da Parma (1523-79). To the left is the 16C *Palazzo Comunale,* reconstructed since 1945 almost from the foundations. The *Museo Comunale* (entrance at back) contains a collection of antiquities.

Via Vittorio Emanuele continues S. to the 18C church of *San Martino* (l.) with a Madonna of 1308 behind a high-altar tabernacle. After a bend to the right and Piazza Mazzini a road continues S. to Piazza Umberto I. In a small square to the left is the entrance to the CATHEDRAL (*San Clemente*), a 13C church built on the remains of a Roman basilica many times altered, and rebuilt in 1660. It has been patched up since the war and its remaining points of interest have to be sought for amid the conflicting styles.

The basilican INTERIOR has a rebuilt 13C apse and a restored ceiling, with a huge painting (1954) by Angelo Canevari. The windows have recently been filled with stained glass in a strong modern style at variance with the remainder of the present decoration. The Baldacchino is surmounted by a Cosmatesque tabernacle. On the right of the 17C high altar is a candelabrum attrib. to *Iac. Sansovino*. In the second chapel on the right is a Madonna and Child by *Antoniazzo Romano*. At the end of the left aisle a Renaissance doorway (1483) leads past a fine wall lavabo into the *Sacristy*, in which is a Byzantine painting of the Saviour.—The entrance to the MUSEO CAPITOLARE is beneath the portico. Among the paintings are versions of the Madonna by *Gentile da Fabriano* and *Antoniazzo Romano*. 13. Fragments of an *Exultet* (School of Montecassino; 12C); 14. Story of the Passion (late 13C; English); *16. Jewelled 12C Byzantine cross-reliquary; *42. Ornamental parts of the chasuble of Benedict XI (1303-4).

Just beyond the Cathedral the road leaves the town by the Porta Napoli, flanked by cylindrical towers; the railway station lies to the left.

Via dei Laghi (p. 344; Rte 23B) leads back to Rome.

# 24  PALESTRINA

ROAD. VIA CASILINA, 38 km. (return by VIA PRENESTINA, 37 km.). Frequent buses from Viale Castro Pretorio and P.za dei Cinquecento along Via Casilina in 1 hr viâ S. Cesareo. AUTOSTRADA DEL SOLE, 27 km. to S. Cesareo, then 10½ km. E. to Palestrina.

RAILWAY from *Rome* (Termini) to *Palestrina*, 37 km. in 1 hr.

Rome is left by Porta Maggiore (Pl. 6; 8). The right-hand road of the two main roads beyond the gate is Via Casilina. For the first 18½ km. the road passes through perhaps the most unpleasant suburbs of Rome.— 5 km. *Tor Pignattara* (45 m; somewhat hidden to l., behind a school), all that remains of the tomb of St Helena (d. c. 330), mother of Constantine. It is circular outside and octagonal, with niches, in the interior. The modern name is taken from the terracotta amphoræ (*pignatte*) introduced into the vaulting to diminish the load. St Helena's sarcophagus is in the Vatican (p. 310). No. 643, next door, is the entrance to the *Catacombs of SS. Pietro and Marcellino* (3-4C), the most pictorially decorated in Rome.—7½ km. *Centocelle;* on the right is the military air station of that name and beyond can be seen the arches of the Aqua Claudia; on the left are the Tiburtine and Prenestine Hills; to the N. the Monti Sabini and to the N.W. Monte Soratte.—This route crosses the Rome Circular road before (11½ km.) *Torrenova,* adjoining the old Borghese Palace.—At (18½ km.) *Finócchio* by-roads lead S. to Frascati (p. 339) and N. to the Via Prenestina (see below).—Beyond (20 km.) *Pantano Borghese* station, the road ascends and becomes more attractive. It passes on the left the *Tenuta di Pantano,* which comprises two dried-up lakes: *Lago Regillo,* drained in the 17C, and the *Lago di Castiglione,* reclaimed in the 19C.

The BATTLE OF LAKE REGILLUS, in 496 B.C., was a victory for the Romans over the Latins led by the Tarquins and ended the last attempt of the Tarquin dynasty to recover the kingship of Rome. The Romans are said to have been miraculously assisted by the Dioscuri, Castor and Pollux, in whose honour a temple was accordingly built in the Roman Forum. Between the two lakes is the ancient line of the Via Prenestina, with the ruins of Gabii (see below).

26 km. Road r. to (1 km.) *Colonna,* the northernmost of the Castelli Romani (p. 338). This little town is situated on a park-like hill (343 m), with numerous vineyards; a road, the Via Colonna, leads s.w. to Frascati.—At (30 km.), a road from Monte Cómpatri and Frascati comes in from the right (bus, see p. 342).—31 km. *San Cesareo.* This route leaves Via Casilina 2 km. farther on, and Via Prenestina Nuova continues (l.)—33½ km. Road l. for **Zagarolo** (2½ km.; 303 m), a town of 11,500 inhabitants, recorded in the 12C under the name of Gazzarolo and a fief of the Rospigliosi from the 17C. The wines from its vineyards are renowned.

The medieval part of the town is entered through a gateway erected by the Rospigliosi (and including Imperial Roman fragments). The Piazzetta delle Tre Cannelle has a pretty group of houses and a fountain made up from a Roman sarcophagus. Beyond lies P.za Indipendenza with the imposing *Palazzo Colonna* (Palavicini) with two red granite columns supporting two sarcophagi. Via Fabricci continues past the church of *S. Pietro,* a fine Baroque building, to P.za Marconi. Here the church of *San Lorenzo* (containing a triptych in the manner of Antoniazzo Romano) faces two scenographic palazzi, fine works attrib. to Maderno.

The road ascends. At 36½ km. it is joined on the right by the Olmata di Palestrina a road leading to the Via Casilina near Palestrina station (6½ km.). The hill of Palestrina suddenly comes into view, with Castel San Pietro Romano near the top.

38 km. **PALESTRINA** (12,400 inhab.), the ancient *Prœneste,* occupies the s. slope of Monte Ginestro, a spur of the Monti Prenestini. Its steep narrow streets are often stepped. It is renowned for its Temple of Fortune, a masterpiece of Roman architecture, important elements of which were revealed by the clearance of buildings destroyed by bombing in 1944. Palestrina is one of the six suburbicarian sees.

*Praeneste,* one of the oldest towns of Latium, is said to have been founded by Telegonus, son of Ulysses and Circe. It was a thriving place as early as the 7C B.C. Strongly fortified, it long resisted the attacks of the Romans, but in 499 B.C. it joined its traditional enemy. Later it revolted and took a prominent part in the Latin War of 340-338, after which it became subject to Rome. Refuge of the younger Marius, it was besieged in 82 B.C. by the troops of Sulla. Sulla destroyed the town after its capture but he later made amends by building the Temple of Fortune. Its oracle, which delivered the 'Prænestinæ sortes', became famous, and its influence survived until the 4C A.D. In the golden age of Rome 'cool Præneste', as Horace calls it, became a retreat of the patricians from the heats of summer.

In the Middle Ages a town called *Città Prenestina* was built over the abandoned temple. In 752 this town was occupied by Astaulph, king of the Lombards. Later it passed to the counts of Tusculum and in 1043 to the Colonna; it thus became involved in the feuds of the Guelphs and Ghibellines, being several times destroyed and rebuilt. In 1630 Francesco Colonna sold it to Carlo Barberini, brother of Urban VII. The most famous native was Giov. Pierluigi da Palestrina (1524?-94), the father of polyphonic music.—In the history of art Palestrina is noted for its cistæ or bronze caskets of a type seldom made elsewhere.

Via degli Arcioni passes large blocks of tufa which supported the First Terrace of the temple and, beyond, the battlemented 17C *Porta del Sole.* Viale Duca d'Aosta swings round to the entrance to the town (left) by Viale della Vittoria.

The **Temple of Fortune** is of such vast extent that the whole of the medieval town is contained within its bounds and its ruins are seen on every side. It is a replacement of an older temple destroyed by Sulla in 82 B.C. Sulla, believing himself to be an especial favourite of Fortune, ordered its construction.

M

Sulla's temple was an immense edifice, laid out in a series of terraces conforming to the slope of the hill and connected by ramps. The lowest terrace had a frontage of 366 m; it was 152 m below the level of the rotunda that once crowned the temple summit. The total area was c. 32 hectares. The shrine of the oracle, on the second terrace, claimed to foretell the future by delivering to inquirers *sortes,* or lots, which were pieces of wood with letters carved on them. When the town was bombed in 1944, the houses covering the third terrace were destroyed. The homeless but reluctant citizens were rehoused on the outskirts of Palestrina and the work of clearance and discovery began. Some indication of the results of subsequent work is given below, but much study has still to be carried out by the experts.

Viale della Vittoria ends in Piazzale Santa Maria degli Angeli, from which Via Anicia continues to the central Piazza Regina Margherita, which occupies the site of the *Forum* and the central section of the SECOND TERRACE. In the middle of the square is the monument to Palestrina, by Arn. Zocchi (1921); the composer was born in a little house in the neighbouring Vicolo Pierluigi. The **Cathedral,** dating from the 5C, was rebuilt in the Romanesque style in the 12C and altered again later. The façade presents an interesting ensemble of ancient fragments. Beneath the sanctuary excavations in 1974 have revealed part of a pagan Roman edifice in tufa, and a stretch of Roman road (visible through a grille at the end of the right aisle; opened by the sacristan). In the left aisle is a copy of Michelangelo's famous Pietà of Palestrina (comp. below).—Outside, on the right of the Cathedral (below ground level) are further remains of the Roman road and the steps of the Roman building known as the Iunonarium. Behind rises the high wall of the *Seminario* which incorporates four Corinthian half-columns from the façade of the Apsidal Hall (see below).

The so-called *Santuario Inferiore* is at present closed to the public. It is still not clear how this group of buildings were related to the main temple area. They are reached through the portal of the Seminario. The *Aerarium,* or treasury, contains busts, votive offerings, and architectural fragments. Beyond the *Area Sacra,* a spacious clearing carved out of the hillside, is the *Antro delle Sorti* (Shrine of the Oracle), a small cave with three niches whence appeared the lettered *sortes* (see above). Extensive remains of a coloured *Mosaic depict an Egyptian seascape, possibly the port of Alexandria. On the other side of the court is an *Apsidal Hall* (now a convent). This is a rectangular room in opus incertum, with an apse and a frieze of metopes and triglyphs, and niches framed in half columns. Here was found the Barberini mosaic (see below).

From the piazza Corso Pier Luigi da Palestrina leads to P.za Liberazione. Below the gardens of the Villa Comunale can be seen a long stretch of the wall of the first terrace and part of a Roman road.

Steps in the right corner of the square which correspond to one of the ancient ramps, ascend to the *THIRD TERRACE, called Via del Borgo. Two great ramps, constructed on rubble, converge on the terrace, which is supported by a massive wall and divided into halves by a central staircase. Along the back of each half ran a Doric colonnade, the line of which was broken by a monumental hemicycle, also colonnaded. Over the hemicycles was a barrel-vaulted roof carried on Ionic columns; part of the roof is still in place.

The *View from the terrace embraces all the points of the compass: w. Rome, with Soracte in the far distance; N. the Monte Tiburtini; E. the Monti Ernici; S. the Monte Lepini; S.W. the Campagna as far as the Tyrrhenian Sea.

The central staircase ascends to the next level, also adorned with a colonnade; above is the FOURTH TERRACE, originally the courtyard in front of the rotunda that crowned the temple. This terrace, called Piazza

della Cortina, once had side porticoes. A flight of steps leads up to
**Palazzo Colonna-Barberini,** occupying the site of the rotunda. The
palace was built by the Colonna in the 11C and, after many vicissitudes,
was given its definitive form in 1640 by Taddeo Barberini. The modernized interior now contains the ***Museo Nazionale Archeologico
Prenestino** (9–14; closed Mon). Although many antiquities from
Praeneste have been dispersed to Rome and elsewhere, the museum
offers as complete a picture as possible of local civilization from the 8C
B.C. to the 4C A.D.

On the GROUND FLOOR may be seen traces of the temple walls in opus incertum.—R. I. Sculpture fragments from the Roman town.—R. II. 26. Cippus of two
praetors (2C B.C.?).—R. III. *27. Large fragment of a statue of Fortune in grey

Oriental marble (Hellenistic Rhodian school).—R. IV. Among the funerary altars:
40. Votive altar to the Di Manes (Flavian period).—R. V. 44-45. Marble plinths
dedicated to Security and Peace by the emperor, and consecrated by the council
and people of Praeneste (first half of 1C A.D.); 52. Base of a candelabrum, with
Dionysos, a maenad, and a satyr (neo-Attic.)—R. VI. Portrait busts, fragments of
sarcophagus reliefs.—Stairs lead up past remains of the temple to the FIRST
FLOOR.
R. VII, 62, 63. Two painted Archaic metopes in terracotta (6C B.C.), with scenes
of horses and chariots.—RR. VIII and IX contain mirrors, cistae (p. 353), and
other toilet articles coming from tombs of the 4C B.C. R. VIII. Case III. 64, 65.
Mirrors with Silenus on horseback and Silenus and panther; Case IV, 72.
*Cylindrical cista, with fine graffiti; Case V. 81. Cista with battle between Hercules
and the Amazon Hippolyta, and on the lid, two warriors carrying a wounded man;
82. Oval cista with battle scenes, and a female acrobat on the cover; also, 85-87.

Three strigils (used by athletes).—R. IX. Case VI. 83. Cista with two figures (a third lacking) forming a circle on the cover; Case VII. 89. Bronze statuette of an ephebe (in the style of an Archaic kouros); Case VIII. Bronze mirrors decorated with mythological scenes; Case X. *Cista with Dionysos supported by Pan on the cover.—R. X. 110. Lid of a sarcophagus in peperino, with a frieze of animals; floor mosaics. Model of the Temple of Fortune. R. XI contains decorative fragments and votive objects from the temple. R. XII is used for restoration work; in 1978 work was being carried out here on frescoes detached from the temple.

From R. XI a staircase ascends to R. XIV where is the celebrated *Barberini Mosaic, extensively restored. It depicts an Egyptian scene during the flooding of the Nile, from its source in the mountains of Ethiopia to the Delta. At the bottom is a banqueting scene on a canal overshaded with vines. Here is the Canopus of Alexandria, with the Serapeum to the right, before which are warriors and a priestess. Higher, to the right, is a sacred precinct, with pillars towers and statues; to the left, near a building with obelisks, is a well, perhaps that of Aswan which helped Eratosthenes to calculate the meridian. The highest section shows regions of cataracts and deserts, inhabited by tropical animals.

The left-hand staircase descends; here can be seen the circular *Shrine, once sheltering the well which stood before one of the hemicycles at the back of the third terrace of the temple.

To the W. of the palace is the charming little church of *Santa Rosalia* (1660) which once contained the Pietà of Michelangelo, now in the Galleria dell'Accademia in Florence.

FROM PALESTRINA TO CAPRÁNICA PRENESTINA, 12 km.; bus in ½ hr. This road, a continuation of Via Pedemontana, climbs in spirals to (3½ km.) *Castel San Pietro Romano* (752 m), a hamlet on the site of the citadel of Praeneste. Its church of San Pietro has an altarpiece by Pietro da Cortona. On the top of the hill is the ruined *Castle of the Colonna*. The *View is magnificent, reaching all the way to Rome and beyond.—The road continues to climb. 12 km. *Capránica Prenestina* (914 m).—Beyond this point the road gradually descends in a huge curve round the E. side of the Monti Prenestini and across the Monti Tiburtini to (29½ km.) *Tivoli* (Rte 25).

FROM PALESTRINA TO TIVOLI (41½ km.). Via Prenestina leads out of Palestrina and at 8 km. a turn (r.) leads to *Gallicano nel Lazio*, situated on a high tufa rock between two valleys, probably on the site of the Latin city of *Pedum* conquered by Rome in 338 B.C. The present village dates from the 10C, and has picturesque roads leading off the central street.—18½ km. *Poli*, a pretty town with a Conti palace (frescoes by Giulio Romano).—25½ km. *Casape*, in the wooded folds of the Prenestine Hills.—28½ km. *S. Gregorio da Sassola*, a charming hill town with a 15C castle, later converted into a baronial palace. From here the road, clinging to the hill-side, passes through olive groves with views to the plain towards Rome on the left.—41½ km. Tivoli (Rte 25).

The return to Rome may be made by Via Prenestina (37 km.).—8 km. Turning r. for *Gallicano nel Lazio*, and other attractive hill towns on a road to Tivoli (see above).—At (8½ km.) *Santa Maria di Cavamonte* there is a cross-roads. To the left is Zagarolo (p. 353); to the right, Tivoli (18½ km.) From here the narrow straight Via Prenestina leads back to Rome, through gently rolling country. The road passes a long stretch of Roman pavement on the approach (16½ km.) to the ruins of *Gabii* (r.), which gave the road its original name, the *Via Gabina*. It passed through Gabii and Praeneste (Palestrina) and joined the Via Latina at Anagnina (Anagni). The ancient Latin town of Gabii was guilefully captured by Tarquinius Superbus. The ruins (conspicuous to the r. of the road near a tower) include those of a Temple of Juno Gabina, and a sanctuary in which a vast number of bronze statuettes were found in 1976. In the neighbourhood are the stone quarries from which parts of Rome were built.—22 km. *Ponte di Nona*, at the 9th (Roman) milestone, a fine Roman bridge of the Republican era, in excellent preservation; it has seven arches and is 72 m long.—30 km. *Tor de' Schiavi* (l.; Tower of the

Slaves) is a circular building which, with the ruins of an octagonal hall, formed part of a 3C villa of the Gordiani.—37 km. This route rejoins Via Casilina, just outside Porta Maggiore to return to the centre of Rome.

# 25   TIVOLI.   HADRIAN'S VILLA.   SUBIACO.

Tivoli bears a name that is famous all over the world; Hadrian's Villa, the most important of its kind, lies in a plain below Tivoli, some 6 km. s.w. of that resort. Subiaco, of particular significance in ecclesiastical history, is normally reached from Rome by the road—Via Tiburtina—running through Tivoli and following the valley of the Aniene.

## A   From Rome to Tivoli

ROAD (VIA TIBURTINA), 31½ km. Buses of ACOTRAL every 30 min. from Via Gaeta, N.E. corner of Piazza dei Cinquecento, to Tivoli (Largo Nazioni Uniti) in 50 min. Buses for Hadrian's Villa depart from P.za della Repubblica 20 min. past every hour. There is also a bus service every 20 minutes between Tivoli and Hadrian's Villa.—The Motorway (A 24, for l'Aquila) passes well s. of Tivoli, and has little advantage over the Via Tiburtina.

RAILWAY. A somewhat roundabout route from *Rome* (Termini) to *Tivoli* viâ *Guidónia*, on the Rome–Pescara line (40 km. in c. 1 hr.).

VIA TIBURTINA, or Highway 5, on the line of the old Roman road to Tibur (Tivoli), starts from Porta San Lorenzo (Pl. 6; 5, 4). The road passes the huge Campo Verano Cemetery (p. 198) on the right, and then crosses the railway (Rome Tiburtina station, l.). The next 10 km. traverse a dreary factory area, and the Aniene is crossed by (8 km.) the *Ponte Mammolo,* successor (1857) to the ancient *Pons Mammeus,* dating from the Republican era and rebuilt by Julia Mammæa, mother of Alexander Severus. On the left is a road leading to Via Nomentana.

The river **Aniene,** the classical *Anio,* rises in the Monti Simbruini, to the E. of Subiaco. It flows past Subiaco and Tivoli, where it forms the noted cascades, and joins the Tiber N. of Rome, near the Ponte Salario. In antiquity its waters were conveyed to Rome by two aqueducts—the *Anio Vetus* (43 m.), begun in 273 B.C., and the *Anio Novus* (59 m.) begun in A.D. 36 (p. 217).

The Rome Circular Road is crossed just before (13 km.) *Settecamini* (48 m). Farther on, a road leads s. to *Lunghezza,* with a 13C castle. Here is the site of *Collatia,* where archæological material dating from the Iron Age has come to light.—19½ km. *Le Tavernúcole;* on the left is the crenellated *Castell' Arcione,* probably erected in the 12C on ruins dating from the Imperial era, and restored in 1931. Beyond it are the three summits of the Monti Cornicolani with Monte Gennaro rising behind them; ahead are Tivoli and the Monti Tiburtini; to the right the Monti Prenestini and the Alban Hills.—21½ km. Turning (l.) for Guidónia.

22½ km. **Bagni di Tivoli** (80 m), with the *Stabilimento delle Acque Albule,* which uses the waters of two lakes. The smell of sulphuretted hydrogen is all-pervading.

The hot springs, the Roman *Aquoe Albuloe,* are charged with sulphuretted hydrogen, and are beneficial in skin, throat, and urinary affections, etc. The establishment can accommodate 1000 bathers in four baths, the largest of which is called the Spiaggia di Tivoli. The two lakes that feed the baths are c. 2 km. N. The *Lago della Regina,* or *Solfatara,* is the larger. From its depths the water bubbles up at a temperature of 24°C. At times the water takes on a vivid blue colour. To the s. are remains of Roman thermæ. To the E. is the smaller *Lago delle Colonnelle,* also bright blue in colour. To the N. is the Lago di San Giovanni.

Having crossed the railway the road passes through a region of travertine quarries that furnished stone for the Colosseum, St Peter's, and many other buildings in ancient and modern Rome. The stone is the 'lapis tiburtinus' which hardens after cutting. The Aniene is crossed near (26 km.) the five-arched *Ponte Lucano,* a Roman bridge named after Lucanus Plautius and rebuilt at various times from the 15C to the 19C. Immediately beyond the bridge is (r.) the tower-like *\*Tomb of the Plautii,* of the Augustan period and resembling the Tomb of Cecilia Metella on the Appian Way.

At (28 km.) *Bivio Villa Adriana* (41 m) the road to (1½ km.) Hadrian's Villa branches off to the right. Via Tiburtina now begins its long serpentine climb to Tivoli, passing through a beautiful olive grove. The town is entered by Via Nazionale.—31½ km. **Tivoli** (230 m).

**TIVOLI** (44,500 inhab.), the classical *Tibur,* stands on the lower slopes of the Sabine Hills at the end of the valley of the Aniene, which here narrows into a gorge between Monte Catillo (348 m) on the N. and the Colle Ripoli (484 m) on the S., and discharges the celebrated cascades. The river makes a bold loop round the town and borders it on three sides. Surrounded by olive groves and overlooking the Roman Campagna, Tivoli is delightfully situated, and, though poor and severely damaged in the last war, is justly renowned for its Roman and medieval monuments and enhanced by the tradition that is associated with its name.

**History.** *Tibur* is fabled to have been founded, four centuries before the birth of Rome, by the Siculi, who were later expelled by Tiburtus and his brothers, grandsons of Amphiarus. It was captured by Camillus in 380 B.C., and by the end of the 1C B.C. it had become a holiday resort for the wealthier Romans, who erected their famous temples to Vesta, Hercules, and other deities. Marius, Sallust, Cassius, Catullus, Mæcenas, Quintilius Varus, and, later, Trajan and Hadrian all had sumptuous villas at or near Tibur. It was a spot sacred to the cult of the Sybil Albunea, a favourite haunt of Augustus and the poets Horace, Catullus, and Propertius, and later on a place of confinement for state prisoners such as Syphax and Zenobia. In Hadrian's time its splendour was extraordinary, and in the 6C Totila, the Ostrogoth, after sacking the place rebuilt it as his capital. By the 10C it had recovered its prosperity. It stood a siege by Otho III, became independent as an imperial free city, was occupied by the Caraffas in the 16C and did not lose its autonomous character till 1816. Among its natives were Munatius Plancus (consul 42 B.C.), the founder of Lyons, and Popes Simplicius (468-83) and John IX (898-900).

Via Tiburtina enters the town from the S.W. as Via Nazionale and ends at Largo Garibaldi, a busy traffic centre. On the left is the shady Giardino Garibaldi, which commands a splendid *\*View* of the open country below. To the N.W. is the air station of Guidonia, with the Monti Cornicolani villages above it; almost due W. is Rome; to the S.W. the Campagna extends to the sea.

Viale Nazioni Uniti leads out of the right side of the square up past the bus station to the imposing **Rocca Pia** (adm. 9-12.30, 15-18.30), a castle built by Pius II (1458-64) to overawe the natives of Tivoli. Exhibitions are held here. It is rectangular in shape and has four crenellated cylindrical towers, two large and two smaller. The castle was built over the ruins of a Roman amphitheatre, best seen from Vicolo Barchetto to the N. Viale Trieste continues to Porta San Giovanni, now the entrance to a hospital. Here is the little church of *San Giovanni Evangelista,* containing good frescoes by Antoniazzo Romano.

From the other side of Largo Garibaldi (comp. above) Via Boselli leads to Piazza Trento outside the church of *Santa Maria Maggiore,* a Romanesque structure with a fine rose-window attributed to Angelo da Tivoli above the later Gothic narthex (which contains a 13C fresco of the Madonna and Child, in a fine tabernacle).

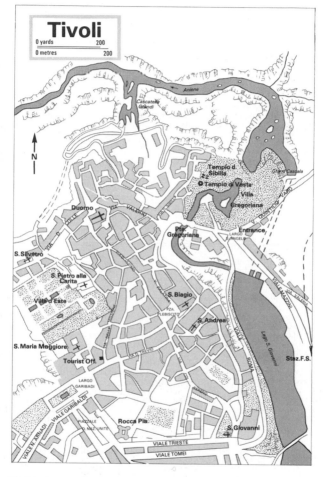

The interior contains remains of the original floor at the E. end. In the presbytery are two triptychs, the one on the r. dates from the 16C, and the one on the l. is signed by Bart. Bulgarini of Siena (14C). Above the latter, Madonna and Child, by Iac. Torriti. Over the high altar is a Byzantine Madonna (12C?). In the r. aisle, Crucifix attrib. to Baccio da Montelupo.

Adjoining the church, on the right, is the entrance to the *Villa d'Este* famous for its incomparable garden with its many fountains. The garden is open (exc. Mon) 9 to dusk (1000 lire, Sun free); the water pressure diminishes between 12 and 14.30 when the fountains are less impressive. From May to early October the gardens are floodlit and open from 20.30 or 21 to 23.30 or 24 (exc. Mon). The villa, closed in 1978, is to reopen shortly.

Originally a Benedictine convent, the property became the Governor's residence after confiscation. In 1550 Card. Ippolito II d'Este was installed here as governor; he commissioned Pirro Ligorio to transform the convent into a sumptuous villa, which his successors embellished. In the course of time it passed by bequest to the House of Austria, but after 1918 the Italian Government resumed possession and undertook a general restoration. The top floor was the Italian headquarters of Franz Liszt (1811–86) from 1865 to the year of his death; from this base he travelled to many parts of Europe and, while here, he composed the third book of his *Années de Pélerinage,* one of the most popular pieces in which is *Les Jeux d'Eau à la Villa d'Este.*

Beyond the entrance is a court which was the cloister of the convent, with the entrance to the *Appartamento Vecchio,* ten frescoed rooms containing minor paintings. A staircase at the end descends to a pavillion, fitted with a bar and commanding a fine view. From here there is access to the walk in front of the villa, below which is the *Fontana del Bicchierone,* by Bernini. A path descends to a lower walk and (left) the *Grotto of Diana,* with stuccoes. Another path leads (r.) to the ROMETTA ('Little Rome'). This has a model of the Tiber with an islet (represening the Isola Tiberina) in the form of a boat, on which is an obelisk. Behind are a seated statue of Rome, with the wolf suckling Romulus and Remus, and miniature reproductions of the principal buildings of ancient Rome. From the Rometta the *Viale delle Cento Fontane* leads right across the garden, parallel to the villa. It is skirted by a long narrow basin with scores of jets and overgrown with maidenhair fern and moss. At the end is the *Fontana dell'Ovato,* by Pirro Ligorio, with the end of a conduit from the Aniene, one of the water supplies for the fountains. In the hemicycle of the fountain are statues of nymphs, by G. B. della Porta. To the right is the *Fontana di Bacco;* to the left is the architectural *Fontana dell'Organo Idraulico,* named after a water-operated organ which was one of the garden's features in the 16C.

Going a little towards the villa, a path turns right into an avenue, half-way along which (l.) is the *Fontana dei Draghi,* by Pirro Ligorio, recalling the dragons that formed part of the coat-of-arms of Gregory XIII, a guest of Card. Ippolito d'Este in 1572. At the end of the avenue are the *Fontana di Proserpina* and the curious *Fontana della Civetta e degli Uccelli,* once noted for producing alternately by water power the screech of an owl and the song of birds. Leading away from the villa, a path passes (r.) the fishponds and (l.) the ruined *Fontana di Arianna,* and, at the end of the garden, reaches the *Fontana della Natura,* with a statue of Diana of the Ephesians. Opposite the gate, beyond, the central avenue leads back towards the villa; in it is the *Rotonda dei Cipressi,* once a circus with some of the mightiest cypresses in Italy. It is now sadly reduced to a hemi-cycle since some of the ancient trees, struck by disease, have had to be felled.

From the fishponds there is a superb view (l.) of the cascades descending from the Organo (see above). From here paths reascend to the terrace in front of the villa, and a spiral stair beyond the bar (r.), emerges into the *Appartamento Nobile,* ten frescoed rooms. The Great Hall has ceiling paintings by the School of Muziano and Fed. Zuccari. From here there is access to the *Loggia dello Scalone,* by Pirro Ligorio, the finest part of the garden façade; the view of the garden is enchanting. A vaulted passageway leads back to the entrance.

The church of *San Pietro alla Carità,* outside the garden to the N.E., contains ten cipollino columns, probably from a Roman villa, and an interesting crypt (open Sun mornings; otherwise ring at the base of the campanile).

From Largo Garibaldi Via Pacifici and Via Trevio lead towards Piazza del Plebiscito (comp. the Plan), the town centre. On the right is the church of *San Biagio,* dating from the 14C and rebuilt in the neo-Gothic style of 1887 (14-15C paintings and frescoes). To the s., in Via Sant'Andrea, is the church of *Sant'Andrea,* with a Romanesque campanile. From the square Via Palatina and Via Ponte Gregoriano, with interesting medieval houses, lead to Piazza Rivarola, an important traffic centre. From here Via San Valerio leads left to the **Duomo** (San Lorenzo), rebuilt in 1650 but retaining a Romanesque campanile of the 12C.

INTERIOR. RIGHT AISLE, 4th chap. (light on r.), *Descent from the Cross, a 13C group of five carved wooden figures, and a copy of the triptych (comp. below); 3rd chap. (l.) so-called *Macchina del Salvatore,* containing a precious 11C or 12C triptych, painted in tempera, with silver and gilt decoration of the 15C and 16C. It is shown only on High religious festivals (copy in the adjoining chapel). Also in the left aisle are two episcopal tombs (late 15C and early 16C).

From P.za Duomo the medieval Via del Duomo (partly stepped) leads past (No. 78) the entrance to the *Ponderarium,* containing two tables with measures of capacity, used by Roman Inspectors of weights and measures.

In Piazza Tani, outside the side entrance to the Cathedral, is a pretty fountain made up from a medieval sarcophagus. From here the narrow Via del Colle (impracticable for cars) descends steeply past medieval houses and remains of ancient buildings through one of the most picturesque parts of the town. It passes the romanesque church of *San Silvestro* (if closed ring to r. of façade at No. 2), recently restored. Inside are interesting 12C or 13C frescoes and a wooden figure of St Valerian of 1138 (r. wall). At the end of the street, outside Porta del Colle, is the *Sanctuary of Hercules Victor* (second half of 1C B.C.), a large area, with arches and vaults, until recently occupied by a paper-mill. It is now being excavated and studied and there are plans to open it to the public.

From Piazza Rivarola (comp. above) Via della Sibilla leads N.E. to the so-called *Temple of Vesta,* a famous land-mark. It is not known to whom the temple was dedicated; it is circular peripteral and dates from the last years of the Republic. Situated on the edge of the cliff dominating the valley, it was converted in the Middle Ages into the church of Santa Maria della Rotonda. Ten of its eighteen fluted Corinthian columns survive, and there is a frieze of bucrania, garlands, rosettes, and paterae. The doors and windows of the well-preserved cella are trapezoidal.—Close by is an earlier temple, known as the **Temple of the Sibyl,** but also of uncertain attribution. It is rectangular with a tetrastyle Ionic façade. Until 1884 it was the church of *San Giorgio.*

From Piazza Rivarola Ponte Gregoriano leads over the Aniene to an open space by the *Porta Sant'Angelo,* a busy traffic centre. Here is the entrance to the *Villa Gregoriana,* a natural park enclosing that reach of the Aniene where it plunges down in the cascades (adm. daily 9.30-dusk).

The park commemorates Gregory XVI, who took vigorous steps to put an end to the periodic local flooding, which in 1826 had seriously damaged the town. On his accession to the papacy in 1831, he instructed the engineer Folchi to build a double tunnel under Monte Catillo, to ease the flow of the river. This tunnel (300 m and 270 m) became known as the *Traforo Gregoriano,* or *Emissario Gregoriano,* and the water plunged down from it in a new waterfall, thenceforth known as the Great Cascade.

From the ticket office a path bears a little right, following the direction post ('Grande Cascata') to a terrace, with a view of the temples of Vesta and of the Sibyl across the valley. Farther on the path reaches a parapet overlooking the crest of the Great Cascade. Steps lead down to another terrace from which the mouth of the tunnel may be seen. Here the aniene makes a leap of 108 metres as it emerges from the Traforo Gregoriano. The tunnel (no adm.) bears inscriptions recording the visits of popes and kings. From the first terrace a path marked 'Ruderi della Villa-Grotte della Sirena, di Nettuno, e Cascata Bernini' descends to another terrace planted with ilexes, at the end of which is a tunnel which passes through remains of a Roman villa. At the exit a path continues to descend with a good view of the *Little Cascades* and of the *Bernini Cascade.* Farther down, a little square is reached marked with two signposts, to the right of which there is a viewpoint about half the height of the Great Cascade, which enables one to appreciate its volume, its noise and the rainbow colours of its spray. From the little square a path follows the signpost marked 'Grotte Nettuno e Sirena, Cascata Bernini', descending for some distance and bearing sharp left at a signpost marked 'Ingresso Grotta della Sirena' to reach the fantastic *Grotto of the Siren,* a limestone cavern in which the water tumbles down a narrow ravine. The other side of the valley may now be climbed. From a fork marked 'Grotta di Nettuno e Tempio di Vesta', a path turns left, passing through two tunnels lit from the side. At another fork a descent (l.) leads to the *Grotto of Neptune,* through which the Aniene originally flowed. From the last-named fork the other path (r.) leads to the exit-gate close to the temples.

From Porta Sant'Angelo Viale Mazzini leads s. to the Station. Here, in a park, the tomb of Vestalia Cossinia has recently been set up.

VIA DELLE CASCATELLE (3 km.). From Porta Sant'Angelo Via Quintilio Varo winds between olive plantations, and passes several times beneath the viaducts of the Rome-Tivoli railway. It soon reaches the \**Belvedere,* with a fine view of the Great Cascade, and, after crossing beneath the railway for the last time, there is a wonderful \*View of the Great Cascade, the Cascatelle, the town of Tivoli, and the Campagna. The road passes the church of *Sant'Antonio* (l.) and the ruined arches of the *Aqua Marcia.* This aqueduct, 58 km. long and dating from 144 B.C., ran from Via Valeria to Rome. Farther on (½ km.) a by-road (left; unsignposted) diverges from the main road and leads down past a group of houses to the conspicuous *Santuario di Santa Maria di Quintiliolo,* near the ruins of a Roman villa, said to have been that of Quintilius Varus.

The road soon deteriorates and becomes less interesting. Farther on it crosses the *Ponte dell' Acquoria* over the Aniene, and, going straight on, begins to climb the *Clivus Tiburtinus,* partly levelled by Constantine. On the right, is the so-called *Tempio del Mondo,* with a large interior chamber and farther on, also on the right, is a Roman building known as the *Tempio della Tosse.* This is most probably a tomb, and is circular without, octagonal within, and may have been adapted for Christian worship (traces of Byzantine decoration). The road passes round the ruins of the Temple of Hercules Victor (comp. p. 361).—It re-enters Tivoli by Porta del Colle.

From Tivoli to *Subiaco,* see Rte 25C; to *Palestrina,* see p. 356.

# B  Hadrian's Villa

ROAD, 28½ km. Tivoli buses (see above) from Rome stop at the *Bivio Villa Adriana.*

RAILWAY. The nearest station is at *Bagni di Tivoli* (see Rte 25A), 7 km. from the Villa.

From Rome by the Via Tiburtina to (27 km.) the *Bivio Villa Adriana,* see Rte 25A. At the bus stop the road leads to the right (s.; signpost). The entrance to Hadrian's Villa (1½ km.) is a good 15 min. walk from here. The villa is open daily from 9 to dusk except Mondays; visitors are recommended to bring a picnic.

\***Hadrian's Villa,** the largest and richest imperial villa in the Roman Empire, was the chosen residence of Hadrian, who became emperor on the death of Trajan in 117. He began to build the villa in 125 and completed it ten years later; but he enjoyed it for only a brief period before ill-health constrained him to move south to Baiæ, where he died in 138. It is one of the most evocative classical sites left in Italy.

It is difficult to understand why Hadrian, with all the resources of the Empire at his disposal, should have lit on such an unprepossessing spot for his magnificent estate. Though little over 5km. from the scenic health resort of Tivoli, the surroundings of the villa are flat, low-lying, and devoid of charm. In the emperor's day they were not even salubrious. One reason adduced for the choice of ground is the fact that its owner was the Empress Sabina; another suggested reason is the emperor's desire to keep himself apart from his courtiers, many of whom owned villas on the hills around Tivoli. Parts of a smaller country house of the 1C B.C., overlooking the 'Vale of Tempe', were incorporated into the emperor's villa.

The idea underlying the construction of the villa was the emperor's wish to reproduce those places that had most impressed him during his prolonged travels in the Empire. These were the Lyceum, the Academy, the Prytaneum, and the Stoa Poikile in Athens; the Canopus of the Egyptian Delta; and the Vale of Tempe in Thessaly. To these he added even a representation of Hades, as conceived by the poets. His successors enlarged and embellished the villa, but it is said that Constantine despoiled it to beautify Byzantium. Barbarian invaders plundered the site, and in course of time it became a quarry for builders and lime-burners. Until the Renaissance the ruins continued to be neglected or abused.

The first excavations were ordered by Alexander VI and Card. Aless. Farnese. Soon after he had begun to live at the Villa d'Este in 1550, Card. Ippolito II d'Este took many of the newly-discovered works of art to adorn his Tivoli villa. Excavations continued in the 17-19C and yielded many valuable discoveries; the engraver G. B. Piranesi (1720-78) left a plan of the ruins and engravings of the buildings and sculptures (comp. p. 171). A successful attempt to improve the amenities of the site was made in 1730 by Count Fede by the plantations of cypresses and pines. In 1870 the Italian Government acquired most of the site and excavation was systematically planned. It is still, however, far from complete and important discoveries are still being made. The works of art discovered in the villa (more than 260) are scattered in museums and galleries all over Europe. In Rome they are to be found in the Museo Nazionale Romano, the Capitoline Museum, the Egyptian Museum in the Vatican, and elsewhere.

The general plan of the villa is capricious though the buildings individually are quite regular. These are grouped round four principal structures: the Poikile, the Canopus, the Academy, and the Imperial Palace. Guide-posts indicate the names of the buildings and in some instances give a few details about them. The visitor to Hadrian's Villa cannot fail to be impressed by its vast size. A walk round the estate takes some hours; half a day is needed for even a cursory inspection.

From the ticket entrance, a short drive leads on to the car park (Rfmts.). A building here displays a model of the villa. The entrance to the ruins is through the massive N. wall of the **Poikile** (*Pecile*).

The *Stoa Poikile* (painted porch) was a building in Athens famous alike for its varied paintings by Polygnotos and Panainos and for its association with the Stoic philosophers. Hadrian's reproduction is a rectangular peristyle (232 x 97 m) with the ends slightly curved. The huge N. wall (9 m high), running almost due E. and W., still exists. On the S. side the wall has vanished, but there are remains of a pavilion with three exedræ and a fountain. On both sides of it ran roofed colonnades, so that sun or shade could be enjoyed at any hour and warmth or freshness at any season. In the middle of the rectangle the fish-pond has been restored. The free area round it was possibly used as a racecourse. On the S.W. the Poikile had as a substructure a wall with three rows of small chambers, now called the *Cento Camerelle,* which are supposed to have accommodated the Prætorians.

At the N.E. angle of the Poikile, a few steps lead up to the *Philosophers' Hall* (17 x 9 m), with an apse, seven niches for statues, and four side-doors; adjacent is a series of baths. Beyond is a charming circular building, with an Ionic marble peristyle, known as the *Naval Theatre* (*Teatro Marittimo*), but more probably a retreat in which the emperor sought occasional solitude. A circular moat (3½ m broad), lined with Luni (Carrara) marble, encloses an island on which stand an atrium with fluted Ionic columns in an intricate design, and a series of living-rooms. It could be reached only by a revolving bridge. A reconstruction of one part of the building is displayed on the S. side.

On the E. side stairs lead up to the first complex of buildings belonging to the **Imperial Palace,** which is disposed parallel to the Vale of Tempe (see below); its elements are grouped round four peristyles. The COURT OF THE LIBRARIES (*Cortile delle Biblioteche*), is now a secluded olive plantation; its N.W. side is flanked by the so-called *Greek and Latin Libraries,* now identified as summer *Triclinia,* with towers. Behind them new excavations have revealed part of a delightful garden.

To the N. of the Cortile are the OSPITALI (*Guest rooms*), the best preserved part of the Palace complex, with ten small rooms leading off either side of a wide corridor. Rectangular alcoves indicate space for a bed, and the lighting of each room was provided by the high openings. The rooms are decorated with well-preserved mosaics.—Steps lead down to the TRICLINIUM with (l.) some capitals with a lotus motif, and a mosaic floor. To the right is a long corridor with oblique openings in the vault, to allow the light of midday to enter. This leads to the PADIGLIONE (*Pavilion*) which overlooks the Vale of Tempe.

From here steps lead up to a path (S.) to the GREAT PERISTYLE of the palace, with a private library and other small rooms overlooking the Court of the Libraries. Here also is the *Room of Three Naves,* a delightfully proportioned room with two rows of small columns. Near by, stairs lead underground to a *Cryptoporticus,* with well-lit corridors. At the other end of this central nucleus of the palace is the *Room of the Doric Pilasters,* with a fine entablature. The *Barracks of the Vigiles* are beyond the apse of the basilican hall (r.) To the left is the *Nymphæum* which had two round fountain basins, and from here a path leads to the **Piazza d'Oro,** a rectangular area at the S.E. end of the Palace. It was so named because excavations here yielded such rich finds.

It is entered through the fine octagonal *Vestibule.* The peristyle was formed of alternate columns of cipollino and granite in two rows. On the far side (S.E.) is an intricate series of rooms, the central one being the most interesting design, a Greek cross with alternate convex and concave sides. A dome used to rest over the four walls nearest the centre.

A path continues W. past the back of the Barracks of the Vigiles and a *Quadriporticus* with a pool and a portico of fluted composite columns. Beneath is an extensive Cryptoporticus.

A path descends to a clump of mighty cypresses and the **Small Thermæ** and the **\*Great Thermæ.** The small baths are well-preserved, with a large rectangular hall, perhaps the frigidarium, and an octagonal hall with a domed vault. The large baths contain a circular hall, with cupola and skylight. A huge *Sala Absidata* has a superb cross-vault, mostly collapsed. Opposite is another cross-vaulted room (closed; but well seen from the S.E.) decorated with exquisite stucco reliefs. On the E. is a swimming-bath, bounded on the N.W. side by a *Cryptoporticus* on the ruined walls of which are numerous graffiti of the 16C and 17C. This gives access to the so-called *Proetorium,* a tall edifice which was divided into three storeys by wooden floors. It is thought to have been used as a warehouse.

The **\*Canopus** was designed to imitate the famous sanctuary of Serapis, that stood at the 15th milestone from Alexandria.

Hadrian dug a hollow (185 by 75 m), in which he constructed a canal, bordered on one side by a block of 20 rooms and a portico, and on the other by a heavy buttressed wall (238 m long), against which were set entertainment booths. The Canopus has for the most part been restored to its old aspect. Around the curved N. end of the canal reproductions of statues found on the site have been set up between marble columns surmounted by an epistyle arched over alternate pillars. Along the right side are reproductions of Caryatids and Sileni.

At the s. end of the canal is a nymphæum, commonly called the *Serapeum*, where most of the Egyptian sculptures in the Capitoline and

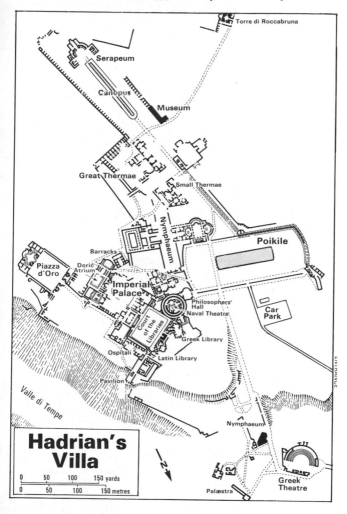

Vatican museums were found. An excellent survey of the greater part of the villa may be obtained from the hill behind.

On the N.W. side of the hollow is the **Museum**, housing finds from more recent excavations. ROOM I. Decorative fragments.—R. 2. Bust of Caracalla and other portraits; Venus, copy of a work by Praxiteles.—R. 3. Wounded Amazons, one a mutilated copy of a Polykleitan original, the other a fine replica of the famous original by Pheidias; portrait of Verres, spoiler of Sicily; Athena, from a mid-5C original.—R. 4. Mars also from a mid-5C original; two athletes.—R. 5. Crocodile; tondo of a satyr (bas-relief).—R. 6. Four marble caryatids, copies of the 5C originals on the Erechtheion at Athens; two Sileni.

About 4 min. w. of the entrance to the Canopus is the *Torre di Roccabruna* (view), a belvedere or pharos, rectangular externally and circular within. This is possibly an imitation of the Tower of Timon of Athens, which stood near the Academy. It stands in the Oliveto Roccabruna, which is famous for the size of its olive trees, one of them (the 'albero bello') being reputed the largest in the Tivoli district.

To the s.e., within an olive-grove, is the so-called **Accademia,** a complex of buildings which some authorities, however, prefer to identify as a secondary palace. The group includes a round basin, styled the *Temple of Apollo,* a peristyle, and the remains of three rooms with delicate stucco ornamentation. About 300 m. s.e. are the remains of an *\*Odeion* or *Theatre* (45 m in diameter) with the imperial box in the centre of the cavea. To the e. of the Odeion a path descends to a hollow (150 m long), hewn in the tufa and overshadowed by thick vegetation, which leads to a semi-circular vestibule (once perhaps guarded by an image of Cerberus). This was the entrance to **Hades** or the **Inferi,** represented by a quadrangle of four subterranean corridors, 5½ m wide and 91 m in total length, with 79 apertures for light. Smaller tunnels connected Hades with various parts of the Villa.

A broad main path returns towards the entrance. To the right, just before the Poikile, is a court with three apses and a large connecting room. The *Nymphæum* beyond adjoins the *Quadriporticus* (see above). A path leads back across the Poikile to the entrance. From here a fine avenue of cypresses leads n. to the Greek Theatre, passing the Casino Fede (now the excavation office), built on part of the ruins of the so-called *Nymphæum.* Here the *Temple of Venus* was restored in 1959. Beyond, to the right, a walk leads to the modernized *Fontana di Palazzo,* near which are a few traces of the *Paloestra.* Beyond this lies the *Valle Pussiana,* the Emperor's Vale of Tempe, with a streamlet to represent the Peneios. Descending (l.) through olives and cypresses, the path passes the **Greek Theatre,** c. 36 m in diameter; its cavea or auditorium is carved out of the hill-side. Visitors without cars may continue past the theatre back to the ticket entrance; those with cars return up the cypress avenue to the car park.

# C   From Rome to Subiaco

ROAD, viâ Tivoli, 74½ km. Frequent bus services in c. 2 hrs viâ Castel Madama, and in c. 1½ hrs viâ Vicovaro; from the Castro Pretorio.
RAILWAY from *Rome* (Termini) viâ Tivoli to Mandela-Sambuci, 54 km. in c. 1 hour.—Buses connect with the trains from *Rome,* to *Subiaco,* 25 km., in 40 minutes.

From Rome to (31½ km.) *Tivoli,* see Rte 25A. On reaching Tivoli the through buses by-pass the town, taking Viale Trieste, Viale Roma and Viale Giuseppe Mazzini, forking left just before the railway station. The road, still N5, is now called Via Valeria.

The VIA VALERIA, one of the great Roman roads across the Apennines, passed through Carseoli (Carsoli) and Corfinium (near Sulmona) to Aternum (Pescara), on the Adriatic. Thence it followed the coast-line to Castrum Truentium (near San Benedetto del Tronto), where it joined the Via Salaria.

Beyond Tivoli the road accompanies the Rome-Pescara railway as it winds N.E. between wooded hills up the Aniene valley, followed, farther on, also by a new autostrada (A 24; for Aquila).—36 km. *San Polo* station (*S. Polo de' Cavalieri,* with a medieval Rocca, is 7 km. along a branch road left).—40 km. Castel Madama station lies 3 km. below *Castel Madama* whose Orsini castle, on top of a green hill (453 m), is prominent to the right.

Remains of arches of the Aqua Marcia are seen here and there. The valley widens and the scenery increases in charm; chestnut trees, olive groves, and vineyards abound.—46 km. **Vicovaro** (3051 m; 3700 inhab.) occupies the site of the citadel of *Varia,* a town of the Aequi. The little church of *Sant' Antonio* has antique columns in its portico. The *Orsini Palace* dates from the 13C. The *Tempietto di San Giacomo,* an octagonal Renaissance chapel by Domenico da Capodistria (c. 1450), has a rich porch by Giov. Dalmata.—Beyond the little town the *Monastery of San Cosimato* rises to the right.

After several sharp bends in the road, a lovely road diverges left through the valley of the turbulent Licenza (the ancient Digentia). To the r. is the beautiful hill-town of Mandela (see below), and on the l. *Roccagióvine* with an Orsini castle. Before (8 km.) Licenza, an unmade road on the left and a footpath lead to the ruin of **Horace's Sabine farm.**

From the car park is the entrance to a series of rooms with magnificent mosaic pavements; the first one is the most sumptuous, with an area of different mosaic design for a bed. The rooms are raised above an oblong garden with a swimming-pool in the centre. They are grouped round an open court with a square pool; parts of the original lead piping used to channel the water from it can be seen under the floors of neighbouring rooms. On the w. side of the site (most recently excavated) are baths with later Imperial and medieval extensions. Further s. is a 2C aquarium, which was later covered by the church of a medieval convent.—The custodian keeps a small collection of fragments of mosaic, glass, and ceramics found during the excavations.

The spring or *'Fonte di Orazio',* presumed to be the Bandusian Spring apostrophized in one of Horace's odes (iii, 13), can still be seen up the rise to the s.w. of the site (from which its sound can be heard). Farther up is the *Ninfeo* constructed by the Orsini, probably replacing a similar edifice of Horace's time (fragments of which are in the museum in Licenza). The unmade road continues up the valley (although the main road gives easier access) in which stand the two spectacular hill-towns of (8 km.) **Licenza** and (10 km.) **Civitella di Licenza.**

The route continues along the main road. At 48 km. another turning left leads to the village of *Mandela* which stands on the spur of a hill to the N. Its position affords magnificent views of the valleys on either side, which are glimpsed down its narrow streets. The castle belonged to the Orsini.—Beyond, a road on the r. leads to the village of *Sambuci,* 4 km. s. of the main road. The valley of Subiaco—Valle Santa—soon comes into view.

56 km. Turning right for **Antícoli Corrado.** The by-road crosses the Aniene and in 2 km. reaches this small town, beautifully situated on a hill side.

The road climbs up to a spacious main square with a Noah's Ark fountain by Arturo Martini. On the l. is the 11C church of *San Pietro,* well-preserved, with early frescoes recently uncovered, the most primitive of which were painted over in several succeeding centuries. From the opposite corner of the piazza, a road leads through the ancient gate of the city up to the *Museum of Modern Art* (damaged by fire in 1974), housed in an old villa, used as a prison in the 16C. The small collection has been donated over the last 50 years by artists of all nationalities who have worked in Antícoli, as well as those who were born here. The story is told of a group of artists in the early 19C travelling to Subiaco, stopping on the way at Antícoli and falling in love with its charm and most of all its beautiful women, using them as models in their work. An artistic community has remained, and the collection is impressive.

At 58 km. this route leaves Via Valeria and turns right into the beautiful wooded Subiaco road (Via Sublacensis), following the course of the Aniene upstream, with the Monti Simbruini on the left. On the right can be seen the hill town of Marano Equo. In this area are springs, which are the source of the Aqua Marcia (p. 362), and still supply Rome with water.—64 km. *Agosta* (l.) is a hamlet founded by the monks of Subiaco.—From (68½ km.) *Madonna della Pace,* a secondary road, the Via Empolitana, leads w. to Tivoli past the conspicuous hill-top village of *Rocca Canterano* (747 m).

74 km. **SUBIACO** (408 m; 8700 inhab.) lies near the head of the narrow Aniene valley, on the w. slopes of Monte Livata. It is famous as the birthplace of western monasticism under the rule of its founder St Benedict. Modern buildings are fast encroaching on the medieval aspect of the town.

**History.** Subiaco, anciently *Sublaqueum* ('under the lakes') appears to owe its origin as a town to the necessity of accommodating the workmen employed by Nero to build here a grandiose villa, with an extensive lake in its grounds. There were already in existence three small lakes—the *Simbruina Stagna* mentioned by Tacitus—the level of which was raised by the building of a dam across the Anio. Tacitus relates that at a banquet in the villa the table before Nero was struck by lightning. Nero's lake disappeared after flood waters had breached the dam in February 1305, but traces of his villa survive.

A monastery dedicated to St Clement, was founded at Subiaco early in the history of the church. Towards the end of the 5C Benedetto da Norcia (St Benedict; 480-543?), a rich youth, revolting against the dissolute life of his contemporaries, decided to live in a cavern on the slopes of Monte Taleo. Here he dwelt, in prayer and contemplation, for three years. The fame of his saintliness spread all over Italy and multitudes journeyed to Subiaco to see him. His cavern was known as the *Sacro Speco* (Holy Grotto). Later, persuaded by his twin sister Scholastica, he built a monastery near the ruins of Nero's villa. This was followed by others, of which only two still exist. After a time, harassed by the persecution of a monk called Fiorenzio (Florentius), St Benedict, guided by three tame ravens, moved to Monte Cassino, where in 529 he founded a new monastery.

Some of his companions stayed behind with the abbot St Honorius, and built the convent of SS. Cosmas and Damian (now St Scholastica) and other retreats. Most of these were destroyed by the Lombards. The golden age of the surviving convents was in the 11-12C, but the ambition of the monks, earthquakes, and the plague of 1348 contributed to their decay. In the 16-18C the monastery was ruled by powerful prince-abbots, first of the Colonna family and later of the Borghese and Barberini, until, in 1753, Benedict XIV abolished the temporal power of the abbots.

Arnold Pannartz and Conrad Sweynheim, pupils of Fust, from Mainz, set up the first printing press in Italy, in the Convent of St Scholastica, in 1464. They soon quarrelled with the scribes in the monastery, and in 1467 transferred their press to Rome (comp. p. 78).

Outside the town, to the right of the road and reached by a tiny 14C hump-backed bridge (new bridge under construction downstream) is the church of *San Francesco.* Over the high altar is a triptych signed and dated 1467 by Antoniazzo Romano. A wooden altar frames a painting of St Francis receiving the stigmata, attrib. to Seb. del Piombo. In the 3rd chap. on the left are frescoes attrib. to Sodoma, and an altarpiece of the Nativity attrib. to Pinturicchio. The 2nd chap. contains a wooden Crucifix by Piazza (1685).—At the town entrance is the conspicuous *Arch of Pius VI,* erected in 1789 in honour of the Pope, who, as Card. Braschi, had been abbot Subiaco and had done much for its inhabitants.

The 'one-way' main street leads to the *Cathedral* (St Andrew), built by Pius VI, heavily damaged by bombing, and now rebuilt. In the apse is a

16C Crucifix and in the r. transept a large painting of the Miracle of the Fishes by Sebastiano Conca. The altars in the transepts incorporate antique marbles from a Roman villa. On the left a road leads up through the medieval part of the town to the *Rocca Abbaziale,* founded in 1073. Pius VI converted the castle, which dominates this part of the town, into a stately dwelling for high ecclesiastical dignitaries.

The monasteries outside the town are reached by the Ienne road (or on foot by mule track which crosses and recrosses the road). The road passes the round chapel of *San Mauro* and continues to ascend. It skirts the ruins of *Nero's Villa;* on the right of the road is the lake (now dried-up) formed by the dam that Nero built across the river.

The road continues to climb to reach (2½ km.) the **Convento di Santa Scolastica** (500 m; shown by a monk 10-12, 16 18.30), a vast establishment comprising a church and three monasteries. In the middle ages it became a powerful abbey, with feudal privileges. The convent was badly damaged in the war; the rebuilt façade bears the Benedictine motto 'Ora et Labora' over the door. The *First Cloister,* likewise restored, was built in 1580, and contains fragments from Nero's Villa.

To the right are the *Library* and *Archives* (open to scholars). There are 380 MSS. and over 30,000 printed books (among them 90 incunabula), as well as papal bulls, royal and imperial edicts, and other rare documents. It also contains the first two books printed in Italy, Cicero's De Oratore and a Lactantius of 1465.—Between the first and second cloisters is a fresco of James Stuart, the Old Pretender.

The *Second Cloister* is entered through a Gothic arch (1450) with statuettes of German workmanship. The cloister is one of the earliest Gothic works in Italy, and has a crude bas-relief (8C) and a tablet recording the property of the abbey in 1052. There is a fine view of the campanile. In the porch are Cosmatesque fragments.—The *Church of St Scholastica,* built in 975, was reconstructed for the fourth time in 1777 by Giac. Quarenghi. This is the only work in Italy by this architect who lived in Russia and built much of Leningrad. Here are two pillars in cipollino from Nero's villa. Frescoes from the earlier church (1426) are preserved in the vault (visible only with special permission). Beneath the church is the Cappella degli Angeli, with an altar recomposed from Cosmatesque fragments, and an urn containing the ashes of St Scholastica. A corridor from a 9C porch which supports the Campanile, leads to the *Third Cloister* a fine work by the Cosmati (1208-30; signed 'Cosmas et filii'). The walls have over-restored frescoes.

The road continues to the *Convento di San Benedetto, or *Sacro Speco* (640 m; open daily 9-12.30, 15-17.30), consisting of two superimposed churches, chapels, and grottoes, naturally formed in or artificially hewn out of the mountainside. From the car park an easy path leads up through a venerable ilex grove to the entrance gate, above which is an ancient watchtower. A small Gothic door opens into a loggia decorated with 15C Umbrian frescoes. Beyond are two more rooms (the first with frescoes of the school of Perugino) leading into the upper church.

The UPPER CHURCH (c. 1350) has an aisleless nave and a chancel. The cross-vaulting is noteworthy. The nave is adorned with 14C frescoes, mainly of the school of Siena. Outstanding among these are The Kiss of Judas and the Way of the Cross (left wall), the Entry of Christ into Jerusalem (right wall), and the Crucifixion (front wall). The Sacristy has a 15C Crucifixion, two panels of the Sienese School, and a fresco of St Benedict, by Consulus (Consolo) a late-13C master who did much work in the covent. A painting of the Madonna with the prophets on wood by the school of Pinturicchio, has been removed for safety.—Steps before the altar lead down to the LOWER CHURCH, comprising a remarkable series of chapels at different levels. The stairway is decorated with frescoes by Consulus. After a second flight of steps, the level of the **Sacro Speco** is reached, which gave the convent its alternative name. The Holy Grotto is a small dark natural cavern in the rock. Here is a marble statue of St Benedict, by *Ant. Raggi* (1657). The walls of the grotto are lined with cipollino from Nero's villa. Outside it are frescoes by Consulus illustrating the life and death of the saint.

From the landing a little spiral staircase leads up to the *Chapel of St Gregory*, with further frescoes by Consulus, and a \*Portrait of St Francis, without halo or stigmata, painted at the time of his visit to the convent (c. 1210) and claimed to be the first example in Italy of a genuine portrait.—From the landing begins the *Scala Santa*, so called because it is on the line of the path taken by St Benedict on his way to and from his cavern. The stairway is decorated with macabre 15C frescoes depicting Death. It leads to the 14C *Chapel of the Madonna*, covered with contemporary frescoes and, farther down, to the *Grotta dei Pastori*, a small cave where St Benedict is said to have preached to the local shepherds. It contains the oldest fresco in the convent, an 8C or 9C work representing the Madonna with St Luke and another saint. Outside the cave is a small terrace from which can be seen the great columns and arches supporting the convent buildings. Here is the *Holy Rose Tree*, subject of a miracle performed by St Francis on the occasion of his visit. Centuries before, St Benedict, to mortify his flesh, had lain down on a bramble; St Francis turned the aged bramble into a rose tree. It still blooms today. The *Refectory* (no adm.) contains interesting 15C frescoes of the Umbrian school.— Outside, to the right, paths lead through delightful woods with views.

# 26   VIA FLAMINIA AND THE TIBER VALLEY

ROAD (Via Flaminia) to (42 km.) *Sant'Oreste (Civita Castellana*, 57 km.). Return by Via Tiberina and Via Salaria, 52½ km.

RAILWAY from Rome (Piazzale Flaminio) by electric trains (Ferrovie del Nord), stopping at nearly all stations to S. Oreste (41 km.) in 1 hr, to Civita Castellana (57 km.) in 1½ hr. The railway follows the Via Flaminia as far as Civita Castellana.

Via Flaminia, Via Tiberina, and Via Salaria are taken as central points for this route, but many of the interesting places described are several kilometres to the w. or E. Although not well known, or of major importance, this area with its charming medieval villages and often spectacular countryside is typical of the most unspoilt parts of the Roman campagna.

The terminus in Rome of the Ferrovie del Nord is in an extension of Piazzale Flaminio (Pl. 11; 7), just N. of the Porta del Popolo. **Via Flaminia** runs almost due N. (see p. 257), while the railway tunnels under the Parioli Quarter, emerging just before (3 km.) *Acqua Acetosa*. It then crosses the Tiber, passes on the left the Tor di Quinto racecourse, and beyond (7 km.) *Due Ponti*, rejoins Via Flaminia.

The VIA FLAMINIA, the old great North Road, traverses Umbria and reaches the Adriatic at Fano, from where it continues as N 16 to Rimini. It was named after C. Flaminius, censor and afterwards consul, who was killed at the battle of Lake Trasimene in 217 B.C.

At (7½ km.) the road passes the so-called *Tomb of the Nasoni* (l.) and several other tombs. *Grotta Rossa,* with pozzolana quarries.—The road passes under the Rome Circular road which crosses the Tiber and Via

Salaria beyond. Here also is the Fosso di Valchetta, which flows past Veio (p. 373).—At (12 km.) *Prima Porta* this route leaves the Tiber.

Via Tiberina branches to the right (see below). At the road fork an inscription (1912) commemorates the battle of Saxa Rubra where Constantine defeated Maxentius in 312, after being converted to Christianity by a vision of the flaming Cross with the words ἐν τούτῳ νίκα (conquer by this).

On the hill between the roads are the ruins of the imperial **Villa of Livia** (*ad Gallinas Albas*), the wife of Augustus and mother of Tiberius. The path to the villa leads to the right beyond the houses (guide-post). The fine statue of Augustus of Prima Porta, now in the Vatican, was found here in 1863, as were the frescoes now in the Museo Nazionale Romano.

Beyond the fork, the huge *Cimitero di Prima Porta* extends on the right as far as Via Tiberina.—19½ km. *Sacrofano Station.*

A longer but more scenic road leads N.W. to (7½ km.) *Sacrofano,* a picturesque medieval town at the foot of the prominent Monte Musino. The road continues to (15½ km.) *Campagnano di Roma,* a larger medieval town. A beautiful road from Campagnano runs E. (12 km.) to rejoin the Via Flaminia 1½ km. N. of *Morlupo Station* (see below).

The more direct route N. along Via Flaminia from Sacrofano Station passes (25½ km.) a turning r. to *Riano* (2 km.), with a Ruspoli castle.— At (28 km.) *Castelnuovo di Porta* (r.), an ancient fortress remodelled into a palace in the 16C (no adm.) dominates the town, which is becoming spoilt by modern buildings.—30½ km. *Morlupo Station.* Turning right for *Morlupo* (2½ km.), of ancient origins. This road leads in 13½ km. viâ Capena to Via Tiberina (see below).

Via Flaminia, joined by the road from Campagnano di Roma, continues through (39 km.) *Rignano Flaminio,* which preserves the ruins of a Savelli stronghold. The ancient church of Sant'Abbondio, outside the village to the E., has a campanile and other relics of the 11C.—42 km. **Sant'Oreste.** The village, 5 km. E., is the best base for an ascent of *Monte Soratte* (691 m) with its long isolated ridge, the Soracte of Horace and Virgil. The view from the summit takes in southern Etruria and the fertile Sabine hills, with the Apennines behind them across the Tiber valley.—The road from here to *Civita Castellana* (10½ km.) and the country to the N. are described in the 'Blue Guide to Northern Italy'.

The return to Rome may be made by Via Tiberina and Via Salaria, following the Tiber valley. A somewhat tortuous small road leads from Sant'Oreste Station to **Via Tiberina,** joining it at (15½ km.) *Fiano Romano.* This old town, overlooking the Tiber valley, used to have its own river-port and ferry boat in Roman times.—19½ km. **Lucas Feroniæ.** Here excavations are in progress of the ancient town, famed in antiquity for its Temple of Feronia, founded in the 6C or 5C B.C., and sacked by Hannibal in 211 B.C. A Museum is being arranged near the entrance to the site. So far the *Forum* and *Amphitheatre* have been unearthed. Some distance away (also approached from the service area on the Autostrada del Sole, prominent to the left) is the *Villa of Gens Vulusia,* one of the most important private villas near Rome, discovered in 1961. Two of the three floors survive and some of the rooms have fine mosaics. Just beyond, a road leads r. to *Capena* (5 km.) on the site of an

Etruscan city thought to have been the chief town of the Capenates, an Italic tribe subject to Veii.

At (23 km.) *Girardi* the road crosses the autostrada and Tiber to (26 km.) *Torremancina* on **Via Salaria.** It turns s. to (28½ km.) *Monterotondo-Mentana Station.* Here a road diverges s.e. viâ *Monterotondo* (2½ km.), with a town hall in a former Orsini palace, to *Mentana* (5½ km.), on the approximate site of the ancient *Nomentum.* Piazza San Nicola is picturesque. Near by the Garibaldians were defeated by French and Papal forces in 1867.—Via Salaria returns towards Rome, passing *Marcigliana,* near (36 km.) *Settebagni.* This was the ancient *Allia,* scene of a disastrous defeat of the Romans by the Gauls in 390 B.C. Castel Giubileo, a medieval fortalice, stands above the bank of the Tiber.—40½ km. (l.) *Villa Spada* on the site of the ancient *Fidenoe.* A colony of Veii, it was taken by Mamercus Aemilius in 440 B.C., resettled by the Emperor Tiberius, and destroyed by the Lombards.—42½ km. *Urbe Airport* (r.) surrounded on three sides by the Tiber. The Aniene is crossed near its confluence with the Tiber at Ponte Salario, and Rome entered at Piazza Fiume, on the site of the vanished Porta Salaria.

# 27  VEIO AND LAKE BRACCIANO

ROAD (VIA CASSIA), N 2. 18 km. Veio.—40 km. Bracciano.
BUSES from Via Palestro and P.za Risorgimento for Bracciano. C.I.T. tours viâ Bracciano to Cervéteri and Tarquinia. Bus No. 201 from Piazzale Ponte Milvio for Isola Farnese (Veio).
RAILWAY from *Rome* (Termini), Viterbo line. To *La Storta-Formello,* for Veio (slow trains only), 27 km. in c. 1 hr; to *Bracciano,* 52 km. in 1-2 hrs.

From Porta del Popolo (Pl. 11; 7) Via Flaminia and Viale Tiziano lead to Piazza Apollodoro, from where Corso di Francia turns off to the right to cross the Tiber by Ponte Flaminio. At the end of the Corso this route branches left into Via Cassia Nuova.

The VIA CASSIA, originally an unmade road connecting Rome with Etruria, was paved by C. Cassius Longinus, consul in 107 B.C., and was named after him. Now Highway 2, it is a beautiful road which runs through Viterbo, Siena, and Poggibonsi to Florence.

The road undulates between gardens and parks, with lofty pines and oak-trees, and almost continuous ribbon development. To the left, soon after the junction with the old Via Cassia, is the *Scots College* (1962).— 9½ km. On the left, half-hidden in a clump of cypresses, is the tomb of P. Vibius Maranus (2C A.D.), commonly called the *Tomb of Nero.*

Beyond (13 km.) *La Giustiniana* the Viterbo railway approaches on the left.—17 km. *La Storta* is a former posting stage, dominated by its large modern church. Near by, a chapel commemorates a vision of Christ vouchsafed here to St Ignatius in 1537.—17½ km. *Madonna di Bracciano* is a chapel at a road fork.

The left-hand road, the Via Claudia, leads to Bracciano (see below). To see Veio it is necessary to continue for another ½ km. on the Via Cassia. A by-road here leads E. (sign-posted 'Isola Farnese e Veio') to *Isola Farnese* (2 km.); an alternative route for Veio is 1½ km. farther along the Via Cassia.

Isola Farnese is a tiny hamlet beneath a medieval castle in a pretty position. The  •
church contains interesting frescoes.

**Veio,** one of the most famous of the Etruscan cities, was built on a triangular plateau (124 m) bounded by two streams, the Fosso di Formello-Valca and the Fosso di Valchetta, the ancient Cremera. At the confluence the sides are precipitous; on the promontory above it was the citadel, now called the *Piazza d'Armi.* The city was directly accessible only from the N.W. angle.

Veio was one of the twelve cities of the Etruscan Confederation and apparently the largest of them all. Its walls had a circuit of 11 km. and its territory (*Ager Veiens*) was extensive, reaching to the Tiber on the S., E., and S.W. It controlled the salt-works at the mouth of the Tiber. On the W. its neighbour was Caere. Veio reached the zenith of its power between the 8C and the 6C B.C. and its position brought it into frequent conflict with Rome during the period of the kings and the early days of the Republic. It took the side of the deposed Tarquins in their attempt to return to Rome.

In the year of his third consulship (479 B.C.) the patrician L. Fabius Vibulanus, after a disagreement over the treatment of the plebeians, quitted Rome, and, at the head of 306 members of his gens, marched towards Veio. The Fabii established themselves on a hill to the right of the Formello-Valca, and harassed the Veientines for two years. In 477 they were trapped in an ambush near the Cremera and all were killed, save one, from whom all the later Fabii were descended. In 396, after a historic siege of ten years, M. Furius Camillus tunnelled through the rock and captured the city. It was destroyed and remained in ruins until Julius Cæsar planted a colony, which Augustus elevated into a municipium. But the new Veio did not flourish; it was moribund even in Hadrian's time and soon disappeared from history. Excavations on the site began in the 18C; the work has now been carried out systematically. Many of the discoveries are in the Villa Giulia in Rome, among them the celebrated Apollo of Veio.

Below Isola Farnese a steep narrow road descends right; it deteriorates as it approaches a barn near the Mola torrent. This can be forded on foot above the waterfall. A path leads up (r.) to the *Portonaccio* gate and the ticket entrance (admission 9-13, 16-19 exc. Mon). Beyond, on a terrace, are remains of the *Temple of Apollo,* a cistern, and a rock-hewn tunnel. Outside the enclosure, and above it to the east, is the *West Gate* of Veio. Here, besides remains of walls, are a large cistern and the foundations of a rectangular building (possibly a temple).

Other remains are widely dispersed over the site; a whole day is needed for a complete tour. Since the area is now under cultivation it is difficult to explore without a guide.

Beyond the ruins of the Roman city (on the S.) stands (2½ km.) the *Citadel,* which is separated from the rest by a slight depression. Here the sides of the plateau are sheer and rise 60 m above the torrents, and from the promontory can be seen Rome and the semicircle of the Alban, Tiburtine, and Sabine hills beyond. Then, descending to the E. into the Cremera valley, a path leads left and comes first to the ruins of Roman baths, and then (on the right) the *Grotta degli Inglesi* or *Tomba Campana.* This (discovered in 1843) is a chamber-tomb of the late 7C cut in the rock, and one of the earliest painted tombs in existence. It consists of a deep-cut approach flanked by lions (two of which remain) and two quadrilateral chambers. The arch is of a transitional type between the beehive and the keystone systems, and on the walls are archaic paintings representing Mercury conducting the dead, also fantastic animals. A path continues W. up the valley with the city to the left, to reach the *Ponte Sodo,* a broad gallery cut by the Etruscans to open a passage for the torrent (one of the most romantic spots in the Campagna). From there a path continues up to the level of the city and so to Isola; or (easier but longer) the valley may be followed to the Ponte di Formello, where it is necessary to cross the torrent and bear left to reach the Fosso di Valca at Ponte di Isola, 1 km. N.W. of Isola Farnese, and so continue back to the main road.

It is necessary to return to the crossroads (see p. 372), and take Via Claudia (r.) for Lake Bracciano. By a tavern, just beyond (24 km.) the prominent radio station of the Vatican, a by-road (l.) leads to Santa Maria di Galéria.

**Santa Maria di Galéria** is a tiny hamlet with a delightful piazza. A fine gateway leads to a courtyard with old houses and the 15C church of *Santa Maria in Celsano,* with a good portal. The interior is divided by wide low arches supported by four columns; the two on the l. have fine Corinthian capitals. It has a painted ceiling, and frescoes on the right wall (probably 16C; restored), and in the two side apses (much damaged).

Just before the ascent to the piazza, a road forks below to the right. The first unmade road to the r. leads to the ruins of *Galéria.* Situated above a beautiful wooded river valley, the castle, with a long history from before the 9C to the 19C, is a magnificent ruin. It stands on the site of the Etruscan *Careiæ;* more remains can be seen across the river Galera.

Via Claudia continues to (40 km.) **Bracciano** (280 m; 10,400 inhab.), a small town on the s.w. shore of the Lago di Bracciano. It was associated with the Orsini family from the 14C until 1696. From the station (fine view) a broad road leads direct to the **\*Castello degli Orsini** (1470-85), a magnificent and perfectly preserved example of a Renaissance baronial castle, now belonging to the princely Odescalchi family. It has five crenellated round towers supporting the superb pentagonal structure. It was the first place that Sir Walter Scott wished to visit on his arrival in Rome.

Visitors are conducted every hour, 9-12, and 15-17.

A steep ramp leads up to the entrance; on the wall to the right are frescoes by Antoniazzo Romano (1491). The vaulted kitchen off an imposing triangular interior courtyard, has huge fireplaces.

FIRST FLOOR. R. I (*Library*) is decorated with frescoes by the Zuccari.—R. III has a wooden ceiling painted by Antoniazzo Romano and pupils and a 15C bed. In R. IV (*Sala del Trittico*) are the panels of a large triptych (late 15C), with a Crucifixion in the manner of Giotto and an Annunciation.—R. V is frescoed with scenes from the Renaissance legend of the Fountain of Youth.—R. VI. Large fresco by Antoniazzo Romano showing episodes in the life of the Orsini.—R. VII (*degli Orsini*) contains busts (by G. L. Bernini) and portraits of the Orsini and Medici families. The paintings in R. VIII (*Sala del Leone*) are of the 15C. The ceiling of R. IX (*Camera Rossa*) is again painted by Antoniazzo.

SECOND FLOOR. R. XI has a 15C water-clock.—R. XII has a frieze of the Labours of Hercules (15C) and a collection of arms. Noteworthy in R. XIII (*Sala d'Armi*) are three suits of tournament armour: one Milanese (15C), and two German (16C).—R. XVI contains a collection of finds from the cemeteries at Cervéteri and Palo.—R. XVII gives out on to a loggia from which an enchanting view of the lake can be enjoyed by taking the *Cammino di Ronda,* the rampart walk.

In the town the *Collegiata* (Santo Stefano) has a Baroque façade and a campanile of 1500. Inside are paintings by Trevisani and Domenichino, and a gilded wooden triptych of 1315 by Gregorio and Donato d'Arezzo.

The **Lago di Bracciano** (164 m) is the classical *Lacus Sabatinus,* named after the Etruscan town of *Sabate.* A pre-historic village was found here in 1977. It occupies an almost circular crater in the volcanic Monti Sabatini, with a diameter of 9½ km., an area of 58 sq. km. and a maximum depth of 160 m. It teems with trout, trench, eels, and other fish. Its outlet, the Arrone is on the s.e. side, near Anguillara Sabazia. The *Aqua Traiana,* built by Trajan c. 110, from the Lacus Sabatinus to Rome, was reconditioned by Paul V in 1615 to supply some of the fountains in Rome, e.g. the Fontana Paola.

The waters of the lake, as well as those of the Lago di Vico and the Lago di Bolsena, are harnessed to a great hydro-electric scheme.—To the E. of Lake Bracciano is the much smaller *Lago di Martignano* (Alsietinus Lacus), another crater-lake (207 m).

The upper road out of Bracciano (the lower one leads only to the lake-side) skirts the entire lake. This beautiful road passes *Bagni di Vicarello,* with springs which were used in Roman times, to (52 km.) *Trevignano Romano*, a picturesque village reached through the old town gate. Cars should be left in the modern part of the village just outside the gate, or on the lake-side.

A narrow road leads up to the church of the *Assunta*, just below the ruined Orsini castle. Here there is a magnificent view of the lake over the roofs of the village. The interior has a striking fresco (1517) of the death and coronation of the Virgin, by the School of Raphael, beautifully designed to fit the curved apse. On the entrance wall is a stoup of 1541, and over the 1st altar (l.), a 13C triptych of Jesus enthroned with the Madonna and St John. Over the 2nd altar, a fine 16C fresco of the Madonna with Saints, and on the altar, a marble 16C Pietà.

The road now skirts a small crater lake with a good retrospective view of the village, and passes *Grotta del Pianoro*. —57 km Road fork left to join the Via Cassia (see above; an alternative route back to Rome). The lower road to the right leads on to (63½ km.) *Anguillara Sabazia* on high ground above the lake. The church of the *Assunta*, with an interesting 18C façade, has a magnificent position above the lake. The growing town can be well seen from the road leading on to Bracciano, now passing through more hilly and wooded country. Soon after *Vigna di Valle* (with a Museum of Military Aeroplanes) the road recrosses the railway to rejoin (70 km.) Via Claudia.

The return to Rome may be made by Via Claudia and Via Cassia, or, if time permits, along the sea via *Cervéteri* (Rte 28).

# 28   ROME TO CERVÉTERI

ROAD. Via Aurelia (N 1), 45 km.—The coastal Autostrada, A 16 which follows roughly the same route as the railway, diverging from the Fiumicino highway (Rte 21c), runs conveniently close to Cervéteri (57 km.).

BUSES. From Viale Castro Pretorio, or from Termini (Via Giolitti). C.I.T. tours via Bracciano, and including Tarquinia.

RAILWAY (part of the main line from Rome to Pisa, Genoa, etc.). To *Cervéteri-Ladíspoli* (51 km.) in c. 1 hr.

The modern Via Aurelia, from its beginning in Largo di Porta Cavalleggeri (Pl. 1; 6), diverges from Viale Vaticano to cross the Vatican and Viterbo railways. Beyond (3½ km.) the church of *Madonna del Riposo* (l.) the road crosses Piazza Irnerio.—Near (8 km.) the *Villa Troili* it joins Via Aurelia Antica, from the Porta San Pancrazio.

The road, fringed with pines, planes, oleanders, and cypresses, undulates towards the w. crossing the Rome Circular Road.—Before (14½ km.) *Malagrotta* it crosses the Fosso la Galeria, where the Anguillara are said to have slain a dragon that once ravaged the countryside.—20½ km. *Castel Di Guido* is on the site of *Lorium*, where Antoninus Pius built a magnificent villa, in which he lived and died (in 161); it was a favourite resort of his successor Marcus Aurelius. Farther on the Arrone is crossed, flowing from Lake Bracciano to the Tiber.

Here a road (l.) leads to the attractive little seaside resort of *Fregene* (10 km.), with a noted pinewood. It occupies the site of the Etruscan *Fregenæ*, colonized by the Romans in 245 B.C.

Via Aurelia ascends to *Casale Bruciato*, with fine views of the mountains and the sea. On the right is the isolated *Torrimpietra*, followed by a descent, crossing to seaward of the autostrada, to (25 km.)

the *Ponte Tre Denari.* Here the railway comes in from the left.—30 km. *Palidoro,* on the site of the ancient Bæbiana.—Near (32½ km.) *Casale di Statua,* a ruined 13C castle, are remains of a Roman bridge.

A little farther, on the right, a by-road leads N. to (8 km.) *Ceri,* a village on a hill (105 m), formerly *Cære Novum,* founded in the 13C after the exodus of the inhabitants of Cære Vetus (see below). It has an old castle of the Anguillara.

37 km. *Palo Laziale* station. On the left is Palo, a fishing village on the site of *Alsium,* a port of Caere, colonized by the Romans in 247 B.C. It has a 15C castle, and in the neighbourhood are several chambered tumuli. Remains of a large Roman villa, with good polychrome mosaics were discovered here in 1974. A Museum is being arranged here. A road leads (l.) to *Ladíspoli* (2 km.), a popular seaside resort founded by Prince Ladislao Odescalchi in the 19C. The coast to the N. is dotted with old defence-towers.

Beyond *Borgo Vaccina* the road crosses (41 km.) the Fosso di Vaccina, the Amnis Cæritis mentioned by Virgil. A second road leads left for Ladíspoli (3 km.), but this route turns right for Cervéteri (3½ km.).

**CERVÉTERI** (9400 inhab.), a medieval stronghold on a round tufa hill (81 m), derives its name from *Cære Vetus.* The immediate neighbourhood is renowned for its Etruscan tombs.

Caere, called by the Greeks *Agylla,* was a Pelasgic city, capital of Mezentius who was expelled by his subjects for his cruelty. It became one of the most important towns of the Etruscan Confederation and had three seaports.—*Pyrgi* (Santa Severa), *Alsium* (Palo Laziale), and *Punicum* (Santa Marinella). Early in its history it was closely allied with Rome. When Rome was taken by the Gauls in 390 B.C., Caere gave refuge to the vestal virgins. The city became a dependency of Rome in 351 B.C., but without full rights of citizenship. From then onwards it declined. In the early middle ages Caere was the seat of a bishop and a redoubtable fortress. In the 13C its inhabitants abandoned it on account of malaria and founded *Cære Novum* (Ceri). In the later middle ages the town became populated again. It was surrounded with walls, still partly existing, and provided with a castle by the Orsini.

A full inspection of the tombs requires 5-6 hours, but the most interesting can be visited in 2-3 hrs.

Passing the road up to the Necropolis on the left, the road continues to the medieval city, with appreciable remains, including walls and towers. The old Orsini (later Ruspoli) castle dating from the 16C was donated in 1967 as a *Museo Nazionale di Cervéteri* (adm. 9-13, 16-19). It stands in an attractive piazza.

The Museum is excellently displayed chronologically with groups of objects from individual tombs in two long halls. Below, pots and objects from burials of the 8-6C B.C., including protocorinthian ware; continuation upstairs with sarcophagi, sculpture, wall-paintings, terracottas, and two superb groups of black-figured and red-figured *Vases.

From the main square below the castle a road (sign-posted to the Necropolis) leads right; a minor road soon branches right to ascend in 2 km. to the **Necropolis.** At the car park is the ticket office and the entrance to the MONUMENTAL ENCLOSURE (adm. daily exc. Mon 9-13, 16-19; winter 10-16).

This vast cemetery, occupying an area of 270 hectares, not counting isolated groups of tombs, has its nucleus on the tufa hill known as *Banditaccia,* to the N.W. of Cervéteri. All types of interment are represented: from the earliest *pozzetto* or *fossa* graves to the later tumuli, some of them colossal, with diameters exceeding 40 metres. These contain several hypogea, with chambers modelled in the rock in the

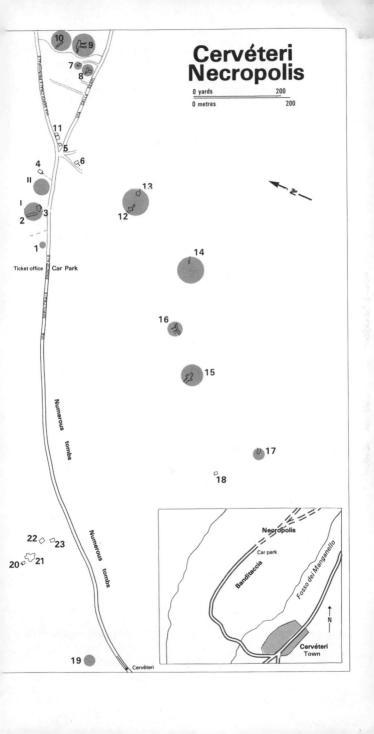

# Cervéteri
# Necropolis

0 yards          200

0 metres         200

10
9
7
8

VIA SEPOLCRALE PRINCIPALE
VIA DEL MANGANELLO

11
5
6
4
II
I
3
2
1

Ticket office    Car Park

VIA SEPOLCRALE

13
12
14
16
15
17
18

Numerous tombs

Numerous tombs

22
23
20
21

19    Cervéteri

Necropolis

Car park

Banditaccia

Fosso dei Manganello

N

Cervéteri
Town

form of Etruscan dwellings (which were built in wood). The tombs are especially interesting for their architectural design. From the tombs (dating from the 7th to 1st centuries B.C.), and their contents it has been found possible to obtain the fullest picture yet available of Etruscan civilization.

The site, which contains hundreds of tombs, is beautifully planted. Only some of the tombs are fully excavated and lit; those which may be entered are described below (and numbered according to the Plan on p. 377).

On the right of the ticket office VIA SEPOLCRALE PRINCIPALE (r.) leads S.E. between various tombs. The first tomb on the left which is open (and lit) is the *Tomb of the Capitals* (1), dating from the mid-6C B.C., with carved capitals and a roof imitating the wood roof of a house. Beyond a path which diverges left there follow two huge tumuli (II and I). The first contains four tombs probably all belonging to the same family and constructed over a period of nearly two centuries. Two of these may be visited: the *Tomb of the Thatched Roof* (2; approached by iron steps on the far side of the tumulus) excavated in the tufa to imitate a hut (mid-7C B.C.), and the *Tomb of the Greek Vases* (3; entered from the side nearest Via Sepolcrale). Beyond the second tumulus, in an opening, steps (guarded by a wood fence) lead down to the TOMB OF THE STUCCOES (4), or of the Bas-Reliefs (closed for restoration since 1977), a single chamber with numerous loculi or niches hewn out of the walls; the ceiling is supported by two columns; the walls are decorated with stuccoes and reliefs of arms, utensils, domestic animals, and mythological subjects (end of 4C B.C.), an important revelation of Etruscan civilization of the period.

Via Sepolcrale continues to a cross-roads where several minor roads meet. In front is the *Tomb of the Little House* (5; no adm.); the road on the extreme right (Via della Cornice) leads in a short way to (l.) the *Tomb of the Cornice* (6; approached up a short flight of wooden steps) so-called because of a heavy cornice which decorates the rooms. From the Tomb of the Little House, Via Sepolcrale (here with conspicuous cart tracks cut in the tufa rock) diverges left (comp. below) while VIA DELLE SERPE continues (r.) to the NEW AREA OF EXCAVATIONS opened in 1977.

Beyond a short flight of steps the road passes blocks of tombs constructed *a dado* or in cubes, a form of burial which was begun at the end of the 6C B.C. The area to the left, traversed by Via dei Monti della Tolfa and the parallel Via dei Monti Ceriti is interesting as an example of 'urban' planning and the symmetrical tombs have fine entrances. The tombs are unlit but may be entered; they have regular plans with small chairs on either side of the entrance. At the end of a long tufa wall a path leads left between a tumulus (l.) and a series of cubicle tombs (r.) and curves round to end at a flight of tufa steps which lead up to the *Polychrome Tumulus* (7), built of various materials including peperino and tufa. Adjacent is the larger *Maroi Tumulus* (8) which may also be visited. Via delle Serpi continues to the fence which marks the end of the enclosure; some metres before the fence five iron steps lead up past two small tumuli to a path which leads round to the left towards the two largest tumuli in this enclosure (near a group of three cypresses) known as the *Mengarelli Tumulus* (9; approached by a steep flight of steps) and the *Colonel's Tumulus* (10; the path passes beneath an iron bridge which leads into the entrance). Opposite this tumulus a short flight of steps leads up to a path which continues (viâ another flight of steps) to the Via Sepolcrale (comp. above). This may now be followed (l.) back towards the entrance past the *Tomb of Marce Ursus* (11; with its two entrances facing on to the road) just before the cross-roads (comp. above) where Via Sepolcrale forms a fork with Via delle Serpe.

Outside the enclosure an unmade-up road (poor surface) continues for c. 500 metres to an unenclosed area known as *Bufolareccia,* excavated in the 1960s by the Fondazione Lerici. Here the tufa rock has been uncovered and the tombs left unrestored; the oldest (and simplest) tombs can be seen on the surface (round or oblong sepulchres), while the later tumuli appear on a lower level since they were excavated in the rock when no more surface space was available. The conspicuous track marks are from ploughs which have worked the surface of the earth over the centuries. An impressive tufa rock face can be seen across the valley, and along to the right, the present town of Cervéteri.

Just beyond, the road ends on an open hill-side from which a good idea of the site of the necropolis surrounded by low hills can be gained. Here VIA DEGLI INFERI curves down to the right between the rocks. This was the first part of the Via Sepolcrale which led from the city to the necropolis. It is practicable on foot for several hundred metres and has conspicuous cart ruts. On the right, at the beginning, is the *Tomb of the Doric Columns* (unlit) with two Doric columns (4C B.C.).

The other tombs, widely scattered over the Necropolis, can be seen only with a guide (sometimes available at the ticket office) who will unlock them and turn on the light (although most of them are unlit and a torch is needed). Some of these tombs are more or less permanently flooded.

In a tumulus E. of the Monumental Enclosure are the *Tomb of the Painted Lions* (12) and the *Tomb of the Chairs and Shields* (13). The former has a fine ceiling decoration and traces of colour on the walls; in the latter the walls are decorated with reliefs of shields and the vestibule has two rock-hewn chairs. Other large tumuli to the S.W. contain the *Tomb of the Painted Animals* (14), the *Tomb of the Ships* (15), and the *Tomb of Giuseppe Moretti* (16). This is the largest tomb yet known with an atrium with Doric columns and ten rooms (difficult to see as it is normally flooded). Farther S. are the *Tomb of the Tablino* (17), and the *Tomb of the Waves* (18), with traces of painted decoration.

Another important group of tombs (all unlit) lies to the N.W. of the road which leads up to the Monumental Enclosure (comp. the Plan). These include the *Tomb of the Five Chairs* (19); the *Tomb of the Alcove* (20), with a pillared vestibule and a flight of steps leading up to a rock-hewn alcove with a nuptial bed; the *Tomb of the Tarquins* (21), so called because of the names inscribed in it; the *Tomb of the Sarcophagi* (22); and the *Tomb of the Triclinium* (23), with traces of paintings of a funeral banquet.

On a hill c. 2½ km. S. of Cervéteri is the famous **Regolini-Galassi Tomb** (unlit) the oldest of all (late 7C B.C.) discovered in 1836. Named after its discoverers, it is a circular tumulus 48 m in diameter, surrounded by a double wall and surmounted by the typical conical grass-grown top. Its hypogeum, of two compartments, is divided by a wide corridor with a ceiling of overlapping stone blocks. Its most valuable contents are exhibited in the Etruscan Museum of the Vatican.—In the same area (Ripe Sant'Angelo) rock tombs of the 4C B.C. have recently been discovered. These can be seen carved in the rock face with 'mock' doors.

About 1½ km. N.E., on Monte Abetone, is the *Campana Tomb* (unlit) with remarkable carvings imitating household furnishings; 1½ km. farther on is the *Tomb of the Round Vestibule,* with a noteworthy fan vault.—To the S.E. of Monte Padula is another tomb, covered by a kind of pyramid, containing a vestibule, two side chambers, and a central room with two biers and a throne carved in the rock. Close by is the *Torlonia Tomb* (more or less permanently flooded), with a vestibule having columns in the Greek style, and two chambers, of which the first contains 54 loculi.—From this point the Monte Cucco track leads direct to (6½ km.) Cervéteri.

Via Aurelia and the autostrada continue N. to *Civitavecchia* (72 km; see 'Blue Guide to Northern Italy'), the modern port of Rome and a base of sea communications with Sardinia. If time permits the road inland can be taken for (17½ km.) *Bracciano* (Rte 27), and the return to the capital made by Via Claudia.

# LIST OF THE PRINCIPAL ITALIAN ARTISTS

whose works are referred to in the text, with their birthplaces or the schools to which they belonged. — Abbreviations: A = architect, engr. = engraver, G. = goldsmith, illum. = illuminator, min. = miniaturist, mos. = mosaicist, P. = painter, S. = sculptor, stuc. = stuccoist, W. = woodworker.

## ABBREVIATIONS OF CHRISTIAN NAMES

| | | | | | | |
|---|---|---|---|---|---|---|
| Agost. | = Agostino | Des. | = Desiderio | Ipp. | = Ippolito |
| Aless. | = Alessandro | Dom. | = Domenico | Laz. | = Lazzaro |
| Alf. | = Alfonso | Elis. | = Elisabetta | Leon. | = Leonardo |
| Ambr. | = Ambrogio | Fed. | = Federigo | Lod. | = Lodovico |
| And. | = Andrea | Fel. | = Felice | Lor. | = Lorenzo |
| Ang. | = Angelo | Ferd. | = Ferdinando | Mart. | = Martino |
| Ann. | = Annibale | Fil. | = Filippo | Matt. | = Matteo |
| Ant. | = Antonio | Fr. | = Francesco | Mich. | = Michele |
| Baldas. | = Baldassare | G. B. | = Giambattista | Nic. | = Nicola |
| Bart. | = Bartolomeo | Gasp. | = Gaspare | Pell. | = Pellegrino |
| Batt. | = Battista | Gaud. | = Gaudenzio | Raff. | = Raffaele |
| Bened. | = Benedetto | Giac. | = Giacomo | Rid. | = Ridolfo |
| Benv. | = Benvenuto | Giov. | = Giovanni | | |
| Bern. | = Bernardino | Girol. | = Girolamo | Seb. | = Sebastiano |
| Cam. | = Camillo | Giul. | = Giuliano | Sim. | = Simone |
| Ces. | = Cesare | Gius. | = Giuseppe | Stef. | = Stefano |
| Crist. | = Cristoforo | Greg. | = Gregorio | Tim. | = Timoteo |
| Dan. | = Daniele | Gugl. | = Guglielmo | Tom. | = Tomaso |
| Dav. | = Davide | Iac. | = Iacopo | Vinc. | = Vincenzo |
| Def. | = Defendente | Inn. | = Innocenzo | Vitt. | = Vittorio |

## ABBREVIATIONS OF THE NAMES OF TOWNS AND PROVINCES

| | | | | | |
|---|---|---|---|---|---|
| Anc. | = Ancona | Lig. | = Liguria | Pist. | = Pistoia |
| Are. | = Arezzo | Lomb. | = Lombardy | Rav. | = Ravenna |
| Ass. | = Assisi | Mant. | = Mantua | Rom. | = Romagna |
| Berg. | = Bergamo | Mil. | = Milan | Sett. | = Settignano |
| Bol. | = Bologna | Mod. | = Modena | Trev. | = Treviso |
| Bres. | = Brescia | Nap. | = Naples | Tur. | = Turin |
| Crem. | = Cremona | Orv. | = Orvieto | Tusc. | = Tuscany |
| Emil. | = Emilia | Pad. | = Padua | Umbr. | = Umbria |
| Faen. | = Faenza | Parm. | = Parma | Urb. | = Urbino |
| Ferr. | = Ferrara | Pav. | = Pavia | Ven. | = Venice |
| Fies. | = Fiesole | Per. | = Perugia | Ver. | = Verona |
| Flor. | = Florence | Piac. | = Piacenza | Vic. | = Vicenza |
| Gen. | = Genoa | Pied. | = Piedmont | | |

ABATE, NIC, DELL' (1511-71), P.,
    Mod. - 82, 157, 179
AGRESTI, LIVIO (c. 1580), P., Forli. -
    80
ALBANI, FR. (1578-1660), P., Bol.
    Sch. - 69, 83, 148, 158, 169
ALBERTI, CHERUBINO (1553-1615), P.
    Sansepolcro. - 96
ALBERTI, LEON BATT. (1404-72), A.
    Flor. - 62, 72, 74, 170, 174, 265,
    346
ALBERTI, MICH. (fl. 1535-68), P.,
    Sansepolcro. - 62
ALBERTONI, PAOLO (18C), P. - 149
ALGARDI, ALESS. (c. 1602-54), S.,
    Bol. - 62, 73, 79, 83, 103, 104,
    110, 148-9, 159, 176, 204, 213,
    244, 270-1
ALLEGRI, see Correggio
ALLORI, ALESS. (1535-1607), P., Flor.
    - 148, 168
ALUNNO, see Foligno
AMATRICE, COLA DELL' (1489-1559),
    P., Abruzzi. - 69, 286
AMERIGHI, see Caravaggio
AMMANNATI, BART. (1511-92), A. &
    S., Sett. - 101, 149, 152, 163, 244,
    258
ANESI, PAOLO (fl. 1725-66), P.,
    Rome. - 186-7
ANGELICO, FRA (Giov. da Fiesole or
    Beato Angelico; 1400-1455), P.
    Flor. sch. - 97, 178, 284, 293
ANGELINI, GIUS. (1735-1811), S.
    Rome. - 90
ANGELIS, DOM. DE (18C), P., Rome.
    - 299, 301
ANGELO DA TIVOLI (15C), S., Tivoli.
    - 358
ANGUISSOLA, SOFONISBA (c. 1530-
    1629), P., Crem. sch. - 82
ANSALDO, AND. (1584-1638), P.,
    Gen. - 241
ANTONIAZZO ROMANO (Aquilio; fl.
    1460-1508), P., Rome. - 85-6, 95-
    7, 105, 178, 205, 216, 244-5, 352-3,
    358, 368, 374
ARPINO, see Cesari
ARRIGUCCI, LUIGI (fl. 1620-30), A.,
    Flor. - 76, 88
ASPRUCCI, ANT. (1723-1808), A.,
    Rome. - 156
AVANZO, IAC. DA BOLOGNA (or
    Avanzi; 14C), P., Bol. - 169
AVERULINO, see Filarete
AZEGLIO, MASSIMO D' (1798-1866),
    P., Tur. - 160, 345, 347
AZZURRI, FR. (1831-1901), A.,
    Rome. - 178, 196

BACHIACCA, IL (Fr. Ubertini; 1490-
    1557), P., Flor. - 73
BACICCIA (or Baciccio, G. B. Gaulli;
    1639-1709), P., Gen. - 74, 82, 84,
    99, 100, 103, 106, 149, 170-2, 177,
    241

BAGLIONI, GIOV. (1571-1644), P.,
    Rome. - 140, 157
BALDI, LAZZARO (c. 1624-1703), P.,
    Pistoia. - 177
BARBIERI, see Guercino
BARIGIONI, FIL. (1690-1753), A.,
    Rome. - 271
BAROCCI, FED. (Il Baroccio; 1526-
    1612), P., Urb. - 79, 96, 159, 171,
    179, 311
BAROCCI, IAC. see Vignola
BARONZIO, GIOV. (da Rimini; fl.
    1345-before 1362), P. - 178
BARTOLINI, LOR. (1777-1850), S.,
    Flor. - 101, 160
BARTOLOMEO, FRA (della Porta or di
    San Marco; 1475-1517), P., Flor.
    - 158, 179
BASAITI, MARCO (fl. 1490-1521), P.,
    Friuli. - 148, 159
BASILE, ERNESTO (1857-1932), A.,
    Palermo. - 152
BASSANO (Fr. Giambattista da Ponte,
    the Younger; 1549-92), P., Ven.
    sch. - 104
BASSANO (Giov. da Ponte; 1553-
    1613), P., Vic. - 171
BASSANO (Girol. da Ponte; 1566-
    1621) P., Vic. - 171
BASSANO (Iac. da Ponte; 1510-92), P.,
    Ven. sch. - 148, 159, 168, 171, 179
BATONI, POMPEO (1708-87), P.,
    Lucca. - 100, 158, 169, 172, 186,
    190, 241, 286
BAZZANI, CES. (1873-1939), A.,
    Rome. - 160, 257, 340
BECCAFUMI, DOM. (Mecarino; 1485-
    1551), P. Siena. - 149, 179
BELLI, PASQUALE (1752-1833), A.,
    Rome. - 93
BELLINI, GENTILE (1429-1507; son of
    Iac.), P., Ven. - 68
BELLINI, GIOV. (1430-1516; son of
    Iac.) P., Ven. - 68, 73, 148, 159,
    286
BELLOTTO, BERN. (1720-80;
    sometimes called Canaletto, q.v.),
    P., Ven. - 179
BELTRAMI, LUCA (1854-1933), A. -
    284
BENVENUTI, G. B., see Ortolano
BERLINGHIERI, BONAVENTURA (fl.
    1235-75), P., Lucca. - 178
BERNINI, GIAN LOR. (1598-1680), A.,
    P., & S., Nap. - 62, 73-4, 79, 80,
    83, 95, 97-8, 103, 105, 141, 148,
    152, 154-5, 157, 159, 169-70, 172,
    177-8, 180, 182, 202-3, 213, 218,
    238, 244, 247, 249, 252, 258, 264,
    266-8, 270, 271, 273, 277, 296,
    299, 301, 348, 350, 360, 362, 374
BERNINI, PIETRO (1562-1629), S.,
    Flor. - 80, 157, 173, 204
BERRETTINI, see Cortona
BIANCHI, PIETRO (1694-1740), P.,
    Rome. - 169, 271
BIANCHI-FERRARI, FR. (Il Frarè; c.
    1457-1510), P., Mod. - 179

BICCHIERARI, ANT. (1706-30), P., Rom. - 186-7

BICCI, NERI DI (1418-91), P., Flor. - 180

BIGIO, NANNI DI BACCIO (d. 1568), S. & A., Flor. - 96, 102, 155

BIONDI, ERNESTO (1855-1917), S., Frosinone. - 350

BIONDO, GIOV. DEL (fl. 1368-92), P., Flor. - 284

BISTOLFI, LEON (1859-1935), S., Casale Monferrato. - 161

BIZZACCHERI, CARLO FR. (fl. 1700-17), A., Rome. - 86

BOCCACCINO, BOCCACCIO (c. 1467-1524), P., Crem. (Ven. sch.). - 148

BOLGI, AND. (1605-56), S., Carrara. - 244, 268

BOLOGNA, VITALE DA (c. 1289-1359), P., Bol. - 284

BOLTRAFFIO, GIOV. ANT. (1467-1516), P., Lomb. sch. - 246

BONDONE, see Giotto

BONIFACIO VERONESE (or de' Pitati; 1487-1553), P., Ven. - 168

BONITO, GIUS. (1707-89), P., Nap. - 242

BONSI, GIOV. (fl. 1366-71), P., Flor. - 284

BONVICINO, see Moretto

BORDONE, PARIS (1500-70), P., Treviso (Ven. sch.). - 169, 171, 253, 286

BORGIANNI, ORAZIO (d. 1616), P. & engr., Rome. - 82

BORGOGNONE, IL (Guglielmo Courtois; c 1628-79), P., St Hippolyte. - 177, 187, 350

BORROMINI, FR. (1599-1667), A., Rome, born at Como. - 79-81, 83, 99, 103-4, 172-3, 177-8, 213, 225, 243, 269, 341

BOSCO, MASO DEL (Tom. Boscoli; 1503-74), S., Flor. - 79, 200

BOSIO, PIETRO (fl. 1813-27), A., Milan. - 93

BOTTALLA, G. M. (1613-44), P., Gen. - 69

BOTTICELLI (Sandro Filipepi; 1444-1510), P., Flor. - 158, 169, 295

BRACCI, PIETRO (1700-73), S., Rome. - 157, 172, 269

BRAMANTE, DONATO (1444-1514), A. & P., Umbr. - 76, 80, 101-3, 154, 225, 244, 253, 264-7, 277, 286, 292, 299, 313

BRAMANTINO (Bart. Suardi; c. 1455-1536), A. & P., sch. of Bramante. - 95, 289

BREGNO, AND. (And. da Milano; c. 1421-1506), S., Rome, born at Osteno (Como). - 70, 75-6, 79, 90, 96-7, 153-5, 170, 183, 200, 202, 208, 212, 214, 221, 264, 295

BRESCIANINO, IL (And. Piccinelli; c. 1485-after 1529), P., Bres. - 158

BRONZINO (Agnolo di Cosimo Tori; 1503-72), P., Flor. sch. - 149, 158, 168-9, 171, 179

BUGIARDINI, GIUL. (1475-1554), P., Flor. - 169

BUONACCORSI, see Vaga

BUONARROTI, see Michelangelo

BUONVICINO, AMBR. (c. 1552-1622), S., Mil.-Rome. - 96-7

BUSELLI, ORFEO (1600-67), S., Rom. - 169

BUSI, GIOV., see Cariani

CABIANCA, VINC. (1827-1902), P., Ver. - 160, 188

CADES, GIUS. (1750-99), P , Rome. - 159, 170

CAFFI, IPP. (1809-66), P., Rome. - 100, 160, 241

CAGNACCI, GUIDO (1601-81), P., Forlì. - 171

CALABRESE, see Preti

CALANDRA, DAVIDE (1856-1915), S., Tur. - 152, 156

CALIARI, CARLETTO (son of Paolo Veronese; 1570-?96), P., Ven. - 171

CALIARI, PAOLO, see Veronese

CAMAINO, TINO DI (fl. c. 1285-1338), S., Siena. - 94

CAMBIASO, LUCA (1527-85), P., Gen. sch. - 69, 158, 179

CAMBIO, ARNOLFO DI (c. 1245-1302), A. & S., Colle Val d'Elsa. - 73, 94, 204, 207, 214-5, 238, 268

CAMERINO, IAC. DA (fl. c. 1290), mos., Rome. - 215

CAMPI, PAOLO (fl. 1702-35), S., Rome. - 103

CAMPORESE, GIULIO (1754-1840), A., Rome. - 93, 310

CAMUCCINI, VINC. (1771-1844), P., Rome. 94, 270

CANALETTO (Ant. Canale; 1697-1768), P., Ven. The name is applied also to his nephew, Bellotto (q.v.). - 169, 171, 241

CANEVARI, ANT. (1681-c. 1750), A., Rome. - 220

CANEVARI, G. B. (1789-1876), P., Gen. - 172

CANONICA, PIETRO (1869-1959), S., Tur. - 149, 156, 271

CANONICO, GREG. (d. 1591), A., Rome. - 66

CANOVA, ANT. (1757-1822), S., Possagno. - 57, 100-1, 157, 160, 162, 170, 172, 234, 269, 270-1, 305

CANTARINI, SIM. (da Pésaro; 1612-48), P., Bol. sch. - 73, 158, 169

CAPODISTRIA, DOM. DA (d. at Vicovaro before 1464), A. - 367

CAPPONI, LUIGI (fl. 1485-98), P., Mil-Rome. - 79, 97, 103, 105, 201, 208, 212, 221

CAPRINA, MEO DEL (or Amadeo di Fr.; 1430-1501), A., Sett. - 96, 200, 332

CARADOSSO (Crist. Foppa; c. 1452-1527), medallist, Lomb. - 200

CARAVAGGIO (Michelangelo Amerighi da; c. 1569-1609), P., Lomb. - 69, 82, 104-5, 147, 154, 158-9, 179, 241, 286

CARAVAGGIO, PASQUALE DA (fl. 1485-95), A., Rome. - 103

CARAVAGGIO, POLIDORO DA (Caldrara; fl. c. 1500-c. 1543), P., Lomb. - 100, 176, 253, 292

CARBONE, GIOV. BERNARDO (1614-83), P., Gen. - 241

CARDI, see Cigoli

CAROSELLI, ANGELO (1585-1652), P., Rome. - 269

CARPI, GIROL. DA (1501-56), P., Ferr. - 81, 100, 157, 179

CARPACCIO, VITT. (1455/6-1525/6), P., Ven. - 159

CARRÀ, CARLO (1881-1966), Alessandria. - 294

CARRACCI, AGOST. (1557-1602), P., Bol. - 81, 168

CARRACCI, ANN. (1560-1609), P., Bol. - 69, 79, 81-2, 99, 148, 157-9, 168-9, 178, 180, 245, 343

CARRACCI, ANT. (son of Agost.; 1583-1618), P., Rome. - 69, 83, 177

CARRACCI, LOD. (1555-1619), P., Bol. - 148

CASONI, ANT. (1559-1634), A. & S., Ancona-Rome. - 101

CASORATI, FELICE (1886-1963), P., Novara. - 172

CASTELLI, DOM. (Il Fontanino; d. 1657), A. - 140

CASTELLO, VALERIO (1625-59), P., Gen. - 241

CASTIGLIONE, GIOV. BENED. (Il Grechetto; 1617-70), P., Gen. - 241

CATENA, VINC. (c. 1470-1531), P., Treviso. - 148

CATI, PASQUALE (c. 1550-? 1621), P., Rome. - 188, 239

CAVALLINI, PIETRO (fl. 1250-1330), P. & mos., Rome. - 88, 94, 236, 238-9, 269

CAVALLINO, BERNARDO (1622-54), P., Nap. - 242

CAVALLUCCI, ANT. (1752-95), P., Rome. - 242

CAVAROZZI, BART. (called Crescenzio; c. 1600-25), P., Rome. - 82

CECCARINI, GIOV. (d. after 1829), S., Rome. - 340

CELLINI, BENVENUTO (1500-71), G. & S., Flor. - 79, 247, 249-50, 252, 273

CERQUOZZI, MICHELANGELO (1620-60), P., Rome. - 82

CESARI, GIUS (Arpino, Il Cavalier d'; 1568-1640), P., Rome. - 62, 158, 171, 176, 189, 202, 204, 215, 224, 245, 254, 268, 286, 340

CHIARI, GIUS. (1654-1727), P., Rome. - 168, 207

CHIRICO, GIORGIO DE (1888-1978), P., Volo. - 162, 294

CIAMPELLI, AGOST. (before 1577-1642), P., Flor. - 218

CIGOLI (Lod. Cardi; 1559-1613), A., San Miniato. - 100, 104, 157, 204

CIPOLLA, ANT. (1822-74), A., Nap. - 150

CITTADINI, PIER. FR. (1616-81), P., Bol. - 241

COGHETTI, FR. (1804-75), P., Berg. - 94

COLI, GIOV. (1636-81), P., Lucca. - 168

COLLE, RAFFAELLINO DEL (c. 1490-1566), P., Umbr. - 292

CONCA, SEB. (1680-1764), P., Nap. - 99, 149, 171-2, 208, 242, 307, 369

CONCA, TOM. (before 1770-1815), P., Rome. - 157

CONTE, IACOPINO DEL (1510-98), P., Flor. - Rome. - 88, 104

CONTUCCI, see Sansovino

COPPI, GIAC. (1523-91), P., Flor. - 200

CORBELLINI, SEB. (fl. 1689-95), P., Rom. - 109

CORNACCHINI, AGOST. (1685-1740), S., Tusc. - 267

CORREGGIO (Ant. Allegri; 1489-1534), P., Emilian sch. - 147, 159

CORTONA, PIETRO BERRETTINI DA (1596-1669), P. & A., Cortona. - 57, 69, 74, 79-80, 83, 100, 102, 104, 109-10, 149, 153, 158, 169, 172, 177, 179-80, 201, 218, 242, 269, 286, 293, 340, 348, 356

COSIMO, PIERO DI (pupil of Cosimo Rosselli; 1462-1521), P., Flor. - 158, 178, 295

COSMATI (12-14C), family of A., S., & mos., Rome. - 87, 91, 183, 211, 214-5, 224, 369

COSMATI, GIOV. (di Cosma; d. c. 1300), S., Rome. - 96, 204, 222

COSSA, FR. DEL (c. 1438-c. 1481), P., Ferr. sch. - 284

COSTA, LOR. (1460-1535), P., Ferr. sch. - 85, 180

COSTANZI, PLACIDO (1688-1759), P., Rome. - 169, 270

COTIGNOLA, G. B. (Cassignola; d. c. 1600), S., Lomb. - 105

COZZA, FR. (1605-82), P., Rome. - 169

CREDI, LOR. DI (1459-1537), P., Flor. - 158, 169, 171, 286

CREMONA, GIROL. DA (fl. 1467-75), illum., Siena. - 73, 141

CRESPI, GIUS. MARIA (Lo Spagnuolo; 1665-1747), P., Bol. - 78, 242

CRETI, DONATO (1717-49), P., Crem. Bol. - 73

CRISTOFARI, P. P. (1685-1743), Mos., Rome. - 270

CRIVELLI, CARLO (1430/5-1495), P., Pad. & Ven. sch. - 252, 284

CRIVELLI, VITT. (d. c. 1500), P., Ven. - 284

CROCETTI, VENANZO (b. 1913), S., Teramo. - 267

DADDI, BERN. (fl. 1317-50), P., Flor. - 284

DALMATA, GIOV. (Duknovich or Giov. da Traù; 1440-after 1509), A. & S., Dalmatia. - 73-4, 97, 154, 204, 208, 275, 295, 367

DIAMANTE, FRA (c. 1430-98), P., Terranova in Valdarno. - 295

DIANA, BENED. (Rusconi; fl. 1482-1524), P., Ven. - 73

DOLCI, CARLO (1616-86), P., Flor. - 158, 241

DOLCI, GIOV. DE' (fl. 1450-86), W. & A., Rome. - 294

DOMENICHINO (Dom. Zampieri; 1581-1641), P. Bol. - 69, 75, 81, 83, 104, 158, 176, 180, 182, 190, 200, 221, 239, 245, 269, 286, 340, 343, 374

DONATELLO (Donato de' Bardi; fl. 1386-1466), S., Flor. sch. - 70, 273

DOSSI, DOSSO (Giov. Luteri; 1480-1542), P., Ferr. - 68, 148, 157, 159, 168, 254

DUCA, IAC. DEL (fl. 1540-1600), S., Sic. - 136, 216

DUCCIO, AGOST. DI (1418-81), S., Flor. sch. - 97

DUGHET, GASPARE (1613-75), P., Rome. - 104

DUPRÉ, GIOV. (1817-82), S., Siena. - 160

ESTE, ALESS. D' (1787-1826), S., Rome. - 171

FABRIANO, GENTILE DA (c. 1370-1427), P., Umbr. - 284, 352

FABRIS, GIUS. DE (1790-1860), S., Vicenza. - 99, 245, 265, 269, 302

FANCELLI, COSIMO (1620-88), S., Rome. - 102, 150

FATTORI, GIOV. (1825/28-1908), P., Flor. - 160

FERRABOSCO, GIROL. (c. 1631-after 1675), P., Pad. - 242

FERRABOSCO, MARTINO (fl. 1616-23), A., Rome. - 177, 267

FERRARI, ETTORE (1845-1929), S., Rome. - 89

FERRARI, FR. (1634-1708), P., Ferr. - 179, 221

FERRARI, GIOV. AND. DE (1598-1669), P., Gen. - 241

FERRATA, ERC. DE (1610-86), S., Como. - 88

FERRI, CIRO (1634-89), P. & A., Rome. - 73, 80, 82, 103, 172, 177, 269

FERRUCCI, FR. (1437-93), S., Fies. - 75

FERRUCCI, POMPEO (c. 1566-1637), S., Flor. - 340

FETTI, DOM. (or Bastiano Feti; 1589-1624), P., Mantua. - 148, 242

FIASELLA, DOM. (Il Sarzana; 1589-1669), P., Gen. - 82, 241

FIESOLE, MINO DA (1431-85), S., Flor. sch.; born at Poppi. - 73-4, 97, 154, 170, 237, 275, 295

FILARETE (Ant. Averlino; c. 1400-69), A. & S., Flor. - 267

FIORI, MARIO DE' (Nuzzi; c. 1603-73), P., Rome. - 168

FOLIGNO, NIC. DA (L'Alunno; c. 1430-1502), P., Umbr. - 168, 178, 186, 252, 284

FONTANA, CARLO (1634-1714), A., Rome, born Mendrisio, Como. - 99, 149-50, 169, 154, 229, 239, 244, 266, 269, 272

FONTANA, CARLO (1865-1956), S., Carrara. - 161

FONTANA, DOM. (1543-1607), A., Lomb. - 89, 153, 176-8, 187, 203-4, 212-3, 215, 264, 277, 298-9

FONTANA, FR. (son of Carlo; 1668-1708), A., Rome. - 169

FONTANA, GIOV. (brother of Dom.; 1540-1614), A., Rome. - 104, 244

FONTANA, GIROL. (fl. 1690-1714), A., Rome. - 168, 340

FONTANA, LAVINIA (1552-1614), P., Bol. - 82, 158

FONTANA, LUIGI (1827-1908), P. & S., Ascoli Piceno. - 170

FONTEBUONI, ANASTASIO (c. 1580-1626), P., Flor. - 91

FOSCHINI, ARNALDO (b. 1884), A., Rome. - 94

FRANCAVILLA, PIETRO (Pierre Franqueville; 1553-1615), S., Flor., born at Cambrai. - 180

FRANCIA (Fr. Raibolini; c. 1450-1517), P., Emil. - 68, 159, 179

FRANCIA (Giac. Raibolini; c. 1487-1557), P., Bol. sch. - 178

FRANCIABIGIO, MARCANTONIO (Fr. di Crist. Bigi; 1482-1525), P., Flor. - 158, 179

FRANGIPANI, NIC. (fl. 1555-1600), P., Padua. - 148

FRANZONI, FR. ANT. (1734-1818), S., Rome. - 306

FUGA, FERD. (1699-1781), A., Flor.-Rome. - 177, 203, 216, 240

FURINI, FR. (? 1604-46), P., Flor. - 82

N

GADDI, TADDEO (1300-66), P., Flor. - 252

GAGLIARDI, PIETRO (1809-90), P., Rome. - 105

GALILEI, ALESS. (1691-1736), A., Flor.-Rome. - 80, 213-4

GALLETTI, STEF. (1833-1905), S., Rome. - 198, 255

GALLORI, EMILIO (1846-1924), S., Flor. - 245

GANDOLFI, GAETANO (1734-1802), P. & A., Bol. - 242

GARBO, RAFFAELLINO DEL (c. 1466-c. 1524), P., Flor. - 96

GARÓFALO (Benv. Tisi; 1481-1559), P., Ferr. - 68-9, 73, 79, 148, 157, 159, 179, 286

GATTA, DON BART. DELLA (1448-1502 or 3), A. & P., Flor. - 295

GEMIGNANI, LOD. (1643-97), P., Rome. - 102, 176

GEMITO, VINC. (1852-1929), S., Nap. - 162

GENNARI, BENED. (1633-1715), P., Bol. - 344

GENTILE, FR. DI (15C-16C), P., Ancona. - 284

GENTILESCHI, ARTEMISIA (Lomi; 1590-1642), P., Pisa. - 82

GENTILESCHI, ORAZIO (Lomi, father of above; fl. 1565-1638), P., Pisa-Rome, d. London. - 82, 241, 286

GENTILI, ANT. (c. 1519-1609), G., Rome. - 273

GERINI, NIC. DI PIETRO (fl. 1368-1415), P., Flor. - 69

GHERARDI, ANT. (d. 1702), A. & P., Umbr. - 239

GHERARDI, FIL. (1643-1704), P., Lucca. - 168

GHINI, SIM. (1407-91), G., Flor. - 208, 214

GHIRLANDAIO, DOM. (Dom. di Tom. Bigordi; 1449-94), P., Flor. - 295

GHIRLANDAIO, RID. (1483-1561; son of Dom.), P., Flor. - 158

GIAMBERTI, see Sangallo

GIAMBOLOGNA (Jean Boulogne or Giov. Bologna; 1529-1608), S., Flor. sch. (a native of Douai), - 73

GIAQUINTO, CORRADO (? 1699-1765), P., Apulia. - 216

GIMIGNANI, GIACINTO (1611-81), P., Pistoia. - 104

GIOCONDO, FRA (Giov. Monsignori; 1457-1525), A., Ver. - 266

GIORDANO, LUCA (Luca fa presto; 1632-1705), P., Naples. - 83, 187, 242

GIORGETTI, ANT. (d. 1670), S., Rome. - 229

GIORGIONE (Giorgio Barbarelli; c. 1478-1510), P., Ven. - 73, 159, 168

GIOTTO DI BONDONE (1266-1336), P., Flor. (perhaps a native of Vespignano in the Mugello). -

213, 267, 284

GIOVANNI, MATT. DI (c. 1435-95), P., Siena. - 171

GIOVENALE, G. B. (1849-1934), A., Rome. - 238

GIULIO ROMANO, see Romano

GOZZOLI, BENOZZO (1420-97), P., Flor. sch. - 73, 84, 284

GRANDE, ANT. DEL (d. 1671), A., Rome. - 147, 168, 172

GRASSI, GIUS. (1757-1838), P., Udine. - 171

GRASSI, ORAZIO (1583-1654), A., Rome. born at Savona. - 150

GRECA, FELICE DELLA (c. 1626-77), A., Rome. - 151

GRECHETTO, see Castiglione

GRECO, EMILIO (b. 1913), Catania. - 172, 271

GREGORINI, DOM. (c. 1700-77), A., Rome. - 216

GRIMALDI, FRA FR. (1606-80), P., Bol. - 75

GRIMALDI, GIOV. FR. (1560-c. 1641), A., Potenza. - 177, 241

GUERCINO (Giov. Fr. Barbieri; 1591-1666), P., Bol. sch. - 69, 73, 79, 82-3, 105, 148, 158, 168-9, 172, 180-1, 186, 200, 241, 270, 286

GUIDI, DOM. (1625-1701), S., Rome, born at Carrara. - 83, 103

GUIDO, see Reni

GUTTUSO, RENATO (b. 1912), P., Palermo. - 162, 188, 294


HAYEZ, FR. (1791-1882), P., Ven. - 160, 172


IACOMETTI, IGNAZIO (1819-83), S., Rome. - 203, 216

IBI, SINIBALDO (c. 1475-1550), P., Per. - 141

IMOLA, INN. DA (Francucci; 1494-c. 1550), P., Imola. - 169

IUVARRA, FIL. (1685-1736), A., Messina. - 81


LANDINI, TADDEO (c. 1550-96), A. & S. Flor.-Rome. - 83

LANFRANCO, GIOV. (1582-1647), P., Parma. - 69, 75, 83, 157-8, 168, 177, 204, 241, 269-70

LAPICCOLA, NIC. (c. 1730-90), P., Rome. - 187

LAURETI, TOM. (c. 1508-92), A. & P., Palermo. - 62, 292

LEGA, SILVESTRO (1826-95), P., Flor. - 160

LEONARDO, see Vinci

LEONI, LEONE (Il Cavalier Aretino; 1510-92), S., Lomb. - 73, 180

LEVI, CARLO (1902-75), P., Tur. - 162, 188, 294

LICINIO, BERN. (d. c. 1556), P., Ven. sch. - 147

LIGORIO, PIRRO (c. 1500-83), A. & P., Nap.-Ferr. - 88, 96, 167, 213, 258, 266, 277, 315, 360

LIPPI, ANN. (fl. 1563-81), A., Umbr. - 174

LIPPI, FILIPPINO (son of Filippo; 1457-1504), P., Flor. sch. - 96, 149

LIPPI, FILIPPO FRA (c. 1406-69), P., Flor. - 174, 178, 284

LOCATELLI, AND. (1695-c. 1741), P., Rome. -172

LOMBARDI, CARLO (c. 1554-1620), A., Arezzo. - 141

LONGHI, LUCA (1507-80), P., Rav. - 169

LONGHI, MARTINO (The Elder; fl. 1570-d. 1591), A., Rome. - 79, 86, 102, 152, 171, 341

LONGHI, ONORIO (c. 1569-1619), A., Rome. - 153

LONGHI, SILLA (fl. 1568-1619), S., Rome. 204

LORENZETTO (Lor. di Lotti; 1490-1541), S. & A., Flor. - 99, 154, 237, 247

LORENZO, BICCI DI (1373-1452), P., Flor. - 148

LORENZO, FIORENZO DI (1445-1522/25), P., Per. - 252

LOTTO, LOR. (1480-1556), P., Ven. sch. - 147, 149, 158, 168, 254

LUCIANI, see Piombo

LUDOVISI, BERN. (c. 1713-49), S., Rome. - 74

LUTERI, see Dossi

LUTI, BENED. (1666-1724), P., Rome. - 169, 172

LUZZI, LUZIO (da Todi; called Luzio Romano; fl. 1528-73), P. & stuc., Rome. - 251, 254


MACCARI, CES. (1840-1919), P., Siena. - 255

MACRINO D'ALBA (Gian Giac. de Alladio; c. 1470-1528), P., Pied. - 69

MADERNA, CARLO (1556-1629), A., Ticino. - 75, 80, 83, 94-6, 101, 103, 150-1, 153, 176-8, 181, 202, 205, 216, 221, 244, 264, 266, 269, 340, 347, 353

MADERNA, STEF. (1576-1636), S., Como. - 94, 238, 315

MAGNASCO, ALESS. (Lissandrino; 1681-1747), P., Gen. - 241

MAIANO, BENED. DA (1442-97), S., Flor. sch. - 73

MAIANO, GIUL. DA (1432-90), A. & S., Flor. sch. - 72, 74

MAINI, G. B. (1690-1752), S., at Rome, born in Lomb. - 103

MANCINI, FR. (c. 1694-1758), P., Pésaro. - 270

MANCINI, ITALO (b. 1897), A., L'Aquila. - 182

MANZÙ, GIAC. (Manzoni Giacomo; b. 1908), S., Bergamo. - 162, 188, 198, 267, 272, 336

MARAINI, ANT. (b. 1886), S., Rome. - 93, 277

MARATTA, CARLO (1625-1713), P., Ancona. - 68, 73-4, 79, 91, 96, 153-4, 168, 171, 177, 190, 216, 241-2, 247, 271-2, 286, 348

MARCHETTI, G. B. (1730-1800), A. & P., Siena. - 157, 159

MARCHIONNI, CARLO (1702-86), A. & S., Rome. - 274

MARCHIS, TOM. DE (1693-1759), A., Rome. - 90

MARCONI, ROCCO (fl. 1504-29), P., Trev. - 73

MARGARITONE (d'Arezzo; fl. c. 1262-75), P., Are. - 284

MARIANI, CAMILLO (1556-1911), S. & P., Vicenza. - 181

MARINI, MICH. (b. 1459), S., Fies. - 97

MARTINI, A. (1889-1947), S., Trev. - 162, 198, 367

MARTINI, FR. DI Giorgio (1439-1502), A., S. & P., Siena. - 171

MARTINI, SIMONE (c. 1283-1344), P., Siena. - 178, 284

MARUCELLI, PAOLO (1594-1649), A., Rome. - 104

MASCHERINO, OTTAVIO (1524-1606), A. & P., at Rome. born at Bol. - 101, 177, 247, 340

MASOLINO DA PANICALE (Tom. Fini, master of Masaccio; 1383-1447), P., Flor. - 210, 284

MATTEO, GIOV. DA CITTÀ DI CASTELLO (fl. 1566-1616), A. - 79

MATURINO (da Firenze; ?1490-?1528), P., Flor. - 100

MAZZOLA, FR., see Parmigianino

MAZZOLINO, LOD. (c. 1480-1528/30), P., Ferr. - 68, 148, 159

MAZZONI, GIULIO (?1525-?1618), S. & P., Piac.-Rome. - 81, 244

MELI, GIOSUÈ (1807-93), S., Berg. - 141

MELOZZO DA FORLÌ (son of Giul. di Melozzo degli Ambrogi; 1438-95), P., Forlì - 74, 96, 99, 169, 177, 217, 284

MEMMI, LIPPO (fl. 1317-47), P., Siena. - 273

MENICUCCI, GIOV. BATT. (d. 1690), A., Rome. - 153

MESSINA, ANTONELLO DA (c. 1430-79), P., Ven. - 159

MESSINA, FR. (b. 1900), S., Catania. - 269

MICHELANGELO (Buonarroti; 1475-1564), A., S. & P., Flor., b. at Caprese, near Arezzo. - 56, 62, 75, 80-1, 96, 155, 163, 170, 172, 174, 182, 190, 195, 200, 204, 251, 266, 269, 274, 288, 295, 297, 354

MOCHI, FR. (1580-1646), S., Montevarchi. - 73, 100, 268

MODENA, BARNABA DA (14C), P., Mod. - 69

MODENA, GIOV. DA (fl. 1420-51), P., - 73

MOLA, PIER FR. (1612-68), P., Mendrisio. - 69, 157, 168-9, 171, 177, 242, 286

MONACO, LOR. (Fra Lor. degli Angioli; c. 1370-1425), P., Flor. sch. - 284

MONTAGNA, BART. (1451-c. 1523), P., Vic. sch. - 252

MONTANO, G. B. (1534-1621), A., Mil. - 110

MONTAUTI, ANT. (d. c. 1740), A. & S., Flor. - 214

MONTELUPO, BACCIO DA (1469-1535), A. & S., Flor. sch. - 73, 259, 359

MONTELUPO, RAFF. DA (1503-70), S., Flor. sch. - 86, 96, 99, 200, 254

MONTEVERDE, GIULIO (1837-1917), S., Alessandria. - 160

MORANDI, GIORGIO (1890-1964), P., Bol. - 162, 172, 188, 294

MORELLI, COSIMO (1732-1812), A., Imola. - 100

MORETTO (Aless. Bonvicino; 1498-1554), P., Bres. (Ven. sch.). - 168, 267, 286

MOSCA, SIM. (Moschini; 1492-1553), A. & S., Sett. - 102, 201

MURATORI, DOM. (1661-1744), P., Rome. - 170

MUZIANO, GIROL. (1528-92), P., Bres.-Rome. - 105, 168, 171, 229, 273, 286-7, 340, 360


NELLI, OTTAVIANO (c. 1375-c. 1440), P., Gubbio. - 73

NERVI, PIER LUIGI (1891-1979), A., Sondrio. - 257, 260, 315

NOVELLI, PIETRO (1603-47), P., Sic. - 159, 168-9, 242

NUCCI, AVANZINO (c. 1552-1629), P., Città di Castello. - 62, 105


ODAZZI, GIOV. (1663-1731), P., Rome. - 170

ODERISI, PIETRO DI LOR. (Oderisio; d. 1299), min. - 94

OGGIONO, MARCO D' (c. 1470-1530), P., sch. of Leonardo. - 158

OLIVIERI, PIER PAOLO (1551-99), A. & S., Rome. - 141, 181, 205, 215

ORSI, LELIO (da Novellara; c. 1511-87), P., Emil. sch. - 73

ORTOLANO (G. B. Benvenuti; 1488-?1525), P., Ferr. - 148, 159

OTTONI, LOR. (1648-1736), S., Rome. - 74


PACETTI, VINC. (c. 1746-1820), S., Rome. - 171

PAGLIA, GIUS. (fl. 1655-82), Sic. - 98

PALMA GIOVANE (Iac. Negretti, grandson of the next; 1544-1628), P., Ven. sch. - 172

PALMA VECCHIO (Giac. Negretti; c. 1480-1528), P., Berg. (Ven. sch.). - 68, 74, 158-9, 168

PALMEZZANO, MARCO (1456-c. 1539), P., Forlì. - 82, 136, 284

PANNINI, GIUS. PAOLO (1691/2-1765), P. at Rome, born at Piacenza. - 100, 171, 186, 241

PAOLO, GIOV. DI (?1403-1482), P. & illum., Siena. - 148, 284

PARMA, ALESS. DA (1523-79), A., Parma. - 351

PARMIGIANINO (Fr. Mazzola; 1503-40), P., Parm. sch. - 82, 148, 159

PARODI, G. B. (1674-1730), P., Gen. - 200

PASSALACQUA, PIETRO (d. 1748), A., Messina. - 216

PASSAROTTI, BART. (1520-92), P., Bol. - 68, 168-9, 179

PASSERI, GIUS. (1654-1714), P. & A., Rome. - 272

PAZZINI, NORBERTO (1856-1937), P., Forlì. - 161, 188

PENNI, FR. (or Giov. Fr.; ?1488-?1528), P., Flor. - 242, 274, 285-6, 288, 292

PERUGINO (Pietro Vannucci; 1446-1523), P., Umbr. - 97, 158, 178, 186, 238, 285, 288, 295

PERUZZI, BALDAS. (1481-1537), A. & P., Siena. - 78, 85, 99, 102-3, 179, 217, 242, 244, 266, 292, 296

PERUZZI, GIOV. SALLUSTIO (son of Baldas.; c. 1510-73), A., Siena. - 255

PÉSARO, SIM. DA, see Cantarini

PIACENTINI, MARCELLO (1881-1960), A., Rome - 189, 198, 256, 258, 260

PIAZZETTA, G. B. (1683-1754), P., Ven. - 171

PICCINELLI, see Brescianino

PIETRASANTA, GIAC. DA (fl. 1452-95), A. & S., Rome. - 105, 277

PIETRO, LOR. DI, see Vecchietta

PIETRO, NIC. DI (Paradisi; fl. 1394-1430), P., Ven. - 178, 284

PINELLI, BART. (1781-1835), S., P., & engr., Rome. - 100, 171

PINTURICCHIO (Bern. di Betto; c. 1454-1513), P., Per. - 97, 154, 158, 238, 285, 293-5, 306, 368, 370

PIOMBO, SEB. DEL (Luciani; 1485-1547), P., Ven. - 149, 154, 242, 244, 253, 368

PIRANDELLO, FAUSTO (b. 1899), P., Rome. - 162, 172, 188

PIRANESI, G. B. (1720-78), A. & engr., Ven.-Rome. - 90, 171, 174, 363

PISA, ISAIA DA (15C), S., Rome-Nap. - 74, 101, 105, 214, 275

PISANO, GIUNTA (fl. 1229-1254), P., Pisa. - 284

PISANO, NIC. (1220-after 1278), A. & S. Apulia. - 73

PISIS, FIL. DE (1896-1956), P., Ferr. - 162, 294

PODESTI, FR. (1800-95), P. & A., Anc. - 94, 288

PODESTI, GIULIO (1857-1909), A., Rome. - 197

POLETTI, LUIGI (1792-1869), A., Modena. - 81, 93, 94

POLLAIUOLO, ANT. DEL (1433-98), S. & P., Flor. sch. - 62, 271, 273

POLLAIUOLO, PIERO DEL (brother of Ant.; 1443-96), P. & A., Flor. sch. - 201

POMARANCIO (Crist. Roncalli da Pomarance; 1552-1626), P., Tusc. - 86, 200, 205, 219-20, 224, 244, 271, 314

POMARANCIO, NICCOLÒ (1517-96), P., Pisa. - 190, 311

PONTELLI, BACCIO (Bart. di Fino; c. 1450-92), A. & W., Flor. - 102, 170, 240, 247, 264, 332, 337

PONZIO, FLAMINIO (1560-1613), A., Rome. - 105, 150, 127, 203-4, 230, 244

PORTA, BART. DELLA, see Bartolomeo

PORTA, G. B. DELLA (1549-97), S., Como. - 360

PORTA, GIAC. DELLA (1539-1602), A. & S., Lomb. - 56, 74-5, 80-1, 83, 95-7, 100, 103-5, 151, 155, 181, 199, 204-5, 213-4, 224, 253, 261, 266-7, 271, 274, 340

PORTA, GUGL. DELLA (1516-77), A. & S., Lomb. - 158, 204, 249-50, 270

PORTA, TOM. DELLA (the Elder; c. 1520-67), S., Lomb. - 153

POSI, PAOLO (1708-76), A. at Rome, born Siena. - 105

POZZO, AND. (or Pozzi; 1642-1709), A. & P. at Rome, born Trento. - 150, 242

PRETE GENOVESE, see Strozzi

PRETI, MATTIA (Il Cavalier Calabrese; 1613-99), P., Nap. - 74, 82, 147-8

PRINI, GIOV. (1877-1958), S., Gen. - 160-1, 188

PROCACCINI, AND. (1671-1734), P. & A., Rome. - 272

PULIGO DOM. (1492-1527), P., Flor. - 158, 169

PULZONE, SCIPIONE (before 1550-98), P., Rome. - 158, 168-9, 176, 179

QUARENGHI, GIAC. (1744-1817), A., Rome. - 369

QUATTRINI, ENRICO (1863-1950), S., Todi. - 255

QUERCIA, IAC. DELLA (1371-1438), S., Siena. - 254

RAGGI, ANT. (Il Lombardo; 1624-86), S., Rome. - 175, 177, 370

RAGUZZINI, FIL. (1680-1771), A., Benevento. - 150

RAIBOLINI, see Francia

RAIMONDI, MARCANTONIO (c. 1480-c. 1534), engr., Bol. - 171, 213

RAINALDI, CARLO (son of Girol.; 1611-91), A., Rome. - 75, 79, 83, 103, 147, 153, 203

RAINALDI, GIROL. (1570-1655), A., Rome. - 56, 80, 103, 126, 153

RAPHAEL (Raffaello Sanzio; 1483-1520), P., Urb. - 75, 80, 99, 101-2, 105, 144, 147-8, 154-5, 158, 171, 173, 240, 242-3, 256, 264, 266, 271, 285, 287, 289-92, 375

REAME, MINO DEL (fl. 1463-77), S., Nap.-Rome. - 204, 222, 239

RECCO, GIUS. (1634-95), P., Mil. - 242

RENI, GUIDO (1577-1642), P., Bol. sch. - 68-9, 79, 82-3, 100, 104, 148, 152, 157, 168-9, 172, 176-7, 180, 204, 221-2, 238, 241, 270-1, 286-7, 298, 344

RIBERA, GIUS. (Lo Spagnoletto; 1590-1652), P., Nap. - 147, 168, 172, 186, 242

RICCI, G. B. (1537-1627), P., Rome. - 271

RICCI, SEB. (1659-1734), P., Belluno. - 169

RIDOLFI, CLAUDIO (1570-1644), P., Ven. - 245

RIGHI, TOM. (1727-1802), S. & stucc. - 90

RIMINI, GIOV. FR. DA (d. 1470), P., Umbr. - 178

RINALDI, RINALDO (1793-1873), S., Pad. - 94

RIPANDA, GIAC. (fl. 1490-1530), P., Bol. - 62

ROBBIA, LUCA DELLA (1400-82), S., Flor. - 176

ROCCA, MICH. (1670/5-1751), P., Parma. - 99

ROMANELLI, GIOV. FR. (1616-62), P., Viterbo. - 168, 178-9, 190, 270-1

ROMANELLI, RAFF. (1856-1928), S., Flor. 177

ROMANO, GIULIO (Pippi; c. 1492-1546), A. & P., Rome. - 94, 99, 102, 158, 174, 179, 187, 202, 220, 242, 252, 256, 274, 285-6, 288, 292, 340, 356

ROMANO, PAOLO (Salvati; fl. 1404-17) S., Rome. - 224, 237

RONCALLI, see Pomarancio

RONDINELLI, NIC. (1450-1510), P., Rav. - 148

ROSA, ERCOLE (1846-93), S., - 174

ROSA, SALVATOR (1615-73), P., Nap. - 68, 80, 168-9, 172, 190, 242

ROSATI, ROSATO (c. 1560-1622), A. & P., Macerata. - 83

ROSSELLI, COSIMO (1439-1507), P., Flor. - 295

ROSSELLI, MATT. (1578-1650), P., Flor. - 168

ROSSELLINO, BERNARDO (Gambarelli; 1409-64), S., Sett. - 72, 265

ROSSI, MARIANO (1731-1807), P., Rome. - 156

ROSSI, ANG. DE (1671-1715), S., Gen. - 270

ROSSI, GIOV. ANT. DE (1616-95), A., Rome. - 99, 105, 147

ROSSO FIORENTINO (G. B. Rosso; 1494-1541), P., Flor. - 158

RUGHESI, FAUSTO (fl. 1605), A., Rome. - 79

RUSCONI, CAMILLO (1658-1728), S., Rome. - 269

RUSUTI, FIL. (fl. 1300-20), P. & mos., Rome. - 203

RUTELLI, MARIO (1859-1941), S., Palermo. - 189, 245


SACCHI, AND. (1599-1661), P., Rome. - 90, 100, 159, 179-80, 212, 215, 270-1, 274, 286

SACCONI, GIUS. (1853-1905), A., Marches. - 93, 99

SALIMBENI, VENTURA (c. 1568-1613), P., Siena. - 179

SALMEGGIA, ENEA (Talpino; c. 1558-1626), P., Bergamo. - 168

SALVI, see Sassoferrato

SALVI, NIC. (1697-1751), A., Rome. - 169, 179

SALVIATI, FR. (1510-63), P., Flor. - 76, 88, 90, 102, 154, 168-9, 295-6

SANCTIS, FR. DE (fl. 1725), A., Rome. - 173

SANCTIS, GUGL. DE (1829-1911), P., Rome. - 100

SANGALLO, ANT. DA (the Elder, Giamberti; 1455-1537), A. & S., Flor. - 337

SANGALLO, ANT. DA (the Younger, Cordiani; 1483-1546), A., Rome. - 76, 79-81, 96, 102, 104-5, 154, 226, 246-7, 250, 252, 256, 266, 277, 296-7

SANGALLO, GIUL. DA (Giamberti; 1443-1517), A. & S., Flor. - 201, 203, 265-6

SAN GIOVANNI, GIOV. DA (Mannozzi or Manozzi; 1592-1636), P., Flor. sch. - 211, 241

SANO DI PIETRO (1406-81), P., Siena. - 148, 284

SANSOVINO, AND. (Contucci; 1460-1529), S., Tusc. - 102, 105, 154, 220, 294

SANSOVINO, IAC. (Tatti; pupil of And.; c. 1486-1570), A. & S., Flor. - 73, 79-80, 97, 105, 150, 216, 239, 352

SANTI, GIOV. (father of Raphael; d. 1494), P., Urb. - 285

SANZIO, see Raphael

SARACENI, CARLO (1585-1620), P., Ven. - 82, 102, 147, 177, 179

SARDI, GIUS. (c. 1680-1753), A., Pésaro. - 99

SARTO, AND. DEL (Vannucchi; 1486-1531), P., Flor. - 82, 148, 158, 179

SARTORIO, GIULIO ARISTIDE (1860-1932), A., Rome. - 152, 172, 188

SASSOFERRATO (G. B. Salvi; 1605-85), P., Umbr. - 73, 90, 148, 158, 169, 172, 208, 241, 286

SAVOLDO, GIROL. (fl. 1508-48), P., Bres. - 68, 158

SCARSELLINO (Ipp. Scarsella; 1551-1620), P., Ferr. - 68, 159, 179

SCHERANO, ALESS. (fl. 1537), S., Sett. - 200

SCIPIONE, VANNUTELLI (1834-94), P., Genazzano. - 188

SEGNA, NIC. DI (son of Segna di Buonaventura; fl. 1331), P., Siena. - 73

SEITZ, LOD. (1844-1908), P., Rome. - 102, 199

SELLAIO, JACOPO DEL (1442-93), P., Flor. - 169

SENESE, MICHELANGELO (c. 1470-c. 1520), S., Siena. - 102, 239

SERMONETA, IL (Girol. Sicciolante; 1521-c. 1580), P., Rome. - 104, 169, 179, 204, 253

SERRA, LUIGI (1846-88), P., Bol. - 182

SIENA, BARNA DA (fl. c. 1369-81), Siena. - 214

SIGNORELLI, LUCA (c. 1441-1523), P., Cortona. - 186, 252, 295

SIGNORINI, TELEMACO (1835-1901), P., Flor. - 160

SIMONETTI, MICHELANGELO (d. 1787), A., Rome. - 277

SIRANI, ELISABETTA (1638-65), P., Bol. - 69

SODOMA (Giov. Ant. dei Bazzi; 1477-1549), P., Vercelli. - 179, 242, 368

SOGLIANI, GIOV. ANT. (1491-1544), P., Flor. - 69

SOLARI, see Lombardo

SOLARIO, AND. (fl. 1490-1530), P.,
sch. of Leonardo. - 179
SOLIMENA, FR. (1657-1747), P.,
Nocera. - 73, 242
SORIA, G. B. (1581-1651), A. & W.,
Rome. - 83, 181, 221, 236
SORMANI, LEON. (d. c. 1589), S.,
Savona. - 181, 204
SPADA, LIONELLO (1576-1622), P.,
Bol. - 158
SPADARINO (Giov. Ant. Galli; fl.
1615-45), P., Rome. - 140
SPAGNA, LO (Giov. di Pietro; c.
1450-1528), P., died at Spoleto. -
100, 169, 285
SPAGNOLETTO, LO, see Ribera
SPANZOTTI, GIOV. MARTINO (c. 1456-
1526/8), P., Pied. - 147, 252
SPECCHI, ALESS. (1668-1729), A.,
Rome. - 173
STEFANO, GIOV. DI (fl. 1366-91), A.
& S., Siena. - 214
STEFANO, GIOV. DI (son of Sassetta;
1444-1506), S., Siena. - 213
STEFANO, TOMMASO DI (Lunetti; c.
1495-1564), P. & A., Flor. - 179
STOCCHI, ACHILLE (early 19C), A. &
S., Rome. - 151
STROZZI, BERNARDO (Prete
Genovese; 1581-1644), P., Gen.
sch. - 241
SUARDI, BART., see Bramantino
SUSINI, ANT. (d. 1624), S., Flor. - 73,
157, 169, 180

TACCA, PIETRO (1577-1640), S. & A.,
Carrara. - 73
TACCONE, PAOLO (d. 1477), S., Sezze.
- 75, 247, 257
TADDEO DI BARTOLO (1362-1422), P.,
Siena. - 284
TADOLINI, ADAMO (1788-1868), S.,
Bol. - 74, 265
TASSI, AGOSTINO (1566-1644), P.,
Per. - 69, 100, 104, 177
TATTI, see Sansovino
TEMPESTA, ANT. (1555-1630), P.,
Flor. - 219, 301
TENERANI, PIETRO (1789-1869), S.,
Massa. - 101, 160, 213, 241, 271
TESTA, PIETRO (1611-50), P., Rome. -
69, 82
TIBALDI, PELL. (Pellegrino Pellegrini;
1527-96), A., S. & P., Bol. - 104,
150
TIEPOLO, G. B. (1696-1770), P., Ven.
- 241
TINTORETTO, DOM. (son of Iac.;
1562-1637), P., Ven. - 68, 168, 179
TINTORETTO, IAC. (Robusti; 1518-94),
P., Ven. - 147, 168-9, 179, 186
TISI, see Garófalo
TITIAN (Tiziano Vecellio or Vecelli;
1477-1576), P., Ven. sch., born at
Pieve di Cadore. - 68, 82, 147,
159, 169, 171, 179, 286

TITO, SANTI DI (1538-1603), A. & P.,
Flor. sch. - 311
TORI, see Bronzino
TORNIOLI, NIC. (fl. 1622-40), P.,
Siena. - 82
TORREGIANI, BART. (d. 1675), P.,
Rome. - 148
TORREGIANI, PIETRO (1472-1522), S.
& P. Flor. - 104
TORRESINI, ATTILIO (b. 1884), S.,
Ven. - 188
TORRIANI, ORAZIO (16C-17C), A.,
Rome. - 84
TORRIGIANI, SEB. (d. 1596), S., Bol. -
273
TORRITI, IAC. (fl. late 13C), P. &
mos. - 90, 203, 215, 359
TOSI, ARTURO (1871-1956), P., &
engr., Varese. - 162
TRAU, see Dalmata
TREVISANI, FR. (1656-1746), P.,
Rome. - 82, 172, 242, 374
TREVISO, GIROL. DA (Girol.
Pennacchi; 1497-1544), P., Ven.
sch. - 159
TRIBOLO, NIC. (Pericoli; 1485-1550),
S., Flor. - 102, 172

UBERTINI, see Bachiacca
UDINE, GIOV. DA (Nanni, or dei
Ricamatori; ?1457-1564), A. & P.,
Udine. - 99, 242, 253, 256, 285,
292, 294
UTILI, G. B. (1495-1516), P.,
Ravenna. - 284

VACCA, FLAMINIO (1538-1605), S.,
Rome. - 181
VAGA, PERIN DEL (Pietro
Buonaccorsi; 1500-47), P., Flor. -
82, 99, 141, 150, 158, 173-4, 220,
251, 253, 288-92, 294, 296
VALADIER, GIUS. (1762-1839), A.,
Rome. - 78, 100, 106, 153, 169-70,
174, 250, 257, 266
VALLE, FIL. (1697-1768), S., Flor. -
100, 150, 170, 269
VALSOLDO, IL (Giov. Ant. Paracca;
fl. 1572-1628), Rome. - 204
VALVASSORI, GABRIELE (1683-1761),
A., Rome. - 147
VANNUCCHI, see Sarto
VANNUCCI, see Perugino
VANVITELLI, GASP. (Gaspar van
Wittel; father of Luigi; 1653-
1736), P., in Rome from 1693,
born at Amersfoort, Netherlands.
- 62, 148, 172, 187, 190-1
VANVITELLI, LUIGI (1700-73), A.,
born in Naples. - 105, 169
VASANZIO, GIOV. (Jan van Santen of
Utrecht; 1550-1621), A., engr. &
S., - 156, 229, 341

VASARI, GIORGIO (1512-74), A., P., and art historian, Are. - 88, 158, 163, 244, 286, 296, 298

VASSALLETTO, Roman family of sculptors (12C-13C). - 95, 215

VASSALLETTO, PIETRO (fl. 1154-86), S. & mos. - 94

VECCHI, GIOV. DE' (1536-1615), P., Sansepolcro, d. in Rome. - 244, 261

VECCHIETTA (Lor. di Pietro; c. 1412-80), S. & P., Siena. - 154

VENETO, BART. (early 16C), P., Crem. (Ven. sch.). - 179

VENEZIANO, ANT. (late 14C), P., Ven. - 284

VENEZIANO, PAOLO (fl. 1335-60), P., Ven. - 73

VENUSTI, MARCELLO (1512-79), P., Rome, born at Como. - 96, 103, 171, 176, 179, 215

VERONESE, PAOLO (Caliari; 1528-88), P., Ven. sch. - 68-9, 159, 168-9, 286

VESPIGNANI, FR. (1842-99), A., Rome. - 215, 239, 244

VESPIGNANI, VIRGINIO (1808-82), A., Rome. - 81, 182, 200, 203

VIGNOLA, IL (Iac. Barocci; 1507-73), A. & P., Mod. ; founder of the Baroque school. - 74, 105, 126, 163, 213, 258, 266, 274, 341

VINCI, LEONARDO DA (1452-1519), A., P. & S., Flor. sch., born near Empoli. - 286

VINCIDOR, TOM. (d. c. 1536), P. & A., Bol. - 287

VITERBO, ANT. DA (fl. 1478-1509), P., Viterbo. - 62, 238, 294

VITTORIA, ALESS. (1528-1608), S. & A., Trento. - 73

VIVARINI, BART. (brother of Ant.; fl. 1450-99), P., Murano, Ven. sch. - 169

VIVIANI, ANT. (1560-1620), P., Urb. - 222, 284

VOLTERRA, DANIELE DA (Ricciarelli; 1509-66), A., S. & P., Flor. sch. - 105, 150, 173, 244, 296

VOLTERRA, FR. DA (Capriani; d. 1588), A. & S., Rome. - 79, 101, 204, 214, 221

ZAMPIERI, see Domenichino

ZAVATTARI, AMBR. & GREG. (Brothers; fl. 1453), P., Mil. - 252

ZEVIO, STEF. DA (1393-c. 1450), P., Ver. sch. - 169

ZOCCHI, ARNALDO (1862-1940), S., Flor. - 354

ZUCCARI, FED. (1542-1609), P., Pésaro. - 68, 73, 76, 80, 90, 100, 171, 179, 202, 241, 296, 311, 340, 360, 374

ZUCCARI, GIAMPIETRO (fl. 1584-1621), W., Urb. - 340, 374

ZUCCARI, TADDEO (1529-66), P., Pésaro. - 86, 90, 99, 158, 174, 186, 296, 340, 374

ZUCCHI, FR. (c. 1570-1627), P., Bergamo. - 217, 261

ZUCCHI, IAC. (c. 1541-1589), W. & A., Parma. - 298

# INDEX

Topographical names are printed in **bold type**, names of eminent persons in *italics*, other entries in Roman type. The tombs of popes (given in the List of Popes, page 20), and the building activities of popes and emperors have generally been ignored.

Abbreviations 10
**Accademia dei Lincei** 242
„ **di S. Luca** 171
**Acqua Acetosa** 258, 370
„ **Claudia** 217
„ **Felice** 181, 218
„ **Julia** 218
„ **Marcia** 218, 262, 367-8
„ **Tepula** 218
„ **Traiana** 374
„ **Vergine** 170
*Adrian I* 87, 213, 225
*Adrian III* 212
*Adrian IV* 220, 348
*Adrian VI* 102, 266
**Aedes Caesarum** 135
**Ager Vaticanus** 246
**Agosta** 368
*Agrippa, M. Vipsanius* 14, 97, 170, 324
**Agro Pontino** 320, 335
Airports 33
**Alba Longa** 347
**Alban Hills** 338
*Albani, Card.* 57
**Albano, Lake** 344
**Albano Laziale** 348
*Alexander III* 12, 213
*Alexander VI* 16, 75, 79, 203, 240, 248, 250, 252, 277, 294, 337, 363
*Alexander VII* 98, 102, 113, 147, 151, 255, 266, 270, 347
*Alexander VIII* 247, 270, 298-9
*Alexander Severus* 142
*Alfonso XIII* 79
**All Saints'** 173
**Allia** 372
**Alsium** 376
*Altieri, The* 84
American Church 189
American Military Cemetery 338
**Amphitheatrum Castrense** 217
**Anaglypha Trajani** 113
*Ancus Marcius* 11, 13-14, 243
**Anguillara Sabazia** 375
**Anio or Aniene, The** 184, 357
**Anio Novus** 217
**Antemnae** 185
**Antícoli Corrado** 367

**Antiquarium Comunale** 70
„ **Forense** 124
„ **of Forum Augustus** 139
„ **Palatinum** 133
**Antium** 336-7
*Antoninus Pius* 15, 122, 151, 247, 375
*Antony, Mark* 11, 112, 125, 128, 201
**Anzio** 336
**Aprília** 336
Aqua, *see* Acqua
**Aquae Albulae** 357
**Aqueduct of Nero** 217
**Ara Pacis Augustae** 106, 305
**Ara Pietatis Augustae** 67, 174
**Arcadia** 243
*Arcadius* 19
**Arch of Augustus** 116
„ „ **Claudius** 61, 151
„ „ **Constantine** 144
„ „ **Diocletian** 150
„ „ **Dolabella and Silanus** 220
„ „ **Drusus** 225
„ „ **Gallienus** 205
„ „ **Janus** 88
„ „ **San Lazzaro** 90
„ „ **Septimius Severus** 15, 114
„ „ **Tiberius** 115
„ „ **Titus** 124
„ „ **Trajan** 137
**Archives, Municipal** 79
„ **State** 99
„ **Vatican** 298
**Archivio dei Castelli** 255
**Arcus Argentariorum** 88
**Ardea** 336
**Area Palatina** 132
**Argiletum** 111
**Aríccia** 349
*Arnulph of Carinthia* 246
*Arquati, G. T.* 236
**Arx** 56
*Astaulph, King* 353
*Atticus* 234, 337
**Auditorium of Mæcenas** 206
**Auguratorium** 127
*Augustus* 11, 14, 84-5, 106-7, 109, 112-14,

125, 128-9, 135, 153, 197, 218, 322, 334, 351, 358, 373
**Aula of Isis** 132
*Aurelian* 15, 18, 95, 222, 248
**Aurelian Wall** 15, 18, 95, 175, 181, 218, 222, 248
**Aventine, The** 89

**Bagni di Tivoli** 357
**Bagni di Vicarello** 374
*Bainbridge, Card.* 81
*Ballantyne, R. M.* 92
**Banditaccia** 376
**Bandusia, Fountain of** 367
**Baptistery of St John** 212
*Baronius, Card. Ces.* 224
**Basilica Aemilia** 111
„ **Argentaria** 137
„ **of Constantine** 123
„ **Eudoxiana** 200
„ **Julia** 115
„ **of Maxentius** 123
„ **Ostiense** 93
„ **di Porta Maggiore** 217
„ **of St Valentine** 257
„ **Ulpia** 136
Basilicas, Patriarchal 45
**Bastione del Sangallo** 226
**Baths of Agrippa** 95
„ „ **Caracalla (Thermae Antoninianae)** 222-3
„ „ **Constantine** 176
„ „ **Diocletian** 189
„ „ **Septimius Severus** 134
„ „ **Tiberius** 132
„ „ **Titus** 145
„ „ **Trajan** 145, 201, 206
*Bede, Venerable* 142
*Belisarius* 175, 226
*Bell, John* 92
*Bembo, Pietro* 96, 99
*Benedict II* 98
*Benedict XIV* 68, 98, 104, 142, 203, 216, 247, 249, 269, 297, 368
*Benedict XV* 265, 270-1, 275
**Benedictine Seminary** 91
*Bernis, Card. de* 150
*Bessarion, Card.* 170, 224, 257

*Biagio da Cesena* 296
Biblioteca Corsiniana 242
„ Lancisiana 247
„ Nazionale 197
„ Vallicelliana 79
Bocca della Verità 87
*Bonaparte, Joseph* 101, 150
*Bonaparte, Letizia* 147, 240
*Bonaparte, Louis* 101-2
*Bonaparte, Lucien* 150, 341
*Boni, Giac.* 126
*Boniface IV* 98, 115
*Boniface VIII* 12, 99, 213, 262
*Boniface IX* 56
*Borghese, Pauline* 157, 182
*Borghese, Scipione, Card.* 155-6, 176, 341
Borghetto 343
Borgo, The 246
Borgo S. Spirito 247, 264
Borgo Vaccina 376
Borsa 151
Bosco Parrasio 243
Bosco Sacro 229
Botanical Gardens 240
Bovillæ 347
Bracciano 374
*Bristol, Earl of (Bp of Derry)* 348
British Embassy 182
British Military Cemetery 92, 336
British School 162
*Browning, R.* 152, 173
*Bruno, Giordano* 76
*Burckhardt, H.* 75
Buses 41
*Byron, Lord* 59, 173, 231, 305

Cabum 345
*Cadorna, Gen. Raff.* 13, 182
Cælian, The 219
Cære 376
Caffè Greco 173
*Cairoli, Brothers* 174, 257
Calcografia Nazionale 171
*Caligula* 14, 117, 125, 217, 246, 264, 337, 346
*Calixtus I, St* 239
*Calixtus II* 12, 87, 268, 275
*Calixtus III* 79
Camaldoli 341
*Camillus, M. Furius* 110, 358, 373
Campagna, The 320
Campagnano di Roma 371
Campania Romana 320

Campi d'Annibale 345
Campidoglio 55-6
Camping 36
Campo di Carne 336
„ dei Fiori 76
„ Vaccino 109
„ Verano 198
Camposanto Teutonico 315
Campus Martius 95
Campus Sceleratus 197
Cantoniera 339, 343
Capannelle 219, 343-4
Capena 371
Capitoline Hill 55
Cappellette, Le 342
Cappuccini 180
Capránica Prenestina 356
*Caracalla* 15, 89, 98, 114, 222
Carceri Nuove 80
Careiæ 374
*Carissimi, Giac.* 344
Casa del Burcardo 75
„ dei Cav. di Rodi 138
„ dei Crescenzi 86
„ di Dante 236
„ della Fornarina 240
„ di Lor. Manilio 84
„ dei Mattei 237
„ di San Paolo 83
Casal Rotondo 234
Casale di Statua 376
*Casanate, Card.* 214
Casape 356
Casino dell' Aurora 181
Casino Borghese 156
Casino Rospigliosi-Pallavicini 176
*Cassius* 358
Castel Fusano 333
„ Gandolfo 347
„ Giubileo 372
„ di Guido 375
„ di Leva 235
„ Madama 366
„ San Pietro 356
„ Sant'Angelo 247
„ Savelli (Borghetto) 343
„ Savelli (Castel Gandolfo) 350
Castell' Arcione 357
Castelli Romani 338
Castelnuovo di Porto 371
Castrimmoenium 344
Castro Pretorio 197
Catacombs 227
„ of Commodilla 92
„ Jewish 183
„ of Nicomedes 183
„ of Panfilo 185
„ of Praetextatus 229
„ of Priscilla 185
„ of St Agnes 184
„ of St Calixtus 228
„ of St Domitilla 230
„ of S. Ermete 185
„ of S. Felicità 185

„ of S. Pancrazio 244
„ of SS. Pietro and Marcellino 352
„ of St Sebastian 229
„ of S. Valentino 257
„ of Trasone 185
*Catanei, Vannozza* 199
*Catiline* 110
*Cato the Censor* 109, 341
*Cato of Utica* 342
*Catullus* 358
*Catalus, Q. Lutatius* 125
*Celestine IV* 134
*Cenci. The* 84, 244
Centocelle 352
Ceri 376
CERVETERI 376
Chamber of Deputies 152
*Charlemagne* 12, 265, 266
*Charles I of England* 285
*Charles V, Emp.* 12, 236
*Charles of Anjou* 70
*Charles of Bourbon* 351
*Charles Emmanuel IV of Savoy* 168
*Charles Stuart ('Young Pretender')* 170, 271, 340
*Charlotte of Cyprus* 275
*Chateaubriand* 152
Chiesa Nuova 79
*Chigi, Agost.* 154, 242
*Christina of Sweden* 155, 174, 240-1, 243, 269, 275, 298
Churches 45, 51
Churches and Basilicas, *see under* Saint, etc.
Ciampino 344
*Cicero* 125, 257, 322, 337, 341
Cimitero Maggiore 184
Cinecittà 339
Circular Road 226
Circus of Flaminius 84
„ of Maxentius 231
„ Maximus 89
„ of Nero 246
„ Varianus 217
Cispian Hill 201
Città Leonina 246
Civitavecchia 380
*Claudius, Emp.* 14, 126, 322, 334
*Claudius, Appius* 226
*Clement V* 12, 213
*Clement VII* 12, 96, 247, 252, 256, 266
*Clement VIII* 96, 188, 204, 213, 251, 268, 271, 276
*Clement IX* 98, 149
*Clement X* 149, 203, 270
*Clement XI* 149, 170, 207, 271, 315
*Clement XII* 58, 149, 170, 213-4, 301, 339

*Clement XIII* 270, 277, 301, 347
*Clement XIV* 277, 304, 310
Clivus Capitolinus 110, 112
,, Martis 227
,, Palatinus 126
,, Sacer 112, 122
,, Victoriae 127
Cloaca Maxima 88
*Clodius, P.* 125
*Cloelia* 236
Collegio dei Gesuiti 149
,, di Propaganda Fide 172
,, Romano 149
Colonna 353
*Colonna, The* 12, 98, 342, 345, 368
*Colonna, Marcantonio* 70, 226
*Colonna, Vittoria* 176, 344
Colonnacce, Le 138
Colosseum 142
Columbarium of Pomponius Hylas 225
*Columbus, Christopher* 203
Column of M. Aurelius 151
Column of Phocas 115
Column of Trajan 136
Comitium 112
*Commodus* 234
Concert Halls 46
Conciliazione, La 13, 95, 261-2
*Consalvi, Card.* 99
*Constans II, Emp.* 98
*Constantia* 183-4, 310
*Constantine* 12, 15, 89, 123, 144, 198, 201, 212, 257, 265, 275, 322, 334, 371
*Constantine II* 220
*Constantius II* 212
Consulates, British and American 44
Corbio 342
*Corelli, A.* 104
*Coriolanus* 336
Corso, The 147
Corso d'Italia 181
Corso Vittorio Emanuele 74
*Crassus, L. Licinius (orator)* 125
*Crassus, M. Licinius* 11
*Crescentii, The* 86, 104
Cristo Re, Ch. of 256
*Cromwell, Thos.* 81
Cryptoporticus 129
Curia 113
*Cybo, The* 154

*Damasus I* 203

*d'Annunzio, Gab.* 341
*Dante* 70, 213, 236, 296, 303
*De Gasperi, A.* 198
*Della Rovere, The* 154
*Diaz, Marshal* 190
*Didius Julianus* 197
*Diocletian, Emp.* 11, 15, 109, 113, 115, 189
Domine Quo Vadis? 227
*Domitian* 14, 56, 97, 110, 113, 117, 126, 129, 132, 138, 144-5, 347
Domus Augustana 133
,, Aurea 144
,, Flavia 129
,, Gelotiana 134
,, Publica 122
,, Tiberiana 126
*Doria, And.* 149
Due Ponti 370
*Duphot, Gen.* 240

*Easton, Card. Adam* 237
Embassies, British and American 44
Emporia 92
English Church 173
*Eratosthenes* 356
Esquiline, The 201
*Este, Ippolito d'* 360, 363
*Eudoxia, Elder & Younger* 200
*Eugenius III* 203, 276
*Eugenius IV* 98, 101, 213, 246, 315
E.U.R. 258
*Eutropius* 234
*Evelyn, John* 81
Explanations 10

Fabian gens 373
Facchino, Il 150
*Farnese, The* 126
Farnese Gardens 126
Farnesina, Villa 242
*Faustina, Empress* 122, 151
*Felix IV, St* 140
*Ferdinand and Isabella of Spain* 203, 243
*Ferdinand II of the Two Sicilies* 301
Ferro da Cavallo 225
Festivals 45
Fiano Romano 371
Fidenae 372
Finocchio 352
Fiumicino 334
*Flaminius, C.* 370
*Flaxman, J.* 173
*Fonseca, Gabriele* 152
Fontana dell'Acqua Felice 181
,, della Barcaccia 173

,, di Egeria 222
,, dei Fiumi 103
,, del Moro 103
,, delle Naiadi 189
,, Paola 244
,, delle Tartarughe 83
,, di Trevi 170
,, del Tritone 180
Fontanella del Facchino 150
Fontanella delle Api 180
Food and Wine 38
Forma Urbis 123
*Formosus, Pope* 246
Foro Italico 256
Forum, The 108
Forum of Augustus 137
,, Boarium 86
,, of Caesar 137
,, Holitorium 85
,, of Nerva 138
,, of Peace 123
,, of Trajan 136
,, of Vespasian 138
Fosse Ardeatine 230
*Francis I of France* 12, 76
*Francis I of Bourbon Parma* 126
*Francis II of Austria* 12
Frascati 339
Frattocchie 347
*Frederick Barbarossa* 12, 246, 342
Fregene 375
French Military Cemetery 257
French School of Art 174

Gabii 356
Gabinetto delle Stampe 243
*Gaius Caesar* 106, 112
*Galileo, Galilei* 97, 174
*Galla Placidia* 93
Galleria Borghese 156
,, Capitolina 68
,, Colonna 168
,, Comunale d'Arte Moderna 188
,, Doria-Pamphilj 147
,, Nazionale 178
,, Naz. d'Arte Antica 178
,, Naz. d'Arte Moderna 160
,, Pallavicini 176
,, di S. Luca 171-2
,, Spada 82
Gallicano nel Lazio 356
*Gallienus* 235
Garbatella Quarter 92
Gardens of Sallust 182
*Garibaldi, Gius.* 105, 236, 243, 245, 257
*Gelasius II* 87, 202
Genzano 351

George IV 271
Germalus 125
German Military Cemetery 336
Germanicus 115
Gesù, Church of 74
Gesù e Maria, Ch. of 153
Geta 88, 114
Ghetto 84
Gibbon, Edw. 70, 119, 144, 197
Gibson, John 92
Gilberto Pio of Savoy 68
Giostra, La 235
Glossary of Art Terms 52
Goethe 102, 153, 347
Gogol, Nikolai 174
Gracchus, C. 110
Gracchus, Tib. 109
Gregory I, St (the Great) 221, 248, 268, 271, 275
Gregory II 221
Gregory III 98
Gregory IV 322, 332
Gregory VII 12, 93, 203, 246, 248
Gregory XI 141, 203, 276
Gregory XIII 149, 269, 339, 341, 347
Gregory XV 173
Gregory XVI 93, 142, 181, 269, 277, 279, 297, 302, 311, 315, 361
Grotta del Pianora 375
Grotta Rossa 370
Grottaferrata 342
Grotto of Egeria 229
Guiscard, Robert 12, 207, 220, 246, 248

Hadrian 14, 97, 126-7, 135, 141, 144-5, 175, 247-8, 362
Hadrian's Villa 362
Hannibal 11, 345
Hare, Augustus 322
Harvey, Wm. 81
Hawthorne, Nathaniel 59
Heliogabalus 119, 126, 135
Henry IV, Emp. 246
Henry VII, Emp. 142
Henry Stuart, Cardinal York 170, 239, 271, 340, 345
Herodes Atticus 229
Holidays 51
Holy Year 262
Honorius, Emp. 19, 93, 181, 217-8, 226
Honorius I 123, 141, 183, 261
Honorius III 89, 94, 140, 198, 261
Horace 201, 335, 337, 350, 353, 358, 367, 371
Horatii and Curiatii, The 347, 349

Horatius 236
Horrea Agrippiana 118
Horrea Piperataria 123
Hortensius 125
Hospitals 44
Hotels and Pensions 34-6
House, see also Casa and Domus
House of Card. Bessarion 324
„ „ the Griffins 132
„ „ John Keats 173
„ „ Livia 128
„ „ Raphael 101
„ „ Romulus 128
„ „ SS. John and Paul 221
„ „ the Vestals 119
Howard, Card. 81
Howitt, Wm. and Mary 92
Humbert I 99
Hunt, J. Leigh 173
Hypogeum, see Tomb

Ibsen, Henrik 350
Imperial Fora 135-9
Imperial Rostra 114
Indipendenza Quarter 197
Ine, King 247
Innocent II 239, 250
Innocent III 12, 214, 216, 247
Innocent IV 70
Innocent VIII 75, 268, 271, 277, 306
Innocent X 103, 148-9, 213
Innocent XII 149, 228, 269, 337
Isaeum Campense 95
Isola Farnese 372
Isola Sacra 332
Isola Tiberina 84
Istituto Centrale del Restauro 199
Istituto Naz. d'Archeologia e Storia dell'Arte 73
Istituto di S. Michele 238

James Stuart ('Old Pretender') 170, 271, 341, 369
Janiculum 243
John I 224
John VII 117
John VIII 93, 246
John XIX 343
John XXIII 262, 271, 275, 279, 283
John XXIII, antipope 248, 276
Jugurtha 110
Julian, Emp. 220

Julius I, St 239, 257
Julis II 12, 16, 80, 170, 183, 246, 253, 265, 277, 289-91, 295, 302, 307, 332, 343
Julius III 163, 258, 275
Julius Cæsar 11, 14, 75-6, 85, 108, 112-4, 135, 137, 335, 373
'Julius Cæsar' 128
Justinian II 273

Kauffmann, Angelica 172, 347
Keats, John 92, 173
Kesselring, F. M. 339

Labicum 342
Lacus Curtius 116
Lacus Juturnæ 116
Lacus Sabatinus 374
Ladíspoli 376
Lago di Castiglione 352
Lago Regillo 352
Lago Traiano 334
Lapis Niger 112
Largo Argentina 75
Largo Magnanápoli 175
Lars Porsena 236
Lateran, The 215
Latium 320
Lavinium 336
Lazio 320
Leo I, St (the Great) 200, 213, 270
Leo III 12, 93, 224, 265, 298, 315
Leo IV 117, 246
Leo X 12, 16, 76, 80, 96, 219, 228-9, 242, 246, 250-2, 266, 277, 285, 291-4, 335
Leo XI 174, 271
Leo XII 17, 93, 142, 269-70
Leo XIII 152, 214, 277, 293, 298
Le Roy, Thomas 76
Liberius, Pope 202
Licenza 367
Lido di Ostia 333
Liszt, Franz 360
Livia 106, 128-9, 371
Livy 14, 89
Lorium 375
Lost Property 44
Louis XII 173
Louis XIV 174
Louis XVIII 173
Lucius Cæsar 106
Lucius II 216
Lucullus, L. Licinius 174
Lucus Feroniæ 371
Ludovisi, Card. 181
Ludovisi Collection 181
Ludovisi Quarter 180

Ludus Magnus 207
Lunghezza 357
Lupercal 128
Luther, Martin 155

Macao, Caserma del 197
Maddalena, La 99
Madonna di Bracciano 372
Madonna dei Monti 199
Madonna del Sacro Cuore 104
Madre di Dio 257
Maecenas 201, 358
Maidalchini, Olimpia 104, 148
Malagrotta 375
Mameli, Goffredo 82, 198, 244
Mamertine Prison 110
Manara, Luciano 244
Mandela 367
Manlius, T. ('Torquatus') 185
Marcellus 85
Marcellus II, Pope 275
Marcigliana 372
Marconi, Gugl. 256, 315
Marcus Aurelius 15, 151, 375
Margaret of Parma 104, 256
Margherita of Savoy 99, 181
Maria Christina of Sardinia 341
Marino 344
Marius 11, 322, 358
Marius the Younger 353
Markets of Trajan 137
Martignano, Lago di 374
Martin V 12, 168, 213-4
Massaia, Card. 340
Matilda of Tuscany 269
Mausoleum of Augustus 106
„ „ Hadrian 247
„ „ Lucilius Peto 185
Maxentius 15, 123, 141, 144, 231, 257
Maximian 189
Mazzini, Gius. 13, 236
Menenius Agrippa 184
Mengs, Raphael 172, 186, 206, 242, 264
Mentana 372
Merenptah 153
Messalina 174
Meta Sudans 144
Metropolitana 42
Mezzocammino 321
Mezzofanti, Card. 245
Milliarium Aureum 114
Milton, John 81
Mithræum 91, 210
Mohammed Ali 93
Monastero di Tor de'

Specchi 85
Mons Albanus 345
Mons Sacer 184
Montaigne 102
Monte Cavallo 176
„ Cavo 344
„ Cómpatri 342
„ Giordano 101
„ del Grano 339
„ Mario 256
„ di Pietà 83
„ Porzio Catone 342
„ Sacro 184
„ Savello 85
„ Testaccio 92
Montefeltro, Federico da 298
Monterotondo 372
Monteverde Quarter 244
Monument, Bersaglieri 182
„ Cairoli 174
„ Dogali 196
„ Marconi 259
„ Victor Emmanuel II - 71
Morlupo 371
Munatius Plancus 358
Mundus, Palatine 132
Munoz Ant. 90, 190, 211
Muro Torto 175
Museo dell'Alto Medio Evo 260
„ di Arte Orientale 206
„ delle Arti e Tradizioni Popolari 259
„ Barracco 77
„ dei Bersaglieri 182
„ Canonica 156
„ Capitolino 58
„ della Civiltà Romana 260
„ Etnografico 259
„ del Genio 256
„ dei Gessi 198
„ Nazionale Romano 190
„ Preistorico 259
„ del Risorgimento 72
„ di Roma 100
„ Tassiano 246
„ Torlonia 240
„ della Via Ostiense 91
„ di Villa Giulia 163
Museum, Copernican 256
„ Geological 181
„ of Medical History 247
„ of Musical Instruments 217
„ Napoleonic 101
„ Numismatic 182
„ Postal 255
Museums 47-50
Mussolini 13, 72, 95, 144, 175, 183
Mutius Scaevola 236

Napoleon 12, 173, 272, 283, 299
Napoleon III 126, 133
Necropolis, Archaic 122'
Necropolis, Vatican 275
Nemi 345
Nero 14, 126, 129, 137, 141, 144, 153, 201, 212, 219, 246, 322, 334, 337, 368-9
Nero, Tomb of 372
Nerva 14, 106, 137
Nettuno 337-8
Nicholas I of Russia 94
Nicholas IV 203, 213
Nicholas V 61, 219, 248, 257. 265, 277, 298
Nome di Maria, Ch. 136
Nomentum 372
North American College 246
Nova Via 112, 119, 122
Numa Pompilius 11, 118, 243

Obelisks 95, 106, 152-3, 173, 175-6, 178, 196, 204, 212, 264
Observatory 256
Octavia 106
Odoacer 12, 126
O'Donnell, Roderick 244
O'Neill, Hugh 244
Opera House 46, 189
Opimius, L. 110
Oppian Hill 144, 201
Oratorio dei Filippini 79
Oratorium Marianum 205
Oratory of the Forty Martyrs 117
Orsini, The 12, 85, 98, 101, 345, 367, 374
Orsini, Giordano 344
Orsini, Matteo 134
Orto Botanico 240
Ospedale di S. Spirito 247
Osteria Belvedere 231
Osteria del Malpasso 336
Osteria dell'Orso 102
Osteria del Vermicino 339
OSTIA 14, 321
Otho II, Emp. 271, 276
Otho III 358
Oudinot, Marshal 243-4

Pædagogium 134
Palace of Domitian 129
Palatine, The 125
Palazzetto degli Anguillara 236
„ Massimi 78

,, dello Sport 257
,, di Venezia 72
Palazzina of Pius IV 167
Palazzo Altemps 102
,, Altieri 74
,, Antonelli 175
,, Baldassini 105
,, Balestra 170
,, Barberini 178
,, Bonaparte 147
,, Borghese 105
,, Brancaccio 206
,, Braschi 100
,, Caffarelli 66
,, della Cancelleria 76
,, Capranica 99
,, Carpegna 171
,, Cenci 84
,, Chigi 151
,, Colonna 167
,, dei Congressi 259
,, dei Conservatori 61
,, della Consulta 177
,, dei Convertendi 264
,, Corsini 240
,, Costaguti 83
,, Doria 147
,, del Drago 178
,, dell'Esposizione 188
,, Falconieri 80
,, Farnese 81
,, Fiano 152
,, Giustiniani 104
,, di Giustizia 255
,, del Governatorato 315
,, del Governo Vecchio 101
,, Lancellotti 101
,, Madama 104
,, Marescotti 95
,, Margherita 181
,, Massimo alle Colonne 78
,, Mattei 83
,, di Montecitorio 151
,, Odescalchi 147, 167
,, Pamphilj 103
,, dei Penitenzieri 264
,, Pio 76
,, Rospigliosi 176
,, Ruspoli 152
,, Sacchetti 80
,, Sacripante 101
,, Salviati 147, 243
,, di S. Calisto 239
,, Sanseverino 153
,, del Sant'Uffizio 265
,, della Sapienza 99
,, Sciarra-Colonna 150
,, Senatorio 56
,, Sforza Cesarini 79-80
,, Simonetti 150
,, Sora 78
,, Spada 81
,, di Spagna 172
,, dello Sport 260
,, Taverna 101
,, Torlonia 263

,, Turci 101
,, Valentini 175
,, di Venezia 72
,, Vidoni 75
,, del Viminale 189
,, Wedekind 151
PALESTRINA 352
Palestrina, G. P. da 271, 353-4
Palidoro 376
Palo Laziale 376
Pannartz, Arnold 78, 368
Pantheon 97
Parco di Porta Capena 222
Parco della Rimembranza 257
Parco Savello 89
Parco Virgiliano 184
Parioli Quarter 185
Paschal I, St 202, 220, 228, 237, 298
Paschal II 12, 153, 207, 211, 220
Pasquino 98, 101
Passeggiata del Gianicolo 245
Paul I 140
Paul II 72, 262, 275
Paul III 56, 81, 249-50, 252, 265-6, 270, 277
Paul V 17, 105, 123, 138, 184, 202, 204, 266, 277, 287, 297, 299, 303, 374
Paul VI 93, 262, 283
Pelagius I 169
Pelagius II 198
Pensions 34-6
Pepin the Frank 12
Petrarch 63, 213
Phocas, Emp. 98
Piazza d'Aracœli 55, 56
,, Augusto Imperatore 106
,, Barberini 180
,, Bocca della Verità 86
,, Campidoglio 56
,, Cavour 255
,, dei Cinquecento 196
,, Colonna 151
,, dell'Indipendenza 197
,, Minerva 95
,, Navona 103
,, del Popolo 153
,, di Porta Capena 222
,, della Repubblica 189
,, della Rotonda 97
,, S. Pietro 264
,, Ss. Apostoli 175
,, di Spagna 172
,, Venezia 55
,, Vitt. Emanuele 206
Piazzale Flaminio 155
,, Giardino 256
,, Napoleone 175
,, Ostiense 91
Piccola Farnesina 76

Pincio 174
Pineta, La 334
Piso, C. Calpurnius 212
Pius I, St 201
Pius II 257, 268, 358
Pius IV 72, 98, 182, 190, 249, 252, 296, 315
Pius V, St 218, 265, 302
Pius VI 12, 173, 176, 272, 274-5, 277, 283, 307, 335; 368
Pius VII 12, 142, 153, 176, 257, 271, 277, 297, 299, 303
Pius VIII 271, 315
Pius IX 13, 17, 93, 100, 142, 173, 177, 183, 199, 214, 239, 245, 257, 265, 277, 288, 297, 347
Pius X, St 257, 271, 298
Pius XI 262-3, 267, 269, 277, 283, 298
Pius XII 167, 198, 262, 269, 275
Plutei of Trajan 113
Poli 356
Police Station 44
Policlinico 197
Pomezia 336
Pompey 11, 76, 201
Pons Aelius 247
,, Aemilius 87
,, Janiculensis 240
,, Milvius 257
,, Sublicius 92
Ponte Aventino 92
,, Cavour 153
,, Cestio 85
,, Fabricio 84
,, Flaminio 257
,, Lucano 358
,, Mammolo 357
,, Margherita 153
,, Milvio 257
,, Molle 257
,, di Nemi 344
,, Nomentano 184
,, di Nona 356
,, Palatino 87
,, Principe Amadeo 246
,, del Risorgimento 256
,, Rotto 87
,, Salario 185
,, Sant'Angelo 247
,, Sisto 83, 240
,, Sublicio 92
,, Umberto I 101
,, Vitt. Emanuele 247
Pontifex Maximus 119, 122
Pontine Marshes 335
Pope, Alex. 99
Popes, List of 20
Porta Appia 226
,, Asinaria 216
,, Aurelia 244
,, Capena 222

„ Flaminia 155
„ Furba 339
„ Latina 225
„ Maggiore 217
„ Magica 206
„ Mugonia 126
„ Nomentana 182
„ Ostiensis 91
„ Pia 182
„ Pinciana 181
„ del Popolo 155
„ Portese 238
„ Prenestina 217
„ Salaria 184
„ S. Giovanni 216
„ S. Lorenzo 218
„ S. Pancrazio 244
„ S. Paolo 91
„ S. Sebastiano 226
„ S. Spirito 246
„ Settimiana 240
„ Tiburtina 218
Portico of the Dii
  Consentes 110
Porticus Julia 112
„ of Octavia 84
„ of Pompey 76
Porto 334
Portus Romae 333
Post Office 43, 152
Poussin, Nicolas 152
Praeneste 353
Prati Quarter 255
Pratica di Mare 336
Prima Porta 371
Priorato di Malta 90
Propertius 201, 358
Protestant Cemetery 92
Psammetichus II 152
Pyramid of C. Cestius 91
Pyrgi 376

Quattro Fontane 178
Quirinal 176-7

Rabelais, Fr 102
Railway Stations 33, 196
Rameses II 153
Rampolla, Card. 238
Regia 122
Regillus, Lake 352
Regina Coeli 243
Restaurants 36
Riano 371
Rienzo, Cola di 12, 56,
  60, 70, 84, 109, 150,
  203, 212, 248, 344
Rignano Flaminio 371
Rocca Canterano 368
Rocca di Papa 344
Rocca Priora 342
Roccagióvine 367
Roma Quadrata 125, 127
Roma Vecchia 234
Romulus 11, 88, 112
Rosary, Ch. of 256

Rossi, G. B. de' 228, 297
Rostra 114
Rostra ad Divi Julii 112
Ruspoli, The 345

Sabate 374
Sabina 363
Sacchetti, Card. 68
Sacra Via 111
Sacrofano 371
St Anacletus, Pope 265
St Anastasius 216
St Anicetus, Pope 265,
  275
St Augustine 221
St Augustine of Hippo
  322
St Aurea 332
St Bartholomew of
  Rossano 342
St Benedict 237, 368, 370
St Benedict Labre 199
St Bernard 260
St Caesarius 216
St Catherine of Siena 12,
  96-7
St Cecilia 228, 237-8
St Charles Borromeo 153
St Dominic 89, 224
St Francis 238, 370
St Francis Borgia 149
St Gregory Nazianzen
  269
St Helena 215, 268, 310,
  352
St Hilary 212
St Honorius 368
St Ignatius of Antioch
  142
St Ignatius Loyola 74,
  372
St Jerome 207
St John the Evangelist
  225
St John of Matha 220
St Laurence 122, 152,
  198
St Mark, Pope 74
St Maximus 238
St Melchiades 212
St Monica 322, 332
St Nilus 342
St Paul 92-4, 150, 214,
  260
St Paul of the Cross 220
St Peter 92, 110, 140,
  200, 202, 214, 224,
  227, 243, 246, 265-9,
  275
St Philip Neri 79, 245
St Scholastica 368
St Siricius, Pope 204
St Symmachus 201, 207
St Tiburtius 238
St Valerian 237-8
St Zosimus 207

Sallust 182, 358
S. Adriano 113
S. Agata dei Goti 188
S. Agnese in Agone 103
S. Agnese fuori le Mura
  183
S. Agostino 105
S. Alessio 90
S. Ambrogio, Oratorio di
  153
Ss. Ambrogio e Carlo al
  Corso 153
S. Anastasia 88
S. Andrea delle Fratte
  172
S. Andrea al Ponte
  Milvio 257
S. Andrea al Quirinale
  177
S. Andrea della Valle 75
S. Andrea della Via
  Flaminia 258
S. Andrew's 178
S. Angelo in Pescheria 84
S. Anna dei Palafrenieri
  318
S. Anselmo 91
S. Antonio Abate 205
S. Antonio dei
  Portoghesi 105
Ss. Apostoli 169
S. Balbina 222
S. Bartolomeo 84
S. Bartolomeo dei
  Bergamaschi 151
S. Benedetto 237
S. Bernardo 181
S. Bibiana 218
S. Caesarius, Oratory of
  133
S. Carlo ai Catinari 83
S. Carlo alle Quattro
  Fontane (S. Carlino)
  177
S. Caterina dei Funari 83
S. Caterina da Siena 175
S. Cecilia in Trastévere
  237
S. Cesareo 224
S. Clemente 207
S. Cosimato 239
Ss. Cosma e Damiano
  140
S. Costanza 184
S. Crisogono 236
S. Croce 257
S. Croce in Gerusalemme
  216
Ss. Domenico e Sisto 175
S. Eligio degli Orefici 80
S. Eugenio 167
S. Eusebio 206
S. Eustachio 99
S. Francesca Romana
  140
S. Francesco a Ripa 238
S. Giacomo in Augusta
  153

S. Giacomo degli
  Spagnoli 104
S. Gioacchino 255
S. Giorgio in Velabro 88
S. Giovanni Decollato 88
S. Giovanni dei
  Fiorentini 80
S. Giovanni in Fonte 212
S. Giovanni dei Genovesi
  238
S. Giovanni in Laterano
  212
S. Giovanni in Oleo 225
Ss. Giovanni e Paolo 220
S. Giovanni della Pigna
  95
S. Giovanni a Porta
  Latina 225
S. Girolamo della Carità
  81
S. Girolamo degli
  Schiavoni 106
S. Giuseppe dei
  Falegnami 110
S. Gregorio Magno 221
S. Gregorio da Sassola
  (Lazio) 356
S. Ignazio 150
S. Isidoro 180
S. Ivo 180
S. Lorenzo fuori le Mura
  198
S. Lorenzo in Damaso 76
S. Lorenzo in Lucina 152
S. Lorenzo in Miranda
  115
S. Lorenzo in Panisperna
  188
S. Luca e S. Martina 109
S. Lucia del Gonfalone
  80
S. Luigi dei Francesi 104
S. Marcello 150
S. Marco 74
S. Maria degli Angeli 190
„ dell'Anima 102
„ Antiqua 117
„ in Aracoeli 70
„ Aventinense 90
„ in Campitelli 83
„ in Campo Marzio 105
„ in Cannapara 115
„ in Cappella 237
„ di Cavamonte (Lazio)
  356
„ della Concezione 180
„ della Consolazione 86
„ in Cosmedin 87
„ in Domnica 219
„ Egiziaca 86
„ di Galeria (Lazio) 374
„ di Galloro (Ariccia)
  350
„ Liberatrice 117
„ di Loreto 136
„ Maggiore 202
„ ad Martyres 97
„ sopra Minerva 95

„ dei Miracoli 153
„ di Monserrato 79
„ in Montesanto 153
„ in Montecelli 83
„ della Navicella 219
„ Nova 140
„ dell'Orto 238
„ della Pace 102
„ del Popolo 153
„ del Priorato 90
„ Rotonda 97
„ della Scala 240
„ Scala Coeli 261
„ dei Sette Dolori 243
„ in Traspontina 263-4
„ in Trastévere 239
„ in Vallicella 79
„ in Via 151
„ in Via Lata 149
„ della Vittoria 181
S. Marta 149
S. Martino ai Monti 201
Ss. Nereo ed Achilleo
  223
S. Nicola in Carcere 85
S. Nicolo da Tolentino
  181
S. Onofrio 245
S. Oreste (Lazio) 371
S. Pancrazio 244
S. Pantaleo 78
S. Paolo alle Tre
  Fontane 261
S. Paolo fuori le Mura
  93
S. Paul's 189
S. Peter's 265
Ss. Pietro e Paolo 260
S. Pietro in Carcere 110
S. Pietro in Montorio
  243
S. Pietro in Vincoli 200
S. Polo de' Cavalieri
  (Lazio) 367
S. Prassede 201
S. Prisca 91
S. Procula Maggiore
  (Lazio) 336
S. Pudenziana 204
Ss. Quattro Coronati 211
S. Rocco 106
S. Saba 91
S. Sabina 89
S. Salvatore in Lauro
  101
S. Salvatore in Onde 83
S. Sebastiano 229
S. Sebastiano al Palatino
  135
S. Silvestro in Capite 152
S. Silvestro al Quirinale
  176
S. Sisto Vecchio 224
S. Spirito in Sassia 247
S. Stefano degli Abissini
  315
S. Stefano Rotondo 219
S. Susanna 181

S. Teodoro 88
S. Thomas of Canterbury
  81
S. Tomaso in Formis 220
Ss. Trinità dei Pellegrini
  82
S. Urbano 229
Ss. Vincenzo ed
  Anastasio 171
Ss. Vincenzo ed
  Anastasio (Tre
  Fontane) 261
S. Vitale 189
Ss. Vito e Modesto 204
Sancta Sanctorum 216
Santuario del Divino
  Amore 235
Saxa Rubra 371
Scala Santa 215
Scalae Caci 127
Scarlatti, Aless. 172
School of the Praæcones
  134
Scipios, The 225, 304
Scots College 180, 372
Scottish Churches 178,
  180
Scott, Sir W. 374
Scuderie Pontificie 177
Sejanus 197
Senate 104
Senate House 113
Sepolcreto Ostiense 92
Septimius Severus 15, 84,
  88, 98, 114, 118, 126,
  324, 348
Septizonium 134
Sergius III 213
Servian Wall 18, 91, 175,
  197, 206, 222
Servius Tullius 11, 14,
  18, 199, 201
Sessorium 216
Sette Sale 206
Settebagni 372
Seven Hills 18
Severn, Joseph 92
Shakespeare 128
Shelley, P. B. 92, 152,
  173, 222
Simon Magus 141
Sixtus III 203, 212
Sixtus IV 57, 102, 124,
  153, 224, 246, 273,
  277, 298, 315
Sixtus V 15, 17, 153, 177,
  204, 215, 218, 246,
  262, 264-5, 277, 298-9,
  335
Smaragdus 115
Sobieska, Clementina 271
Spanish Academy 244
Spanish Steps 173
Stadio Flaminio 257
Stadio dei Marmi 256
Stadio Olimpico 256
Stadium 134
Statue of Garibaldi 245

,, ,, **Marcus Aurelius** 56
,, ,, **Pompey** 76, 82
**Stazione Termini** 196
*Stephen III* 12, 152
**Storta, La** 372
**Student Hostels** 36
**Subiaco** 368
**Subura** 199
**Sudario, Ch.** 75
*Suetonius* 109
*Sulla* 11, 56, 109, 113, 322, 353
*Sweynheim, Conrad* 78, 368
*Sylvester I, St* 201, 217, 265
*Symonds, J. A.* 92
Synagogue 84
**Syphax** 358

**Taberæ Novæ** 111
**Tabularium** 57
*Tacitus* 368
**Tarpeian Rock** 86
*Tarquinius Priscus* 11, 14
*Tarquinius Superbus* 11, 14, 356
*Tasso, Torquato* 245
**Teatro Argentina** 75
**Teatro Goldoni** 102
**Teatro dell'Opera** 189
*Tebaldeo, Ant.* 150
**Tellene** 235
**Tempietto di Bramante** 244
**Temple of Antoninus and Faustina** 122
,, ,, **Apollo** 128
,, ,, **Apollo Sosianus** 85
,, ,, **Augustus** 117
,, ,, **Bacchus** 123
,, ,, **Castor** 116
,, ,, **Claudius** 219
,, ,, **Concord** 110
,, ,, **Cybele** 127
,, ,, **Deus Rediculus** 228
,, ,, **Fortuna Virilis** 86
,, ,, **Hadrian** 151
,, ,, **Isis** 95, 132
,, ,, **Janus** 112
,, ,, **Julius Cæsar** 112
,, ,, **Jupiter Capitolinus** 55
,, ,, **Jupiter Stator** 135
,, ,, **Jupiter Victor** 128
,, ,, **Mars Ultor** 138
,, ,, **Minerva** 138
,, ,, **Minerva Medica** 218
,, ,, **Romulus** 122
,, ,, **Saturn** 144
,, ,, **Serapis** 168
,, ,, **the Sun** 135, 152
,, ,, **Veiovis** 57
,, ,, **Venus Cloacina** 112
,, ,, **Venus Genetrix** 137
,, ,, **Venus and Rome** 141

,, ,, **Vespasian** 110
,, ,, **Vesta** 86
,, ,, **Vesta (Forum)** 118
*Thackeray, Miss* 174
**Theatre of Marcellus** 85
**Theatre of Pompey** 76
Theatres 46
*Theodoric* 126, 248
*Theodosius I (the Great)* 93, 118, 141
*Theodosius II* 142
Thermæ, *see* Baths
*Thorvaldsen, B.* 99, 102, 173, 187, 271, 280
**Tiber, The** 236
*Tiberius* 14, 110, 112, 115-6, 125, 135
**Tibur** 358
*Titus* 14, 111, 142, 201, 217
**TIVOLI** 358
**Tomb of the Aureli** 218
,, ,, **the Baker** 217
,, ,, **Cæcilia Metella** 231
,, ,, **Julius II** 200
,, ,, **Romulus** 112
,, ,, **St Peter** 275
,, ,, **the Scipios** 225
,, ,, **Seneca** 234
**Tombs of the Via Latina** 343
**Tor Pignattara** 353
,, **di Quinto** 370
,, **de' Schiavi** 356
,, **Vaianica** 338
**Torraccio del Palombaro** 235
**Torre Colonna** 175
,, **dei Conti** 199
,, **delle Milizie** 137
,, **in Selce** 235
**Torremancina** 372
**Torrenova** 352
**Torrimpietra** 375
*Totila* 89, 358
**Traforo Principe Amedeo** 246
**Traforo Umberto I** 172
*Trajan* 11, 14, 89, 113, 136-7, 144-5, 201, 322, 334, 358, 374
Trams 42
Transport 41
**Trastévere** 235
**Tre Fontane** 260
*Trelawny, Edw.* 92
**Trevignano Romano** 375
**Tribune of Benedict XIV** 216
**Trinità dei Monti** 173
**Trinità dei Pellegrini** 82
**Trionfale Quarter** 255
**Tropaion of Gaius** 275
**Trophies of Marius** 56
**Tullianum** 110
*Tullius Hostilius* 11
**Tumulus Cæsarum** 106
*Turner, J. M.* 346

*Turnus* 336
**Tusculum** 341

**Umbilicus Urbis** 114
Underground 42
**Università Gregoriana** 170
**University of Rome** 198
Unknown Soldier 71
*Urban VII* 96
*Urban VIII* 17, 98, 100, 149, 170, 173, 178, 199, 212, 238, 243-4, 249, 255, 266, 268, 270, 347
**Urbe** 372
*Ursinus, antipope* 203

*Valentinian II* 93
*Valentinian III* 142
**Valle Giulia** 163
*Varallo, Card.* 183
**Varia** 367
*Varro, M. Terentius* 201
*Varus, Quintilius* 358, 362
**Vascello** 244
**Vatican City** 261, 314
**VATICAN PALACE** 276
Borgia Rooms 293
Braccio Nuovo 299
Chiaramonti Gallery 303
Library 298
Loggia of Raphael 292
Museums:—
Christian Antiquities 282
Christian Art 297
Egyptian 302
Ethnological Mission-ary 283
Etruscan 311
Gregorian 278
Historical 283
Modern Religious Art 294
Pagan Antiquities 278
Pio Christian 282
Pio-Clementino 304
Picture Gallery 283
Sistine Chapel 294
Sistine Hall 299
Stanze of Raphael 288
Veio 373
**Velabrum** 88
**Velia** 125
**Velletri** 351
*Vercingetorix* 110
*Vespasian* 14, 56, 60, 110, 123, 142, 145, 217
Vestal Virgins 119
**Via Appia** 218, 226

Via Appia Nuova 216, 347, 350
Via Appia Pignatelli 228
Via Ardeatina 228, 230
Via Aurelia 244
Via Casilina 217, 352-3, 357
Via Cassia 372
Via Cavour 199
Via della Conciliazione 263
Via Condotti 173
Via dei Coronari 101
Via del Corso 147
Via Flaminia 370
Via dei Fori Imperiali 109, 135
Via Gabina 356
Via Giulia 80
Via del Governo Vecchio 101
Via Labicana 339
Via Lata 147
Via Latina 339, 343
Via Laurentina 336
Via della Lungara 240
Via del Mare 321
Via Margutta 173
Via Nazionale 188
Via Nomentana 183
Via Olimpica 258
Via Ostiense 92
Via Ostiensis 321
Via Pontina 335
Via Portuensis 334
Via Prenestina 217, 356
Via Quattro Novembre 175

Via della Ripetta 105
Via Sacra (Mte. Cavo) 345
Via Salaria 184, 372
Via Scelerata 199
Via Severiana 321
Via Sistina 174
Via del Teatro di Marcello 85
Via Tiberina 371
Via Tiburtina 357-8, 362
Via del Tritone 172
Via Tuscolana 339
Via Valeria 366
Via Vitt. Veneto 180
Viale Regina Margherita 183
Viale Trastévere 236, 238
Viale Vaticano 261
Vicarello, Bagni di 374
Vicovaro 367
*Victor Emmanuel I* 168
*Victor Emmanuel II* 99, 177, 341
*Victor Emmanuel III* 13, 180, 185
Vicus Jugarius 114
Vicus Tuscus 88, 115
Vigna di Valle 375
Vignola, La 222
Villa Ada 185
„ Aldobrandini 188
„ Borghese 155
„ Celimontana 220
„ Colonna 168
„ Doria Pamphilj 244
„ d'Este 359
„ Farnesina 242

„ of Gallienus 235
„ Giulia 163
„ Glori 258
„ Ludovisi 181
„ Madama 256
„ Mario Mellini 256
„ Mattei 220
„ Medici 174
„ Paolina 182
„ di Papa Giulio 163
„ of the Quintilii 234
„ Sciarra 244
„ Senni 343
„ Spada 372
„ Torlonia 183
„ Torlonia (ex-Albani) 186
„ Wolkonsky 216
Villaggio Olimpico 257
*Virgil* 201, 371
*Virginia* 112
Volcanal 114

Wadding, Luke 180
Waldensian Church 175
Walls of Rome 18
War Graves Commission 183
*Wilhelm II* 341
*Winckelman, J. J.* 186, 347
Wines 38
*Wiseman, Card.* 81, 205

Zagarólo 353
*Zenobia, Queen* 358
Zoological Gardens 159

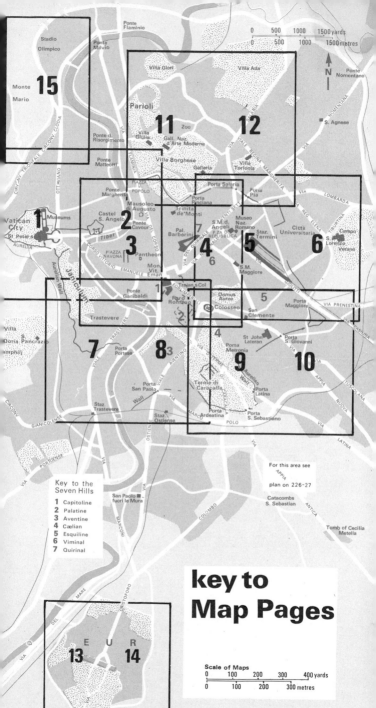

# key to Map Pages

**Key to the Seven Hills**
1 Capitoline
2 Palatine
3 Aventine
4 Caelian
5 Esquiline
6 Viminal
7 Quirinal

For this area see
plan on 226-27

| Scale of Maps | | | |
|---|---|---|---|
| 0 | 100 | 200 | 300 400 yards |
| 0 | 100 | 200 | 300 metres |

0   500   1000   1500 yards
0   500   1000   1500 metres

N

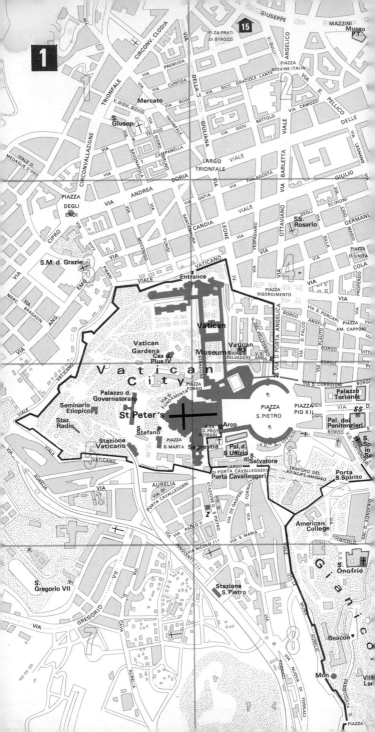

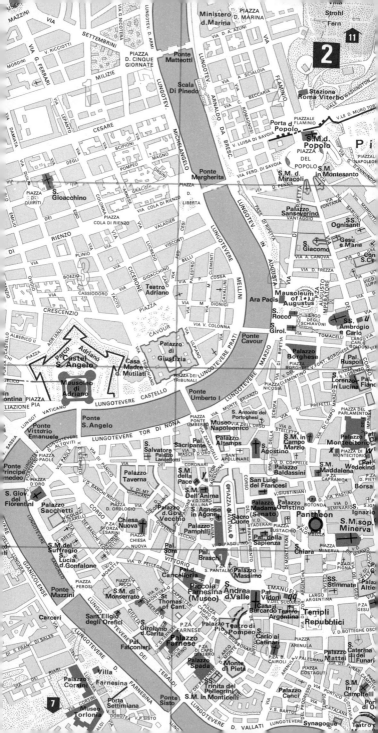

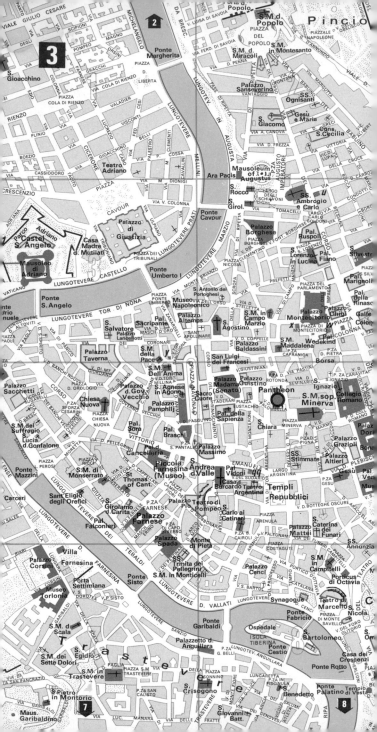

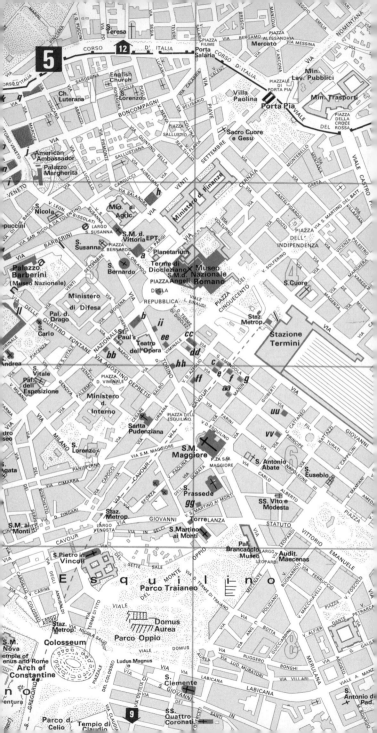

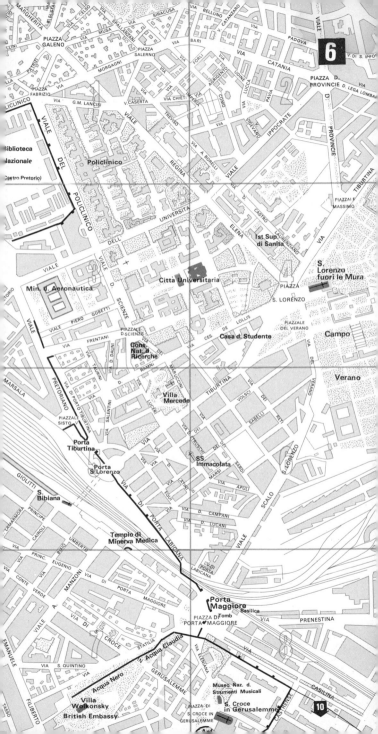

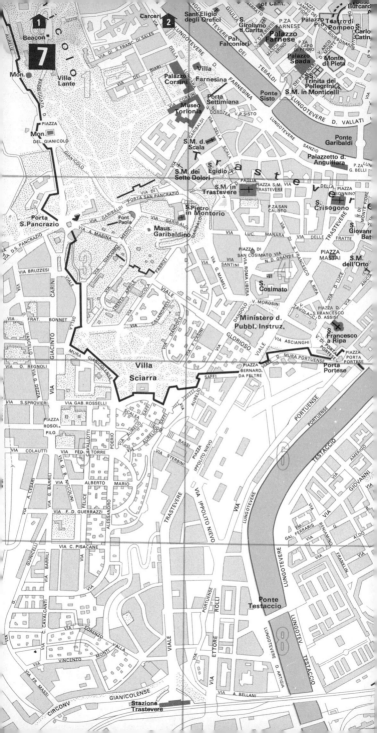

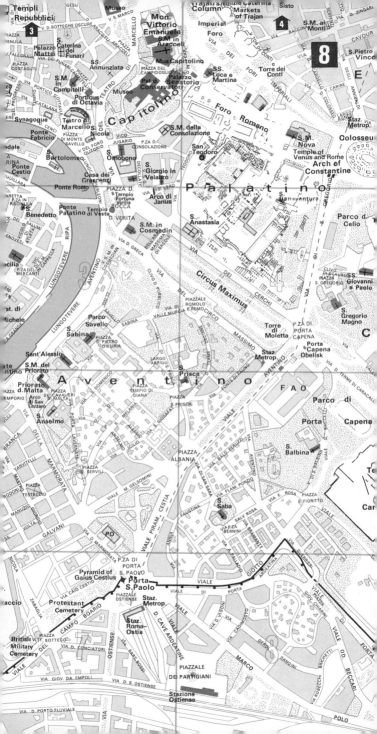

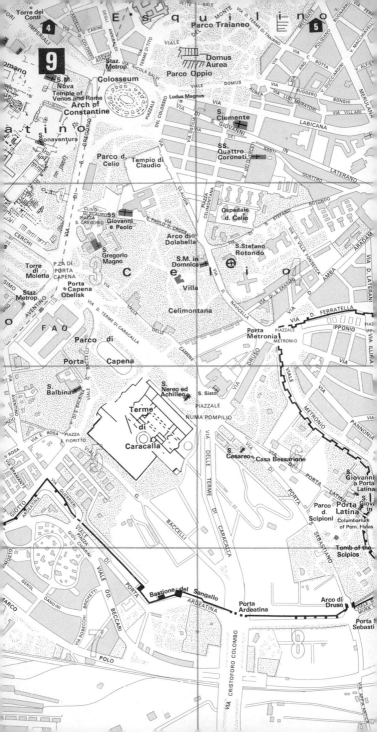

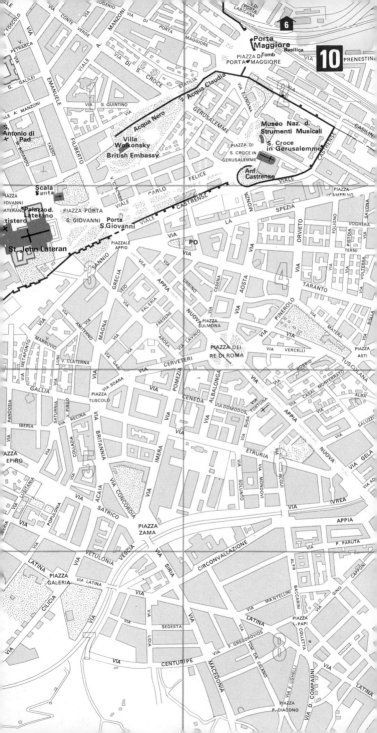

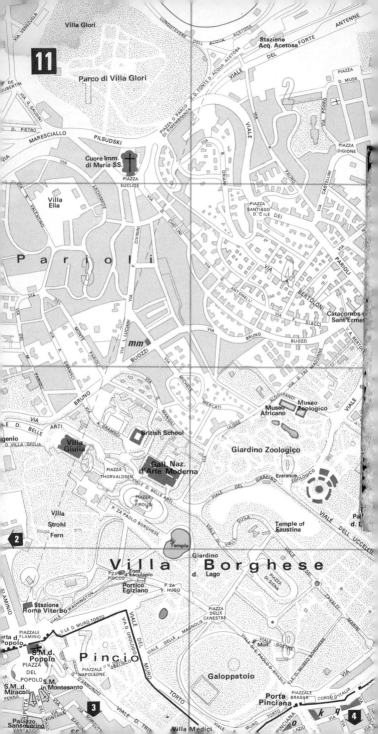

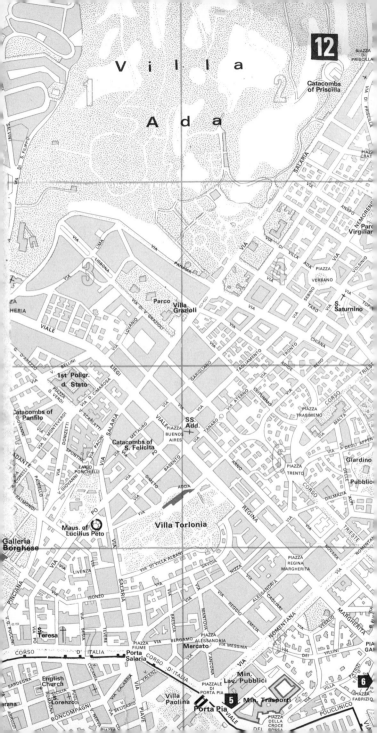

**12**

PIAZZA DI PRISCILLA

Catacombs of Priscilla

V i l l a

A d a

Parco Virgiliar

PIAZZA CRAT

VIA DI PRISCILLA

VIA SALARIA

ANAPO

VIA DI VILLA ADA

VIA NEMORENS

Parco Virgiliar

PIAZZA VERBANO

VOLSINO

VIA

VIA LIMA

VIA PANAMA

VIA LISBONA

Parco Villa Grazioli

VIA DI V. GRAZIOLI

VIALE

GIOVANO

SEBINO

TARO

VIA

S. Saturnino

CHIANA

VIA TOPI

HERIA

VIALE

G. D'AREZZO

V. BELLINI

LIEGI

GARIGLIANO

TAGLIAMENTO

ADIGE

TRONTO

NERO

CORSO TRIES

1st Poligr. d. Stato

V. DONIZETTI

V. SCARLATTI

V. PACINI

VIA SALARIA

VIALE

PIAZZA BUENOS AIRES

VIA ATERNO

CHIRIMO

VIA

METAURO

TANARO

PIAZZA TRASIMENO

MALTA

Catacombs of Panfilo

V. G. MONTEVERDI

SPONTINI

V. GIOVANNI

CHISONE

BASENTO

PO

ARNO

PIAZZA TRENTO

DRECE

VIA DEGLI APPEN

Giardino Pubblico

Catacombs of S. Felicita

LARGO PONCHIELLI

SIMETO

ADDA

VIA

REGINA

CORSO

DALMAZIA

Villa Torlonia

TRIESTE

Galleria Borghese

Maus. of Lucilius Peto

PO

VIA SALARIA

VIA DI VILLA ALBANI

SAVOIA

PIAZZA REGINA MARGHERITA

NOMENTAN

VIA

PINCIANA

LIVENZA

ISONZO

SAVOIA

NIZZA

REGGIO EMILI

ALESSANDRIA

CAGLIARI

NOVARA

MARGHERITA

S. Teresa

V. PUCCINI

TEVERE

SESIA

BRESCIA

MANTOVA

NOMENTANA

VICENZO

VILLINI

GAR

CORSO

D'ITALIA

Porta Salaria

PIAZZA FIUME

Mercato

PIAZZA ALESSANDHIA

VIA MESSINA

DEI

PIA

English Church

S. Lorenzo

BONCOMPAGNI

PIAVE

Villa Paolina

PIAZZALE DI PORTA PIA

Min. Lav. Pubblici

VIA

VILLA

PIAZZA FABRIZIO

**6**

**5** Min. Trasporti

Porta Pia

PIAZZA DELLA CROCE ROSSA

POLICLINICO

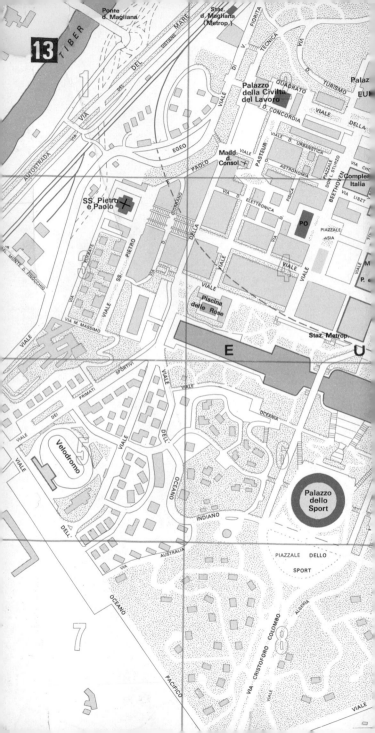